WESTERN NEVADA COLLEGE
3 1439 00079 5503

T3-AOR-588

The Greenwood Encyclopedia of Daily Life

2 THE MEDIEVAL WORLD

The Greenwood Encyclopedia of Daily Life

A Tour through History from Ancient Times to the Present

Joyce E. Salisbury
GENERAL EDITOR AND VOLUME EDITOR

GREENWOOD PRESS
Westport, Connecticut • London

Library of Congress Cataloging-in-Publication Data

The Greenwood encyclopedia of daily life : a tour through history from ancient times to the present / Joyce E. Salisbury, general editor.
p. cm.
Includes bibliographical references and index.
Contents: v. 1. The ancient world / Gregory S. Aldrete, volume editor; v. 2. The medieval world / Joyce E. Salisbury, volume editor; v. 3. 15th and 16th centuries / Lawrence Morris, volume editor; v. 4. 17th and 18th centuries / Peter Seelig, volume editor; v. 5. 19th century / Andrew E. Kersten, volume editor; v. 6. The modern world / Andrew E. Kersten, volume editor.
ISBN 0–313–32541–3 (set: alk. paper) — ISBN 0–313–32542–1 (v. 1: alk. paper) — ISBN 0–313–32543–X (v. 2: alk. paper) — ISBN 0–313–32544–8 (v. 3: alk. paper) — ISBN 0–313–32545–6 (v. 4: alk. paper) — ISBN 0–313–32546–4 (v. 5: alk. paper) — ISBN 0–313–32547–2 (v. 6: alk. paper)
1. Manners and customs—History—Encyclopedias. I. Salisbury, Joyce E.
GT31.G74 2004
390—dc21 2003054724

British Library Cataloguing in Publication Data is available.

An online version of *The Greenwood Encyclopedia of Daily Life* is available from Greenwood Press, an imprint of Greenwood Publishing Group, Inc. at: http://dailylife.greenwood.com (ISBN 0–313–01311–X).

Library of Congress Catalog Card Number: 2003054724
ISBN: 0–313–32541–3 (set)
0–313–32542–1 (vol. 1)
0–313–32543–X (vol. 2)
0–313–32544–8 (vol. 3)
0–313–32545–6 (vol. 4)
0–313–32546–4 (vol. 5)
0–313–32547–2 (vol. 6)

First published in 2004

Greenwood Press, 88 Post Road West, Westport, CT 06881
An imprint of Greenwood Publishing Group, Inc.
www.greenwood.com

Printed in the United States of America

The paper used in this book complies with the Permanent Paper Standard issued by the National Information Standards Organization (Z39.48–1984).

10 9 8 7 6 5 4 3 2

Everyday life consists of the little things one hardly notices in time and space. . . . Through the details, a society stands revealed. The ways people eat, dress, or lodge at the different levels of that society are never a matter of indifference.

~Fernand Braudel, *The Structures of Everyday Life* (New York: Harper and Row, 1979), 29.

ADVISORY BOARD

CONTENTS

TOUR GUIDE: A PREFACE FOR USERS

What did people, from the most ancient times to the most recent, eat, wear, and use? What did they hope, invent, and sing? What did they love, fear, or hate? These are the kinds of questions that anyone interested in history has to ask. We spend our lives preoccupied with food, shelter, families, neighbors, work, and play. Our activities rarely make the headlines. But it is by looking at people's everyday lives that we can truly understand history and how people lived. *The Greenwood Encyclopedia of Daily Life* brings into focus the vast majority of human beings whose existence is neglected by the standard reference works. Here you will meet the anonymous men and women of the past going about their everyday tasks and in the process creating the world that we know.

Organization and Content

The Greenwood Encyclopedia of Daily Life is designed for general readers without a background in the subject. Articles are accessible, engaging, and filled with information yet short enough to be read at one sitting. Each volume provides a general historical introduction and a chronology to give background to the articles. This is a reference work for the 21st century. Rather than taking a mechanical alphabetical approach, the encyclopedia tries something rather more elegant: it arranges material thematically, cascading from broad surveys down to narrower slices of information. Users are guided through this enormous amount of information not just by running heads on every page but also by "concept compasses" that appear in the margins: these are adapted from "concept mapping," a technique borrowed from online research methods. Readers can focus on a subject in depth, study it comparatively through time or across the globe, or find it synthesized in a way that provides an overarching viewpoint that draws connections among related areas—and they can do so in any order they choose. School curricula have been organizing research materials in this fashion for some time, so this encyclopedia will fit neatly into a modern pedagogical framework. We believe that this approach breaks new ground in the structuring of reference material. Here's how it works.

Level 1. The six volumes of the encyclopedia are, naturally, arranged by time period: the ancient world, the medieval world, 15th and 16th centuries, 17th and 18th centuries, the 19th century, and the modern world.

Level 2. Within each volume, information is arranged in seven broad categories, as shown in this concept compass:

Level 3. Each of the introductory essays is followed by shorter articles on components of the subject. For example, "Material Life" includes sections on everything from the food we eat to the clothes we wear to the homes in which we live. Once again, each category is mapped conceptually so that readers can see the full range of items that make up "Material Life" and choose which ones they want to explore at any time. Each volume has slightly different categories at this level to reflect the period under discussion. For example, "eunuchs" appear under "Domestic Life" in volume 2 because they served a central role in many cultures at that time, but they disappear in subsequent volumes as they no longer served an important role in some households. Here is one example of the arrangement of the concepts at this level (drawn from the "Domestic Life" section of volume 1):

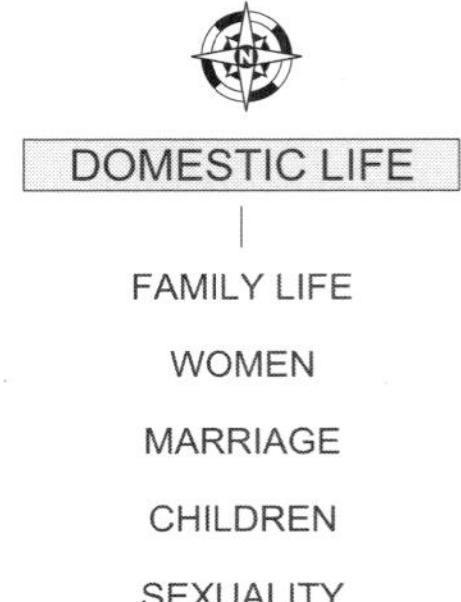

Level 4. These conceptual categories are further subdivided into articles focusing on a variety of representative cultures around the world. For example, here users can read about "Children" in Egypt, Greece, medieval Europe, and 16th-century Latin America. Here is an example of a concept compass representing the entry on money in Ancient India:

The articles at each level can stand alone, but they all also offer integrated information. For example, readers interested in food in ancient Rome can focus right in on that information. If curious, they can look at the next conceptual level and learn how Roman food compares with that of other cultures at the same time, or they can see how food fits into material life in general by looking at the highest conceptual level. Readers may also decide to compare ancient Roman food with menus in Italy during the Renaissance; they need only follow the same process in another volume. Readers can begin at any of the levels and follow their interests in all directions: knowledge is linked conceptually in these volumes, as it is in life. The idea is to make it easy and fun to travel through time and across cultures.

This organization offers a number of advantages. Many reference works provide disparate bits of information, leaving it to the reader to make connections among them. More advanced reference tools assume that readers already have the details and include articles only on larger conceptual issues. *The Greenwood Encyclopedia of Daily Life* assumes no previous knowledge but recognizes that readers at all stages benefit from integrated analysis. The concept-mapping organization allows users to see both the details of the trees and the overall shape of the forest. To make finding information even easier, a cumulative subject index to the entire encyclopedia appears at the end of each volume. With the help of detailed running heads, concept compasses, and an index, anyone taking this "Tour through History" will find it almost impossible to get lost.

This encyclopedia is the work of many contributors. With the help of advisory boards, specialists in daily life around the world wrote the detailed articles in the "level 4" concept category. Many of these experts have published books in Greenwood's award-winning "Daily Life through History" series, and their contributions were crafted from those books. Each volume's editor wrote all of the many higher-level conceptual articles that draw connections across the topics, thus providing a consistent voice and analysis throughout the volume.

Coverage

The chronological coverage of this encyclopedia is consistent with the traditional organization of history as it is taught: the six volumes each take on one of the standard periods. But in reality, history is messy, and any strictly chronological organization has flaws. Some societies span centuries with little change, whereas others change rapidly (usually because of cross-cultural interactions). We have addressed these questions of change and continuity in two ways. Sometimes, we introduce cultures in one volume, such as the Australian Aborigines in volume 1, and then we do not mention them again until they were transformed by colonial contact in volume 4. In these entries, readers are led by cross-references to follow the story of the Australian indigenous peoples from one volume to another. At other times, cultures have experienced enough change for us to introduce many new entries. For example, volume 5, devoted to the 19th century, includes many entries on Muslim lands. But some aspects of the 19th-century Muslim world (e.g., education) had long remained largely unchanged, and in these instances readers are led by cross-references to entries in earlier volumes. This network of cross-references highlights connections and introduces users to the complexities of change and continuity that form the pattern of the social fabric.

We also depart from the chronological constraints of each volume when describing cultures that left few written records. Borrowing from anthropological methods, we sometimes (cautiously) use evidence from later periods to fill in our understanding of earlier lives. For example, colonial observers have at times informed our description of earlier indigenous cultures in many parts of the world.

The geographic scope of this encyclopedia reflects the relatively recent recognition that culture has always operated in a global context. In the Stone Age, bloodstone from Rhum, an inaccessible island off the stormy coast of Scotland, was traded throughout Europe. Domesticated plants and animals from Mesopotamia spread to Africa through Nubia in the third millennium B.C.E., and throughout the ancient world the trade between China and the Mediterranean was an essential part of life. Global history is woven throughout these volumes.

We do not attempt to document every one of the thousands of societies that have arisen throughout history and around the world. Our aim—to provide a general reference source on everyday life—has led to a careful focus on the most studied and representative cultures of each period. For example, ancient India is introduced in volume 1 and then reappears in the complexities of a global society in volumes 5 and 6. Nubia, the path from Egypt to sub-Saharan Africa, is introduced in volume 1, but the range of African cultures is addressed in depth in volume 4 and again in volume 6. Muslim cultures are introduced in volume 2 with the birth of the Prophet, reappearing in volume 3 with the invigorated society of the Turks and then again in volumes 5 and 6 with modern Muslim states. This approach draws from archaeological methods: we are taking deep samples of cultures at various points in time. The overall picture derived from these samples offers a global perspective that is rich and comprehensive. We have covered every area of the world from Australia and the South Pacific to Viking Scandinavia, from indigenous cultures to colonial ones, from age-old Chinese civilization to the modern United States.

Another issue is that of diversity within some dizzyingly complex regions. Africa, China, Polynesia, and India, for example, all contain many cultures and peoples whose daily life is strikingly diverse. Rather than attempt exhaustiveness, we indicate the range of diversity within each entry itself. For instance, the many entries on Africa in volume 4 recognize that each society—Yoruba, Swahili, Shona, and all the others—is unique, and each entry focuses on the cultures that best represent trends in the region as a whole.

The United States is yet another complex region. It grew from its inception with a mingling of European, Native American, African, and other cultural groups. Instead of treating each individually, we combine them all within the entries on the United States. For example, as volume 4 discusses Colonial New England, it weaves a description of Native American life within the entries showing the full range of social interaction between native peoples and colonists. This organization recognizes the reality that all these groups grew together to become the United States.

Features

This work has been designed by educators, and pedagogical tools help readers get the most out of the material. In addition to the reader-friendly organization already described, we have added the following special features:

- *Concept compasses*. Each section of each volume contains a concept compass that visually details the contents of that section. Readers are immediately able to see what topics are covered and can decide which ones they want to explore.
- *Illustrations*. The illustrations drawn from primary sources are in themselves historical evidence and are not mere ornament. Each shows some aspect of daily life discussed in the text, and the captions tell what the picture illuminates and what readers can see in it.
- *Maps*. Maps give readers the necessary geographic orientation for the text. They have been chosen to reinforce the global perspective of the encyclopedia, and readers are consistently offered the view of the parts of the world under discussion.
- *Chronologies*. In addition to geography, students can quickly lose track of the chronology of events. Each volume offers a list of the major events of the periods and of the cultures covered in the volumes. These chronologies serve as a quick reference that supplements the historical introduction.
- *Snapshots*. The fascinating details of the past engage our curiosity. Each volume is scattered with boxed features that highlight such evidence of past life as a recipe, a song, a prayer, an anecdote, or a statistic. These bits of information enhance the main entries; readers can begin with the snapshot and move to more in-depth knowledge or end with the details that are often designed to bring a smile or a shocked insight.
- *Cross-references*. Traditional brief references point readers to related entries in other volumes, highlighting the changes in daily life over time. Other "See" references replace entries and show readers where to find the information they seek within the volume.
- *Primary documents*. The encyclopedia entries are written to engage readers, but nothing brings the past to life like a primary source. Each volume offers a selection of documents that illustrate the kinds of information that historians use to re-create daily life. Sources range widely, from the unforgettable description of Vikings blowing their noses in a water basin before they wash their faces in it to a ration book issued by the United States government during World War II.

- *Bibliography*. Most entries are followed by a section called "For More Information." These sections include recommended readings, as one might expect in a bibliographic attachment, but they often provide much more. For this media age, the authors recommend Web sites, films, educational videos, and other resources.
- *Index*. Even in the 21st century, a comprehensive index is essential. Concept compasses lead readers from one topic to the next, but an index draws connections among more disparate entries: for example, the history of the use of wine or cotton can be traced across many volumes and cultures. A cumulative index appears in each volume to allow fast and easy navigation.

The Greenwood Encyclopedia of Daily Life: A Tour through History from Ancient Times to the Present has been a labor of love. At the end of the day, we hope that readers will be informed and entertained. But we also hope that they will come to a renewed appreciation of an often-spoken but seldom-felt reality: at the most basic level all humans, across time and space, share concerns, pleasures, and aspirations, but the ways these are expressed are infinite in their range. The six volumes of this encyclopedia reveal both the deep similarities and the fascinating differences among people all over the world. We can participate in our global village more intelligently the more we understand each other's lives. We have also learned that people are shown at their best (and sometimes their worst) in the day-to-day activities that reveal our humanity. We hope readers enjoy taking this tour of people's lives as much as we have enjoyed presenting it.

~Joyce E. Salisbury

1

HISTORICAL OVERVIEW

In 476 C.E., the Roman Empire in the West fell. What was to come next to replace the greatest empire of the ancient world? The short answer is violence and decentralization—a time historians call the Middle Ages, or the medieval world. This period spans the time from about the 5th century C.E. to the 15th century. During the Renaissance in Europe (beginning in the 14th century), some European scholars believed they had introduced a new way to look at themselves and their world. They claimed that this new approach was better than anything that had been seen since the greatness of the Roman Empire; thus they defined what had gone before as the "Middle" or "Dark Ages." Although these scholars may have been rightly proud of their new vision, they were unduly simplistic in rejecting the previous thousand years. In Europe, the Middle Ages were exciting times that spawned great monarchies, new technologies, vibrant trade, religious complexities, and the rising middle class that would create the very Renaissance that rejected this thousand years.

From a global perspective, the "Middle Ages" is an even more artificial division: the Tang dynasty in China represented an organic development from previous ages; the Islamic religious revolution took place, changing the lives of a huge number of people; and indigenous people in Polynesia continued as they had for hundreds of years before. Nevertheless, Renaissance definitions of the Middle Ages have found their way into modern methods of organizing the past, and thus we keep it for this volume.

This introduction offers a brief historical overview of the main political and cultural events of the societies that are included in the present volume. This will provide a background for the entries that follow. At the end of this overview is a chronological list of the major events of the era. This chronology will allow readers to compare the time of events among the various cultures under discussion.

Europe

Medieval Europe is traditionally divided into three parts: the early Middle Ages, the High Middle Ages, and the late (or decline). The early Middle Ages begins about the 5th century C.E., when the Germanic tribes of the north and east invaded the western part of the Christian Roman Empire and established kingdoms in the transformed empire. The main kingdoms included the Anglo-Saxon ones in Britain, the Visigothic in Spain, the Ostrogothic (and later Lombard) in Italy, and the Franks in Gaul (France and southern Germany). All the kingdoms struggled with similar problems: How would they blend the Christian, Roman, and Germanic cultures of their territories? How would they bring order and law to the violent clans that inhabited their lands? How would they establish centralized monarchies with people who were used to decentralized control?

The most successful resolution of all these problems came about in Gaul, in the kingdom of the Franks. The first important Frankish king was Clovis of the Merovingian family. Clovis ruthlessly united many of the clans and recognized the importance of the Catholic Church as a unifying force. He converted to Christianity and began a long-standing alliance between the Franks and the popes in Italy. The Merovingian dynasty lasted 200 years, but during that time real power lay in the hands of the "mayor of the palace"—a sort of prime minister who ran the kingdom in the name of the Merovingian dynasty. By the beginning of the 8th century, one family—the Carolingians—dominated the office of Mayor of the Palace. A new dynasty was in the making.

The most famous of the early Carolingians was Charles Martel (later called "the Hammer" for his military exploits). Charles Martel led the victorious force against the Muslims who had crossed the Pyrenees into the Frankish kingdom in 732. This great victory stopped the Muslim threat to the north, but it also won Charles tentfuls of treasure captured from the retreating Muslims. The Carolingians were well placed to expand their influence. Charles Martel's son, Pepin the Short, received the endorsement of the pope to take the title king of the Franks, and the Carolingian dynasty began.

The greatest of the Carolingians was Charlemagne (Charles the Great). Charlemagne represented the high point of the early Middle Ages. He conquered neighboring tribes and united all of northern Europe into an empire. He was crowned emperor of the Franks in Rome, which once again established an emperor in the west and created a precedent of a Holy Roman Emperor that would last until World War I. He fostered learning to such a degree that his reign has been called the "Carolingian Renaissance." It appeared that all the problems created by the early Germanic invasions had been resolved and that Europe was unified. However, this was not to last.

Charlemagne's grandsons engaged in civil war and ended up dividing the great empire into three kingdoms: roughly, France, Germany, and Italy. Furthermore, the kingdoms confronted pressure from new invaders: Muslims from the south attacked coastal areas; Magyars (Hungarians) from the east swept into the European plains, and most serious, Scandinavian Vikings from the north raided and established their own kingdoms in England, Normandy in France, Sicily, and Russia. Decentralization and violence once again descended on northern Europe.

The year 1000 saw the beginnings of order and prosperity return to Europe. The pagan Vikings had converted to Christianity and settled down, and kings began to

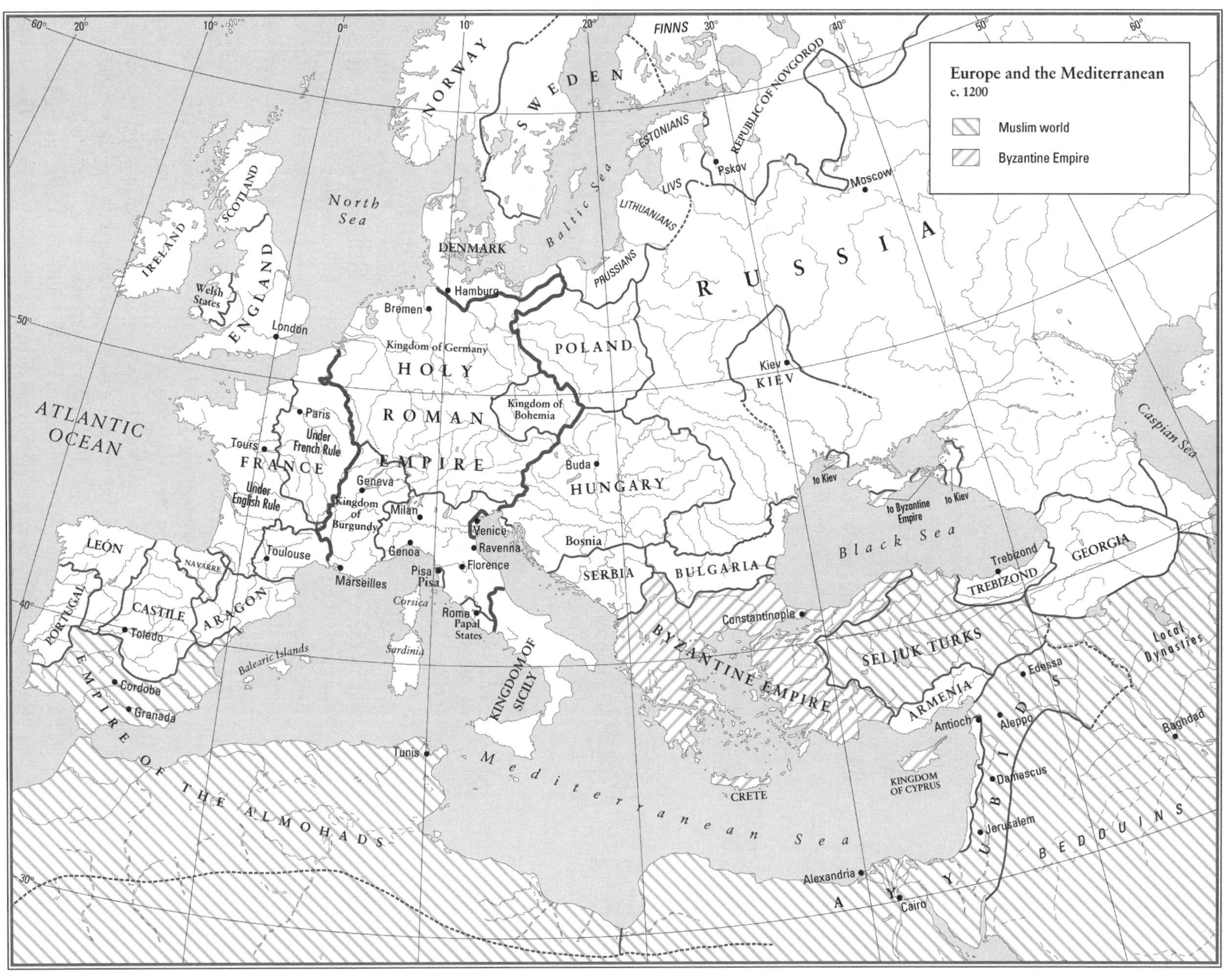
Europe and the Mediterranean
c. 1200
Muslim world
Byzantine Empire
NORWAY
SWEDEN
FINNS
ESTONIANS
LIVS
LITHUANIANS
PRUSSIANS
REPUBLIC OF NOVGOROD
Pskov
Moscow
RUSSIA
Kiev
KIEV
to Kiev
to Byzantine Empire
Caspian Sea
Black Sea
North Sea
Baltic Sea
IRELAND
SCOTLAND
ENGLAND
Welsh States
London
DENMARK
Hamburg
Bremen
Kingdom of Germany
HOLY ROMAN EMPIRE
POLAND
Kingdom of Bohemia
Buda
HUNGARY
Bosnia
SERBIA
BULGARIA
ATLANTIC OCEAN
Paris
Under French Rule
Tours
FRANCE
Under English Rule
Toulouse
Geneva
Kingdom of Burgundy
Milan
Genoa
Venice
Ravenna
Florence
Pisa
Marseilles
Corsica
Sardinia
Rome
Papal States
KINGDOM OF SICILY
LEÓN
NAVARRE
PORTUGAL
CASTILE
Toledo
ARAGON
Balearic Islands
Cordoba
Granada
EMPIRE OF THE ALMOHADS
Tunis
Mediterranean Sea
Constantinople
BYZANTINE EMPIRE
CRETE
Trebizond
TREBIZOND
GEORGIA
SELJUK TURKS
ARMENIA
Edessa
Antioch
Aleppo
Damascus
Jerusalem
KINGDOM OF CYPRUS
Alexandria
Cairo
AYYUBIDS
BEDOUINS
Baghdad
Local Dynasties

restore order to their kingdoms. Perhaps most important, technological innovations such as water mills, exploitation of new iron mines, efficient horse collars, and agricultural innovations allowed for an increase in population that freed people from subsistence farming. Europe in the year 1000 was poised to expand in many ways, and it certainly did.

Trade networks expanded, and cities grew larger and more prosperous. Urban life developed structures such as guilds and city communes to conduct their business, and increasingly, the wealth of the middle class began to be felt in society as a whole. In England, for example, by the 13th century, merchants sat in Parliament to advise the king, and the roots of participatory government were established. King John of England was forced to sign the Magna Carta in 1215 as a guarantee that kings were not above the law, and this important document formed one of the pillars of modern legal theory.

The church grew more centralized, and the popes claimed a universal sovereignty over Christian Europe. Crusaders pushed back Islam in Spain and the Holy Land as Western armies established Crusader states in Jerusalem and the surrounding territories. Kings such as Richard the Lion-Hearted from England and Frederick Barbarossa of Germany and Louis IX of France have been long remembered for their battles in the east against Muslim forces led by equally able rulers such as Saladin. Fighting religious orders such as the Knights Templars rose to protect pilgrims traveling to the Holy Land, and they became powerful bankers as well.

Western Europeans expanded intellectually as well. Universities grew up in the large cities, and philosophers and theologians made dramatic intellectual accomplishments especially after the acquisition of Muslim and Jewish commentators of classical texts such as those of Aristotle. Scholars such as Thomas Aquinas forwarded the search for systems to understand everything from God to the physical world.

This golden age of medieval life lasted about two hundred years; by the beginning of the 14th century, however, a series of disasters occurred that transformed the medieval order. First, bad weather triggered a series of famine years beginning in 1315. Then the weakened population was buffeted by the bubonic plague that spread from Mongol China through western Europe, destroying between one-third and one-half of the population. People's faith in a unified Christendom under one pope was shattered when the Great Schism (split) turned a contested election of popes into two popes reigning, each condemning the followers of the other. Late in the 14th century, the social order itself was overturned when violent peasant revolts broke out in England, France, and Spain.

Even the military order of the Middle Ages—dominated by armored knights and walled castles—broke down in the 14th century. The Hundred Years' War between England and France revealed the weaknesses of the medieval military order. Mounted knights were defeated by new weapons—English longbows, Swiss pikes, and at the end of the century, gunpowder—and generals saw the benefits of hiring mercenary soldiers instead of relying on their noble armies of knights. The Hundred Years' War ended in 1453—appropriately, the same year that cannons broke through the walls of Constantinople, bringing down the Byzantine Empire. The Middle Ages in Europe ended, and out of the destruction, a new order was ready to appear.

FOR MORE INFORMATION

Butt, J. J. *Daily Life in the Age of Charlemagne*. Westport, Conn.: Greenwood Press, 2002.

Rily-Smith, J., ed. *The Oxford Illustrated History of the Crusades*. New York: Cambridge University Press, 1995.

Tuchman, B. W. *A Distant Mirror: The Calamitous Fourteenth Century*. New York: Ballantine Books, 1987.

Whitelock, D., ed. *English Historical Documents, c. 500–1042*. London: Eyre and Spottiswoode, 1955.

Vikings

In 793 C.E., Alcuin, a scholar in Charlemagne's court school recorded an unexpected and ferocious raid on the church and monastery on the tiny island of Lindisfarne off the northern coast of England. He wrote that "never before has such terror appeared in Britain as we have now suffered from a pagan race, nor was it thought that such an inroad from the sea could be made" (Whitelock, 776). Alcuin was right; something new had appeared on the European scene. Northern Europeans from the Scandinavian regions—Danes, Norwegians, and Swedes—began systematically to travel from their homeland in ships that were technologically superior to anything else at the time. They traveled, traded, raided, and plundered with a ferocity that reportedly led people throughout Europe to pray, "From the fury of the Northmen, O Lord, deliver us" (www.ancientsites.com).

In the three centuries that followed, Scandinavians crisscrossed half the world in their longships. In the East, they navigated down the great rivers of Russia to the Caspian and Black Sea and even to the borders of China. In the West, they sailed along the Atlantic coasts, past Muslim Spain, through the Strait of Gibraltar and over the Mediterranean. Unlike southern sailors who hugged the coasts, intrepid Scandinavians sailed out across the Atlantic to settle Iceland, Greenland, and North America. This period of Scandinavian expansion from about the 9th century through the 11th century is known as the Viking Age. After the 11th century, Vikings settle down and become part of the tapestry of European society.

Present-day Scandinavians tend to look upon the Viking Age as a golden age, when the three Scandinavian kingdoms—Denmark, Norway, and Sweden—took shape, towns were established, trade routes were organized, Christianity was introduced, and new lands were discovered. Whereas the ancient texts emphasize the Viking violence, modern scholars emphasize their achievements in fields such as government, law, and culture, as well as their technological skills and their contribution to the knowledge of geography and navigation.

The most important impact of the Vikings lay in their settlements. About 830, Vikings known as the Rus staked out settlements in the region that would become Russia (probably named after the intrepid Rus). They founded trading cities in Novgorod and Kiev, from which their influence was felt throughout the East. By 866, a Danish army had landed in eastern England and established a permanent settlement.

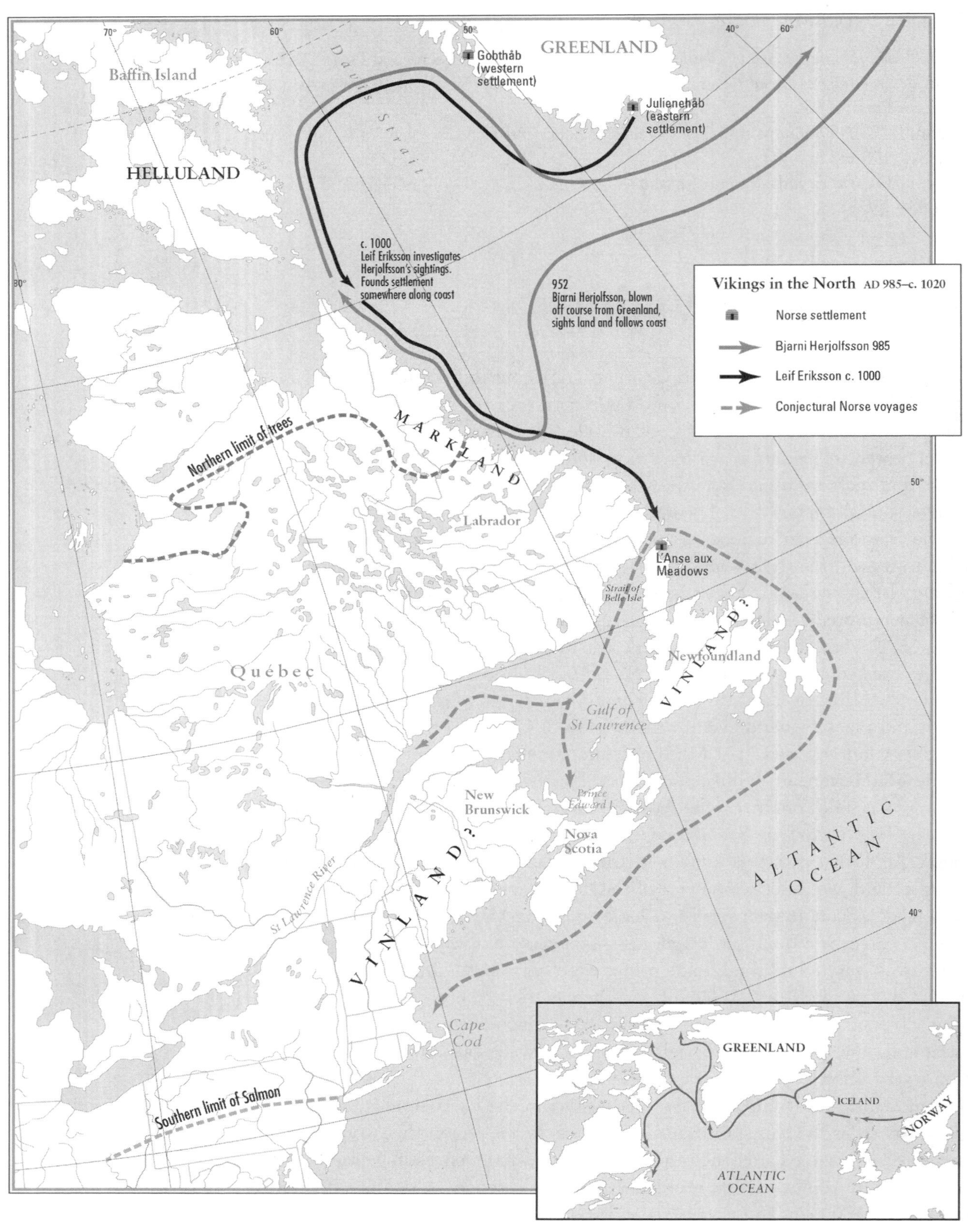

Vikings in the North AD 985–c. 1020
Norse settlement
Bjarni Herjolfsson 985
Leif Eriksson c. 1000
Conjectural Norse voyages
GREENLAND
Gobthåb (western settlement)
Julienehåb (eastern settlement)
Baffin Island
HELLULAND
Davis Strait
c. 1000 Leif Eriksson investigates Herjolfsson's sightings. Founds settlement somewhere along coast
952 Bjarni Herjolfsson, blown off course from Greenland, sights land and follows coast
MARKLAND
Northern limit of trees
Labrador
L'Anse aux Meadows
Strait of Belle Isle
Newfoundland
VINLAND?
Québec
Gulf of St Lawrence
New Brunswick
Prince Edward I.
Nova Scotia
St Lawrence River
VINLAND?
ATLANTIC OCEAN
Cape Cod
Southern limit of Salmon
GREENLAND
ICELAND
NORWAY
ATLANTIC OCEAN

On the continent, the Viking Rollo secured from the French king the territory that would come to be called Normandy (from the name Northmen). In the 9th century, Vikings settled Iceland and later, Greenland. Iceland continues to be a vibrant Scandinavian country today, whereas the Scandinavian impact on Greenland and North America ended with difficulties of sailing to those remote regions.

In the 11th century, the violence at last spent itself. The traditional Scandinavian farming and trading life was easier to conduct in peace than in war. The Scandinavians also eventually converted to Christianity, thus becoming fully integrated into Christian Europe. King Olaf Sigurdson converted the Norwegians by force of arms and his own charisma in the early 11th century; Leif Erikson introduced Christianity to Iceland and Greenland about the same time. Canute, who ruled England, Denmark, and Norway in 1016, converted to Christianity and brought priests from England to complete the conversion of the Northmen.

The Vikings may have settled down by the 11th century, but the centralization that had been established by Charlemagne unraveled. In the wake of the violence, people bound themselves to local lords, and the medieval European feudal system was entrenched.

FOR MORE INFORMATION

NOVA. "The Vikings." <http://www.pbs.org/wgbh/nova/vikings/>.

China

The Sui dynasty (581–618) unified China after nearly four centuries of division. Despite that monumental achievement, the second ruler of the Sui squandered the state's resources, human and material, on three disastrous campaigns of conquest against northern Korea in 612, 613, and 614. Those debacles caused widespread disaffection and rebellions throughout northern China. In the face of mounting insurrections, the Sui court fled south to Yangzhou. After the emperor abandoned his capital Luoyang in the north, one of his commanders, Li Yuan—the duke of Tang, known posthumously as Gaozu—rose in revolt. Li led his armies out of his base at Taiyuan and marched southwest to seize the western capital, a feat that he accomplished in late 617.

On June 18, 618, Gaozu assumed the throne, adopted the name Tang as the title of his new dynasty, and changed the name of the western capital to Changan. His declaration of sovereignty was audacious and premature because he had not yet subjugated other anti-Sui contenders for power or conquered all of China. Not until 624 did Tang forces defeat his last major rivals. Soon after assuming the throne, Gaozu set to work restoring the imperial government that he had inherited from the Sui. At the apex of it were the chief ministers, the most powerful bureaucrats in the country. They served on a council responsible for making policy decisions.

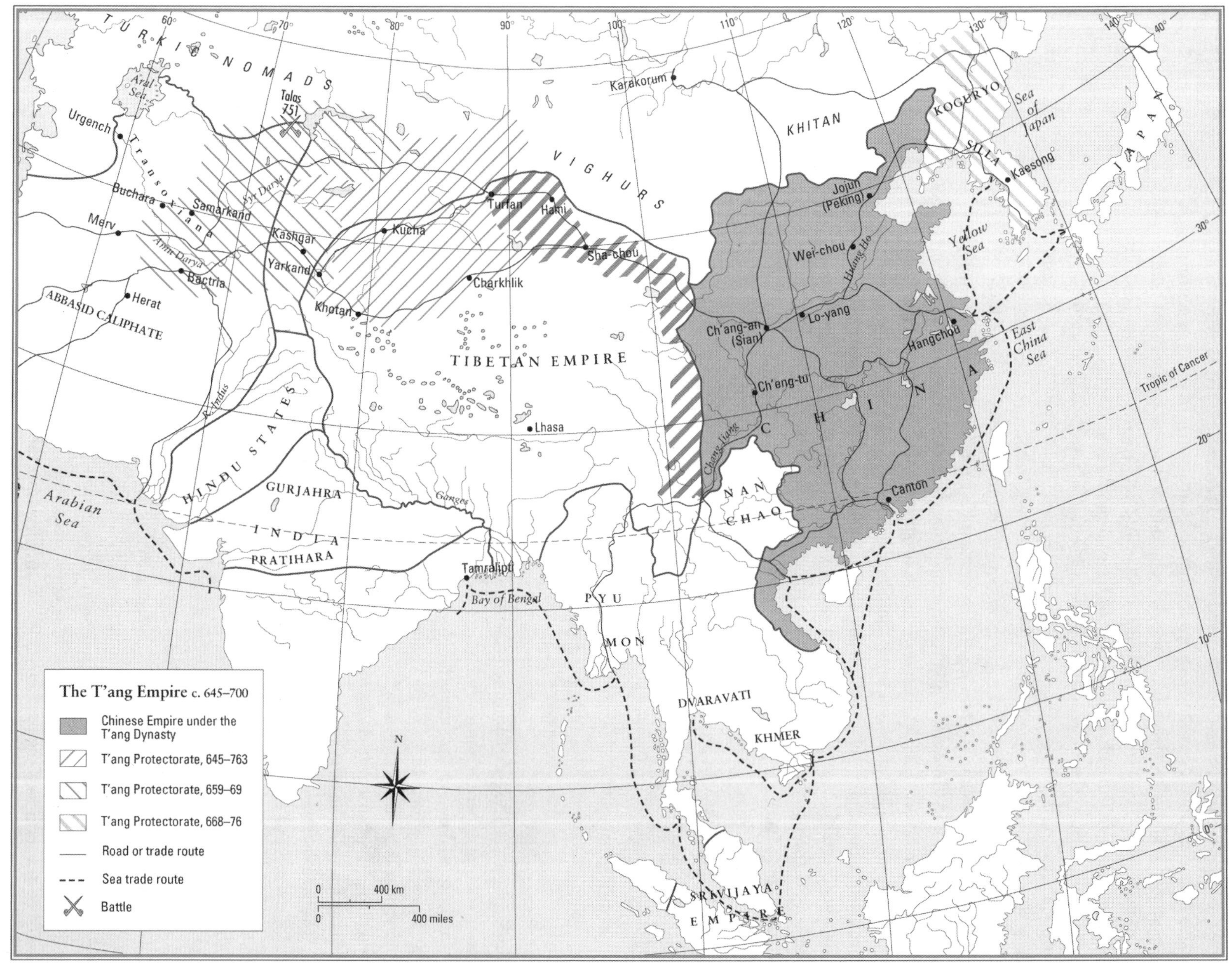
The T'ang Empire c. 645–700
Chinese Empire under the T'ang Dynasty
T'ang Protectorate, 645–763
T'ang Protectorate, 659–69
T'ang Protectorate, 668–76
Road or trade route
Sea trade route
Battle
0 400 km
0 400 miles
N
TURKIC NOMADS
Aral Sea
Urgench
Transoxiana
Bukhara
Samarkand
Merv
Amu Darya
Syr Darya
Bactria
Herat
ABBASID CALIPHATE
Talas 751
Kashgar
Yarkand
Khotan
Kucha
Turfan
Hami
Sha-chou
Charkhlik
VIGHURS
Karakorum
KHITAN
TIBETAN EMPIRE
Lhasa
R. Indus
HINDU STATES
GURJAHRA
INDIA
PRATIHARA
Ganges
Tamralipti
Bay of Bengal
Arabian Sea
PYU
MON
DVARAVATI
KHMER
SRIVIJAYA EMPIRE
NAN CHAO
CHINA
Ch'ang-an (Sian)
Ch'eng-tu
Lo-yang
Wei-chou
Huang Ho
Chang Jiang
Jojun (Peking)
Hangchou
Canton
KOGURYO
SILLA
Kaesong
Sea of Japan
JAPAN
Yellow Sea
East China Sea
Tropic of Cancer
60°
70°
80°
90°
100°
110°
120°
130°
140°
40°
30°
20°
10°
0°

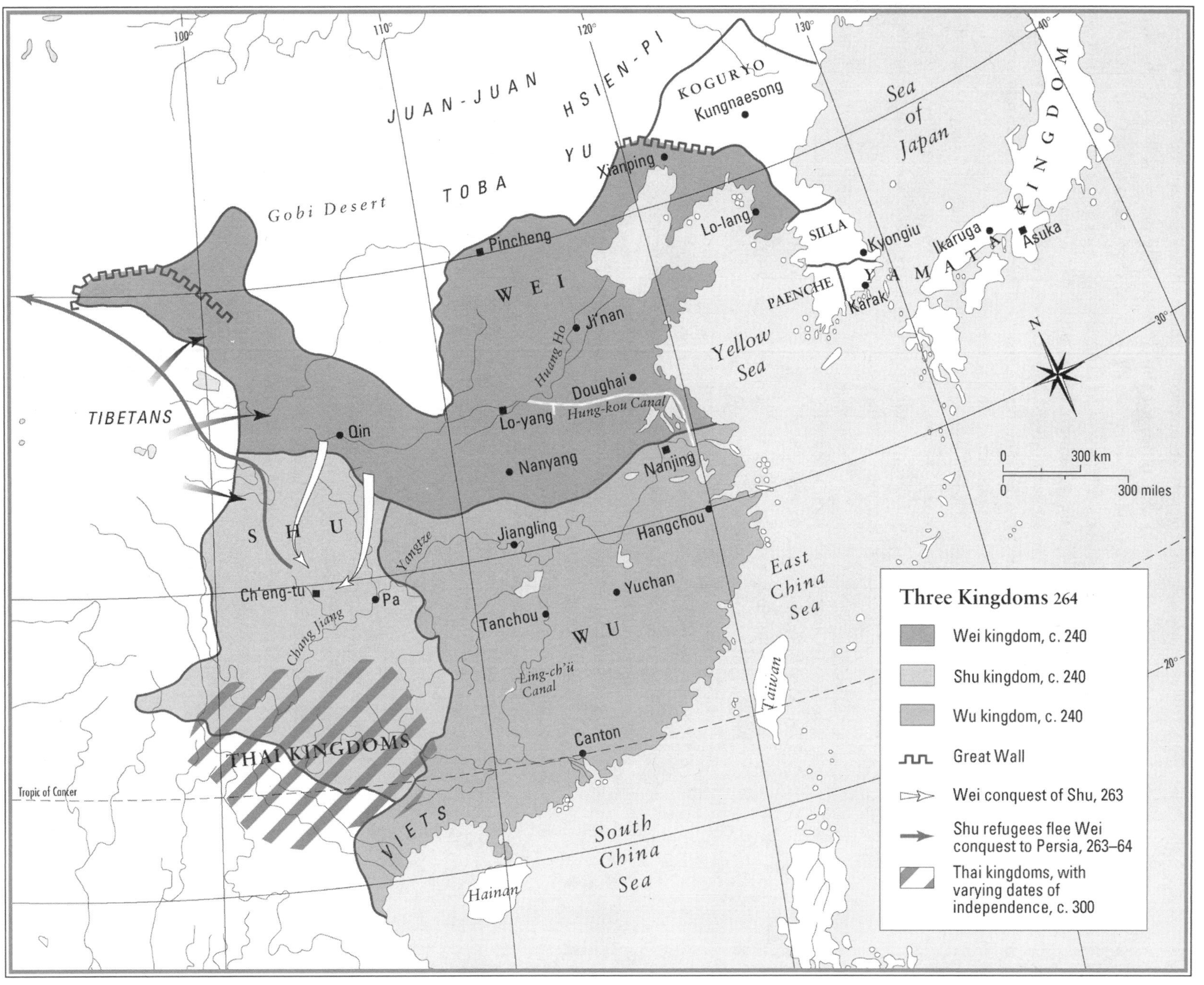
Three Kingdoms 264
Wei kingdom, c. 240
Shu kingdom, c. 240
Wu kingdom, c. 240
Great Wall
Wei conquest of Shu, 263
Shu refugees flee Wei conquest to Persia, 263–64
Thai kingdoms, with varying dates of independence, c. 300
0 300 km
0 300 miles
N
100°
110°
120°
130°
40°
30°
20°
Tropic of Cancer
JUAN-JUAN
HSIEN-PI
YU
TOBA
Gobi Desert
KOGURYO
Kungnaesong
Xianping
Lo-lang
SILLA
PAENCHE
Kyongiu
Karak
YAMATO KINGDOM
Ikaruga
Asuka
Sea of Japan
Yellow Sea
East China Sea
South China Sea
Taiwan
Hainan
WEI
Pincheng
Ji'nan
Huang Ho
Doughai
Hung-kou Canal
Lo-yang
Nanyang
Nanjing
Qin
TIBETANS
SHU
Ch'eng-tu
Pa
Chang Jiang
Yangtze
Jiangling
Hangchou
Yuchan
Tanchou
WU
Ling-ch'ü Canal
Canton
THAI KINGDOMS
VIETS

The sound administration established by the early Tang emperors did not prevent periodic rebellions and difficulties for the dynasty. The period following the death of the third Tang emperor on December 27, 683, was unique in the annals of Chinese history because a remarkable woman, Empress Wu, ruled the empire in her own right. Gaozong, her husband, suffered from a chronic illness, perhaps a stroke, that left him subject to dizziness, paralysis, and impaired vision. He was also weak willed. Taking advantage of the situation, the empress assumed the power behind the throne by 660 and became monarch in reality if not in name. After Gaozong's death, she deposed her eldest son, Zhongzong, and sent him into exile. Then she installed her second son, Ruizong, on the throne and governed for the next six years as a regent, the manner by which women in traditional China took control of the government. In 690, she deposed Ruizong, overthrew the Tang, assumed the throne, and established her own dynasty, the Zhou (690–705). She was the only woman in Chinese history to accomplish such a feat. In 705, Tang loyalists deposed Empress Wu and restored Zhongzong to the throne.

The golden age of the Tang dynasty (712–55) was introduced during the long reign of Illustrious August (Xuanzong), as he was known popularly. Illustrious August's reign was probably the most prosperous age in the Tang for the vast majority of the people. It was a period of low inflation, land reclamation, and an expansion of the canal system that allowed goods to move through the empire more cheaply. Furthermore, the emperor's government efficiently maintained law and order so that there was little banditry. Travel was safe, and trade flourished.

The halcyon age of Illustrious August came to an end with the rebellion of An Lushan. An's father was a Sogdian, an Indo-European people who lived in a kingdom far to the northwest of China, and his mother was a Turk. In the summer of 756, Illustrious August made a disastrous decision. He ordered the imperial forces that occupied a formidable defensive position at a pass on the Yellow River to advance and confront An Lushan's armies. The frontal assault turned into a debacle when the rebel troops ambushed the national armies on July 9. The way to Changan was open, and there was nothing left to defend the city. Consequently, Illustrious August with his heir apparent, Yang Guifei, Chief Minister Yang, and a small escort of troops skulked out of the capital in the predawn hours of July 14. They were captured, and the emperor was forced to abdicate. Although the Tang recovered its capitals in 757 and finally suppressed An Lushan's successors in early 763, the effects of the rebellions were devastating.

The half century following the outbreak of An Lushan's rebellion was a dismal time of great suffering for the dynasty and its subjects. The rebellion wrought destruction throughout northern China. Rebel armies destroyed libraries, stole art treasures, and abducted entertainers—singers, dancers, musicians, and acrobats. Changan and Luoyang suffered repeated lootings and became dangerous places to live from 756 to 786. Mutinies and assassinations occurred frequently in both loyal and separatist armies during those 30 years, and warfare laid waste to many areas of northern China. The latter caused many people, especially peasants, to migrate south, where peace and prosperity prevailed.

In 805, an aggressive and vigorous emperor, Xianzong, ascended the throne. He was bent on reestablishing central control over the recalcitrant autonomous provinces. Xianzong conducted seven major military campaigns against the autonomous, recalcitrant provinces between 806 and 819 and managed to reassert imperial authority over all but two of them. That meant that the throne recovered its powers to appoint military governors (that is, hereditary succession came to an end) as well as local officials in those areas. Xianzong's successors, unfortunately, proved less capable than he. The first two spent much of their time indulging in hunting, polo, and other forms of diversion. The third was frugal and more serious. He enjoyed reading and studying. However, neither he nor his predecessors could control the eunuchs or instill awe in the most powerful mandarins at the capital. The eunuchs held enormous sway over the emperor in the palace, while the mandarins led factions that caused strife in the bureaucracy.

The final decline of the Tang dynasty began when a large-scale rebellion broke out in a region southeast of the Yangtze River between 859 and 860. The government quickly suppressed it, but the revolt was the outcome of disaffections that had been growing for years in the south. Half of the rebels, who numbered more than 30,000 at one time, were peasants who had abandoned their lands because of oppressive taxation and had turned to banditry for their survival. The dynasty was losing the support of the region that had been staunchly loyal since the An Lushan rebellion and had been the major source of its revenue. It was precisely in the region between the Yellow and Yangtze Rivers that the rebellion that broke the back of the Tang originated.

In 878, Huang Chao, who excelled in swordsmanship and mounted archery, took command of an army of insurgents and, in the face of stronger imperial forces, decided to head south—pillaging, burning, and slaughtering as he went. In 879, he took Canton, the great entrepôt of overseas trade, and slaughtered most of its 200,000 inhabitants. In late 880, Luoyang fell to him without a fight. Changan succumbed on January 5, 881. Emperor Xizong and his court fled to Chengdu in modern Sichuan province. Huang declared the establishment of a new dynasty, and the magnificent Tang dynasty was ended.

The Tang dynasty (618–907) is worthy of special treatment because it was the golden age of Chinese culture, at least in the opinion of many later Chinese. They have esteemed two of its poets as the greatest in their history, and an anthology of 300 Tang poems compiled in the 18th century is still the primer for children when they begin their study of verse. One of its painters was regarded as the greatest of all time for centuries after his death, even though few of his works survived the fall of the dynasty. The Tang was also one of the greatest, if not the greatest, periods in the development of music, song, and dance during Chinese history. Its law code, promulgated in 637, remained in force until the Ming dynasty (1368–1644) revised it in 1397. Forty percent of it survived until the fall of the Qing dynasty (1644–1911). It also served as the basis for the law codes of premodern Japan, Korea, and Vietnam. Two new forms of historical compilations emerged during the Tang and became standard genres in later dynasties. The dynasty was the first to compile a national compendium of medicinal substances, a text that was also the first to have illustrations. Both printing, including the first printed illustrations, and gunpowder—developments that profoundly affected the emergence of the modern world—were invented during the period. The Tang was also the golden age of Buddhism. The religion attracted large numbers of adherents, amassed immense wealth, and exerted great influence at court. It also produced the only uniquely Chinese sect of the religion, Chan (Zen). Finally, tea became the national drink during the dynasty (Benn, 1–18).

After the collapse of the Tang dynasty, warlords ruled a decentralized China until the Song dynasty restored centralized rule in the late 10th century. Although it survived for more than three centuries (from 960 to 1279), the Song dynasty was never very powerful. It placed little emphasis on the military and concentrated on civil administration, education, and the arts. The Song survived until the onslaught of the Mongols in the 13th century (see the section on Mongols later in this chapter), but the astonishing achievements of the Tang dynasty continued to influence the world long after the Middle Ages.

FOR MORE INFORMATION

Benn, C. *Daily Life in Traditional China: The Tang Dynasty.* Westport, Conn.: Greenwood Press, 2002.

Medieval China. <http://www.auburn.edu/english/gb/gbsite/china/medieval%20china/medievalchina.html>.

Islamic World

"Islam" is the name of the religion that began in the 7th century C.E. and that has turned into a vibrant world religion; its followers are called Muslims. According to Islamic tradition, Islam began about the year 610 with a revelation from God to Muhammad in the brackish oasis settlement of Mecca in western Arabia. The 40-year-old Muhammad understood his visions to be from the one God, Allah, delivered through the angel Gabriel. Muhammad presented oral recitations of his visionary revelations, and in time his followers wrote down these visions, and they became the Qur'an (Koran)—the holy book of Islam.

Muhammad's prophetic career can be divided into two approximately equal periods. The first took place in his home town of Mecca from about 610 to 622. By 622, he had fallen out of favor with the leaders of Mecca and negotiated a move for himself and his followers to the oasis settlement of Medina some 250 miles to the north. This move from Mecca to Medina in 622 is referred to as his Hijra (*Hegira*) (migration) and is of such importance to his prophetic career that the year 622 of the Gregorian Christian calendar marks the year 1 of the Muslim calendar. Those early Meccan converts who moved to Medina with Muhammad are referred to as *Muhajirum* (emigrants). The people of Medina who embraced Muhammad and his message and who welcomed him to Medina are referred to as *Ansar* (helpers). These

Expansion of Islam
624 – c. 750
Arab advance
Battle (with date)
Under Mohammed's control
Under the Umayyads (661–750)
VISIGOTHIC KINGDOMS
FRANCE
BERBERS
IFRIQIYA
Agadir
Carthage 698
Kairouan 670
Tripoli 647
Mediterranean Sea
Sahara Desert
Tropic of Cancer
LIBYA
EGYPT
Alexandria 646
Fustat 670
Faiyum
Heliopolis 640
Nile
Rhodes 654
Cyprus 649
SLAVS
BYZANTINE EMPIRE
Constantinople 673–7, 717–18
Black Sea
BULGARS
KHAZAR EMPIRE
ALANS
ARMENIA
Tiflis
Derbend
Caspian Sea
Erzurum
AZERBAIJAN
Tabriz
Ardabil
Tarsus
Edessa
Antioch
SYRIA
MESOPOTAMIA
Mosul 641
Euphrates
Damascus 635
capital from 658
Ramla
Yarmuk 636
Fihl
Jerusalem 638
Ajnadain 634
Jalula
Kerbela 680
Baghdad
Ctesiphon
Kufa
Susa
Qadisiya 636
Nehavend 642
Rai
GURGAN
KHURASAN
Nishapur 651
Merv
Herat
Isfahan
SASANIA
PERSIA
Basra 656
FARS
Istakhr 648
KIRMAN
BAHRAIN
Persian Gulf
YAMAMA
Tabuk
HEJAZ
Badr 624
Medina
Mecca 622
ARABIA
Red Sea
Nejran
YEMEN
Aden
HADHRAMAUT
OMAN
Suhar
Muscat
Aral Sea
Syr Darya
Amu Darya
TRANSOXIANA
Bukhara 710
Samarkand 710
Talas 751
FERGHANA
Balkh 664
Kabul 664
SEISTAN
MAKRAN
Arabian Sea
SIND
Indus
PUNJAB
Multan 711
HINDU STATES
INDIAN OCEAN
Dongola
NUBIANS
Soba
ALWA
KINGDOM OF AXUM
N
0°
10°
20°
30°
40°
50°
60°
70°

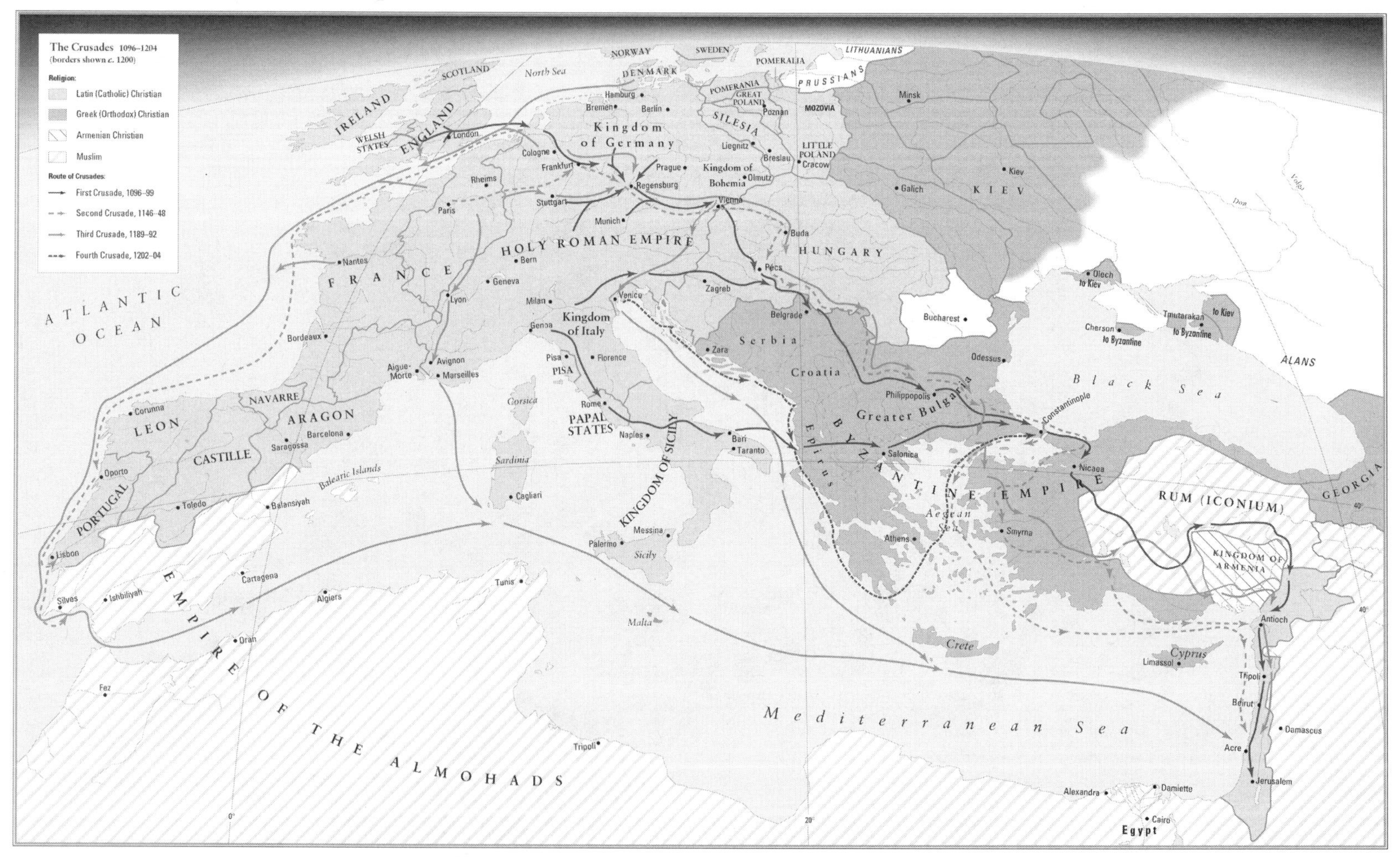

The Crusades 1096–1204
(borders shown c. 1200)
Religion:
Latin (Catholic) Christian
Greek (Orthodox) Christian
Armenian Christian
Muslim
Route of Crusades:
First Crusade, 1096–99
Second Crusade, 1146–48
Third Crusade, 1189–92
Fourth Crusade, 1202–04
ATLANTIC OCEAN
IRELAND
WELSH STATES
ENGLAND
SCOTLAND
London
North Sea
NORWAY
SWEDEN
DENMARK
POMERALIA
LITHUANIANS
PRUSSIANS
POMERANIA
GREAT POLAND
MOZOVIA
SILESIA
LITTLE POLAND
Hamburg
Bremen
Berlin
Poznan
Liegnitz
Breslau
Cracow
Kingdom of Germany
Cologne
Frankfurt
Prague
Kingdom of Bohemia
Olmutz
Regensburg
Rheims
Paris
Stuttgart
Vienna
Munich
Buda
HOLY ROMAN EMPIRE
HUNGARY
Nantes
Bern
Pécs
FRANCE
Lyon
Geneva
Milan
Venice
Zagreb
Kingdom of Italy
Genoa
Belgrade
Bordeaux
Serbia
Croatia
Avignon
Aigue-Morte
Marseilles
Pisa
PISA
Florence
Zara
NAVARRE
ARAGON
Corunna
LEON
Barcelona
Saragossa
CASTILLE
Corsica
Rome
PAPAL STATES
Naples
Bari
Taranto
Oporto
PORTUGAL
Balearic Islands
Sardinia
Cagliari
KINGDOM OF SICILY
Toledo
Balansiyah
Messina
Palermo
Sicily
Lisbon
Silves
Ishbiliyah
Cartagena
Algiers
Tunis
Malta
Oran
EMPIRE OF THE ALMOHADS
Fez
Tripoli
Minsk
Kiev
Galich
KIEV
Don
Volga
Oloch
to Kiev
Bucharest
Chersan
to Byzantine
Tmutarakan
to Kiev
to Byzantine
ALANS
Odessus
Black Sea
Philippopolis
Greater Bulgaria
Constantinople
Epirus
Salonica
Nicaea
BYZANTINE EMPIRE
RUM (ICONIUM)
GEORGIA
Aegean Sea
Athens
Smyrna
KINGDOM OF ARMENIA
Antioch
Crete
Cyprus
Limassol
Tripoli
Beirut
Damascus
Mediterranean Sea
Acre
Jerusalem
Alexandra
Damiette
Cairo
Egypt
0°
20°
40°

two groups and their descendants played major roles in the course of Islamic history both during Muhammad's career in Medina and after his death in 632.

By the time Muhammad died in 632, he had established tributary alliances with a number of the outlying tribes in Arabia. At his death, Muhammad's senior associates (his companions) came to a consensus about a successor to Muhammad and proclaimed his close friend, early convert, and father-in-law—Abu Bakr—as the head of the community, or *caliph* (which means deputy). As such, he enjoyed all of Muhammad's authority save that of prophethood.

Abu Bakr's principal objective during his short reign (632–34) was to subdue a rebellion in Arabia among the tribes who believed that their compacts with Muhammad died with him or who did not think that Abu Bakr was worthy of their allegiance. Abu Bakr and Muhammad's companions obviously disagreed. For them, the tribes' submission to Muhammad during his lifetime was equal to their submission to God; therefore, they did not have the option to secede from the new political and religious community. Hence, the wars to subjugate the Arabic-speaking tribes of the peninsula are referred to as the *Ridda* Wars—or the Wars of Apostasy, although not all of those who were compelled to accept Islam and submit to Muslim political authority were actual apostates. That is, some had never been Muslims nor had they submitted to Muhammad's authority during his lifetime. Within a year, Abu Bakr had forced the clans to recognize the faith of Islam and the rule of the caliph. Then the forces of Islam began to sweep from the boundaries of Arabia.

Between 633 and 651, the Arabian Muslim armies seized Byzantine Syria and Palestine and took most of Mesopotamia. During the 640s, they swept through Byzantine Egypt and North Africa; in 651, they incorporated Persia into their expanding empire; and in 711, they conquered the Hindu kingdom in northwestern India. Between 711 and 718, they crossed the Strait of Gibraltar, conquering most of the Visigothic kingdom of the Iberian Peninsula, and crossed the Pyranees Mountains into the Frankish kingdom.

It seemed as if nothing could stop the onslaught, but in 732, at a battle near Poitiers in west-central France (known as the Battle of Tours), the Muslims were finally defeated by a force of Franks under the command of Charles Martel. Thus, by 732, three great cultures confronted each other around the Mediterranean and beyond: the Germanic kingdoms of western Europe, the Byzantine Empire centered on the great city of Constantinople, and the Muslim world that extended from Spain, through North Africa, and east to India. Medieval society and culture developed through the interactions of these cultures.

As impressive as the spread of Islam was, there were forces of disunity within the faithful. Disagreements over succession led to the emergence of the Shiʿite (Shia) sect (as opposed to the majority Sunni Muslims). The Shiʿite sect began when a group supported Muhammad's cousin and son-in-law, ʿAli, as the first caliph. However, the support for Abu Bakr was stronger, and ʿAli's enemies assassinated ʿAli. Shiʿite Muslims remain a minority today, preserving doctrines and rituals distinct from the Sunnis.

After the assassination of ʿAli, the Umayyad dynasty was established. They were the most prominent of Meccan merchants, and they established a strong, centralized

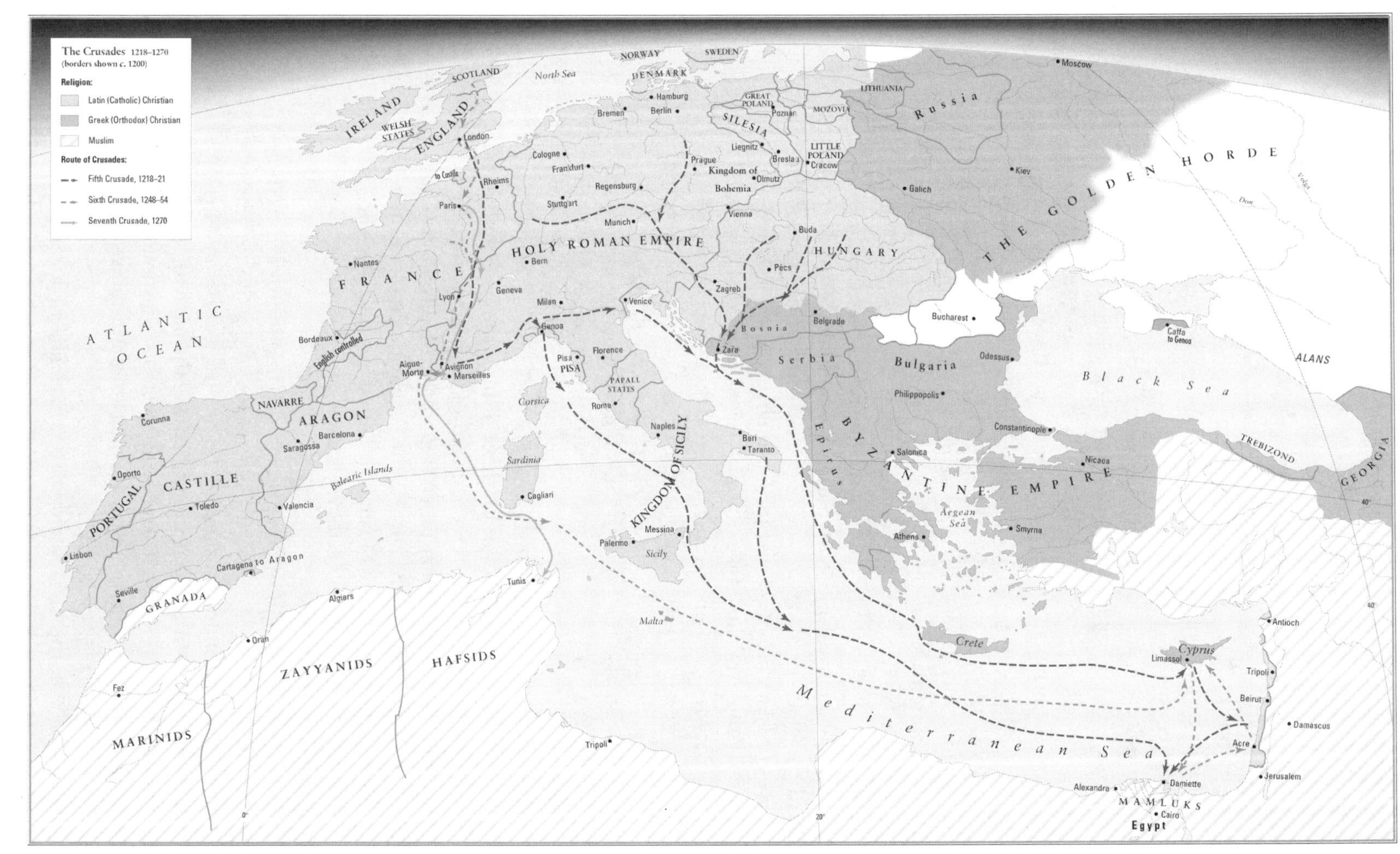

The Crusades 1218–1270
(borders shown c. 1200)
Religion:
Latin (Catholic) Christian
Greek (Orthodox) Christian
Muslim
Route of Crusades:
Fifth Crusade, 1218–21
Sixth Crusade, 1248–54
Seventh Crusade, 1270
ATLANTIC OCEAN
IRELAND
SCOTLAND
WELSH STATES
ENGLAND
London
North Sea
NORWAY
SWEDEN
DENMARK
Hamburg
Bremen
Berlin
GREAT POLAND
Poznan
MOZOVIA
LITHUANIA
SILESIA
Liegnitz
Breslau
LITTLE POLAND
Cracow
Prague
Kingdom of Bohemia
Olmutz
Russia
Moscow
Kiev
Galich
THE GOLDEN HORDE
Volga
Don
to Castile
Rheims
Paris
Cologne
Frankfurt
Regensburg
Stuttgart
Munich
Vienna
Buda
HUNGARY
Pecs
Zagreb
HOLY ROMAN EMPIRE
Bern
Geneva
Nantes
FRANCE
Lyon
Milan
Venice
Bordeaux
English controlled
Aigue-Morte
Avignon
Marseilles
Genoa
Pisa
PISA
Florence
PAPAL STATES
Rome
Corsica
Sardinia
Cagliari
Naples
Bari
Taranto
KINGDOM OF SICILY
Messina
Palermo
Sicily
Malta
Bucharest
Belgrade
Bosnia
Zara
Serbia
Bulgaria
Odessus
Philippopolis
Constantinople
Caffa to Genoa
Black Sea
ALANS
TREBIZOND
GEORGIA
Epirus
BYZANTINE EMPIRE
Salonica
Nicaea
Aegean Sea
Athens
Smyrna
Crete
NAVARRE
ARAGON
Barcelona
Saragossa
Corunna
Oporto
PORTUGAL
CASTILLE
Toledo
Valencia
Balearic Islands
Lisbon
Cartagena to Aragon
Seville
GRANADA
Tunis
Algiers
Oran
ZAYYANIDS
HAFSIDS
Fez
MARINIDS
Tripoli
Mediterranean Sea
Antioch
Cyprus
Limassol
Tripoli
Beirut
Damascus
Acre
Jerusalem
Alexandra
Damiette
MAMLUKS
Cairo
Egypt
0°
20°
40°

rule. They moved their capital to Damascus, which allowed them to maintain communication (and profitable trade) with the far-flung reaches of the empire. The Umayyad's favored an ethnically Arab elite, and in time their luxurious, high-handed policies generated discontent.

In 750, the Umayyad rule was brought to an end by a rebellion in Persia led by Abu al-Abbas, a descendant of Muhammad's uncle. He brought together Sunni and Shi'ite Muslims and introduced the 'Abbasid dynasty. The 'Abbasids encouraged cultural and economic development and in 762 moved the capital to the newly built magnificent city of Baghdad. The high point of the 'Abbasid dynasty came during the reign of Harun al-Rashid, who traded with the Western emperor Charlemagne. Harun was a patron of the arts, and Baghdad was a center of intellectual achievement.

After Harun's Caliphate, the 'Abbasid empire began to decline as a result of civil war among Harun's sons. Provincial governors began to act independently of the caliphs, and by the 860s and 870s many petty states had established themselves under Muslim rulers in North Africa and Spain to the west and in modern-day Iran and lands farther east. Some of these had even declared full autonomy from the 'Abbasid caliphs in Baghdad. By the early 900s, the 'Abbasid caliphs really only ruled in central and southern Iraq.

From 945 onward, the 'Abbasid caliphs remained subordinate to a series of Muslim warlord regimes until 1258, when the invading Mongol armies sacked Baghdad and brought an end to the 'Abbasid Caliphate. Despite the failure of the political ideal of a single community of believers under the universal government of the successors of the Prophet, it was during the 10th to the 15th centuries that we see Islam's capacity to expand, both geographically and in the intellectual, cultural, and economic spheres.

FOR MORE INFORMATION

Ahsan, M. M. *Social Life under the Abbasids*. New York: Longman, 1979.

Inalcik, H. *The Ottoman Empire: The Classical Age, 1300–1600*. Translated by N. Itzkowith and C. Imber. New York: Palgrave Macmillan, 1973.

Lindsay, J. *Daily Life in Medieval Islam*. Westport, Conn.: Greenwood Press, forthcoming.

Peters, F. E. *Muhammad and the Origins of Islam*. Albany, N.Y.: SUNY Press, 1994.

Byzantium

During the late Roman Empire, emperors recognized the strategic and economic advantages of the eastern portion of their empire. In 330 C.E., the emperor Constantine moved his capital from Rome to the old city of Byzantium and renamed it Constantinople. This city became the keystone of the eastern Roman Empire. During the turbulent 5th and 6th centuries, when the western part of the empire fell to Germanic tribes, the eastern empire held firm, in large part because of the fortified

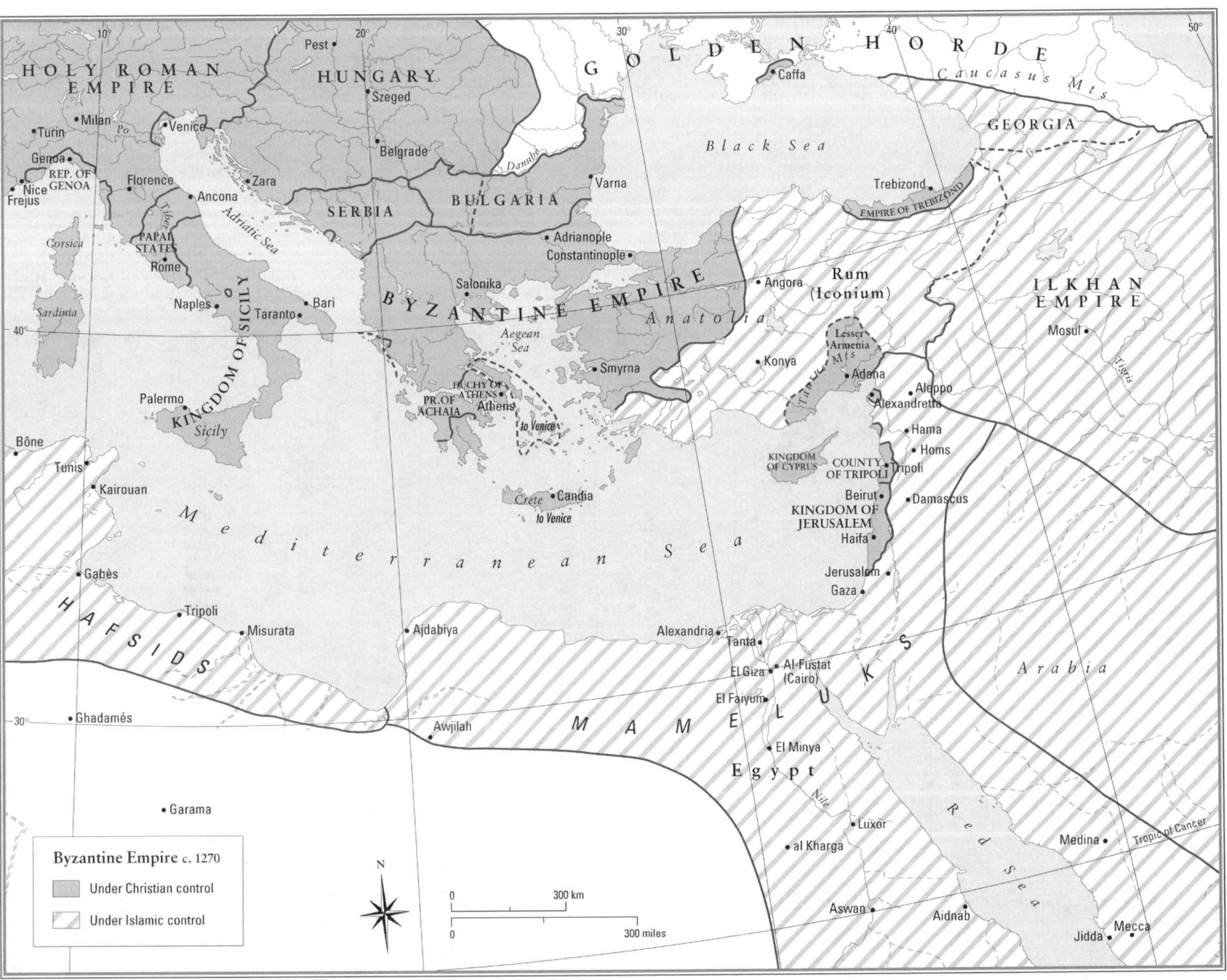

Byzantine Empire c. 1270
Under Christian control
Under Islamic control
HOLY ROMAN EMPIRE
HUNGARY
GOLDEN HORDE
GEORGIA
ILKHAN EMPIRE
SERBIA
BULGARIA
BYZANTINE EMPIRE
KINGDOM OF SICILY
PAPAL STATES
REP. OF GENOA
EMPIRE OF TREBIZOND
Rum (Iconium)
Lesser Armenia
KINGDOM OF CYPRUS
COUNTY OF TRIPOLI
KINGDOM OF JERUSALEM
DUCHY OF ATHENS
PR. OF ACHAIA
HAFSIDS
MAMELUKS
Egypt
Arabia
Anatolia
Black Sea
Mediterranean Sea
Aegean Sea
Adriatic Sea
Red Sea
Caucasus Mts
Taurus Mts
Danube
Tiber
Po
Tigris
Nile
Corsica
Sardinia
Sicily
Crete
to Venice
Tropic of Cancer
Pest
Szeged
Belgrade
Milan
Turin
Venice
Genoa
Nice
Frejus
Florence
Ancona
Zara
Rome
Naples
Taranto
Bari
Palermo
Varna
Adrianople
Constantinople
Salonika
Athens
Smyrna
Candia
Caffa
Trebizond
Angora
Konya
Adana
Aleppo
Alexandretta
Hama
Homs
Tripoli
Beirut
Damascus
Haifa
Jerusalem
Gaza
Mosul
Bône
Tunis
Kairouan
Gabès
Tripoli
Misurata
Ajdabiya
Awjilah
Ghadamés
Garama
Alexandria
Tanta
El Giza
Al-Fustat (Cairo)
El Faiyum
El Minya
Luxor
al Kharga
Aswan
Aidnab
Medina
Jidda
Mecca
N
0
300 km
300 miles
10°
20°
30°
40°
50°

city. In the 5th century, inhabitants of Constantinople watched from the safety of their wall as smoke rose from villages set aflame by the Germanic tribes and Huns surging westward. The wall continued to protect the new capital for almost a thousand years until it was breached by Turkish cannons in 1453. The empire that stood a thousand years after the fall of the western Roman Empire has come to be called the Byzantine Empire—named after the original city that had lured Emperor Constantine.

The rulers of the Byzantine Empire considered themselves the heirs to the Roman Empire, so they continued to rule by Roman law, and indeed, the Emperor Justinian in the 6th century ordered a famous codification of Roman law—the *Corpus Iuris Civilis* (The Body of Civil Law)—compiled. In this form, Roman law survived and was revived in western Europe. The rulers were also Christian, and the emperors took an active role in leading the church through controversies concerning doctrine and policies.

At the same time, the Byzantine Empire took a different direction from the western kingdoms. The emperors and administration began to use Greek as the official language (instead of Latin, as in the west), and this served to split the two sides of the Mediterranean. The two branches of the Christian church also began to separate: Greek became the official language of the Eastern Church, and the emperors continued to exert leadership over the Eastern Church, while popes in the West claimed religious sovereignty. These religious separations led to controversy that finally caused the two branches to split in 1054—from then on the Christian world was split into the Catholic West and the Greek Orthodox East.

In the 7th century, the armies of Islam made serious encroachments into Byzantine territory: The empire lost Syria, the Holy Land, Egypt, and North Africa. From the 7th century onward, the Byzantine Empire faced a constant threat from the armies of Islam in the east and south. Despite the losses to Islam, the 9th-century Byzantine Empire entered into a second "Golden Age." The imperial government was centralized and ordered, trade enriched the courtly coffers, and the Orthodox Church expanded.

On its northern borders, the Byzantine Empire faced tribes of Slavs—Serbs, Croats, Avars, Bulgars, and so on—who had settled there. The Orthodox Church sent missionaries—Cyril and Methodius—north to convert the Slavs, and they were profoundly successful. As part of their missionary work, they created an alphabet based of Greek letters to record the Slavic languages, and this "Cyrillic alphabet" (named after the missionary) remains the alphabet in Russia and many of the other Slavic lands. The cultural influence of the Byzantine Empire had a lasting impact on the modern nations in these lands north of the great city.

As Islam grew stronger in the 11th century, the Byzantine Empire felt more threatened, and the emperors turned to the West for help. Emperor Alexis I Comnenus sent a call for mercenary soldiers, but he got more than he bargained for. This appeal led to the series of crusades that established Western crusader states in the Holy Land and lasted sporadically for 200 years until the Muslims retook the crusader outposts. The Fourth Crusade in 1204 took the city of Constantinople itself, and Western Christians raided and killed their Eastern counterparts. Western crusaders held the city until 1261, when the Byzantine rulers reestablished their reign.

The Byzantine rulers never really recovered from the looting of Constantinople in 1204. Its territory was continually shrinking, and internal disorders regularly interfered with trade and centralized control. Yet Byzantium's great walls and the prestige and intellectual achievements of the Byzantine scholars continued to hold disaster at bay until the 15th century. As the Turks besieged Byzantium, the emperor once again sent to the West for help, but it was too late. Technology finally outstripped the defenses, and Turkish canons breached the wall and Constantinople fell in 1453. The bastion of Greek Orthodoxy had fallen, and the empire became Muslim.

FOR MORE INFORMATION

Byzantium: Byzantine Studies on the Internet. <http://www.fordham.edu/halsall/byzantium/>.
Cavallo, G. *The Byzantines*. Chicago: University of Chicago Press, 1996.
Conte, F. *The Slavs*. New York: Columbia University Press, 1995.

Mongols

The great grasslands of central Asia produced many nomadic peoples, who herded grazing animals (especially sheep and horses, but also cattle, goats, and camels) and moved as their animals thinned the vegetation. They were extremely skilled in living in this difficult land, but they always sought trade with settled peoples, and there was always a brisk trade between the steppes and the agricultural regions. The nomadic peoples were strongly linked to kinship groups, which made it difficult for them to join together into larger social groups. During the early 13th century, however, the Mongols under a brilliant leader changed that and formed the largest empire the world had ever seen.

The Mongols were united by Temüjin, who was born about 1167 to a noble family. Using diplomacy, ruthlessness, and great talent, Temüjin eventually brought all the Mongol tribes into a single confederation. In 1206, an assembly of Mongol leaders proclaimed him "Chinggis (Genghis) Khan," which means "universal ruler," and it is by this title that history remembers this great leader.

Chinggis Khan rearranged the old tribal organization and forced men of fighting age to join new military units loyal only to him. Similarly, he chose his officials for their loyalty rather than because of tribal affiliations, and he established a capital at Karakorum (about 186 miles west of the modern Mongolian capital of Ulaanbaatar). Now a Mongolian state was established with a center that was clearly superior to any clan or tribe.

Once he had united the Mongols, Chinggis Khan turned his formidable army to the settled societies of central Asia. He attacked the peoples in Tibet, northern China, Persia, and the central Asian steppes. The conquest of China began in 1211; by 1215, the Mongols had captured the capital near modern Beijing. Now

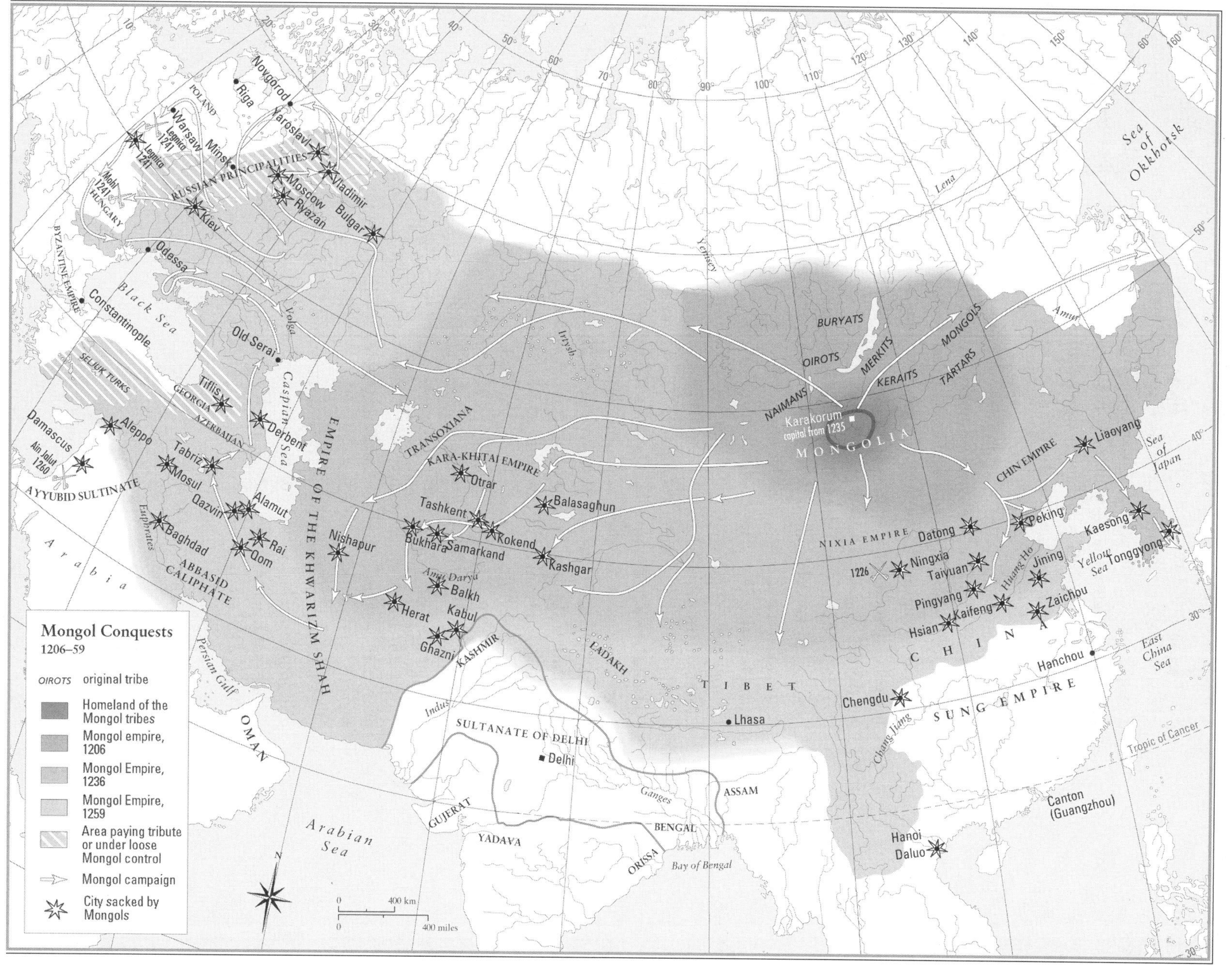

Mongol Conquests
1206–59
OIROTS original tribe
Homeland of the Mongol tribes
Mongol empire, 1206
Mongol Empire, 1236
Mongol Empire, 1259
Area paying tribute or under loose Mongol control
Mongol campaign
City sacked by Mongols
0 400 km
0 400 miles
N
Sea of Okkhotsk
Novgorod
Riga
POLAND
Warsaw
Legnica 1241
Minsk
Yaroslavl
RUSSIAN PRINCIPALITIES
Vladimir
Moscow
Ryazan
Bulgar
Kiev
Mohi 1241
HUNGARY
BYZANTINE EMPIRE
Odessa
Constantinople
Black Sea
Volga
Old Serai
Caspian Sea
SELJUK TURKS
Tiflis
GEORGIA
AZERBAIJAN
Derbent
Damascus
Ain Jalut 1260
Aleppo
AYYUBID SULTINATE
Tabriz
Mosul
Qazvin
Alamut
Rai
Qom
Baghdad
Euphrates
ABBASID CALIPHATE
Arabia
Persian Gulf
OMAN
Arabian Sea
EMPIRE OF THE KHWARIZM SHAH
TRANSOXIANA
KARA-KHITAI EMPIRE
Otrar
Tashkent
Bukhara
Samarkand
Kokend
Balasaghun
Kashgar
Nishapur
Amu Darya
Balkh
Herat
Kabul
Ghazni
KASHMIR
Indus
SULTANATE OF DELHI
Delhi
GUJERAT
YADAVA
ORISSA
BENGAL
Bay of Bengal
Ganges
ASSAM
LADAKH
TIBET
Lhasa
Irtysh
Yenisey
Lena
Amur
BURYATS
OIROTS
MERKITS
MONGOLS
NAIMANS
KERAITS
TARTARS
Karakorum capital from 1235
MONGOLIA
NIXIA EMPIRE
1226
Datong
Ningxia
Taiyuan
Pingyang
Kaifeng
Hsian
CHIN EMPIRE
Liaoyang
Peking
Jining
Huang Ho
Zaichou
Kaesong
Tonggyong
Yellow Sea
Sea of Japan
CHINA
Hanchou
East China Sea
Chengdu
Chang Jiang
SUNG EMPIRE
Tropic of Cancer
Canton (Guangzhou)
Hanoi
Daluo

known as Khanbaliq ("city of the khan"), this became the Mongol capital in China. By the time of his death in 1227, Chinggis Khan had established a vast and mighty empire that extended from China in the east to Persia in the west. Chinggis Khan's death touched off a struggle for power among his sons and grandsons, and eventually they divided his extensive empire into four regional empires. The great khans ruled China—the wealthiest region—and were nominally superior to the other khans, although they were seldom able to exert their authority over the others.

Kublai (or "Khubilai") Khan, one of Chinggis Khan's grandsons, consolidated Mongol rule in China. He not only ruthlessly suppressed his opponents; this talented leader actively sought to improve the lot of his subjects. He promoted Buddhism and gave religious freedom to Daoists, Muslims, and Christians in his land. In 1279, he proclaimed himself emperor and established the Yuan dynasty, which ruled China until its collapse in 1368.

The Mongols in China resisted assimilation to Chinese cultural traditions by staying aloof from their Chinese subjects and outlawing intermarriage between Mongols and Chinese. Kublai encouraged foreign trade and brought administrators from far away: the Mongols' administrative staff included Arabs, Persians, and even Europeans—the Venetian Marco Polo was one of the most famous visitors in the court of the Great Khan.

As Kublai Khan consolidated his hold on east Asia, his cousins and brothers established a firm control on land to the west. Mongols known as the Golden Horde overran Russia between 1237 and 1241. They did not occupy Russia, but they extracted tribute from the Russian cities. The Golden Horde controlled Russia until the mid-15th century, when the princes of Moscow managed to break free.

Kublai's brother Hülegü conquered the Muslim ʿAbbasid empire and established the Mongol il-khanate of Persia. In 1258, he even captured the ʿAbbasid capital of Baghdad. While Kublai worked to keep Mongols aloof from Chinese culture, the Mongols in Persia took a different tact. They allowed the Persians to administer the il-khanate and simply deliver the tax revenues to their new overlords. Over time, the Mongols even assimilated to Persian cultural traditions, and in 1295 Il-khan Ghazan converted to Islam and introduced a large-scale massacre of Christians and Jews.

By the late 13th century, the four powerful khanates began to experience serious difficulties. The il-khanate in Persia suffered severe financial difficulties because of overspending, and factional struggles plagued the leadership. When the last of the Mongol rulers died without an heir in 1335, the il-khanate itself simply dissolved. Local administrators simply took over the government, a state of affairs that lasted until late in the 14th century, when Turkish peoples reintroduced an effective central government.

The Yuan dynasty of China also confronted serious economic problems as well as factional skirmishes. During the 1330s, plague erupted in China that spread throughout China and central Asia (and from there moved to Europe as the Black Death). In the course of the disruption brought by plague and famine, in 1368 rebel forces captured Khanbaliq, and the remaining Mongols returned to the steppes.

The Mongols continued to be a strong presence in central and western Asia, and the great empires they created served to stimulate the imagination of conquerors that would follow.

FOR MORE INFORMATION

Adshead, S.A.M. *Central Asia in World History*. New York: Palgrave Macmillan, 1993.
Morgan, D. *The Mongols*. Oxford: Blackwell, 1986.

Polynesia

The term *Polynesia* refers to a cultural and geographical area in the Pacific Ocean, an area bounded by what is commonly referred to as the Polynesian Triangle—from Hawai'i in the north to New Zealand in the southwest to Easter Island in the southeast. Thousands of islands are scattered throughout this area, most of which are currently included in one of the modern island states of American Samoa, Cook Islands, French Polynesia, Hawai'i, New Zealand, Samoa, Tonga, Tokelau, Tuvalu, and Wallis and Futuna. Some—Easter Island, Nauru, Niue, and Pitcairn, for example—still remain only isolated islands. With the exceptions of Hawai'i and New Zealand, all are inhabited by a majority population of Polynesian descent, a population that first began the settlement of these islands some three thousand years ago.

The great settlement of the islands in the Pacific Ocean began by human migrants who entered Australia and New Guinea at least 60,000 B.C.E., when hunting-and-gathering peoples left mainland Asia in boats. Agriculture came to these island when seafarers brought yams, taro, pigs, and chickens to the island of New Guinea. Equipped with portable food crops, a sophisticated maritime technology, and courage and curiosity, mariners settled all the inhabitable islands in the south Pacific.

The settlement of Polynesia proper originated in southeast Asia when, about 3000 B.C.E., Austronesian groups sailed out into the open ocean. Pushing out in their large, double-hulled, oceangoing canoes, these ancient Polynesians sailed vast distances to reach the Marquesas Islands by the 2nd century B.C.E., and from the Marquesas they settled other islands in an area referred to as eastern Polynesia—Hawai'i, Cook Islands, Tuvalu, Tokelau, French Polynesia (Society Islands), Easter Island, and New Zealand. In some instances, islands were settled several times by new waves of immigrants from neighboring archipelagos. By 1000 C.E., almost all of the islands and atolls within this triangle were inhabited, and for the next 600 years, these island people developed, in relative isolation, complex political, social, religious, and cultural characteristics that formed a sophisticated and unique Neolithic society. As these societies developed in relative isolation, they grew diverse in language and customs.

Having no written language, Polynesians passed down through generations of time their oral traditions, most of which have been lost with the exceptions of a few volumes recorded in the 19th century by European missionaries and scholars, or later

Societies of Oceania

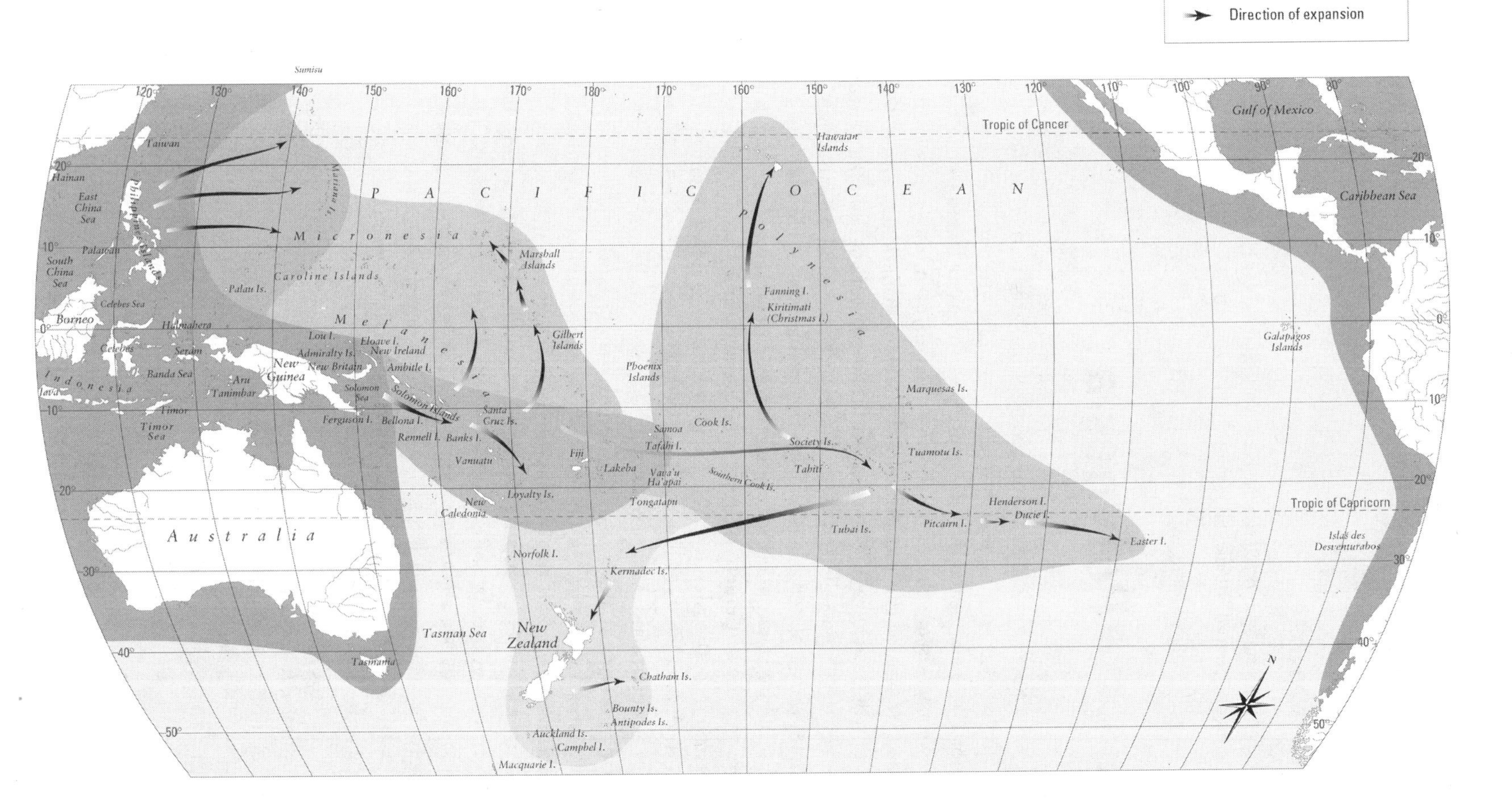

by indigenous writers educated by Westerners. These stories provide tales of gods and heroes that rival any classical Greek and Roman mythology, but unfortunately, they provide less detail on the specific history of their own ancient society.

Polynesian peoples established hierarchical chiefdoms in the Pacific Islands, and contests for power frequently caused tensions. Indeed, the spread of Austronesian peoples throughout the Pacific Islands took place in part because of population pressures and internal conflicts. Their migration is regarded as one of the most daring navigational exploits in all of human history and would not be matched until the 16th-century explorations by the Chinese and Europeans. The European contacts would transform the traditional Polynesian societies. For more on the European contacts with these societies, see Australia entries in volume 4 of this series.

~*Joyce E. Salisbury*

FOR MORE INFORMATION

Bellwood, P. *The Polynesians: Prehistory of an Island People*. London: Thames and Hudson, 1978.

Craig, R. *Historical Dictionary of Polynesia*. Lanham, Md.: Scarecrow Press, 2002.

Kirch, P. V. *The Evolution of the Polynesian Chiefdoms*. Cambridge: Cambridge University Press, 1984.

Chronology of the Medieval World

All dates are given according to the Gregorian Christian calendar.

2000 B.C.E.–700 C.E.	Austronesian migrations to Pacific islands
485–511	Clovis, king of the Franks converts to Christianity, establishing a long-standing alliance between the Frankish kings and the popes
527–65	Justinian and Theodora rule the Byzantine Empire
ca. 570	Muhammad is born in Arabia
581–618	Sui dynasty unifies China after nearly four centuries of division
ca. 610–22	Muhammad is called to prophethood and preaches in Mecca
618–907	Tang dynasty rules China
622	Muhammad makes his Hijra [*Hegira* (migration)] from Mecca to Medina; the Hijra marks the official beginning of the religion of Islam and this year counts as year 1 of the Muslim calendar
628–32	Islam is consolidated and expands within Arabia
632	Death of the prophet Muhammad; Abu Bakr is proclaimed first caliph
638	Muslim conquest of Jerusalem
650s	Compilation of the Qur'an (Koran), the Islamic holy scripture
661	Assassination of ʿAli ibn Abi Talib; Muʿawiya ibn Abi Sufyan (r. 661–80) establishes the Umayyad dynasty

661–750	Umayyad Caliphate is based in Damascus
680	Martyrdom of Husayn at Karbala'; Husayn becomes the model of protest and suffering for Shi'ite Muslims down to the present day
690s	Muslims conquer Byzantine North Africa
691	Completion of the Dome of the Rock in Jerusalem; the venerated mosque is built on the site of the original Jewish Temple
705–15	Construction of the Umayyad Mosque in Damascus
711	Muslim conquest of most of Iberia
712–55	Reign of Emperor Illustrious August (Xuanzong) marks the golden age of China's Tang dynasty
732	Battle of Tours; the Frankish leader Charles Martel halts the expansion of Islam into western Europe
744–50	Third civil war in the Islamic World leads to the defeat of the Umayyads by the 'Abbasids
750–1258	'Abbasid Caliphate marks the golden age of Islamic civilization
762	Baghdad is founded and becomes the capital of the 'Abbasid Caliphate
768–814	Charlemagne, the king of Franks and emperor of the Romans, unites northern Europe for the first time since the fall of the western Roman Empire
786–809	Reign of Harun al-Rashid marks the height of the 'Abbasid Caliphate
ca. 790	Viking raids of Europe begin
800	Charlemagne is crowned emperor of the Romans
ca. 830	Vikings found settlements in Kiev, which will later become the state of Russia
833–945	Emergence of regional states within 'Abbasid territories
836	'Abbasid capital is moved from Baghdad to Samarra
843	Treaty of Verdun divides Charlemagne's kingdom among his grandsons and roughly establishes the early divisions of Europe into France, Germany, and Italy
ca. 858–67	Cyril and Methodius make missionary journeys from Byzantium to convert the Slavs; their efforts result in creation of the Cyrillic alphabet
886	Vikings take portions of northern England, establishing the "Danelaw"
907–60	Fall of the Tang dynasty in China introduces a period of decentralization with warlords dominating regions of China
909–969	Fatimid Caliphate rules in North Africa
945	Buyid dynasty occupation of Baghdad; end of direct rule by 'Abbasid caliphs
960–1279	Song dynasty is established in China
969–1171	Fatimid Caliphate of North Africa also rules Egypt and Syria
988	Kievian Rus convert to Christianity

ca. 1000	Viking Leif Erikson travels to North America
1016	Norwegian king Canute converts to Christianity, thus converting the Scandinavians of his kingdoms of England and Denmark
1038–1194	Seljuk dynasty rules in Iraq and Iran
1054	Schism (split) in Christian Church establishes the Roman Catholic Church in the West and the Greek Orthodox Church in the East
1066	Norman conquest of England establishes a French/Norman dynasty in England; this becomes the last time England was conquered by foreign invaders
1071	Turks crush a Byzantine army at the Battle of Manzikert, forcing the Byzantine emperor to ask for help from the West
1081–1115	Reign of Byzantine emperor Alexius I Comnenus
1095	Pope Urban II calls First Crusade to recover Jerusalem from the Turks
1099	Crusaders capture Jerusalem and establish Latin Kingdom of Jerusalem
1171	Muslim ruler Saladin conquers Egypt, leading to a renewed call for crusades in the West
1187	Saladin defeats Franks at the Battle of Hattin and reconquers Jerusalem for Islam
1204	City of Constantinople is sacked by crusaders
1206–27	Reign of Chinggis (Genghis) Khan, who unites nomadic Asiatic tribes and establishes the formidable Mongol Empire
1215	King John of England is forced to sign Magna Carta, which establishes that kings in England are not above the law
1219–21	Mongol conquest of Persia
1237–41	Mongol conquest of Russia
1250–1517	Mamluk dynasty rules in Egypt and Syria
1254–1324	Venetian travelers Marco Polo and his family visit the Mongol court in China to trade
1258	Mongols sack Baghdad
1260	Mamluks defeat Mongols at ʿAyn Jalut in Palestine
1261	Constantinople is retaken from crusaders by Byzantines
1264–94	Reign of Kublai (Khubilai) Khan, grandson of Chinggis Khan, who centers Mongol rule in China
1279	Mongol conquest of Song dynasty of China
1279–1368	Yuan (Mongol) dynasty rules in China
1281–1924	Ottoman Empire, a rejuvenated Muslim empire is established in Asia Minor (see volume 3 for more on the Ottoman Turks)
1291	Mamluk conquest of Acre, last Frankish stronghold in Syria, ends crusader presence in the Holy Land
1330s	Plague erupts in China and spreads west
1337–1453	Hundred Years' War between England and France is fought in France; the ongoing violence helps end the medieval feudal order

1348	Outbreak of bubonic plague in Europe; the Black Death claims one-third to one-half of the population of Europe
1368	Rebel forces capture Yuan capital of Khanbaliq, and remaining Mongols return to the steppes, ending Mongol dynasty
1431	Joan of Arc is burned to death for witchcraft and heresy by the English; she had rallied French forces against England during the Hundred Years' War
1453	Ottoman conquest of Constantinople ends the Byzantine Empire; 1453 becomes the traditional date for the end of the Middle Ages

HISTORICAL OVERVIEW: WEB SITES

http://eawc.evansville.edu/mepage.htm
http://history.boisestate.edu/westciv/medieval/
http://www.ancientsites.com
http://www.euratlas.com/atlag.htm
http://www.historylink101.com/middle_ages_europe/middle_ages_maps.htm

2

DOMESTIC LIFE

DOMESTIC LIFE

KINSHIP

MARRIAGE

WOMEN

EUNUCHS

CHILDREN

OLD AGE

The center of daily life is the home and, more important, the people who inhabit our domestic space. Domestic life can be defined as relationships with the humans who share our private spaces, as distinct from our friends and acquaintances with whom we interact in the public worlds of work, politics, and sometimes recreation. However, even this definition of domestic life is a little slippery, because it includes family members within our private sphere even if they live in separate homes and join us on the holidays and for celebrations that mark our domestic life. Over time, the definitions of those who are our intimates have changed. Who are the people who might share our domestic life?

The first ties are a married couple with their children. But even these relationships defy clear definition. Throughout history, children have often depended on the kindness of strangers to raise them, whether they were orphaned or fostered or fed by wet nurses. All these people share the domestic intimacy of home life. In addition, households included others outside the nuclear family, from relatives to servants to slaves. In ancient Rome, the head of the family (the *paterfamilias*) was responsible for family, relatives, slaves, and freed slaves, and he also cared for clients who put themselves in his charge. Families might also include unmarried partners or even roommates who combine living space for convenience or necessity, or concubines who shared the private life of rulers. The relationships that make up domestic life are impossible to define perfectly, but (like art) we recognize them when we see them.

A study of domestic life not only involves the people who create a private sphere, but it also encompasses the roles they play—including at times the emotional functions they fill. Fathers of 19th-century families were to be distant and angry, while mothers accessible and nurturing. Mothers in ancient Rome, by contrast, were stern disciplinarians and teachers of values, while the nursemaids handled the nurturing. Here in the domestic life, societies define the roles of men, women, children, and everyone else who shares this space. It is here that we learn early on who we are and how we are to act and feel.

Everywhere in the Middle Ages, kinship was the central bond of society, and domestic life began with extended family life. The bonds of kin were so important that families everywhere arranged marriages; marriage was too important to be left to the whims of love and passion felt by youth. Marriage was to link families together and create a new generation, and if the couple grew to love each other, that was only a bonus.

Women's roles during this time varied according to the degree to which kinship ties were bound to property and inheritance. In traditional Mongol and Polynesian societies, women had high status and shared much of the work that had to be done. In Europe, the Islamic world, and China, on the other hand, high-born women's roles tended to be focused on creating the next generation in a clearly defined bloodline through the father. This preoccupation led some societies—such as Byzantium, China, and Islam—to restrict women's freedom of movement to ensure their sexual purity. The higher the status of the woman, the more secluded she was in these cultures. The seclusion of these women led to the proliferation of eunuch slaves to watch over women. Eunuchs served an important part of domestic life in these societies, and eunuch slaves were highly prized from China to Islam to Byzantium. Societies that cared a great deal for female purity also institutionalized—or at least ignored—prostitution, and the entry on China "Women" reveals how prostitution was central to the life of the city.

Perhaps the largest difference in the domestic life of the Middle Ages compared with ours is their lack of privacy. In the households of the rich and the poor, people of all ages lived closely together. Whole families might sleep together in a bed, with the women and girls on one side and the men and boys on the other. Indeed, a traveler in Europe during this time who stayed at an inn for the night could expect to share a bed with a stranger. Even royal couples who shared a marital bed expected any number of servants to sleep in the same bedroom. When couples sought privacy for sexual encounters, they more often looked outdoors than indoors.

Domestic households, then, were full of people—family members, extended family members, children, stepchildren, foster children, servants, and people simply passing through. People mingled with those of all ages; the elderly expected to be cared for by the rest of the family members, and children grew up intimately aware of all aspects of life.

~Joyce E. Salisbury

FOR MORE INFORMATION

Veyne, P., ed. *A History of Private Life*. Vols. 1 and 2. Cambridge, Mass.: Harvard University Press, 1987.

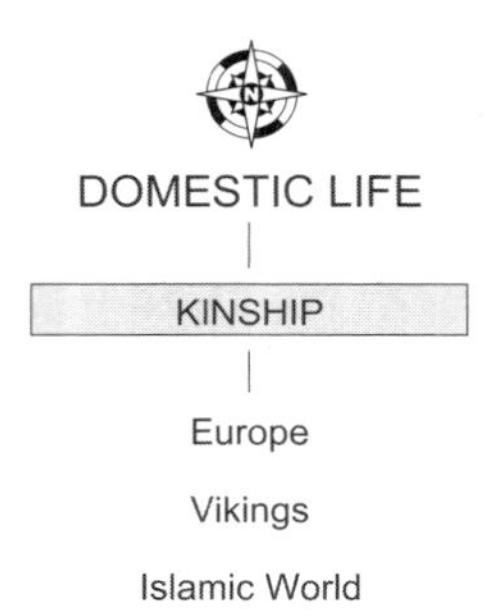

Kinship

Kinship was the most important organizing principle for the thousand years covered in the present volume. Without connections to family, tribe, and clan, people were lost and disconnected. Furthermore, one's family offered protection, affection, financial security, and identity. When strangers met—whether to trade or fight—they often first asked for a genealogy so they would know the full social context of the connection.

This strong kinship identification meant that the importance of the individual was reduced. It did not matter, for example, whether you loved the spouse chosen for you; what mattered was whether the selection was good for the family. Nor did personal choice in such things as profession matter; for example, in Europe if a child was selected to go into a monastery for the good of the family, that decision was not questioned.

Honor, too, was a matter for the whole family. In ancient Arabia, families rigorously prided themselves on their reputation for hospitality or courage or other values. If anyone violated these values, the whole clan was shamed, which would have been intolerable. In early Europe, the slightest insult was grounds for revenge—if a man pushed another off his horse or if he spied on a woman urinating behind a bush, either money or blood had to be exchanged to restore the honor lost by the family. Viking explorers often sought new lands to escape the feuds generated by families in the old land.

Of course, this vigorous code of kinship honor brought with it certain problems, not the least of which was incessant fighting. Throughout this period, we can see the tension between loyalty to kin and loyalty to larger bodies, whether religious or political. The most successful cultures in the Middle Ages were those that were able to shift their allegiances successfully from family to state.

In Europe, it took centuries for kings and the church to break the kinship ties. As nobles moved to primogeniture (dispossessing younger sons and daughters), kings began to claim a fidelity that had nothing to do with blood ties. The church also broke kinship loyalties by imposing regulations of clerical celibacy to be sure priests and bishops felt tied to the church rather than to families. By the end of the Middle Ages, people began to feel tied to nations instead of kin, and the way was paved for modern states.

In Arabia, the prophet Muhammad confronted even more deeply entrenched clans and tribes. The stunning success of Islam was in part a result of Muhammad and his followers' ability to forge the fierce clans of the desert into a large tribe bound together by religion. The Muslims continued to identify with tribes and clans, but they had an overarching loyalty that bound them together in the service of Allah.

The Mongols, too, forged a huge empire on the breakdown of kinship ties. The Mongol peoples were loosely connected in tribes, but there were a number of ways to be joined that did not depend on blood. Some joined in sworn brotherhood, which was a fictive kinship that became as strong as blood ties. Men so joined found reason to fight for leaders even if they were not family. The flexibility of definitions of kinship allowed Chinggis (Genghis) Khan (like Muhammad before him) to create a large multi-ethnic empire.

The history of the peoples discussed in this volume reveals the complex tension between ties to kin and to larger loyalties. Kinship relations remained critically important throughout the period, but societies expanded in direct proportion to people's abilities to set aside family loyalties. In the future, families became more narrowly defined, and loyalties to religion and state increased, but the full flowering of that development would only occur after the Middle Ages had ended.

~*Joyce E. Salisbury*

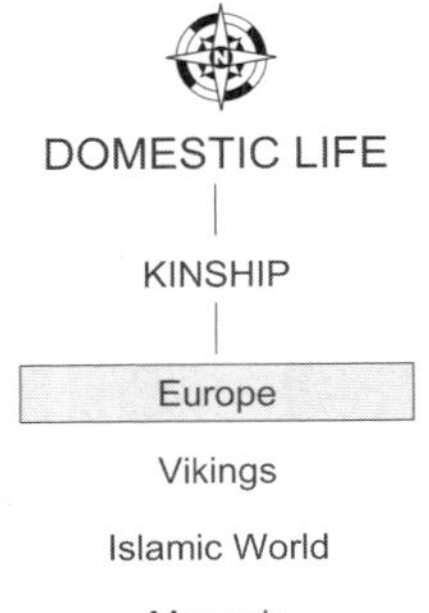

EUROPE

With the fall of the Roman Empire, the Germanic tribes established their kingdoms in Europe. These were tenuous states that were actually ruled by tribes and clans of kinfolk, who jealously guarded their rights. Ties of kinship were highly respected as society was organized horizontally with men and women joined with siblings, cousins, uncles, and aunts in bonds of loyalty. Much of the violence of the early Middle Ages stemmed from seemingly endless feuds as kin sought revenge for everything from violence to insults.

The early Germanic law codes show the early attempts to regulate the feuding families and to try to impose an order other than that of kin. Laws regulated feuds by placing limits on the occasions for which vengeance was allowed. For example, a family was not permitted to seek revenge if one of their number was killed while committing a crime. Nor could a family strike back before an offender from another family was proven guilty. (See the Europe entry in the section "Law" in chapter 6 ["Political Life"] of this volume.) Through the 8th century, rulers tried to slowly place themselves and their royal officers between feuding families, but the process was slow. Through the 9th century, individuals' fortunes were intimately linked with those of their family members.

The poignant repercussions of unfortunate family ties can be seen in the life of a Carolingian family—Bernard, his wife, Dhuoda, and their two children, William and Bernard—who were caught up in the civil wars among Charlemagne's grandsons. While Dhuoda lived quietly away from the centers of power, Bernard showed himself to be singularly inept at negotiating the tricky political situation. Accused of treason, Bernard lost his positions, but his relatives, too, paid dearly for his transgressions. His sister, a nun, was sealed in a wine cask and thrown in the river to drown. His brother was blinded and imprisoned, and his 14-year-old son, William, was given as hostage to Charles the Bald. Eventually, Bernard was executed, and his son was killed while trying to avenge his father. In early medieval families, the political was always personal, and the challenge for kings trying to bring order was to break the power of kinship.

In the 11th century, a new pattern of kinship began slowly to appear in Europe. Gradually, the horizontal grouping of kinship began to be replaced by a vertical arrangement organized through the male line. Fathers began to introduce primogeniture in which only the eldest son inherited the land. The other children had to find other means of a livelihood—enter the church or monastery, become a warrior for some other lord, or try to find land of their own. Records from the mid-11th century hint tellingly of youths forced to leave their homes and of others who took up arms against their fathers or uncles. Brothers killed each other, and contemporaries complained that the youth no longer had any respect for their elders (Duby, 93).

The movement toward linear kinship of primogeniture was a revolution in the organization of families, and it is not surprising that it came with some resistance, but the old pattern of inheritance had also spurred violence. For example, when Charlemagne's grandsons inherited, their grandfather's empire was divided among the three of them, and they were left fighting civil wars (the ones that consumed Bernard's family) to determine who might emerge as the most powerful. By the 12th century, eldest sons inherited; their younger siblings had to marry an heiress or go somewhere else and carve out a kingdom for themselves. It is not surprising that popes found many willing younger sons to go on crusade to get their own lands.

Full-length portrait of John of Gaunt, duke of Lancaster. His costume bears the lion of England and the French fleur-de-lis. He holds a table of coats of arms, with a Latin inscription above. Through the late Middle Ages, the European aristocracy were increasingly interested in proving the nobility of their ancestry, and they proudly displayed coats of arms that traced their genealogy. © The British Library/Topham-HIP/The Image Works.

The focus on lineage also left its mark on the medieval practice of heraldry—the science of depicting one's genealogy by coats of arms. By late in the Middle Ages, old families proudly wore the evidence of the nobility of their kinship, and the very display marked the reduction of the close-knit horizontal kinship ties that facilitated the rise of centralized kingdoms.

The 11th-century church was also involved in breaking the old kinship networks. In this century, the Cluniac monks and popes began a reform movement that ended up insisting on clerical celibacy for churchmen. Although this has been seen as a restriction of sexuality, it was as much an attempt to insist that churchmen be loyal to the church, not to family. Previously, clerical marriages and marital alliances involved the preservation and transmission of church property for one's heirs, but with the imposition of celibacy, churchmen had to renounce kinship ties and remain loyal only to the church organization.

Throughout the Middle Ages, the church also slowly added new kinds of fictive kinship ties to replace the old. Godparents who sponsored a child at baptism were considered relatives, and bans on incestuous marriage applied to godparents as well as blood relatives. These ties further weakened the old strong families.

In the millennium that marks the Middle Ages, dramatic changes took place in the kinship structure. At the beginning, people's loyalty lay primarily—indeed only—to one's family. By the end of the Middle Ages, loyalty was to emerging nation states ruled by kings.

~*Joyce E. Salisbury*

FOR MORE INFORMATION

Dhouda. *Handbook for William: A Carolingian Woman's Counsel for Her Son*. Translated by C. Neel. Lincoln: University of Nebraska Press, 1991.

Duby, G. *The Knight, the Lady, and the Priest*. New York: Pantheon Books, 1983.

Frassetto, M. *Medieval Purity and Piety*. New York: Garland, 1998.

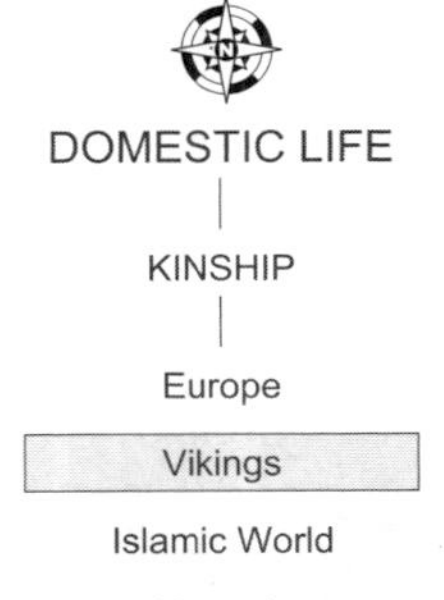

VIKINGS

The kinship system in Viking Age Scandinavia was a bilateral and not a patrilinear one. Men erected memorials to their relatives by marriage; many of the inscriptions include the name of the wife or mother of a dead man, and in some, a husband, when commemorating his wife, names her father and occasionally her grandfather. This type of kinship system is confirmed by medieval Scandinavian laws. Their rules of inheritance show that kinship was traced through both sexes and acknowledge that women have a right to inherit. Admittedly, sons were given a stronger claim than their sisters, but daughters had priority over their uncles and grandfather. What is more, women could inherit land from children who died without descendants. The absence of husbands on raids or their deaths abroad leaving minor heirs may at least in part have contributed to this, since the needs to secure family property were better served by partnerships between sexes than by patriarchy.

The nuclear family (a social unit comprising husband, wife, and their children) was the predominant domestic group in Viking Age Scandinavia. This is clear from rune stones, most of which were raised in memory of people by their closest relatives—by spouses for each other, by children for their parents, or by siblings for each other. The two 10th-century Jelling stones in Jutland, for example, were raised by King Gorm in memory of his queen and by their son Harald in memory of his parents.

Extended families (the addition of one or more relatives other than children) and especially multigenerational families were less common. The reason for the latter is obvious: the average life expectancy was somewhere between 30 and 40 years at most, and only a small percentage of people lived long enough to enter the role of grandparent. One may assume, however, that there was considerable local variation. In sparsely populated areas, and especially in areas with intensive animal husbandry, grand families—that is, two or more nuclear families living together in the same dwelling—were probably not uncommon and would seem to have been financially advantageous; by practicing joint ownership of a farm, families could avoid splitting up the means of production and could pool family labor. The narratives known as the Sagas of Icelanders and Icelandic laws report several instances of such complex families.

Persons living alone and all persons living in the same dwelling, biologically related or not, constitute a household. Nuclear family and household were often identical units, especially among the lower classes of farmers. Because, however, servants, lodgers, and relatives quite often lived with nuclear families, households tended to be larger social units than the nuclear families. It is difficult to give estimates for the mean household size in the Viking Age, but 10 to 13 persons have been suggested by several researchers. As for the size of nuclear families, five or six persons is probably a fair average, but because there was a high rate of infant mortality, many more children were no doubt born.

Despite the predominance of the nuclear family structure, family ties extended well beyond the immediate family to include almost the entire clan on both the paternal and maternal sides. The family was a powerful unit of protection. It was from the family that a person would receive assistance or support if he or she got into trouble, and it was to the family that a person owed his or her obligations. This is clear from the laws concerning wergild (compensation made to the injured party for the killing of a man). Both the payment and receipt of wergild were divided among the families of the perpetrator and the victim in amounts that grew smaller as the degree of kinship became more distant. In Scandinavia, this extended far into the branches of the family, and in Iceland as far as to fourth cousins, that is, to people sharing a great-great-great-grandfather.

The family was a powerful unit of protection within the larger, less clearly defined community. Men and women depended on family in time of need—whether economic, political, or other help. In return, each person owed support to all family members. This relationship formed the core of Viking society.

~*Kirsten Wolf*

FOR MORE INFORMATION

Brondsted, J. *The Vikings*. Translated by K. Skov. Harmondsworth, England: Penguin, 1971.
Wolf, K. *Daily Life of the Vikings*. Westport, Conn.: Greenwood Press, forthcoming.

ISLAMIC WORLD

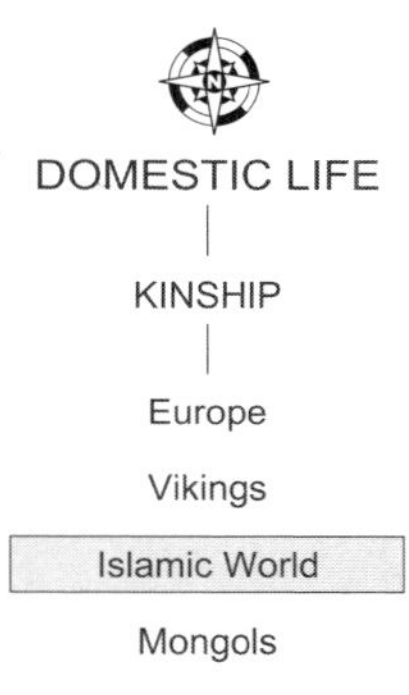

Whether one was an oasis dweller, a resident of the highlands of Yemen, a pastoral nomad, or someone whose way of life fell somewhere between settled and nomad, it was kinship—one's family, one's clan, one's tribe—that defined who one was. The issue of kinship remained important even in the cosmopolitan urban world of 12th-century Damascus and remained so to the end of the Middle Ages and beyond. In 7th-century Arabia, the concern with kinship entailed more than just knowing the identity of one's parents, grandparents, uncles, aunts, and cousins. It provided the means by which a family's position in relation to its clan, a clan's position in relation to its tribe, and a tribe's position in relation to other tribes were made clear. In short, one's name and the genealogy contained in it served to locate a person in a complex pecking order of overlapping relationships.

The need for protection against myriad potential threats from neighbors as well as from the harsh physical environment tended to foster cooperation and only served to strengthen the bonds of kinship, at least on the local level. Because there was no state police or state judicial system to which one could appeal, it necessarily fell to one's kin to provide sustenance, protection, and the arbitration of disputes. Moreover, because the relationships between families and groups were negotiated on the basis of kinship, ensuring the honor and the purity of the family tree were absolutely essential.

These kinship values are also apparent throughout the biographical literature on the life of Muhammad in the context of the two oasis settlements of Mecca (ca. 570–622) and Medina (622–632). For example, Muhammad's biographers went to great lengths to establish a genealogy for Muhammad that went back to Abraham through Ishmael to demonstrate that not only did Muhammad come from *honorable* stock but he, like Abraham and the other ancient prophets, came from *prophetic* stock. Another rather obvious example is that when Muhammad was orphaned as a young boy, he was taken in and raised by his uncle, Abu Talib. Although it may seem perfectly normal to us that a family member would help out in such circumstances, in Muhammad's case it was customary that it be his *father's* brother who took him in. Moreover, it was his uncle's protection as the leader of the Banu Hashim clan that made Muhammad's early prophetic career possible.

The importance of a clan's protection is also seen in how Muhammad's followers in Mecca were treated. Although Muhammad did have some converts who were members of important clans in Mecca, many of his followers at this stage of his career fell outside this kinship system. And because the leaders of Mecca could not afford to hurt Muhammad or their own kin who had accepted his call, they began to persecute (even kill) those of his converts—slaves, orphans, and outcasts of various sorts—who did not have the protection of a clan. Because he could not protect his followers, Muhammad sent those without the protection of a clan on what is called the first Hijira [*Hegira* (migration)] to seek the protection of the Christian negus (or king) of Abyssinia. The reason that Muhammad sent these followers on the Hijra was that he simply could not protect those who had no kin to protect them.

Once Muhammad reached Medina, and in his role as the messenger of God and the arbitrator of all affairs, he established a new social order that is described in what modern scholars call the "Constitution of Medina." The key to membership in this new community (*umma*) in Medina was right belief not kinship. In particular, the *Muhajirum* (those Meccan converts who immigrated to Medina) were to be equal to the *Ansar* (Muhammad's Medinese supporters), not clients under the *Ansar*'s protection as was customary in such circumstances. While Muhammad sought to replace the bonds of *blood* kinship among his followers with the bonds of spiritual kinship, one of the opening passages of the Constitution of Medina makes clear that the new order in Medina embraced the fundamental values of vengeance, retribution, and mutual aid so common in Arabian society. This new order was a genuine departure from the norm and would prove to be very costly to some for it meant that they now had an absolute duty to support their fellow Muslims come what may, even against their own kin who had rejected Muhammad's message.

Because of his force of personality and his standing as the messenger of God in the eyes of his followers, Muhammad's vision of a community in which the bonds of right religion superseded the bonds of blood kinship remained largely intact during his lifetime. It would continue to be the ideal that Muslim scholars have long venerated as well. However, as the sources make abundantly clear, the tug of blood kinship remained very strong even during Muhammad's lifetime, and upon Muhammad's death the early community plunged immediately into intertribal strife as the *Ansar* of Medina argued with the *Muhajirum* of Mecca for leadership of Muhammad's community even while Muhammad's corpse was being prepared for burial. In the end, the Meccans prevailed. Abu Bakr was proclaimed the first caliph, and all the subsequent caliphs in Islamic history traced their ancestry to one of the clans of

Mecca. Nevertheless, tensions within and among the various kinship groups in early Islamic history led to many a conflict, at times breaking out in open civil war.

To read about family life and kinship in the Islamic World in the 19th century, see the Islamic World entry in the section "Family Life" in chapter 2 ("Domestic Life") of volume 5 of this series.

~James Lindsay

FOR MORE INFORMATION

Lindsay, J. *Daily Life in Medieval Islam*. Westport, Conn.: Greenwood Press, forthcoming.

MONGOLS

Family relations, inheritance, and authority were complex matters with the Turco-Mongol tribes of the Eurasian steppes, the more so once they had risen to power with the advent of Chinggis Khan. Men were permitted a number of wives, economics being the limiting factor, so there was a resulting rivalry among the siblings of the various wives, especially when a "major" wife had not been clearly appointed. Add to this the widespread acceptance of the principles of Tanistry (election of the strongest or worthiest of the ruling family) among the steppe people, and it becomes clear why empires and dynasties based on or arising from the steppe lands of Eurasia have not been noted for their longevity or stability.

Rules and principles did exist to regulate social life and to determine inheritance rights, but they were extremely flexible. This can be seen in tribal institutions, in inheritance practices, and in the assumption of leadership.

People were divided into clans and tribes, although these were rather loosely organized institutions and not restricted to blood relationships. Most tribal groupings claimed common heritage, but this was generally agreed to be a political device to engender common cause and unity with little basis in reality. The loose tribal structure enabled Chinggis Khan to radically reorganize the tribal structure of the nomadic Eurasian and so to enforce his own discipline and chain of command on his extraordinarily disparate unruly tribal people. As units before and certainly after this radical reconfiguration of the clans, these Turco-Mongol tribes were not linguistically, racially, or religiously united polities.

Within these tribes, the clans formed a subdivision, but even at this level, blood ties did not necessarily take precedence, and the institution of *andas* (sworn brotherhood) was commonplace. An exchange of blood accompanied the swearing of allegiance, loyalty, and trust when two friends declared themselves *anda*, as was the case with the young Chinggis Khan (then called Temüjin) and his boyhood friend, Jamuqa. *Anda*-ship was recognized as an equal, although voluntary, relationship to a blood tie and could be used as such as when Temüjin called on his late father's *anda*, the powerful leader of the Kereit tribe, Toghrul, to honor this relationship and come to his *anda*'s son's aid. Another voluntary relationship that involved renouncing other blood ties was the position of the *nöker*, which can be loosely translated as "comrade" or "associate," although with a suggestion of "follower" attached to the term. The subordinate status of the *nöker* became more pronounced later, until eventually the term was used to denote a servant or lackey. Many of Chinggis Khan's greatest generals began their careers as his *nökers*. The openness of the clan was further ensured by the strict practice of exogamy, or marriage without the clan or tribe. One of the results of the constant warfare that characterized pre-Chinggis steppe society was the incorporation of various tribes by their conquerors and the parceling out of the men and women as slaves or concubines. These people and their offspring could eventually be assimilated into the tribe, adding to its ethnic, religious, and linguistic mix.

Inheritance conventions among the Mongol tribes were also flexible. The father's *ordu* or camp and possessions, including wives and slaves, were inherited by the youngest son of the chief wife, although it should be added, not the son's actual mother. In the case of Hülegü Khan, Mongol ruler or il-khan, of Iran (r. 1256–65), his inherited wife, Dokuz Khatun, became his principal wife. By convention, the eldest son would retain seniority but would inherit the *ulus* (subject people and effectively, lands) farthest from the family homelands. Other *ulus* would be granted other sons until the youngest would inherit the homelands or homestead itself. With Chinggis Khan, this pattern was followed with Jochi, his firstborn, receiving lands to the west "as far as Mongol hoof had trod," and Tolui receiving the lands of the Mongol steppes. However, when Jochi died, just before his father, it was his younger son Batu who inherited his father's lands and position. Traditions existed, but flexibility and adaptability ruled.

The laws governing inheritance of kingship were also flexible to a degree and were influenced by the tribal custom of Tanistry. During the debate over Chinggis Khan's succession, his son Ögödei (r. 1229–41) expressed reservations first because "in accordance with Mongol custom, it is the youngest son from the eldest house that is the heir of his father" (Juwaynī, 186) and second because he had elder brothers and uncles whose familial seniority gave them priority. In this case, the ruling and choice of Chinggis Khan himself was followed, but in later cases the precepts of Tanistry, nemesis of would-be steppe dynasties, where kingship fell to the strongest aspirant, were followed. The principle of Tanistry awarded the leadership of the tribe to the "best-qualified" member of the ruling family by a meeting of tribal elders. Disputes frequently led to civil war and the breakup of the tribe. With two succession traditions very much alive, patrilineal following father to son and lateral, which followed familial seniority through uncles and brothers and so on, disputes were inevitable. Such disputes eventually split the Mongol Empire. The Mongol Il-khanid dynasty of Persian lands (roughly modern-day Iran) (1256–1335) followed an often-bloody mixture of these traditions, the kingship passing from father to son to brother to uncle through rarely smooth successions.

Kinship was a valued and important factor in Mongol society. However, it was a far more flexible institution than its adherents possibly realized. Although blood links were considered important, tribal and clan and even close family relationships could be manipulated, changed, manufactured, and created without undue controversy. Chinggis Khan's rise to power was in part a result of his ability to mold the ties of kinship within Turco-Mongol society to his own ends.

~George Lane

FOR MORE INFORMATION

Fletcher, J. *Studies on Chinese and Islamic Inner Asia.* Aldershot, U.K.: Variorum, 1995.

Jackson, P. "The Dissolution of the Mongol Empire." *Central Asiatic Journal, Wiesbaden* (1978): 186–244.

Juwaynī, ʿA. M. *Genghis Khan: The History of the World Conqueror.* Translated by J. A. Boyle. Manchester, U.K.: Manchester University Press, 1997.

Marriage

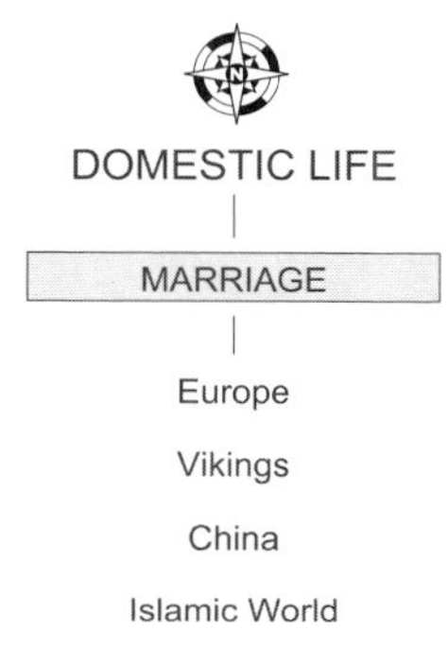

In all the cultures of the Middle Ages, marriages were key to joining and perpetuating the kinship organization that formed the structure of societies. Marriages brought economic and social ties that united families, and the states and religious organizations were as interested in overseeing and regulating these ties as were the families who were united by them.

All the societies discussed here regulated (either formally or informally) who might be permitted to marry, and in these regulations one can see some rather surprising differences among the cultures. For example, in Europe by the 13th century, the church prohibited marriages between people who shared a great-great-grandfather. In America in most places, marriages between first cousins are banned as a way of reducing the probability of genetic disorders in the children, but the European ban was not for health considerations. Instead, these bans were designed to try to break up the kinship ties among old families so that centralized monarchies might exert more authority. (Nonetheless, these prohibitions of consanguinity were violated almost as often as they were enforced.) In early Muslim lands, on the other hand, first cousins frequently married. This allowed families to keep property within the family and to reinforce tribal and clan ties. In both extremes, marriage was about political and economic ties even more than considerations of progeny.

As befitting such an important ritual, marriages were arranged by elder, male family members; it was too significant a tie to be left to the whims of youthful passion. Throughout Europe—from the south to the Scandinavian north—fathers entered into negotiations to find suitable matches for their offspring. By the 12th century in Europe, lords of large land holdings had to approve the marriages of the men and women tied to them in contractual arrangements—whether they were fighting knights or peasants. In China, fathers hired matchmakers to act as go-betweens to examine the suitability of prospective spouses. This allowed negotiations to end without any embarrassment on either side.

The age at marriage varied rather widely among the cultures discussed here. Considerations of age were determined by two main variables: economic status and ability to procreate. If the new couple was expected to be financially self-reliant, the age of marriage was higher—for example, European peasant newlyweds were usually in their twenties and merchant men were in their late twenties. This makes sense because it would take that long for a young man to establish himself and have a reliable income. In noble families, whether in Europe or in China, people were younger—Chinese law, for example, required that boys be at least 14 years old and girls 12. European noble girls married shortly after puberty. This was intended to guarantee that the woman was a virgin at her wedding and thus that subsequent heirs were clearly the husband's.

Once parents agreed to the match, they usually settled on a contract to solidify the relationship. (Of course, among the wealthy and propertied this contract was more elaborate and formal than among the peasantry.) The contract was solidified by an exchange of gifts; engagement rings are a remnant of this exchange of gifts, and like today, if the parties decided not to marry, the gifts were forfeit. In all cultures, women brought with them a dowry—that is, a sum of money or property that they contributed to the household economy. This dowry remained theirs throughout the marriage and offered some security that they were not totally dependent upon their husband's generosity. Women whose families had no such resources not only found it hard to find a suitable husband but were also more dependent within the marriage.

Marriages everywhere were celebrated with public joy. In Europe, couples were usually married at the church door with the community as witness to the public joining of the two families. In China, the woman was taken with ceremony to the groom's household amid the public accolades. In some places—including Scandinavia—the wedding party would last for several days.

In the Middle Ages, marriages brought economic and social ties that united families. The most important part of medieval wedding ceremonies in Europe took place in front of the church door when the groom presented a ring to the bride in the presence of the whole community. © The Art Archive/ Bibliothèque Municipale Laon/Dagli Orti.

Today in America, we expect marriages to be monogamous, and indeed, we prosecute bigamy. This was not always the case. In Europe during the early Middle Ages, kings and the wealthy might take several wives, but by the 11th century, the church was able to impose a requirement of monogamy on everyone. In Islam, on the other hand, the Prophet took a situation in which tribesmen took many wives and instead restricted men to four wives, and this many only if the husband could support them. Mongols took many wives, although each had her own hut. Even where there were requirements of monogamy, societies accepted the presence of concubines—essentially unofficial wives—in the household. Charlemagne of the Franks had several concubines who bore him children, and everywhere from China to Byzantium to Muslim lands, concubines lived in the households of the mighty.

No matter how much care matchmakers and concerned family members gave to selecting a suitable match, sometimes marriages did not work out. What options did people have to undo what had been so carefully and publicly done? These cultures offered a range of choices. Under Islam, divorce was possible and indeed relatively easy and available to both partners. In Europe by contrast, once the church had made marriage a sacrament, it was permanent. Incompatible couples could move apart, but neither could legally remarry. (For the wealthy and influential, the church offered "annulment" as an option, which pronounced that the original marriage had been invalid, so they were free to contract another.) In China, men could obtain divorces for reasons as varied as adultery to "talkativeness."

In modern society, marriage remains a cause for ceremony and celebration as two previously separate people establish a new committed household. In ancient times, marriages were even more important because they marked a joining of extended families and economies in a way that was meant to provide for generations to come.

~Joyce E. Salisbury

EUROPE

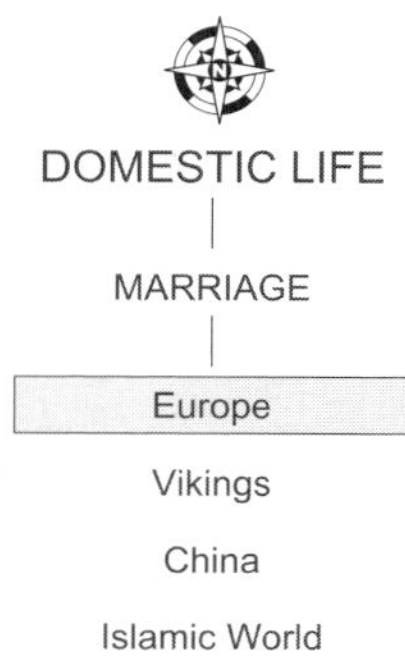

Across the social spectrum in Europe, full entry into adult society generally came with marriage and the establishment of a household of one's own. For men, this only became possible after acquiring the means to support a family, such as a landholding, a workshop, or a business. Because husbands had primary responsibility for supplying the family's livelihood, they were generally older than their wives. Reliable statistics are rare for the Middle Ages, but the evidence suggests that the typical age of marriage among the peasantry was the late twenties for men and the early twenties for women; similar ages probably applied for the urban laboring classes. The ages decline, particularly for women, further up the social scale. Among prosperous urban families, the marriage age for women was typically the late teens; the age varied widely for men. In the aristocracy, ages in the midteens for women and early twenties for men seem to have been common.

Marriage in the Middle Ages was a complex affair that combined economic, folkloric, and religious elements. At all levels of society, it involved a major economic commitment, and both parties were expected to consider carefully the likely economic consequences of the union. Because the man was usually the main source of household income, the woman needed to find a husband whose economic prospects met her expectations. The economic criteria for the man depended in part on his class. Among commoners, the woman was often a significant contributor to the household finances, so a man wanted a wife who was skilled and industrious. In the upper classes, where the woman was less likely to contribute to household income directly, it was more important that the bride bring with her a substantial dowry of land or money from her family. Such considerations also played a role among ordinary people. A peasant might significantly enhance his economic status by marrying a woman who stood to inherit land in the village. The economics of the marriage were often settled beforehand through an agreement witnessed between the two sides, stipulating the property to be brought by the wife into the marriage, as well as the property bestowed by the groom on his wife to support her in case of his death.

The legal dimension of marriage fell under the jurisdiction of the church, which had its own requirements. The prospective couple were not permitted to be close relatives. The appropriate distance was debated for centuries, but as of the early 13th century, it was fixed at four degrees, meaning that a couple who shared a great-great-grandfather could not marry. This relationship also included godparentage, which made the determination of kinship more complex. A preexisting marriage, or even a prior marriage agreement, also prevented marriage. To forestall prohibited marriages, the prospective match had to be announced in the parish church of both parties on three successive Sundays. These announcements, called banns, gave the local communities a chance to bring forward any possible impediments to the union.

The ceremony itself was celebrated at the door of the church, with the priest officiating and the community as witness. The wedding service of the Middle Ages included many of the same elements as mainstream Christian ceremonies of today, including the request that any impediments be brought forward and the mutual exchange of vows. The church emphasized the importance of the consent of both partners as essential to the validity of the marriage. There was only a single wedding ring, given by the man to the woman. After the ceremony, the company proceeded into the church for a nuptial Mass.

The wedding ceremony was followed by popular celebrations, depending on local folk customs. A feast was commonly held, and in some places a procession of neighbors accompanied the couple to their home. One 13th-century story mentions a French custom of casting grain over the couple as they crossed the threshold, shouting "Abundance, Abundance!" although the priestly author notes cynically that many wedded couples soon find themselves living in want and misery (Singman, 29).

Not every marriage followed these formalities. According to canon law, marriage could be contracted either by a vow of marriage expressed in the present tense or by a statement of future intent to marry, followed by sexual consummation. The latter sort of marriage in particular could take place without the participation of church or community. Such marriages were illegal but not invalid: although the couple might be prosecuted in the church courts, they remained married. Some couples took advantage of this as a means to elope without the approval of their families, clear evidence that love—or at least desire—could also play a part in the decision to marry.

Once the marriage took place, the couple was joined for life, and they were legally required to cohabit. Neither partner was permitted to enter a monastery, or even become celibate, without the consent of the other. Divorce as such was not permitted, although a marriage might be annulled in certain situations, especially if the marriage was invalid in the first place (for example, because of a prior contract or close kinship), or if it was never consummated by sexual union. It was also possible to secure an official separation in cases such as adultery or cruelty. In this situation, the couple was no longer required to cohabit, but they remained legally married. If one partner in a marriage died, remarriage was freely permitted. According to church doctrine, procreation was the sole purpose of marriage, and contraception and abortion were forbidden, as were all sexual acts that did not lead to conception. Of course, the very condemnation of these acts suggests that they were indeed practiced, and this is confirmed by records of legal actions against transgressors.

The relationship between husband and wife was complex, reflecting both broad cultural patterns and customs specific to the time and place. In principle, a wife generally stood in a position similar to that of a servant or child, as a subordinate and dependent member of her husband's household. It was even considered appropriate for a husband to use corporal punishment to discipline his wife, just as he might use it with a child or servant. Actual brutality was not condoned, but the line between discipline and brutality is always problematic in corporal punishment. Whether it was actually common for husbands to beat their wives is another matter. In practice, there were a number of factors that permitted her a measure of unofficial independence and influence. Unlike the servant or child, a wife had relatives of her own, comparable in social status to her husband, who might take an interest in her well-being. She might be capable of earning money in her own right, and many women among the working classes brought additional money into the household by hiring out their labor, or selling goods produced at home. Aside from these economic principles, the sources always indicate that marriage remained a complex, human relationship (Singman, 27–30).

To read about marriage and family life in Elizabethan England, see the England entry in the section "Life Cycles" in chapter 2 ("Domestic Life") of volume 3; for 18th-century England, see the England entry in the section "Marriage" in chapter 2 ("Domestic Life") of volume 4; for Victorian England, see the England entry in the section "Family Life" in chapter 2 ("Domestic Life") of volume 5 of this series.

FOR MORE INFORMATION

Singman, J. L. *Daily Life in Medieval Europe*. Westport, Conn.: Greenwood Press, 1999.

VIKINGS

In pre-Christian times, marriage in Scandinavia was essentially a commercial contract between two families. The prospective bride and groom were expected to be of similar status in birth and means, although the Sagas of Icelanders suggest that wealth could compensate for social prestige. In such cases, the woman usually married someone of lower status. Emotional attachment or love appears not to have played any particular role in a man's choice of a woman.

The arrangement of a marriage consisted of two steps: the betrothal and the wedding. The initiative was taken by the man or by his father; the woman's father could do nothing to initiate the marriage of his daughter but had to wait for a suitor to appear. If the suitor seemed acceptable, negotiations took place, in which the prospective groom or his spokesman promised to pay a sum known as the bride-price, and the woman's father or guardian agreed to hand over at the wedding a dowry, the sum of the woman's inheritance. When the agreement had been reached, the conditions were repeated in front of witnesses, and the date of marriage was fixed. The woman was absent from all negotiations; female consent to marriage was not required until Christian times, when a woman could choose to become a nun.

The wedding took the form of a feast at either the bride's or the groom's house, which often lasted several days. The climax, but not necessarily the end, of the feast was the bedding of the bride and groom. The Old Norse term for the marriage ceremony is *brud(h)laup*, a compound word of which the first element means "bride" and the second "leap" or "run." The origin of the word has been debated, but it may imply a pre-procreative movement of the groom toward the bride, a ritual that emphasizes the reproductive purposes of marriage, or it may refer to the journey of the bride to her new home. However, the word also calls to mind an image of a woman trying to escape, and it is known that during their expeditions abroad Viking men obtained women through force, some of whom they brought home as wives.

There is little in the way of documentary evidence regarding age at marriage during the Viking Age, but the fact that the Sagas of Icelanders contain a considerable number of cases in which girls married at the age of 12 or in their early teens is indicative and makes it clear that there was no normative resistance to such a practice.

Marriage precluded other sexual outlets for women. A wife's adultery was a serious crime; according to some of the Danish and Swedish provincial laws, it gave a husband the right to kill both her and her lover if they were caught in the act. Although Norwegian and Icelandic laws treat unfaithfulness of husbands as a crime also, men generally seem to have been free to have extramarital relationships. Indeed, polygyny was practiced by many of the Scandinavian kings, including the Norwegian king Harald Hairfair (d. ca. 940), about whom it is told that he dismissed nine mistresses before marrying the Danish princess Ragnhild. There is nothing to indicate that concubinage or extramarital affairs in general were regarded as improper at any social level before the church condemned them as sinful, and if a man publicly acknowledged a child born to him out of wedlock, he could give it gifts, which essentially meant that the child became entitled to a share in the inheritance, although with some restrictions.

Heterosexuality was the norm in Viking Age Scandinavia, but that homosexual relations between men were recognized as social phenomena is clear from Old Norse Icelandic literature, especially the Sagas of Icelanders, in which they are regarded as signs of unmanliness and immorality. As in many societies with a distinct masculine disposition, and particularly where this disposition is combined with the requirements of warfare, homosexuality was equated with effeminacy and cowardice, and it was epitomized by the man who passively tolerated sodomy. Although the later secular laws do not mention homosexuality per se, they do mention verbal accusations of (passive) homosexuality, which were considered a serious crime and punishable by law.

The sources suggest that divorces were relatively common and that they were easy to obtain for both men and women. In the pre-Christian period, a formal declaration before witnesses was probably sufficient. In Christian times, divorce was granted only at the bishop's discretion for, according to the Christian Church, marriage was a not a financial agreement between two parties but a sacrament and a monogamous union that could not be dissolved because the couple had promised faithfulness to one another for life. After a divorce, the woman would typically return to her family with her personal belongings, her dowry, and also the bride-price, if her husband was the cause of the divorce. The purpose of the return of the dowry, the function of which was to provide maintenance for the wife, was clearly to ensure that a divorced woman did not become financially destitute.

~*Kirsten Wolf*

FOR MORE INFORMATION

Brondsted, J. *The Vikings*. Translated by K. Skov. Harmondsworth, England: Penguin, 1971.
Wolf, K. *Daily Life of the Vikings*. Westport, Conn.: Greenwood Press, forthcoming.

CHINA

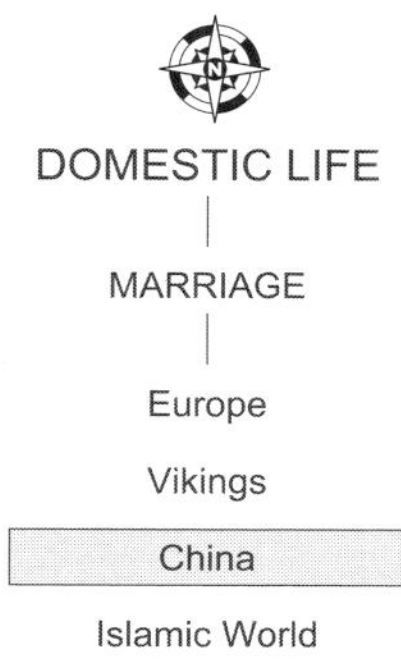

Marriages in China were almost always arranged. Two men, usually close friends, might reach an agreement to engage their children when the children were infants, but in almost all cases, families relied on outsiders to arrange marriages. The expert at providing such services was a matchmaker, who was always a woman. As such, she held an advantage over a man because she had access to the women's apartments in homes. The matchmaker could enter the inner quarters, converse with the mother, and examine the prospective bride. Afterward, she would convey the information she gleaned there to the intended groom's father.

There was also a more compelling reason for employing matchmakers. The Tang code of laws required it, for the state had an interest in preventing fraud and violations of its laws. Fraud might involve misrepresenting the age of the prospective bride or groom. Legally, the marriageable age was 14 for males and 12 for females. Furthermore, a man could not marry a woman who was half his age or younger. Further deceit might involve a false claim that one of the pair was an adopted child or the child of a concubine instead of the wife's child. Finally, one of the families might conceal their child's disability. As defined in Tang statutes, the impaired included the blind (in one or both eyes), the deaf, the dumb, dwarfs, hunchbacks, the insane, and the dismembered (loss of one or two limbs). A matchmaker could prevent such duplicity because she could examine the pair physically and question the family about their status.

Once the matchmaker completed the arrangements, the "marriage master" (normally, the father, grandfather, uncle, or older brother of the prospective groom) drew up a contract and sent it to the woman's family. Her senior male relative signed and returned it. If thereafter the woman's family broke the agreement, her marriage master was liable for a punishment of 60 blows with a thick rod. If the man's family canceled it, its marriage master suffered no punishment, but he could not keep betrothal gifts. The prospective groom's family sent betrothal gifts, tokens of good faith, to the prospective bride's home when they received the signed contract or shortly thereafter. In Tang times, betrothal gifts included symbolic articles: glue and lacquer for cementing the relationship, a pair of stones for establishing a firm base, silk floss for ensuring meekness, and two mats for assuring that the will would submit.

Acceptance of the presents was a legally binding pledge of engagement even when there was no contract established between the two parties.

Normally, a family of means sent the bride to the groom's home in a carriage. She arrived there veiled and immediately became a member of his family although she retained her surname. The groom did not see her face until the evening of the wedding day. To celebrate the occasion, his father threw a banquet that only men attended.

Tang society was monogamous. A man could have only one wife, but that did not mean that he could not install other women in his household. In fact, it was customary for patricians to do so. Because affection was rarely a basis for matrimony and fidelity to a wife was not one of their virtues, men took concubines, sometimes a large number of them. Under Tang law, the distinction between a wife and a concubine was that the latter could be bought and sold.

The Tang law code declared that the union of husband and wife was unalterable throughout their lives and that they must dwell together even in the grave. That was the ideal marital state, but the law also recognized that divorce was acceptable and even desirable under certain circumstances. Divorce was a male prerogative only; a woman who left her husband without his consent was subject to two years of penal servitude if apprehended.

The law recognized seven legitimate grounds for such separations. Failure to bear children was the first. That rule applied specifically to sons because sons carried on the family line and were in charge of maintaining sacrifices to ancestors. Daughters did not count because they left the family upon marriage. A man could divorce a wife for barrenness only when she reached the age of 49 and had failed to produce a son. However, he need not divorce her because he could legally make the eldest son born to one of his concubines his heir. If he had no male offspring, he could adopt a son, in which case the boy or man had to be related to him by blood.

The second ground for divorce was adultery. An extramarital affair was unacceptable because the woman might bear a child that was not of the husband's bloodline. The third justification for divorce was a wife's refusal to serve her in-laws. Obedience to the will of a husband's parents or grandparents was as important as, if not more important than, obedience to him. It was difficult for a man who detested his wife to divorce her when his parents were fond of her.

The fourth ground was talkativeness. According to a Tang ballad, a young, newly married woman wandered alone in the market, insulting her husband and abusing her in-laws, so he divorced her with her consent. Women were outsiders who might also spread discord in the family by pressing the interests of their husbands against those of his brothers, so wives were to be silent. The fifth ground was jealousy. It was considered a cause of disharmony. Because men took concubines, contention between those women and his wife could easily develop as they competed for his affection and favor. The sixth ground was theft, particularly of her in-laws' property. The last was contracting an incurable disease. A woman with such an ailment was not permitted to prepare food for offerings to the dead and therefore could not carry out her duty with regard to the rites performed for her husband's ancestors.

Even if a husband had legitimate grounds for divorce, there were three instances when he could not renounce his wife: she had observed the 27-month mourning period for his parents; she had married into the family when its status was humble or poor, and it subsequently acquired higher status or wealth; or she had no family of her own to which she could return. A man who divorced his wife under those circumstances was subject to a beating of 100 blows with a thick rod and was compelled to take her back (Benn, 243–48).

FOR MORE INFORMATION

Benn, C. *Daily Life in Traditional China: The Tang Dynasty*. Westport, Conn.: Greenwood Press, 2002.

ISLAMIC WORLD

In pre-Islamic Arabia, when a man wanted to marry, he paid a dowry, or bride-price, to the father or male guardian of the girl or woman to whom he was betrothed, in part as compensation for the loss of her value as a laborer in his household. According to the Qur'an (Koran), the bride-price became the wife's property that she would bring into the marriage, not the property of her male guardian.

> Give women their dowry as a free gift; but if they choose to make over to you a part of it, you may regard it as lawfully yours. (Qur'an 4:4)
>
> If you wish to replace a wife with another, do not take from her the dowry you have given her even if it be a talent of gold. That would be improper and grossly unjust; for how can you take it back when you have lain with each other and entered into a firm contract. (Qur'an 4:20)

Because a man was supposed to provide for every member of his household out of his own resources, the husband was to have no recourse to this wealth. It became the wife's property solely to dispense with it as she saw fit. She could, of course, make a part of it over to her husband, but he could not lawfully take it away from her on his own.

Despite the fact that marriage under this Qur'anic scenario became a contract between a man and a woman (not between a man and a woman's male guardian), most marriages resulted from some sort of arrangement between families. As such, each family had a vested interest in the prestige and economic status of the other as well as the success of the union. Of course, most families of a lower status would be happy to improve their position by marrying their daughters to men (or their sons to girls or women) from more prestigious families; however, the families of higher standing might not be as accommodating about their sons or daughters "marrying down" and the implications that such unions would have for the kinship group as a whole.

Because families generally arranged a marriage, the ideal union was between cousins. Such an arrangement ensured that both parties were from good families. In addition, it meant that the bride and groom were likely to have known each other for some time prior to their wedding night because they may have played together as children and as kin it was permissible for them to have greater social interactions after the onset of puberty.

The purpose of marriage in the Qur'an as well as the medieval Islamic world was the procreation of children and the strengthening of ties between two extended families. In principle, the man or the woman was able to decline a proposed match, but rarely was there an opportunity for such an arrangement to be entered into on the basis of mutual affection or common interests, and certainly not after a period of courtship as in the modern American ideal of the institution. Another way in which marriage differs from the modern American model is that according to the Qur'an, a man may take up to four wives at the same time, with the proviso that he maintain each wife equally:

According to the Qur'an, a man may take up to four wives at the same time.

> If you fear that you cannot treat orphan [girls] with fairness, then you may marry other women who seem good to you: two, three, four of them. But if you fear that you cannot maintain equality among them, marry one only or any slave-girls you may own. This will make it easier for you to avoid injustice. (Qur'an 4:3)

Scholars interpreted this passage to mean that if a man took more than one wife, he had to maintain each wife equitably in *separate* residences. Given the expense involved, having more than one wife was a luxury that only the wealthier classes could afford.

Whatever the class, a wife was obligated to obey her husband in return for his provision. If a wife was not obedient, her husband was allowed to chastise her and even to beat her into submission:

> Men have authority over women because God has made the one superior to the other, and because they spend their wealth to maintain them. Good women are obedient. They guard their unseen parts because God has guarded them. As for those from whom you fear disobedience, admonish them and send them to beds apart and beat them. Then if they obey you, take no further action against them. Surely God is high, supreme. If you fear a breach between a man and his wife, appoint an arbiter from his people and another from hers. If they wish to be reconciled God will bring them together again. Surely God is all-knowing and wise. (Qur'an 4:34–35)

In addition to wives, wealthy men could keep concubines as part of their household. Indeed, to the Sharia (Islamic law), a concubine had certain legal protections not afforded to a wife. Once a concubine bore a child, she was henceforth classified as an *umm walad* (mother of a child). Unlike the American slave system, the child of a free Muslim man and a slave woman received the status of the father, not the mother. Thus the child was a legally free Muslim and bore no stigma of illegitimacy. Initially, such offspring tended to be seen as inferior (although not illegitimate) largely because their mothers were not of Arabian stock. However, as the importance of Arabian purity began to be contested vigorously in the 8th and 9th centuries, this sense of inferiority waned considerably. In fact, the mothers of many of the caliphs and sultans in Islamic history were *umm walads*. In addition, once a slave woman had borne a child, she could not be put out of the house, she could legally expect maintenance and support, and she had to be granted her freedom upon the death of her owner. A wife, on the other hand, could bear her husband 14 children and he could divorce her at will.

The Qur'anic procedures under which a man could divorce his wife were fairly simple—he merely needed to say three times that he is divorcing her, and the marriage was dissolved. "Divorce may be pronounced twice, and then a woman must be retained in honor or allowed to go with kindness" (Qur'an 2:229). Nonetheless, the woman had certain protections and rights should her husband decide to divorce her. Because her property was always hers throughout the marriage, whatever property she had at the time of the divorce remained hers to do with as she chose.

> It is unlawful for husbands to take from them anything they have given them, unless both fear that they may not be able to keep within the bounds set by God; in which case it shall be no offence for either of them if the wife ransoms herself. These are the bounds set by God; do not transgress them. Those that transgress the bounds of God are wrongdoers. (Qur'an 2:229)

The woman was also owed maintenance after the divorce for the purpose of determining whether she was pregnant:

> Those that renounce their wives on oath must wait four months. If they change their minds, God is forgiving and merciful; but if they decide to divorce them, know that God hears all and knows all. Divorced women must wait, keeping themselves from men, three menstrual courses. It is unlawful for them, if they believe in God and the Last Day, to hide what God has created in their wombs: in which case their husbands would do well to take them back, should they desire reconciliation. Women shall with justice have rights similar to those exercised against them, although men have a status above women. God is mighty and wise. (Qur'an 2:226–28)

Muslim scholars devoted a great deal of attention to the meaning of this passage, and as good lawyers, they spent much time addressing all sorts of possibilities. Was the waiting period the same for a Muslim man's Muslim wives as it was for his wives who were Jews or Christians? What if the marriage was never consummated? What if the woman did not menstruate (either because she was too young or because she had already gone through menopause) but had had sexual relations with her husband? In general, the practice came to be that if a woman was pregnant, she was owed maintenance until the delivery of the child, and both she and the child were owed maintenance until the weaning of the child (generally around age two).

As the Sharia developed, provisions were made for women to seek a divorce as well. However, it was much more difficult for a woman to divorce her husband, and the procedure required the services of a court. Legitimate causes for divorce included the husband having some sort of disgusting disease, a husband's intolerable cruelty, and a husband's abandonment—ranging from 10 to 90 years depending on a woman's family and status. Needless to say, few women lived long enough to be granted a divorce on the grounds of abandonment in those courts where the husband had to have been gone missing for 90 years.

To read about marriage and family life in the Islamic World in the 19th century, see the Islamic World entry in the section "Family Life" in chapter 2 ("Domestic Life") of volume 5 of this series.

~James Lindsay

FOR MORE INFORMATION

Lindsay, J. *Daily Life in Medieval Islam*. Westport, Conn.: Greenwood Press, forthcoming.

Women

In the Middle Ages, much more than today, women's roles were heavily determined by biology: Both men and women were acutely aware that the next generation depended on women bearing children. Furthermore, a man wanted to be sure that the children a woman bore were his, and the more property a man had to leave to his heirs, the more he wanted to be certain they were of his blood. Many of the regulations surrounding women's activities derived from this desire of fathers to know their children. The seclusion of Muslim women both within the household and under heavy veils represented a desire to keep them pure during their reproductive years.

In Viking Scandinavia, women were not secluded, and commentators remarked on the independence and strength of Viking women. Questions of paternity and property in the cold northern lands were put aside, so both men and women could work to ensure the family's survival.

In most of Europe, on the other hand, the desire to ensure paternity led to many men being suspicious of women's infidelities. Literature was full of stories about women who deceived their husbands with lovers, and the most popular medieval romantic poem—*The Romance of the Rose*—was a handbook of how to seduce women. However, some wise observers realized that seclusion was not the way to ensure fidelity. The author of the romance *Tristan and Isolde* wrote of a king who tried to spy on his wife to keep her faithful, but to no avail. As the author pointed out: "Yet, when all is said, to whatever lengths you take it, surveillance is wasted on a woman in that no man has the power to guard a vicious one. A virtuous woman does not need to be guarded; she will guard herself" (Gottfried von Strassburg, 276). This was the wave of the future in the West—women became responsible for their own virtue.

One way to secure the purity of some women was to provide prostitutes to satisfy men. Prostitution has been called the oldest profession, and we do have records of women acting as prostitutes throughout history. The South Bank in London contained one of the oldest districts of prostitution in Europe; it had been there from the Roman occupation through the theaters of the Renaissance. Changan in China also had a large brothel district, where women entertained men and made substantial profits.

Women were never simply sex objects and child bearers. There was just too much work in the medieval household for women of all classes to be exempt from the labor force. The most aristocratic women—whether in China, Europe, or Byzantium—could rely on servant labor, but other women had to work. Women were primarily engaged in the seemingly endless production of clothing. European women sheared sheep, spun wool, and wove cloth; Chinese women tended silkworms and wove the precious silk; and Mongol women cured leather and sewed it into clothing. Rural women from Europe to China tended animals and milked goats and cows to provide food for their families. (Mongol men, however, milked mares themselves to make an intoxicating fermented beverage.)

In the cities, whether Byzantium or Paris or Changan, women engaged in the brisk trade in the shops. Muslim women were unlike their other counterparts; their seclusion prevented their working in the stores of Baghdad. The middle-class activity of urban women was part of family-owned enterprises in which all members of the household made sure the business was a success.

During the Middle Ages, some women rose to be rulers. China and Byzantium saw the rule of several empresses, and some European queens, such as Eleanor of Aquitaine, made a dramatic impact on society. The Ostrogothic queen Amalasuintha ruled Italy and engaged in complex diplomatic correspondence with the Byzantine emperor Justinian. Extraordinary women pepper the political history of the medieval years. There was less opportunity, however, for Muslim women to rise from their segregation to the zenith of rule.

Again, with the exception of Islam, some women from Europe to China devoted their lives to religion. In no churches could women officiate in a leadership role, but religious women could become nuns and dedicate themselves to following Christ or Buddha. Many such women were highly educated, and abbesses such as Hildegard of Bingen and Hrostvit of Gandersheim have left profound literary contributions.

In sum, women around the world faced many of the same restraints. They were responsible for bearing and raising children, feeding and clothing their families, and nurturing those in their care. Countless anonymous women plainly lived full and rich lives fulfilling these functions. At the same time, women contributed to the public lives of these dynamic cultures—working, praying, and at times even ruling. In these broad arenas, women of the past were not that much different from those of the present as they support their families and contribute to their world.

~Joyce E. Salisbury

FOR MORE INFORMATION

Gottfried von Strassburg. *Tristan*. Translated by A. T. Hatto. New York: Penguin, 1982.

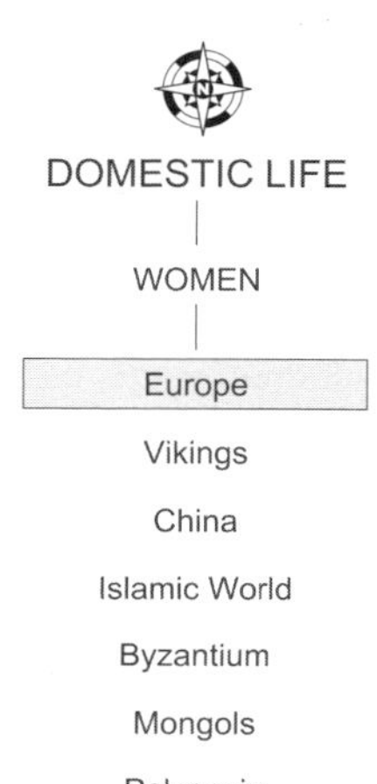

EUROPE

Medieval social life in Europe was organized by function—that is, what people did for society as a whole. There were three functions—called "orders"—that medieval people identified: those who pray, those who fight, and those who work. Medieval women belonged to the orders that bound their fathers and husbands to their functional place in society—noble women were to produce heirs and warriors, nuns were to pray and serve God, and peasant and townswomen worked. However, in every case, women were officially seen as standing in a position of subordination to men, and their powers of choice were always circumscribed to a greater or lesser degree by both official social structures and unofficial customs.

The official constraints on women were probably least restrictive among commoners. In a laboring household, women were generally assigned roles pertaining directly to the home itself, while the man engaged in more external work. A woman's domestic responsibilities included maintaining the house, preparing food, mending clothes, and raising children. She also contributed directly to provisioning the household by raising poultry, dairying, and tending the garden; she might also engage in moneymaking labor within the home, such as spinning and brewing. Among the peasantry, it was quite common for women to take part in field labor during harvest time, and there is evidence that women were hired for a wide variety of agricultural work.

A central job for women of all classes was preparing clothing. Here, women are depicted carding wool (separating the fibers) and spinning it into thread. © The Art Archive/British Library/British Library.

Sustenance and income were also provided by the woman's dairying work during the milking season. Dairy animals included cows, sheep, and goats, depending on local dairying customs. This milk was a valuable source of nutrients for the peasant family, but because milk goes sour quickly in the absence of refrigeration, the woman had the task of making it into butter and cheese, both of which could be kept for a significant period of time. This labor-intensive work must have occupied a significant part of the peasant woman's time during the dairying season. Brewing was another predominantly female activity that provided both nutrition and income for the household. Because a single household could not necessarily consume a full batch of ale before it went sour, there was usually a surplus to sell.

Finally, the female householder often generated additional income by spinning. The production of thread to make cloth involved an enormous amount of labor—each thread had to be spun by hand—but the work itself was not difficult and could be carried out with the simplest equipment. A woman using a drop spindle could produce thread while she was busy doing her other household chores. This thread would be sold to agents who purchased it to send to the weaver.

For peasant women as for men, social status often depended on access to land. A woman could come into a holding by marrying a landholder, with whom she might be a joint tenant, depending on local custom, or she might inherit land in her own right. A daughter inherited land only if there were no sons, but this was not an especially rare situation in families where the average number of children was only two or three. A married couple was generally considered joint tenants of the landholding, with the husband as the official head of the household, but an heiress's holding continued to be recognized as her inheritance.

Not every peasant woman was a householder. Like the men, many women ended up as laborers, and their role in the hired workforce was scarcely less important than that of the men. One 13th-century tract on estate management recommends hiring women because they can be paid lower wages, and later sources indicate that women were hired for such tasks as road repair, manuring, thatching, sheapshearing, weeding, mowing, transporting grain, and even plowing, which was normally thought of as man's work.

Women in the city, like their counterparts in the countryside, were active participants in the economic life of their community. Like the peasant woman, the urban wife was responsible for household affairs such as cooking, cleaning, and raising children, but she might have also earned money through a trade. The Parisian tax records yield many examples of householding tradeswomen, always a minority, but still significant in number. The wife of a journeyman stud maker in Paris and other medieval cities was allowed to practice the craft if her husband had been a journeyman for a year and a day. A lace maker's wife could also practice the craft and even help her husband to train apprentices. The labor of women was less valued than that of men, and even crafts that permitted wives to practice often placed restrictions on them. In some cases, a wife was not allowed to train apprentices or engage in the trade after the death of her husband or if she remarried someone who did not belong to the trade.

Some trades could be practiced by a woman in her own right. The regulations of the poulterers of Paris allowed women to purchase the right to practice the trade as freely as a man in all things. The daughter of a currier could be apprenticed to the trade, and a currier's widow was permitted to take apprentices of her own. The regulations of the linen drapers made provisions for female journeymen, trained in a six-year apprenticeship. In some cases, a husband might even learn his trade from his wife. Some trades were practiced principally by women, including the spinners of silk thread, the makers of silk ribbon, and veil makers. Such trades might be governed jointly by male and female overseers, as in the case of the silk ribbon makers, or by women alone, as for the veil makers. At the lower end of the social scale, many women earned their living as laborers. Heavy physical labor was generally reserved for men, but there was always domestic work for women as chambermaids and laundresses, and as hired workers performing the unskilled labor required in tradesmen's shops.

All women worked hard, a fact recognized in many of the sources. For example, one advocate of monastic life for women offered this vivid, albeit biased, vignette of the pressures of a woman's domestic life around the year 1200: "When she comes in the house, the wife hears her child screaming, sees the cat at the bacon, and the dog gnawing her hides; her biscuit is burning on the stone, and her calf is sucking up her milk; the crock is boiling over into the fire, and the husband is scolding" (Singman, 14). This author suggests that the life in the cloister was more desirable than filling all the occupations expected of women.

How did women fare in monastic life? Because women could not become priests, they were cut off from a large part of the activity of the church. The only clerical route open to women was in the regular clergy, living the monastic life as nuns, or, from the 13th century onward, joining one of the female orders associated with the mendicants. The life of such women, like that of the monks, was restricted by the rules of their order, which for women tended to be even more restrictive than for men. Yet women in the cloister might achieve a level of education not usually available to women at the time, and they were free from direct and constant male authority to a degree uncommon in medieval society in general. Many women achieved extraordinary influence as abbesses, including the 12th-century German abbess Hildegard of Bingen, who became a mystic and communed with God directly, and was respected enough that she corresponded with popes and kings offering her advice.

The higher one was on the social scale, the less pressure there was to earn a living and the more the preoccupation with proper social roles grew. An aristocratic woman might have enjoyed more power because of her social station, but she was at the same time more limited by the constraints of her class. An aristocratic wife, like her commoner counterpart, might have had particular responsibility for running the household, and during her husband's absence might even have administered the family estates. However, she did not normally participate in the aristocratic work of warfare or government. One of the standard courtly skills of the aristocratic woman was needlework, an extremely time-consuming activity whose prominence in the lady's routine suggests that she had an excess of idle hours to fill (Singman, 13–15, 80–82, 166, 177–78).

Snapshot

Rape and Violence in 13th-Century England

In the 12th century, the office of the coroner was established in England to examine crime. The coroners' rolls are a perfect source of information on daily life in the Middle Ages. Here is one example of a record of rape and violence:

> In 1270, Emma, daughter of Richard Toky of Southill went to gather wood. Walter Garglof came, carrying a bow and a small sheaf of arrows. He took hold of Emma and tried to throw her to the ground and deflower her, but she immediately shouted and her father came. Walter immediately shot an arrow at him, giving him a mortal wound. Seman of Southill came and asked him why he wished to kill Richard, and Walter shot an arrow at him, killing Seman. Walter then fled. Later, Emma, Richard's wife, came and found her husband wounded to the point of death and shouted. The neighbors came and took him to his house. He had the rites of the church, made his will, and died at twilight on the same day. (Ant, 189)

To read about the roles of women in Elizabethan England, see the England entry in the section "Women's Roles" in chapter 2 ("Domestic Life") of volume 3; for 18th-century England, see the England entry in the section "Men and Women" in chapter 2 ("Domestic Life") of volume 4; and for Victorian England, see the England entry in the section "Women" in chapter 2 ("Domestic Life") of volume 5 of this series.

FOR MORE INFORMATION

Ant, E. *Women's Lives in Medieval Europe: A Sourcebook.* New York: Routledge, 1993.

Sharpe, R. R., ed. *Calendar of Coroners' Rolls in the City of London, A.D. 1300–1378.* London: Richard Clay and Sons, 1913.

Singman, J. L. *Daily Life in Medieval Europe.* Westport, Conn.: Greenwood Press, 1999.

VIKINGS

In marriage, men and women during the Viking Age had well-defined, distinct roles. Basically, women managed those affairs of the couple that pertained within the house, while men were in charge of everything outside and represented the family in society at large. Only men enjoyed legal or judicial responsibilities, and only men could witness and prosecute in law. Only men fought, and only men could speak at the assemblies.

The primary duty of a wife was to provide her husband with offspring, preferably male offspring. In the absence of any reliable method of birth control, there would be little opportunity for respite between pregnancies, and the care of infants and small children must have occupied most of a woman's time. The high mortality of young women in the Viking Age has often been attributed to frequent pregnancies and complications associated with childbirth, but this may be an oversimplification, especially in light of the fact that women had as one of their particular tasks the nursing of the elderly and the sick, which obviously meant increased exposure to infectious diseases.

In addition to fulfilling reproductive needs, a woman also fulfilled labor requirements. Upon marriage, a husband would typically turn over the running of the household to his wife. The specific tasks involved in running a household depended on a couple's social status and whether the couple lived in the countryside or in towns. Little is known about women in urban communities, but presumably, wives of craftsmen and merchants took some part in their husbands' businesses.

We are better informed about women in the countryside, especially those married to landowning men, although the circumstances of women also varied in the farming communities. The smaller the farm, and consequently, the smaller the size of the household, the greater the amount and variety of work were required of husband and wife. In areas where fishing and handicrafts were subsidiary occupations, women typically did most of the heavy work. On larger farms with a larger household, many jobs, especially the less desirable ones, such as cleaning the pens or milking the cows or sheep, could be delegated to servants or slaves.

Indoor work included the preparation and preservation of food and drink, cleaning and laundering, and the manufacturing of cloth and the production of garments or hangings. The last-mentioned tasks—spinning and weaving—were laborious, and it is likely that men participated in the work. Although linen was produced, wool was by far the most common woven cloth. The first step was the shearing or plucking of the sheep or goats, followed by the cleaning and grading of the wool. Next, the wool was carded with fingers or a special comb to straighten it and separate the fibers. The spinning was done by attaching the carded wool to a distaff. The wool was then teased onto a weighted spindle. By twisting and turning the spindle as it was thrown to the ground, the yarn was rolled onto the spindle. When sufficient yarn had been spun, it was removed from the spindle and wound into a ball, unless it had to be dyed, in which case it was wound onto a wooden reel to form a skein (although some cloth was presumably dyed after it had been woven). At this point in the process, the weaving could commence.

The most common loom was the so-called warp-weighted loom, which is known throughout the world. Although the loom found in the Oseberg ship burial in Norway—the only loom to survive from the Viking Age—is a two-beam vertical loom, most likely it is atypical; indeed, loom weights, required to tension the warps on an upright loom, are common finds. During weaving, the weft was straightened by the use of a weaving batten. Detailed patterns were made with the help of small combs, thread pickers, and pin beaters. After the cloth was cut from the loom, it was sometimes felled, that is, soaked and pressed in a mixture of fermented urine and hot water. This process caused the cloth to shrink and thicken and also reduced the oil content of the wool.

Although women's work pertained to the house, it does not follow that all tasks were performed indoors. Men were generally the ones who tended the animals, but women were in charge of dairy operations. Men were also the ones who sowed and fertilized the home fields, but women, especially in poor families, participated in field work during harvest. The task of collecting berries, mosses, herbs, seaweed, wild fruit, and eggs from birds, whether domestic or wild, also fell to women, as did the washing of clothes, which was typically done in streams, and the fetching of water for drinking, cooking, and bathing.

In this age of high mortality, widowhood was not an uncommon state. Because it was difficult for a single person to work a farm, rapid remarriage was often a practical necessity if the widow was young and had small children to care for. Older widows, on the other hand, probably enjoyed considerable freedom, at least if they were women of high or moderately high social status. An older widow was no longer under the authority of her husband, and her sons were usually grown and gone. Her dowry and bride-price guaranteed her economic security, and she was in charge of her husband's property.

The Sagas of Icelanders contain several examples of independent and powerful older widows. The most famous of these is Unn (alternatively called Aud) the Deep-minded, wife of a Norse king in Dublin and daughter of a Norwegian chieftain who went to the Hebrides as an agent for the Norwegian king Harald Hairfair. About 900, Unn's husband was killed in battle in Ireland, and her son was killed fighting in Scotland. Accordingly, Unn was left responsible for a large number of grandchildren. *Laxdoela saga* (Saga of the People of Laxardal) reports that because of the hostilities between the Scots and the Norsemen, Unn felt that her grandchildren's future prospects in the British Isles were rather dim and so resolved to emigrate to Iceland, where two of her brothers were already living.

Unn had a ship built secretly in the forest. When it was finished, she made the ship ready and set out with substantial wealth. She took along all her kinsmen who were still alive, and the saga writer praises her ability to escape from such a hostile situation with as much wealth and as many followers. She was indeed an outstanding woman. The saga proceeds to relate that Unn cleverly married her granddaughters to sons of prominent men in the Orkney and Faroe Islands, whose authority she managed to escape by continuing to Iceland, where she laid claim to a large area of land, of which she gave portions to family members and followers. She lived until she had arranged for a suitable wife for her favorite grandson, to whom she bequeathed all her property. She died with dignity during the wedding feast. The resourcefulness and independence exhibited by Unn and others may well have been fostered by the many responsibilities with which women were left when their husbands were away on trading voyages and military expeditions.

Of course, not all women married. Unmarried daughters, who were not needed at home, could choose to work on another farm or in towns. On farms, a woman could hire herself for specific tasks for a specific period of time. The income was probably small, among other reasons because there were slave women, who for the most part had to be content with lodging, food, and clothes in return for their labor. Towns offered a wider range of employment. The trades in which women engaged were typically female ones: washing, cleaning, baking, brewing, and cloth making.

Viking women were as strong and independent as their men.

Viking Age graves indicate that women, especially older ones, commanded considerable respect. Many of the richest burials in Scandinavia are of women, the most famous being the Oseberg ship burial in Norway. That they also enjoyed a measure of freedom of action is suggested, among other things, by the fact that several rune stones in Scandinavia were raised at the initiative of women and some, moreover, by women in memory of women. A famous example is the stone from Dynna just north of Oslo, which was erected by a woman in memory of her daughter. The stone is clearly a work from the early Christian period. Its inscription reads:

> Gunnvor, Thrydrik's daughter, made a bridge in memory of her daughter Astrid. She was the most skilful girl in Hadeland. (Page, 52)

Other stones were raised by men in memory of women. The women named in the inscriptions on these stones are usually wives and mothers, and the men typically pay tribute to the deceased woman's fine housekeeping and other traditionally female skills, as exemplified by the mid-11th-century stone from Hassmyra, Sweden, raised by the farmer Holmgaut in memory of his wife Odindis:

> A better housewife will never come to Hassmyra to run the farm. Red Balli carved these runes. She was a good sister to Sigmund. (Jesch, 65)

In addition, several women were buried with pairs of scales as symbols of good housekeeping or with keys to the meal or treasure chest as symbols of their authority in the home.

Foreigners were evidently so struck by the independent behavior of Scandinavian women that they considered it worthy of comment. Al-Ghazal, a 9th-century poet and diplomat from Andalusia (Muslim Spain), who was sent on a mission to an unspecified Viking court (possibly the court of the King Turgeis of Norway in Ireland or the royal seat in Lejre in Denmark) emphasizes the frankness and flirtatiousness of high-ranking Norse women and the legal freedom women had to leave an unsatisfactory marriage. His comment on women's right to divorce is echoed by Ibrahim b. Ya'qub al-Turtushi, a 10th-century merchant or diplomat also from Andalusia, who visited what is probably Hedeby in South Schleswig. Clearly, such conduct and practices were in stark contrast to what these men were accustomed. Viking women were as strong and independent as their men.

~Kirsten Wolf

FOR MORE INFORMATION

Brondsted, J. *The Vikings*. Translated by K. Skov. Harmondsworth, England: Penguin, 1971.
Jesch, J. *Women in the Viking Age*. Rochester, N.Y.: Boydell & Brewer, 1991.
Page, R. I. *Runes*. London: British Museum Publications, 1987.
Wolf, K. *Daily Life of the Vikings*. Westport, Conn.: Greenwood Press, forthcoming.

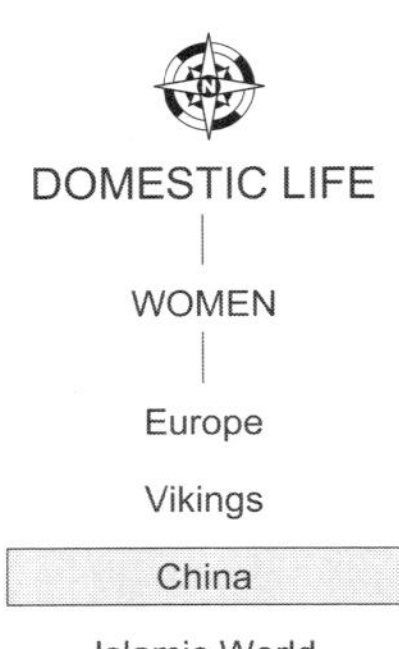

CHINA

Most of the women in Tang China have been forgotten in the sources. Although husbands and sons sometimes wrote eulogies praising these quiet and no doubt hard-working women who cared for households and families, the details of most women's lives have been lost. However, there are some notable exceptions, drawn from the extremes of the social spectrum—empresses and courtesans.

The period following the death of the third Tang emperor on December 27, 683, was unique in the annals of Chinese history. It was singular because a remarkable woman, Empress Wu, ruled the empire in her own right. Gaozong, her husband, suffered from a chronic illness, perhaps a stroke, that left him subject to dizziness, paralysis, and impaired vision. He was also weak willed. Taking advantage of the situation, the empress assumed the power behind the throne by 660 and became monarch in reality if not in name. After Gaozong's death, she deposed her eldest son, Zhongzong, and sent him into exile. Then she installed her second son, Ruizong, on the throne and governed for the next six years as a regent, the manner by which women in traditional China took control of the government. In 690, she deposed Ruizong, overthrew the Tang, assumed the throne, and established her own dynasty, the Zhou (690–705). She was the only woman in Chinese history to accomplish such a feat.

The daughter of a lumber merchant, Empress Wu was extremely gifted and intelligent and had a natural gift for politics, a superb ability to judge men, and an exceptional talent for manipulating them. However, she also was singularly ruthless and cruel. After a rebellion against her regime broke out in Yangzhou during 684, she initiated a reign of terror that grew in intensity over the next decade. She established a secret service to ferret out her enemies, or those supposed to be her foes, and in 690 established a special investigative office at a gate in Luoyang where her agents subjected suspected traitors to unspeakable tortures. The persecution culminated in the exile and executions of thousands.

In 705, Tang loyalists deposed Empress Wu and restored Zhongzong to the throne. For the next eight years, women enjoyed unprecedented power in court politics, and a dramatic upsurge in corruption occurred. Empress Wei, the wife of Zhongzong, who assumed the throne in that year, enjoyed his favor because she had given him steadfast support and talked him out of committing suicide while he was in exile between 684 and 698. Taking advantage of his goodwill and weak disposition, she promoted the rights of her daughters and sought to acquire for them the same privileges that royal princes enjoyed. At her insistence, Zhongzong established offices with staffs of officials—previously granted only to sons of the emperor—for his sister and his daughters in 706. In 709, Wei requested that Zhongzong grant women the right to bequeath hereditary privileges to their sons, previously a male prerogative only.

The princesses also pressed their causes. In 706, Princess Anle, the emperor's favorite daughter, asked him to name her heir apparent in place of his son, a request that he ignored despite his weak will. She, her sisters, and other women in the empress's clique granted themselves the right to make appointments to their staffs without going through bureaucratic channels. Those commissions came at a price: the women charged 300,000 coppers per title. They made a princely sum from the enterprise, selling more than 1,400 appointments. They also peddled official ordination certificates to the Buddhist and Daoist clergy for 30,000 coppers apiece (Benn, 6). In 714, the authorities discovered that the women had fraudulently ordained 12,000 monks and priests. As time went on, their behavior became even more outrageous. They stole gold, jade, and priceless pieces of calligraphy from the palace treasury. The princesses also sent their servants out to abduct the children of commoners to enslave them for service in their households.

Empress Wei had pretensions of emulating Empress Wu and planned to assume the throne in her own right. In 710, she had poison inserted into one of her husband's pastries. After he died, she placed a boy on the throne. Tang loyalists, however, were not about to endure another usurpation of the throne. Eighteen days after the enthronement, they stormed the palace and slew the empress and Princess Anle. For three more years, another woman, Princess Taiping, the daughter of Empress Wu, wielded great power at the imperial court. She, too, was brought down by Tang loyalists in the summer of 713 and was forced to commit suicide.

At the other end of the social spectrum, some women were courtesans who entertained men for a price. There was one special district, the North Hamlet, in Changan reserved for high-class courtesans who mainly served nobles, officials, graduates of the civil service examinations, and occasionally, rich merchants. Prized more, or at least as much as, for their talents as entertainers at feasts than for their sexual services, they resembled Japanese geishas. They were official entertainers who had to register with the government and over whom the mayor of the capital exercised control.

The North Hamlet was in the northeast quadrant of a ward that was adjacent to the eastern market, across from the August Enceinte and east of the national colleges. It had three winding alleys. The courtesans living in the North Alley were inferior in skills to those residing in the Central and Southern Alleys, who held them in contempt. Newly appointed officials sauntered incognito there, looking for pleasure. The bordellos on those alleys were large and tranquil. They had three or more salons for receiving guests, as well as smaller rooms hung with several layers of drapes. Flowers and shrubs grew in front of and behind the dwellings, where there were ponds with strangely shaped rocks.

Some courtesans had been raised as beggars in their youth, and some had been indentured to poor families in rural hamlets. Others came from good (i.e., wealthy or patrician) families that had betrothed them to obtain a bride-price from unscrupulous men. Those scoundrels then sold the girls to madams in the North Hamlet, where the girls had no means of extricating themselves. When the girls entered the bordellos there, they took the surnames of their foster mothers. After training, at the age of 11 or 12, they received splendid gowns, a gift that signified they were fully fit to receive guests.

An important role for the courtesans was to supervise feasts. They were at ease with nobles, high-ranking officials, and candidates for the civil service examinations but were especially punctilious in following the rules of propriety when receiving court officials who carried gold insignia. Whatever the case, the best of them were skilled conversationalists, poets, and singers who knew the rules of drinking games and kept a party convivial. They were also not above telling a guest that he talked too much when he was bragging about his accomplishments and spoiling the banquet for others.

The normal fee for a feast at a bordello in North Hamlet was 1,600 coppers, and double that for a guest who was a newcomer and for a party that went on after the first candles sputtered out. Musicians who lived near North Hamlet were ready to perform for a feast at a moment's notice. The musicians charged 1,200 coppers for each round of drinks, but 2,400 if the revelry went on after the first candles died. When a guest came up short on the required fee to a madam, she might seize his carriage and clothes in lieu of payment.

Some courtesans were not happy with their lives in North Hamlet and yearned to leave it. If they were lucky, a rich man might marry them, present them with gold and silk as a bride-price, and take them away from North Hamlet. Nobles might, with the approval of their wives, take them as concubines (Benn, 4–6, 64–67).

FOR MORE INFORMATION

Benn, C. *Daily Life in Traditional China: The Tang Dynasty*. Westport, Conn.: Greenwood Press, 2002.

ISLAMIC WORLD

In principle, at least, the role and status of women in Islamic thought were governed by three concepts: (1) the dynamics of patrilineal kinship; (2) a woman's moral and spiritual responsibility and autonomy; and (3) the principle that a man must provide for every member of his household—wives, children, servants, and slaves—out of his own resources. These three principles shaped women's roles through subsequent Muslim history.

The principle that women are subordinate to men certainly was not unique to pre-Islamic Arabia. It was extremely common throughout the ancient Near East and the Mediterranean world as a whole. While this principle is taken for granted in the Qur'an, it is clear that many of the modifications to existing practices set forth in the Qur'an do in fact represent what we might call improvements in women's status. One of the most important elements of the whole system of patrilineal kinship is paternal certainty, for without it the entire system would fall apart. According to this system, female chastity before marriage and fidelity in marriage are absolutely essential to guarantee paternal certainty. Sexual activity by a woman outside the bonds of marriage was not a matter of individual choice but a violation of family honor as well as the Qur'anic sexual ethic that embraced it.

In theory, the Qur'anic requirements of chastity and fidelity applied equally to men and women; however, the physical consequences of sexual activity by a man outside the bonds of marriage were less readily apparent, and the punishments less strictly enforced. In short, the reason that women were the guardians of the purity and honor of a kin's lineage concerned basic biology. That is, while a child's mother's identity was known to her as well as to the midwives who helped deliver the child, the identity of the father could rarely be attested to by outside eyewitness testimony.

Related to female chastity is the issue of modesty. One of the most important practices designed to ensure female chastity was the requirement that women be segregated from men who were not part of their households. Modern Americans tend to distinguish between private space and public space, or a person's private life and his or her public life. Although this division between private and public is applicable to the medieval Islamic world, a more accurate distinction would be between appropriate behavior among one's kin and appropriate behavior among those outside one's kin group. For example, in what we would call the private space of a home, segregation of the sexes could consist of women's actual physical separation from men when men not of the family were guests in the common area of the home. In such instances, women might be segregated in the women's quarters of a dwelling or they could be segregated from men who were not their kin by appropriate female dress. However, neither type of segregation was necessary among men who were close relatives.

Segregation of the sexes did not apply to prepubescent girls and boys for the simple reason that they were not considered sexual beings because they were physically unable to reproduce. Likewise, many of these restrictions on women were not applied as strictly to widows or to women whose children were adults. Such women had far greater freedom of activity, especially in the public sphere, for reasons of biology and perceived sexuality. That is, postmenopausal women were no longer considered to be sexual beings because they could no longer bear children. As such, they were no longer seen as illicit temptresses (*fitan;* singular, *fitna*) of men nor could they produce illegitimate offspring, which would bring shame to their families.

In reality, such universal cloistering of women was nearly impossible for all but the wealthiest of families in the towns and cities. Less-wealthy families as well as rural and pastoral communities generally needed their women's labor. Nevertheless, the principle of modesty and separation of the sexes was observed in the public sphere—that is, essentially everywhere outside of the home and apart from one's kin. In the public sphere—especially the most prominent of public spaces, the market—this separation of the sexes consisted of the physical separation of women from men by means of modest dress. This principle of the separation of the sexes was particularly important in larger oasis settlements and towns and later in major urban centers, where the residents were not all close kin and where the likelihood that women would encounter strangers was a virtual certainty.

The preceding discussion of the role and status of women in Islamic thought has focused on how things were supposed to be according to the Qur'an. In the medieval Islamic world, as in any society, there were disparities between the ideal and the real in daily life. In the countryside and especially among the pastoral nomadic populations, for example, local custom tended to outweigh the dictates of Islamic law on these issues, even though they are set forth clearly in the Qur'an itself. If a bride-price was paid to a guardian or inheritance rights were withheld or divorce protections were not honored, to whom could a woman appeal? Moreover, if a woman decided that she wanted to make a fuss about these issues, her brothers and other male relatives could always coerce her by refusing to find her a husband, much less a suitable one. Faced with the choice of spinsterhood or worse, most women in such circumstances chose to forgo their marriage and inheritance rights, if in fact they knew they had them at all. In a major city, however, a woman—especially an educated upper-class woman—could appeal to a court and have confidence that a judge would rule in her favor. Moreover, she could have confidence that the judge would not only seek to but also have the authority and means to enforce his ruling with the backing of the ruler who had appointed him judge, even in the face of possible opposition from her husband or other relatives.

A woman's position in her family was carefully defined to preserve chastity and honor for her kin and guarantee legitimacy for her children. Whether these ideals were enforced by Islamic law or by a woman's family, they formed an overriding determinant of women's lives.

~James Lindsay

FOR MORE INFORMATION

Lindsay, J. *Daily Life in Medieval Islam*. Westport, Conn.: Greenwood Press, forthcoming.

DOMESTIC LIFE
WOMEN
Europe
Vikings
China
Islamic World
Byzantium
Mongols
Polynesia

BYZANTIUM

Byzantine views of women were complex and contradictory. The importance of motherhood and the family were celebrated as representing both their highest achievement and only proper place in society. Individual women were regarded as irresolute and weak, yet at the same time they presented men with dangerous sexual distractions. This apparent ambiguity stems in large part from inherent biases in the surviving literary sources, whose authors were almost exclusively male. One of the few known documents written by a woman, the *Alexiad* of Anna Komnene, offers a valuable perspective of the imperial household but has less to say about broader gender roles, especially at lower social levels. The understanding most women had of their place in the world remains unknown.

In late antiquity, women were not infrequently found in the public sphere. Contemporary sources indicate that aristocratic and imperial women were active as heads of extended households, church members, and artistic patrons. The tumultuous 7th and 8th centuries brought a new inward focus to the Byzantine family, with a sharp divide separating the public male world from the enclosed domestic sphere of women and children. The 11th-century ideal expressed by the moralist Kekaumenos sees the family unit as a defensive outpost within society. In this view, only immediate family members could be truly trusted; women were under constant threat, needed to be kept apart from male visitors, and should be veiled and escorted when venturing outdoors. Attendance at games, exhibitions, and performances was discouraged, and limitations on public appearance became more restrictive with social rank. As a result, church services and festivals became some of the most important occasions for activity outside the home.

The importance of the nuclear family to Byzantine social stability ensured that women occupied a key position within the home. Their principal occupation was motherhood; its centrality was visually underscored by the many icons depicting the Virgin Mary in the company of her son. A woman's proper responsibilities included managing the household, attending family finances, and raising the children. The primacy of her domestic authority and maternal responsibility appears throughout Byzantine history and at all social levels. It is reflected in the wide popular support enjoyed by the empresses Eudokia Makrembolitissa and Anna Dalasene, who succeeded their husbands and ruled briefly on behalf of their young sons. The ultimate deposition of these and other surviving imperial spouses also makes clear the limits of authority even they could command.

The wider domestic world was rarely recorded by male observers. Predictable daily routines included acquiring water and fuel, preparing food and serving meals, and making, mending, and laundering clothes. Women played a vital role in maintaining the health of family members and negotiating social transitions from birth to death. Firsthand experience in childbirth led women to assist relatives and neighbors as midwives, which for some could expand into informal nursing careers. When there was a death in the household, women were expected to wash and prepare the body for burial. Practical information about health, hygiene, and sex would have passed from mother to daughter. Women naturally played an important part in educating their children, with most of their efforts apparently directed toward their sons.

Women often were directly involved in arranging the marriage of their children. The nominal age of marriageability was 12 years, but this rule was often overlooked by coercion or abduction. The woman's status within the family received legal protection in the tightening of civil and canon laws on divorce and the recording of dowries and wills. The dowry (*proika*) was offered by the parents of the bride and was met by a corresponding wedding gift from the groom. The dowry clearly was intended to function as a hedge against unforeseen financial catastrophe for family and children; it could consist of land, houses, shops, jewelry, or other tangible assets. Upon the husband's death, the estate normally was divided between the woman and her children; in cases of divorce by consent, she retained her dowry.

Public careers for women were very limited and certainly were discouraged by both the church and wider male sentiment. The 12th-century charter of the Pantokrator monastery in Constantinople mentions the appointment of midwives and women physicians to the staff of its hospital (*xenon*), although at half the salary of male doctors. Domestic spinning and weaving had long been regarded as the only honorable craft pursuits. Some women, after providing for their household's wardrobe, managed to produce surplus goods that they sold in the market; an annual festival in Constantinople mentioned by Michael Psellos in the 12th century apparently commemorated the role of women in this tradition. Women in late Byzantium are known to have run household businesses and operated bakeries, fruit and vegetable stands, taverns, and other small shops in Constantinople and elsewhere. The countryside presumably presented women with fewer social restrictions on such activities. Many village women would have worked family gardens and orchards, selling their produce in the local market. Others wove baskets and made ceramic pots for use by themselves and their neighbors.

The world of public entertainment offered some women unconventional opportunities for fame and wealth. Mime and pantomime suffered from disapproval by churchmen and the emperor and were banned in late antiquity. Criticism of women performers is reflected in the continuing notoriety of the stage, which was seen as closely related to prostitution, concubinage, and other subversions of the Byzantine family. Apart from these public spectacles, dancing remained an important part of seasonal festivals and wedding celebrations, especially in rural areas. Women dancers also routinely performed within homes for weddings and other occasions.

In such an environment, religion afforded a important avenue of social engagement. Visits to chapels and attendance at worship services were regarded as legitimate occasions for public interaction. While the institutional church offered women only the minor role of deaconess, it encouraged them to support its programs by making charitable donations. Wealthy widows founded a large number of monasteries, especially in later Byzantine times. A growing emphasis on celibacy led some women to forgo marriage and assume monastic vows; others sought the refuge of a convent following divorce, the husband's death, or the departure of children. The surviving records of women's monastic experiences suggest that outside of her original family, it was in the convent that many Byzantine women felt most at home.

~Marcus Rautman

FOR MORE INFORMATION

James, L., ed. *Women, Men, and Eunuchs. Gender in Byzantium*. London and New York: Routledge, 1997.

Talbot, A.-M. "Women." In *The Byzantines*, edited by Guglielmo Cavallo. Chicago: University of Chicago Press, 1992.

MONGOLS

Women enjoyed a high status in Mongol society and were involved in most aspects of life, including battle, along with their men folk. This is apparent with even a cursory look at the genealogical tables of the Mongol Great Khans, which reveal extended periods during which women effectively ruled over the whole Mongol Empire. Between 1241 and 1246, the Great Khan Ögödei's widow, Töregene, ruled as regent, and between 1248 and 1251 the Great Khan Güyük's widow, Oghul-Qaimish, became regent until Möngke was installed as the new great khan. After Chinggis Khan's youngest son, Tolui, died (1231–32), his formidable wife, Sorghaghtani Beki, resisted attempts to remarry her to Ögötei's son Güyük. Instead, she ruled her late husband's domains herself and eventually was able to successfully promote her own sons as heirs to the Mongol throne. The high status women enjoyed in Mongol society found reflection in the lands under their control, and both the Iranian provinces of Shiraz and Kirman experienced extended periods of rule by powerful women. Qutlugh Terkān Khātūn (r. 1257–83) of Kirman maintained close personal, political, and cultural links with her Mongol overlords in the Iranian Mongol capital of Maragheh during her two decades of rule over this southern Persian province. The period over which she resided as queen is considered a golden age in Kirman's history. Her namesake in the neighboring province of Shiraz, although not as illustrious nor so well regarded nor indeed so long serving, was a powerful female monarch and reflected the Mongol influence on the society of the time.

However, Mongol society was clearly a society in which some women were more equal than others, as a mission of Franciscan friars observed on a journey to the Mongol Empire in 1245–47:

> [The Mongols] have as many wives as they can afford, and generally buy them, so that except for women of noble birth they are mere chattels. They marry anyone they please, except their mother, daughter, and sister from the same mother. When their father dies, they marry their step-mother, and a younger brother or cousin marries his brother's widow. The wives do all the work, and make shoes, leather garments, and so on, while the men make nothing but arrows, and practice shooting with bows. They compel even boys three or four years old to the same exercise, and even some of the women, especially the maidens, practice archery and ride as a rule like men. If people are taken in adultery and fornication, man and woman alike are slain. (Skelton, Marston, and Painter, 94)

The friars were no apologists for the Mongols, and other reports suggest that women generally enjoyed more equitable treatment within the tribe. After Chinggis Khan's first wife, Börte, was kidnapped, Chinggis spared no effort to get her back; once safely within his *ordu* (camp), she resumed her position of chief wife, and her unborn child, Chinggis's firstborn, Jochi, was later awarded the respect due to the firstborn son of the Great Khan despite his questionable parentage.

Although women participated in all aspects of Mongol life, there were particular tasks assigned them. They were generally expected to drive the large wagons, so essential for these nomadic tribes, on which the family placed all their tents, dwellings, and household goods. William of Rubruck, the cleric who traveled among the Mongols between 1253 and 1255, claimed that one woman would drive up to 30 connected wagons. One noble's dwelling could demand 200 wagons, and one noble with many wives could possess many dwellings. Because the terrain was relatively flat, many wagons could be lashed together in sequence. The woman driver would sit on the front of an ox- or camel-pulled wagon, and the rest would follow. If the terrain became difficult the animals with their individual wagons could quite easily be separated and led one at a time. Women would also load and unload the wagons themselves.

When camp was struck, it was the woman's duty to saddle the horses and apportion the packs and loads to the camels and horses. When a suitable site for a camp was chosen, it was the women who were expected to erect the tents and dwellings. The dwellings were pitched with the doorway facing south, the master's couch at the far end of the tent or yurt, and his wife's on the east side to her husband's left. The wife would place her own doll-like felt effigy on the wall over her head. By the entrance to the dwelling on the woman's side was placed another effigy. This effigy used a cow's udder and was considered protection for the woman, the cow milker. On the man's side of the door there was placed a mare's udder, representing the man's responsibilities for making *kumis* (alcoholic mare's milk). Each wife would have her own residence, called *curia*, which might include a smaller dwelling, placed behind, for her maids. The chief wife would pitch her *curia* at the westernmost end, and the others would then position their own dwellings accordingly, "a space of one stone's throw between [them]" (William of Rubruck, 74), until the last wife would have her own tent or yurt at the eastern end of the camp. William of Rubruck is not alone when he states that these family units resembled small cities when they were finally assembled, although he adds that an absence of men was noticeable within their confines.

Milking the cows, although not the *kumis*-yielding mares, was considered women's work, as was making butter and curds. Both men and women tended the sheep and goats, and both would on occasion milk these animals. Skin curing and leather preparation was a task left to the women, as was shoe making and the stitching and manufacture of all leather garments. Women also made other clothes, such as socks and jerkins.

The stories that have endured idolizing the daughter of Kaidu (d. 1301), a great-grandson of Chinggis Khan and an upholder of traditional Mongol values and virtues, suggest an aspirational ideal for Mongol women and an idealized wife or daughter or even sister for Mongol men. Kutulun, daughter of Kaidu Khan, cherished her reputation for martial prowess while at the same time cultivating her beauty and her attraction to men, attributes recorded by Marco Polo. She would accompany her father into battle and gained fame for her fighting skills, fearlessness, and ferocity. She steadfastly refused to take a husband unless that man should first force her submission through unarmed combat. Many failed in the attempt. If Kutulun represented the ideal, then the perfect Mongol woman would have been proud and brave, valuing physical strength and stamina. She would have felt at home in the saddle and enjoyed time spent as a warrior, preferring the open spaces to the camp. Kaidu fought a losing battle to retain traditional, pastoral Mongol values, a passion that his daughter shared. Neither survived.

~*George Lane*

FOR MORE INFORMATION

Rossabi, M. *Khubilai Khan*. Berkeley: University of California Press, 1988.

Skelton, R. A., T. E. Marston, and G. D. Painter. *The Vinland Map and the Tartar Relation*. 2nd ed. New Haven, Conn.: Yale University Press, 1995.

William of Rubruck. *The Mission of William of Rubruck.* Translated and edited by P. Jackson, with D. Morgan. London: Hakluyt Society, 1990.

POLYNESIA

The status of Polynesian women was much superior before the introduction of Western ideas and cultures into Polynesia in the 18th and 19th centuries. Even at that, ancient Polynesian societies were not egalitarian, and men held more dominant and important positions than women.

Almost all Polynesian islands adhered to a patriarchal order of governance. High chiefs and other rulers governed because they were descended through senior blood-lines (primogeniture) from other high-ranking individuals. Generally, the longer and more impressive the genealogical pedigree, the higher the ranking of the individual. There are numerous examples, however, where high-ranking chiefs did not rule a more important or larger geographical territory. Prestige and ranking did not always coincide. In large island groups such as Tonga, Hawai'i, and Samoa, for example, women played a major role in the transmission of rank. Chiefs could claim status and rank through their more important mother's line, and on a few occasions a high-ranking woman might hold prestige and status far above her sovereign. Such a woman could enter aggressively into politics, maintain her own court, and become as influential as her husband. A case in point is King Kamehameha I of Hawai'i (1758–1819) who, when visiting his wife Ka'ahumanu (1768–1832), had to enter her dwellings on his hands and knees because she far outranked him genealogically. After Kamehameha's death in 1819, Ka'ahumanu continued her domineering status as *kuhina nui* (great sovereign) over the next two Hawaiian kings, Kamehameha II and III. High-ranking women like these were treated with utmost respect by chiefs and commoners alike, and their wishes were carried out as consistently as that of a high-ranking male.

Common women, on the other hand, assumed roles and duties highly regulated by custom and *kapu* (things being forbidden to them), just as *kapu* determined the duties and functions of every other individual in Polynesian societies—chiefs, priests, commoners, and so on. The origin of this complex *kapu* system is hidden through the mists of time, but it continued up until the 19th century when, in most cases, it met its death blow with the introduction of Christianity.

Anciently, women were forbidden to participate in public religious ceremonies, eat with the men, cook their own food, touch their husband's fishing equipment, or eat various types of food—coconuts, some bananas, certain fish, dog, pork, sea turtles, and whales. Each month during their menstrual period, women had to live in separate dwellings by themselves because they were considered unclean.

Traditional customs also regulated the division of labor between men and women. Men's work consisted of house building, temple construction, canoe and weaponry making, weaving *sennit* (rope), fishing beyond the lagoons, collecting mountain plantains, hunting pigs, and strenuous gardening. Women essentially reared the children at home (assisted in most cases by her eldest daughter), fished in the lagoons and shallow waters, produced tapa used in the construction of clothing and decorative coverings (discussed in chapter 5, under "Fabrics"), plaited all the mats for the floors and ceilings (some fine mats took up to nine months of a woman's time), wove various types of baskets, gathered fire wood for their daily meals, and in many instances, helped in the family's garden. Women were not expected to participate in military battles, but many accompanied their husbands and often fought side by side with them. In the absence of the men during wartime, women were prepared to defend their villages against enemy attack. Women also accompanied their husbands on long, perilous oceangoing voyages of discovery. They participated freely in music and dance, they traveled freely, and they competed together with men in swimming and surfing contests.

Women were not considered chattels, and they had a large amount of freedom in their choice of husbands or in divorcing one. Many had the will to strike back verbally when needed. If all else failed, they could willingly pick up and live with another relative or an immediate family member. Women were a scarcity in many areas of Polynesia where infanticide was practiced—male children were usually preferred and were allowed to survive more often than girls. A beautiful woman, therefore, was highly prized and much sought after in marriage.

Life was hard in ancient Polynesia, and both women and men spent a good deal of their day in subsistence living. Although they possessed a Neolithic technology and lived in formidable insularity, the Polynesians created a larger and more complex way of life than achieved by many other peoples in the world. A typical woman's day might unfold like this. Everyone in the household arose shortly after dawn and proceeded to a nearby stream or the ocean, where they had a vigorous bath, often despite the cold water so early in the morning. Mothers would attend to the washing of the smaller children and make sure the older ones were spotlessly clean.

Returning home, the adults would roll up the tapa sleeping cloth and woven mats they had used as beds and store them in the rafters of the house. After eating a few leftovers from the previous day's meal, the father would set out to fish or gather various foods for the main meal, which he would plan to cook in the early afternoon. The children would venture out to play with others in the neighborhood, and the mother would then set about her regular duties. First, perhaps, she might join a group of other women in gathering shellfish or octopus in the shallow lagoons. Polynesian women often worked in groups, and their friendly conversations likely made work that much easier. After having caught sufficient seafood, the women would return to the village and gather food plants and firewood for their daily meal. The rest of the morning would be devoted to the never-ending task of tapa production (see the Polynesia entry in chapter 5, under "Fabrics"). A common sound heard throughout Polynesian villages was that of the tapa mallets beating out cloth against a hard wooden anvil. The women would continue their tapa production or perhaps weaving of mats and baskets while the men prepared the meal in an underground oven (discussed further in the section "Food" in chapter 5). Most regulations prevented food prepared by women from being eaten by men. After about two hours, the men would retrieve the prepared food from the oven and serve the women, who would then eat with their smaller children, separately from the adult men.

Invariably after the main meal of the day, Polynesians took a one- to two-hour nap. The work in the morning, the high quantity of food consumed, and the heat of the day triggered the need for such a rest. After awakening, some women resumed their pressing chores, while others resorted to more leisure time activities of conversing, visiting friends, playing games, or love making. By evening, mothers would gather their children up and bathe once again either in the stream or ocean. A light supper consisted of leftovers from the noon meal (Polynesians cooked only once a day). Late evenings might be taken up with chitchat, gossiping, telling humorous stories, singing and dancing—normally done together in groups—or listening to professional entertainers who might be in the vicinity. By nightfall, the mats would be removed from the rafters once again and rolled out, and the family settled down for another night's rest.

~Robert D. Craig

FOR MORE INFORMATION

Cunningham, S. *Hawaiian Religion and Magic*. St. Paul, Minn.: Lewellyn Publications, 1995.
Oliver, D. *Ancient Tahitian Society*. 3 vols. Honolulu: University of Hawai'i Press, 1974.
Reed, A. W. *An Illustrated Encyclopedia of Maori Life*. Auckland: A. H. and A. W. Reed, 1963.

Eunuchs

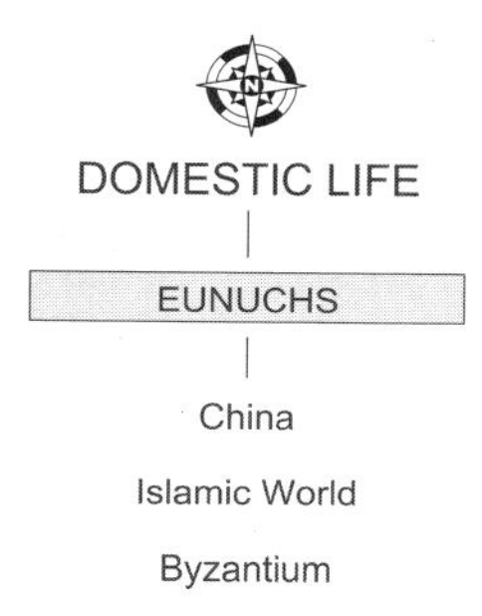

Before the Middle Ages, many parts of the world used castrated men—eunuchs—to serve as slaves. In addition to being shocked by this kind of cruelty, we tend to focus on this as a sexual act, designed to prevent the slave from being involved in reproductive activity. However, the ancient world saw it less as restricting sexuality than as breaking the loyalty ties to family. As the ancient Greek historian Herodotus wrote: "For it is among the barbarians [Persians] that eunuchs fetch a much higher price than whole men, because they are trustworthy in every respect" (Ayalon, 14).

Why would eunuchs be more trustworthy? In a world in which domestic life was dominated by loyalty to kinship groups, rulers and those in power at any level feared the conflicting loyalty that family ties brought. Why would one steal if not to enrich one's children and grandchildren? Why betray a king if not to place a relative in his place? The castration knife broke all those ties.

It would also seem, however, that a eunuch would harbor such anger at his owner that he could not be trusted. This problem was solved in two ways. First, the owner usually bought a slave that had already been castrated in faraway slave markets. In addition, eunuchs were generally scorned by the surrounding society, so a eunuch's only support was his owner. Loyalty to his owner was often rewarded by trust, power, and respect that he could get nowhere else. Thus the institution persisted in parts of the medieval world.

Most boys were castrated before the age of puberty; the sources say between ages 6 and 10. Sometimes merchants wanted to create eunuchs for use as homosexual prostitutes, in which case they castrated them after puberty so they would experience sexual reactions (Ayalon, 303). There were two kinds of castration: "complete," in which both the penis and testicles were removed, and "partial," which removed only the testicles. Eunuchs in the Islamic world and China were usually complete eunuchs, for they were the only ones who were trusted in the harems. In Byzantium, they favored partial eunuchs.

The surgery for complete eunuchs was by far the most dangerous. After the surgery, a tube was placed in the urethra to prevent it from closing during the healing process. Infections were frequent and mortality high. Only about one-third of the boys who had been completely castrated survived.

Christians in western Europe banned castration. Probably the most famous eunuch in the West was the brilliant church father Origen, who castrated himself in the 3rd century. The famous ancient historian, Eusebius, wrote that Origen's act was "proof of a mind youthful and immature, but at the same time of faith and self-mastery," for he took literally the phrase, "there are eunuchs who made themselves eunuchs for the kingdom of heaven's sake" (Eusebius, 245). Origen was a teacher who taught boys and girls, and he claimed he did not want any suspicion to fall on him because of the proximity between him and his students. Origen lived in the eastern part of the Roman Empire and no doubt knew of Persian eunuchs. The church's rejection of Origen's act set the stage for further prohibition. The Council of Nicaea in 325 proclaimed that a man who had been castrated for medical reasons—such as testicular cancer—or violently mutilated in warfare could remain a cleric. However, "if anyone in good health has castrated himself," he could not become a cleric, and he would be removed from office if he already was a churchman (Murray, 74).

Of course, religious prohibitions alone would not end the practice of castration. After all, Islam also prohibited castration, and the Byzantine Empire was Christian. Byzantine Christians even castrated their own sons to serve in the court. In western Europe during the Renaissance, boys began to be castrated to preserve their beautiful high singing voices. Most likely, castration in the medieval West went out of practice as the decentralization of the Germanic kingdoms did away with large-scale household slavery. In the east all the way to China, on the other hand, powerful rulers in powerful courts relied on the loyalty of tens of thousands of men who had been castrated to ensure their loyalty.

~Joyce E. Salisbury

FOR MORE INFORMATION

Ayalon, D. *Eunuchs, Caliphs, and Sultans: A Study in Power Relationships*. Jerusalem: Magnes Press, 1999.

Eusebius. *The History of the Church*. Translated by G. A. Williamson. Harmondsworth, U.K.: Penguin, 1965.

Murray, J. "Mystical Castration." In *Conflicted Identities and Multiple Masculinities: Men in the Medieval West*. Edited by J. Murray. New York: Garland, 1999.

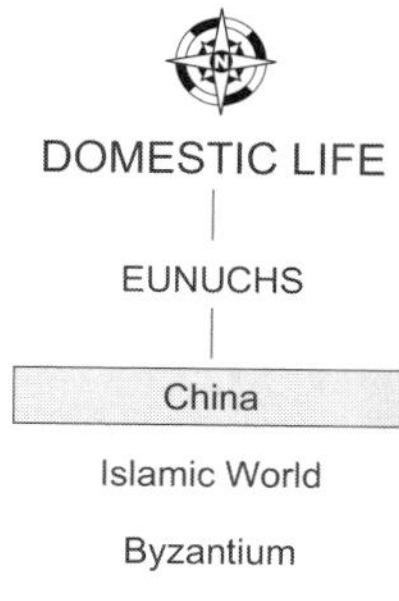

CHINA

Imperial eunuchs constituted a small class of the privileged in China. They probably numbered no more than 5,000 at any given time during the dynasty, but they had tremendous power and influence. Although by the mid-9th century, the throne required all regions to submit castrated boys, most came from regions along the southeast coast. The majority of them were sold by their parents and emasculated in their youth, before they were sent to the capital. After the boys arrived in Changan, a senior eunuch of the Service for Palace Attendants adopted them and gave them his surname. He also taught them whatever duties the throne assigned them. By and large, eunuchs were illiterate, and most performed menial duties in the innermost, private quarters of the emperor. Some, however, had enough education to teach palace ladies the Confucian classics, Daoist philosophy, history, mathematics, law, poetry, calligraphy, and board games.

In the early years of the dynasty, the throne restricted the number, power, and privileges of the eunuchs. In the late 7th century, Empress Wu eased the restraints. Eunuchs began to acquire mansions in the capitals, as well as estates in the nearby countryside, take "wives," and adopt uncastrated children of both sexes so that they could bequeath their titles and property to their heirs.

Eunuchs were the guardians of the imperial harem, so employed because they could not spawn offspring that were not the emperor's. By the middle of the 8th century, the number of women in the seraglio of Emperor Illustrious August soared to 40,000, with about 1 eunuch for every 10 women. Because they governed the emperor's household, eunuchs had unique and frequent access to him. Illustrious August's most trusted eunuch slept in a curtained area along the side of the emperor's bedchamber. Eunuchs were solely responsible to and dependent on the emperor but acquired enormous power over officials because of their unique access to him.

By the early 8th century, the throne was employing eunuchs as generals. It sent one to northern Vietnam with orders to suppress revolts by aborigines. Between 722 and 728, this general quelled three rebellions with the help of an army that he recruited from the native peoples. He took more than 80,000 heads and had the bodies of the slain stacked in pyramids, presumably to serve as a warning to men contemplating insurrection. He was a brutal man who terrified the aborigines because he took scalps and cut the skin from the faces of prisoners he had captured. He was not the only eunuch known for his cruelty. The citizens of Changan so despised one who had been a thief catcher in the capital that they stood by the road with bricks and stones to hurl at him when he departed for an assignment in the south. A chief minister at the time had to order market officials to disperse the crowd so the man could leave the city.

It was not until the rebellion of An Lushan that eunuchs began to exert great power over the court and the government. After 800, they came to control the flow of documents to and from the throne. Addresses to the emperor and decrees from him passed through their hands and required their approval before implementation. They became involved in appointments of provincial governors and the operations of capital schools. By the 9th century, the throne had placed eunuchs in charge of the palaces, the postal system, guest houses, the imperial treasury, and temples in the capitals. It also established a council of eunuchs responsible for conducting deliberations on public policy. As a result, the power of eunuchs became so great that they engineered the enthronements of over half of the emperors in that century. Some of the hapless rulers in that epoch became puppets of the eunuchs (Benn, 138–42).

FOR MORE INFORMATION

Benn, C. *Daily Life in Traditional China: The Tang Dynasty*. Westport, Conn.: Greenwood Press, 2002.

ISLAMIC WORLD

At the founding of Islam, people in the Middle East and elsewhere had a history of using eunuchs in many capacities, and the Muslims adopted the practice. However, there were specific conditions in Muslim society that fostered the use of eunuchs and that made the eunuch institution stronger and more essential in Muslim lands than elsewhere. The three most important conditions affecting the use of eunuchs were (1) the extreme seclusion of women and their large numbers in the courts of the rulers, (2) the extensive use of slaves in the military, and (3) the wide boundaries of the lands of Islam, which allowed eunuch slaves to serve far away from their homes.

The seclusion of women fostered the need for trustworthy eunuchs to watch and serve the women. In addition, during medieval Muslim society, there were large numbers of women in the households of the well-to-do in general (including the Muslim clergy). Muslims were allowed to have four wives, and they could also keep an unlimited number of concubines. These women remained secluded in harems, so they needed people to serve them, provide for them, and guard them. Husbands entrusted their concubines to eunuchs—apparently only complete eunuchs, whose penis and testicles had been removed. These were the only men—aside from the owner—who had free access to the women's quarters. Even adolescent sons could not enter. Thus the flow of communication to and from the women was in the hands of the eunuchs.

The numbers of eunuchs who served were staggering. In 908, the ʿAbbasid caliph recorded that he had 11,000 eunuchs—7,000 black and 4,000 white—in his household. Other records suggest that men kept an average of three eunuchs for every woman in their harem (Ayalon, 16–17).

At least officially, Muslims did not castrate the captives themselves; it was done by slave traders before the eunuchs were sold. Boys from the Sudan in Africa were castrated and sold in Egypt, and others on the borders of the extensive lands were also sold into this kind of slavery. The huge numbers of eunuchs who served the caliphs is made more shocking by the texts that suggest that only about one-third of the boys who underwent complete castration survived. Thus, for the 11,000 eunuchs who served one caliph, 33,000 slave boys were castrated.

Eunuchs were not only used to guard the harems. Because they had no family ties, and because they were scorned by the surrounding society, they owed their full allegiance to their owner. Consequently, some eunuchs were placed in charge of the palace treasury as well as in trusted positions close to the person of their owner. Records indicate that some of the highest offices in Muslim courts were sometimes held by influential eunuchs.

Eunuchs began to serve a second critical function for Islam—caring for and training the slaves who would serve in the Muslim armies. Uncastrated boys were captured and placed in training in military schools, and eunuchs served as supervisors, protectors, and trainers of the young boys. During this apprenticeship, the slave boys were slowly molded into becoming good Muslims and good soldiers, and the eunuchs seem to have served as a shield against the homosexual exploitation of the young recruits. Guarding and training the young soldiers seemed a logical extension of the eunuchs' care of the women in the harem.

The relationship between soldier and eunuch forged in the military schools seems to have extended to the battlefield, where some eunuchs served as commanders of the forces they had trained. In 891, for example, the war between Byzantium and Islam produced a famous eunuch commander, Yāzmān, about whom the chroniclers wrote: "The enemy feared him, and Christianity was scared of him even in its own fortress" (Ayalon, 123). This case was not isolated, and throughout the medieval period there is evidence of eunuchs commanding forces and even fortresses.

One of the advantages of the eunuchs for their owners was not really their lack of sexual lust, for the sources all indicate that eunuchs did feel sexual pleasure—both homosexual and heterosexual—and there is evidence that pleasurable relationships formed between eunuchs and women in the harems. In fact, the advantage was that eunuchs did not have family ties—there was no one to compete for their loyalty. However, in violation of this fundamental principle in the eunuch institutions, there is occasional evidence of eunuchs getting married. In 1347, the sultan's favorite eunuch married one of his concubines, much to the disgust of the commentators (Ayalon, 323).

This incident indicates that with an institution as large and far reaching as that of the Muslim eunuchs, the complexities and varieties within the institution are equally varied. Once they had been castrated, the men remained men with all the human desires for greed, power, and love as they had before.

~Joyce E. Salisbury

FOR MORE INFORMATION

Ayalon, D. *Eunuchs, Caliphs, and Sultans: A Study in Power Relationships*. Jerusalem: Magnes Press, 1999.

Marmon, S. *Eunuchs and Sacred Boundaries in Islamic Society*. New York: Oxford University Press, 1995.

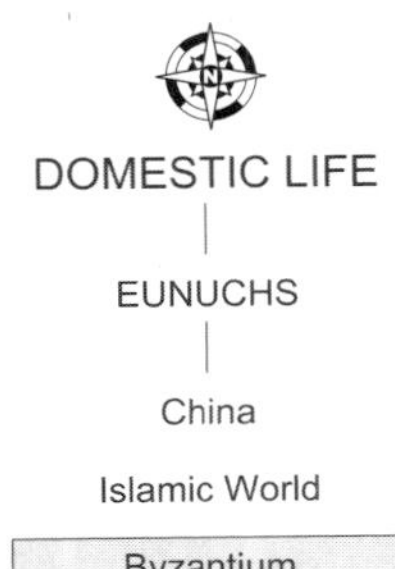

BYZANTIUM

The fundamental sense of order (*taxis*) that underlaid the Byzantine worldview entailed a strict hierarchy of gender roles, political rank, and spiritual status. The definition of these social categories in late antiquity was a major concern of both court and church, which shaped popular perceptions in later years as well. The important place that eunuchs came to occupy in Constantinople between the 4th and 12th centuries reflects the persistent need to bridge the space—between men and women, emperor and subjects, and patriarch and laity—that was fundamental to Byzantine society.

Eunuchs had long been retained as servants at the imperial palace in Rome. Because the castration of Roman males was officially condemned, many of these eunuchs were brought as slaves from neighboring states to the north and east. The 2nd-century physician Galen describes the surgical options, which involved crushing or excising the testicles, while admitting his own reluctance to perform such operations. When castrated as infants or children, eunuchs developed a distinctive adult physique, comportment, and voice. By contrast, adult castrates normally retained their mature physical characteristics, including sexual desire. In all cases, the eunuch's sterility set him outside the conventional gender roles of the Roman family, which was based on procreation as the key to social stability.

By the late Roman Empire, the imperial court in the eastern portion of the empire had been influenced by the practices of the Persians and had come to recognize the advantages of using eunuch slaves in the imperial households. As the Roman Empire was transformed into the Byzantine Empire, the practice continued. During the early centuries, it appears that most of the eunuchs were enslaved foreigners who had been sold as eunuchs to serve as domestic servants in elite households. Because these men had no kinship ties, they were considered perfectly loyal to their masters. The origin of some of the famous eunuchs may be seen in their names: Stephen the Persian served Emperor Justinian II (685), and Damianos the Slav was the chief eunuch of Emperor Michael III (842). In the 10th century, we read of Samonas the Arab who rose to power under Emperor Leo VI (912) (Tougher, 148).

The high positions eunuchs held perhaps explains the shift from foreign slave to family eunuchs. The emperor and empress each had their own corps of eunuchs, who served as caregivers, chamberlains, advisors, and messengers. Many were entrusted with the care of treasuries and with military leadership. Emperor Justinian's great general, the eunuch Narses, was renowned, and some commentators were surprised that a eunuch "raised in the women's quarters and accustomed to a soft life" could serve so courageously (Ringrose, 96).

Eunuchs rose to prominence as special attendants to the emperor in the late 3rd and 4th centuries, and through much of the Byzantine period they filled many important positions at court. They traditionally occupied the various ranks of *koubikoularios*, personal assistants within the emperor's domestic quarters (*kouboukleion*). Most of these positions were responsible for activities that in other Byzantine households were managed by women: cooking, serving meals, tending the wardrobe, writing letters, and managing family finances. Their intermediate gender also permitted eunuchs free access to the restricted women's quarters of the palace, where the empress maintained her own set of *koubikoularioi*. The highest ranking of these palace officials was the *parakoimomenos*, who supervised the personal safety of the emperor by locking himself within his bedchamber at night. Because "beardless men" were thought to pose no threat to the imperial family's power and purity, they functioned as barbers, physicians, trusted advisors, and confidants. They conducted marriage negotiations, attended the birth and education of the imperial children, and arranged burials. In such roles, eunuchs functioned as valued intermediaries between the extended Byzantine bureaucracy and the outside world, their ambiguous status permitting them to cross the boundaries of personal and institutional etiquette. While themselves disqualified from occupying the throne, they clearly were in a position to promote the careers of other family members. More than 30 eunuchs are known to have occupied these important administrative posts during the middle of the 11th century. The official status of eunuchs declined during the 12th century with the establishment of the aristocratic Komnene dynasty and the imposition of its new masculine ideal. Their numbers at court appear much reduced after the Latin Conquest of 1204.

The steady demand for eunuchs in Constantinople was recognized outside the city. Castrated slaves were brought on occasion as diplomatic gifts by ambassadors from Italy, Persia, the Slavic north, and the Caucasus. Aristocratic families are also known to have sent such offerings; the wealthy widow Danelis sent 100 eunuchs to the emperor Basil I in the late 9th century. Such ready availability suggests that the practice was condoned in the Byzantine provinces. Under some circumstances, infant castration could be regarded as an investment in a future career by parents seeking to place their progeny in the official hierarchies. A number of successful palace eunuchs came from the region of Paphlagonia in northern Asia Minor.

Narses, Byzantine general and eunuch; commanded Emperor Justinian I's imperial bodyguard. © Mary Evans Picture Library.

Young castrates were brought up in special quarters within the palace in Constantinople. Older eunuchs were responsible for training new arrivals in the intricate protocol of court ceremony. As a result, this cohort formed an interconnected network that reached across formal civil and clerical boundaries. Their elegant court garb included a white tunic trimmed with gold decoration and a red doublet with gold edging. Eunuchs of the *protospatharios* rank were distinguished by pearls set in a special neck decoration. Others are known to have worn earrings.

In a society that stressed external appearance and social rank, eunuchs were regarded with mixed feelings by many contemporary observers. Their supposed lack of sexual distraction allowed eunuchs to develop formidable intellectual and rhetorical skills. In addition to possessing a distinctive body language, voice, and lack of beard and body hair, eunuchs were said by male observers to have less-stable temperaments, to resemble women in their lack of discipline and self-control. Michael Psellos, writing in the 12th century, praises individual eunuchs as loyal, shrewd, and hard working while he remains wary of their ambiguous, haughty, and "changeable" nature. Readily identifiable in appearance and manner and familiar with esoteric palace routines, eunuchs were sometimes suspected of possessing supernatural skills.

Eunuchs occupied varied positions outside the imperial palace. Military commanders, including the famous 6th-century general Narses, were celebrated as clever field strategists. Others served as provincial administrators and in aristocratic houses. Their equal intimacy with men, women, and children qualified them to work as doctors and teachers on all social levels. They are known to have led careers as musicians, singers, actors, and prostitutes.

Surprisingly, given the Christian disapproval of eunuchs, many Byzantine eunuchs entered the church and served as priests, bishops, and monks. Some (like the famous Christian teacher Origen) had themselves castrated to help them remain chaste. There are even texts that praise eunuchs and liken them as angels—both pure and royal messengers. In fact, dream interpretation texts claimed that if one dreamed of a eunuch, that represented an angel (Tougher, 167). Thus, while eunuchs were scorned by many, they obviously offered an appeal for some.

Most of the eunuchs in Byzantine society seem to have been partial eunuchs, meaning that their penises remained intact. This is a much milder mutilation than the complete eunuchs who were traditionally enslaved in China and Muslim lands. Byzantine commentators indicate that there were various ways to produce eunuchs, and different ages for the operation. Sometimes mothers or nurses crushed infants' testicles to produce eunuchs. In other cases, doctors tied off the testicles to cut off the blood supply and destroy the organs. In these cases, the men grew up retaining childhood voices and more feminine physiques. Sometimes, the testicles were removed after men reached puberty. In this case, they could still feel desire and have intercourse if the surgery was done correctly. Medical texts indicate that surgeons understood anatomy sufficiently to just cut off the supply of semen while retaining normal sexual functioning (much like today's vasectomies). The Byzantines defined these men as eunuchs because they could no longer reproduce.

This range of surgery reveals the degree to which the term *eunuch* referred to men's ability to reproduce rather than to have and enjoy sexual intercourse. Indeed, many texts speak scornfully about eunuchs enjoying the favors of the women they were to be guarding in the harems of the wealthy. However, it seems that in Byzantium, what mattered most was that women would not bear illegitimate children while eunuchs were in charge.

The ambivalent attitude of Byzantines to eunuchs produced a remarkable document from the 12th century. A churchman named Theophylaktos wrote a work called *In Defense of Eunuchs*, ostensibly as a gift to his brother, who was probably a castrated cleric at Hagia Sophia, the great church in Byzantium. The text is written as a dialogue between a eunuch and a noncastrated man on the occasion of the baptism of the eunuch's nephew, who had been castrated. The author, speaking as the noncastrated man, lists all the stereotypes about eunuchs: they are greedy, avaricious, unsociable, licentious, ambitious, quarrelsome, and more. He claims that women teach eunuchs to be lazy and lie. Theophylaktos then turns to the eunuch in his text and allows him to speak in favor of eunuchs. The eunuch argues that some of these stereotypes might be true of Persian and Arabian eunuchs, but not Byzantine ones. He claims that because it is "natural" for some men to remain celibate, it is equally natural to remove the testicles since the body no longer needs them. He goes on to praise in detail eunuchs' skills and argues that they would not have risen to such high estate in church and state if they were not virtuous and talented (Ringrose, 103–7). In this detailed text, we can certainly read many of the arguments families must have used when they decided to castrate their child for his future career.

Eunuchs continued to play a significant role in Byzantine history at least until the beginning of the 15th century. However, after the 13th century, their roles had become less prominent. It may be that once families took over the institution, eunuchs no longer owed allegiance only to their masters. The advantage of having eunuchs was that it broke the power of the family ties that dominated the Middle Ages. Once that was gone, rulers were no longer so eager to procure eunuchs, and then families were no longer so willing to offer the sacrifice of their sons' procreative lives.

~Marcus Rautman and Joyce E. Salisbury

FOR MORE INFORMATION

Ringrose, K. M. "Living in the Shadows: Eunuchs and Gender in Byzantium." In *Third Sex, Third Gender.* Edited by G. Herdt. New York: Zone Books, 1994.

Tougher, S, ed. *Eunuchs in Antiquity and Beyond.* Swansea: Classical Press of Wales, 2002.

Children

Did people in the Middle Ages love children as modern parents do? This question has led to an ongoing debate among historians as they use scarce sources to try to look into the emotional lives of people in the past. We still do not have a full understanding of historical childhood, but the course of the debate has led us to learn more about the ways children and parents in the past were both different and similar to our own times.

One school of thought (begun by the French historian Philippe Ariès in the 1960s) argues that children in medieval Europe were largely invisible. Ariès quite rightly noted that households were crowded places with extended families, retainers, servants, and other strangers, and in such an atmosphere there was little room for children to occupy the center of attention as they so often do today. Furthermore, Ariès argued that because childhood was a dangerous time—many children died from disease and accidents—parents were not invested emotionally until their children were safely grown (Thurer, 87–91).

Other historians have looked at the data differently and argue that while medieval life was hard, parents then as now cared deeply for their children and did the best they could to raise them during hard times. Records offer descriptions of mothers weeping and tearing their hair out in grief at the death of a child, and of a father paralyzed in despair at the loss of a son. Fictional stories evoked great sympathy for lost and abused children; if no one cared, why would these stories be popular? Yes, there was death and dislocation of children as parents died and strangers raised them, but without a doubt, people loved their children.

There are some common threads of childhood across time and cultures: Children love toys, dolls, balls, toy animals, and hoops to roll. In Europe, some children even had small carriages pulled by live mice. Babies played peek-a-boo and struggled to learn to feed themselves whether with a spoon or chopsticks. In Europe beginning in the 12th century, families began to emphasize Christmas and St. Nicholas's Day (December 6) as times to give children presents (Thurer, 124). In all these things, we can see familiar parental care for children and their amusements.

Other child-rearing customs, however, seem very odd to modern readers. In all these cultures, wealthy mothers hired wet nurses, poorer women who had borne an infant and who could breast-feed an additional child. We can immediately see the hazards in this arrangement; a poorer woman might suffer from some malnutrition and might struggle to have enough milk for her own child as well as the nurseling. Sometimes a nursing woman whose own child had died would serve as a wet nurse. These women might move into the noble household, or more often, the infant might be sent to the wet nurse's home to live for a year or two until weaned. This practice violates modern notions that caution against separating a young child from a caretaker.

Another custom that was practiced from Europe to China to Muslim countries was swaddling the infant. Infants were wrapped tightly in strips of cloth, which were removed only once a day for cleaning. People believed this was necessary to mold the infant's limbs into nice straight legs and arms. It also served to keep babies warm in houses that were poorly heated. While some modern commentators have criticized this practice, it was probably the safest way to ensure that infants did not injure themselves in dangerous households with open fires. Throughout most of history, babies grew up with this kind of limited mobility.

Although early cultures shared these practices for feeding and caring for infants, their attitudes toward childhood in general were quite different. In Europe, including Scandinavia, childhood as a stage was quite short. By the age of seven, children were seen as small adults ready to begin to take their place in the world. Peasant boys worked with their fathers in the fields, taking responsibility for chores such as herding the oxen, and girls of all classes learned to spin, weave, and cook. Noble boys were sent to other households to learn the arts of war as squires, and middle-class boys were sent to be apprentices. The games were over, and responsibilities had begun. In China, on the other hand, the state actually identified particular stages of childhood that recognized (as we do today) that growing up is a gradual thing. In China, "childhood" extended from 3 years old to 14, and "adolescence" from 15 to 19. Each stage came with its own expectations of education and behavior. The difference is likely a result of the extended educational system that the Chinese court had implemented to be sure to produce skilled public servants.

The survival of families depended on the next generations. Childhood was difficult largely because of the many childhood diseases that had to be overcome without recourse to antibiotics and injections. But children did grow up and learn to take their place in the world, and despite scarce information, we can get glimpses of the games they played and the love they felt as they grew.

~*Joyce E. Salisbury*

FOR MORE INFORMATION

Ariès, P. *Centuries of Childhood: A Social History of Family Life*. Translated by R. Baldick. New York: Knopf, 1962.

Thurer, S. L. *The Myths of Motherhood*. New York: Penguin, 1994.

EUROPE

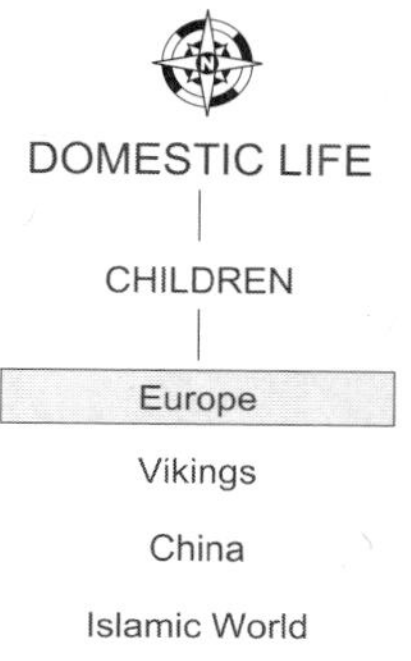

The birth of a child in Europe in the Middle Ages normally took place in bed at the home of the mother. The mother was assisted by her female relatives and friends, and if any sort of medical practitioner was present, it was usually a midwife. Birth was a moment of heightened danger both for the mother and child, with infant mortality about twice as high as that in the poorest countries of the world today. Even if the delivery was successful, the child's prospects remained uncertain. Children have relatively weak immune systems, and the high incidence of disease and limited medical knowledge of the period meant that many children never reached adulthood. During the 13th century, about one child in six may have died in the first year, one in four by age 5; perhaps two-thirds lived to age 20.

The arrival of the new child was marked by the ceremony of baptism. This sacrament was considered vitally important because the church taught that the unbaptized could not enter heaven. At baptism, the child was lifted from the font by its godparents, who undertook to educate the child in the Christian faith. One of the most important elements of the baptismal ceremony was the assigning of a name. The child at baptism received only a single name—the term "Christian name" still survives today.

During the first six years or so of life, the child was almost entirely in the hands of women. Breast-feeding was the only satisfactory means of nourishing an infant since animals' milk was recognized as potentially hazardous. Yet the milk was not always provided by the mother herself. Many wealthy families entrusted their children to the care of a wet nurse, a practice also followed in less-privileged households, whether for the sake of fashion or because the income lost by nursing in person would be greater than the cost of hiring a wet nurse, or for some biological cause that impeded the mother's ability to nurse.

Wealthy families often had the wet nurse live in their home. Alternatively, the family could send the child away and visit from time to time to see that it was doing well. The wet nurse, of course, had to be lactating. In some cases, she was a mother whose infant had died—with the high rate of infant mortality, there were always more lactating women than nursing infants. In many instances, she was probably the mother of an older infant who weaned her child early in order to take on wet-nursing.

During the first few months of its life, the baby spent much of its time in swaddling clothes. Depending on local customs, the swaddled baby might be wrapped mummy-style in long bands of linen, with only its face showing, or in a large cloth with a few bands wrapped around it to hold it in place. Sometimes the wrapping left the arms or upper body free. Swaddling may have helped to keep the infant out of trouble, but its principal purpose was to keep it warm, a very real concern in the drafty living conditions of the time. The mummy-style swaddling bands were also intended to ensure that the limbs grew straight, a purpose based on medieval ideas of physiology, which held that a baby's body was so pliant that pulling or pushing on a body part determined how it grew.

The practice of swaddling cannot have made infant hygiene very easy. The linen swaddling cloths were washable, but keeping the baby clean was a challenge that was not always very satisfactorily met. Contemporary doctors emphasized the importance of regular bathing of the infant, and some recommended as many as three baths a day and changes of swaddling whenever the baby soiled itself. But such cleanliness was probably not very common, especially among poorer people who had less time for child care.

Woman holding a swaddled child. Notice how tightly the child is wrapped for warmth and restricted movement. Illustration by Jeffrey Singman (after Maciejowski Bible).

Over the course of the baby's first few months, its swaddling was reduced, and eventually swaddling was dispensed with altogether. The toddler wore a shirt and gown, which must have greatly facilitated hygiene. While learning to walk, the child wore a padded bonnet to help protect his or her head against injury.

As the baby entered the second year of life, he or she was weaned. A nursing baby might already have been introduced to other liquids such as water, honey water, or beer. Eventually, the baby received soft solids such as mashed or prechewed food, bread soaked in honey water, wine, or soup, or a pap of flour and milk flavored with honey. Honey was often used to stimulate the child's appetite, although it may have been too expensive for a poor family. By age two, the child had its milk teeth and was fully ready for solid food.

Medieval people also recognized that children had a natural inclination for play. Already as infants, they were given simple toys like rattles, and as they grew, their repertoire of toys and games grew. Medieval toys included dolls, clay figurines, hobby-horses, carts, tops, and whistles.

About age seven, children began to be actively prepared for the expectations imposed by their assigned place in society. Girls remained under female tutelage, learning the skills appropriate to their class. For most girls, this meant helping their mothers with tasks around the home, assisting with the care of younger children, and eventually learning the full range of a woman's household responsibilities. Many aristocratic and urban girls learned to read and write. Boys, meanwhile, began the transition from the world of women to that of men. For the overwhelming majority, this meant beginning to participate in the work of agriculture. Boys in the aristocracy headed in one of several directions. Many were prepared for a position in the warrior class by training for knighthood. A boy on this track was usually sent away from his family to the household of some greater lord, where he would learn aristocratic manners and the arts of war. Other boys might be groomed for a life in the church and would learn reading, writing, and related skills. Urban boys might become apprentices to learn a trade (Singman, 17–23).

To read about children in Elizabethan England, see the England entry in the section "Children" in chapter 2 ("Domestic Life") of volume 3; for 18th-century England, see the England entry in the section "Children" in chapter 2 ("Domestic Life") of volume 4; and for Victorian England, see the England entry in the section "Children" in chapter 2 ("Domestic Life") of volume 5 of this series.

FOR MORE INFORMATION

Orme, N. *Medieval Children*. New Haven, Conn.: Yale University Press, 2003.
Singman, J. L. *Daily Life in Medieval Europe*. Westport, Conn.: Greenwood Press, 1999.

VIKINGS

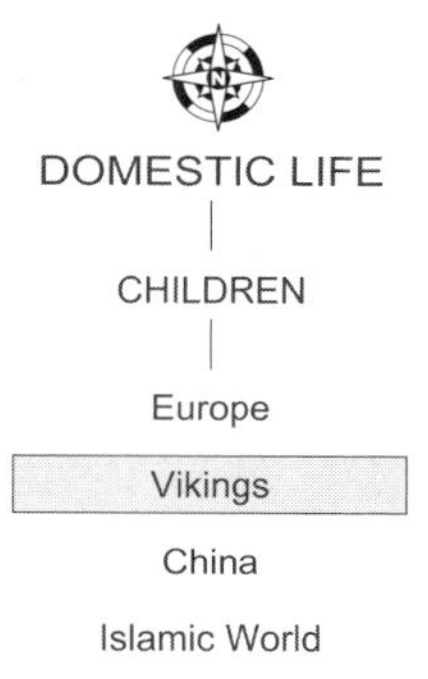

The birth of a baby was exclusively a female affair during the Viking Age. The helpers were always women, trained or untrained, although on more isolated farms, the husband assisted. The birth typically took place in the bath chamber or other separate place, evidently to provide the prospective mother with privacy and to limit the risk of infection. The normal birth position was for the woman to kneel on the floor. As the birth progressed, she would shift to a knee-elbow position, and the child would be received from behind. Birth chairs appear not to have been used in Scandinavia.

Childbirth was a risky matter in the Viking Age. Although there are no figures for childbirth deaths in this period, it is certain that they were considerably higher than they are now. One reason was marriage at an early age; young and often not fully grown females have a particularly marked pregnancy-related mortality. In the pre-Christian period, runes and charms were offered as remedies for painful labor and difficult births; in Christian times, appeals were made to the Virgin Mary and Saints Margaret and Dorothy.

Infant mortality was also high and must be seen in light of poor hygienic standards, causing frequent acute gastroenteritis and epidemics of dangerous intestinal diarrheal diseases including dysentery and typhoid fever. Epidemics of other children's diseases, such as measles, diphtheria, whooping cough, and scarlet fever, no doubt also took their toll.

Despite the desire for offspring, some babies were unwanted. Such babies were exposed to the elements and left to their fate. The fact that this practice was prohibited in some Scandinavian laws compiled in the 12th and 13th centuries suggests that it continued well after the introduction of Christianity; indeed, some laws permitted exposure when a baby was deformed. Runic inscriptions naming the children of a couple show that daughters were considerably fewer than sons. Sons were more useful in the home than daughters, who had to be provided with a dowry to attract a suitable husband, and there are reasons to believe that couples deliberately attempted to limit through exposure or neglect the number of girls allowed to live.

Shortly after birth, the baby was given a name, and this was the first formal event in a baby's life. The naming of the baby signified its inclusion in society and—in Christian times—the church. Even in pre-Christian times, the ceremony appears to have involved sprinkling the baby with water and giving it a present (another gift was given when the baby cut its first tooth). The choice of a name was an important matter because name, personal qualities, and good fortune were all considered to be closely related. Rune stones and Old Norse-Icelandic literature show that parents often reproduced name elements in different combination with each child, as with the children of the 9th century Norwegian Vegeir, who were named Vebjorn, Vedis, Vegest, Vemund, Vestein, Vethorm, and Vethorn; or they repeated the name of a recently deceased relative, commonly a paternal grandparent.

Babies were breast-fed for a long time, and during the first years of their life children were in female care, although obviously under the authority of their fathers. The appearance in children's graves of bronze jingle bells, small ornaments, and infant clothing testify to the tender feelings of parents for their little ones and, of course, sentimentality and grief at the loss of a young child. There are, however, no rune stones raised in memory of children, and nothing is known of beliefs about children's afterlife.

The life of children was a combination of learning and play. There is archaeological evidence of model weapons, boats, and animals, and these toys allowed children to imitate the activities of adults. Ball games and other outdoor activities were no doubt also common. But childhood was brief in the Viking Age, and from an early age children were actively guided toward their anticipated places in society. For girls of the privileged classes, this might mean learning the skills required for household management; for the less privileged, it would mean cooking, laundry, spinning, and other domestic skills. Boys might be given the tasks of herding or caring for domestic animals, or, if they were of royal or well-to-do families, they were taught the arts of hunting and riding and the basics of combat and sailing. The mentors were presumably the children's parents, although the practice of fosterage, that is, having one's child—especially son—raised in another family, was common. Often this was a "political" arrangement between the child's father and the foster father, and, like marriage, it was a way of supplementing blood kinship relationships with nonblood kinship bonds to develop new alliances or strengthen existing ones.

~Kirsten Wolf

FOR MORE INFORMATION

Brondsted, J. *The Vikings*. Translated by K. Skov. Harmondsworth, England: Penguin, 1971.
Wolf, K. *Daily Life of the Vikings*. Westport, Conn.: Greenwood Press, forthcoming.

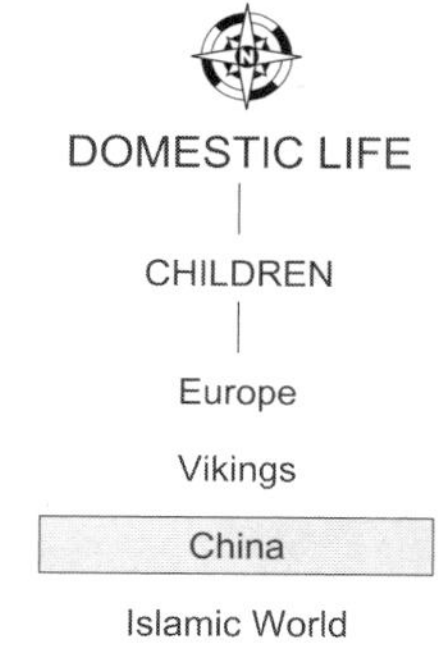

CHINA

Procreation was the paramount duty of husband and wife in medieval China. To ensure that they would conceive a child, a Tang medical text recommends that they each drink a cup of rainwater before retiring to the bedchamber. Men in traditional China seem to have had a great deal of anxiety about their potency, which led herbalists to suggest various remedies to treat the problem. One claimed that pistachio nuts were a marvelous treatment for impotence. He recommended extracting the juice by frying and then bathing the genitals in it. The repute of that cure was so great that by the 8th century, men often applied it before bedtime.

In most cases, mothers were responsible for child care. If a mother died in childbirth or thereafter, a relative might take over the task. In the homes of the well-to-do, wet nurses took over the duty of suckling infants and in some cases nursed children for years. Physicians warned families to avoid choosing women with obvious maladies: goiters, swellings, eczema, scabies, baldness resulting from fungal infections, stuffy noses, deafness, and body odor. The connection between a child and his or her wet nurse was intimate and enduring, especially when the mother did not attend to the child's upbringing or died when he or she was young. Other alternative caretakers were stepmothers. They might be loving substitutes for the natural mothers who had died, but they could also be abusive, unjustly thrashing their stepchildren or even attempting to murder them. They could be cruel because they did not have the maternal affection of a birth mother but also because they saw the eldest son of the first marriage, the husband's heir, as an impediment to the interests of their own sons.

After the birth of an heir, the father threw a feast to celebrate his good fortune. According to an ancient and revered classic source on rites, the banquet took place on the third day after the birth and was the first time that the father held his son in his arms. At some point after the infant's third month, the father selected a given name for the baby. The choice was never haphazard, for the words affected the future fortune of the child. The given name was taboo, that is, not used by family or outsiders. Children never referred to their parents by their personal names in speech or in writing. A son would have to decline an appointment to a political post whose title contained a character from his father's or paternal grandfather's given name. If he did not, he was subject to one year of penal servitude. The punishment for using the emperor's given name was much greater: three years of penal servitude. To avoid using it, writers used synonyms as substitutes.

The state divided childhood into three periods: infancy (1 to 2 years of age), childhood (3 to 14), and adolescence (15 to 19). Some fathers believed that discipline should begin as soon as a child could recognize the facial expressions of adults that expressed approval or disapproval of its behavior. They favored training the infant to be obedient and started using a bamboo rod to instill obedience at a fairly young age. Strictness tempered with tenderness led children to be respectful. Other fathers were indulgent, preferring love to discipline, praise to blame. Some moralists, however, contended that that sort of upbringing produced arrogant scoundrels.

Education began during the second period, usually about the age of six, and continued through the third, adolescence. Peasants passed on their agricultural knowledge to their sons orally, and artisans taught their sons their crafts by training them on the job. Some of the latter—brewers, swordsmiths, and the like—whose crafts involved various forms of technology, often swore their progeny to secrecy because disclosure entailed the loss of their monopoly on production and the income derived therefrom when competitors acquired their secrets and sold their goods at market. The child of a patrician learned the rudiments of reading, writing, and arithmetic. A precocious child might learn to write poetry at the age of five or six and master it by nine years of age. Sometimes the instructors were fathers, many of whom had high expectations for their sons. Some fathers were harsh in their discipline. For example, one governor found his son's knowledge of the classics wanting and had his son beaten with a thin rod, imprisoned him for a time, and forced him to stand at the city's gate as a demonstration of his own rectitude in dealing with his kin.

Adolescence for boys came to an end with "capping" at the age of 19. The father took his son to the ancestral shrine, if he had one, on an auspicious day and placed a cap on him before the spirits of the family's forebears. Capping was a rite of manhood. After the ritual concluded, the son took a new name that he usually used in signing his literary works. The end of adolescence came earlier for girls, with "pinning" at the age of 14. Their mothers did their daughters' hair up on top of their head and inserted a hairpin to keep it there. It was a rite of womanhood that signified the girl was eligible for marriage. Females also took new names at age 14 (Benn, 248–54).

FOR MORE INFORMATION

Benn, C. *Daily Life in Traditional China: The Tang Dynasty*. Westport, Conn.: Greenwood Press, 2002.

ISLAMIC WORLD

Childhood in the medieval Islamic world was generally defined as lasting from birth to the onset of puberty. In the absence of any physical signs of maturity, 15 was the generally accepted age of majority by which adulthood was defined. Such a determination was important because neither sexual segregation nor the requirements for women to wear the veil applied to prepubescent girls for the simple reason that girls and boys were not considered sexual beings until they were physically able to reproduce.

The four stages of childhood were generally defined as follows:

1. birth to teething
2. teething to about age 7, or the age of discernment
3. ages 7 to 14
4. age 14 to the onset of puberty, a transitional phase to adulthood

Medieval treatises on marriage admonished parents to receive the births of boys with restrained joy and to avoid demonstrating disappointment at the birth of girls. They also emphasized the importance of breast-feeding, which was the basic right of an infant for the first two years of its life.

Child mortality rates were high in the medieval Islamic world, as they were in all premodern societies. It was common for parents to lose one or more children in infancy or later to childhood diseases. For instance, in the 14th century, outbreaks of plague (Black Death) hit the medieval Islamic world especially hard.

Shortly after a child was born, it was customary to whisper in its ear the call to prayer (*adhan*) and the Islamic statement of faith (*shahada*)—"There is not god but God; Muhammad is the Messenger of God." Seven days later, when the child's prospects for survival were more certain, a public feast was held during which the child was named and had some of its hair cut; a sheep or goat was also slaughtered to express gratitude for the child's birth. The public nature of these ceremonies confirmed the father's parentage and his responsibility to provide for the child.

Some scholars argued that boys should be circumcised at this time as well, but the general practice was to perform the circumcision about age seven (when the boy began his formal education) or later as a right of passage to mark the onset of puberty and in preparation for adulthood and marriage. At whatever age it was performed, the circumcision of boys was in some sense an act of ritual purification (*tahara*). Moreover, it was a public and festive occasion and a nearly universal practice among Muslims in the Middle Ages.

Girls were also circumcised as an act of ritual purification prior to the onset of puberty, but the practice seems to have been less widely observed than it was with boys. Whereas the circumcision of boys was a public affair and often performed by the local barber, the circumcision of girls was a private affair without any public celebration and surrounded by many negative connotations. Some of the rationales for female circumcision included the preservation of chastity and the inhibition of sexual desire, but many people also believed it promoted fertility and ensured the birth of sons.

Although people believed children were able to discern right from wrong, children were generally seen to have certain legal disabilities that paralleled those imposed on persons who were mentally deficient. For example, children could not make binding contracts, nor were they subject to the same punishments for criminal offenses as adults. In addition, most jurists argued that children were not required to fulfill the rituals of Islamic worship—prayer (*salat*), fasting (*sawm*) during Ramadan, paying alms (*zakat*), or making the pilgrimage (*hajj*) to Mecca. Rather, children were to be taught these as part of their religious education in preparation for adulthood.

While the training of children received a great deal of attention in medieval treatises on education, even the great teachers recognized that childhood required more than study. Scholars recommended that childhood also include play. The kinds of games and toys mentioned in the medieval sources include puppet theater, games with balls, toy animals, and toy birds on strings.

The marriage age for females tended to coincide with the onset of puberty, but it was not uncommon for prepubescent girls to be given in marriage. While there is evidence of marriages being arranged between children, most males married after they had entered into adulthood and tended to be older than their brides. It was not uncommon for much older men to marry young girls. In fact, when Muhammad was in his fifties, he contracted a marriage to his favorite wife, ʿAʾisha, when she was six years old (some accounts say she was nine years old).

Children in the Muslim world were highly valued because they represented the continuity of the family. Their births were celebrated, their childhood was carefully tended, and they were much beloved by their families.

~*James Lindsay*

FOR MORE INFORMATION

Giladi, A. *Children of Islam: Concepts of Childhood in Medieval Muslim Society*. New York: St. Martin's Press, 1992.

Lindsay, J. *Daily Life in the Medieval Islamic World*. Westport, Conn.: Greenwood Press, forthcoming.

POLYNESIA

Among the peoples of Polynesia, the raising of children was largely the role of women. See the Polynesia entry in the section "Women" in this chapter.

Old Age

How old is old? When we study societies in which life expectancy was only about 40 years old, did that mean that people were not aware of the elderly? Not at all. The life expectancy figures are skewed by the high childhood mortality rates; if people lived through their youth (and for women, through their child-bearing years), they could expect to live into their sixties. People in the Middle Ages knew the elderly and—since no one imagines themselves succumbing to illness or accident—expected to grow old.

In medieval Europe, some thinkers divided the ages of humans into stages that are remarkably similar to our own. For example, one 13th-century author identified four stages: (1) childhood—from birth to age 20, (2) youth—from 20 to 40, (3) middle age—from 40 to 60, and (4) old age—from 60 to 80 (Shahar, 15). These breakdowns are fairly consistent across cultures. This is not to say everyone died at 80, of course. A Christian leader of the Fourth Crusade against the Muslims was in his nineties.

In the Middle Ages, people recognized retirement ages. In medieval Europe, a knight no longer had to serve in the military when he was past 60 years of age. This was also true of peasants and women. This figure is rather astonishing considering how physically hard fighting and labor were; people assumed the elderly would remain fit into their sixties. China had a slightly different retirement age; peasants had to retire at 59 years old, and this mandatory retirement was intended to make sure the younger generations inherited the land. Bureaucrats had to stay in office until the age of 69. As in Europe, we have accounts of vigorous elderly in China—for example, a general who conquered northern Korea was 74.

The elderly in the past, as now, faced particular problems—notably, health and resources. In Europe, working people had to set resources aside for their old age, and in most households—whether peasant or noble—the family was expected to care for their elderly relatives at home until they died. In the absence of family, the church offered charity to the aged poor, and support of widows had been a major function of the church since its inception. In China, care for the aged was regulated by law. For example, the elderly were provided caretakers to satisfy their needs. The state also ensured that the elderly were supported financially.

In China more than Europe, children were raised to respect and care for the elderly, and this deeply ingrained attitude went a long way toward ensuring that people not only received care in their old age but also received respect. In Europe, on the other hand, attitudes toward the elderly were more ambivalent: even while writers praised wisdom and perspective gained by the elderly, they noted that the aged were feeble—both mentally and physically—and often anxious. In fact, in Europe with rare exceptions, the elderly were marginalized and outside the centers of power. In the harsh northern lands of Scandinavia, sometimes the elderly infirm were killed in a form of euthanasia.

Western medicine followed the classic physicians in noting that old age was accompanied by a cooling of the body—its vital heat that had burnt so brightly during youth was rapidly fading. Thus physicians recommended foods that were warming—for example, a little red wine—rest in a warm, sunny room, and moderate exercise to keep the limbs warm. Although the medical analysis is different from our own views, the advice was sound for retaining one's health into old age. Chinese medicine recommended balanced food, herbs, and a more radical cure when the elderly were sick: a family member should cut off some of his or her own flesh and cook it to feed to the ill relative. The bodily strength in the young flesh was thought to restore the old.

The presence of the elderly in society is not new. The aged always brought their memories, perspective, and wisdom to society. All societies had also to care for the aged who could no longer work and try to make sure their last days were tranquil. Many societies have been judged by how well they care for the helpless among them, whether children or the elderly.

~Joyce E. Salisbury

FOR MORE INFORMATION

Shahar, S. *Growing Old in the Middle Ages*. New York: Routledge, 1997.

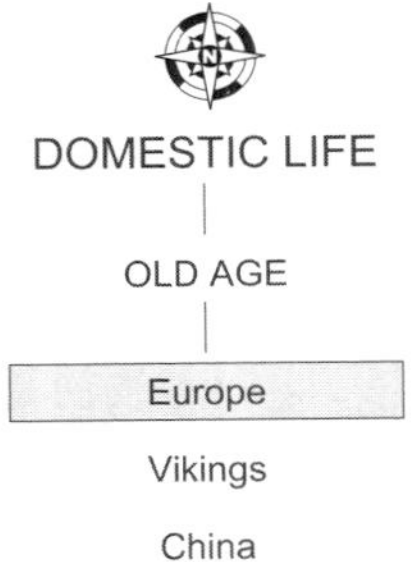

EUROPE

Life expectancy at birth was relatively short in Europe, probably about 40 years, but this figure is skewed by a high incidence of mortality among children and teenagers and generally reflects the effects of disease rather than the natural life span. Once a person reached 20 or 30 years of age, he or she had passed the period of highest susceptibility to disease and had a reasonable likelihood of reaching 60 or more. The bodies of medieval people were not much different from ours today and presumably aged at about the same rate. This conjecture is confirmed by medieval customs pertaining to old age. Legal requirements imposed on the able-bodied, such as military service and taxation, commonly remained in place until the age of 60. Services of the mind rather than the body, such as the responsibility for serving on a manor court or providing political counsel to one's feudal lord, were often required up to age 70. Such figures closely correspond with the modern practice of retirement somewhere between 60 to 70 years of age.

Records exist of some astonishingly vigorous elderly men and women. The papal legate who accompanied crusaders during the Fourth Crusade in 1204 was in his nineties. Ramon Lull, a 13th-century scholar (and author of a book on chivalry) went to North Africa to try to convert Muslims when he was in his seventies, and when he was 76, he survived a shipwreck by swimming ashore. The vigorous who survived the hazards of childhood might expect to live a long life.

However, like now, old age was a time of heightened economic vulnerability. Most people supported themselves through some sort of physical work, and as their physical abilities declined, so did their earning power. Society provided no safety net for the elderly, who were obliged to find their own means of keeping body and soul together.

For people at the top of the social scale, security in old age was not a problem. Aristocrats who were supported by the profits from their lands and merchants who lived by commerce had the means to support themselves, and their families also had sufficient surpluses to look after their less-wealthy members as well. Important followers of wealthy men, such as the steward of a baronial estate, might also expect support from their patrons. Farther down the scale, a more modest property holder might exchange his holding for financial support. Many villagers surrendered the use of their lands to their heirs, if there were any, in exchange for housing and a regular payment of cash or goods to support them. When Thomas Bird of Romsley in England took over a cottage holding from his mother in 1281, he promised to provide her with a suitable dwelling 30 feet long and 14 feet wide, with three doors and two windows, with stipulated allowances of fuel and food. The owner of an urban tenement sometimes donated or promised to bequeath his property to a church institution such as a monastery in exchange for support; in some cases, the donor took up residence on the property of the monastery, receiving food from the monastic kitchen.

Those with neither property nor connections were at greater risk. The income of a wage laborer was not enough to support investment in long-term sources of income such as property, and those who lacked family to support them, unless they died early, could expect only an impoverished old age. Many were doubtless obliged to beg for a living. Women were particularly at risk. Because it was common for wives to be significantly younger than their husbands, many experienced long periods of widowhood, and because the earning capacity of women was lower than that of men, a widow was particularly vulnerable to poverty.

The church helped care for those who were indigent or who lacked family to care for them. The earliest records of the church show that widows were listed on the roles of those who received regular charity, and each parish church throughout the Middle Ages provided a portion of its income to care for the poor elderly. Finally, monasteries sometimes provided a haven for those who wanted to take vows at the end of their lives and live in the care of the community while they prayed for a better life after death (Singman, 30–31).

To read about old age in Elizabethan England, see the England entry in the section "Life Cycles" in chapter 2 ("Domestic Life") of volume 3; and for 18th-century England, see the England entry in the section "Aging and Death" in chapter 2 ("Domestic Life") of volume 4 of this series.

FOR MORE INFORMATION

Lull, R. *Book of Knighthood and Chivalry (and The Anonymous Ordene de Chevalerie)*. Translated by B. R. Price. New York: Chivalry Bookshelf, 2001.

Singman, J. L. *Daily Life in Medieval Europe*. Westport, Conn.: Greenwood Press, 1999.

VIKINGS

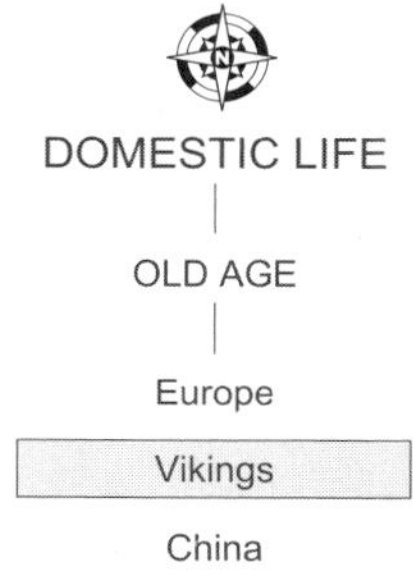

Because the average age at death in the Viking Age is usually put below 40, few people reached what we would now consider old age. Retirement did not exist as an official institution, but we occasionally hear of the head of the household transferring his or her property to a son or grandson. Such was the arrangement made by the Icelandic poet and farmer Egil Skallagrimsson, who died shortly before 1000. In his biography, *Egil's Saga*, it is told that after his wife died, Egil gave up farming and turned over the estate to his son Thorstein, but because he did not care much for Thorstein, he went to live with his stepdaughter Thordis and her husband. We have no means of knowing the fate of elderly or infirm servants or slaves, and it is difficult to know how old age was viewed by the elderly or by the younger generation(s). The impression given by *Egil's Saga* is that old age was undesirable for men; Egil is portrayed as receiving little sympathy or assistance as he suffered increasing infirmity, including, finally, blindness.

In his poem, Egil may well represent other Viking Age men who reached old age; indeed, according to pagan Scandinavian religion, it was considered nobler to die by the sword than from sickness and old age. The lack of sympathy for old-age infirmity, which is given clear expression in the comments made by the female servants in *Egil's Saga*, may also have a basis in reality, and there are indications that some old people were as unwanted or superfluous as some infants. Although there is no documentary evidence of the exposure or killing of old people, the *Ynglinga Saga* (Saga of the Ynglings) tale, as related by the Icelandic historian and poet Snorri Sturluson in the 1230s, about the ancient King Aun of Uppsala, Sweden, hints at such practice. According to Snorri, Aun had struck a bargain with Odin that the god would grant him 10 years of life for every one of his sons that he sacrificed. He had sacrificed nine of them and grown so old and feeble that he was bedridden and drank out of a horn like an infant. But when it came to the tenth son, the king's subjects said no, and Snorri adds that it was later called Aun's disease when a man died of old age without any sickness. It is also known that in Sweden there was a tradition of "family cliffs," from which men and women were pushed or hurled themselves in times of famine, and of "family cudgels," with which the elderly were knocked on their heads. Viking society was harsh and practical, and there was no room for the helpless.

~*Kirsten Wolf*

FOR MORE INFORMATION

Hreinsson, V., ed. *The Complete Sagas of Icelanders Including 49 Tales*. 5 vols. Reykjavik, Iceland: Leifur Eiriksson, 1997.

Wolf, K. *Daily Life of the Vikings*. Westport, Conn.: Greenwood Press, forthcoming.

DOMESTIC LIFE
OLD AGE
Europe
Vikings
China

CHINA

According to Tang statutes, the mandatory age of retirement was 59. That regulation, however, applied only to peasants and was the measure that the state used to redistribute land to the younger generation. The law did not apply to merchants and artisans, who could not own land. By law, mandarins had to remain in office until the age of 69. Those ranked fifth grade or higher could then personally submit a request to the throne for release from duty. In special cases, the emperor rejected such appeals. The Department of Personnel submitted such requests for lower-ranking bureaucrats. Officials who remained fit could continue to serve in their posts past 69. The general who conquered northern Korea in 668 was 74 at the time. In one case, the throne would not accept an eminent minister's resignation until he was 80. In another, a general who participated in the Korean campaign and later rose to become a chief minister died in office at the age of 83.

In most instances, families were responsible for the care of their aged. That was both a traditional and a legal obligation. According to Tang statutes, everyone 79 to 88 was to be furnished with an attendant; those aged 89 to 98 with two; and those over 99 with five. The caretakers were first selected from the elder's adult children or grandchildren. If there were no adults, then adolescents served. If the seniors had neither, then close relatives assumed the burden. If they had no kinsmen at all, then the state appointed an adult or adults from the community to undertake the assignment. The government was reinforcing deeply rooted social mores and conventions with that law. Families inculcated respect for elders, especially parents and grandparents, in their children from a very early age. Men and women procreated in part to provide themselves with social security in their old age.

This is not to say that the state did not provide for the welfare of the aged. Although in theory a farmer lost 80 percent of his fields by his sixtieth birthday, Tang land statutes set aside 40 percent of his land as an allotment for his care until his death. As long as he remained vigorous, he presumably cultivated it. When he was no longer able to work, his sons apparently assumed the task. The law provided for the maintenance of the disabled in the same manner. The regulations also provided for widows, who received 30 percent of their husband's allotment unless they were the head of a household, in which case they received 40 percent.

A woman cuts her arm to cook some of her flesh to feed to her ailing elder, pictured on the right. Illustration by Charles Benn.

Sometimes the throne bestowed direct assistance on the old. The occasions for dispensing such philanthropy included imperial progresses and the proclamations of Great Acts of Grace. Usually, age was a determining factor in the qualification of the elders so blessed. For example, Emperor Illustrious August once ordered officials to present three lengths of silk cloth (money) and three-and-a-half bushels of grain to caretakers of all men and women 79 to 98 years old and five lengths of silk cloth and five bushels of grain to those tending seniors 99 years or older. Other gifts included canes, quilted coats, ale, and felt frocks.

Sometimes the throne invited the elderly to the palace for a feast. At other times, it sent agents to inquire after the health of the old. In rare instances, the emperor personally undertook the task himself. In 645, Taizong visited the hut of a man who claimed to have attained the ripe old age of 145 years by ingesting gold. The intent of bestowing the gifts was less to furnish support for the old than to provide an example of the emperor's veneration of the aged and his benevolent concern for them. The court often restricted the recipients to a small number of subjects living in one locality. Even when it presented gifts to "all people of the empire," the number who acquired the gifts must have been very small, given the restrictions on age, usually 79 and older.

Aging usually involved illness of some sort, and the responsibility for nursing elders fell to their sons, daughters, daughters-in-law, or other family members. The obligation to care for parents in their later years was deeply rooted in the psyche of Tang Chinese. Some dutiful children went to extremes in preparing medicine for their elders. A pharmacologist in the early 8th century declared that human flesh was a remedy for ailments. At that time and later, sons and daughters sometimes carved muscle from their body to feed their parents. The preferred location was generally the thigh, although sometimes it was the arm. One man sliced off three-quarters of a pound from his hip to prepare a remedy for his mother, who was suffering from tuberculosis. Some intellectuals decried the custom, but the children who sacrificed themselves enjoyed the respect of their contemporaries for their devotion to their parents. The throne bestowed honors and rewards on 29 people for mutilating themselves in that manner (Benn, 261–64).

FOR MORE INFORMATION

Benn, C. *Daily Life in Traditional China: The Tang Dynasty*. Westport, Conn.: Greenwood Press, 2002.

DOMESTIC LIFE: WEB SITES

http://ccat.sas.upenn.edu/~rs143/map.html
http://www.bbc.co.uk/history/ancient/vikings/women_01.shtml
http://www.luc.edu/publications/medieval/emsv12.html
http://www.pitt.edu/~asian/week-10/week-10.html
http://www.u.arizona.edu/~kari/intro6.htm

3

ECONOMIC LIFE

The basic principle of economic life is that men and women must work to provide for themselves. Of course, throughout history it has always been that some have to work harder than others, but this does not violate the basic importance of work; it only reveals the complexities of economic life, which includes everything from the production of income to trade to its unequal distribution throughout society.

At the basic level, people work on the land to produce their food and other items they need. However, even at this simplest level, people trade goods among themselves. Thus economic life moves from the work that we do to the exchange of the products of our labor. This diversification contributes to increasing variety in society, as some work on the land living in villages and farms while others move to urban areas that grow ever larger throughout history. The patterns of farm, village, and urban life exist all over the world and help define the lives of the people who work within them.

During the Middle Ages, most people worked on the land. The age produced some quite striking advances in agriculture—paddy rice fields in China, planting new legumes in western Europe in a three-field crop-rotation system, new irrigation methods developed in the Muslim world, and windmills from Persia that spread all over western Europe. Nevertheless, these innovations only served to allow the population to grow; they never produced enough surplus food to free most people from the land. Therefore, the basic structure of economic life during the medieval centuries was agriculture conducted by peasants, most of whom lived their whole lives in villages clustered near their fields.

Despite the preponderance of rural life in the Middle Ages, urban life (so central in the ancient world) never died out. Cities remained administrative and small commercial centers, and when the world economy improved, urban life flourished. Asia and the Muslim Middle East were first in fostering a vibrant city life, and by the 12th century, Europe was beginning to catch up. People in the cities needed to invent new ways to govern themselves, and these new structures offered a degree of freedom and flexibility unknown in the countryside. During the Middle Ages, some of the great cities of the modern world grew into prominence, and studying the rise of London, Paris, Changan, Byzantium, and Baghdad reveals much about the dynamic growth of urban life during these centuries.

Commerce, or the exchange of goods, is as central to human economic life as the production of goods in the towns and countryside. From the beginning of town life in Mesopotamia, the excitement generated within shops lining a street is palpable in the sources. Merchants hawking their wares and shoppers looking for the exotic as well as the ordinary form a core of human life. Merchants (and merchandise) have always ranged far beyond local markets as people moved their goods across large areas. Even during the prehistoric late Stone Age, domestic animals native to the Middle East moved down the Nile valley to sub-Saharan Africa, and plants native to the Euphrates valley moved as far east as China. Our global marketplace is only the logical extension of the constant movement of people and things that goes on as people engage in their economic life.

Travel was difficult during the Middle Ages. Roads were rough and plagued by bandits; sea routes were limited by shipping technology and remained slow and hazardous. Most goods were traded locally—within a radius of about 25 miles, or one day's travel. Nevertheless, long-distance trade remained so lucrative that some merchants braved the hazards. People such as Marco Polo traveled from Venice, Italy, all the way to China to the court of the Mongol emperors and brought back riches and tales of exotic places. The movement of goods throughout Eurasia generated an exchange of ideas that served to stimulate further growth. For example, at the end of the Middle Ages, gunpowder developed in China would bring down the knights in shining armor that had defined the age and prepare the world for a new kind of warfare. The increased desire for goods from far away stimulated the exploration of the new world that finally ended the predominantly provincial medieval world.

All societies have been in part defined by people at work. They have built societies with divisions of labor, of city and country, and of class as some people grow richer than others. To study daily life through history is in large part to understand people at work.

~*Joyce E. Salisbury*

FOR MORE INFORMATION

Braudel, F. *The Wheels of Commerce*. New York: Harper and Row, 1979.
Wallerstein, I. M. *Historical Capitalism*. London: Verso, 1983.

Europe
Vikings
China
Islamic World
Byzantium

Urban Economic Life

City life is one in which there is a division of labor; it differs from village life in which everyone farms and everyone makes the things they need for their households. From the time of their founding, cities always existed in a necessary but often tense relationship with the surrounding countryside. City dwellers were often disdainful of the "backward" country folk who seemed so much less sophisticated than they. But at the same time, the city depended on the countryside to bring in their wares to feed the urban population. In the 11th century, for example, one estimate suggests that a town of 3,000 inhabitants required the land of some 10 villages to support it (Braudel, 486), and this suggests how many villages needed to contribute to the survival of the larger cities of 300,000 or more. In return, cities often carted "night soil" or human solid waste to the nearby fields to use as fertilizer.

In their turn, peasants believed (probably correctly) that they would be robbed or at least cheated when they came to town. One account of a medieval transaction at a market told of a man who was invited to look into a deep barrel to be sure the produce was as advertised. As the purchaser leaned in, he was pushed into the barrel and trapped until he was willing to pay a ransom to be released. Then as now, people had to watch their person and their purses as they went to town, and yet they did not stay away. There was money to be made in the cities and goods to buy. Thus the exchange between city and country fostered a vibrant economic life.

Despite the fact that commerce lay at the heart of the cities, there were several ways that cities grew. Some arose rather organically because of their location on the banks of rivers or on caravan routes, which facilitated trade. These cities, including London, Paris, and Mecca, had served as commercial routes since ancient times and continued to do so. Other cities were established by rulers who then grew even richer from the commercial life of the city they fostered. Cities such as Changan, Baghdad, and Constantinople (Byzantium) owed their founding to imperial design and yet developed an economic life of their own.

Markets in the cities were regulated in various ways. First, sections of the cities were devoted to particular trades to facilitate oversight and comparison shopping. This was true in Byzantium, China, European cities, or Muslim ones. In most of the large cities—east or west—the center was dominated by a religious structure, whether a cathedral or a great mosque. The markets arranged themselves around the religious center. In Muslim towns, the shopping streets, the *souks*, were arranged in winding circles around the mosque, and the locations of the shops reflected notions of cleanliness: For example, the perfume and incense merchants were nearest to the mosque, and the blacksmiths, curriers, and others who worked with animals were at the outer edge of the town. At the gates themselves, the ever-scorned peasants came to sell food products (Braudel, 509).

Markets in European towns were regulated by the merchants themselves through their guilds, instead of being regulated by religious directive. In China, the government controlled all urban markets through market commandants who regulated everything from location of the market to quality control. The Byzantine government, too, carefully regulated the markets of its cities.

After the fall of the Roman Empire, the great urban life of the Mediterranean world declined, and in most parts of the west the countryside seemed to prevail. In the Muslim world and the east, on the other hand, cities such as Byzantium and Baghdad continued to foster the trade that had always brought them wealth. By the 12th century, however, trade again flourished in Europe, which began to join the Muslim world in a great expansion. With the burgeoning trade, cities again grew important, and it is in these economic centers of the Middle Ages that our modern society was born.

~*Joyce E. Salisbury*

FOR MORE INFORMATION

Braudel, F. *The Structures of Everyday Life*. New York: Harper and Row, 1979.

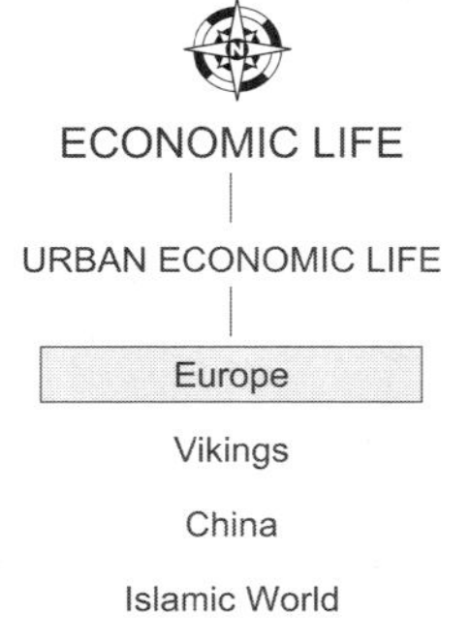

EUROPE

Some medieval towns and cities served as administrative centers for their regions, but the heart of urban life was commerce. Urban life flourished in direct proportion to the growth of trade, and ready access to transportation was crucial to urban development. Transportation not only furnished necessary foodstuffs but also connected towns to its customers; thus most of the medieval cities were located along rivers that offered ready transportation by boats and barges. Smaller towns offered commercial services for the hinterland, providing goods for rural buyers, particularly manufactured items such as clothing and household wares, and receiving from them the agricultural produce needed to sustain the urban population. Larger towns engaged in the same sort of trade, but they were also involved in interurban commerce, exchanging commodities over longer distances with other urban centers.

The important function of trade also shaped the structure of the town itself. Trades were clustered in neighborhoods. In some cases, the location of shops was influenced by local conditions or opportunities. Tradesmen who served travelers were often found near the gates on important roads. Horse sellers and tavern keepers, for example, clustered near the northern gates of Paris by the main road toward St. Denis, and innkeepers lined the rue St.-Jacques on the left bank. Taverns were often clustered near markets or near the principal entry points into cities. There were many other clusters of trades for which no external influence can be identified, but in all cases clustered trades helped facilitate administration and quality control. Many of the core trades that supported city life, such as the sellers of foodstuffs and clothing, and politically or economically important trades, such as armorers, sword makers, and goldsmiths, were found in large numbers in the center of cities, close to the centers of regulation.

Each trade in the city had its own structure, with rules governing its practice, customs as to the tradesmen's rights and responsibilities, and a greater or lesser degree of communal self-government. These trade associations had their roots among urban social fellowships called guilds that appeared in the 11th century. Early guilds provided town dwellers with some of the social functions that were furnished by village and kinship communities in the country, such as arranging social feasts and religious festivals, and providing charitable services for their members, especially funerals and support for widows. In the 12th century, guilds began to appear that were restricted to the practitioners of a certain craft, and by the 13th century the institution of the trade guild was well established.

Trade guilds tended to be grouped by their raw materials as much as by their products. In Paris, a distinction was made between the makers of iron buckles and those who made them of copper or brass. There were separate regulations for the various makers of prayer beads, depending on whether they worked in bone and horn, coral and shell, amber and jet, or copper and its alloys. The structure of trade guilds varied, but usually each craft was overseen by one to three guild masters, in some cases assisted by a couple of journeymen. The guild masters were generally assisted by a body of jurors who helped adjudicate matters of controversy. The bakers had some 12 jurors, chosen by the guild master, who were chosen from among "the most judicious men of substance . . . who are good at assessing bread." The jurors of the bakers were required to swear upon holy relics "that they will look after the trade well and faithfully, and that in judging bread they will not spare either kinsman or friend, nor will they condemn anyone wrongfully for hatred or ill-will" (Singman, 194).

Merchants or tradesmen bartering in the Middle Ages. © North Wind/North Wind Picture Archives.

The trade guilds continued to fulfill some of the social and charitable roles of the earlier guilds, such as supporting the elderly who could no longer work. Guild regulations also related directly to the work of its members. Each guild had its own rules regarding the process of admission to the trade and guaranteed product quality, particularly in such essential trades as baking. The master of the bakers was expected from time to time to summon the jurors of the craft to accompany him on a tour of inspection of the city's bakers. The bakers were one of the most highly regulated trades in a medieval town because their product was the community's main staple food. Bread was to be sold in loaves at specific prices: halfpenny bread, penny bread, and twopenny bread. The actual weight of the bread varied with the price of grain according to an official schedule of weights and prices. To prevent the selling of underweight loaves, each baker was required to keep a set of approved standard weights. Inspectors also looked for adulterated bread: unscrupulous bakers were known to include sand in their loaves to increase weight at less cost.

Some guilds also regulated the terms of competition. The makers of purses and belts were not permitted to leave their shops to show their merchandise to a customer who was at a neighboring shop; the cooks were forbidden to call to a customer at a neighbor's stall or shop; and the saddle makers were forbidden to shout or gesture. Cooks were also forbidden to make false criticisms of one another's food.

Many regulations concerned the training of apprentices. The regulations themselves emphasize the time and attention needed to train an apprentice, but such laws also served to limit access to the trade, lest a glut of tradesmen lower the value of their work. Yet the guild might take a real interest in the treatment of apprentices. An apprentice linen weaver who left his master because of inappropriate treatment might complain to the guild or send a friend to do so on his behalf. If the charges were justified, the guild might summon the offending master and order him to "treat the apprentice honorably like the son of a proper householder, providing him clothing and shoes, and drink and food, and all other things, within the next two weeks," and if the master failed to satisfy them, a new master would be found (Singman, 196).

Guilds also exercised authority over the tradesman's work schedule. Regulations restricting the hours of work served in part to prevent masters from overworking their staff. Several by-laws specifically mention the journeyman's right to rest. The makers of metal thread even allowed their journeymen to take a month's leave from work in August—probably not an actual holiday but an opportunity to make higher wages working at the harvest. Prohibitions against nighttime work also helped ensure product quality.

In time, the guilds came to be dominant forces in city government. Some cities, such as London, developed a municipal government in which a number of guilds participated. Others were dominated by a single guild, most often the guild of merchants, who were among the most wealthy and powerful guildsmen in the town. This was the case in Paris, where the water merchants' control over Parisian trade on the Seine brought them to prominence in the 12th and 13th centuries. In 1221, they were assigned authority over petty justice and the salt and grain measures in the city. In 1260, the king constituted the four jurors of the water merchants as the city's magistrates, and the guild of water merchants effectively became the municipal government of Paris. To this day, the symbol of Paris is a medieval ship derived from the seal of the water merchants.

Snapshot

Wages and Prices in 13th-Century England

What one day's wages bought in 13th-century England (compiled from Burnett):

	Wages	Purchases
Unskilled laborer	2 pennies	1 gallon ale = 1/2 penny 1 hen = 1/2 penny 2 loaves bread = 1 penny
Carpenter	3 pennies	Above items plus 1 pound candle wax
Only for the rich:		Wine (one quart) = 166 pennies One Pike (fresh fish) = 80 pennies Pepper (one pound) = 34 pennies

The presence of a public marketplace—whether an indoor hall, an open square, or just a wide city street—was one of the defining characteristics of the town. Small market towns held their markets one day each week. Large cities had multiple marketplaces and hosted markets several days a week, perhaps even daily. Some wares were sold by wandering vendors, but established guildsmen were always suspicious of the wandering salesmen and regulated them firmly. As time passed, merchants saw more advantages in arranging periodic markets for larger numbers of customers. These markets grew into fairs that were held at specific times and brought goods together from larger trade areas.

The right to hold a fair, like the right to hold a market, was bestowed by the feudal lord. It was not accorded to every town. Larger towns were more likely to have a fair, and some of them even had more than one. The fair took place each year at the same time, usually lasting three days to a week, and in some cases lasting several weeks. Some fairs attracted vendors from great distances. Those in the Champagne region in northeastern France served as one of the principal centers for European commerce in the 13th century, and even fairs of less importance were visited by merchants from all over western Europe. They were also frequented by local country folk, who often preferred to buy their household goods at fairs because they offered a better selection and more competition than the local weekly markets.

While the economy of these towns slowly increased to bring in substantial revenue, most of the medieval thinkers ignored these urban dwellers, thinking them peripheral to the feudal organization of medieval life. However, the future lay with these enterprising town dwellers who, as they sought to make profits, changed the world (Singman, 183, 193–200).

To read about urban life in Elizabethan England, see the England entry in the section "City Life" in chapter 3 ("Economic Life") of volume 3; and for Victorian England, see the England entry in the section "Urban and Rural Environments" in chapter 3 ("Economic Life") of volume 5 of this series.

FOR MORE INFORMATION

Burnett, J. *A History of the Cost of Living*. Harmondsworth, England: Pelican, 1969.
Lilley, K. D. *Urban Life in the Middle Ages*. New York: Palgrave, 2002.
Singman, J. L. *Daily Life in Medieval Europe*. Westport, Conn.: Greenwood Press, 1999.

VIKINGS

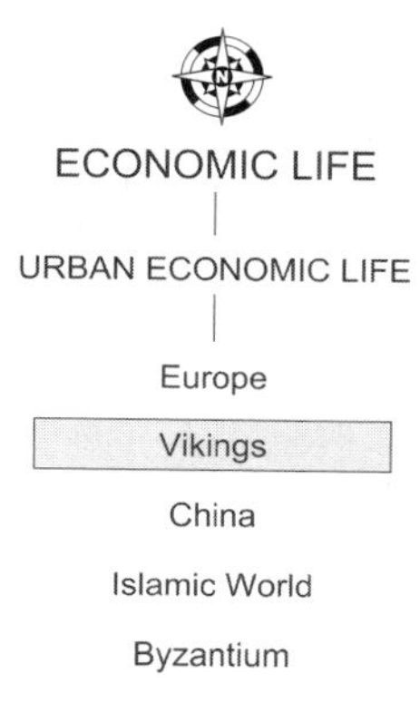

With the rapid growth in trade during the Viking Age, small trading centers came into existence. These trading centers gradually grew into towns, although any real tendencies toward urbanization cannot be detected until the 9th and 10th centuries. Most towns were craft and mercantile centers from whence goods came and went throughout the Vikings' extensive trade networks. Not surprisingly, the successful towns were located by the sea or rivers, and Scandinavia's deep fjords offered shelter for burgeoning towns along their shores. Given the violence of the Viking Age, it is also not surprising that the towns were fortified. Birka and Hedeby, for example, had semicircular walls around the landward side, and the waterfront was protected by palisades. Sometimes artificial harbors, now known as Salviksgropen, were built to provide suitable and safe anchoring places.

Vikings also founded trading centers and towns in their colonies abroad. Dublin in Ireland was founded by the Vikings shortly before the middle of the 10th century, and it soon became an exceedingly prosperous and powerful trading center for the merchants of the North Atlantic. The Dublin Vikings appear to have engaged especially in slave trade, and it is believed that Dublin was the prime slave market of western Europe, furnishing customers in the British Isles and the Scandinavian countries and Iceland. Other towns in Ireland—including Limerick, Cork, Wexford, and Waterford—also owe their existence to the Vikings, although they never became as important as Dublin.

In England and on the Continent, the Vikings settled themselves in already-existing towns. The capital of the Vikings in England was York, which was captured by the Vikings in 866. In eastern Europe, the Scandinavians had established trading centers in the south Baltic before the Viking Age. They include Wolin at the mouth of the Oder River, Truso on the Vistula in Estonia, and Grobin near modern Liepaja on the Latvian coast.

The inhabitants of towns made their living from a full range of trades and crafts. Most of our information about crafts and industries comes from archaeological finds, and while they give a detailed and broad picture of production and products they provide little information about the producer, the artisan, and his workshop.

The Scandinavian crafts and industries were, of course, largely determined by available resources and demand. Metalworking was clearly an important trade, and the smith was a vital part of every community, for only he had both the skills and the equipment for manufacturing and repairing metal goods. Iron, which could be found in Scandinavia, was the most common metal and was used for tools, weapons, domestic utensils, nails and rivets, and riding equipment. Some of the smiths were evidently also highly skilled artists. Some of their products—especially sword hilts, spurs, and stirrups—are decorated with elaborate patterns and motifs. Encrustation, that is, covering a surface with silver or copper wire pressed and hammered to form a pattern, was clearly quite common.

A variety of metals was used for jewelry and other decorative items, such as buckles, keys, and tableware. Gold and silver were imported, but copper was mined in Sweden. The copper was alloyed with other metals, such as lead and tin, which may have been imported. Bronze was especially common, and bronze casting was carried out all over Scandinavia. Several clay and iron molds used for casting bronze ornaments have been found. These clay molds obviously had to be broken open to release the casting, quite unlike the molds of stone and antler used for casting silver, tin, lead, and pewter, for which lower temperatures are needed. Other tools used by the jeweler included crucibles for smelting, bellows, tongs, molds for ingots, light hammers, dies, metal shears, pinches for filigree work, dies for impressing foils, and engraving and chasing tools.

The quarrying of steatite, a rock also known as soapstone, which is quite soft when quarried but which hardens in the air, and the manufacture of soapstone vessels and pots, molds, crucibles, loom weights, and other artifacts were a major industry in Norway, from whence the products were exported. In many parts of Norway and Sweden, there were also rocks from which high-quality whetstones could be made. These were necessary for sharpening weapons, knives, and tools and were distributed throughout Scandinavia and even exported.

The production of bone, horn, and antler objects was yet another important industry and was most likely carried out by professional craftsmen. The antlers of red deer were widely used to make combs. The method used was to cut a pair of long, flat, and relatively thin plates to form the back of the comb, and between these plates a number of smaller plates were fastened, into which teeth were cut. Antler was also used for many other products, such as arrowheads, handles for knives and tools, gaming pieces, dice, and vices. Animal bone was used for skates, pins, spindle whorls, handles, bodkins, and the like. Animal horn was used especially for drinking vessels, which might also be decorated with carving. In contrast to wood carving, carving in bone, horn, and also tusk was limited to small objects by nature of the size of the material. Nonetheless, the same methods of carving are found in bone, horn, and tusk as in wood carving: incised work, openwork, relief, and sculpture.

Amber and glass were used mostly for ornamental objects. Amber was available in the southern Baltic and along the coast of southwest Jutland. It was used for making small objects such as pendants, beads, and gaming pieces. The raw material for glass was imported from abroad. The preserved glass objects are mostly beads. As the archaeological remains show, the urban craftsmen produced many products that fueled the long-distance trade that so dominated the Viking Age and beyond.

~*Kirsten Wolf*

FOR MORE INFORMATION

Wolf, K. *Daily Life of the Vikings*. Westport, Conn.: Greenwood Press, forthcoming.

CHINA

Some cities in medieval China were more than seats of government. They were also centers of economic activity. The greatest of them in the Tang dynasty was Yangzhou, located on the Grand Canal close to the Yangtze River, where commodities from the interior of China and overseas were transshipped and sent to northern metropolises. It was also the headquarters for the national salt monopoly as well as the greatest industrial town in the period. It produced admirable bronze mirrors, fine felt hats that citizens of Changan esteemed, sugar refined from cane, boats that sold for 5 million coppers, elegant, expensive furniture, and beautiful silk textiles. Canton was the greatest entrepôt of foreign trade. There, ships from Persia, Arabia, and southeast Asia off-loaded rare perfumes, woods, jewels, plants, drugs, dyes, and other goods that Chinese merchants sent north to satisfy the tastes of the rich and powerful in the capitals. Chengdu in the southwest was the greatest center for the production of paper and printed books, both of which were Chinese inventions. It also served as a haven for emperors fleeing rebels who attacked and seized Changan.

In China as elsewhere, commerce depended on transportation. Most Tang cities lay on flatlands next to rivers that served as the cheapest routes for transportation. To further facilitate the movement of goods and people, canals were built in many cities, especially in the south, which had more watercourses than the north. The great metropolis of Yangzhou, which was crisscrossed with canals, had more boats than carriages. Changan had five canals, all but one of which delivered water to parks in the outer city, to lakes in the gardens of patricians, and to the grounds of imperial palaces.

In theory, every city had a market, but small and impoverished counties probably did not. Those that did were official markets ruled by market commandants appointed by the central government. In 707, the throne issued a decree forbidding the establishment of markets outside cities. There were, however, exceptions. The state operated periodic markets along the northern frontier, mainly to purchase horses from nomadic, pastoral peoples. There were also unofficial rural markets, called "markets in the grass" (northern China) or "markets in the wilds" (south China). They arose spontaneously in the countryside to serve the needs of peasants living more than a day's ride from a city. The farmers traded their produce for goods—the most important of which was salt, which was not available in many places—supplied by traveling merchants. At first, they had no stores, shops, or warehouses, but toward the end of the dynasty some of them acquired such facilities.

The government controlled all urban markets through the agency of market commandants and their small staffs. The duties of the commandants were to register merchants and their establishments; to inspect weights and measures to ensure that they met government standards; to weed out counterfeit coins; and to prevent the sale of inferior goods that did not meet official requirements for size, weight, and quality of materials or workmanship. The statutes required market officials to send all weights and measures to the imperial treasuries in the capitals or the offices of prefectures and counties in the eighth moon of every year so they could be tested to ensure their accuracy and stamped with a seal. It was the responsibility of market officials to issue certificates of purchase for slaves, horses, cattle, camels, mules, and donkeys within three days after the transactions. In addition, it was their duty to prevent price fixing, monopolies, and other unfair market practices by merchants. According to regulations, they had to set the prevailing prices for all commodities every 10 days. If they fraudulently acquired goods by setting the prices higher or lower than their real value at the time, the government ordered them to resign, stripped them of all their bureaucratic and aristocratic titles for a period of six years, and forced them to pay double the value of the property involved.

The nine sectors of Changan's markets, as well as other urban bazaars, were subdivided into lanes (*hang*), each of which was devoted to a single commodity and was required by law to erect at its entrance a sign with a title that designated its specialty. All retail shops or stalls that sold a given product were located in the lane with the appropriate sign. Warehouses and wholesale outlets lined the outer walls of the market. Only a dozen or so of the names for the *hang* in the capitals and other cities have survived in Tang literature: Meat (where a man once purchased the head of a white cow to concoct a nostrum for curing some ailment); Iron (where one could find a clever fortune-teller); Apothecary (where an emperor once ordered ingredients for a Daoist elixir meant to ensure his immortality); Ready-Made Clothes; Pongee (low-grade silk); Axes; Steamed Buns; Bridles and Saddles (which had a tavern); Weights and Measures; Gold- and Silversmiths; Fishmongers; and Greengrocers. Given that the eastern market of Changan alone had 220 lanes, these titles represent a minute fraction of the goods and services offered in the lanes.

By the beginning of the 9th century, a large increase in trade led to new developments in urban markets. Protobanks—there was one in the western market of Changan—emerged that offered a safe-deposit service. For a fee, they took custody of gold, silver, and coins to protect them from theft. The firms issued checks to their customers, who could use them to draw funds from their stored valuables. The checks were the ancestors of the world's first paper currency, which a provincial government in China issued during 1024. Gold- and silversmiths also issued such promissory notes.

The hours for trading at markets throughout the empire were restrictive. According to a Tang statute, markets opened at noon with a tattoo of 300 beats on a drum and closed an hour and three quarters before dusk with 300 beats on a gong. However, night markets must have flourished in residential wards because the gates of the central markets closed before nightfall. There is little information about them, but no doubt they served the needs of customers who had neglected to purchase essential items during the day at central markets. The throne banned the night markets in Changan in 841, but like many such edicts, that decree was probably ineffective because the bazaars were critical to the lives of urban dwellers.

Not all trading took place in the great urban markets. By the 9th century, some retail establishments, such as shops that sold fine silk textiles, existed in residential quarters. Furthermore, throughout the Tang, peddlers roamed the wards of Changan. A hawker who acquired the nickname Camel because he was a hunchback pushed a small cart from which he sold pastries in the streets. Once he crashed into an overturned wagon of bricks and spilled his snacks on the ground. When he removed the bricks with a mattock, he found a pot of gold. He became a wealthy man and purchased a mansion in the capital.

The markets had their complement of taverns, but there were also pubs scattered throughout the cities. In Changan, westerners operated taverns, favored by poets, in the wards along the southeast wall of the city. They employed white-skinned, green-eyed, blond women from central Asia to sing and dance so that patrons would spend more money on ale. Aside from the taverns inside Changan's walls, there were pubs where villagers living along some 19 miles of the eastern road outside the city sold ale to travelers. Sojourners called the drinks that those establishments purveyed "goblets for dismounting the horse." Since the Chinese rarely drank without eating, pubs were also restaurants or snack shops (Benn, 53–58).

To read about urban life in 19th-century China, see the China entries in the sections "Work" and "Urban and Rural Environments" in chapter 3 ("Economic Life") of volume 5 of this series.

FOR MORE INFORMATION

Benn, C. *Daily Life in Traditional China: The Tang Dynasty*. Westport, Conn.: Greenwood Press, 2002.

ISLAMIC WORLD

While the Islamic religion had its origins in the oases of western Arabia, what historians call Islamic civilization began to emerge in the new garrison towns established during the Islamic conquests of the 7th century, especially Basra (established 637) and Kufa (established 638) in southern Iraq, and Fustat (established 642) in Egypt, near where Cairo would be established in 969. In the wake of the conquest of Syria, the Muslim forces set up camps at Ramla in southern Palestine and at the old Ghassanid capital, al-Jabiya, in the Golan. However, both were quickly replaced by Damascus as the administrative center of Syria. Initially, these and other garrison towns were little more than military bases and administrative centers for the conquering forces. In time, they developed into full-fledged urban centers with governors, military commanders, soldiers, and their families, as well as mosques, markets, merchants, craftsmen, scholars, religious strife, political dissent, beggars, gangs, and what we would call organized crime.

Daily life in the medieval Islamic world revolved around its markets and its mosques—two institutions essential to the hustle and bustle of daily life of every city and town. It was in the local markets that goods were manufactured and food was bought and sold. In the major cities such as Damascus, Baghdad, Cairo, and others, everything imaginable from all over the Abode of Islam and beyond could be found as well. The main congregational mosque—the center of official religious and political life—was always located within or next to a market. In those instances where new congregational mosques were constructed in new garrison towns such as Basra and Kufa or in new palace cities such as Baghdad and Cairo, new markets soon sprung up adjacent to the principal gathering place for the faithful.

One example of the thriving urban life of the Muslim world (and the abundance brought by trade) may be seen in Naser-e Khosraw's glowing description of one of the markets near the mosque of ʿAmr ibn al-ʿAs:

> On the north side of the mosque is a bazaar called Suq al-Qanadil [Lamp Market], and no one ever saw such a bazaar anywhere else. Every sort of rare goods from all over the world can be had there: I saw tortoise-shell implements such as small boxes, combs, knife handles, and so on. I also saw extremely fine crystal, which the master craftsmen etch beautifully. [This crystal] had been imported from the Maghreb, although they say that near the Red Sea, crystal even finer and more translucent than the Maghrebi variety had been found. I saw elephant tusks from Zanzibar, many of which weighed more than two hundred pounds. There was a type of skin from Abyssinia that resembled a leopard, from which they make sandals. Also from Abyssinia was a domesticated bird, large with white spots and a crown like a peacock's. (Thackston, 53)

This description shows that from the very beginning, Muslim urban life was organized around commerce and that cities blossomed with the prosperity that came with the bustling trade.

Because at any given time one could find coins in the markets of the medieval Islamic world from Damascus, Baghdad, Cairo, Cordoba, Constantinople, Genoa, and a host of other mints, it should come as no surprise that one of the most important men in any market was the *sayrafi*. *Sayrafi* is usually translated as money changer, but his job was more than simply making change; rather, it was to determine the value of a coin. How else was a merchant in 12th-century Fustat supposed to know the value of a dinar minted in Isfahan or a gold coin minted in Venice?

The standard way for a *sayrafi* to determine the value of a coin was to measure its bullion content by weighing the coin itself.

Like the *sayrafi*, the *muhtasib*, or market inspector, was essential to the smooth functioning of markets, long-distance trade, and the overall economy in any given region. His job was to ensure that the weights and measures in the market (including those used by the *sayrafi*) were correct and that business was transacted honestly, but it was also his job to make sure that public morality in the very public space of the market was upheld. Market inspectors were to check scales and prices and to make sure that weights were accurate so that no fraud occurred in the markets.

Maintaining the integrity of the marketplace was one of the foundations of the state, so Muslims believed the sultan had to support his market inspectors and ensure the integrity of the markets in his realm. The only way that a sultan could ensure that his markets were honest was to appoint market inspectors who were beyond reproach and who could not be bought off. The best candidates for the job were men who did not have anything to gain by corruption. A nobleman was a good candidate, but even better would be a eunuch or an old Turk, who would be feared by nobles and commoners alike. The rigorous regulation of the markets stimulated the trade and economic prosperity of the cities in the Muslim world.

~James Lindsay

FOR MORE INFORMATION

Lindsay, J. *Daily Life in Medieval Islam*. Westport, Conn.: Greenwood Press, forthcoming.

Thackston, W. M. *Naser-e Khosraw's Book of Travels*. New York: Persian Heritage Association, Bibliotheca Persia, 1986.

BYZANTIUM

Byzantium was a predominantly agricultural state, yet it was within its cities that cultural life attained its highest expression. The largest urban centers were located along the Mediterranean coast, communicating readily with each other by sea and controlling access to their productive hinterlands. Cities of the interior occupied similarly strategic sites on major rivers and highways. Over the long life of the empire, Byzantine cities assumed very different architectural, administrative, and economic characteristics. Constantinople, as the capital and the only true megalopolis, always occupied a special place among them.

Most late antique cities continued with little change the physical framework of their Roman predecessors. The urban plan normally consisted of an orderly network of roads that was adjusted to fit the local topography. A centrally located business district included an open forum or agora that was surrounded by public buildings and churches. In provincial capitals, the administrative offices and governor's residence presumably were located nearby. Larger cities might have a hippodrome, stadium, or theater for sporting events and popular entertainments. Broad streets, often flanked by covered porticoes, stretched outward from this urban core to connect neighborhoods with their own plazas, fountains, and monuments. Numerous small shops opened on to these public squares and street colonnades, which became the main focus of economic life. Urban blocks were filled by densely built houses, which ranged from elegant residences of local elites (*curiales*) to the ramshackle dwellings occupied by most city dwellers.

The more elaborate houses included rooms for reception, dining, and other specialized functions, which were arranged around an open court. Perhaps the most distinctive feature of late antique cities was their fortification walls, many of which had been hastily built to confront military threats in the 3rd and early 4th centuries. The transfer of government from Rome to Constantinople encouraged the growth of cities across the east Mediterranean. Large centers such as Alexandria, Antioch, and Ephesus may have reached their greatest physical extent in the 5th and 6th centuries.

The crises of the 7th and 8th centuries transformed the appearance of all Byzantine cities. In many cases, new defenses were built to enclose a much smaller area, often with a reinforced hilltop complex (*kastro*) serving as place of refuge for inhabitants of the countryside. Rather than constituting major population centers, these reduced settlements typically functioned as military stations, gathering points for local tax revenues, and market towns for regional exchange. Monumental building projects apart from fortifications were rare. Many churches and other public structures were abandoned or rebuilt on a smaller scale. The few houses that are known from this period consisted of small clusters of loosely interconnected rooms facing onto irregular roads and alleys. Many of these places revived with the empire's economic expansion during the 10th and 11th centuries. In some cases, shops of related function were gathered in rows around a central courtyard (*aule*); the entire complex might be variously owned or leased by one or more proprietors. Districts for the manufacture or sale of specific goods are only infrequently mentioned. Markets usually were found around the port and near major gates in the city walls. Periodic markets associated with saint's festivals, such as the fair of St. Demetrios at Thessaloniki, took place on the plains surrounding the settlement.

The prosperity of most Byzantine cities was based on regional agricultural production and supplemented to varying degrees by manufacturing and trade. The yield of the surrounding territory was organized by rural villages and forwarded as taxes to the provincial capitals. Basic processing of mined materials and crops took place in the countryside, but a concentrated labor force offered advantages for secondary processing and manufacture. Within the cities, most work was done in small workshops (*ergasteria*), whose owners employed a few slaves, family members, or other helpers. The *Book of the Eparch* provides an extensive list of commercial ventures operating in Constantinople in the 10th century, including bakers, grocers, butchers, tavern owners, textile weavers, dyers, and tailors, furriers, and smiths who worked copper and silver. Other shops were occupied by goldsmiths, notaries, and money changers, whose activities in later times extended into the realm of banking. Many of these activities were also found in larger cities, including Thessaloniki, Thebes, and Corinth.

Evidence for large-scale urban industry is limited primarily to late antiquity. Most of the fine table pottery and ceramic lamps used between the 4th and 7th centuries came from a few specialized production sites in North Africa, western Asia Minor, and Cyprus, which may have been located near major cities. The manufacture of glass vessels and lamps may have followed a similar pattern. Pottery for routine household use was made on the regional, neighborhood, and even household levels. The large-scale production of bricks and roof tiles is not well understood but likely took place on the urban outskirts. Later sources mention the organization of government workshops for metals, textiles, and equipment for the Byzantine army. State operations in Constantinople provided silk embroideries, jewelry, and manuscripts for use by the imperial and patriarchal courts, as well as minting coins for public circulation.

Under favorable conditions, the countryside yielded an agricultural surplus that could be directed to wider markets within the empire and with neighboring states. Intercity trade was especially important for the economies of coastal cities. The extent of long-distance exchange is clear from the literary sources and in the discovery of goods, especially pottery, far from their place of origin. Pottery, glass, metalwork, and luxury goods presumably were shipped together with bulky agricultural commodities. The scope of this commerce remains unknown, as are the sponsoring roles played by the church and state. The interruption of long-distance exchange by the 7th-century Arab campaigns contributed to a serious monetary contraction and the physical decline of cities. Not until the 10th and 11th centuries did the Byzantine economy recover from these shocks.

~*Marcus Rautman*

FOR MORE INFORMATION

Dagron, G. "The Urban Economy, Seventh–Twelfth Century." In *The Economic History of Byzantium*, edited by Angeliki Laiou. Washington, D.C.: Dumbarton Oaks, 2002.

Oikonomides, N. "Entrepreneurs." In *The Byzantines*, edited by Guglielmo Cavallo. Chicago: University of Chicago Press, 1992.

Great Cities

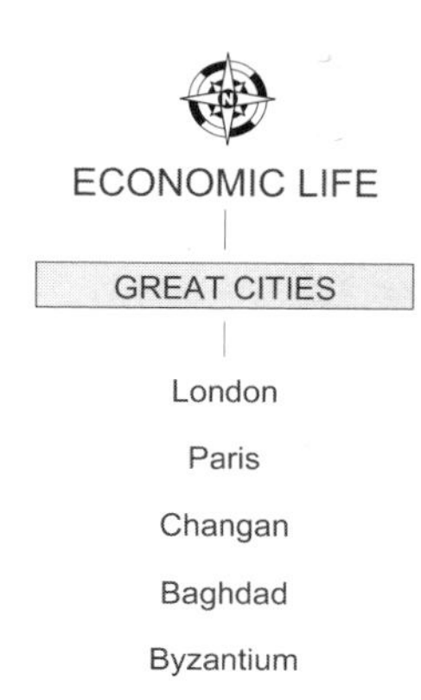

What makes a city great? From the beginnings of civilization in Sumeria (see volume 1), humans have constructed cities, places in which many people can live and engage in specialization of labor. Urban dwellers might plant small gardens, but they buy most of their food from the countryside as they specialize in some craft to make enough money to satisfy their other needs. History is full of cities that have grown up and then disappeared, and archaeologists spend time and money excavating long-dead cities. Some cities, however, have lasted for thousands of years and have earned their reputation in people's memories as great cities. What was their advantage?

Like any good real estate, great cities have great locations. The basic function of cities was commerce, so cities had to have ready access to water, which until the industrial age was the best means of transportation. London was situated on the river Thames, which flowed handily from the interior to the sea; Paris was on the Seine; Baghdad on the Tigris and Euphrates; and Changan on the Yellow River. These rivers formed the arteries through which the lifeblood of the cities flowed. Byzantium was located on the Golden Horn leading into the Black Sea and the Mediterranean, so like the ancient cities of Carthage and others, the sea was its pathway. To facilitate communication and transportation within the cities, the largest—Baghdad and Changan—built canals linking the waterways and providing rapid arteries through the cities themselves.

Because cities also depended on produce from the countryside for their survival, all great cities had to be located within regions that were sufficiently productive to supply their food needs. Of course, this distance changes over time; for example, Rome depended on the grain from Egypt and North Africa to supply its needs, and modern cities are supplied by goods from all over the world. One principle remains constant: cities have to be close enough to their food supply to get goods before it spoils.

To survive, cities also have to be in defensible locations, and geography often helped. Byzantium was surrounded on three sides by water, which aided its defense, but the great cities of the medieval world were surrounded by walls. In fact, a dictionary from the 17th century defines cities as "the home of a large number of people which is normally enclosed by walls" (Braudel, 492). Walls were built of brick or—more effectively—stone. To protect a city, any wall had to be high and thick. If the wall were too low, it would be too easy to storm; if too narrow, it would prevent defenders from moving effectively along the top. The great medieval cities met these standards, but the height of the wall indicated the degree to which the cities were threatened by the outside. London, Paris, and Changan were content with walls 18 feet high, Byzantium, ever-threatened by invaders, raised its barricades to 30 feet high, and Baghdad overwhelmed all invaders with walls 112 feet high.

Curiously perhaps, one of the characteristics of great cities of the medieval world is *not* the layout of the city. Changan was the only city that had any town planning. There, streets were laid out in a grid pattern with carefully designated quarters of the city. The other cities—from London to Baghdad—grew up in a random design within the city walls. Space was at a premium, so narrow streets wound haphazardly around structures that were built randomly. The only part that was regulated was the commercial districts, but for residences, mansions adjoined hovels.

All the great cities of the medieval world shared the same problems—many of which still plague modern cities. First was to ensure a reliable food supply, a problem that was made even more evident when towns were besieged within their enclosing walls and citizens struggled to find food. More towns were starved into submission than conquered any other way during the Middle Ages. A second problem was eliminating the waste from the large populations. The rivers that served as vital lifelines also served as sewers, receiving everything from bodily waste to food refuse. Consequently, diseases were always a problem, and the mortality rates in the teeming cities was always higher than that in the countryside.

One would think that the high death rates would lead to depopulation of these cities, but that was never the case. The last characteristic of great cities is that people long to go there. They always drew those who wanted to be a little more free than elsewhere, who wanted a chance to grow wealthier, and who even wanted the excitement of novelty. The great walled cities served as a lure to many in the medieval world.

~Joyce E. Salisbury

FOR MORE INFORMATION

Braudel, F. *The Structures of Everyday Life*. New York: Harper and Row, 1979.

LONDON

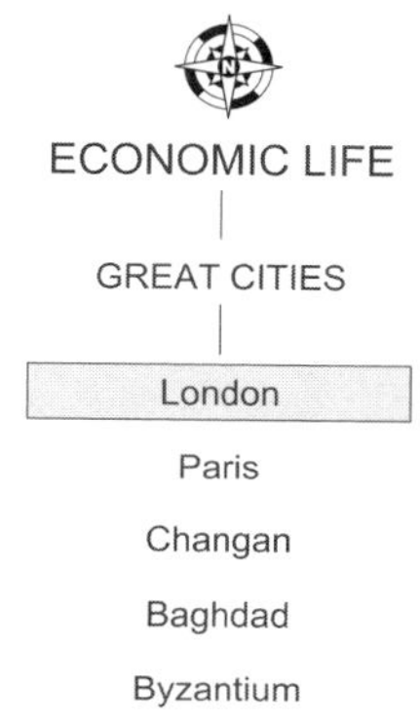

From Roman times, and probably before, the site of London was a perfect spot for a city. Located in England, along a bend of the great river Thames, the city offered easy access to the sea and to the interior of the island. Goods—and armies—moved from the Continent and the Mediterranean to the rich lands of England. Of course, the river made it essential that this access be well guarded. The important location of London shaped its development into one of the great cities of medieval world.

The Anglo-Saxon kings of England recognized the strategic position of London, held court there. The last Anglo-Saxon king, Edward the Confessor, built Westminster Abbey there to serve as the royal church. It was recently completed in 1066 when Edward died and was buried there. The results of the struggle for succession after Edward's death profoundly shaped the development of medieval London. On Christmas day in 1066, William the Conqueror was crowned king of England at Westminster Abbey.

As William began to consolidate his victory, he first had to face the citizens of London itself. To ensure their support, William granted London special privileges and freedoms, essentially allowing them to continue their trade unencumbered by royal control. This allowed him to focus his attention on the countryside. However, William needed to make sure this critical bend of the Thames was secure both from Londoners and from foreign invaders, so he built a castle in the southeast corner of the city. This castle (known as the "White Castle") was expanded by later kings until it became the complex now called the Tower of London. The tower was the secure royal residence, and it contained the royal mint, treasury, and the beginnings of a zoo. In 1097, William II began to build Westminster Hall, near Edward the Confessor's abbey, and it was the basis for a new royal residence. (Today it serves as the seat of parliament.)

The city that we generally call London, today, is really two cities: the old city of London itself, which maintains a tradition of merchants governing themselves, and Westminster, the neighboring seat of royal government. When William II died under suspicious circumstances, his brother Henry I needed the support of London merchants to secure his reign. In exchange, he gave city merchants the right to levy their own taxes and to elect a sheriff. In 1191, Richard I acknowledged the right of London to govern itself, which confirmed the separate roles of the two parts of what was rapidly becoming a great city.

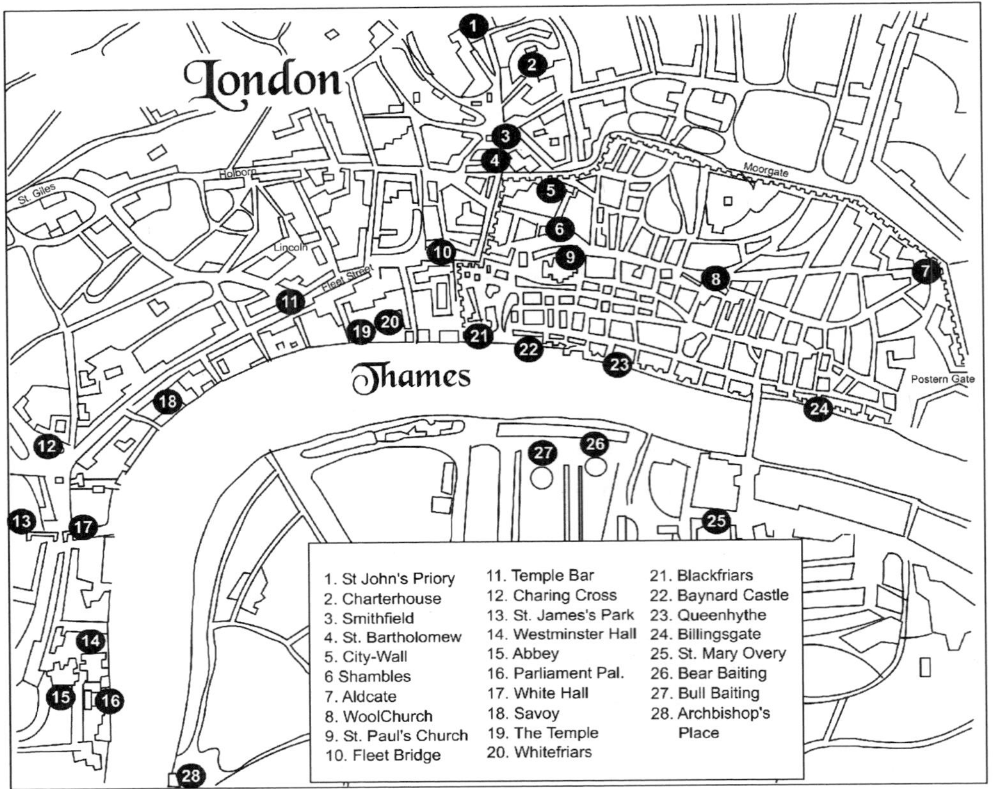

Map of Late Medieval London.

While Westminster was guarded by the king in the Tower of London, the city (like other medieval cities) was surrounded by walls. The walls were about 18 feet high, and gates gave access to the city during the day, although they were locked at night. The gates were fitted with double swinging doors of heavy oak, reinforced with iron.

The government of the city of London itself was by a lord mayor and a city council elected from the merchant guilds (see the previous section, "Urban Economic Life," for a discussion on how guilds governed cities). Each guild had its own hall and its own coat of arms and regulated its own trade, but they all met in common at the Guildhall. (The 15th-century Guildhall can be visited today.) Many of the streets in the city were named after the particular trade that was practiced there. For example, Threadneedle Street was in the tailor's district, Bread Street had the bakeries, and Milk Street allowed people to buy fresh milk from the cows that were milked on site.

The main problem of any city on a river is transportation across. In 1176, the first stone London Bridge was built very near the site of the old Roman wooden bridge. This bridge remained the only pedestrian crossing for the next 600 years. It was narrow and crowded with shops lining both sides and was so congested that most travelers preferred to hire boatmen to row them across or up and down the river. The banks of the Thames housed many enterprising boatmen ready to serve people from all classes.

The city was a maze of twisting streets and lanes. Most of the houses were made of wood, wattle, and daub. Many were whitewashed with lime, and others were painted—usually red, blue, and black—with paint made of pitch and linseed, which was highly flammable. Not surprisingly, the threat of fire was constant, and in the 13th century, a law was passed that required new houses to use slate for roofing instead of the more flammable straw, but slate was too expensive, and the law was often ignored. Rich people had houses of hewn blocks of stone bonded together by cement. People loved decorations on their houses—stone houses had saw-tooth ornamentations and elaborate moldings, and wooden houses imitated similar decorations. Windows and doors were embellished with curved carvings. Nearly all the smaller houses were in solid rows extending down the street. The lower floors of such houses had shops for tradesmen who lived with their families upstairs.

Common people's houses were small and not suitable for entertainment. Therefore, people gathered at "public houses"—or "pubs"—after work to eat, drink, and meet their friends. The pubs also accommodated travelers who needed a place to rest.

The city of London was also a city of churches and monasteries. The great cathedral—St. Paul's—was built in the 12th century and dominated the city just as Westminster Abbey dominated the royal environs. At one point, there were 13 monasteries in the city, and while they were disbanded during the Reformation, their names still dominate regions of London—Greyfriars, Whitefriars, and Blackfriars.

Medieval town planners (such as they were) like today's tried to separate undesirable elements from the best parts of town, so the south bank of the Thames became the refuge for activities frowned on by the better folk. Here in Southwark people could find prostitutes in the bathhouses, and here also they could go to bet on bear baiting, dog fights, and other violent and popular amusements. It was in this area that theater began, for the great Renaissance theaters, including Shakespeare's Globe were built. Spectators to all these unsavory entertainments could see the spire of St. Paul's Cathedral across the river reminding them of respectable lives to which they would return when the boatman ferried them back across the river.

In the 14th century, the poet Chaucer wrote the famous *Canterbury Tales* in which pilgrims leaving London going to the shrine of Thomas Becket in Canterbury told stories to pass their time. Chaucer had his pilgrims leave from a pub in Southwark as they began their journey, and medieval readers who saw this designation would know from the unsavory part of town that the tales would include lively bawdy stories of common folk, just the kind people liked to exchange in the pubs in the evening after work.

Modern visitors to medieval London would have been overwhelmed by the smells and dirt. There was no provision for disposing sewerage, and people dumped their chamber pots in the muddy streets. The river was used to dispose of all kinds of waste, from household wastes to remains of slaughtering animals to sell for meat. The air was smoky, the water polluted, and the streets filthy. There were always beggars and thieves in the narrow streets and safety was in one's own hands. Not surprisingly, diseases took a heavy toll in cities such as London. Nevertheless, London was an exciting place to be. Goods and people came from far away, and people in the pubs shared adventures and ideas that would have been unheard of in the villages of the countryside.

To read about London life in Elizabethan England, see the England entry in the section "City Life" in chapter 3 ("Economic Life") of volume 3; and for Victorian England, see the England entry in the section "Urban and Rural Environments" in chapter 3 ("Economic Life") of volume 5 of this series.

~*Joyce E. Salisbury*

FOR MORE INFORMATION

Britain Express. "London History—Medieval London." <http://www.britainexpress.com/London/medieval-london.htm>, accessed 6 October 2003.

Holmes, U. T. *Daily Living in the Twelfth Century*. Madison: University of Wisconsin Press, 1966.

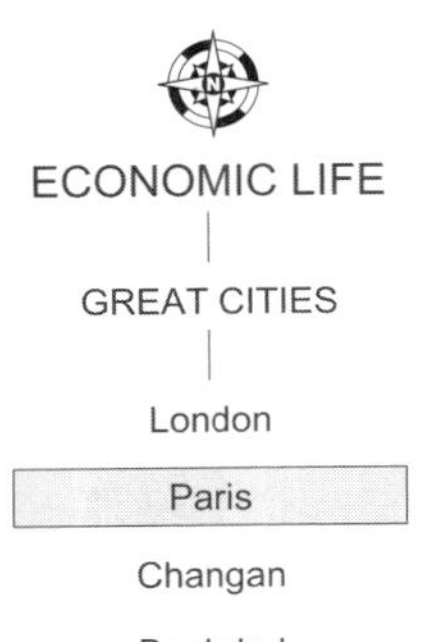

PARIS

Paris was already a substantial city in the Roman period, and by the 13th century it had become a leading political, religious, cultural, and economic center and arguably the most important city in Europe north of the Alps. Very little of medieval Paris survives after centuries of warfare, political turmoil, and economic development, but a rich body of documentary evidence allows a fairly detailed glimpse of Parisian life.

Like most ancient cities, Paris had grown up along a major river—the Seine—which facilitated transportation and trade. The Seine is one of France's principal rivers, wide enough to carry a great deal of traffic. Upriver is a network of waterways connecting Paris to the rich agricultural lands that provided much of the city's grain and wine; downriver are Normandy and the English Channel.

The center of the city was the Île de la Cité, an island in the middle of the Seine that had been the heart of Paris since Roman times. There was a main north-south street (called the rue de la Juiverie) that had once formed one of the axes of the Roman city, and sections of the old Roman ramparts were probably still visible around the edges of the island. The location of the Île de la Cité served an obvious military purpose, since the water constituted a natural barrier to an attacking force. In fact, the Île de la Cité had survived a yearlong siege by the Vikings in 885, but by the 13th century it constituted only a small part of the urban area of Paris. The bulk of the Parisian population now lived on the right bank of the Seine, to the north of the Île de la Cité, with a less-populous, but equally large, urban area on the left bank.

As an island, the Île de la Cité had ready access to water, but the island itself also facilitated land transportation. The site of riverside towns such as Paris was often determined by the availability of a crossing. Sometimes the crossing was in the form of a ford, reflected by the many towns in Europe with names such as Oxford and Frankfurt. In other places, including Paris, it was based on the suitability of the site for construction of a bridge. The Île de la Cité made the Seine easier to bridge by reducing its breadth and dividing it into two branches, making Paris an important crossroad in France's inland transportation system. To the north was the smallest, a wooden footbridge called the Planches de Mibray (Mibray Planks). To the south was the Petit-Pont (Small Bridge), which led to the left bank. The third, to the northwest, was the Grand-Pont (Great Bridge), the main route to the right bank.

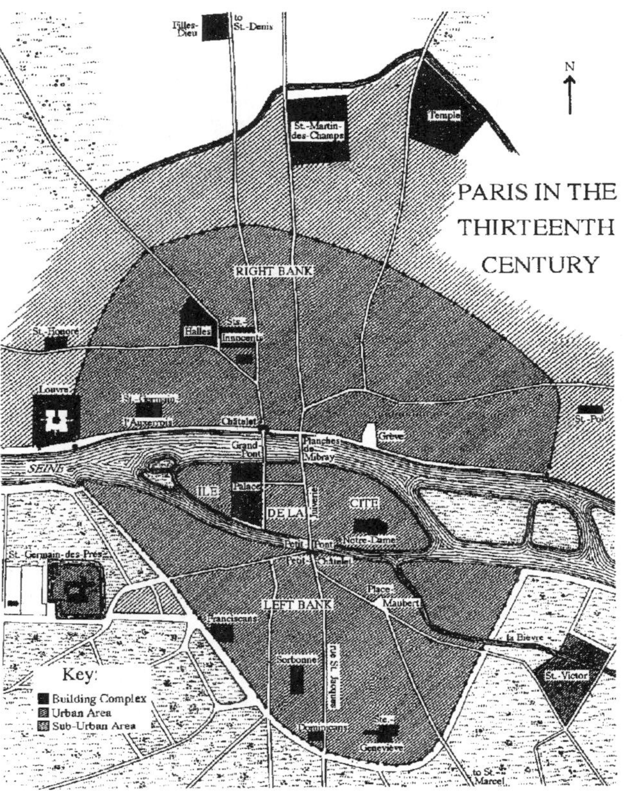

Map of Paris in the 13th century. Illustration by Jeffrey Singman (after Géraud).

These bridges were not merely thoroughfares but important commercial properties. The Grand-Pont and the Planches de Mibray supported a large number of watermills that harnessed the power of the Seine to grind flour for the Parisians' bread. The Grand-Pont and Petit-Pont were lined with commercial buildings along each side of the bridge itself. Bridges were important features of many towns, either joining its various quarters, as in Paris or Florence, or connecting the city to the world beyond, as in London, where London Bridge led to the road toward Dover and the Continent. As in Paris, these bridges were often substantial stone structures built wide to accommodate housing, and real estate on these key points of transportation was some of the most expensive in town. A bridge was an expensive installation, and many charged some sort of passage: the Petit-Pont, for example, levied a toll on merchandise brought across the bridge.

The population in the Île de la Cité was particularly dense, and people lived in a network of small streets lined with tightly packed houses. The layout of the streets in this part of Paris was fairly regular, in part reflecting the street patterns of the Roman city. Outside of the Île de la Cité, the streets were more haphazard, the product of centuries of evolution rather than distinct stages of urban planning. Although some medieval cities had an area where the older Roman street system survived, few were dominated by the gridwork layout typical of the planned cities of the Roman or modern world. Growth in the medieval city tended to be by accretion, with neighborhoods clustering around important centers such as major streets, water supplies, and markets.

Many of the core trades that supported city life, such as the sellers of foodstuffs and clothing, and politically or economically important trades, such as armorers, sword makers, and goldsmiths, were found in large numbers in the Île de la Cité and on the right bank near the Châtelet, close to the centers of regulation. The Juiverie was one of the better-appointed streets in Paris. Many city streets, like those of smaller towns and villages, were simply dirt and tended to become muddy in wet weather. The better streets were cobbled with stones or bricks, usually slanting toward a gutter in the middle. The Île de la Cité still had Roman foundations under its streets, but centuries of dirt and refuse had covered them over by the late 12th century. A chronicler of the reign of Phillip Augustus offers an account of the king's decision to improve the streets of Paris:

> King Phillip Augustus was staying at Paris, and was pacing around in the royal hall meditating on the affairs of the kingdom. He came to the windows of the palace, where he liked sometimes to watch the river Seine to revive his spirit, but the horse-drawn carts that traveled through the city, churning up the mud, raised an intolerable stench. The king, pacing about in his hall, was unable to bear this, and he conceived of a very arduous but necessary plan, which none of his forebears had dared to approach because of the great difficulty and expense of the work. He called together the burgesses and provost of the city, and ordered by the royal authority that all the streets and roads of the whole city of Paris should be laid with hard and strong stones. (Singman, 187)

The project was not an unqualified success. One chronicler remarks that the burgesses "would have done it with much more joy had it not been at their own expense" (Singman, 187). In fact, the paving of Paris was a gradual process, beginning with the principal streets of the Île de la Cité, like the Juiverie, and major thoroughfares, such as those leading to the city gates. At any given time, only a portion of the city streets were paved, and new urban development always brought with it new unimproved streets.

Important streets were fairly wide, sometimes wide enough to accommodate a market. Others were narrower, and many were no more than alleys: Unicorn Alley (ruelle de la Licorne) and Four-Basset Alley (ruelle du Four-Basset) off the Juiverie were each about four feet wide. There were no street signs. Street names were never official and could change over time. Many street names reflected a clustering of crafts: the Heaumerie (Helmery) was heavily populated by armorers, the Peleterie (Furriery) was home to many furriers, the Selerie (Saddlery) had numerous saddle makers and other makers of riding gear, the rue aux Ecrivains (street of Writers) had a concentration of parchment makers. Individual houses were not numbered as is the modern custom, but some had names reflecting the building's appearance, use, or current or former owner. Many were known by the name of a decorative emblem on the facade; some houses named in 13th- and 14th-century sources included the Rose, the Scales, the Lantern, and the Unicorn.

The state of Parisian streets that prompted Phillip Augustus's interest in paving was just one part of the problem of medieval urban sanitation. Even contemporaries sometimes complained of the bad air of the city: one wrote, about 1200, "He who lives amidst stench no longer perceives it; he must depart and return for the stench to affect him. . . . This can be proven by the inhabitants of Paris who forget its evil odor and only notice it when they return from a journey" (Singman, 188). Households made use of cesspits and rubbish pits on their property for disposal of waste, and the excess was sometimes carted outside of the city for disposal elsewhere, but much of the city's refuse ended up in the streets. Inadequate drainage meant that towns were often subject to flooding, so that waste in the streets could easily contaminate drinking water.

The sanitation conditions in the cities were made worse by the omnipresence of animals. Horses, oxen, and donkeys were common in the streets since they were essential to transportation. Many houses kept pigs, dogs, or poultry. Pigs and dogs were a serious hazard for young children because they were often left to roam the streets and entered open houses, sometimes attacking unattended infants. The animal population was no respecter of persons: in 1131, Prince Phillip, heir to the throne of France, was riding through Paris when his horse was startled by a pig; rider and horse fell to the ground, and the prince died of his injuries.

The concentrated population supported other animals even less subject to human control. Rats and mice were common, as were flies, fleas, and lice, all agents for the propagation of disease. The fleas and rats eventually brought devastation by transmitting the plague that came to Europe in 1347. The plague killed some 25 to 50 million people in its first three or four years, representing about a quarter to a third of the total population. The plague was the greatest demographic catastrophe to strike medieval Europe, but even before its arrival, disease was a chronic feature of urban life (Singman, 172–89).

FOR MORE INFORMATION

Singman, J. L. *Daily Life in Medieval Europe*. Westport, Conn.: Greenwood Press, 1999.

CHANGAN

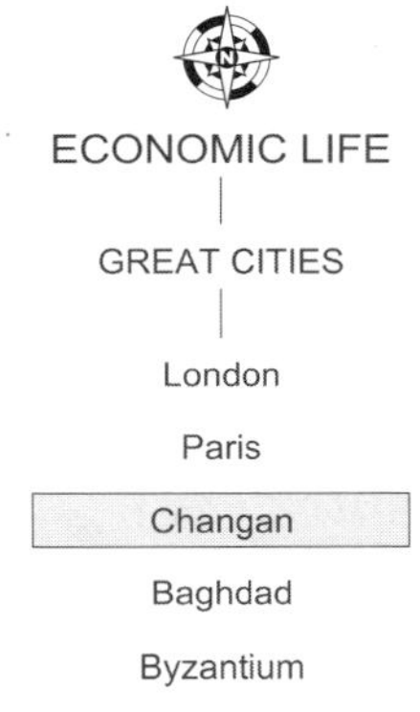

The greatest of the city in Tang China was the capital, Changan, which had been the main seat of the Tang since its founding in 618 and was probably the largest city in the world at the time, with a population of perhaps 2 million. Its prestige was so great that the Japanese adopted its layout for their imperial metropolis at Nara in the 8th century. This great city was laid out in a grid pattern, with wide thoroughfares (that served as effective firebreaks). The great imperial palace was on the western edge, and the city itself was dotted with lakes, parks, temples and markets. This bustling city was the center of civilization of the magnificent Tang dynasty.

The city was surrounded with walls about 18 feet high, which encompassed an area some 5 miles by 6, about 30 square miles. The purpose of the ramparts was to provide security for the residents within. They were barriers for preventing intrusions by assassins and bandits, but not insurmountable obstacles, as Tang law recognized. Climbing over the walls of Changan was an offense punishable by one year of penal servitude. As defensive bulwarks for impeding attacks by foreign invaders and indigenous rebels, the ramparts were less than satisfactory. They rarely withstood prolonged sieges, and emperors usually abandoned their capitals at the first signs of imminent military attack. Furthermore, the efficacy of walls as impediments was somewhat dubious, for wild animals sauntered into cities from time to time. In 769, a tiger settled in the ancestral shrine of a chief minister in Changan, and a general dispatched by the throne slew it with a crossbow. Another tiger entered a ward of the city in 782 and wounded two men before it was captured. In 830, a bear lumbered into a Buddhist monastery in Changan. Deer were also frequent intruders at the capital.

The walls of Changan had three gates each in the east, south, and west walls, as well as a dozen or so in the north that opened onto imperial parks and palaces. Each gate had three portals, and because traffic traveled to the right in Tang times, men, horses, and carriages entered Changan through the right portal (as one faced the gate from outside) and departed through the left. The middle opening was no doubt reserved for imperial or ritual processions.

The Gold Bird Guards were charged with maintaining law and order within the city, and they patrolled the thoroughfares day and night. Every intersection had a police post with 30 guards at major crossroads and five at minor ones. All gates had such posts with 100 men at the most important and 20 at the least important. The Gold Bird Guards were not always effective in carrying out their duties. In 838, some highwaymen shot at Chief Minister Li as he was making his way to an audience with the emperor in the predawn hours. Li suffered a slight wound, his retainers fled in all directions, and his startled horse raced back to his mansion. The thugs intercepted Li at the gate of his ward, assaulted him, and cut the tail off his horse. He barely escaped with his life. The emperor commanded army troops to take over guarding the streets of the capital. It was several days before calm returned to Changan.

Drainage ditches 11 feet wide and 7 feet deep flanked both verges of the avenues and streets in Changan. The installation of the drains naturally entailed the construction of bridges, four at all intersections. The ditches were not sewers. Human waste was a commodity carted to the countryside and sold to farmers, who used it as fertilizer for their crops. There was a family in Changan that for generations had engaged in collecting such "night soil" from dwellings in the city and had become wealthy from the trade. They had a beautiful mansion replete with fine furniture, a staff of slaves to do their bidding, elegant clothes for their women to wear, and herds of domestic animals to supply meat for their table.

From the founding of Changan in 582, emperors had trees planted—elms and junipers and pagodas—alongside the ditches to provide shade and elegance for the metropolis. Citizens were probably most pleased when the throne ordered the planting of fruit trees along the avenues in 740, an act that enriched their diets as well as their surroundings. Emperors periodically had to order the replanting of trees. Gales occasionally uprooted them. In 835, a great wind blew down 10,000. Heavy snow and rainfall in 820 also toppled many. In addition, citizens chopped down trees for fuel and building materials in times of unrest when the authorities governing towns were unable to enforce the laws.

In the capital there were 11 avenues running from north to south and 14 streets running from east to west. The roads were constructed of rammed earth and, being unpaved, turned to muddy bogs when it rained. The narrowest were 82 feet wide, those terminating in the gates of the outer ramparts were 328 feet wide, and the imperial way located in the exact center of the city, running from north to south, was 492 feet wide.

These avenues and streets divided the city into square or rectangular wards—Changan had 110 of them—similar to blocks in modern towns. Unlike their modern counterparts, however, they were far larger and walled with barricades of rammed earth, 9 or 10 feet high. The function of ward walls was to provide internal security by preventing the movement of people. In Changan, the size of the smallest ward was 68 acres, and that of the largest was 233 acres. The wards encompassed houses, mansions, government offices, monasteries, temples, parks, workshops, and inns. In Changan, newly rebuilt in the late 6th century, the southernmost wards, four to the east and west of the main north–south avenue, had no great dwellings, at least in the early 8th century. Farmers raised crops there. In both capitals, there were also gardens for cultivating medicinal herbs used in the palace, growing vegetables served at imperial feasts and sacrifices, and raising bamboo to supply the Department of Agriculture. The southern portion of one ward in Changan had no dwellings at all, only graves. Ironically, although the region surrounding Changan was overpopulated, the capital itself was underpopulated.

Roads divided wards into quarters. The quarters had alleys that were crooked or serpentine, so the grid pattern favored by Chinese city planners since antiquity broke down at that point. A few names of the alleys—Felt Alley and the Alley of the Jingling Harness—survive in Tang sources and suggest that shopkeepers populated these alleys (Benn, xiii, 46–58).

FOR MORE INFORMATION

Benn, C. *Daily Life in Traditional China: The Tang Dynasty.* Westport, Conn.: Greenwood Press, 2002.

BAGHDAD

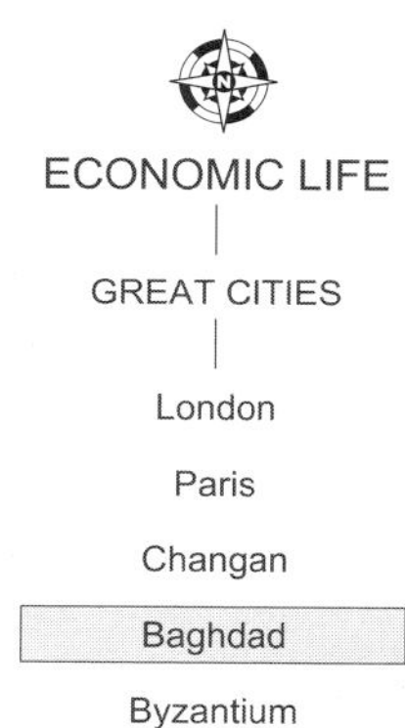

> Baghdad, in the heart of Islam, is the city of well-being; in it are the talents of which men speak, and elegance and courtesy. Its winds are balmy and its science penetrating. In it are to be found the best of everything and all that is beautiful. From it comes everything worthy of consideration, and every elegance is drawn towards it. All hearts belong to it, and all wars are against it. (Clot, 151)

The medieval Arabic commentator's praise for the city of Baghdad was not exaggeration. The city was founded in 762 by Caliph Mansour, and within 50 years it was the biggest city in the world, with a population of about a million people. The phenomenal success of the city was a result of the site of the city and the growth of Islam that fostered it.

Baghdad is located where the land narrows between the Tigris and Euphrates Rivers. The land surrounding the city is seldom flooded, and the two rivers are close enough together there for canals to be readily built linking the two rivers. The location is on the traditional trade route between the Mediterranean basin and central Asia, India, and the Far East, so goods from all over came through the city bringing variety and uncounted wealth.

The caliph's original plan was to build a city-fortress in which he could centralize his power, and it was built in the form of a circle nearly two miles across. Thus it was referred to as the Round City, although it was actually composed of concentric circles—a deep moat surrounding three huge, sloping walls. Of these three barriers, the middle one was the largest, measuring some 112 feet in height, 164 feet thick at the base, and 46 feet wide across the top. It was fortified with lookout towers. The round city at the center was the administrative center of the empire.

At the very hub of the round city was the caliph's palace, a magnificent building of marble and stone. Next to it was the Great Mosque. The palace had two striking features: a golden gate, and a green dome that rose to a height of 120 feet, covering the caliph's main audience hall. On the summit of the dome was a large statue of a soldier on horseback; later, legend would say that the figure swiveled and pointed to any area of the empire where danger threatened.

The city soon grew to be much more than the administrative center. Mansour first gave land to his followers in the center of what was called the Round City. While Mansour's original plans contained no provision for extending the metropolis, expansion soon became necessary to accommodate the flood of immigrants who started arriving as soon as the caliph took up residence.

The market was set up in the southwest of the city, and this section quickly became the commercial center. Each trade had its own section where merchants arranged their wares in shops, stalls, and courtyards so shoppers could compare as their strolled along. Merchants shouted their prices and urged buyers to stop, and the commercial district was a loud vibrant region. People could buy goods from all over Europe and Asia. Some merchants grew so wealthy they could even lend money to the caliphs themselves.

Soon the right bank of the Tigris, where the Round City was located, became overcrowded, and the city overflowed onto the east bank. This new quarter sprang up around the caliph's palace, and as the rich gathered there, so did those who offered services to them. By the end of the 8th century, there were 23 palaces in Baghdad, and the city sprawled on both sides of the river.

Most great cities of the Middle Ages were adjacent to rivers, and transportation was key to their success. Three pontoon bridges linked both sides of the city, but these were not enough to handle all the traffic of the bustling metropolis. The town was intersected by a network of canals, and both goods and people moved mostly by water. Two-thirds of the properties were on waterways, and people more often than not moved by boat. A local saying was that everyone "should have an ass in the stable and a boat on the river" (Clot, 156). The canals were crossed by many small pedestrian bridges and crowded with barges and smaller boats. Caliphs had huge, elaborately decorated processional barges, and everyone moved out of the way when they came by.

There was no town planning, so mansions grew up side by side with hovels. Following ancient techniques for the region, houses were built of sun-dried or kiln-fired bricks. The poorest dwellings were just pounded earth. The bricks of the rich were plastered over or covered with ceramics. Baghdad was the world center for glazed ceramics, and they were decorated with beautiful patterns. Roofs were flat, and people slept on them during the hot summer nights.

As appropriate for all great Muslim cities, there were many mosques in the capital. Arab historians make extravagant claims about the number of mosques in the capital, some even suggesting as many as 60,000 (Clot, 168). In addition to the great mosque by the palace, there were several other great mosques that were used for midday prayer on Fridays, but all the local small mosques were used for the daily prayers. People also gathered at the mosques for conversations, meetings, and quiet reflection. The streets of Baghdad always rang out with the muezzins calling the faithful to prayer from the mosques.

The great city stood until 1258, when the Mongols swept through the region. They laid siege to Baghdad and took it almost without a fight. Tens of thousands of people were massacred; the caliph was killed, and the magnificent palace with the green dome was reduced to smoking ruins. The heart of Islam would move from Baghdad where it had ruled for so long, and other great cities replaced it.

~*Joyce E. Salisbury*

FOR MORE INFORMATION

Clot, A. *Harun al-Rashid*. New York: New Amsterdam, 1986.
Stewart, D. *Early Islam*. New York: Time-Life Books, 1967.

BYZANTIUM

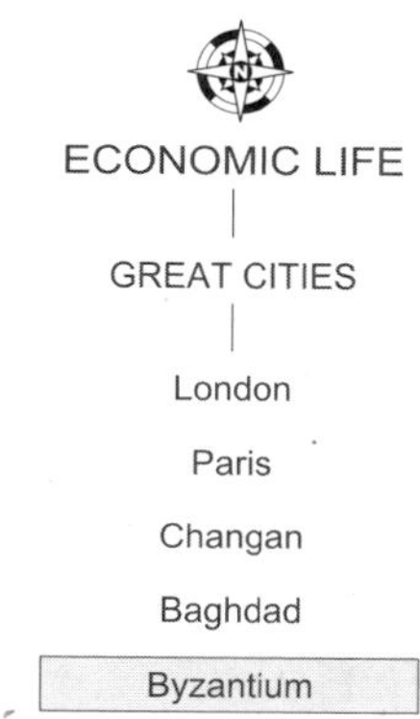

Where the waters of the Black Sea flow out toward the Mediterranean, they run through a narrow strait, then open into the Sea of Marmara, from where the waters narrow again before flowing into the Mediterranean Sea. This is a crucial communication link between the Mediterranean basin and Asia through the Black Sea. Furthermore, at the southwest end of the first strait, an arm of the sea projects four miles into the European peninsula forming a perfect sheltered harbor. The ancient Greeks called this curved arm of the sea the "Golden Horn." Thus the city that grew up on this site would be surrounded on three sides by water and needed only to be defended from attack by land on one side.

According to legendary accounts, a man named Byzas was leading colonists from Greece to found a new city. He had been told by the Delphic Oracle to settle "opposite the blind," and they traveled, wondering how to find a location to satisfy the oracle's recommendation. When they reached the Sea of Marmara, they discovered a colony on the Turkish side. Byzas thought they had been foolish—indeed, blind—to have ignored the harbor of the Golden Horn. Thus he believed he found the land they sought, and they crossed the Bosporus and founded Byzantium. For centuries, it exploited its perfect location and thrived as a Greek maritime city.

In 340 B.C.E., Philip of Macedon besieged the city, but the light of the moon gave away his attempted night attack, and Byzantium was saved. In gratitude, the Byzantines adopted the crescent moon as their symbol. Two thousand years later, the Turks borrowed this crescent for their own symbol when they made Byzantium part of their empire and renamed it Istanbul. However, that would happen much later. The city's fortunes really prospered under the Romans.

The emperor Constantine in 324 C.E. decided he needed a new capital. He chose Byzantium as the site for his New Rome—which he called Constantinople but which never lost its old name, Byzantium. The city had about as many hills as the original Rome, it was located in the heart of the wealthy eastern portion of the empire, and it was perfectly defensible. He brought settlers and promised them free grain as they had enjoyed in the old Rome, and he gathered art objects from all over to beautify his city. He built a wall across the land side of his triangular city, but the city soon outgrew it. On May 11, 330, Constantine dedicated his city.

Almost a century later, as Goths sacked Rome and threatened the whole empire, Emperor Theodosius II ordered a new wall built a mile and a half west of Constantine's. The frightened citizens hurried to make the wall, and 16,000 volunteers worked beside the hired masons. The wall was 13 to 15 feet thick, 30 to 40 feet high, and four-and-a-half miles long, with 96 towers. This wall guarded the city for another thousand years until the Turks attacked with cannons.

The defenses were complete with the addition of a huge chain that was stretched across the mouth of the Golden Horn, with winches to raise and lower it. With the chain raised, ships could not enter the harbor to threaten the city. The chain did not always serve as a deterrent, however. In the early 11th century, the Viking Harald Hardraad, who had served as a mercenary soldier in Byzantium, was trying to escape the city in two Viking longships filled with chests of stolen coins and jewels and a Byzantine princess. When faced with the chain, Harald ordered everyone to rush to the back of the boats with all the treasure as the rowers propelled the ships as fast as they could. The front ends of both ships rose to the top of the chain. One ship broke in two on the hard metal, but Harald's ship held firm. He then quickly moved everyone to the front of the ship, which duly lowered to the sea over the impeding chain. Harald returned safely to Norway with enough Byzantine treasure to ensure his kingship. Only the light Viking ships could perform such a maneuver; others were kept away from the well-defended city.

Within the walls, the city was periodically threatened by its own citizens. A particularly violent riot took place in the 6th century in the reign of Justinian and Theodora. Factions within the city were polarized along political and religious lines, but they identified themselves with chariot racing teams—the Greens and the Blues. In 532, the Greens and the Blues rioted against Justinian, in what is called the "Nika riots," because the rioters shouted "Nika," which means "victory." In the course of the brutal uprising, much of the city burned to the ground. After suppressing the riot, Justinian began to rebuild the city. At this time he left his most enduring legacy—the Church of Hagia Sophia—Holy Wisdom.

The church is an enormous domed structure. The central dome, with its diameter of 101 feet, is the largest such structure in the world. Two half-domes double the interior length of the church to 200 feet. The church was so magnificent when completed that Justinian reputedly claimed he had outdone Solomon, who had built the temple in Jerusalem. In 987, the Russian envoys were so dazzled by the church they reported back to their prince, "We no longer knew whether we were in heaven or on earth" (Sprague de Camp, 431). After the conquest by the Turks in 1453, Hagia Sophia became a mosque; it is now a museum. It remains the most extraordinary building in a remarkable city.

Byzantium remained a center of power, learning, and culture throughout the Middle Ages. The city withstood attacks from Muslims and Goths and was noted as one of the great cities of the medieval world.

~*Joyce E. Salisbury*

FOR MORE INFORMATION

Sprague de Camp, L. *Great Cities of the Ancient World.* New York: Dorset, 1972.

Rural Life

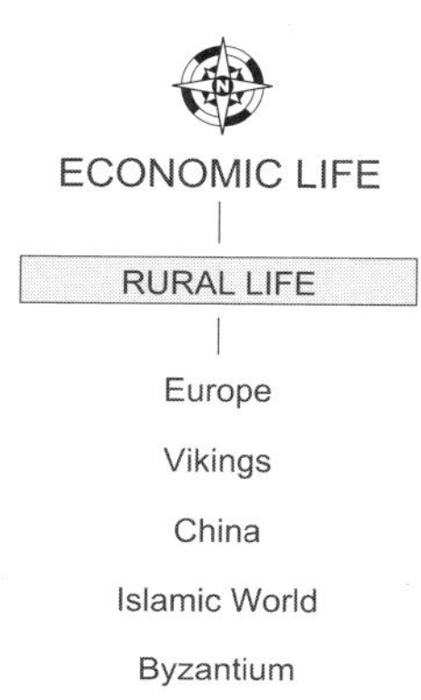

Most of the people throughout the world during the Middle Ages were *peasants*, a term that has a very specific meaning among anthropologists. Peasants are rural agricultural workers, but that is not all that characterizes their lives. Peasants work the land, but not only for themselves—they are ruled to some degree by an elite society, whether rulers or city dwellers, who depend on the produce of their land. In this way, peasants differ from tribes, who might be equally rural but who are more free in that they are responsible to no one but themselves. Within this general definition, all the rural workers considered in this volume were peasants, and as such they had many things in common, whether they lived in China, the Byzantine Empire, England, or the Middle East.

Peasants lived in villages in houses near one another and went out to the fields to work the land. (This is in contrast to farmers who lived in isolation surrounded by their fields and who periodically went into town for supplies. Farmers' lives followed a different pattern from that of peasants.) Village life was essential to the peasants who resided there; it was the center of their social, religious, and economic worlds. Each person's well-being and indeed survival was seen to be linked to the others in the village, and their culture was shared by the villagers. It is here in the village that peasants shared their suspicions of the surrounding larger culture—the urban dwellers who would cheat them, the rulers who would exploit them.

A second characteristic of peasant culture is that they not only produced a variety of crops and animals but they processed all or most of their food and other products for their own consumption or for sale in very local markets. Animals might be slaughtered by traveling specialists, but it was done at the peasant's home; wheat was threshed nearby, and vegetables were stored and fruit was preserved in the household. Beyond food, women spun and wove the their cloth in the household, and men made simple wood artifacts and even metal tools. The peasant economy, then, was highly diversified and self-sufficient. The family consumed most of the goods it produced.

The self-sufficiency of the peasant household contributed to the isolation of the peasant culture. Villagers had little need of outsiders, who tended to bring nothing but trouble in their minds. Traditionally, peasants, therefore, traveled very little. Many people in the Middle Ages never traveled more than 20 miles from their homes, so their view of the world was parochial. Peasants tended to be inherently conservative, as well. In their eyes, their village had survived since before their memories and there was no need to change the practices that had led to its survival.

Medieval texts repeatedly tell of conservative peasant reluctance to adopt new technologies. Indeed, in the peasant view, change was seldom to their direct advantage. For example, the import of the horse collar into Europe allowed horses to pull a plow and turn considerably more land than the ox had before. The peasants, however, also had to move faster behind the plow, so like their animals, they, too, had to work harder to produce more. The motive to change came from above, which signals another characteristic of peasant society: peasants never lived wholly self-sufficiently; they owed rents and services to landlords. Therefore, peasants were part of a larger society made up of mutually dependent parts, so anthropologists call elites and peasants "part-cultures" of the whole, a term that is intended to emphasize both the separateness and the interdependence of peasants and their lords.

Landlords everywhere required labor and rents from the peasants. Villagers had to produce more than they needed to supply the tax collectors with their due. The system required middlemen to serve as liaison from the part-culture of the village to the ruling culture that governed them. Tax collectors, merchants, and even local priests served as these critical connectors between the two parts of the total society. In return, the peasants were supposed to receive protection, although the bargain was never to the peasants' advantage.

For most of history, the system worked; peasants worked the land so that aristocrats did not have to. Villages operated quasi-independently, running their own affairs as much as possible and hoping most to be left alone. This pattern persisted whether peasants were growing wheat in Europe or rice in China.

~Joyce E. Salisbury

FOR MORE INFORMATION

Anderson, R. T. *Traditional Europe: A Study in Anthropology and History*. Belmont, Calif.: Wadsworth, 1971.

Potter, J. M., M. N. Diaz, and G. M. Footer. *Peasant Society: A Reader*. Boston, Mass.: Little, Brown, 1967.

Tree of the Wooden Clogs. Directed by Ermanno Olmi. Fox Forbes, 1979. Videocassette.

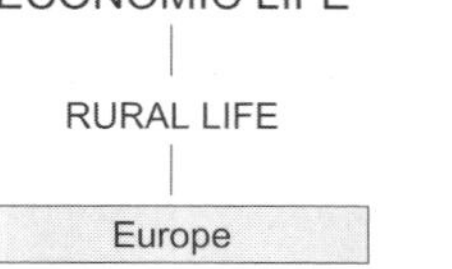

EUROPE

The work of the peasant family lay at the heart of medieval Europe and indeed was the foundation of the economic structure. The peasant economy depended on the work of the whole family, and all members recognized that. While there was some general division of labor, everyone recognized that all the work had to be done; thus if there was a shortage of men or women, then all participated in all forms of work. Men—and their sons—generally worked in the fields to produce mainly the grain crops. Women—and their daughters—performed the household work of preparing food and clothing. Women also were generally responsible for a vegetable garden and for caring for small animals such as goats, sheep, chickens, and so on. Women gathered eggs, milked the goats and cows (and occasionally domestic deer), sheared the sheep, and helped slaughter the pigs. Children as young as six years old cared for infants and toddlers in the home while parents worked; other young children might take the animals to pasture, or spend their days in the field driving birds away from newly planted grain.

Beyond all this labor that the family needed to do for its own subsistence, medieval peasants owed obligations to their lords. (For more information, see the Europe entry in the section "Social Structure" in chapter 6.) Men did everything from building roads and castles to farming on the lord's lands, while women spun and wove for the lady of the manor. This general catalog of work serves to indicate how the peasant family's work filled their lives. The remainder of this entry discusses some specific details about the labor on the manors of medieval Europe.

The most important part of the peasant economy was the cultivation of cereal crops. By the 11th century, the production of grains in most villages was done collectively on the basis of the three-field system. Before that, many areas only used a two-field system—one under cultivation and one fallow. In the three-field system, one field was planted in the spring in rye (or wheat), another was planted in early fall in oats (or barley), and the third was left fallow to restore the land's fertility. In some mountainous areas or regions with difficult soil, peasants planted spelt, a grain that was more forgiving than wheat, which needed good conditions to grow.

Men and women harvesting grain; the grain is cut by hand with sickles, which requires the men and women to bend over as they walk cutting the wheat. Illustration by Jeffrey Singman.

Most of the fields were arranged in long strips; a peasant family would own one or more strips distributed throughout the field. This arrangement (which seems so peculiar to modern eyes used to a different ownership pattern) grew up as medieval peasants adopted a large wheeled plow that had a strong fixed moldboard able to turn heavy clay soils of northern Europe. This plow needed to be pulled by a team of six to eight oxen—too many for any one household to own. Thus the village gathered its oxen and plowed collectively. Small square plots would have been inefficient because the large plow needed a wide area at each end of the field to turn around. Long strips solved the problems, and villagers had to work together throughout the season in their fields.

The lack of fertilizer was a perennial problem for peasants. They used animal manure on the fields, but they never had enough. Some villages that were near cities collected "night soil," human excrement from the urban areas, to spread on their fields.

The garden, near the peasant house, was fenced, and it was here that plants that needed intensive care were cultivated. Families grew turnips, peas, beans, cabbages, leeks, and other vegetables along with some herbs such as dill. These gardens were usually fenced to keep out wandering animals. The gardens provided an essential part of peasants' diets.

In some areas, peasants produced grapes for wine, which was a relatively lucrative crop in areas near growing urban regions. It became one of the most important sectors of the peasant economy along the rivers Thine, Moselle, Neckar and Main, and in France along the Rhône and the Loire. Locating the wine production areas along rivers allowed for the wine to be transported readily, which let peasants produce much more than needed for local consumption.

In the 11th century, there appeared a number of significant innovations that led to a small agricultural revolution. The increased use of the three-field system brought more land into cultivation, but there were other improvements as well. By the 12th century, Europeans had learned to use a new kind of horse collar (that may have spread to Europe from China). This collar rested on the horse's shoulders instead of its neck (like oxen yokes do), so a horse could lower its head to pull without choking itself. This new harnessing system allowed horses to pull plows and do more heavy labor. This was a great advantage because horses work about 50 percent faster than oxen and can work one to two hours longer during the day. Horses pulling the plow allowed more land to be cultivated by the same numbers of peasants, which increased the food produced.

In the 12th century, more iron became available in Europe. This allowed horses to be shod and plows to be equipped with iron plowshares, both of which improved the production of the all-important grain. However, iron had other less-obvious advantages: iron cooking pots became more prevalent, and when people cook in iron some leeches into the food, offering an advantageous supplement to people whose diets where often iron deficient. This particularly helped menstruating women, and women's health improved noticeably, so much so that by the 13th century, contemporary observers were noticing that there were more women than men in the population.

Diets were also improved by the more widespread planting of legumes—beans, peas, and related plants. These were wonderful plants because they offered iron and protein to the villagers, who did not eat as much meat as the nobility. They also improve the soil because they are nitrogen-fixing plants that fertilize the soil as they grow.

These agricultural improvements that began in the 11th century spread throughout Europe and allowed the medieval population to grow dramatically between the 12th and the 14th century. However, at the beginning of the 14th century, the population had grown so much that peasants could no longer grow enough to support everyone. People began to cultivate marginal lands that gave less grain in return for the labor, and pasturage was plowed to grow grain. This made peasants have to slaughter more animals, so there was less manure for fertilizer. When the weather turned cold for some years beginning in 1315, crops failed, and a severe famine spread through Europe. The 14th century saw the failure of the medieval peasant economy to keep pace with the changing times.

To read about rural life in Elizabethan England, see the England entry in the section "Rural Life" in chapter 3 ("Economic Life") of volume 3; for 18th-century

England, see the England entry in the section "Agriculture" in chapter 3 ("Economic Life") of volume 4; and for Victorian England, see the England entry in the section "Urban and Rural Environments" in chapter 3 ("Economic Life") of volume 5 of this series.

~*Joyce E. Salisbury*

FOR MORE INFORMATION

Rösener, W. *Peasants in the Middle Ages*. Chicago: University of Illinois Press, 1992.

VIKINGS

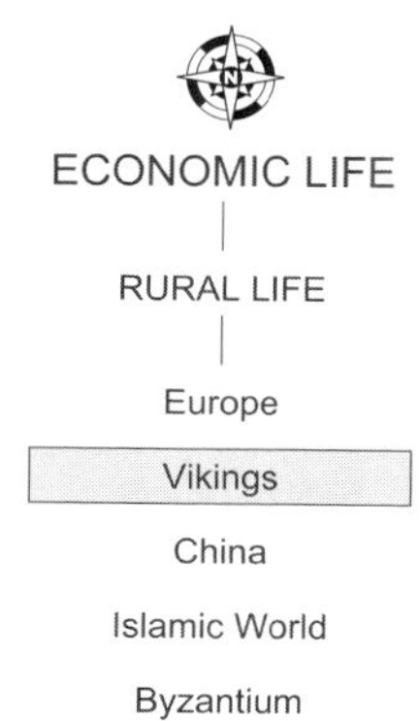

The economy of the Scandinavian countries was dependent on and conditioned by the local ecology. Agriculture was the mainstay of the economy in most areas, although the farming conditions of Denmark differed considerably from those of, for example, northern Norway and Sweden, for Scandinavia is divided into different ecological zones with different resources. These differences are clearly reflected in the settlement patterns of Scandinavia. Denmark and most of the Swedish coastlands were dominated by village settlements, that is, a cluster of three farms or more. These were generally situated on easily cultivated land. In most of Norway, the Swedish interior, and also the Norse colonies in the North Atlantic, the normal pattern of settlement took the form of separate or individual farms.

One typical example of a rural settlement dating from the 8th century was the village of Vorbasse, which had seven farms on fenced-in square plots, each with a wide gateway to a communal street. Six of the farms were of approximately the same size, but the seventh was larger. In layout, however, they were all similar. Each farm had a main building situated in the middle of the yard containing both dwelling and byres. The main building was surrounded by smaller buildings, some situated along the fence. These buildings were probably storage places for food and winter fodder, workshops, and dwellings for servants and slaves. In addition, there was a hayloft and some sunken buildings, and some of the farms also had a smithy and a well.

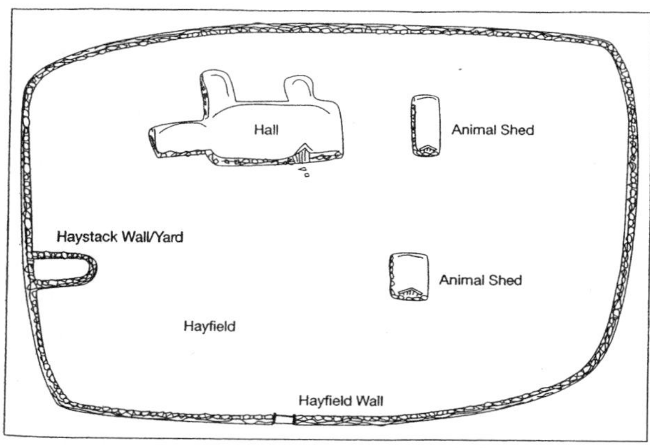

Farm layout of a traditional Viking farm. Note that these residents did not live in a village as traditional peasants in Europe had done. This shows an isolated farmstead.

In the small barns of the Vorbasse village, traces of stall partitions show that there had been room for 20 to 30 animals in each farm, which suggests that the economy was based on animal husbandry. Indeed, livestock breeding appears to have occupied a strong position not only in Denmark but also in Sweden and Norway. For dairy farming, cows were the most important animals, although goats were also used as milk-producing animals. Pigs were raised for their meat especially in the southern part of Scandinavia, and sheep were bred in some areas for wool and meat. In addition, hens, ducks, and geese were kept; they provided eggs and meat, and their feathers were used for pillows and eiderdowns. Horses were used primarily for transportation and as draft animals, although in pagan times horse meat was eaten. In the mountainous areas of Norway in particular, the practice developed during the Viking Age of transferring cattle, sheep, and goats to the mountain pastures—shielings—during the summer months, where the animals could graze on uncultivated land not immediately accessible from the farm. In the fall, the animals were then sorted and driven home, where some would be slaughtered and others kept for the winter.

Cultivated fields were found around the Vorbasse village, and grain appears to have been grown throughout Scandinavia in the Viking Age, especially in Denmark. Barley was the most important crop, although rye and oats were also popular. In addition, peas, beans, cabbage, hops, hemp, and flax were cultivated; the last-mentioned was used for linen making. The smaller fields were cultivated by picks and hoes with iron blades on wooden shafts. On larger fields, an ard—a plow without moldboard—was used, which scratched the surface of the soil with a downward-directed point pulled by one or more oxen or horses. It is not known when the proper plow was introduced, but it must have been known in Denmark in the second half of the 10th century. During the next two centuries, it spread to western Sweden and southern Norway. Corn harvesting was done with sickles and haying with scythes consisting of iron blades fitted with wooden handles. Rakes and pitchforks, other tools needed for hay making, have not survived, so most likely they were made of wood. Other agricultural tools included broad-bladed knives to cut foliage, axes, whetstones, and objects associated with animal husbandry, such as sheepshears.

The various tools and implements were fabricated locally. Many farms had their own smithies for working iron smelted from bog ore. Norway and Sweden had great resources of bog iron, which became the basis for a considerable iron trade in the Viking Age and of great economic importance. It is known that smiths enjoyed much prestige in Viking Age Scandinavia, and some of the wealthiest graves in Scandinavia are those of iron workers. Such craftsmen had their own tools necessary for the trade, including bellows, furnace stones (to protect the nozzle of the bellows used to raise the heat of their furnaces), tongs, hammers, metal shears, files, and an anvil.

~*Kirsten Wolf*

FOR MORE INFORMATION

Wolf, K. *Daily Life of the Vikings*. Westport, Conn.: Greenwood Press, forthcoming.

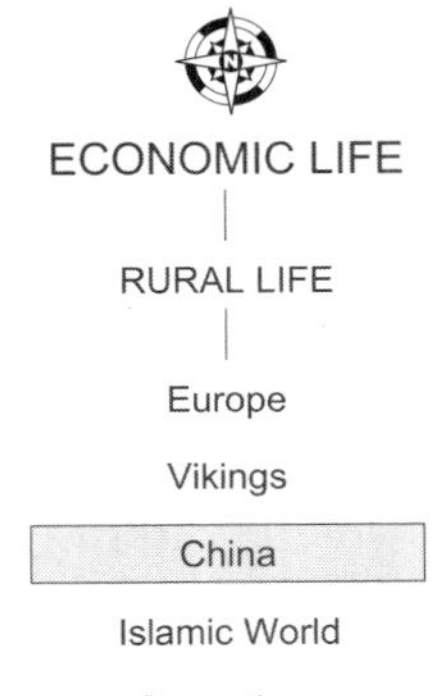

CHINA

By the Tang dynasty, the Chinese had developed a rich agricultural tradition that supported its large population and which consumed the time of the many peasants who worked the land in the rural areas. Peasants cultivated various grain crops. In the north, millet, wheat, and sorghum dominated, whereas in the south, rice was the overwhelming crop. Peasants also cultivated taro, melons, greens bamboo shoots, ginger, chestnuts, and various fruits.

The Chinese peasant had various agricultural implements. (See the section "Technology" in chapter 5.) Since the Han dynasty, there were many iron tools, including the spade, shovel, pick, hoe, and sickle. They also had iron plowshares that could be adapted to various soil types, from the light sandy soils to the heavy clay of the south.

Oxen were the main draft animals. One or two oxen were used to pull a plow, while the farmer followed along behind, holding the plow as he drove the oxen. The draft animals also pulled a harrow that broke up the large lumps of earth. After the seed was sown, oxen pulled a leveler to cover the seed and protected the soil against erosion.

Iron sickles were widely used to harvest grains; then the farmers had to thresh the grains to remove the husks and winnow it to separate the husks from the grain. Most of the time, the grain was beat to thresh it, but in some places archaeologists have found threshing machines, which were operated by a foot pedal that worked a hammer to pound the grain. Large mills, run either by water or animal power, ground the grain into flour.

About 2000 B.C.E., rice spread from India to southern China. There are several kinds of rice, and tombs from the Han dynasty indicate three kinds of rice were available—short grain, long grain, and glutinous rice. Some rice can grow on dry lands, but the most important kind of rice was aquatic rice, which required much irrigation. This rice transformed Chinese society because it could support a large population. However, it is also the grain that needs the most human labor to produce.

The rice roots require a rich supply of oxygen, which stagnant water cannot give, so fields must always have moving water. Chinese peasants developed paddy fields that already by the Middle Ages dotted the landscape in southern China. (The meaning of "paddy" is "rice-in-the-husk.") These fields were divided into small patches divided by earth banks. Water flows through them, often powered by irrigation pumps powered by pedals. The water is muddy, which restores the fertility of the soil (and reduces the malaria mosquitoes). Sluices were designed to allow water to flow from one paddy to the next.

Much organization was needed to make sure the lands were properly irrigated and that there was enough peace to assure the peasant population could tend the fields. It also helped if the villages were close together so the irrigation could be made most efficient. All in all, the rice fields that demanded such intensive human labor also contributed to the highly structured Chinese administration. In return, the rice paddies allowed a population to grow. By 1100, southern China was dominant because of rice, and by 1380, the population of the south was two-and-a-half times that of the north: 38 million to 15 million (Braudel, 149). What rice offered was not yields (the amount of grain harvested); corn and even wheat offer higher yields than a rice plant. Instead, aquatic rice grew so quickly that a hard-working farmer could get two or perhaps even three harvests in a year.

First, a farmer had to plow the muddy, water-filled fields with his plow and oxen. The peasant walked beside his buffalo so his footsteps would not leave hollows in the mud. While he did this, he pulled up weeds and drove away the grabs that infest the deeper waters. Then he planted seedlings that had been previously planted in manure-rich soil. Within three to five months, the rice was ready, and it was harvested and hastily taken to barns to dry. Meanwhile, the farmer rushed to plow the field again and plant the next crop of seedlings to grow while he threshed the rice.

Farms also included domesticated animals. Chinese raised chickens, ducks, and geese for food and eggs. Other domestic animals included horses, cows, sheep, pigs, and dogs. While animals served as food and transportation, animal excrement was also collected to fertilize the fields. In the north, camels were domesticated by the Han dynasty to help in transportation.

Despite the low technology, Chinese population boomed primarily on a diet of rice. This miraculous grain demanded much labor from the peasant cultivator, but in return it provided enough sustenance to feed the large population that its cultivation demanded.

To read about rural life in 19th-century China, see the China entries in the sections "Work" and "Urban and Rural Environments" in chapter 3 ("Economic Life") of volume 5 of this series.

~Joyce E. Salisbury

FOR MORE INFORMATION

Braudel, F. *The Structures of Everyday Life*. New York: Harper and Row, 1979.
Zhongshu, W. *Han Civilization*. New Haven, Conn.: Yale University Press, 1982.

ISLAMIC WORLD

While the Arabian Peninsula (Jazirat al-ʿArab or "Island of the Arabs") is named after the ʿ*Arabs*—that is, the nomads or Bedouin who lived there and in the deserts that extend northward into Syria and Iraq (and even into the Sinai and Egypt east of the Nile)—the vast majority of the population of the region even in antiquity has always lived some sort of settled existence. These settled populations lived in disparate environments and supported themselves in a variety of ways determined to a great extent on the availability of water. Yemen (the Arabia Felix or "Happy Arabia" of the classical geographers) was exceptional in just about everything. Unlike the Bedouin who lived in tents or the residents of the oasis settlements of the Hijaz who lived in dwellings that we might call simple huts, many of the people of Yemen lived in villages and towns made up of multistory tenements.

The people of Yemen built dams in the valleys in order to catch the annual monsoon rains. In the highlands that reached as high as 10,000 feet, they built extensive terraces for the same purpose. As the rains poured down these terraces, the water soaked deep into the soil and deposited nutrients that it brought with it from terrace to terrace. Such water catchment practices produced an agricultural bounty of wheat and barley, as well as fruits, vegetables, dates, and vineyards that was simply impossible elsewhere in the peninsula.

The sparse annual rainfall in the rest of the region (no more than 8 to 10 inches, and in most areas fewer than four) was simply nowhere near sufficient to sustain the extensive agriculture practiced in the south. The largely date palm agriculture that was practiced in much of the rest of the region was dependent on natural springs or wells that were dug to tap underground reservoirs. Eastern Arabia along the Persian Gulf benefited greatly from its extensive underground reservoirs. Parts of the Hijaz in northwest Arabia had sufficient water to cultivate a range of crops as well as irrigate massive palm groves with millions of trees. However, many oasis settlements throughout the region were extremely small and could only sustain a handful of people.

Nomadic Bedouin came to oasis settlements throughout Arabia to trade the surplus from their flocks and herds such as milk, clarified butter, wool, hides, and skins for the produce of the oases such as grains, dates, oil, clothing, wine, arms, cooking pots, and other items that their smiths produced.

Camels, like sheep and goats, were bred as sources of milk, meat, and wool but also as indicators of wealth and status as well. In fact, in the southern deserts and across the Bab al-Mandib straits in Somalia most of the camel herders bred their beasts primarily for their milk, and few actually used them intensely for transportation or as beasts of burden.

In the northern lands of the Muslim world, there was far greater agricultural diversity. These lands were especially renowned for horses, soap, chains, leather straps, cotton, balance scales, and a preserve called *qubbayt* made from locust fruit and nuts. Some villages were renowned for grains, honey, dried meats, coal, fats, cheese, honeydew, sumac, pomegranate seeds, pitch, iron, metal buckets, knives, arrows, salted fish, and chains; others were known for chestnuts, dried fruits, scales, inkstands, rods for fulling carpets, and many other products. This rich diversity of rural production helped fuel the great trade networks of the Muslim world.

~*James Lindsay*

FOR MORE INFORMATION

Lindsay, J. *Daily Life in Medieval Islam*. Westport, Conn.: Greenwood Press, forthcoming.

BYZANTIUM

The Byzantine Empire was a predominantly agricultural state and most of its subjects lived in the countryside. The lives led by these rural inhabitants varied in important ways with location, time, and social status. At its greatest extent, the empire of Justinian stretched from the Near East to embrace much of Italy and even part of Spain. Within these boundaries, extensive lands were cultivated along the Nile River, in north Syria, and across North Africa to supply the growing population of Constantinople. During the 7th and 8th centuries, these productive regions were lost to the Arab Umayyads, which left the later Byzantine Empire confined primarily to the east Mediterranean region. Steep mountains and a unifying sea characterize much of this landscape, with fertile inland plains in Anatolia and the upper Balkans, and narrow valleys opening on to the rocky Aegean coast. Most peasant farmers and pastoralists lived in small villages and market towns, as well as growing estates owned by aristocratic families and monasteries. Within these shifting boundaries, the constant factors of topography, geography, and climate ensured the basic continuity of rural life throughout the Middle Ages.

Information about Byzantine village life is very uneven. Most authors lived in Constantinople or provincial cities and paid little attention to the countryside, which they regarded with suspicion and disdain. Saints' lives sometimes set their moralizing stories against a rustic backdrop of colorful incident but dubious reliability. The controversial *Farmers Law,* which apparently dates from the 7th or 8th century, gives a detailed picture of rural customs in some parts of the empire; the 10th-century compilation known as the *Geoponika* similarly records much traditional information on farming practices. Archaeology brings a special perspective to this poorly understood subject: field surveys can map the regional distribution of settlements, which in many places expanded during the 4th to 6th centuries, withered between the 7th and 9th centuries, and revived during later Byzantine times. Excavations that have been carried out at a few sites provide further information about the appearance and operation of individual settlements. The variety of recovered artifacts gives a sense of the daily activities of their residents.

Most land workers or peasants (*georgike*) lived in villages known as *komai* or *choria*. Considerations for establishing these small settlements included a safe or defensible location, the availability of water, and proximity to fields, vineyards, orchards, and woodlands. Because few villages were fortified, most inhabitants relied for safety on their distance from the coast or a hilltop location overlooking major roads. In times of military peril, people could flee to the safety of a regional castle (*kastro*). Brigands and pirates were a frequent concern even during peacetime. Villagers drew water from perennial springs and wells and often built cisterns to conserve resources during the dry summer months. Agricultural strategies were influenced by local topography, climate, and politics. Kitchen gardens demanded constant tending and were located closest to home. Cereal crops, which needed little attention during the growing season, could be located at a walking distance of one or two hours. Threshing took place on circular platforms (*alonia*) in the fields or around the village periphery, where donkeys or oxen dragged a specialized sled (*doukane*) over the scattered sheaves. Milling was done by hand, with animal labor, or in water-driven mills. Olives and grapes could be raised on terraced slopes, yet needed 8 to 10 years of regular care before yielding a marketable crop. Presses for both crops were found across the countryside. Crop irrigation was not usually practiced on a large scale.

Permanent settlements varied greatly in their physical appearance but shared many features. The most important buildings included a community center (*kathedra*) and one or more churches.

Chapels and churches normally were modest basilicas that stood near the habitation center. Additional churches might be built as a settlement grew, with each new foundation establishing a neighborhood focus and attesting its prosperity.

Their prominence after the 9th century reflects the growing role that the church and its clergy played in rural life. These freestanding buildings sometimes faced onto an open plaza, from which narrow alleys and paths led through densely built residential quarters to the nearest road. Houses were built of local materials such as fieldstone, mudbrick, timber, and thatch; in some areas, fired bricks and roof tiles were also used. Most village properties were enclosed by buildings or a low perimeter wall. Two or three rooms would look onto an open yard where animals were kept. Meals were prepared at a hearth in one room, which also could serve for sleeping quarters; another room was used for food storage in bags, baskets, and large storage jars (*pitharia*) that were recessed into the earthen floor. In larger houses, animals could be stabled indoors while the family slept upstairs.

Most villages were home to fewer than a thousand people. Families of four to six members owned property in small, scattered plots that could include a house, kitchen garden, vineyards, orchards, and arable fields together with wells and springs. Pastures, woodlands, streams, lakes, and seashores were held in common by the village community. Most villagers concentrated on raising a variety of market crops, especially grain, olives, and grapes, to cover the community's tax assessments and rents. Any shortfall by individual farmers had to be made up by the community as a whole. Many of these families also kept livestock, mainly sheep and goats but sometimes poultry, pigs, and cattle. Hunting, fishing, and beekeeping helped supplement the local economy. Individual families specialized in essential crafts including metalworking and smithing, weaving and sewing, and making sandals and shoes. Carpenters produced domestic furnishings and storage barrels. Neighborhood potters made a variety of domestic vessels for table use and storage; their importance is recognized in the *Geoponika*, which calls the pot maker one of the most essential artisans of the countryside. Such craft specialization is a feature of larger settlements and in later Byzantine times may have supported exchange among neighboring villages at periodic markets and festivals. In smaller villages, such basic needs were met within the household itself.

~*Marcus Rautman*

FOR MORE INFORMATION

Bryer, A. "Byzantine Agricultural Implements: The Evidence of Medieval Illustrations of Hesiod's *Works and Days*." *Annual of the British School at Athens* 81 (1986): 45–80.

Kazhdan, A. "The Peasantry." In *The Byzantines*, edited by Guglielmo Cavallo. Chicago: University of Chicago Press, 1992.

Rautman, M. *Daily Life in Medieval Byzantium*. Westport, Conn.: Greenwood Press, forthcoming.

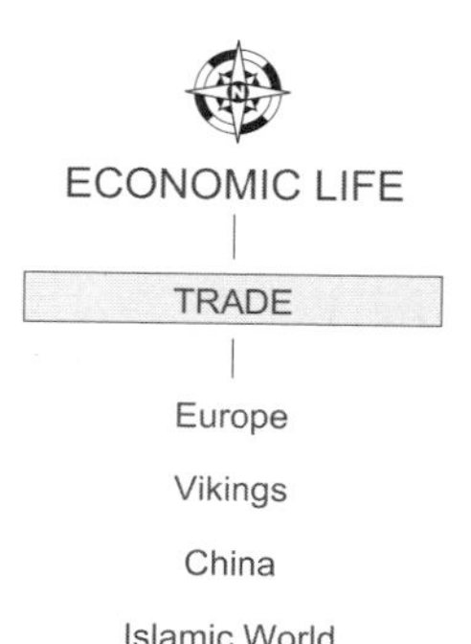

Trade

One of the overriding features of the high part of the Middle Ages was a prodigious expansion of trade across Europe and Asia. In part, this trade was facilitated by the presence of large empires that brought relative peace in their borders. In part, the trade was a continuity of the long-distance trade that had marked the ancient world. In any case, goods from far away traveled east and west, and people expanded their ideas of the world as surely as they came in contact with new, sometimes exotic, goods.

The Muslim empire under the ʿAbbasids was the first to really take advantage of the burgeoning trade. When the caliphs moved their capital to Baghdad in the Tigris-Euphrates valley, they did so consciously to take advantage of being in the heart of a prosperous trade route. From about the end of the 8th century, the worldwide supply of precious metal in circulation increased with new supplies of gold from the Sudan, sent by caravan across the Sahara Desert and into Egypt, Syria, and Mesopotamia. Backed by these resources, the Muslim dinar became the prevailing currency throughout the Muslim world and along with the Byzantine *nomisma* assured reliable financial standards for trade. The Muslim world was well situated to exploit an astonishing trade, and Muslim merchants were dynamic in their pursuit of this trade.

The Byzantine Empire, too, had remained centralized, and they were able to take advantage of the growth in trade as well. Situated between the vibrant trade routes of Islam and the growing Western markets, Byzantine merchants made sure a steady flow of goods came through the great capital.

The Chinese empire under the Tang dynasty had always sustained a rich long-distance trade, and when the Mongols established their far-flung empire in the 13th century, the trade networks only increased. Merchants such as Marco Polo traveled from Italy to the Mongol court in China and back again, aided by the great expanses of the Mongol Empire. They brought with them a wealth of spices and exciting tales to tell.

Even western Europe, although late to enter the game on a large scale, was not left behind. By the 11th and 12th centuries, Europeans had established two prosperous trading zones—north and south—and had developed great fairs in France to connect the two. While European Christians tended to be a bit suspicious of merchants and their way of life, we have evidence that in the 12th century, their disapproval waned in the face of the growing nexus of trade. There is even an account of a merchant who became a saint—Saint Godric—and the account of his life offers testimony to a growing appreciation of trade. Godric's biographer writes that the merchant sailed "to and from between Scotland and Britain, and he traded in many divers wares and, amid these occupations, learned much worldly wisdom. . . . Hence he made great profit in all his bargains, and gathered much wealth in the sweat of his brow; for he sold dear in one place the wares which he had bought elsewhere at a small price" (Coulton, 415–19). Here we can see the essence of the merchant's trade—buy low and sell high. The western Europeans were learning.

The Vikings from Scandinavia were also intimately involved in long-distance trade, although it was often hard to tell the difference between their trading and their raiding. If the former failed, they brought back goods from the latter. In their quest for trade with the wealthy Byzantine Empire, the Vikings established a settlement along the Dnieper River that became the start of Kiev—later to become the Russian Empire. Archaeological finds of Byzantine and Muslim coins in Scandinavia testify to the Viking skill at trade.

All this vibrant activity should not obscure the real hardships of trade in the Middle Ages. Most roads were terrible—rutted and muddy in spring and in the north frozen in winter. The main roads in China were reasonably well maintained, but secondary roads remained terrible. Europeans favored horses and carriages, but it was not unusual for horses to be up to their hocks in mud and the carriages stuck. Overland 3 miles an hour was a good speed, and 20 miles a day was considered a full day's journey. Marco Polo and his family took three-and-a-half years by horseback to get to the Mongol capital of China. After the breakup of the Mongol kingdom in the 14th century, travel became even slower.

The hardships of trade can only remind us of the huge benefits people expected to get from long-distance trade. Not only did some people get rich from the trade, but everyone benefited from the exchange of knowledge that always accompanies an exchange of goods. The way to the great explorations of the Renaissance were prepared by the enterprising merchants of the Middle Ages.

~Joyce E. Salisbury

FOR MORE INFORMATION

Coulton, G. G. *Social Life in Britain from the Conquest to the Reformation*. Cambridge, England: Cambridge University Press, 1918.

EUROPE

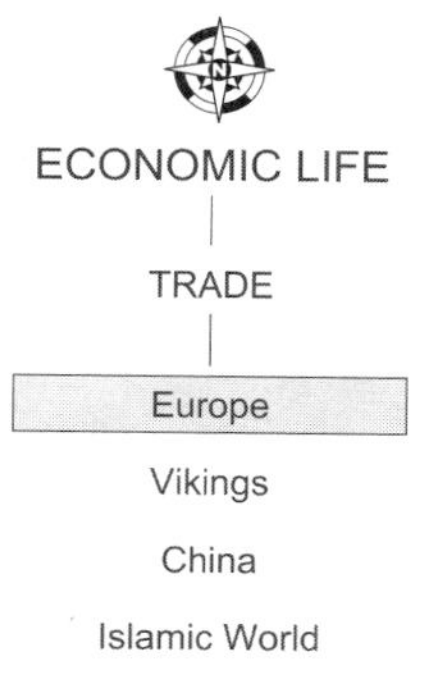

During the early Middle Ages, the vibrant economy of the Roman Empire had crumbled along with its political, legal, and military structures. Even those locations that were cities in the Roman Empire were generally reduced by the 7th century to small markets with limited commercial production and almost no export to distant locales. By the 8th and 9th centuries, most markets were local, but the Carolingians began to encourage long-distance trade. Pepin the Short ordered designated market days in the cathedral towns, for specified markets were the best way to control trade, and regulated trade provided taxes. It was for this reason that markets of certain goods were set for specific days, and toll gates were erected on roads and into towns. Any goods carried into or out of a market town would be taxed. In 802, Charlemagne forbade the sale of goods after dark or anywhere other than in public locations, again because the trade of goods needed to be seen to be taxed (Butt, 96).

The major impediments to long-distance trade were transportation and safety. Carts and wagons, usually pulled by horses or oxen, were more restricted by the condition of the roads, but under good conditions they were more efficient than pack animals. A four-wheeled wagon with a pair of horses could haul as much as 1,300 pounds about 25 miles a day. Like horses, carts and wagons could be hired, usually with a driver to operate them; the cost in the late 13th century was about four pennies a day. Aristocratic ladies sometimes traveled in covered wagons; the experience must have been rough, as these wagons do not appear to have had much in the way of a suspension system. Large trains with substantial numbers of carts, such as an army or an aristocratic household with its possessions, tended to move slowly and might cover only 10 to 12 miles in a day.

The rate of travel depended on the nature and condition of the roads. Many Roman roads were still in use, but they had decayed from centuries of inadequate maintenance, and their stone foundations were covered by a thick layer of soil. More recent roads were not as well constructed, and many routes were served by little more than dirt tracks. In adverse weather, roads became muddy and difficult to pass. Riders particularly lost their advantage of speed when the road was poor or when they left the road for rougher country.

Trade in a seaport of the Mediterranean, 15th century. The Venetian merchants were in the forefront of the long-distance trade that linked Europe to China. © North Wind/North Wind Picture Archives.

Routes of travel were highly sensitive to natural topography. Rivers were major obstacles, and roads were sited to take advantage of such crossings as were available. Bridges were comparatively rare since even a wooden bridge was expensive to build and maintain. Most bridges were built near major settlements that had the means to sustain them. Where bridges were lacking, the river might be forded at a shallow point. This could be risky; sometimes the current proved too strong, and men, beasts, and goods were lost in the water. In some places, a ferry carried passengers for a fee. Mountains also impeded traffic, obliging travelers to wind their way laboriously up and down each side. Travel routes tended to follow the contours of the land, running along river valleys rather than across them; a village might be in closer contact with a town some distance away in the same valley than with one closer to hand but on the other side of a substantial river or mountain ridge.

The challenges of travel were heightened by the danger of attack. Many roads passed through thinly populated areas that served as havens for highwaymen. For safety, it was generally considered prudent for travelers to find companions for the journey; many people traveled in the company of relative strangers for the sake of mutual protection, although there was always some risk in taking up with unknown company. Those who could afford it hired armed escorts to ensure their security. In some cases, security was provided by the feudal lords through whose territory the roads passed, since it was in their interest to encourage commerce and travel through their lands. Some lords even recompensed merchants for losses sustained at the hands of highwaymen. To reduce the risk of attack, the sides of the road might be cleared of trees and brush, depriving highwaymen of convenient hiding places: an English law of 1285 required that the roads between market towns be cleared for 200 feet on either side, although the law was probably not effectively enforced.

Travel by water was a less common experience than travel by land. Swimming was an unusual skill, and travelers generally chose land routes when they were available. Yet some journeys could not be made safely or quickly by land, and for the transportation of large quantities of goods, boats were often the fastest, cheapest, and most reliable option. A boat could carry far more cargo than a cart, it could travel in the rain when dirt roads became little more than mud baths, and with favorable winds and currents it could be self-propelling. The rivers of medieval Europe were busy highways, constantly plied by small merchant boats; when winds and currents were adverse, the boats were towed by draft animals on the shore. A boat might cover 80 miles in a day traveling downstream.

Medieval seagoing vessels were tiny by modern standards. A typical merchant vessel might have a displacement of 100 tons, measuring some 60 feet from stem to stern and 20 feet across, roughly comparable to a modern tugboat. Many were even smaller, although some of the largest Mediterranean ships reached 800 tons. Most had square-rigged sails, limiting their ability to sail toward the wind, but many were also equipped with oars. The rate of travel depended on the weather, but with favorable winds a ship at sea might sail 100 miles in a day. The crossing from England to the west coast of France might take four days, and the journey from Venice to Jaffa (the port that served Jerusalem) lasted a month (Singman, 214–17).

Despite these hazards, trade was profitable enough to make it worth while. By the 11th century, two major trade zones had emerged: The southern zone was dominated by the Italian cities and specialized in luxury goods that came from Byzantium, the Muslim lands, and as far away as China. At the same time, northern cities such as Bruges and Ghent developed and supplied fine wool cloth to all of northern Europe. These cities acted as a supply center for Scandinavian products—particularly furs and hunting hawks—that were in demand all over Europe.

Early in the 12th century, the French count of Champagne saw an opportunity to make a large profit by hosting fairs in his lands at which merchants could sell goods from both the northern and southern trade routes. Like the Carolingians before him, he realized the benefits of taxation that came with commerce.

In the late 13th century, many cities in northern Germany created the Hanseatic League, an association that united to capitalize on the prosperous northern trade. The cities formed a political as well as an economic power, and they were able to acquire a monopoly on the Baltic trade, replacing Flanders as the center of the northern trading zone. At its height, the Hanseatic League included 70 or 80 cities, led by Lubeck, Bremen, Cologne, and Hamburg. By the 14th century, they offered their own great fairs that replaced the French fairs. Thus, by the late Middle Ages, long-distance trade had overcome the hazards of transportation and had become a major feature of the economic landscape.

To read about trade in 18th-century England, see the England entry in the section "Trade" in chapter 3 ("Economic Life") of volume 4; and for Victorian England, see the England entry in the section "Trade" in chapter 3 ("Economic Life") of volume 5 of this series.

~*Joyce E. Salisbury*

FOR MORE INFORMATION

Butt, J. J. *Daily Life in the Age of Charlemagne*. Westport, Conn.: Greenwood Press, 2002.
Singman, J. L. *Daily Life in Medieval Europe*. Westport, Conn.: Greenwood Press, 1999.

VIKINGS

Some of the agricultural products or products derived from hunting served as trade goods for the Vikings. Little, if anything, is known of local trade, but most likely it was fairly extensive and comprised not only perishable commodities but also minerals, from which tools, jewelry, and other items could be fashioned, as well as rocks used to make whetstones and grindstones. Iron and soapstone in particular seem to have been in demand in the home market.

Luxury goods—especially fur—were traded over long distances, and about this kind of international trade we are better informed. Fur was probably the main export in the Viking Age, and fur trade is referred to in records as early as the 9th century. Some Vikings collected taxes from the Sami or Lapps in the form of furs and whale and sealskins. Viking traders then took these goods to main marketplaces farther south, in Norway or in what is now Germany.

Another important commodity was slaves. Slave trade is mentioned in several literary works, and Arab accounts of the Scandinavian traders living on the Volga make it clear that slaves were among the most important trading commodities. Scandinavians bought or captured slaves in Russia and sold them in western Europe or in the east, and it is also known that Viking raiders took prisoners in western Europe and sold them in Scandinavia.

In addition, the Scandinavians traded fish, honey, timber, down, amber, walrus ivory, hide ropes, and a variety of foreign artifacts acquired either as loot or through gift exchange. The main imports were salt, spices, wine, cloth of wool and silk, pottery, glass, semiprecious stones, weapons, and silver in the form of coins. Pottery, glass, and woolen cloth were bought in western Europe. Cloth of silk was imported from Byzantium. Silver was obtained from the Arabs and was one of the primary imports, especially in the form of dirhams (also called Kufic coins because of the inscriptions after the town Kufah southwest of Baghdad in Iraq). Indeed, more than 85,000 Arab coins dating from the 9th and 10th centuries have been found in Scandinavia. Many of the coins were melted down and transformed into jewelry, but the presence of broken or cut silver (hack silver) in many hoards, that is, cash reserves of precious metal concealed in the ground, shows that silver in any form was used as a medium of exchange and—at least within Scandinavia—treated as bullion (rather than currency), which was weighed on scales.

The main period of import of Kufic coins was approximately between 870 and 960. After the end of the 10th century, they were not imported, probably because of a "silver crisis" in the East, as a result of which fewer coins were issued, and these were often of debased metal. Although these coins played a significant role as means of payment in Scandinavia, they were far from the only coins used. French deniers, Anglo-Frisian *sceattas*, and Anglo-Saxon pennies have also been found in Scandinavia. The last-mentioned became especially common at the end of the 10th century and during the first half of the 11th century for clear reasons: around this time Viking armies attacked England and forced King Aethelred the Unready (r. 978–1016) to pay tribute (Danegeld) to the invaders. More than 40,000 Anglo-Saxon coins from the latter half of the 10th and the 11th centuries have been found in Scandinavia, which is more than what has been found in England.

Moreover, coins were struck within Scandinavia starting about 825. These were anonymous imitations of French deniers minted in the Frisian town of Dorestad and made no doubt in Hedeby. An abbreviated form of Carolus (Charlemagne) and Dorestad is found on several of these Danish coins. Other coins are stamped with animals, ships, and the like. It was not until around 1000, however, that pennies were issued in the names of Scandinavian kings: Sven Forkbeard (r. 985–1014) of Denmark, Olaf Tryggvason (r. 995–1000) of Norway, and Olaf Skotkonung (r. ca. 995–1022) of Sweden. Gradually, the Scandinavians became accustomed to using coins. Jewelry, hack silver, and ingots or rods cease to appear in the hoards. Toward the end of the Viking Age, foreign coins disappeared and came to be replaced by native coins, which became the only legal tender.

Little is known about the actual trade routes during the Viking Age. Descriptions of some can be found in the literary sources. The so-called eastern route begins at Hedeby and ends across the Baltic in Truso in the Gulf of Danzig (probably Elbing) in what is now Poland. The "western route" extends south along the Norwegian coast to southern Norway and beyond to Denmark and open sea.

Goods were brought to Norway from the Rhine area, which was an economically advanced part of Europe in the Viking Age. Dorestad, which lay at the junction of the river Lek and an arm of the Rhine right in the center of the Netherlands, was the main trading center toward the North Sea. From here, goods were transported by land or sea to Hedeby. The Frisian and German traders probably used land routes, whereas the Scandinavian merchants, who were primarily seafarers, were more likely to sail the goods along the Frisian coast and across Jutland to Hedeby. All traffic from Hedeby northward and eastward almost certainly went by sea and appears to have been controlled exclusively by Scandinavians. Similarly, the trade routes west were sea routes. Danes and Norwegians regularly crossed the North Sea to England from the Limfjord area in Jutland and western Norway, respectively, and it is known that Scandinavians sailed directly from Ireland to Iceland and from Norway to Greenland.

A northern route reached the upper Volga and Bulgar (near today's Kazan). It was in this region that Scandinavians came into contact with the Arabs, who referred to them as Rus. One of these was Ibn Fadlan, who gave an account of an embassy sent by the caliph in Baghdad to the Bulgars in the 920s. His account is especially valuable because of its inclusion of an eyewitness description of the Rus merchants he encountered on the Volga. A few Scandinavians continued from Bulgar down to the Caspian Sea and even reached Baghdad, where they could touch the long silk route to China and obtain silk, silver, and spices. The Arab author al-Mas'udi (d. 956) tells of an ill-fated Rus expedition to the Caspian in 912. Rus activity on the Caspian is further mentioned by the historian Ibn Miskawayh (d. 1030).

A southern route went along the river Volkhov to Novgorod and from there to Smolensk and along the Dnieper via Kiev to the Black Sea. The goal here was Byzantium (Constantinople), where silk, fruit, wine, jewelry, and other luxury items could be obtained. An alternate route to the Black Sea went from the Baltic (Gotland) through the Gulf of Riga. That this route was a well-traveled one is clear from the many hoards of coins found in Latvia and Estonia and the number of Baltic objects found in graves on Gotland.

A third eastern trade route, the Polish route, passed through either the Oder or the Vistula to link up with the Mainz-Kiev trade route and to the Danube and the markets of central southern Europe and the Mediterranean. As the trade routes through Russia became less important in the late 10th century, these Polish trade routes became increasingly significant, possibly because of the increased importance of the western silver mines.

This summary indicates the dramatic extent of Viking trade routes. Few parts of the known world were untouched by these intrepid sailors, and the trade they established stimulated much exchange of ideas as well as goods.

~Kirsten Wolf

FOR MORE INFORMATION

Wolf, K. *Daily Life of the Vikings*. Westport, Conn.: Greenwood Press, forthcoming.

CHINA

From the time of the Han Empire (200 C.E.), China was engaged in the lucrative long-distance trade that came to be called the Silk Road and that linked much of Eurasia and North Africa. High-quality silk from China was one of the principle commodities exchanged through the trade, but it was certainly not the only item traded. Spices, including cloves, nutmeg, mace, and cardamom, also traveled west from southeast Asia, China, and India to consumers in central Asia, Iran, Arabia, and the Byzantine Empire. Traders in India exported cotton textiles, pearls, coral, and ivory. The western lands exchanged a variety of manufactured goods and other commodities for the silks and spices they craved. Central Asia produced large horses and jade; the Mediterranean lands supplied glassware, jewelry, perfumes, olive oil, wine, and gold.

There were two routes of the Silk Road: overland and sea-lanes. The overland roads took caravan trade from China all the way to the Mediterranean, often through Byzantium. From Changan, the main Silk Road went west through Mongolia and Turkestan until it arrived at the Taklamakan desert, which is one of the most dangerous regions of the earth. The road then split into two branches that skirted the desert, moving from one oasis town to the other. The branches came together again in the westernmost corner of modern China and proceeded to India, to Iran, and finally to the Mediterranean. Individual merchants did not usually travel from one end of the road to the other. Instead, caravans would travel a portion of the route and then exchange their goods to another caravan, in this way moving the expensive goods slowly overland.

The sea route saw merchants' ships leaving southern China, sailing through the South China Sea to the islands of southeast Asia then to India. From India, ships sailed across the Arabian Sea either into the Persian Gulf or the Red Sea. According to the Greek geographer Strabo, in the first century C.E., as many as 120 ships departed from the Red Sea for India. This ancient route of trade continued for centuries, rising and falling in accordance with the stability of the dynasties in China.

The largest of the oceangoing vessels—some 200 feet long and capable of carrying 600 to 700 men—came from Sri Lanka. They had multiple decks and towed lifeboats. The sailors believed that their rats were divine because the rodents would desert a ship 10 days before it capsized. They also carried homing pigeons that could fly a thousand miles and inform the people in their home ports that their vessels had sunk. Foreign shipbuilders in Southeast Asia did not use nails to build their craft. Instead, they lashed planks together with fibers from palm trees and caulked them with oil derived from a fruit.

Virtually nothing is known about shipbuilding in the Tang until after 756. The rebellions of the mid-8th century destroyed much of the government's shipping along the Grand Canal. The court sent one of its economic wizards south to deal with the problem in 764. He established 10 shipyards at a county on the Yangtze. Their managers competed with one another to construct barges with a capacity of 1,750 bushels of rice at a cost of 1 million coppers each. Over a period of 50 years, the competition drove the price down to 500,000 coppers. For transporting grain to the capital, 10 barges were roped together. By 874, the quality of production at the shipyards had greatly declined. They were building barges with a capacity of only 875 bushels and using cheap, thin wood to make them. The official shipyards manufactured only one type of vessel. There were many other kinds, from small, painted pleasure craft on which courtesans entertained their patrons to the Great Mother Ships that could carry more than 15,750 bushels of grain. The latter had crews of several hundred that spent their entire lives, from birth to death, on board. Those giants made one round-trip a year on the Yangtze and Huai Rivers but reaped enormous profits. All of the navigable rivers in ancient China flowed from west to east. That was an enormous problem for the imperial government, which needed to transport heavy loads of tax revenues from the rich regions of the Yangtze River to the north. Yangdi, the second emperor of the Sui dynasty, solved the problem by constructing the Grand Canal, China's second-greatest engineering achievement next to the Great Wall. He joined older canals and had new branches excavated to form a more extensive system some 1,560 miles in length. It began at Hangzhou on the east coast, south of the Yangtze, and ran north and west to a point east of Luoyang. From there, branches stretched eastward to Mount Tai and northeast to a point southeast of present-day Beijing.

The Tang emperors fostered trade within their empire as well as on the long-distance routes. The Tang had an official road system of perhaps 13,500 miles. The highways ran in all directions but did not reach a large number of cities, especially those directly south of Changan. There must have been roads to those places, but they may have been constructed and maintained at private expense. The method of construction was the same as that for building walls: rammed earth. Roadways were bowed in the center to force rainwater to the verges, and they were lined with trees. In mountainous areas with cliffs, engineers built plank roads by applying fire to the rocks. The heat cracked the stones and created holes. Workers inserted horizontal wood beams into the sockets and laid boards on top to make a pathway on which men and horses could walk. Where highways crossed rivers, local governments built and maintained bridges and ferries. Some spans were made of stone, but there were places with pontoon bridges, favored because they did not wash away during floods. Some pontoon bridges consisted of large boats linked together with iron chains. At crossings on broad rivers such as the Yellow and Yangtze, only ferries would do for transporting men, horses, and wagons. Where the traffic was heavy, the crossings had large numbers of boats.

At strategic places along highways and waterways, the state set up barriers where it collected customs. They were also checkpoints at which officials examined the credentials of travelers. Tang subjects were not free to move as they pleased. The punishment for passing through a barrier without the proper travel permits was one year of penal servitude; for going around a checkpoint, the penalty was one-and-a-half years. Local officials issued such documents. The government was specifically concerned with preventing the movement of soldiers and criminals. Officials at the barriers also inspected baggage, wagons, and other objects to intercept contraband. Prohibited articles included armor, crossbows, long spears, lances, astronomical instruments, star maps, and books on military matters and omens.

Under the Mongol Empire of the 13th century, the great trade routes again flourished. The Mongols worked to secure trade routes and ensure the safety of merchants passing through their territories, and as a consequence, the volume of long-distance trade across central Asia reached new heights.

The most famous western Europeans who visited China along the Silk Road were the Venetians Marco Polo and his father and uncle. During several trading journeys in the 13th century, the Polos traveled all the way to the court of the great Kublai Khan. The journey took them three-and-a-half years by horseback, which shows the difficulties of travel even during the relatively peaceful rule of the Mongols. The Polos served at the Mongol court for 17 years but returned with such a wealth of spices and silks that other Italians followed them along the lucrative trade route. By 1300, there was even a community of Italians living in the Chinese capital.

The skill of the Chinese in fostering the long-distance trade across Eurasia led to much more than the exchange of goods. Ideas, too, traveled the caravan routes,

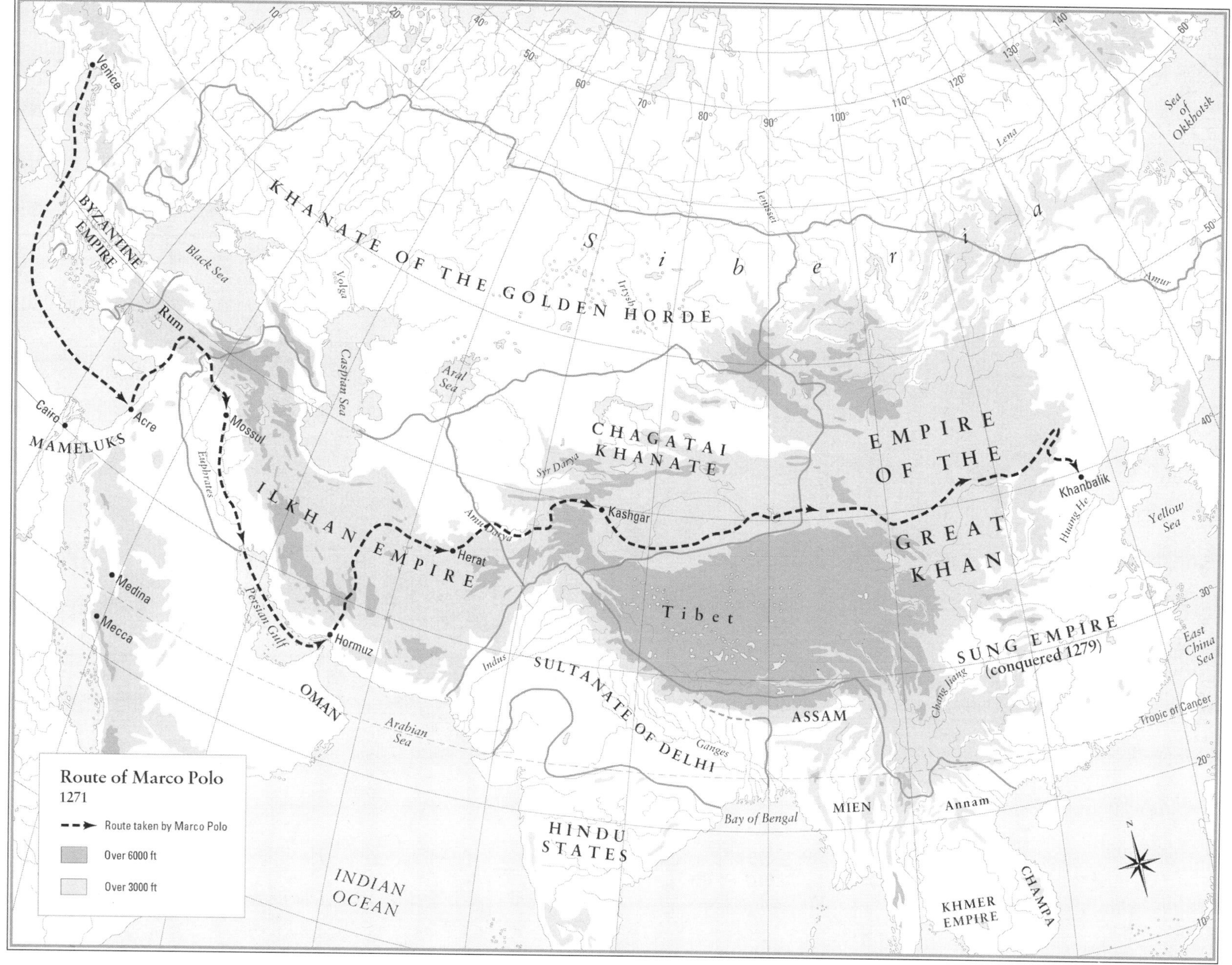
Route of Marco Polo
1271
Route taken by Marco Polo
Over 6000 ft
Over 3000 ft
KHANATE OF THE GOLDEN HORDE
Siberia
BYZANTINE EMPIRE
MAMELUKS
CHAGATAI KHANATE
ILKHAN EMPIRE
EMPIRE OF THE GREAT KHAN
SUNG EMPIRE (conquered 1279)
SULTANATE OF DELHI
HINDU STATES
ASSAM
MIEN
Annam
KHMER EMPIRE
CHAMPA
OMAN
Tibet
Venice
Rum
Acre
Cairo
Mossul
Medina
Mecca
Hormuz
Herat
Kashgar
Khanbalik
Black Sea
Caspian Sea
Aral Sea
Volga
Euphrates
Persian Gulf
Arabian Sea
Bay of Bengal
INDIAN OCEAN
Yellow Sea
East China Sea
Sea of Okkhotsk
Syr Darya
Amu Darya
Indus
Ganges
Irtysh
Jenissei
Lena
Amur
Huang He
Chang Jiang
Tropic of Cancer
N

and Europeans learned of such wonders as coal that burnt and paper money. The lure of the rich and fabulous "East" would stimulate explorers well past the Middle Ages (Benn, 182, 184–85, 187).

To read about trade in 19th-century China, see the China entry in the section "Trade" in chapter 3 ("Economic Life") of volume 5 of this series.

FOR MORE INFORMATION

Benn, C. *Daily Life in Traditional China: The Tang Dynasty*. Westport, Conn.: Greenwood Press, 2002.

Boulnois, L. *The Silk Road*. Translated by D. Chamberlain. New York: E.P. Dutton, 1966.

ISLAMIC WORLD

Because of its location between the Mediterranean world, Africa, Mesopotamia, and India, Arabia inevitably served as a transit point for trade among these regions. Urban settlements along the northern fringes of the desert such as Hatrans of Hatra in northern Iraq, the Nabateans of Petra in southern Jordan, and the Palmyrenes of Palmyra and the Emesenes of Emessa in Syria benefited considerably from trade because of their proximity to Arabia as well as to Rome and Iran. Trade was also favored by the Muslims because Muhammad himself had been a merchant; thus the Muslims never denigrated trading as the western Europeans did for years. Long-distance trade was always a prominent feature of Islamic life.

The camel was critically important to all of the trading cities. Thus, in 137 C.E., the Palmyrenes passed a law that imposed an exorbitant tariff on all goods brought in by cart. Clearly, the Palmyrenes were determined to protect their economic position in the long-distance camel caravan trade in their city from any and all outsiders from the settled areas of Syria where wheeled carts were used. There are other examples of such legislation during late antiquity, and sometime between the 3rd and 6th centuries C.E., the camel replaced wheeled transport throughout nearly all of the Middle East and North Africa. The primary reason for this appears to be the greater efficiency and economic viability of the camel as a means of transportation. Not only could camels go long periods without water (up to one month in the winter), but they could eat just about anything. Fully loaded camels could cover 20 to 25 miles per day; they did not need paved roads at all, could ford rivers easily, and did not need to be shod. Moreover, each camel could carry some 600 pounds, and a single driver could take care of several camels by himself. Compare this with the need for paved roads to operate a cart, the "wasted" weight and expense of the cart itself, the greater needs of water and fodder for oxen, donkeys, mules, or horses to pull a cart, and the fact that it usually took at least one person to operate each cart and team. As one might expect, this near total lack of wheeled transportation throughout much of the medieval Islamic world had major political, social, and economic implications for daily life—especially with respect to urban planning, travel, trade, and the general lack of road construction (although bridges still needed to be built).

Trade fairs were established throughout the peninsula at specified times of the year to bring together goods and buyers. Because these trade fairs were crucial to the welfare of all parties who traded at them, security of person and property was absolutely essential. The security of some fairs was guaranteed by the holiness of the site where the fair took place; others were protected by the strength and prestige of the tribe that administered it; or like the fair of ʿUkaz in the Hijaz (in which Mecca participated), some were held during a holy month. Fairs held during a holy month were especially popular because their duration provided safety of travel to the fair and back and also promoted a kind of festival atmosphere among the participants from far and wide.

While the residents of the oasis and the nomads usually could procure the goods they needed, there was a very mundane but crucially important additional benefit of the trade fair and even smaller scale trade between the nomads and oasis dwellers as well. That is, the nomads' flocks and herds feasted on the fodder left in the farmers' fields after a harvest, while at the same time their droppings fertilized these fields for the next agricultural cycle. Relations between the nomad and the settled populations in Arabia were not always so amicable. In fact, during the more hostile encounter of a raid against an agricultural settlement, the nomads often simply allowed their own animals to graze on the settlement's crops before they made off with whatever booty they could get their hands on—gold, silver, jewels, livestock, and the like.

In the 9th century, the ʿAbbasid caliphs moved their capital from Damascus east to Baghdad. The site was excellently chosen to serve commerce because it dominated the crossroads of the great trade routes, both land and water, that reached from China to the Mediterranean. Even before the caliph selected it as his capital, Baghdad had been the site of monthly trade fairs. The caliphs were right—Baghdad quickly became fabulously wealthy from the trade that flowed through it.

Great caravans and merchant vessels brought the varied resources of the world. From China came silk, ink, peacocks, porcelain, saddles, and spices. India supplied precious stones, rare hardwoods, and dyes. Perfumes came from Arabia, pearls from the Persian Gulf, slaves and gold from Africa, and furs, amber, ivory, and swords from Scandinavia.

The international traffic in goods, and the payments they entailed, led to a new profession—banking, an enterprise that reached a level of sophistication in Islam that was far more advanced than in the West. Banking was a natural outgrowth of the complex monetary system in the Islamic empire. Two kinds of currency were in use: the Persian silver dirham used in the east and the Byzantine gold denarius in the west. These coins fluctuated in value requiring the presence of money changers in every market. Eventually, these men became Islam's bankers.

From the financial system they developed came many of the banking concepts and terms later used in the West, among them the word *check*, from the Arabic *sakk*. They had central banks with branch offices, as well as an elaborate system of checks and letters of credit (Stewart, 83–84).

~James Lindsay and Joyce E. Salisbury

FOR MORE INFORMATION

Lindsay, J. *Daily Life in Medieval Islam*. Westport, Conn.: Greenwood Press, forthcoming.
Stewart, D. *Early Islam*. New York: Time-Life Books, 1967.

ECONOMIC LIFE: WEB SITES

http://myron.sjsu.edu/romeweb/CITIES/art6.htm
http://www.fordham.edu/halsall/source/350palladius-husbandry.html
http://www.britannia.com/church/ch10.html
http://www.chinatown-online.com/cultureeye/highlights/changan.htm
http://www.paris-on-line.com/eng/turisme/historia.htm

4

INTELLECTUAL LIFE

The human mind is an amazing thing in that it allows people to reflect on ideas so abstract that we can imagine things we could never see or touch. We can think about things as complex as philosophical considerations of ethics, justice, and even thought itself. The study of ideas is called intellectual history, and it includes science, philosophy, medicine, technology, literature, and even the languages used to record the ideas.

At the basic level, the capacity for abstraction permits people to impose order on (or to see order in) the astonishingly complex universe. As Stone Age people looked at the dark night sky dotted by millions of stars, they organized the view in patterns of constellations which allowed them to map and predict the movement of the heavens. They then echoed the heavenly order in such earthly monuments as Stonehenge in Britain or the Maya pyramids in Mexico. Through time, this capacity to order extended from the heavens to the submicroscopic particles that dominate 21st-century physics and to the development of mathematics as the language to express these abstractions. An important part of the intellectual life throughout history has been the growing evolution of science, but this is only one aspect of the accomplishments of the mind.

Some people have applied their creative capacity for abstract thought to technology, finding ways to make their lives easier. Technological innovations have spread more rapidly throughout the world than even abstract scientific explanations. Horse collars from China, windmills from Persia, and Muslim medical advances transformed medieval western Europe, while the Internet dominates world culture in the 21st century.

What makes these escalating advances possible is not an increase in human intelligence. Instead, the ability to record abstract ideas in writing and preserve past accomplishments in education have allowed human knowledge to progress. As a medieval thinker (John of Salisbury) noted, if we can see farther than the ancients, it is only because we build on their knowledge. We are as dwarfs on the shoulders of giants, and through our intellectual life, we can look forward to even greater vision.

Some cultures in the Middle Ages—such as the Polynesian, early Germanic, and early Mongol—depended on oral tradition to preserve their intellectual life. People memorized everything from poems to complex historical genealogies and taught these to their descendants. However, the future lay with literate societies who could count on a much richer intellectual tradition.

The medieval world saw a dramatic upsurge in intellectual life. This was in part because of their "giant" predecessors, the Greco-Romans, who left a body of work that served as the basis for subsequent intellectual developments in Europe, Islam, and Byzantium. In the West, scholars founded universities as enduring institutions to transmit and forward knowledge. In China and Islam, rulers established and fostered their own institutions of learning to train an educated workforce. These institutions preserved and built on the wisdom of the past and set the stage for intellectual revolutions that would come later.

Intellectual life also flourished in nonscientific literary works. Poets were prized everywhere from Islam to China to Europe, and the literature they produced continues to delight us today. In Europe, popular literature reflected changes in the languages people spoke. In the ancient Mediterranean world, Greek and Latin prevailed, but by the 9th century, it was clear that Europe would be divided by a number of languages that had developed over time. Southern Europe would speak Latin-derived Romance languages (named for Rome, from which they had come). Northern Europe spoke Germanic languages—less influenced by Latin. Our modern European languages, then, were born in the fertile usages of the Middle Ages. Arabic also began to dominate much of the world as Muslim life built on the Qur'an (Koran)—the holy book written in Arabic. Arabic poetry turned this language into a magnificent instrument of beautiful expression.

People in the Middle Ages—as today—were also preoccupied with their health. Most discoveries in health care during this period took place in the Muslim world, but the enterprise established the idea that health should be something that is studied. Many of the institutions and scientific yearnings of the medieval West and East became the giant ideas on which our modern intellectual life has been built.

~Joyce E. Salisbury

FOR MORE INFORMATION

Tarnas, R. *The Passion of the Western Mind: Understanding the Ideas That Have Shaped Our World View.* New York: Ballentine Books, 1991.

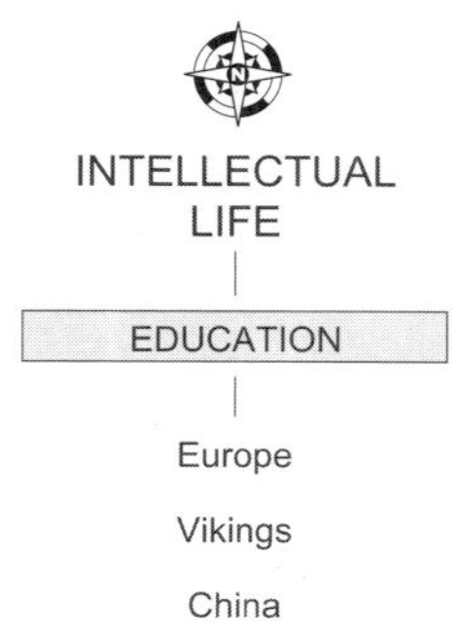

Education

All societies depend on education to prepare their citizens and workers. How they acquire such education, of course, varies. In cultures with an oral tradition (rather than a written language), education took place at home or with an elder and constituted memorizing stories, myths, and histories. With a written language, however, education became more complex because it involved learning to read, write, and master at least a portion of the body of learning that had gone before. All literature cultures have had to determine an appropriate curriculum, how it would be delivered, and where it would take place. This is as true today as it was in the Middle Ages.

Medieval people from the Muslim world to western Europe to Byzantium looked to the previous classical worlds of Greece and Rome for their educational models as well as their curriculum. In western Europe from the 8th century, the curriculum was modeled on the Roman one, and students studied seven liberal arts. First, they learned the "trivium"—grammar, rhetoric, and logic. These three formed the basis for any further education. Grammar referred to Latin grammar, for the great texts were written in Latin, and no further schooling was possible without learning this second language. (In the United States, we still call lower schools "grammar schools" in recollection of the Middle Ages when students began with Latin grammar, even though we have long since given up teaching Latin in the lower grades.) Rhetoric and logic were also considered necessary tools because they let a student learn how to think and argue persuasively. After this basic knowledge, students moved on to the "quadrivium"—music, arithmetic, geometry, and astronomy. While the relationship among these four may not seem immediately obvious to us, medieval thinkers saw these studies as linked in that they revealed a pattern of the universe.

Muslim scholars, too, studied the Greek and Latin classics, and their skill in translating and commenting on the great works of Aristotle, Euclid, Galen, Ptolemy, and others has been essential in preserving these texts. The Muslims emphasized a different curriculum from western Europeans. They considered astronomy to be the noblest science because of its religious applications (in fixing the fasting month of Ramadan, for example). Their studies of the heavens led them to excel in geometry and mathematics as well. The Muslims also emphasized medicine, so much so that the real medical advances outside China in the Middle Ages took place in the Muslim world.

China's curriculum was based heavily on their religious texts of Buddhism, Daoism, and Confucianism. However, their secular studies ranged more widely than those in the West. For example, the Chinese emphasized the study of history, biography, divination, and music, as well as medicine and literature. China's emphasis on education was such that in the 8th century, 25 percent of the population was in school. This is a stunningly high number for the Middle Ages, and no other contemporary culture even came close.

Today, we consider reading to be the main form of education, but in the Middle Ages books were not as accessible. All had to be written by hand, so there were fewer and they were very expensive. Therefore, people relied on different means to receive an education. Students learned to listen to long lectures (several hours at a time) and absorb information that way. They also had to memorize large amounts of material. These two methods prevailed all across Eurasia.

Once the curriculum was determined, people had to decide where education would take place. There were two sources—religious institutions and royal patronage—and both were practiced. In western Europe, monasteries or parish schools took the lead in teaching the foundations of reading, writing, and Latin to promising (mostly upper-class) youth. There were times in Europe when some kings took the lead in stimulating education. Charlemagne and Alfred of England, for example, made great strides in forwarding education in their lands. For the most part, however, the church took the lead. In the 12th century in Europe, universities of higher education grew up at the some of the great cathedrals of the growing cities. Paris, Oxford, Bologna, Salerno, and many others drew advanced students from all over Europe, and knowledge flourished.

In the Muslim world and China, religious institutions also fostered education, but in both the state played a more prominent role. China created many universities to train the bureaucracy that formed the core of the centralized government. In the 9th century in Baghdad, the caliphs built a "House of Wisdom" that served to forward research and translations. Scholars there received a salary, and it drew people from all over the Muslim world to study astronomy, mathematics, medicine, geography, and philosophy.

~*Joyce E. Salisbury*

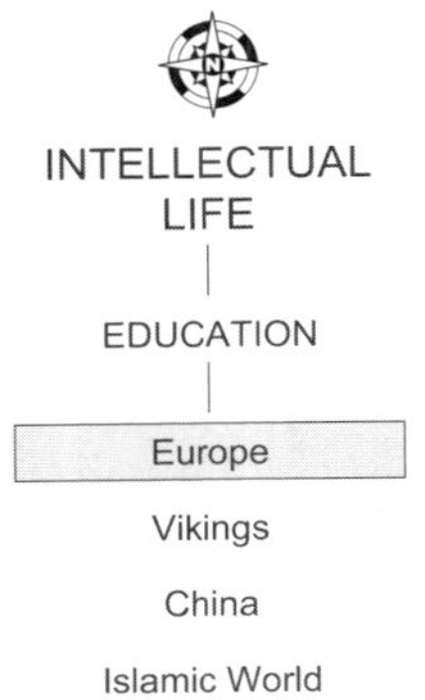

EUROPE

The great emphasis on education during the Roman Empire almost disappeared during the Germanic invasions that transformed western Europe. Even as late as the beginning of the 9th century, education was reduced to a limited study of grammar and, for clerics, a small sampling of theology. Even grammar was beyond most clerics and monks. The reading and writing ability of those who were not entirely illiterate was extremely weak, to the point that their poor knowledge of Latin made it impossible to formulate a proper sentence, let alone a proper document or the performance of a proper church service. Only with the reintroduction of grammar could the church hope to establish a uniformity of service and a literate and functioning clergy.

The 9th-century emperor Charlemagne zealously cultivated the liberal arts and held those who taught them in great esteem and conferred great honors upon them. He revered learning so much that at dinnertime, someone present was expected to read to the others. The educational reforms that were initiated by Charlemagne brought about a number of real changes; for example, he issued a General Admonition in 789, which ordered that schools be established in every church and monastery so that boys might learn to read. Although the most numerous schools were established at the parish level by rural priests, we know very little about these. They have left few records. The schools that have left traces are almost all cathedral or monastic schools.

Whether at a parish, cathedral, or monastic school, a boy would first begin the study of the seven liberal arts with the trivium—grammar, rhetoric, and logic. This had been the core of education in the Roman world, and the Carolingians restored it. Beyond the trivium, there was interest in mathematics, but only at a somewhat more advanced level of learning. The major purpose of mathematics for the Carolingians was to compute the dates of holy days and festivals in the Christian calendar. Computing dates incorporated some mathematics and some astronomy, and a large body of literature concerning this developed in the 9th century. The study of astronomy for the purpose of actually understanding the movement of the heavenly bodies was of little concern to the Carolingians, and geometry was never of much interest because they could not see how it pertained to or advanced the understanding of Christianity.

Musical education was an integral part of the monastic and cathedral training because of its importance in the liturgy. Prior to the 9th century, most Roman chant, often called Gregorian chant, was memorized and transmitted orally and not in a fixed unalterable form. In the 9th century, writing down chant melodies was the only way to ensure that the proper form was being used. Consequently, we have the first large number of musical manuscripts from this period. Whereas previous musical notation had been little more than a reminder to the performer, it now became a nearly complete form of expressing the music, although one quite different from ours today.

To be educated, a boy would be sent to a cathedral or, more often, a monastic school. Although Charlemagne's General Admonition ordered that schools were to be provided for all boys at every church and monastery, a universal education was far from possible. But this did at least establish a kingdomwide policy of education. However, this policy barely outlived Charlemagne, as his son Louis the Pious in 817 ordered that only those who were oblates, or vowed to take orders, should be educated in the monastic schools. Repeatedly in the decades after Charlemagne, there were pleas that education was deteriorating. But during Charlemagne's reign, a limited number of boys from aristocratic families joined small numbers from free or even servile backgrounds in the monastic schools. The numbers were never large, but it was consistent growth over what had existed before. In the smaller monastic communities, the boys who entered were probably assumed to be trained as monks or clerics, but in some of the larger communities there were facilities to train boys who were not intending to stay as monks.

Education for girls varied according to class, as it did for boys. Lower-class girls would be trained to do the same activities as their mothers, such as cooking, cleaning, gardening (for food, not for pleasure), and needlework. Needlework not only was essential to produce all the clothing necessary in a family but was a point of pride for women. Charlemagne insisted that his daughters be trained in needlework, especially the finer types such as spinning, weaving, and embroidery, so that they would learn to do something productive and not become lazy. Girls of the aristocracy were trained not only in needlework but also in household management because they would grow up to run great households of multiple serving people. It was the woman's responsibility to run the household, and this was one area where the male of the house would probably not interfere.

Two boys dressed in loose shirts are being taught by their tutor, who wields a birch rod to "encourage" them to concentrate on their studies. Illustration by Jeffrey Singman (after Manesse manuscript).

Among the aristocracy, girls were occasionally educated to read. Charlemagne's own daughters not only could read but were educated in the same liberal arts as his sons. Those who joined convents, where literacy was useful and encouraged, were often highly literate (Butt, 127–35).

In the early Middle Ages, the church had been dominated by its monasteries, but during the 12th and 13th centuries, the revitalization of urban life was reflected in a renewed vigor in religious institutions rooted in the towns. One of these institutions was the cathedral school. Cathedrals traditionally maintained schools to provide basic training for parish priests, but by the end of the early Middle Ages, these schools had also become centers for the advanced studies that supplied the church with its intellectual leaders. Initially, teaching was in the hands of the cathedral canons, especially the chancellor, but as demand increased, the chancellor licensed other teachers to provide instruction. By the late 12th century, the Parisian masters, or teachers of advanced studies, had coalesced into professional associations—comparable to those of the trade guilds—that represented the faculties in each discipline. By 1200, these associations were collectively termed the University of Paris; the Latin term *universitas* means entirety, and it originally referred to the entire body of teachers in the associations.

The daily lives of the students were largely in their own hands.

Comparable educational institutions appeared in other European cities, especially in the south. Montpellier in southern France and Salerno in southern Italy emerged as leading centers for the study of medicine. The cities of northern Italy excelled in the study of Roman law. In 12th-century England, Oxford emerged as a university on the Parisian model, and Cambridge came into existence in the early 13th century when a conflict with town authorities prompted a number of masters to leave Oxford. There were a few other universities in France but none in Germany or the Low Countries before 1300. In general, the university was found in only a few cities, although a certain measure of advanced learning was available at cathedral schools.

A student arriving in the city to begin his university studies was typically about 14 years old, although some were younger and others older. At Paris, and in northern Europe generally, the student was classed as a cleric, and his education fell under the auspices of the church. Many went on to the priesthood, although for some the goal was an administrative position in the church or a life of scholarship. Prior to his arrival, the student needed to have at least a grammar school education, since courses were conducted in Latin, and this was the principal language of communication among scholars who did not necessarily share any other common language.

On arriving, the student needed to arrange long-term accommodations. The university regulated the teaching activities of the masters, but the daily lives of the students were largely in their own hands. In many cases, a group of students rented a place together, and it became increasingly common for a significant number of students to rent an entire building for a long term, and the dwelling remained in student hands even as the population changed from year to year becoming the first dormitories.

A new student also needed to choose a master. The master was also young, typically in his early twenties, and perhaps pursuing an advanced degree. The master was the student's main source of lectures during his years of study and had general responsibility for seeing that the student fulfilled his requirements for the degree. Because the master-student relationship was so important, the student was well advised to take some care in his choice. The masters, for their part, relied on their students' fees for their income, so they were keen to market their services. It was common to allow a student to sit in as a guest at a few initial lectures to sample the quality of the master's teaching, and many masters even hired older students to visit newly arrived scholars and advertise the master's services.

The first level of university studies for every student, equivalent to the modern undergraduate degree, consisted of the seven liberal arts, inherited from the classical period: grammar, rhetoric, logic, music, arithmetic, geometry, and astronomy. To receive a degree, the student was required to attend lectures on a prescribed curriculum of books in each of these subjects. Within this framework, the student acquired a wide knowledge of medieval scholarship. The lecturing master read the text to his class, expounding on the content as he went. This format allowed for considerable breadth: a lecture on rhetoric might be based on a Roman epic poem and range from versification to geography and classical mythology.

Advanced education in the 12th century was still fairly informal, relying principally on the master-student relationship. By the latter part of the 13th century, a more systematic means of verifying the student's work had taken shape. After about two years, the student was required to certify that he had attended the necessary lectures, after which he underwent an oral examination and took part in a public debate on a set topic. If the masters judged his performance satisfactory, he was granted the status of bachelor, which entitled him to engage in some limited teaching. After two more years, the bachelor was examined by the chancellor, who issued the license to teach; a license from Paris and other accredited institutions was internationally recognized through the authority of the church. Within the following year, if the other masters were satisfied with him, he was admitted to the status of master.

A student who had completed the course in arts might undertake an advanced course of study in one of a few specialized fields. The particular strength at Paris was theology, and the theology faculty at Paris were often called upon to adjudicate important disputes regarding church doctrine. The other advanced fields were medicine, canon law, and civil (i.e., Roman) law. The students in the advanced courses of study, having already been students in the faculty of arts, were generally in their twenties or even early thirties. A degree in medicine required about 6 years of additional study, theology about 15.

The daily routine of the medieval student was built around attendance at lectures. These were much smaller than is often the case today; the lecture hall was usually an ordinary room in a private house and accommodated only a limited number of students. A student typically attended two principal lectures during the day. "Regular" lectures were delivered by the masters in the morning, probably around 6 A.M., and were on the assigned texts of the curriculum. "Cursory" lectures took place in the afternoon. They might be delivered by a master or a bachelor, and they could be on other texts not actually required for the degree. In between lectures, there was time for meals: dinner was taken about 10 A.M., the evening meal about 5 P.M. The school term generally started at the beginning of October and lasted until Easter, with a few days off at Christmas and Easter, and other holidays on major feast days (Singman, 201–5).

To read about education in Elizabethan England, see the England entry in the section "Education" in chapter 4 ("Intellectual Life") of volume 3; for 18th-century England, see the England entry in the section "Education" in chapter 4 ("Intellectual Life") of volume 4; and for Victorian England, see the England entry in the section "Education" in chapter 4 ("Intellectual Life") of volume 5 of this series.

FOR MORE INFORMATION

Butt, J. J. *Daily Life in the Age of Charlemagne*. Westport, Conn.: Greenwood Press, 2002.
Singman, J. L. *Daily Life in Medieval Europe*. Westport, Conn.: Greenwood Press, 1999.

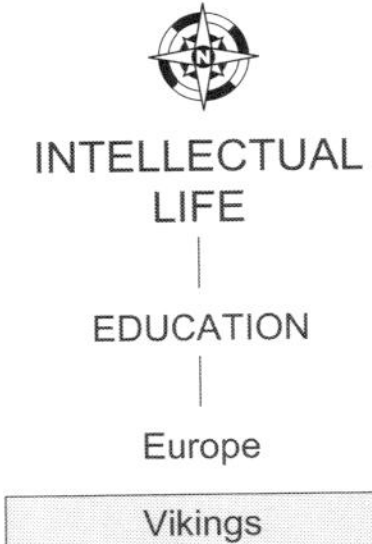

VIKINGS

About training and education in the Viking Age, we know next to nothing. Presumably, home schooling or training in various disciplines was the general practice, but on this matter, as on so many others, the Viking Age Scandinavians have left no traces.

Formal, scholarly education was a late phenomenon that followed in the wake of the introduction of Christianity. The Christian Church was without question the most significant educational institution during the Middle Ages, and it was also the primary employer of educated personnel. Generally, three types of schools may be distinguished: cathedral schools, monastic schools, and town schools. However, it is known that in 11th-century Iceland, a kind of formal home schooling took place; the sources report that learned priests, such as Teit Isleifsson in Haukadal (d. 1110) and Saemund Sigfusson in Oddi (d. 1133), educated young men for the priesthood. Monastic and town schools date from after the end of the Viking Age, and so do most of the cathedral schools, although the year of the establishment of the various cathedral schools is known in only a few cases. One of the cathedral schools in Denmark, that of Lund, now southern Sweden, may date from before the end of the Viking Age; it is first mentioned in 1085 and with certainty in 1123. The two cathedral schools in Iceland appear to have come into existence shortly after the establishment of the bishop's seats at Skalholt in the mid-11th century and Holar in 1106, and records indicate that the bishop of Holar appointed foreign teachers to instruct in reading, writing, Latin, singing, and versification.

The disciplines of the cathedral schools were the liberal arts and more specifically, the trivium, that is, grammar, rhetoric, and logic. To this, courses in Christianity and logic were added. The subjects of the quadrivium, that is, arithmetic, geometry, astronomy, and music, appear to have had low priority, although it is reasonable to assume that in the curriculum, there was much variation, both over time and locally. Although little is known about pedagogic methods and aims, it is reasonable to assume that the education consisted mainly of rote learning and recitation. By modern North American standards, it was rather brutal; corporal punishment, such as birching, whipping, and caning, was considered acceptable and appears to have been common when the pupils broke rules or behaved dishonorably.

The education was a two- to three-year program followed by an additional two-year course under the school's supervision for prospective priests. Although the purpose of cathedral schools was first and foremost to educate priests, the schools also trained pupils for political or civil service positions.

We do not know even approximately how many pupils graduated from a specific cathedral school in a given year. It is reasonable to suppose that only the more prosperous families, who did not need their children's contribution to the family income, could afford to send their children to secondary school. It is also reasonable to assume that girls were excluded from receiving an education. Girls did not need preparation for public life; a girl who would grow up to be a married woman like her mother could obtain her training at home—although it has generally been acknowledged, usually with reference to a charming vignette in the Icelandic monk Gunnlaug Leifsson's (d. 1218/19) biography of Bishop Jon Ogmundarson (*Jons saga helga*) about a certain Ingunn who studied at the cathedral school at Holar, where Latin books were read to her while she sewed or played games, that a few women received the opportunity to study.

~Kirsten Wolf

FOR MORE INFORMATION

Wolf, K. *Daily Life of the Vikings*. Westport, Conn.: Greenwood Press, forthcoming.

CHINA

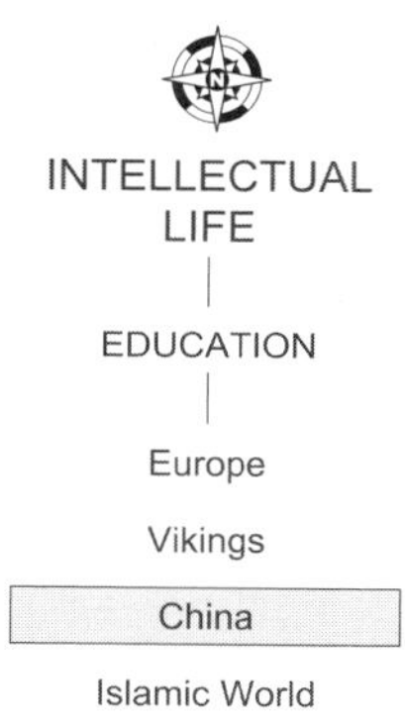

There were at least two forms of institutional education in Tang China. One was religious, based on the written scriptures of Buddhism, Daoism, and Confucianism. The other was secular, based on Confucian classic texts as well as on works on etiquette, divination, medicine, and music; collections of jokes and poetry; short fiction; and dictionaries, almanacs, histories, and biographies. Because of their libraries, monasteries and abbeys became convenient places for lay students to pursue their learning.

The educational opportunities offered by religious establishments paled in comparison to those provided by the state. Eight days after ascending the throne in 618, Emperor Gaozu established three colleges in Changan for somewhat more than 300 students. Six years later, he ordered prefectures and counties to institute schools in their districts. In 738, the emperor vastly expanded the system. He ordered all prefectures and counties to establish schools in their villages and supply them with qualified teachers. By the mid-8th century, the total enrollment of students in the capitals and provinces was about 63,570 (and may not have included pupils in village schools). The total number of students supported by the government—including specialized schools and those for imperial guards, militia, and others—came to about 130,000. The number of the empire's subjects at the time was almost 49 million. That means that students constituted 0.25 percent of the population. By modern standards, the number is small, but it is enormous for premodern societies.

Originally, Tang statutes restricted admission to the three capital colleges to sons of fathers who held high ranks, but in the 8th century access was increased. The colleges accepted young men between the ages of 14 and 19 except for commoners, who could register as late as 25. Age, not social status, determined the rank of a student in the student body. On their first day of class, students had to present their teachers with a gift of silk, jerky, and ale. Afterward, the state provided a stipend in the form of grain and a place to live.

There were two facets to education in the Tang: memorization by the students and lectures by the faculty. Teachers expected students to commit portions of a text to memory before they arrived in the classroom. Professors and assistant professors expounded on the meanings of the assigned passages during class time. In their spare time, students practiced calligraphy and composed trial answers to examination questions. Every 10 days, the masters gave an examination on the materials covered during the week. It consisted of one fill-in question for every 1,000 words of text memorized (students had to supply from memory a passage of which they received only the beginning sentence) and one interpretive question for every 2,000 words of text covered in lectures. A passing mark was given for satisfactory answers to two out of three questions. The faculty also gave a year-end examination to determine the progress of students. It consisted of 10 oral questions. A passing mark consisted of four or more acceptable answers. If a student failed that examination three years in a row or had been in school for nine years without graduating, he was dismissed and sent home.

The government also offered education in specialized fields. The areas of study included medicine, law, mathematics, calligraphy, astronomy, calendrical science, divination, and ritual. The texts for the law school were the Tang code, statutes, ordinances, and regulations. There were 10 textbooks for mathematics that students were expected to master in 14 years. Students of calligraphy studied the classics as engraved in three styles of script on stone tablets, as well as two dictionaries. The course of study had to be completed in six years. Instruction in the remaining fields took place in the appropriate bureaus of the central government.

The aspiration of most young men who received an education was to acquire a government post, civil or military. To achieve that goal, they had to take examinations given by the government. The breadth of Tang examinations was greater than those of any dynasty before or after it. Among other things, it had a test for child prodigies. The state assigned bureaucratic ranks to children nine years old or younger who could recite the *Classic of Filial Piety* and the *Discourses of Confucius* from memory and answer 10 out of 10 questions on the texts. The government did not, however, appoint them to offices at such tender ages. The ranks were presumably entitlements to take posts of those grades when they reached maturity. The state granted degrees, privileges to take political offices, to students who passed examinations in all of the fields already mentioned. The three most important examinations were the classical masters, advanced scholars, and elevated warriors.

Successful passage of a national examination in the capital did not by itself guarantee the graduate an office in the government. He had to remain in the capital and take the "selection examination" with candidates from the provinces. In the fifth moon, governors of prefectures and commandants of counties submitted the names of men they wished to recommend. In the tenth moon, the candidates assembled in the capital, where officials checked their credentials to make sure there were no undesirables, such as merchants, among them. Afterward, the examiners evaluated them on their physique, speech, calligraphy, and judgment. The last part required a written composition and covered all kinds of decisions, not just judicial ones. If all applicants achieved equal ratings, the examiners then ranked them according to their virtue, talent, and merit. Passing that examination might not result in an appointment either. A graduate's chances depended on vacancies in the bureaucracy, and the examination system was not the only avenue to office. In the 680s, an official estimated that only 10 percent of qualified candidates received appointments. If there were no openings, the graduate would have to return home and take the examination another year. The rigorous educational system ensured that the Tang dynasty was served by well-qualified scholars (Benn, 255–58, 261).

To read about education in 19th-century China, see the China entry in the section "Education" in chapter 4 ("Intellectual Life") of volume 5 of this series.

FOR MORE INFORMATION

Benn, C. *Daily Life in Traditional China: The Tang Dynasty.* Westport, Conn.: Greenwood Press, 2002.

ISLAMIC WORLD

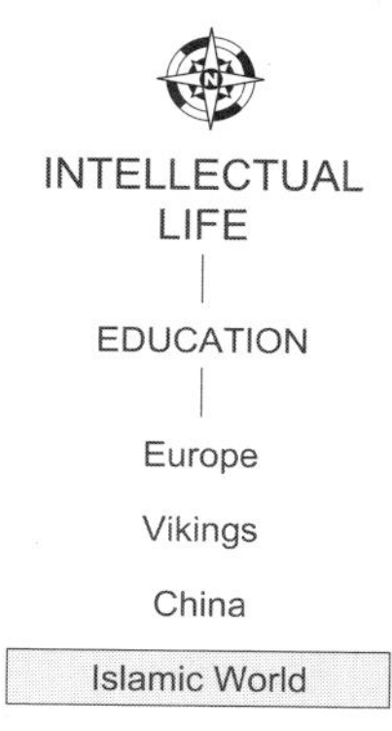

For the vast majority of Muslims, the Qur'an is the eternal uncreated speech of God, flawlessly communicated to mankind through his messenger, Muhammad. The revelations Muhammad received and delivered to the people of Mecca (ca. 610–22) and Medina (622–32) are referred to as Kitab Allah (the book of God) as well as the Qur'an (the recitation). It should come as no surprise then that the Qur'an was the fundamental building block of education in the medieval Islamic world. Nor should it come as a surprise that the medieval Islamic world was a world in which writing was ubiquitous. In addition to pious and laudatory inscriptions on public buildings, coins, swords, textiles, carpets, ceramics, and lamps, one could find inscriptions with far less noble themes as well.

Despite the importance of the written word, it was the word that was committed to memory that was held in highest regard. One could not claim to have studied the Qur'an, or any text for that matter, unless he had committed the text to memory. Therefore, beginning around the age of five or six, children began to memorize the Qur'an and to study the basics of Islamic beliefs and practices with their teachers. In addition, students learned the basics of Arabic grammar, for without a solid understanding of the Arabic language one could not truly understand the speech of God. While paper was introduced to the Middle East during the early Islamic period and eventually made its way to Europe, it was only the wealthiest who could afford to waste it. Therefore, students did their lessons with a reed pen and ink on a washable tablet (usually made of wood).

In the early centuries of Islamic history, elementary education was a very informal affair where children studied with their fathers, uncles, or brothers (and occasionally, mothers, aunts, or sisters) at home or with local scholars in the mosque. More advanced students then moved on to study *hadiths* (anecdotes attributed to or about Muhammad), which along with the Qur'an formed the basis of Islamic jurisprudence and theology. Teachers often sat against a pillar or wall in a mosque with their students sitting in a circle (*halqa*) beside them. The bigger the *halqa*, the better (or more popular) the teacher. Few teachers could actually make a living as a teacher during this period. Most had to support themselves by other means and taught during their off hours.

Some students merely sat in on a lecture. Those intent on mastering the material were expected to faithfully copy and memorize the teacher's lectures, which generally consisted of the teacher reciting a text to which he added his own commentary as well as the commentaries of his teachers. This method of learning from a teacher, who learned from his teachers, who learned from his teachers illustrates the fundamental importance that medieval Muslims placed on direct personal interaction between teacher and pupil. In part because of this emphasis on the interpersonal, we find scholars traveling hundreds, even thousands of miles to study with the leading lights throughout the medieval Islamic world.

Philosophical debate between master and students, from a 13th-century Seljuk Turkish manuscript, *The Best Maxims and Most Precious Dictums of Al-Mubashir.* This shows the Muslim value on education. © The Art Archive/Topkapi Museum Istanbul/Dagli Orti.

The desire to travel in order to study with the masters was often coupled with the obligation to undertake the pilgrimage to Mecca at least once if one were able. In addition to being the means for many to fulfill one of the five pillars of Islam, pilgrimage caravans from such distant places as Spain, West Africa, central Asia, India, and elsewhere functioned as informal traveling universities, which continually added new scholars as they made their way to Mecca each year. As such, these pilgrimage caravans played a very important role in spreading new ideas throughout the Islamic world.

Education in the medieval Islamic world, of course, was not limited to religious subjects. Many ancient Greek, Persian, and Sanskrit works on philosophy, medicine, mathematics, astronomy, and other sciences were translated into Arabic in the 9th century under the patronage of the ʿAbbasid caliphs. Muslim (as well as Jewish and Christian) scholars studied these classics and built upon them. Many of these eventually were translated into Latin and made their way into the medieval European curriculum. Ibn Sina (980–1037) in particular had a tremendous influence on medieval Europe where he was known as Avicenna. His medical text *The Canon of Medicine* was translated into Latin in the 12th century and was a favorite of European doctors and medical schools until the rise of experimental medicine in the 16th and 17th centuries. His proof for the existence of God was equally influential. The great Christian theologian Thomas Aquinas adopted it; so did the great Jewish philosopher and physician Moses Maimonides.

By Ibn Sina's day, we begin to see the emergence of a new institution of Islamic learning—the *madrasa* (literally, place of learning)—in many of the major cities throughout Islamic world. Funded by pious endowments, the madrasa was more than a mere change in venue from the mosque and its informal instruction. The better-endowed madrasas provided salaries for teachers and stipends for students. Most were built with apartments for students and teachers as well. One of Islam's greatest medieval scholars, al-Ghazali (d. 1111), taught at Baghdad's Nizamiyya madrasa, founded by the Seljukid vizier Nizam al-Mulk (d. 1092).

The 12th-century Damascene scholar Ibn ʿAsakir (1105–76) is said to have studied with some 1,300 male teachers and some 80 female teachers during his travels in Syria, Arabia, Iraq, Iran, and central Asia. Although the overwhelming majority of Ibn ʿAsakir's teachers were men, the fact that roughly 6 percent of his teachers were women clearly demonstrates there was no prohibition against women learning to read, write, and even teach. Ibn ʿAsakir was first and foremost a hadith scholar, and it was in the field of hadith studies that women usually made their mark rather than in other subjects. The reason for this is twofold. First, one could hardly argue that women were inadequate to the task of transmitting hadith since ʿAʾisha, Muhammad's favorite wife, was one of the most important hadith transmitters in early Islamic history. Second, when a scholar died, it was common for his sons as well as his daughters to transmit the hadiths that he had taught them.

~*James Lindsay*

FOR MORE INFORMATION

Lindsay, J. *Daily Life in Medieval Islam*. Westport, Conn.: Greenwood Press, forthcoming.

Science

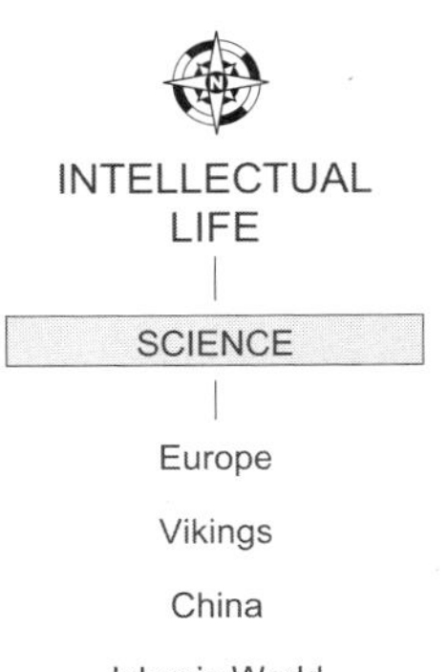

The Middle Ages have been characterized as an "age of faith," as a contrast to the scientific revolution of the 16th century. However, the story of the progress of scientific inquiry is more complicated than that. Indeed, the medieval millennium—in both East and West—established key foundations for the future development of modern science. Furthermore, it established the path upon which western Europe branched off from the rest and headed to the scientific revolution that transformed it. How did this happen?

At the beginning of the Middle Ages, scholars everywhere from England to Baghdad to China carefully preserved scientific knowledge from their ancients. In the West and the Muslim world, authors studied the texts from the ancient Greeks, particularly Aristotle, to shape their view of the world. From these texts, they concluded that the world was made up of four elements—earth, water, air, and fire—and that motion in the world (which is really the study of physics) can be explained by the desire of these elements to seek their own level and remain motionless.

China was equally indebted to its own ancient scholars, and they perceived the world differently. The Chinese had two main systems for categorizing things. The first concerned yin and yang and posited that there were two main forces that governed the world and that the imbalance between these forces caused problems. Second, they believed that the world was made up of five elements—water, fire, wood, metal, and earth. Throughout the Middle Ages, Chinese scholars built on these two venerable traditions.

Byzantium and the Muslim world began the Middle Ages far advanced of the West in their understanding and preservation of classical scientific knowledge. For example, the Muslim astronomer/mathematician al-Tusi (b. 1201) recalculated ancient Greek understandings of planetary orbits with a precision that would not be matched in western Europe until the 16th century. These early advances slowed late in the Middle Ages, just as western Europe began to make dramatic strides in scientific advances. It appears that in both Byzantium and the Islamic world, neither the church nor the state institutionalized the study of natural philosophy and science in a way that fostered its growth. However, both cultures were significantly important in the transmission of the ancient studies. As one scholar of the history of science has written, "The collective achievement of these three civilizations [Greco-Arabic-Latin] . . . stands as one of the greatest examples of multiculturalism in recorded history" (Grant, 206).

Snapshot

Improving Fertility of Agricultural Fields in Anglo-Saxon England

Here is the remedy by which you can improve your fields, if they will not grow properly, or if any harm has been done to them by sorcery or witchcraft:

Take then at night before daybreak four sods from four sides of the land and mark how they stood before. Then take oil and honey and yeast and milk of all the cattle that are on the land, and part of every kind of tree growing on the land, except hard trees, and part of every well-known herb, except burdock only, and pour holy water on them, and then let it drip three times on the bottom of the sods. And then say these words:

Crescite, grow, *et multiplicamini,* and multiply, *et replete,* and fill, *terram,* the earth. (Jolly, 221)

In western Europe, on the other hand, certain features of the Middle Ages established the foundations of modern science that would allow it to flourish during the scientific revolution of the 16th century. Of course, this connection is only seen in retrospect—medieval scholars continued to remain most interested in understanding faith, not science. Nevertheless, the medieval world took the translations of the Greco-Arabic works and institutionalized universities for their study. At the universities, there were for the first time institutions established to study texts. While these institutions became conservative and backward looking, they were nonetheless *there*, and the concept that people should come together and study was significant. The universities produced theologian–natural philosophers such as Roger Bacon who are credited with establishing the roots of the scientific method that would transform the intellectual world.

In addition to establishing the institutions of higher learning, medieval science had other features that would lay the foundations of modern science. Medieval natural philosophy contributed an extensive vocabulary by which to explain, study, and categorize the world. For example, words such as *matter, substance, cause, species, genus*, and others form the heart of modern scientific understandings. The words themselves gave shape to future inquiries.

Medieval thinkers also posed many questions that formed the heart of modern science, for the nature of medieval philosophy was based on inquiry. Many of the questions are disdained by modern thinkers: Such reflections as "How many angels can dance on the head of a pin?" or "Who gets a cannibal's flesh when he is resurrected?" strike modern scientists as foolish at best. However, in their extensive questioning, medieval thinkers also asked things such as "Does nature abhor a vacuum?" Indeed, the freedom to pose all questions—ridiculous or otherwise—is at the heart of modern science.

Thus the age of faith—from China to Europe—tended to be more unified than modern science is. Medieval scholars combined science, philosophy, and theology in their longing to find a unified system to explain everything from the earth to the heavens. In time, however, the West would split that enterprise—faith would go to the theologians, and the world was left to scientists. The modern approach to science was born at that moment.

~Joyce E. Salisbury

FOR MORE INFORMATION

Grant, E. *The Foundations of Modern Science in the Middle Ages*. Cambridge, England: Cambridge University Press, 1996.

Jolly, K. "Father God and Mother Earth: Nature-Mysticism in the Anglo-Saxon World." In *The Medieval World of Nature*, edited by J. E. Salisbury. New York: Garland, 1993.

EUROPE

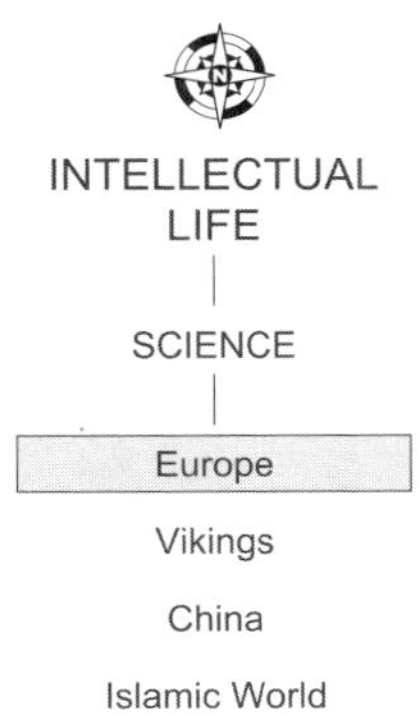

Medieval scholars were deeply indebted to the Greeks and Romans for their approach to science and philosophy, and the most important ancient scholar was Aristotle. Through the early Middle Ages when scholars in the West lost the knowledge of Greek, the only works of Aristotle in Latin were his works on elementary logic. In the 12th century, however, this changed.

In the late 11th century, Spanish Christians made real progress reconquering the Iberian Peninsula that had been held since 711 by the Muslims. They took the capital city of Toledo and discovered that this city had been a major center for study and translating the classic works of Aristotle. Arabic scholars had preserved most of Aristotle's lost treatises, and Western scholars were astounded and excited by the find. By 1160, Aristotle's advanced logic, known as the "new logic," was being used in the university classrooms. By the end of the 12th century, the whole range of Aristotle's scientific works was translated, and he became the authority for Western scholars in almost every field—ethics, psychology, politics, physics, astronomy, meteorology, and zoology. When medieval scholars referred to "the philosopher," everyone knew they meant Aristotle.

Medieval respect for Aristotle at first impeded original scientific inquiry because, although the philosopher had recommended observations and study, medieval thinkers were largely content to read Aristotle. If they wanted to learn about plants, instead of looking at them, they read Aristotle's descriptions. Thus, at the end of the 13th century, medieval scholars held the same view of the physical universe as that of the ancient Greeks. They believed that the earth was composed of four elements—earth, water, air, and fire. They knew that the earth was round, but they imagined it was still, unmoving at the center of the universe. They believed the sun, stars, and planets went around the earth embedded in concentric, crystal spheres.

In Aristotle's universe, each substance desired to reach a state of rest. Thus earth, which was the heaviest, moved down, and fire, the lightest, moved up. This simple physics of motion explained most of the apparent motion on earth, and if any object moved in a direction other than its "natural" one, that meant a force was being applied to it. For example, if a rock sailed through the air, that meant something exerted a force against it to move it.

Attempts to go beyond Aristotle's explanation of the physical world led usually to the pseudosciences of astrology and alchemy. In the former, scholars tried to use the movements of heavenly bodies to predict the future on earth. In alchemy, chemists hoped to change the nature of elements by heating, cooling, and combining them (much as chemists do today). Alchemists, however, were preoccupied with trying to make gold (which they never accomplished).

Despite the failings of 13th-century science, medieval philosophy—called scholasticism—reached its highest point in the 13th century. Philosophers had mastered Aristotle's advanced logic and believed they had the tools to accomplish an astonishing task. They tried to do no less than join faith with reason, which is to understand God through the human mind. The very enterprise reveals the excitement that had been generated by the assimilation of Aristotelian logic—even God's mind seemed now accessible. The greatest of the scholastics was Thomas Aquinas. Thomas Aquinas's huge work—*Summa Theologiae*—represents his summary of all knowledge through which the believer is led to God. Through this long tract full of questions and discussions, he adapted Aristotle's ethics and politics to serve the needs of a Christian society. His thought was so influential that long after the Middle Ages, his philosophy was accepted as the official one of the Roman Catholic Church. However, even in the Middle Ages, Thomas Aquinas's ideas did not go unchallenged, and in the critique, modern science arose.

Some thinkers believed that Thomas Aquinas and the other scholastics were fundamentally wrong to try to approach God through logic. Many felt that the proper way to approach God was through faith alone because God was being limited by being forced into formulas of logic. The most devastating critique came from English Franciscans at Oxford University. These Franciscans approached God and knowledge differently.

Great strides in scientific methodology were made by the Franciscans under the leadership of the English bishop Robert Grosseteste. Grosseteste insisted that his students rely on firsthand knowledge and firsthand observation. Instead of reading Aristotle, people should look at the world. Grosseteste himself made dramatic strides in studying light, which he said could best be represented geometrically. He insisted that physical laws must be represented mathematically, and his own most striking achievement was a sophisticated mathematical explanation of the formation of a rainbow. Grosseteste further developed a scientific method through which hypotheses are tested with evidence. This procedure became the basis of the modern experimental method.

One of Grosseteste's followers, the Franciscan friar Roger Bacon, is even better known than his mentor. Bacon argued that the progress of human knowledge was being impeded by the regard for Aristotle and the other ancients and that all old beliefs should be tested by experimental science. He foresaw the invention of flying machines and mechanically driven ships. Although Bacon was credited for helping medieval scientists move from reliance on the ancients, he did not discover any new scientific laws.

The first major break with Aristotelian physics came in the 14th century with the work of two Parisian philosophers, Jean Buridan (ca. 1300–70) and Nicole Oresme (ca. 1330–82). These two thinkers criticized Aristotle's law of motion that lay at the core of ancient physics. Aristotle believed in the perfection of a motionless universe, so he believed that if a body was in motion, something had to be continuously forcing it to move. For example, when a spear left the thrower's hand, Aristotle held that the initial movement created a disturbance in the air and that the displaced air rushed in behind the spear to fill the space and keep it moving. Of course, this explanation did not satisfactorily explain why the spear eventually stopped. Buridan and Oresme boldly departed from Aristotle in proposing that a moving body acquired "impetus" that kept it going until a counterforce (such as friction) stopped it.

This belief in the idea of impetus made the thinkers believe that God could have placed the universe in motion, then left it alone. Oresme suggested that the idea of heavenly spheres was inaccurate because the heavenly observations could be explained by a spinning earth. Suddenly, here were thinkers who were proposing that movement, not stillness, characterized the universe and that one could understand physics and motion without understanding the mind of God. Science could study the physical world and leave faith to the theologians. The stage was set for the modern scientific revolution.

To read about science in Elizabethan England, see the England entry in the section "Health and Science" in chapter 4 ("Intellectual Life") of volume 3; for 18th-century England, see the England entry in the section "Science and Technology" in chapter 4 ("Intellectual Life") of volume 4; and for Victorian England, see the England entry in the section "Science" in chapter 4 ("Intellectual Life") of volume 5 of this series.

~Joyce E. Salisbury

FOR MORE INFORMATION

Evans, G. R. *Philosophy and Theology in the Middle Ages*. New York: Routledge, 1993.

Jones, W. T. *A History of Western Philosophy: The Medieval Mind*. 2nd ed. Warsaw, Poland: International Thomson Publishing, 1969.

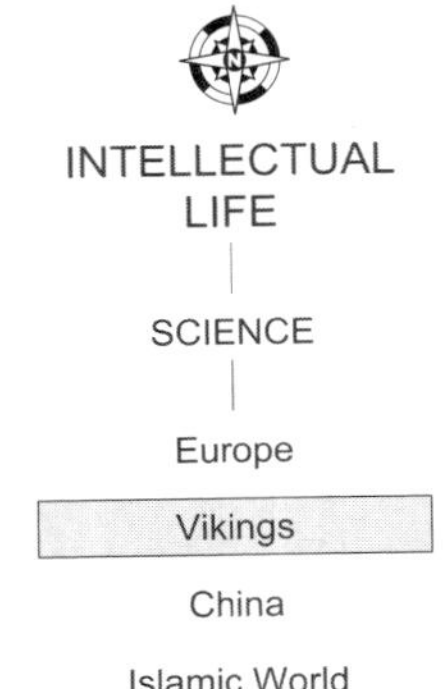

VIKINGS

There is ample evidence that the Viking Age Scandinavians possessed considerable knowledge about the natural world. Old Norse-Icelandic literature testifies to an early interest in geography, zoology, astronomy, medicine, mathematics, and other subjects that are now labeled as scientific, but there is little to suggest deliberate research by the Scandinavians in the Viking Age. Accordingly, the discussion is here limited to the fields of geography and astronomy, in which the Scandinavians may be said to have made independent inquiry.

The Viking Age Scandinavians made no maps and did not leave any artifacts that could be described as maps, but as far as we can tell, their picture of the earth was that of a round one. It was either flat or slightly saucer shaped. Central to it was an inner sea, the Atlantic Ocean and its contiguous waters, and it was surrounded by a land ring. The Norsemen were quite convinced of this, and in many ways it must have been a comforting thought to them that wherever they sailed they were always enclosed by land. From experience, the Viking Age Scandinavians knew that this land ring started somewhere east of northern Norway and went over the White Sea right around the top of the frozen world, came to Greenland, and then proceeded to come down on the other side. When later Latin Christian learning reached Scandinavia, this notion of the earth was somewhat revised, and by the end of the Viking Age, three separate continents, all thought to lie in the Northern Hemisphere, are distinguished: Asia, Africa, and Europe. The Southern Hemisphere was usually thought to be one big unspecified, but inhabited, area. Europe, separated from Africa by the Mediterranean Sea and from Asia by the river Don, included the islands in the Atlantic as well as Greenland, which was joined to Russia by a strip of land, making the Atlantic Ocean a kind of Scandinavian inland sea. The three North American regions named by Leif Erikson, Helluland (Baffin Island), Markland (Labrador), and Vinland (possibly Newfoundland), were considered to be located south of Greenland and to stretch out from Africa.

Astronomy seems not to have been a matter of particular interest until the early 12th century, when it is told that in the north of Iceland a man by the name of Star Oddi Helgason took lunar and solar observations, recording azimuth tables. A little later, another Icelander, Abbot Niculas Bergsson (d. 1159/60), reports in his *Leidarvisir* (Guide), which is an account of his itinerary to the Holy Land, how, by the banks of the Jordan, he laid on his back and used his knee, fist, and thumb to measure the angle of elevation of the Polaris.

Considering the fact that the Viking Age Scandinavians were skilled sailors, it is, however, reasonable to assume use of basic celestial observation in clear skies, that is, when voyaging out of sight of land. On the whole, however, very little is known about the navigational methods used, but it is likely that, for example, courses were steered relative to the Polaris on a clear night and that estimates for directions of north and south were checked at noon with the sun at its highest or in northern latitudes at midnight with the sun at its lowest.

Basic lunar and solar observations obviously determined the Viking Age Scandinavians' conceptions of time. To them, a year consisted of a time of light, summer, and a time of darkness, winter, and both solstices were ritually marked. "Summer" lasted from around mid-April to mid-October, and "winter" from around mid-October to mid-April. A new year was considered to begin at the start of the winter semester, and for this reason people's ages were given in terms of number of winters.

The summer semester was production time; the winter semester was consumption time. This is clearly reflected in the Old Norse names of the months, although months were not months in our sense of the word but rather indicators of seasonal activities. For example, the first month of winter, *Gormanud* (gore month), derives its name from the slaughtering of beasts for winter store, and the third month of winter, *Morsug* (marrow sucker) clearly implies that around this time, people typically ran low on food supplies. The name of the first month of summer, *Varonn* (spring work), shows that activities connected with production began, although during the summer season a division into weeks appears to have been the norm.

The day, too, was divided into a time of light and a time of darkness. The day was defined by the movements of the sun, and this is given clear expression in the Old Norse term for the 24 hours that constitute a day and a night: *solarhring* (sun ring). In addition to the day and night division, the *solarhring* was further divided into *eykt*, that is, intervals of approximately three hours from 6 A.M. to midnight. Each *eykt* had a name, which referred either to a physical fact, such as *hadegi* (midday), or more commonly, to a meal, that is, *dagmal* (day meal) at 9 A.M. or *nattmal* (night meal) at 9 P.M. In Old Norse, *mal* meant also "measure," which shows that meals were considered means of measuring the time of day.

~Kirsten Wolf

FOR MORE INFORMATION

Wolf, K. *Daily Life of the Vikings*. Westport, Conn.: Greenwood Press, forthcoming.

CHINA

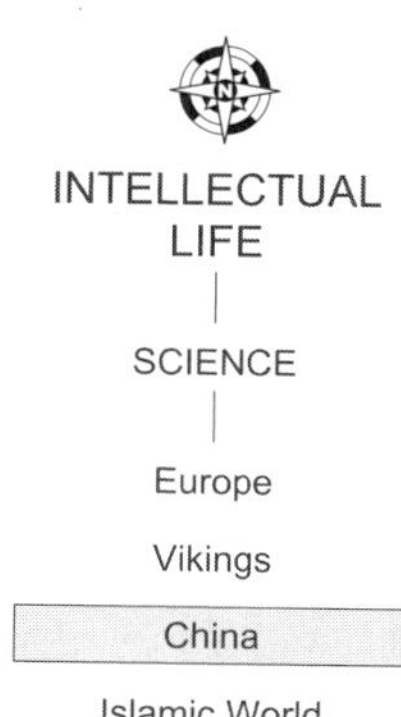

As in other ancient societies, Chinese thinkers did not draw clear lines between science, philosophy, and theology. Thus any discussion of medieval Chinese science includes their total worldview. Tsou Yen, who lived between 350 and 270 B.C.E., is credited with being the founder of Chinese scientific thought. The Chinese *Historical Record* written about the first century B.C.E. reveals something of Tsou Yen's scientific method:

> First he had to examine small objects, and from these he drew conclusions about large ones, until he reached what was without limit. . . . He began by classifying China's notable mountains, great rivers and connecting valleys; its birds and beasts; the fruitfulness of its water and soils, and its rare products; and from this extended his survey to what is beyond the seas, and men are unable to observe. Then starting from the time of the separation of the Heavens and Earth, and coming down, he made citations of the revolutions and transmutations of the Five Powers [Virtues], arranging them until each found its proper place and was confirmed [by history]. (Ronan, 142–43)

This summary reveals that Tsou Yen used some of the best in modern scientific method—he observed, classified, and drew conclusions from what he discovered. He was even willing to depart from traditional wisdom; according to the *Historical Record*, "His sayings were vast and far-reaching, and not in accord with the accepted beliefs of the classics" (Ronan, 142). Thus it is not surprising that his works formed the basis for Chinese scientific thought throughout the Middle Ages.

Scholars who study medieval Chinese science divide up the subject (as the ancient thinkers did) into three theories: first, that of the five elements; second, that of the two fundamental forces (yin and yang); and third, the Book of Changes (*I Ching*). All three theories had the weight of tradition, and Chinese "scientists" were conversant with all of them, choosing one or another as the situation dictated.

The five elements were water, fire, wood, metal, and earth. Tsou Yen systematized the five-element theory, which argued that many systems, from nature to physics to politics, can be understood by the powerful forces of the five elements in motion. Thus, as important as the element itself was the property of the element while it was undergoing change. The qualities of water, for example, its "soaking, dripping, descending" nature, explained and created saltiness (Ronan, 147). By the Middle Ages, the five-element theory became more political than scientific and was used both to explain political change and to prophesy the future. For example, the *Kuan Tzu* book explains: "When we see the cyclical sign *wu-tzu* arrive, the element of Earth begins its reign. If the emperor now builds palaces and constructs pavilions his life will be in danger, and if city walls are built his ministers will die" (Rohen, 148). Over time, the five elements slowly became associated with every category of things in the universe and formed the core of much of Chinese scientific thought.

The theory of the two fundamental forces, yin and yang, is even older than that of the five elements, but it came to be incorporated into the more complex system. The Chinese characters for yin and yang are connected with darkness and light and reveal the idea that the universe is made up of opposites that are in constant struggle for balance. The 4th-century work the *Tao Te Ching* explains that "living creatures are surrounded by Yin and envelop Yang, and that the harmony of their life processes depends on the harmony of the two forces" (Ronan, 160). The struggle for balance and harmony represented by the two fundamental forces formed a continuing basis for Chinese medical thought as well as more abstract philosophical considerations.

The final strand of Chinese science is the system based on the Book of Changes, or *I Ching*. This book may have originated from a collection of peasant omen texts (probably as early as the 7th century B.C.E.), and it ended up as an elaborate system of symbols and their explanations that was recorded in the 3rd century B.C.E. These were then further revised and synthesized through the first century C.E. and preserved by the medieval Confucian scholars. The symbols were supposed to reveal the processes of nature and thus serve as explanations for medical or other natural phenomena.

The *I Ching* shared with the other scientific systems the idea that no state of affairs was permanent. Everything changes, and the vanquished will rise again just as the prosperous will fall. Also like the other systems, the patterns of the *I Ching* were seen to reflect correct bureaucracy and administration on earth, thus reinforcing and serving as a scientific basis for the complicated Chinese political system.

As this summary shows, scientific classification and analysis in China was very old. These venerable ideas were assimilated into the religious and ethical worldviews of Confucius and others and permeated the political and medical wisdom of the times.

~*Joyce E. Salisbury*

FOR MORE INFORMATION

Ronan, C. A. *The Shorter Science and Civilisation in China*. Cambridge, England: Cambridge University Press, 1978.

ISLAMIC WORLD

During the Middle Ages, the Muslim world remained the intellectual center of the Mediterranean world. By the 8th century, the caliphs had collected Persian, Greek, and Syriac scientific and philosophical works and had them translated into Arabic. The ʿAbbasids ruling in Baghdad beginning in the 9th century maintained this support of science by building a "House of Wisdom" in the city. This center included a library, translation center, and a school. The combination of royal support and the presence of texts from the classical world allowed learning to flourish and led to an upsurge in scientific discoveries.

Just as in the West, many scholars focused their attention on philosophy and logic. After all, they were building on the Greek texts—particularly those of Aristotle—which created a method to study all fields of knowledge. Muslim scholars from Baghdad all the way to Toledo in Spain preserved, studied, and wrote commentaries on these influential classical texts. In the 12th century, the Muslim scholar Averroës interpreted Aristotle's works and left extensive commentaries on the ideas. These texts were discovered in Arabic libraries in Spain as Christians slowly reconquered Muslim territories, and the emergence of the commentaries along with the advanced logic of Aristotle served to stimulate a resurgence of learning in the West.

In mathematics, Muslim scholars made advances that transformed the field in the East and the West. Mathematicians brought from India the use of what we call "Arabic" numerals, which are the numerals we use today. These numerals quickly replaced the Roman numerals that had been used throughout the former empire. The major advantage of Arabic numerals was that they included the zero, which makes complex calculations manageable. (One can quickly appreciate the advantage of Arabic numerals by trying to do long division with Roman numerals.) By the 10th century, Muslim mathematicians had perfected the use of decimals and fractions and had invented algebra. The word *algebra* comes from Arabic and means "the art of bringing together unknowns to match a known quantity." Today students all over the world continue to learn this art.

Muslim astronomers, too, built on ancient texts and made great strides in observing the heavens. The Muslim astronomer/mathematician al-Tusi (b. 1201) recalculated ancient Greek understandings of planetary orbits with a precision that would not be matched in western Europe until the 16th century.

Muslim scientists probably made their greatest advances in the field of medicine. Instead of slavishly following the great classical physicians, Hippocrates and Galen, they combined these insights with practical and empirical observation. Islamic rulers required doctors to be licensed, so the practice of medicine was well regulated. Some Islamic physicians wrote extensively and exerted a profound influence on Western medicine. Razi (called Rhazes in the West) wrote more than 100 books on medicine. He was the first to diagnose smallpox and prescribe an effective treatment for it. Muslim surgeons performed remarkably complex operations. They practiced vascular and cancer surgery and developed a sophisticated technique for operating on cataracts of the eyes that involved using a tube to drain the fluid from the cataract. This technique was employed even in modern times.

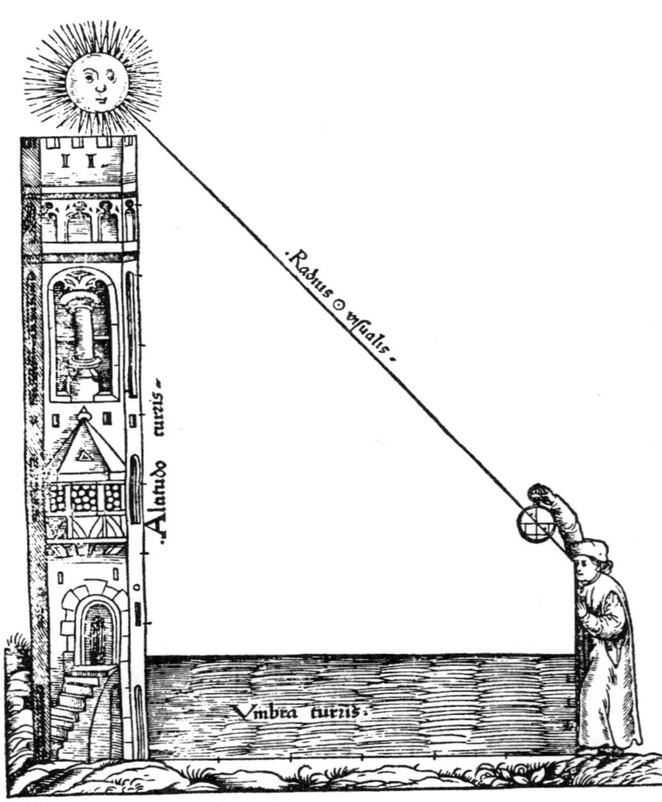

Originating in Constantinople, the astrolabe spread to Europe and influenced sea travel. Here, an astrolabe is being used to fix position—sighting on a building of known elevation—the way a ship's mast would be used at sea. © North Wind/North Wind Picture Archives.

A wide range of anesthetics, from opium mixed in wine to more sophisticated drugs, made surgery tolerable for Muslim patients. Hospitals, too, sprang up throughout the Muslim world and included outpatient treatment centers and dispensaries for the many medicines being developed.

One of the greatest of the medieval Muslim scientists was Ibn Sina, known as Avicenna. As was traditional in Muslim households, young Avicenna had tutors from a young age. The young man showed great intellectual curiosity and talent, and by the age of 10, he had memorized the entire Qur'an. He also studied philosophy, theology, and mathematics. For a while, the avid scholar studied with an Indian surveyor, from whom he learned Indian mathematics using Arabic numerals. Avicenna said he found medicine and natural science so easy that by the age of 16, he was practicing medicine and teaching other physicians. However, it was logic and geometry that most captured his imagination. He was so voracious in studying the works of the ancients that he claimed that by the age of 18, he had mastered all knowledge.

Avicenna wrote treatises on many topics, including arithmetic, music, language, and philosophy. However, what would become his most influential contribution to the future of science was his *Canon of Medicine* (despite his belief that medicine was too easy). This book became the main medical text for more than six centuries and was copied throughout the Mediterranean world. In the West, the *Canon* was probably second only to the Christian Bible in the number of times it was reproduced.

Some scholars suggest that Avicenna's techniques of experimentation and observation gave birth to the modern scientific method. Without any doubt, science and medicine in the Muslim world was a bright light in an otherwise fairly dim scientific world.

~*Joyce E. Salisbury*

FOR MORE INFORMATION

Afnan, S. M. *Avicenna, His Life and Works*. London: Allen and Unwin, 1958.

Language and Literature

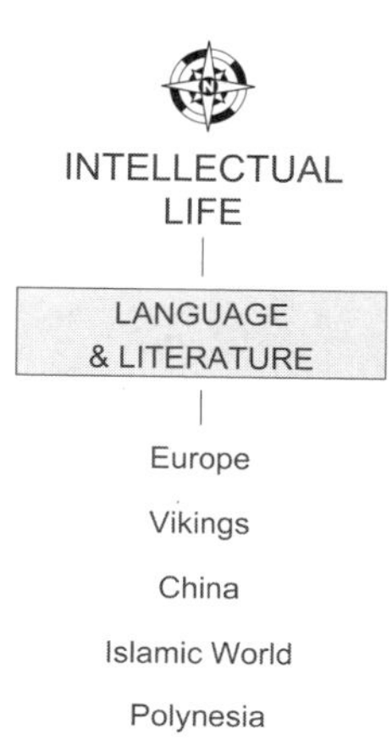

Spoken language is as old as humanity, and through the spoken word, people have preserved their traditions, myths, and histories. When languages were only oral, there was great variation among them. Polynesians spoke 30 closely related languages during the Middle Ages, and their preserved traditions show a complex mythology. The Vikings, too, had a great oral tradition with which they preserved their myths and history. While Vikings had a form of written language with rune stones, in reality, both Polynesians and Vikings only learned to write with the arrival of Christian missionaries—about the 11th century in Scandinavia and the 19th century in Polynesia.

The most important factor that helps civilizations advance is the ability to write. Writing gives some cultures a distinct advantage over others that depend on human memory to recall their achievements. Writing allows the transfer and dissemination of knowledge, which in turn allows people to build on previously acquired advancements instead of continually rediscovering and relearning the same material. Societies that did not have a written language quickly learned of its benefits and adopted one. It is these written texts that historians use as their primary sources.

At the beginning of the Middle Ages, some of the Germanic tribes that invaded the Roman Empire had no written language. Like the Polynesians and Vikings, they preserved their traditions through oral poetry, and like the Polynesians, they learned to write when they came in contact with other cultures who did so. The German tribes learned a phonetic alphabet based on Latin from the Romans and soon recorded their own traditional literature. The Slavic tribes north of Byzantium learned to write from the missionaries Cyril and Methodius, who developed a Slavic alphabet based on their own Greek letters. The modern Russian alphabet is called Cyrillic after the dedicated missionary who developed it. The Chinese used an ancient alphabet based on pictographs or ideographs—that is, drawings that represent an object (similar to the kind of alphabet used by the ancient Egyptians and Sumerians). The Chinese alphabet takes much more time to learn than the phonetic alphabets of the West and Islam, so writing in China remained the skill of the highly educated.

A written language does not necessarily determine the spoken tongue. In western Europe, for example, Latin—the language of ancient Rome—remained the language of the church and of administration long after it was no longer spoken by people. The languages spoken by everyday people are called "vernacular" languages, which simply means the common language of a region. English, French, German, and so forth were the vernacular languages of Europe. However, many regions had spoken dialects of those languages that were different enough to cause confusion to travelers. The educated travelers fell back on Latin as their universal language. China, too, was divided into many languages. The Muslim world was unified linguistically by the fact that it was forbidden for believers to translate the Qur'an into a vernacular language. Therefore, believers had to learn Arabic to read the Qur'an, which then became a unifying tongue. That is not to say that people did not keep their own vernacular languages even in the Muslim world—they certainly did. Just as in Europe, it was common for the educated to speak at least two languages.

With a written language well established, people then chose what kinds of things to record—this forms their literature. Some of the things recorded are mundane administrative items—lists of goods, taxes collected, offices held. However, people also recorded their highest thoughts—their religious understandings, dreams, and myths. In addition, most cultures record their own histories to situate themselves within their past. When the Germans learned to write, among the first things they recorded were the accounts of their heroic past that they had preserved orally through generations. The Vikings did the same. Polynesians recorded the genealogy of their great chieftains. The Chinese of the Middle Ages favored historical writings and even historical criticism to see if the writings were true.

Finally, people write fiction of various sorts. Beautiful poetry—whether Arabic, Chinese, Greek, or any other language—treats language as an aesthetic device to soothe the ear while it engages the mind. In Europe, poems and romances began to be written down in vernacular languages, which preserved people's values while it entertained. There is perhaps no better window into what it means to be human in any particular culture than the literature people produce and the language of its expression.

~Joyce E. Salisbury

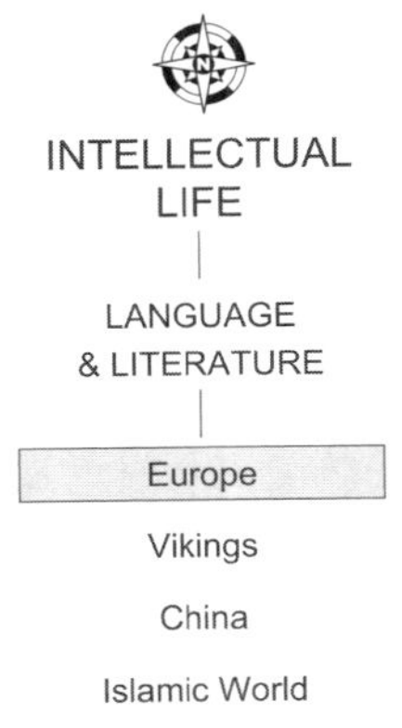

EUROPE

When the Germanic tribes invaded the decaying Roman Empire, they spoke various dialects of Old German and brought this language into the Latin-speaking empire. During the early Middle Ages, the Western kingdoms began to develop different linguistic traditions depending on how many Latin speakers lived in a particular area. Europe began to be split in half on this issue—the north, from England to Scandinavia to Germany, spoke Germanic languages, while the south spoke Romance languages, that is, languages derived from the Romans. Thus Spanish, Portuguese, French, Italian, and Romanian were all derived from dialects of Latin. We have a vivid record of the culmination of this trend in the Treaty of Verdun signed in 843 to divide up Charlemagne's old empire among his grandsons. This treaty had to be written in two languages—Old French and Old German—to reflect the realities of the linguistic divisions.

While the people in the Middle Ages began to use their own regional languages (called "vernacular"), Latin remained the unifying language of the church, governments, and universities. At first in the Middle Ages, all serious literature was written in Latin. Over time, however, more works were written in the vernacular so they could be enjoyed by a wider audience. By the end of the Middle Ages, vernacular languages dominated literature, and Latin became a dead language.

After the fall of the Roman Empire, the Western kingdoms of medieval Europe also inherited a varied body of literature—Roman, religious, and an oral tradition of the songs of the ancient Germanic tribes that had invaded. Scholars of medieval literature have recognized three major stages in the development of a identifiable medieval literature.

In the first stage—which extended from about 400 C.E. to about 800 C.E.—writers concentrated on simply transmitting the rich and varied heritage they possessed. During this age of violence, when the Germanic kingdoms were just being established and the remnants of the Roman empire were falling away, literacy was rare. It was the monasteries of Europe that largely preserved the skills of reading and writing (especially in Latin), and monks and nuns carefully copied ancient manuscripts to preserve the learning. Some great scholars of this early age read Roman classics and compiled the information in ways that were useful to future generations. Isidore of Seville in Spain (560–636), for example, was a prolific encyclopedist of ancient collections. The venerable Bede in England (672–735) wrote a number of educational tracts. For example, in *The Nature of Things*, Bede incorporates much from the Roman encyclopedist Pliny the Elder.

While monastic copiers carefully preserved Roman and early Christian writings, the process was fraught with difficulty. Some nuns and monks knew Latin imperfectly, and because the handwriting of ancient manuscripts was difficult to read, errors crept into the texts. Later scholars would have to sort out these problems. Greek had been forgotten in the West, so Greek texts were unavailable.

During this first stage of medieval literature, Germanic peoples were preserving their own stories and songs of heroic deeds orally as they always had done. Poets in the halls of the warrior tribes composed remarkable songs that needed the memories of the tribes to be preserved.

By about 800 C.E., medieval literature entered into its second stage of development, in which the three elements—Germanic, Christian, and Roman—were blended into a unique body of work. Under Charlemagne, ancient texts were brought out from behind monastery walls and corrected. (Scholars in Charlemagne's court also developed a new handwriting called "Carolingian miniature," which was easier to read and thus helped subsequent transcriptions be more accurate.) Germans had become literate, and some of their ancient stories were written down in the vernacular (with Christian elements sometimes added). At this point, the great heroic epics, including *Beowulf* and the *Nibelungenlied*, were written down.

In the 12th century, the third and most creative stage of medieval literature appeared. Throughout Europe, there was a creation of new kinds of literature (and ideas) that had not been seen before, and these new literary ideas would shape the future of the West. One new form of literature was the *Chanson de Geste*, action tales relating the deeds of feudal heroes. The most famous of these are the French *Song of Roland* and the Spanish *Poem of the Cid*. In these poems, we can see the values of the knights as they praise loyalty to their feudal lords, their faith in God, and their power in war. These works, too, developed the vernacular languages.

Christine de Pisan was a professional writer who hired people to make multiple copies of her writings. Here she presents her book to Isabel of Bavaria, queen of Charles VI of France. © North Wind/North Wind Picture Archives.

At the same time, starting in southern France, a new kind of poetry was developed that introduced a new idea of romantic love. This troubadour poetry held up an ideal love in which a man served a noble lady, doing whatever she wanted, until he received her love in return. These poets promised that lovers would be transformed by this great love and that the excitement of adultery was worth the risks (and social disruption). This romantic literature reached its highest expression in the great romances of the 12th and 13th centuries. Works such as the King Arthur romances by the French poet Chretien de Troyes or the German *Tristan and Isolde* by Gottfried von Strassburg have virtually defined medieval literature. In these works, men and women do anything for love. Some scholars have suggested that this tradition of romantic love that began in the 12th century has separated the West from the rest of the world in a profound way. Love became about individual passion rather than about family ties. Probably the highest expression of this sensibility was the *Romance of the Rose*, which was essentially a seduction manual.

At the end of the Middle Ages, a popular new form of literature—*fabliaux*—bawdy, humorous short tales, reached a new height. Boccaccio in Italy wrote a collection of 100 funny stories in *The Decameron*, and Chaucer in England wrote the well-known *Canterbury Tales*. These two collections marked a new recognition of the power of the individual, the revolutionary impact of humor, and the potential for social criticism in literature. These works were at the dawn of the Renaissance.

To read about language and literature in Elizabethan England, see the England entries in the sections "Language and Writing Systems" and "Literature" in chapter 4 ("Intellectual Life") of volume 3; for 18th-century England, see the England entry in the section "Language and Literature" in chapter 4 ("Intellectual Life") of volume 4; and for Victorian England, see the England entry in the section "Literature" in chapter 4 ("Intellectual Life") of volume 5 of this series.

~*Joyce E. Salisbury*

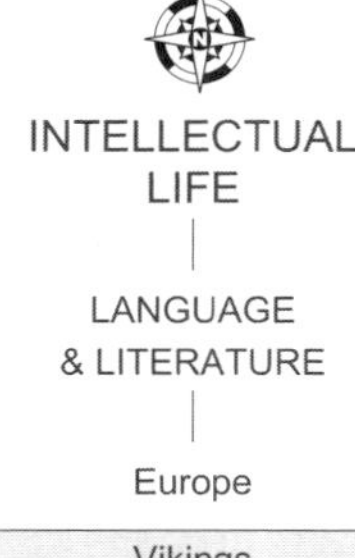

FOR MORE INFORMATION

Taylor, H. O. *The Medieval Mind*. London: Macmillan, 1911.
Wilhelm, J. J. *Medieval Song*. New York: Dutton, 1971.

VIKINGS

Linguists usually refer to the language spoken in Scandinavia in the Viking Age as North Germanic. The term implies that by the beginning of the Viking Age, the language showed sufficient individual traits to distinguish itself from the West Germanic dialect that became Low and High German, Frisian, Dutch, and English, as well as the East Germanic dialect that is mainly known to us through the extinct Gothic.

In the Viking Age, Scandinavian was spoken over an area that comprises what is now Denmark and southern and central Norway and Sweden. As the Scandinavians gradually established themselves in Normandy, the British Isles, the islands in the North Atlantic, Greenland, and the Finnish and Estonian coastal areas, the language came to be spoken also in these regions. Indeed, in the Orkney and Shetland Islands, the Faroe Islands, and Iceland, it became the dominant language, although in the Orkney and Shetland Islands it later yielded to Lowland Scots. In Greenland, Scandinavian died out as a result of the extinction of the Norse colony.

It is often said that the Viking Age Scandinavians were illiterate until they became Christian and the Church of Rome brought to them the art of reading and writing. This is only partially true, because, like other Germanic-speaking peoples, the Scandinavians had their own way of writing, with an alphabet called runic. The origin of the runes has been hotly debated, but most scholars today agree that runic writing was created by the Germanic peoples themselves in the 2nd century C.E. under direct or indirect influence of the Greek and/or Roman alphabets.

The runic characters are made up of vertical and diagonal lines, which make them especially suitable for carving on wood. Curves, which would be difficult to cut in grainy material, are avoided, as are horizontal strokes, which would mingle with the grain. There are, however, many variations in the letter forms of the Germanic runic alphabet, and this makes it virtually impossible to give a standard pattern for the alphabet, which underwent significant changes. Generally, it seems that the Danish runes were used for inscriptions on monuments while the Swedo-Norwegian runes were used for everyday communication, although some inscriptions are mixed.

We do not know if the ability to use and interpret the runes was a privilege of the select few or if there was a general acquaintance with runes among common people. The fact that rune stones were as a rule erected in public places, beside roads and bridges, or at parish or farm boundaries, suggests that they were intended to be seen or read and, by extension, that a good number, if not the majority, of Viking Age Scandinavians could interpret runes.

Rune stones are a hallmark of the Viking Age. There are about 180 Viking Age and early medieval rune stones in what is now Denmark. In Norway, about 45 such monuments are extant. In Sweden, no fewer than approximately 2,500 rune stones have been preserved from this period of time. The 11th century is a particularly rich period for Swedish runes, and in the province of Uppland alone, some 1,300 monuments are recorded. Moreover, a number of Scandinavian runic inscriptions have been found in the Viking colonies; the tiny Isle of Man in particular has a remarkably large collection of rune stones.

The Roman alphabet accompanied the conversion to Christianity, but for some time this alphabet, which was mastered primarily by clerics and the nobility, was used only for writing in Latin. Christians did not disapprove of the runes despite their pagan origin, and Christians themselves used runes on baptismal fonts and memorial stones. It appears that for quite some time, the two alphabets complemented each other and served different functions: texts of a permanent character, such as royal edicts and legal texts, were written in Roman letters on parchment, whereas notes of importance for only a limited time were inscribed with runes on bones or twigs.

After the Scandinavians converted to Christianity, Vikings began to record their oral literature. The earliest literature is poetry, and it falls broadly into two classes, called Eddic and skaldic. The Eddic poems are chiefly of two kinds—mythic and heroic. The former describes the world of gods, and the latter that of heroes and heroines of Germanic antiquity. Both categories, but especially the former, provide useful information about early Norse religion and the social and ethical attitudes of Scandinavians in the Viking Age.

f u þ a r k g w h n i j p ë R s t b e m l ŋ d o
th ng

f u þ ą r k h n i a s t b m l R

f u þ ą r k h n i a s t b m l R

Viking runic alphabet. This written language was used only for ritual inscriptions during the classic Viking Age. Joyce E. Salisbury.

Skaldic poetry differs from Eddic poetry in that it is typically ascribed to named authors and has as its subject recent or contemporary events. The composers of skaldic poetry functioned in a way as historiographers; in their verses, they typically praise a king or chieftain for his courage or generosity either during his lifetime or in a memorial poem after his death, enumerating his battles and other feats of prowess. Several of the skaldic poems rank high as historical sources about the Viking Age.

Prose, too, flourished in medieval Scandinavia. Many of the earliest works, such as sermons and saints' lives, are based on foreign sources, and this is the case also with the 12th-century Icelandic encyclopedic writings. But indigenous composition are found as well, in which Scandinavian authors record in Latin or the vernacular their countries' past or their contemporary world. These writings range from annals and chronicles to historical novels.

The best-known medieval Icelandic prose writings are the Sagas of Icelanders. This is a modern term for approximately 35 to 40 narratives about Icelandic farmer-chieftains from the settlement of Iceland to the mid-11th century. Written in a dry, factual style, they present themselves as history and are often seductively realistic, and from the time they became objects of study until well into the 20th century, scholars generally regarded them as valuable historical sources. However, some of the sagas have been demonstrated to be little more than fiction, and the trend among historians today is to take precautions when relying on information provided by the sagas and use them primarily for the details they give about social mechanisms and mental attitudes. No other sources are as detailed and colorful as the Sagas of Icelanders, and no other sources have had more of an impact on shaping modern conceptions of the Viking Age. Furthermore, few medieval sources are as popular with modern readers as the exciting Sagas of the Icelanders.

~*Kirsten Wolf*

FOR MORE INFORMATION

Hollander, L. M. *The Skalds*. Ann Arbor: University of Michigan Press, 1968.
Snorri Sturluson. *Edda*. Translated by A. Faulkes. London: Dent, 1987.
Wolf, K. *Daily Life of the Vikings*. Westport, Conn.: Greenwood Press, forthcoming.

CHINA

Ancient Chinese written language, like Sumerian and Egyptian, was based on pictographs or ideographs—that is, drawings reduced to bare essentials to represent an object or concept. As the language developed, indirect symbols were introduced: for example, the ideograph *nan*, which represents "male," comes from pictograms for plow and field. As early as the 9th century B.C.E., it was common for pictographs to be combined to form other words. For example, signs for "water" and "fork" could be combined to mean "branching streams." As early as 213 B.C.E., many of these forms were codified, and the first great dictionary appeared in 121 C.E. By this time, there were six ways to form words: (1) pictographs, (2) indirect symbols, (3) associative compound symbols, (4) mutually interpretive symbols, (5) loan characters, and (6) determinative phonetics. The last form (like modern Western alphabets) offers the most flexibility and slowly took over the majority of the characters in written Chinese. By the 18th century, for example, only 5 percent of the characters were pictographs or symbols; the rest were phonetic. Nevertheless, it requires the knowledge of about 2,000 characters to read and write Chinese. The great advantage of the Chinese language is that it has remained largely the same over time, meaning that those who can read modern Chinese have access to the wealth of ancient Chinese writings.

Authors during the Tang dynasty (like those in other dynasties) favored historical writings. In part, this was cultivated by the examination system that required years of historical study to pass the tests, but it was also because of the Chinese inclination to see patterns in the past that explained the present and even forecast the future. The Chinese word *wen* very roughly translates as "patterns and culture," and the Chinese historians used this concept as they studied the past and made elaborate correlations between humans and nature and between moral and physical worlds. Like the religious idea of Dao, historians believed that everything was connected, and to understand one aspect of the universe was to understand others. The historical writers also engaged in historical criticism in which they analyzed other histories to see if they were accurate or useful.

The highly cultured Tang dynasty is also noted for its production of poetry, and poets were as imbued with the past as were the historians. The poets also worked to see patterns between the past and the universe, especially embodied in nature, and the creative weaving of history and nature images is one of the striking features of Tang poetry. One beautiful example, "Song of the Endless Past," captures this tone (Frankel, 348). In this poem, the poet imagines an immensity of time, appropriate to a China that even by the Tang dynasty, had seen itself existing for almost immeasurable ages. This time wears down everything that is created by people, even to a stone bridge or bronze pillars.

The philosophy portrayed by these and many other similar poems is that time itself is the only constant, and nature is almost as certain—mountains and rivers were enduring, and the blossoms of plants promise a rejuvenation of nature. Only people and their products are transitory, but they are connected in the web that links time and nature. This timeless pattern echoes the patterns of the Chinese characters on the page.

To read about language and literature in 19th-century China, see the China entry in the section "Literature" in chapter 4 ("Intellectual Life") of volume 5 of this series.

~Joyce E. Salisbury

FOR MORE INFORMATION

Frankel, H. H. "The Contemplation of the Past in Tang Poetry." In *Perspectives on the T'ang,* edited by A. F. Wright and D. Twitchett. New Haven, Conn.: Yale University Press, 1973.

Ronan, C. A. *The Shorter Science and Civilisation in China.* Cambridge, England: Cambridge University Press, 1978.

ISLAMIC WORLD

The most important contribution to Islam from the pre-Muslim culture was the Arabic language itself. Because the Qur'an was written in Arabic, the faithful all had to learn that language. In fact, early grammarians and, especially, lexicographers spent a great deal of time collecting as much information on the Arabic language in all its complexities, turns of phrase, obscure words, and multiple meanings as they could, for a precise knowledge of the Arabic language was absolutely essential to a proper understanding of the Qur'an and the teachings of Muhammad. Muslim scholars' efforts in the scientific study of the Arabic language during the first Islamic centuries have preserved for us a broad range of early literary sources.

One of the most important sources for 7th-century Arabia is the principal art form of the *qasida* or ode. While the *qasida* was valued for its beauty and as the epitome of Arabic poetry, it was also venerated because, apart from the Qur'an itself, it represented the Arabic language at its purest. Apart from its literary qualities, this poetry provides the modern historian with a clear window onto the values and customs of Arabian tribal society.

The Qur'an is written in beautiful rhymed prose, and its study contributed to a lively appreciation for literature. Muslim writers throughout the Middle Ages would pen magnificent poetry that celebrated beauty, love, and the sensual life. Perhaps the most famous literary collection was the tales of the *Arabian Nights*. This widely admired collection of stories was set in Baghdad in the court of the most famous

ʿAbbasid caliph, Harun al-Rashid (r. 786–809) and has delighted readers in the East and West for centuries.

In the Middle Ages, the Arabic language had become the preferred language of science and learning for nearly every ethnic and religious group under Muslim rule. Arabic served to unite the educated elites in the Islamic world in much the same way that Latin did in medieval western Europe or English does in the modern world. That is, in the 10th century, an educated Jew in Baghdad wrote in Arabic (often with Hebrew characters), while he employed Hebrew for religious purposes and possibly a dialect of Aramaic in everyday speech.

At the same time, ethnic minorities in the far-flung Muslim lands preserved their own vernacular languages. For example, an educated Zoroastrian in Iran could speak and write Arabic but used a dialect of Persian for everyday speech. Educated Christians in Cairo (many of whom served in bureaucratic positions) were fluent in Arabic but used Coptic for religious purposes and possibly everyday speech. The same held true for educated Christians in Damascus. They knew Arabic but used a dialect of Aramaic for religious purposes and possibly everyday speech as well. Similar situations existed among the educated populations of Spain, North Africa, central Asia, and northwest India.

To read about literature in the Islamic World in the 20th century, see the Islamic World entry in the section "Literature" in chapter 4 (Intellectual Life) of volume 6 of this series.

~James Lindsay

FOR MORE INFORMATION

Lindsay, J. *Daily Life in Medieval Islam*. Westport, Conn.: Greenwood Press, forthcoming.

POLYNESIA

Polynesians speak about 30 closely related languages, and their ancient mythologies and legends rival any found elsewhere around the world. The Polynesian languages compose one part of a larger family called Austronesian, spoken throughout Indonesia, the Philippines, Micronesia, Melanesia, Polynesia, Malay, parts of South Vietnam, and extending halfway around the globe to Madagascar, just off the eastern coast of Africa. The Polynesian family of languages itself is divided into three major groups—Tongic (Tongan and Niuean), Samoic (including Samoan, Tokelauan, and Tikopian), and Eastern Polynesian (including Hawaiian, Marquesan, Tahitian, Rarotongan, and New Zealand Māori).

Because of their common origin and because there was little or no communication with foreigners during Polynesia's long history, these languages have remained fairly homogeneous. For example, eastern Polynesians speaking Hawaiian, New Zealand Māori, Tahitian, and Marquesan, can fairly well understand each other's native language by making minor adjustments in the pronunciation of their consonants as shown in the following list:

English	Marquesan	Tahitian	Mäori	Hawaiian
love	kaoha	āroha	aroha	aloha
taro	kalo	taro	taro	kalo
bird	manu	manu	manu	manu
man	kane	tāne	tane	kāne
yes	ae	'ae	ae	'ae
canoe	vaka	va'a	waka	wa'a
fish	ika	i'a	ika	i'a

Of course, not all words in the various Polynesian vocabularies are similar; the ones in the previous list were deliberately chosen to show their similarities. There are many words and expressions that are not identical.

Ancient Polynesian languages were only spoken; they had no written language. When the 19th-century Christian missionaries arrived in the islands, they began the task of introducing a written language to each of the island groups. They did so by using the Roman alphabet with its Latin pronunciation. Similar to the Latin-based languages of Italian and Spanish, for example, Polynesian syllables all end in a vowel (*a, e, i, o, u*), and all vowels are pronounced, either long or short, similar to Latin. The consonants (*b, f, h, k, l, m, n, p, r, s, t, w*) are generally pronounced as they are in English. The Polynesian languages have few letters in their alphabets. Hawaiian, for example, has only 12—the 5 vowels, *a e, i, o, u,* and 7 consonants, *h, k, l, m, n, p, w,* and in most cases every letter is pronounced. Another mark, which is considered a consonant, is the glottal stop, indicated by a reverse apostrophe (ʻ). It appears before some words beginning with a vowel (ʻae) and sometimes between two vowels (iʻa). Apparently, it is the remnant of the consonant *k* spoken originally in a earlier form of the language. The Hawaiian word *oʻo*, for example, is pronounced similar to the English "oh, oh."

Beginning in the later 20th century, Polynesians have become increasingly concerned about the proper spelling and pronunciation of their languages, and a great amount of work has gone into the creation of proper and up-to-date dictionaries. The macron, or the long duration sign over a vowel (ā, ē, ī, ō, ū), and the glottal stop (ʻ) are appearing in almost all serious publications. Their use or absence can cause a drastic difference in translation. Taking Hawaiian again as an example, the word *pepe* means flat, as a flat nose, but the word *pēpē* means a baby; *lolo* means the brain, while *lōlō* means stupid.

Polynesian chants that tell of their ancient mythologies and epics of former heroes and heroines represent some of the richest and most detailed in the whole world. When the first Europeans visited these islands just 200 years ago, they commented on the Polynesian chants that sometimes took several days to relate. Because they had no written language, the Polynesians transmitted their culture from one generation to another verbally. Certain individuals within the society were designated as ceremonial priests, bards, poets, or orators. Their function was to aggrandize the achievements of the rulers and to pass down their sacred lore from one generation to another. Schools were sometimes built to train their novices. Teaching was rigorous and exact, and the student had to memorize not only the details of the chants, but the exact intonation as well. One slip of the tongue during a major ceremony could sometimes cause a major demotion or death sentence for the orator.

Themes of Polynesian chants consist of mythologies, creation chants, epics of gods and heroes, love lyrics, histories, and priestly formulas. These were the stories the Polynesians carried with them as they settled in the far-flung islands of the Pacific. As they settled into their new habitats and were separated from their original homelands, their stories went through local variations and new elements emerged. The stories of their heroes Māui, Kaha'i, Rata, and Tinirau, for example, are known from one end of the Pacific to another, but details of their exploits may vary from one island group to another.

The most widely known hero, of course, is Māui, and a summary of his exploits here gives only a meager sampling of the character of Polynesian legends. The New Zealand chant relates that Māui was prematurely born and was thus thrown into the sea by his mother, Taranga. He was rescued by his divine ancestors, who nourished him until he was grown. He finally returned to his mother, brothers, and sister Hina. He never saw his father, however, and eventually his curiosity got the best of him. One day, he secretly followed his mother to her underground abode, where he first met his father, Makeatutara, and from whom he received a divine blessing. The blessing, however, was faulted, and as a result, Māui was denied full immortality (resembling the story of the Greek hero Achilles).

Māui then set upon a series of adventures for which he is well known. First, he visited his blind grandmother and obtained a magical jawbone to aid him in his quest. His next task was to slow the sun so that his mother's tapa cloths could dry properly out in the sun. (Before Māui's time, the sun traveled much faster around the earth.) He and his brother built a noose from plaited ropes and waited for the sun to rise the next morning. When the sun rose, Māui pulled the snare, captured the sun, and beat him with the jawbone until the sun agreed to travel slower across the sky. Since then, humans have had more time to carry out their daily chores.

His next task was to "fish up" the various islands of the Pacific. One day, he and his brothers went fishing. When they were far out to sea, Māui lowered his magical fishhook and pulled up a large piece of land in the form of a fish. They pulled the "fish" to shore, and Māui set out to seek a priest to bless their catch. While he was away, his brothers became hungry and cut up the "fish." As a result, the land was divided up and slashed in such a manner that mountains and valleys were formed, and this was the origin of the islands of Polynesia.

The origin of making fire was another of Māui's great feats. Up until then, humans had to keep their fires continually burning because they did not known how to rekindle them. Māui decided to remedy the situation. He set out to visit his ancestress, the powerful fire goddess Mahu-ika, in her underground abode. Māui's usual trickery turned into a battle between the two, and in revenge Mahu-ika threw her last sparks of fire into a nearby tree. Since then, humans have been able to rub two tree sticks together whenever they wanted fire.

Māui's last feat was to try to obtain immortality for humans. He set out with his feathered friends, the birds, to visit the night goddess Hina-nui-te-po. To obtain immortality, he had to secretly enter her between her legs and exit out her mouth. He warned his bird friends to be silent while he performed the task. Unfortunately, the little Tiwakawaka bird could not hold its laughter and broke into song. The powerful goddess awoke, saw what was happening, and crushed the hero to death. His fame, however, has remained as one of the most popular heroes of all of Polynesia (Craig, 165–67).

FOR MORE INFORMATION

Craig, R. *Dictionary of Polynesian Mythology*. Westport, Conn.: Greenwood Press, 1989.

Health and Medicine

How to correct illnesses and stay healthy has always been a preoccupation of humans, and the scientific discoveries of the 20th century—including antibiotics, other pharmaceuticals, and surgical techniques—separate us dramatically from ages before. Without these modern cures, healers had to seek other means to help the ill, and the cures depended on their beliefs of the causes of illness.

The oldest societies believed illness was caused by spirits. When the Mongols first appeared, they held this belief, and cures were conducted by shamans who addressed the spiritual world. Polynesian islanders also looked to spirits for cures. China and the Mediterranean world had largely rejected the spiritual approach to illness and looked to other causes. Both, however, believed that the fundamental cause of illness was some kind of imbalance in the body.

Europe, Byzantium, and the Islamic world had adopted the Greco-Roman analysis established by Galen. In this system, the body was composed of four "humors" or fluids that guided the body's functioning. These were blood, black bile, yellow bile, and phlegm. They believed illness was caused by an imbalance among these fluids. For example, if one had a fever and was red and flushed, that indicated an excess of blood, so a physician bled the patient either with leeches or by cutting a vein. This was intended to bring the body back into balance. Anyone at all familiar with modern practice will recognize that in this case, bleeding for a fever is the worst approach. Each of the humors was also identified with a degree of heat, so physicians also tried to bring the body's temperature into balance. Despite its inaccuracies, the advantage of the Galenic approach to health over the spiritual one was that it located cures within the body itself and encouraged perceptive physicians to observe patients' responses. This is the key to medical progress.

Muslim doctors also drew from the classical physician Galen, but they did not slavishly follow his approaches. Instead, they combined this ancient wisdom with practical and empirical observation. Some Muslim physicians wrote extensively and exerted a profound influence on Western medicine. For example, Razi (called Rhazes in the West) wrote more than a hundred books on medicine in the early 10th century and was the first to diagnose smallpox and prescribe an effective treatment for it. Ibn Sina (known as Avicenna in the West) wrote the *Canon of Medicine*, which laid the foundation for experimental science.

The Chinese also believed in a correct balance to ensure health. Instead of focusing on bodily fluids, however, they looked at the body's energy, or *qi*, which flowed through channels in the body. Good health depended on the uninterrupted flow of energy, and physicians tried various means to free blocked energy. Chinese physicians developed acupuncture to insert thin needles at certain points along the channels through which *qi* flowed. While Galenic medicine is no longer practiced, many physicians today in the West as well as the East have reaffirmed the benefits of acupuncture in treating a number of ailments.

As the Mongols expanded, they adopted the medical beliefs of their neighbors. They began to abandon shamanistic practices that located illness in the spiritual world and used physicians trained in Galenic and Chinese medicine. As in so much of their cultural development, they took the best of the worlds they conquered.

Beyond theory, medicine in the medieval world, as now, depended on cures. Intrusive medicine was rarely practiced—the Chinese acupuncture offers an exception to this. Muslim surgeons performed remarkably complex operations. For example, they developed a sophisticated technique for operating on cataracts of the eyes that involved using a tube to drain the fluid from the cataract. Muslims offered a wide range of anesthetics from opium to more sophisticated drugs to make surgery tolerable. In the West, surgery was limited to suturing battlefield wounds or amputations done with little cleanliness nor anesthetic. The Byzantine Empire recognized the need for institutions for health care and began the first real hospitals.

All over the world, most cures involved diet. Whether one was balancing *qi* or humors, people believed changing diet or adding herbs would help bring the body into balance. For example, in western Europe people believed beans were cooling, so they added spices for heat to balance the dish. For the Vikings, food and herbs remained the main medicinal treatment. Physicians and herbalists regularly prescribed changes in diet to bring people back to health. Nutritionists today still recognize the relationship between diet and health as they recommend fruits and vegetables and other dietary modifications.

~*Joyce E. Salisbury*

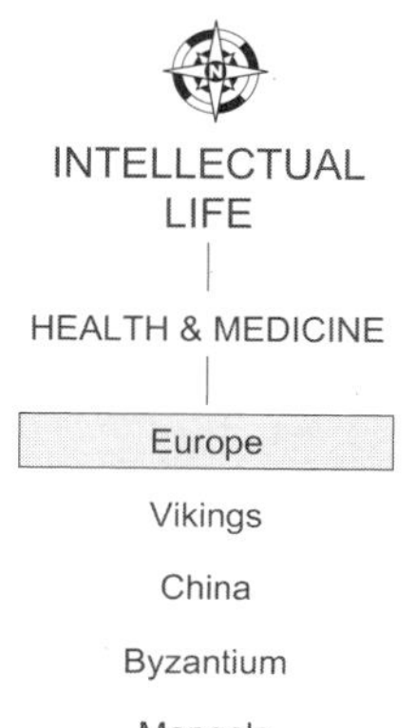

EUROPE

Medieval medicine in Europe was a mixed bag. First, there were many different individuals involved in what we might call medicine: the *medici* (physicians), *rhizotomi* (herb gatherers), *pharmacopolae* (drug or herb dealers), *unguentarii* (salve dealers), *obstetricae* (midwives), and numerous other shadowy figures who specialized in poisoning, abortions, and the like. By the 8th century, medical literature consisted of various letters and pamphlets of medical interest, some as remnants of Greek or Roman medicine, that were read by lay individuals who practiced medicine but who were not fully trained and apprenticed physicians as in the later Middle Ages.

As far as the church leaders were concerned, the structure and function of the human body illustrated the wisdom and goodness of God, and its study was considered to be of real importance. Monastic rules ordered that the sick be carefully attended in all monasteries. Care of the sick was reasonable and humane, with special infirmaries for the sick, extra food portions, greater cleanliness, and resident herb gardens and monks skilled in the use of the herbs. Although the monasteries, in their care for the sick, probably knew as much about medicine and the human body as anyone in the early Middle Ages, their purpose in knowing this was to do God's work and to glorify God, not for the sake of knowledge.

Monastic rules ordered that the sick be carefully attended in all monasteries.

The most important person to transmit classical medical knowledge during this time was Isidore of Seville, who was born around 560. He produced a prodigious amount of writing, including one of the most influential works in the Middle Ages, *The Etymologies*, which acted as a major transmission of information from the classical world to the medieval one. Isidore had clearly read widely and critically and was interested in scientific and medical knowledge even though his primary interest was language, hence the title of the book, which mainly focused on demonstrating the etymologies or origins of words. In doing so, however, he produced an encyclopedia of knowledge intended for the educated public, a very small group. Isidore's medical writings were some of the best medical knowledge available to the Western world in the 7th, 8th, and 9th centuries, yet they were not meant for physicians but for the educated public.

Isidore's medical information was meant to be useful to anyone. In his discussion of disease, he writes that it is an imbalance and is best managed by diet and lifestyle. He held very reasonable thoughts about health and was influenced little by superstition or magic. Isidore absorbed the ancient belief that all matter, including the human body, is composed of four qualities: heat, cold, dryness, and moisture. The health of the human body depended on a balance of these, and disease was a disturbance of that balance. These qualities were also viewed in relation to earth, air, water, and fire, and Isidore discussed the human body as correlating: flesh to earth, breath to air, blood to water, and vital heat to fire. Even though he believed that diet and lifestyle were of utmost importance, he also wrote about diseases that were best treated by drugs or surgery.

Isidore understood the anatomy of the human body rather effectively, describing the nervous system, the spinal cord, the importance of the brain, and the function of the skeleton, tendons, and cartilage. He described accurately the anatomy of the hip joint. The cardiovascular system was probably the least accurately explained, for until the 17th century, arteries and veins were not distinguished, and the circulation of blood was not understood. However, he includes a description of the two chambers of the heart and explains that both contain blood, but one contains more of the vital spirit. Isidore's description is not terribly far off from our modern understanding.

The purpose of the intestines was understood, but not fully the purpose of the liver or kidneys.

Isidore does not cover surgery in great detail except for amputation and cauterization (the burning or scarring of tissue). He does point out that although a patient with cancer cannot be cured, and drugs are ineffective, the patient might live longer if an amputation of the affected limb were performed.

Isidore also describes the use of bandages, compresses, salves, expectorants, enemas, and snake antivenoms. He discusses roundworms, fleas, and lice and mentions leeches and how they become attached to the human body; but he does not mention their medical use for bleeding or any other purpose.

Herbals were intended as practical works. The Greek Dioscorides had written one of the most renowned herbals in the first century C.E. as a practical guide to medicinal herbs. It provides descriptions of the herbs, including the plants' characteristics, habitat, and pharmaceutical use and preparation. This herbal and its variations were intended for use by practicing physicians, but quickly over the years of the early Middle Ages as they were copied, the illustrations became less and less like the original and therefore less useful in finding the plant. In addition, the descriptions gradually were altered, especially as confusion arose over what plant was really meant in regions where there were different plants from those known by Dioscorides (Butt, 140–43).

Unevenness in the diet, poor sanitation, infrequent bathing, and the general hardship of life had health consequences. The lack of fresh fruit and vegetables for much of the year contributed to a high incidence of scurvy. Poor sanitation led directly to the proliferation of disease, as well as fostering vermin that carried disease. The heavy physical work required of urban and rural laborers probably contributed to the arthritis that has been found in many skeletons from medieval burial sites. Infrequent bathing contributed to a high rate of skin disease. Leprosy was recognized as a major problem in the 11th to 13th centuries. In medieval usage, leprosy covered a range of diseases that manifested themselves on the skin, rather than the restricted modern use of the word to designate Hansen's disease. The "falling evil" was another affliction, probably corresponding to what we would call epilepsy or apoplexy. There were various sorts of tumors and cancerous phenomena, known by such names as "apostemes," "fistula," "cancer," and "blains." Many afflictions were simply known as fever—the "quotidian" fever that occurred daily, the "tertian" fever that recurred on alternate days, and the "quartan" fever that recurred on every third day. At the most ordinary level, medieval people were also subject to the head cold, known to them as a "pose." In general, diagnosis was hampered by a very limited understanding of the nature of disease, and their identifications of diseases are not the same as ours.

Personal injury was also a common health risk in the medieval world. The open fire was a feature of every household; many people lived by extremely hard labor under rough conditions; and violence and warfare permeated society more broadly than is the case in the West today. Even recreation was hazardous: the aristocracy was addicted to combat sports, and even the commoner's football game was an extremely rough pastime that often resulted in injury and sometimes even death.

The level of health was affected by the limitations of medieval science. Medieval science was far from primitive; in fact, it was a highly sophisticated system based on the accumulated writings of theorists since the first millennium B.C.E. The weakness of medieval science was its theoretical and bookish orientation, which emphasized the authority of accepted authors. The duty of the scholar was to interpret and reconcile these ancient authorities, rather than to test their theories against observed realities.

In medicine, the fundamental authority was the Greek physiologist Galen (ca. 130–ca. 200), who believed that the body was composed of four humors: choler, phlegm, melancholy, and blood. These humors corresponded to the four elements of which all matter was believed to be composed: earth, water, air, and fire. According to Galenic medicine, illness was principally a result of imbalances in the humors and could best be addressed by medicines that redressed the balance. Astrological influences were also invoked and incorporated into an intricate but orderly system of correspondences among the elements, zodiacal signs, planets, humors, and parts of the body. Medieval scholars produced an enormous body of medical literature detailing ailments, symptoms, and cures according to this system, which made the course of study to become a doctor long and demanding.

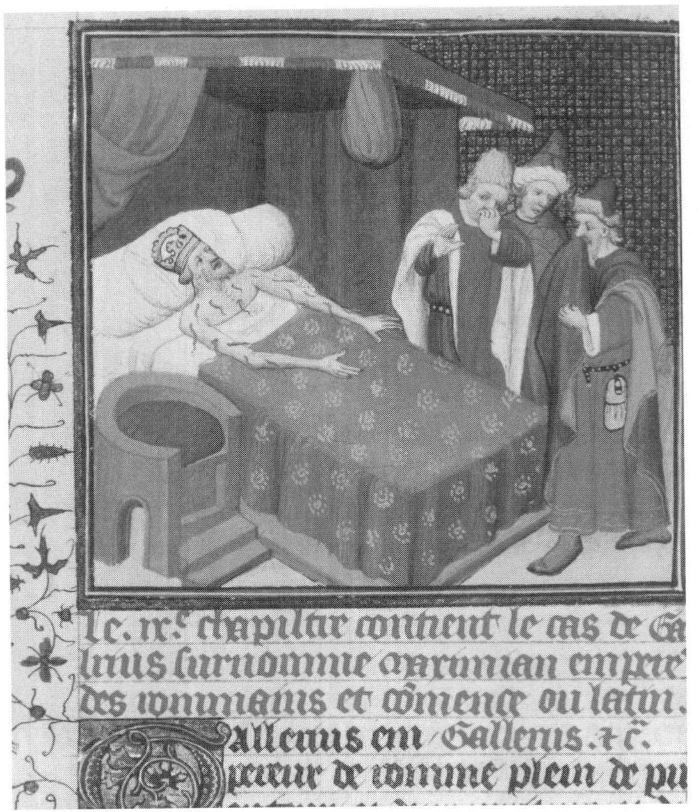

Physicians apply leeches to an ill king. This procedure was intended to reduce the amount of blood in his body to bring down a fever. © Jean-Loup Channet/Science Source/Photo Researchers.

The physician himself was a respected figure in society, educated at a university, and therefore semiclerical in status. His work was principally diagnosis and prescription. The actual preparation of medicine was the work of the apothecary, while physical work on the body itself was left to the surgeon. Both apothecary and surgeon were tradesmen rather than scholars, who learned their craft through apprenticeship rather than university schooling, but their positions, though less lofty than that of the physician, were prestigious and well paid; and they were likely to be literate, and even quite well read.

Most people did not have access to the expensive services of the physician or surgeon. Surgical procedures might be performed instead by a barber, who also extracted bad teeth, in addition to his work trimming hair and shaving beards. For curing diseases, most people likely turned to a practitioner of folk medicine, who might be a professional or a semiprofessional or in some cases, no more than a neighbor or family member. Women in particular learned traditional medical practices as part of their training for running a household. Some of these folk remedies were largely based on superstitions, but others had an element of demonstrable medical value: people knew that it was beneficial to cleanse a wound with wine, even though they did not understand the antiseptic properties of alcohol.

In the 14th century, Europe was confronted by a major medical challenge—the bubonic plague that swept into Italy from China in 1348 and spread rapidly all over Europe in the next few years killing one-third to one-half of the population. The plague was a disease of rodents, and since rats were common in Europe, the disease spread through that population through the fleas that were always a perennial source of discomfort for medieval people. The disease took two principal forms. Initially, it is carried by the flea *Xenopsylla cheopis*, which lives primarily on rats. If the flea transfers to a human host, there is the possibility of an outbreak of bubonic plague, which has a mortality rate of about 50 percent. If the disease enters the pulmonary system, it can become pneumonic plague, an even more deadly and virulent form of the disease that can be transmitted directly from person to person, and has a mortality rate near 100 percent.

Despite dietary problems and the shortcomings of medieval medicine, medieval people were not the stunted grotesques we sometimes imagine them to be. A survey of medieval English graves found mean heights of about 5 feet 7 inches for men and 5 feet 2 inches for women; the figures for a similar survey in Denmark were 5 feet 7 inches for men and 5 feet 4 inches for women. Dental cavities are rare in medieval skeletons, reflecting a diet low in sugar, although tooth loss from other causes was fairly common: one surveyed sample found an average rate of 7.6 percent of teeth missing.

Nor did people die very young, as our estimates of life expectancy indicate. Life expectancy rates derive from an average life span that reflects the high childhood mortality rates. In fact, a fair number of people reached the age of 60 and beyond, and estimates indicate that at any given time some 10 percent of the population were over 60. We have some records of vigorously elderly medieval people: For example, the papal representative on the Fourth Crusade was about 90 years old. Thus, while diseases were rampant and health care sparse, some vigorous people lived long and productive lives (Singman, 55–57; Singman and McLean, 57–58).

To read about health and medicine in Elizabethan England, see the England entry in the section "Health and Science" in chapter 4 ("Intellectual Life") of volume 3; for 18th-century England, see the England entry in the section "Health and Medicine" in chapter 4 ("Intellectual Life") of volume 4; for Victorian England, see the England entry in the section "Health and Medicine" in chapter 4 ("Intellectual Life") of volume 5 of this series.

FOR MORE INFORMATION

Butt, J. J. *Daily Life in the Age of Charlemagne*. Westport, Conn.: Greenwood Press, 2002.

Singman, J. L. *Daily Life in Medieval Europe*. Westport, Conn.: Greenwood Press, 1999.

Singman, J. L., and W. McLean. *Daily Life in Chaucer's England*. Westport, Conn.: Greenwood Press, 1995.

VIKINGS

It is difficult to make an assessment of the health conditions among the Viking Age Scandinavians, and the sources are too few as to give us any concrete idea how they perceived health and sickness, except that there were no clear boundaries between the domains of medicine and religion. Not only did health mean freedom from disease; it also entailed the presence of good fortune. This good fortune could, however, be taken away by sorcery or the ill will of supernatural beings, in which case the restoration of health sometimes involved the aid of a healer, who could identify the sickness and cure it.

Little is known about the types of illnesses that were prevalent among the Viking Age Scandinavians, but poor sanitation and malnutrition were probably the causes of many ailments. Deficiency diseases, such as scurvy, must have been widespread, especially in the winter when food was often scarce. From skeletal evidence, it is also clear that osteoarthritis was common among adults. People frequently lacked one or more teeth, but dental cavities are rarely found (most certainly because of the absence of white sugar in the diet). As for epidemics, tuberculosis, typhus, relapsing fever, leprosy, and dysentery would seem probable candidates. Indeed, it is known that an epidemic of leprosy and bloody discharge occurred among the Vikings in Dublin, Ireland, in 949, and the historian William of Malmesbury (d. ca. 1143) tells of an outbreak of what was probably dysentery among the Danes in Kent, England. However, there is nothing to suggest the occurrence of plague epidemics in the Viking Age that caused severe population reduction in any given area.

Within Scandinavia and in the Norse colonies in the North Atlantic, people lived on farms scattered over a vast area or in small settlements, and the cities were few and far between and relatively small. This type of isolation probably offered some protection against contagious diseases, but it also left the local community unprotected when a new disease was carried in from another community. Once a person had contracted an infectious illness, it was likely to spread rapidly, for the sanitary conditions were deplorable and certainly in the countryside, it was the custom that the whole household slept together in the same room. Some people had farm animals in the houses where they lived, which would tend to increase the number of rats and fleas—both disseminators of disease—living in the immediate proximity of the household. Vikings customarily burned a deceased person's bedstraws, evidently in an attempt to prevent contagious diseases from spreading.

While epidemic disease appears to have been met with passive submission, there is evidence that efforts were made to treat other ailments either through herbal remedies or through diets, steam baths, purges, bloodletting (phlebotomy), or in the case of acute illnesses, surgical intervention. Not to be overlooked in terms of treatment and care is faith healing. In pagan times, such healing efforts involved the recitation of charms, consultation with a religious specialist, or the following of prescribed ritual procedures. In Christian times, they consisted of the invocation of God, Christ, the Virgin Mary, or various saints, especially the Fourteen Holy Helpers (a group of saints known for the efficacy of their intercession against various diseases and especially at the hour of death).

The use of herbal medicine was clearly common. Several herbs from classical Greek and Roman medicine were known and used in Scandinavia in the Viking Age, and to this knowledge was added local tradition and the use of local herbs. In his biography of the Norwegian king Olaf Haraldsson (*Olafs saga helga*), Snorri Sturluson includes an account of a healer's attempt to treat the king's poet by using herbal remedies. The author relates that the king's poet, Thormod, was struck right in the heart by an iron-tipped arrow and that a healer, who ministered to the wounded fighters, offered to treat his wounds. When the healer saw his wounds, she examined the one in his side and noticed that there was a piece of iron in it, although she did not know for certain where the iron had traveled. She gave the wounded man a brew with herbs and strong-smelling leeks to eat in an attempt to find out whether he had serious wounds, because a deep wound would smell like leeks and indicate that Thormod's intestines had been pierced.

Thormod, however, knew the wound was in his heart and not in his stomach, so he refused to eat the mixture with the comment that he did not suffer from "porridge illness." Accordingly, he requested a surgical approach; he instructed the healer to cut away the flesh around the piece of iron and subsequently grasped some tongs and wrenched out the arrowhead himself. Shorty afterward, however, he died—either from the severity of the wound or because of infections resulting from the surgery.

The healer in this story is a female, and in pagan times medical treatment appears to have been the province of women, who relied on their own observations, experiences, and, not least, health advice passed along by word of mouth from previous generations. Indeed, a stanza in the Eddic poem *Havamal* (Sayings of the High One) includes recommendations for the use of a variety of substances to maintain general health, such as oak to prevent constipation, an ear of corn to combat witchcraft, and earthworms for bites or stings. The advice found in *Havamal* is an example of the kind of lore that must have been widespread among Scandinavians in the Viking Age.

Scandinavia appears to have had little in the way of physicians. After the introduction of Christianity, most medical service was provided by men of the church, since many of them had some medical knowledge and were able to practice according to the principles of monastery medicine from central and southern Europe. Indeed, the first hospitals were established in connection with monasteries or churches, but almost all of these date from after the Viking Age.

~*Kirsten Wolf*

FOR MORE INFORMATION

Larrington, C., trans. *The Poetic Edda*. Oxford: Oxford University Press, 1996.
Wolf, K. *Daily Life of the Vikings*. Westport, Conn.: Greenwood Press, forthcoming.

CHINA

According to ancient Chinese thought, the causes of diseases were supernatural, natural, or a combination of both. They were also internal, external, or neither (overindulgence). In general, folklore and religion were the sources for beliefs in supernatural agents. Observations of the environment and human beings were the bases for theories that pathogens originated in nature. Supernatural agents that caused maladies included gods, ghosts, demons, and magic. The long-standing importance of ancient Chinese medicine, however, derived from those who believed that illness sprang from natural causes—a combination of the internal state of the body and environmental forces (not spirits).

The Chinese saw the body as a repository of vital energies and essences. Good health depended on preserving and nurturing those life forces. If people were moderate in their lifestyle and took measures to conserve inner resources, then their skin became an impenetrable husk that prevented energy and essence from leaking out, and an impregnable bulwark that thwarted attacks from external disease-causing agents. Chinese physicians contended that people could expect to live for 120 years in good health if they followed the proper practices. Otherwise, people would suffer from ailments, decrepitude, or senility and would die prematurely.

According to the advocates of the naturalistic conception of disease, the "nurturing of life" and promotion of longevity required the conservation of *qi*, the life force within the body. In humans, *qi* was breath (also thought of as energy). It was the first thing given to a human being at conception and the last thing to depart at death. Between those two poles, *qi* circulated throughout the body, and good health depended on its uninterrupted flow. Many medical treatments involved balancing the flow of *qi*. For example, the theory of acupuncture argues that the body contained a network of invisible conduits, analogous to arteries or the nervous system, through which *qi* flows continuously. The system consists of 12 major channels that run under the surface of the skin from the extremities to the head or chest, plus a web of minor branches connecting neighboring channels. Along the course of the channels, there are minute cavities or pores that serve as regulators of the *qi*'s current. Initially, the medical canon identified 365 points, but by the Tang dynasty, the number had grown to 670. A physician can restore the normal rate of flow and redress imbalances in the network by inserting needles into the cavities or points situated along the ducts.

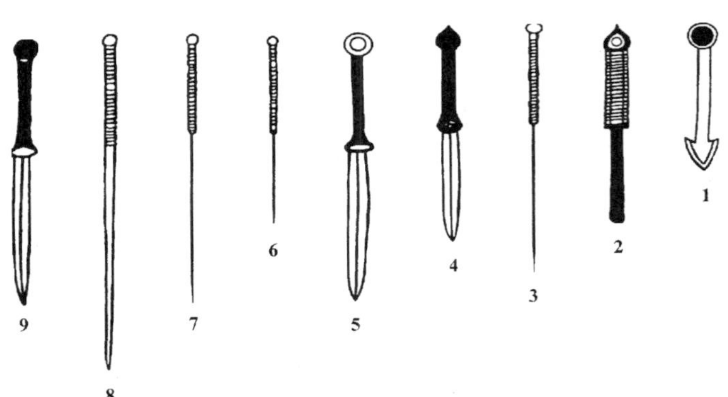

Acupuncture needles. Illustration by Charles Benn.

Moxibustion was a therapy that called for burning cones of dry, powdered mugwort—a shrub with strong-smelling leaves—on acupuncture points to balance the *qi*. The area scorched could not exceed three-tenths of an inch. When it was used to relieve pain, the physician repeated the process until the discomfort ceased. That meant using as many as 50, 100, or more cones. Moxibustion was often employed after acupuncture to enhance its effects. In addition to balancing *qi*, moxibustion was believed to have its own particular therapeutic benefits. Doctors burned the cones on boils and carbuncles to burst them so that their pus would flow out. Whenever a snake bit a person, mugwort was burned on the wound. A single burning would cure the victim immediately if the person acted quickly. If not, the victim would die at once. The cauterization left scars that usually disappeared in a short time.

To determine what sort of treatment he would use for an ailing patient, a Chinese physician made a diagnosis based on careful observation. First, he conducted a visual inspection of the sufferer's physical appearance—face, tongue, lips, and teeth—to find signs of disease. Besides looking for obvious manifestations of a pathological condition, such as ulcers, tumors, rashes, swellings, and the like, he watched for abnormal skin colorations that indicated problems in an organ. For example, a bluish tinge indicated a dysfunction in the liver, and a red tinge indicated a dysfunction in the heart. He checked facial expressions that reflected suffering. In the early 7th century, a disease that caused swellings struck a preeminent official, so the emperor called in a physician to make a diagnosis. After looking the patient over, the doctor declared that the official would die at noon 11 days later. The minister expired precisely on schedule. A diagnosis was sometimes a prognosis as well.

Second, the doctor carried out an auditory and olfactory examination. He listened to the patient's breathing and voice. The physician was interested in detecting coughing, panting, or wheezing, which were symptoms of lung diseases. A feeble voice or delirious speech indicated debilitating illness or madness, respectively. He also took notice of foul body odor, bad breath, and malodorous feces. Some amateurs went to repulsive extremes with regard to the latter examination. In 692, Guo Ba, a sycophantic subordinate of Censor Wei, who was in bed with an illness, paid a visit to inquire after his superior's health. Distressed and alarmed by Wei's appearance, Guo asked to see his stools. After tasting them, Guo declared, "If your excrement had been sweet, then you would probably have had no chance for a cure. However, its flavor is bitter, so you will certainly recover" (Benn, 229).

Unquestionably, the most prevalent remedy for treating illnesses in traditional times was diet, including largely herbal drugs and prescriptions. In 657, the Tang court published the first official *materia medica* in Chinese history. When the emperor commissioned the project, he ordered local officials to have pictures of curative substances in their districts drawn and sent to the capital. The drawings became illustrations for the compilation. By far the greatest factor in the diversity of the Chinese diet, then as now, was the search for substances that could cure illnesses, prolong life, and confer immortality. The search for things to promote health and longevity led medicine men to investigate and classify the benefits of all sorts of animals (dogs, asses, tigers, porcupines, badgers, wolves, hedgehogs, bats, whales, humans), birds (storks, goatsuckers, cuckoos, crested mynahs, goshawks, owls), fish (carp, eels, sharks, cuttlefish, stingrays, sea horses), reptiles (alligators, geckos, pit vipers, sea snakes), amphibians (toads), insects (praying mantises, bombardier beetles, spiders, dung beetles, fireflies, mosquitoes, centipedes, lice), plants (chrysanthemums, camphor, eggplant, hemp, ferns, jasmine), and minerals (gold, silver, mercury, arsenic, mica, copper, iron, lead, jade, coral, pearls). No doubt those who searched for these products were also largely responsible for introducing all sorts of parts from animals and plants into the cuisine of China. For example, the ubiquitous pig yielded its head, lard, brain, heart, liver, spleen, kidneys, pancreas, stomach, bladder, intestines, testicles, feet, snout, lips, tongue, teeth, tail, and nails, as well as various fluids and excreta, such as blood, milk, sweat, bile, and feces, for healing prescriptions. Not all of the substances or parts listed ended up on the table, but many did. A clear distinction between drugs and food did not, and does not, exist in Chinese fare (Benn, 119–26, 219–41).

FOR MORE INFORMATION

Benn, C. *Daily Life in Traditional China: The Tang Dynasty*. Westport, Conn.: Greenwood Press, 2002.

ISLAMIC WORLD

In the Middle Ages, medicine in the Muslim world was intimately tied up with the study of science, and in these enterprises, the Islamic world shone. See the Islamic World entry in the section "Science" in this chapter for a discussion of Islamic science, which includes their medical advances.

INTELLECTUAL LIFE
HEALTH & MEDICINE
Europe
Vikings
China
Byzantium
Mongols

BYZANTIUM

Medical knowledge and practices in Byzantium reflect both classical Greek scientific theories and prevailing social views, encompassing elements of astrology, demonology, folklore, and magic. Most classical treatises and handbooks, including the works of Galen and the encyclopedists of late antiquity, are known today by compilations assembled during the Byzantine period and ultimately translated into Arabic and Latin. Historical chronicles document the availability of specialized medical care among the upper classes, as well as the widespread reputation of Byzantine doctors. Saints' lives, guidebooks, and other vernacular sources provide glimpses of the more limited medical resources and alternative therapies available to most Byzantine subjects. Many of these sources record a basic tension between the roles of medical practice and religious belief in the healing process.

Byzantine medical knowledge rested on familiarity with the works of Hippocrates, who lived in the 5th–4th centuries B.C.E., and Galen of Pergamon, a Greek doctor who wrote a series of theoretical treatises and practical manuals in the 2nd century C.E. The medicinal benefits of various plants were known by the pharmacological writings of Dioscorides, Theophrastus, and other early authors. Byzantine medical writers built on this foundation by evaluating the classical literature and including fresh observations and commentary on the effectiveness of specific remedies. Several medical encyclopedias were produced in late antiquity.

Medical training in Byzantium entailed a period of apprenticeship combined with attending lectures of medical professors (*iatrosophistes*). Alexandria was the most prestigious center for training doctors and attracted students from across the Mediterranean region from Ptolemaic times until the early 7th century. The standard curriculum lasted about four years and covered the basic works of Hippocrates and Galen, which provided a broad theoretical training in anatomy, physiology, etiology, diagnostics, and therapeutics. Later students also referred to medical handbooks written by Oreibasios of Pergamon, Aetios of Amida, and Alexander of Tralles.

Alexander composed his *Twelve Books on Medicine* in the mid-6th century. Drawing on a lifetime of practical experience, the work critically reviews the teachings of classical Greek medical theory and outlines the treatments Alexander found most effective in his practice. He stresses that as a general rule, the therapeutic benefits of diet and hygiene are preferable to treatment with drugs. The importance of maintaining the comfort of the patient is central to his approach, and Alexander concedes the usefulness of amulets, charms, and folk remedies if they are believed to work.

The most important institution in Byzantine medicine was the hospital (*xenon*), which developed from a charitable foundation to become a key feature of urban life. The earliest *xenone* apparently were guesthouses located near thermal springs with fresh air and water, places that were often associated with classical healing sites. Under church sponsorship, such facilities came to play a special role in the care of the poor, sick, and elderly. In the early 5th century, several larger cities are known to have had a special treatment center (*nosokomeion*) staffed by priests, doctors, cooks, and other support staff. By the 7th century, several *xenone* had been built in Constantinople, where they became the main location of medical care. All of these places were administered by clergymen but were staffed by physicians with various specialties. Doctors normally were expected to divide their time equally between providing subsidized health services for hospital residents and caring for private patients. The clearest picture of the operation of an urban hospital is the *xenon* attached to the monastery of Christ Pantokrator in Constantinople, founded in 1136 by the emperor John II Komnenos and his wife, Irene. A walk-in clinic was available for the treatment of minor injuries and ailments. More serious cases resulted in admission by the attending physicians, who then prescribed a course of treatment. Nurses and other medical assistants assisted doctors in carrying out minor procedures and giving medicines. Women were cared for by female physicians and midwives. A further responsibility of medical staff at the Pantokrator *xenon* was to train their children to become the next generation of doctors.

The practice of surgery is known primarily from literary sources. The *Epitome of Medicine*, written by Paul of Aegina in the 7th century, surveys 120 surgical operations as well as the instruments needed to perform them. Later sources tend not to be as comprehensive in scope, which implies that surgery may have become less routine in later times, at least outside of Constantinople. Autopsies and dissections continued to be widely performed. Archaeological excavations in Greece, Egypt, and other parts of the Byzantine Empire have recovered such surgical implements as probes, knives, chisels, and bifurcated tools. Most of these were made of bronze and were finely finished. The written sources suggest that basic instrument shapes remained essentially unchanged.

Public health concerns in larger Byzantine cities focused on maintaining civic sanitation and a safe water supply, especially during the warm summer months. Among the most serious challenges were recurring outbreaks of pandemic disease. The great plague (*loimos*) of the mid-6th century may have originated in East Africa and in 541 arrived in Egypt, from which it spread rapidly across the empire. Cities were depopulated and entire villages were wiped out in its wake. Contemporary observers such as Procopios and John of Ephesus described how corpses were left unburied in streets and plazas and mass burials were common. The population of Constantinople may have been reduced by as much as half during this period. The plague subsided by 545 but recurred throughout the Byzantine and early Islamic Near East through the mid-8th century. Centuries later, the Black Death swept across Asia and devastated Constantinople in 1348–49, before spreading to northern Europe. While mortality estimates are uncertain, both of these great pandemics clearly reduced the empire's human resources and left it seriously weakened.

More pervasive health problems were apparent especially among the lower social levels and often were addressed by miraculous means. The average life expectancy of 35–40 years for men (somewhat less for women) stems in part from shortcomings of the prevailing diet. Food production suffered from recurring drought, floods, hail, insect pests, and political instability, while difficulties of transport and storage led to shortages and famine, especially as grain supplies dwindled in spring. Saints' lives regularly mention the aid of a supernatural intercessor during such critical times. Saints Cosmas, Damian, and other healing saints were known as *anargyroi* (silverless ones) for working cures without charge. Similar remedies could involve visiting or sleeping near a sacred site or tomb, which later sources sometimes referred to as the "free hospital."

~Marcus Rautman

FOR MORE INFORMATION

Miller, T. S. *The Birth of the Hospital in the Byzantine Empire*. Baltimore, Md.: Johns Hopkins University Press, 1985.

Nutton, V. "Medicine in Late Antiquity and the Early Middle Ages." In *The Western Medical Tradition, 800 B.C. to A.D. 1800,* edited by L. I. Conrad, M. Leve, V. Hutton, R. Porter, and A. Wear. Cambridge, England: Cambridge University Press, 1995.

MONGOLS

At the height of their empire in the late 13th and early 14th centuries, the Mongols had access to and use of the major medical systems of Eurasia, namely, Chinese, Korean, Tibetan, Indian, Uighur, Islamic, and Nestorian Christian. Individual princes were accompanied by their own retinue of medical teams selected from this pool of medical expertise and learning. Although they also retained their traditional shamans (holy men), whose role included treatment of disease and physical ailments, the Mongols differentiated between the various medical practitioners and the native shamans. The term *otochi* was applied to the foreign doctors, who were identified as using herbs and drugs, *em,* whereas the Mongol shamans relied on spiritual powers and magic to treat and cure.

On the steppe, it was the shaman whose skills were called upon in cases of sickness and disease; one of his, or even her, first functions was to establish whether the affliction had its origin in natural sources or in malevolent witchcraft. These medieval shamans were sometimes referred to as "physicians" (*t abīb*), although their main skill remained in prophecy. However, with increasing contact with the non-nomadic world, the influence of the shamans, particularly in medical matters, decreased.

Chinese medicine was pervasive in the Mongol Empire, even though evidence of other systems is certainly widespread. With their westward spread, the Mongol commanders took with them Chinese physicians who spread their influence to the local population. Records reveal that all the Mongol rulers who traveled west retained physicians trained in East Asian medicine. The Persian sources from the Il-khanid period (1256–1335), when the Mongols ruled Iran, clearly demonstrate the penetration of Chinese medicine into western Asia. The chief minister for Ghazan Khan (d. 1304) and Öljeitü Khan (d. 1316), the historian and statesman Rashīd al-Dīn started his career as both a chef and a physician. Both occupations were held in great esteem at this time and Rashīd al-Dīn's interest in medicine is reflected both in his writings and in his successful efforts to introduce Chinese medicine to his homeland, Iran. He is commonly known as Rashīd al-Dīn T abīb (the physician), and among his greatest achievements was the establishment of the Rab^{c}-i Rashīdī quarter of Tabriz (northwest Iran), which contained a famous house of healing.

The Chinese introduced various medical practices to the Mongols and hence their subjects in other parts of the empire. These included the use of drugs, various folk medicines and potions, acupuncture, which uses needles to stimulate "power points" and "energy channels" in the body, and moxibustion, which achieves the same results through the use of heat, applied through the dried, powdered, and burnt leaves of the tree *Artemisia moxa*. However, in western Asia and Iran in particular, it was the ancient Chinese technique of "pulse diagnosis" that was most admired, and its introduction to the West can be traced to the Mongols. The papal envoy William of Rubruck spoke highly of the Chinese herbalists and practitioners of pulse diagnosis on his visit (1253–55) to the Mongol capital, Qaraqorum. Various books on the technique were translated into Mongolian.

Although Chinese medical influence was pervasive, there is evidence that the western half of the Mongol Empire also contributed to the health of the Mongol lords and their subjects.

Nestorian Christians had long had an influential presence in East Asia, and some of the Mongol tribes were adherents of the Nestorian creed. Indeed, Dokuz Khātūn, the wife of Hülegü Khan (d. 1265), ruler of Iran (r. 1256–65), was a devout Nestorian Christian. Just as they had in the Muslim west, the Nestorians in the east had a tradition of involvement in the medical profession. They are credited with being the conduit of the Galenic tradition (Galen of Pergumum, d. 217) to the Arabs. The presence of their communities in central Asia and the east facilitated the flow of Western medicine to China and the Turco-Mongol steppe lands. Many central Asian Uighurs were Nestorians, and it was the Uighurs in particular who formed such an influential part of the Mongol administration. West Asian Nestorians received a warm welcome in the Mongol courts. The physician Simeon, named Rabban Ata by the Great Khan, Ögödei, used his medical skills to gain political influence at the Mongol court, which he used to advance Christian communities in the Muslim west. Nestorians became prominent in medical circles under the Yuan dynasty

(Mongol China, 1260–1370). Often their practices, innovations, and infusions were known locally and generically as "Muslim" (*Hui-hui*) medicine, and they would certainly have incorporated the teachings and traditions of the Persian physician Ibn Sina (also known as Avicenna; d. 1037) into their practices.

The physicians of western Asia are thought to have introduced a number of medicines to the east through the agency of the Mongol courts. Two pharmaceutical bureaus (*Hui-hui yao-wu yuan*) were established by the Yuan court to manage the influx of "Muslim" medicines. Mastic (a resin of *Pistacia lentisus*), nux vomica (the seed of the fruit of the strychnine tree), the electuary sherbets, and the compound drug theriaca, used as an antidote for animal and insect venom and later a popular cure-all throughout the empire, are just the best known examples of this West to East travel.

Sherbets were used as refreshment and restoratives and as vehicles to facilitate the ingestion of other medicines; Rashīd al-Dīn mentions their widespread usage by western Asian physicians. They first appeared in China during the Yuan dynasty, and the il-khans of Iran became devotees of sherbet. Nestorians from Samarqand were the earliest recorded sherbet makers in China. Kublai Khan created the office of official sherbet maker, one holder of which was Marsarchis (Mar Sargis), whom Marco Polo encountered in Cinghianfu.

The popular cure-all theriaca, a mainstay of Muslim and eastern Christian pharmaceutical supplies, became a particular favorite with the Mongol elite. Various sources record large rewards being given to suppliers and providers of theriaca by grateful Mongol rulers. One explanation for this attachment to theriaca by these Mongol rulers is probably the concoction's reputation as an antidote to all known toxins and venoms because princes had a well-founded fear of poisoning. The Muslim il-khan of Iran, Ghazan (r. 1295–1304), had his own special antidote made up for him that he honored with his name, *tirāq* [theriaca]-i Ghāzānī.

One result of the Mongols' interest in medicine, their encouragement of various medical disciplines, and their willingness to act as the agency of cross-cultural interaction and exchange, is the existence of a number of medical books and particularly pharmacopoeias. The two traditions, Galenic, based on the theory of humors, and the Chinese, with its yin and yang and five agencies, remained deeply suspicious of each other, but mutual borrowing is evident and the Mongols used freely of both traditions. This can be seen in their pharmacopoeias, which were enriched through the contacts made possible by political union. Scholars such as Rashīd al-Dīn and the Mongol statesman Bolad encouraged and enabled the exchange of medical knowledge, but it was the establishment of the Mongol Empire that created the agency for such an exchange.

~George Lane

FOR MORE INFORMATION

Allsen, T. T. *Culture and Conquest in Mongol Eurasia*. Cambridge, England: Cambridge University Press, 2001.

Boyle, J. A. *The Mongol World Empire 1206–1370*. London: Variorum Reprints, 1977.
Budge, E. A. W., trans. *The Monks of Kūblāi Khan*. London: Religious Tract Society, 1928.

INTELLECTUAL LIFE: WEB SITES

http://icg.harvard.edu/~chaucer/
http://www.amnh.org/exhibitions/vikings/write.html
http://www.china.org.cn/e-gudai/8.htm
http://www.logoi.com/notes/chinese_origins.html
http://www.med.virginia.edu/hs-library/historical/antiqua/texte.htm
http://www.ummah.net/history/scholars/

5

MATERIAL LIFE

MATERIAL LIFE

FOOD

DRINK

HOUSING

CLOTHING

FABRICS

PERSONAL APPEARANCE

FURNISHINGS

TECHNOLOGY

Material life describes all the things we use, from the houses that give us shelter to the food that sustains us, the clothes that protect us, and the items that amuse us. It also includes the luxury items that set us apart from others less fortunate than we. Studying material life is fascinating in the details it provides. We learn that handkerchiefs were a luxury in 16th-century Europe designed to set the wealthy apart from the peasant who used a hat or sleeve, or that underwear was only widely adopted in Europe in the 18th century.

Aside from the delicious details that bring the past to life, the study of material life reveals much about society as a whole. For example, cultures that rely on rice as a major staple have to invest a great deal of labor into its cultivation, whereas societies that thrive on corn (maize), which is not labor intensive, have ample spare time. People who had access to raw materials, such as iron ore, developed in ways different from those who did not, and groups that had domesticated animals or large plows had different organizing principles from others. If we know what a culture uses, we know a great deal about those people's lives.

As we study material life, it is important to remember that humans want much more than the bare necessities of life. Indeed, we are creatures of desire rather than need, and this longing has fueled much of the progress in the world. We want spices to flavor our food, not just nourishment; we want gold to adorn us as much as we want clothing to cover us. Cultures (such as in the West) who have acquired a taste for change in fashion transform themselves (not necessarily for the better) in all areas much more rapidly than those (such as in Asia) who preferred a more conservative approach to clothing. All in all, the details of our daily life matter. From the Stone Age, when humans adorned themselves with cowrie shells as they wielded stone tools, to the modern world shaped by high technology, humans have been defined by the things we use. Our material life reveals and shapes who we are.

During the Middle Ages, people's material life was largely determined by the goods that were locally accessible. Polynesian diet was different from European diet because of what they had. Similarly, people built houses out of bamboo or sticks or stucco or wood or sod, depending on what was available. In modern times, many of us are used to making decisions based on what we want because we can assume that almost everything in the world is available to us.

For food products, because there was no refrigeration, medieval people had to depend largely on local produce—food that could be delivered within one day's travel. Beyond that, people had to try other ways to preserve food. Meat was salted, or in the cold north of Scandinavia, it could be "freeze-dried" by hanging it outdoors in a frigid wind. Some fruits—such as apples—could also be dried to preserve them. However, the easiest way to preserve some food was by fermenting it and turning it into alcoholic beverages. We think of beer and wine as additions to a meal, but peoples during the Middle Ages depended on fermentation to preserve grains and grapes for use as a source of needed calories. The process of fermentation extended to mare's milk among the Mongols of the steppes or date palms in the oases of the deserts.

While all peoples creatively used whatever was available, people in the Middle Ages nevertheless longed for the exotic. This desire stimulated a long-distance trade that although extremely difficult, was sufficiently lucrative to spur merchants on to risk the hazards of travel. With this trade, the rich could set themselves apart through diet—Europeans could add spices from the East to their otherwise bland fare, and Chinese imported dates from Persian palm trees. The rich also set themselves apart by exotic clothing: Europeans longed for silks and cotton from the East, while Chinese paid high prices for fine woolens from Europe. Like today, there is no price too great for some people to pay to acquire what is new and rare. Medieval people, like ourselves, liked to set themselves apart by what they could purchase.

~*Joyce E. Salisbury*

FOR MORE INFORMATION

Braudel, F. *The Structures of Everyday Life*. New York: Harper and Row, 1979.
Diamond, J. *Guns, Germs, and Steel*. New York: Norton, 1997.

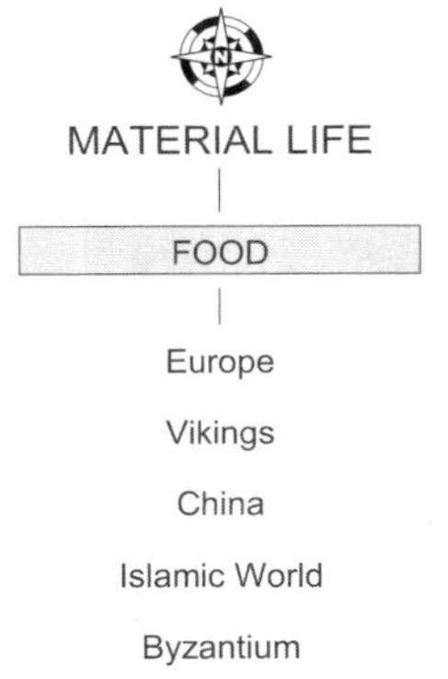

Food

The path to understanding much of human daily life is through the stomach. We are what we eat, and our cultures are organized to feed us. Some aspects of food are universal. We all want diets with enough calories so we don't feel hunger, and beyond that we want diets that provide some balance of the nutrients we need, and this was long before we had experts to tell us what constitutes a balanced diet. People all over the world seek roughly three basic foodstuffs: grains (or other starches), fruits and vegetables, and protein. Beyond these basic needs, people had to select foods from those available to them, and this fact began to separate cultures.

In western Europe and the Byzantine Empire, wheat was the queen of grains. It grew all around the Mediterranean and as far north in Europe as climate permitted. Farther north in Scandinavia, hardier grains predominated: rye, oats, and barley. In China and other parts of Asia, rice reigned supreme. Although wheat had been farmed earlier than rice by about 3,000 years, once rice was cultivated it displaced wheat in many parts of Asia. For comparison, wheat made up 50 to 70 percent of the diet of people who grew it, while rice made up 80 to 90 percent of rice-growing people's diet. Rice also offers much higher yields per acre than wheat (Braudel, 145). Thus rice-growing regions could support higher populations. By the Middle Ages, regions of China used the labor-intensive means of cultivating rice in paddy fields that were highly irrigated and tended constantly to keep the water moving through the plants. Polynesians lacked these grains, so their starches came from breadfruits, taro roots, and yams.

In all these cases, there is no mention of the corn or potatoes that we today take for granted as a rich dietary source. These crops only entered Europe and Asia after the European discovery of the New World that fostered them. Those would only appear after the 15th century.

Fruits and vegetable products were abundant everywhere and always served as an important part of diets. In fact, the poor in Europe and elsewhere ate a larger proportion of vegetables than the wealthy because vegetables were more abundant and thus had diets healthier by our standards than those who ate more meat and sweets. Everything from cabbages to turnips to coconuts to chestnuts supplemented the starchy diets of the world.

Protein consumption tells a more complicated tale of worldwide food intake. Animal protein is expensive compared with vegetable protein, so regions with a high population density (like China) ate diets with less animal protein. Plant protein, however, in the form of beans and other legumes made for better health. The Chinese planted and used soy extensively, and in western Europe in the 12th century, health improved dramatically when people began to regularly plant legumes.

Most people, however, preferred animal protein because it provides the most concentrated form of protein calories. Vikings, for example, ate a large amount of fish, usually salted or dried to preserve it. The Europeans ate the most meat per capita throughout the Middle Ages. There was still land for animals to graze, and game was still relatively abundant. It was only after 1550 that meat consumption in Europe went down.

Despite the volume of meat Europeans ate, however, they were more fussy than most other peoples on what *kind* of meat they consumed. In general, Christian Europe prohibited the eating of carnivores (with the exception of omnivorous pigs). Muslims joined Jews in forbidding the eating of pigs, and thus Christians and Muslims found one more reason to disagree on the proper way to behave. Upper-class Byzantines preferred sheep and goats and considered pork to be a more rustic food source. The Chinese were the most omnivorous of all when it came to protein—reptiles, monkeys, snakes, and bears found their way to the Chinese tables. The Polynesians were more limited in the mammals available for food—pigs and dogs were the only domesticated animals—but seafood was present in abundance. The Byzantines, too, favored the seafood and shellfish that were so available in the Mediterranean Sea.

Once people had satisfied their basic dietary needs, the universal human desire for novelty prevailed. The desire for new tastes would fuel the explorations of the 15th century and beyond, but it also stimulated trade in the Middle Ages. China imported exotic foods such as pomegranates from the West, and Eastern spices were in constant demand on Western tables. The Byzantines discovered sugar from Egypt, and their desserts reflected that delicious taste. Food is more than fuel for the body; it was always seen as a pleasure that people would spare no cost in developing.

~*Joyce E. Salisbury*

FOR MORE INFORMATION

Braudel, F. *The Structures of Everyday Life*. New York: Harper and Row, 1979.
Fiddes, N. *Meat*. New York: Routledge, 1991.
Salisbury, J. E. *The Beast Within: Animals in the Middle Ages*. New York: Routledge, 1994.

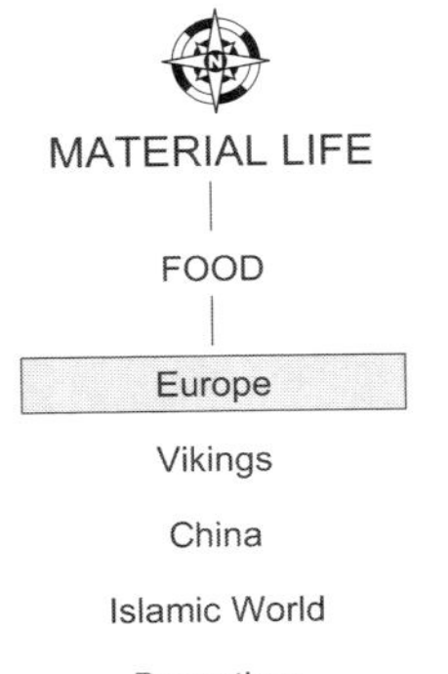

EUROPE

People's social and economic status determined the food they ate. Ironically, the diet of working commoners in Europe may actually have been healthier than that of the aristocracy, at least in terms of nutritional balance. The wealthy were able to indulge a taste for fine and rich foods with higher proportions of red meat, sugar, and fat, whereas the common people consumed more fiber and vegetables. The aristocratic diet also included a great deal of meat, principally beef, followed by pork and mutton, with game and poultry as the smallest component. The medieval aristocracy ate a much greater range of meats than is common today. Not only did they consume domestic livestock such as cows, sheep, pigs, chicken, geese, and ducks, but they also hunted game such as deer, boars, rabbits, and wildfowl. Dairy and egg products were found in the aristocratic diet but were not particularly favored. Neither were vegetables, which mostly appeared as flavorings in the form of leeks, onions, garlic, or herbs. Sweets, including conserves and sugar candy, were also a feature of the aristocratic diet. The daily ration for a person living in an aristocratic household typically included two to three pounds of wheat bread, two to three pounds of meat or fish, and a gallon of ale.

A prosperous peasant might consume two to three pounds of bread, eight ounces of meat or fish, and two to three pints of ale per day. Because meat was expensive, it was not necessarily a regular part of a commoner's diet. Those who could afford it ate the same sorts of meats as the aristocracy, although perhaps somewhat less beef and somewhat more pork and mutton. In place of meat, protein was more likely to be supplied by eggs, butter, and cheese; herring was another inexpensive source of protein. Vegetables figured more prominently here than in the diet of the aristocrat. Beans and bacon were the main food of the peasant. Commoners were generally not supposed to hunt, but they sometimes poached rabbits and wildfowl in defiance of the laws.

Farther down the economic scale, people were more likely to consume their grains boiled whole in pottages, puddings, or gruel, rather than in the form of bread, and depend more heavily on beans and milk products as protein sources. Dairy products were consumed in various forms. Plain milk could be curdled, and the curds either eaten as is or used to make cheese. Cheese was an extremely important staple, as it preserved better than unprocessed milk. The whey, a watery liquid remaining after the curds are removed, was also used as a drink. The diet of the lower classes seems to have improved during this period, as a part of the general rise in the standard of living of the poor following the Black Death in the 14th century. Wage earners during this period were able to negotiate improved rations for their work: one contract from 1397 stipulates a daily ration of two pounds of beef or mutton, four pints of ale, and two pounds of wheat bread (Singman and McLean, 160).

Ordinary people ate their food all at once, but those of social pretensions had it served in a number of courses. Many menus survive for a variety of the more formal sorts of meals, ranging from the dinner and supper of a townsman to the coronation feasts of a monarch. Such menus generally consisted of three to six courses, each being made up of a number of dishes. More elaborate meals might include special dishes between courses (called an "entremess" or "subtlety"), sometimes artfully designed to delight the eye as well as the palate.

The sequence of a medieval menu contrasts markedly from a modern one. Today, we proceed from salad or soup to main course and dessert. Fancy medieval meals were more likely to proceed from the heavier dishes to the more delicate ones. There was no dessert as such, and sweet dishes were mingled among the rest. The diners' status might determine how many of the courses they received. Everyone present was served the first course, but sometimes only the most privileged tables received the last one.

A woman cooks over an open hearth. This was the main cooking method throughout the medieval West. Illustration by Will McLean.

Bread was a staple food for all people and was invariably present at meals. Loaves of bread were always placed on the table to be eaten, in addition to sliced bread used as plates, called trenchers. The type of bread served and its freshness depended on the status of the host and guest. The finest breads were known as *pain-demain*, *wastel*, *cocket*, and simnel; these were made with highly refined wheat flour (although even the finest was not as white as modern white flour). Such flour was finely sifted to extract bran and husk. Less-expensive wheat breads were made with flour that had been sifted less finely and consequently had a higher proportion of bran and husk. This made the flour darker and more coarse but added bulk and significant nutritional value. Less-expensive breads were made from rye, barley, oats, or a mixture of grains. Poor people also ate oatcakes. Biscuits, which had a low water content and therefore preserved well, were useful for long journeys and sea voyages. In times of scarcity, people sometimes had to eat bread made with peas, beans, or even ground acorns. The bread was not baked in pans, so it was typically round in shape.

The range of vegetables was probably less diverse than it is today, especially because of the difficulties of preservation. Onions, leeks, cabbage, garlic, turnips, parsnips, peas, and beans were all staples. Among fruits, plums, cherries, pears, grapes, strawberries, figs, and apples all grew in England. Nuts, particularly walnuts and hazelnuts, were also to be found domestically. Other vegetable foods, such as almonds and dates, were imported.

The actual content of any given meal was much more dependent on the season than is the case today. Fruits and vegetables came into season at specific times of the year, and not all could be preserved for consumption at other times. Meats could generally be preserved, but for many people fresh meat was available for only part of the year.

People also ate a variety of seafood, especially herring and cod; eels, mussels, and oysters were common as well. An important feature of the medieval menu related to "fish days." The church designated certain days as occasions for religious penance. On these days, people were forbidden to eat meat, which in strictest usage included eggs and dairy products but did not include fish or shellfish. Sea mammals such as porpoises were considered fish for these purposes, as were barnacle geese (the name derives from the medieval belief that these birds hatched from barnacles), but such foods were not often found on the tables of ordinary people.

Fish days occurred every Friday and Saturday; they might also be observed on Wednesdays and on the evenings before major feast days. Not everyone observed the Wednesday and Saturday fasts, but they were especially called upon to do so on the "Ember Days." These were the Wednesday, Friday, and Saturday after the first Sunday in Lent (six weeks before Easter), after Whitsunday (six weeks after Easter), after Holy Cross Day (September 14), and after St. Lucy's Day (December 13). Fish days were also in force throughout all weekdays of Lent and, for the pious, during Advent. Exceptions were made for pregnant or nursing women, the very young, the very old, the sick and the poor, and in some cases, laborers. It was even possible to purchase an exemption. Nevertheless, the vast majority of the populace apparently followed the strictures to at least some degree. As a result, people consumed a great deal more fish than is common today.

Medieval people liked their meals strongly flavored, but scarcity of spices prevented their everyday use. Most spices used in 14th-century cooking are still familiar today. It is often suggested that huge amounts of spice were used either to mask spoiled meat or to ostentatiously display wealth, but recent research suggests that this was not really the case. In fact, household accounts of the period suggest that no more spices were used per person than today, and in some cases even less. Spices were much more expensive in the 14th century than they are today, and smaller amounts would have been required to display wealth. Moreover, evidence suggests that imported spices were saved for special occasions. For daily use, people relied on ordinary seasonings such as salt, vinegar, mustard, onions, and garlic. Other domestic herbs included parsley, scallions, cress, and chervil. Another important flavoring agent was verjuice, the juice of sour apples or grapes.

Among imported spices, the most common were pepper, ginger, cinnamon, cloves, and nutmeg; of these, pepper and ginger were the cheapest. Sugar, a fairly expensive commodity, was also used as a spice rather than as a basic ingredient as we use it today. Candies and sweet dishes did exist, but desserts as we know them were not a feature of the 14th-century table. Honey was available domestically but was a relative luxury. For most people, the principal source of sugars was fruit; baked apples would be as close as one would get to what we might call a dessert.

Spices were often used in ways quite different from modern Western cooking: medieval flavorings had more in common with modern Near Eastern and Indian cuisine. Some spices were used primarily or entirely for their coloring effects: saunders (ground red sandalwood) and the root of the plant alkanet gave a red coloring, and turnsole (a Mediterranean plant) yielded blue, for example. Part of the appeal of saffron, which features in many recipes, was the rich golden color it imparted.

The simplest meal was breakfast, which was not normally reckoned as a meal at all: it appears to have been an informal, catch-as-catch-can affair, consisting perhaps of leftovers from the previous day or of a sop, a popular snack consisting of bread dipped in wine, ale, milk, or water. As in England today, fish was sometimes eaten at breakfast. The principal meals of the day were dinner, served around midday, and supper, which took place in the evening. Practice varied as to which was the larger meal of the two. Some people also had a mid-afternoon snack of bread and ale called a "noon-shenche," or nuncheon, ultimately the source of the modern word "luncheon" or "lunch." The truly decadent ate an extra meal late at night called a "rear-supper."

Snapshot

Food Fun in Medieval Europe

Some medieval recipe books included jokes. Some recipes were made of impossible ingredients to give an equally impossible result, as shown here:

> "Prepare a tasty little dish of stickleback stomach and flies' feet and larks' tongues, titmouse legs, and frogs' throats. This way you can live a long and carefree life." (Adamson, 177)

Other recipes produce a trick designed to shock the diners at the table.

The following will make the cooked meat look as if it was full of worms:

> "Cut up tiny pieces of the heart or dried blood of some animals. Strew the particles upon the piece of cooked meat, whose heat will make the raw particles move like worms." (Adamson, 184)

The following recipe will make white wine turn red at the table:

> "In summer, take the red flowers that grow in wheat and dry them so they can be made into powder. Secretly throw them into a glass with the wine, and it will turn red." (Bayar, 130)

In the Middle Ages, people were distinguished by the foods they ate. The variety of choices, the quantities, and the method of presentation all varied according to one's social class (Singman and McLean, 159–64).

To read about food in Elizabethan England, see the England entry in the section "Food and Drink" in chapter 5 ("Material Life") of volume 3; for 18th-century England, see the England entry in the section "Food" in chapter 5 ("Material Life") of volume 4; and for Victorian England, see the England entry in the section "Food" in chapter 5 ("Material Life") of volume 5 of this series.

FOR MORE INFORMATION

Adamson, M. W. "The Games Cooks Play: Non-Sense Recipes and Practical Jokes in Medieval Literature." In *Food in the Middle Ages: A Book of Essays*. New York: Garland, 1995.

Bayar, Tania, trans. *A Medieval Home Companion*. New York: HarperCollins, 1991.

Singman, J. L., and W. McLean. *Daily Life in Chaucer's England*. Westport, Conn.: Greenwood Press, 1995.

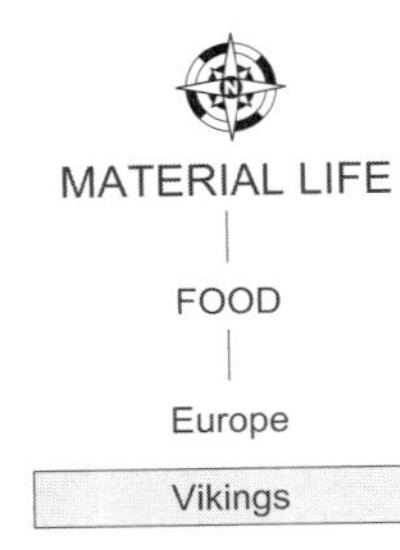

VIKINGS

Viking Age Scandinavians ate two meals a day, one in the morning and one in the evening. The food was served in the main hall, and people ate sitting on the raised platforms along the long walls of the house. Well-to-do people probably had tables and tablecloths.

People normally ate with their fingers off flat wooden trenchers. A short-bladed knife, which they typically carried around with them, was used to chop up the food. Some foods, such as porridge, soups, and stews, were served in wooden bowls and eaten with spoons of wood or antler. Ale and mead were drunk from the horns of cattle, which might be ornamented with metal mounts. One problem involved in drinking from a horn is, of course, that it cannot be put down, so a horn must have had to be drained at once or else circulated. Other beverages were drunk from wooden cups or silver bowls. The latter were probably reserved for wine. Glasses, which had to be imported, were uncommon and used only by wealthy people.

The types of food consumed varied from region to region and depended on available resources, but it is reasonable to assume that the diet was based primarily on dairy products, meat, and fish. Milk from cows, sheep, or goats was drunk, used in the preparation of various dishes, or processed. It was often separated into curds and whey or buttermilk and made into butter and cheese. Whey was a popular drink and was, moreover, used for pickling. Milk and whey were kept in large vats, from which they were ladled into vessels.

In the areas where agriculture was predominant, meat came primarily from domestic animals: pigs, cows, sheep, lambs, goats, and horses. The slaughtering of the animals typically took place in the fall so that they would not have to be fed during the winter. Hens and geese offered the possibility of fresh meat throughout the year and, of course, also provided eggs.

Other birds and animals were hunted. These included seabirds of all kinds, hares, rabbits, wild boar, elk, deer, seals, whales, and, in the north, reindeer. The land mammals were shot by bows or spears, trapped, or chased into trenches. Whales were scared into shallow water by men in small boats and there killed with knives and spears, although a common form of whaling was to cut the blubber off dying or dead whales that had run themselves ashore. Seals were typically killed with clubs and spears when they lay on the ice in the winter or on skerries or shores in the summer. Both whale and seal meat was considered a delicacy, and the oil was used for lamps and, in the case of seal oil, as an alternative to butter.

The meat was prepared in a variety of ways. It might be boiled in a cauldron of iron or soapstone suspended over the open fire from a tripod or hung on chains from a roof beam. It might also be spit roasted or baked in pits filled with hot stones. For preservation, meat was pickled in whey or brine, smoked, dried, or salted. Salt was obtained from boiling seawater or seaweed, after which the crystals were gathered.

Fish nets, hooks, line winders, floats, and weights found in many settlements show that fish played an important part in the diet. Cod and coalfish were the most important fish in Norway, western Jutland in Denmark, and in the Norse colonies in the North Atlantic. In the Baltic and in the Danish waters, herring was the most important fish. When not eaten fresh, herring was typically salted, whereas cod was, at least in northern Scandinavia and in the colonies in the North Atlantic, wind dried. The dried cod was called stockfish because it hung over a rod, or stock, while drying; by the end of the Viking Age, stockfish was exported. Freshwater fish, such as salmon, perch, and pike, was also consumed, as was shellfish such as shrimp, mussels, and oysters.

Barley was the main cereal; indeed, in Iceland it was probably the only grain cultivated. It was used for making porridge and for baking bread. Malted barley was used for making ale, to which hops might be added for flavor. Rye was commonly used for baking bread, as were oats, which were also used for porridge. Although wheat was grown in Scandinavia, it appears to have been rare and expensive, and "white bread" was probably a luxury reserved for the wealthy.

Bread has been found in a number of graves from this era. Some breads were unleavened, while others were leavened with yeast. Barley was the main ingredient, but some breads were mixed with other grains, linseed, pea flour, or pine bark. The flour was ground in hand mills made of local stone or imported lava mills of higher quality. The dough was kneaded in wooden troughs, placed on long-handled, circular pans of iron and baked on the hot ashes of an open fire. Bread might also be baked in dome-shaped ovens made on a framework of wattle. The ovens were heated up and the embers raked out, whereafter the bread dough was put in and baked. Such ovens have been excavated in both Hedeby in South Schleswig and Lund in Sweden and may have been urban phenomena.

Vegetables, fruits, berries, and nuts provided important nutritional supplements. The most common vegetables were probably cabbages, onions, peas, beans, beets, and endives, which were all locally grown. Wild fruits, such as apples, pears, cherries, plums, blueberries, cloudberries, raspberries, blackberries, and strawberries, were found in large areas of Scandinavia and could be picked wherever they grew. They were eaten raw or dried and may also have been used to make fruit wine (real wine had to be imported and was expensive). The only wild nut known in Scandinavia in the Viking Age was hazelnut. Shells of walnuts have been found in excavations, but they are believed to have been imported.

To season the foods, salt, herbs, and spices were used. Cumin, mustard, and horseradish were found in the Oseberg ship burial. In addition to these types of seasonings were probably parsley, dill, cress, mint, marjoram, thyme, angelica, and wild garlic. Other, more exotic spices would have been imported. Honey was the traditional sweetener and was used as the base for sweet, fermented mead.

~Kirsten Wolf

FOR MORE INFORMATION

Wolf, K. *Daily Life of the Vikings*. Westport, Conn.: Greenwood Press, forthcoming.

CHINA

It is probably fair to say that the Chinese have been the most omnivorous people in the history of the world. There are several reasons for this, the most important of which is geographical. The Tang empire stretched from the arid grasslands of Inner Mongolia to the lush, humid tropics of northern Vietnam; from the fish-rich seacoasts on the Pacific Ocean to the fertile plains on the border with Tibet, as well as the deserts and steppes of central Asia. The range of animals, plants, and minerals was greater than that of Japan, Korea, India, Persia, Arabia, Byzantium, and Europe in medieval times. Consequently, the number of edible things was larger than elsewhere, and population pressures often stimulated people to use all their food resources in creative ways.

The major geographic division during the Tang dynasty was that between the north and the south. The relatively arid north favored the cultivation of millet, which had been the major cereal in the Chinese diet from ancient times; barley, which was a preferred ingredient for soups; and increasingly, wheat, which supplied flour for pastas and pastries. Turnips, a northern root vegetable, were delectable when cooked with mutton. Gourmets of the capital prized a summer garlic that flourished in the vicinity of Changan. The best pears, called Phoenix Roost, grew north of Luoyang. Grapes, apricots, peaches, Chinese pears, Chinese apples, persimmons, pomegranates (an import from the West), and jujubes (Chinese blackthorns) were also native to the region. Rhubarb grew in the northwest. The finest hazelnuts came from the region west of Changan; pine nuts, from the east of the capital; and chestnuts (dried, roasted, or ground into a flour) from the northeast. Walnuts, an import from the West, had taken root in northern orchards.

Aside from pork—the most ubiquitous and most often eaten meat throughout the whole of the empire—the meat of choice in the north was lamb. Northerners also enjoyed the flesh of the Bactrian camel, especially the hump, which was broiled or boiled. Bears inhabited the mountain valleys in the region south of Changan but were difficult to catch. A recipe for steamed bear called for boiling the meat and head of the creature until rare and then marinating it in fermented soybean paste overnight; steaming sticky grains that had soaked in fermented soybean paste until they turned a reddish yellow; mixing the meat and cereal with scallions, ginger, dried tangerine peel, and salt; and steaming the mixture. Northeastern prefectures sent bamboo rats, so named because they fed on bamboo roots and were the size of rabbits, for the emperor's table. The peoples of the northwest captured marmots, whose flesh was fatty and savory, to eat. The natives of the northeast ate sea otters, the size of dogs, which had waterproof skins. Eating roasted snow pheasant from an area northeast of Luoyang was said to make one courageous and robust. The natives of Shu (modern Sichuan) in the west ate flying cockroaches.

The south, stretching from the drainage basin of the Yangtze River to the southern border of what is now northern Vietnam, had the greatest variety of fauna and flora because it was warm and moist. The major staple there was rice, most varieties of which grew in flooded paddies that required the great water resources. A palm tree produced another starch, sago flour, that southerners prized for making cakes, although they used rice more often. Bamboo shoots grew everywhere in Tang China, but those of the southern spotted bamboo were the tastiest of all. Yams and taro were southern root vegetables. Several varieties of seaweed were a foodstuff along the seacoast. Overindulgence in eating the purple leaf variety caused stomachaches and gas, but a blue-green variety facilitated urination.

The south was the great homeland of fruits, a paradise of sweets. Bananas grew there, but the crown jewel of the region was the lychee. It had a coarse, reddish skin and a dark pit, its flesh was sweet and aromatic, and court musicians even composed a song in honor of the fruit. Although lychee enjoyed the greatest esteem, it was not the most common fruit. That honor belonged to citrus fruit. Oranges, mandarin oranges, tangerines, kumquats, and loquats all graced the tables of southern diners. As early as the 4th century, markets in the southeast sold rush bags, as thin as silk, filled with reddish-yellow ants that attacked insect pests when hung from mandarin orange trees and saved the fruit from destruction. This is probably the first instance in human history of using insects to control insects.

If the south was the richest region for fruit, it was also the most bountiful area for seafood. Southerners enjoyed jellyfish cooked with cinnamon, Sichuan pepper, cardamom, and ginger; oysters boiled and eaten with ale; fried squid flavored with ginger and vinegar; horseshoe crabs prepared as a sauce or pickle; red crab seasoned with the five flavors (sweet, sour, bitter, salty, and peppery); live shrimp served with vegetables and heavy sauces; and soup prepared from a gelatinous substance obtained from the shells of the green turtle. The natives also ate puffers, fish that Tang men called "river piglet" (although some species also lived in the sea). When frightened, the fish inflate a bladder and float to the surface of the water, where they are easily gathered. The puffer is extremely poisonous, having a sac of toxin near its spine. The Japanese today eat it raw, sometimes with disastrous results; a small number of people die every year when chefs improperly prepare it. However, Tang cooks cleaned and then boiled it in a pot of hot water that presumably leached out whatever poison remained in the flesh.

Mammals, reptiles, and insects also made their way to southern tables. Some, such as the sambar deer, were common and fairly recognizable to northerners. Others were bizarre. The elephant, slain with poison arrows, produced 12 cuts of meat, the best of which was the trunk, whose crispness after cooking made it a favorite for barbecuing. Southerners in pre-Tang times made a broth from the head of the macaque monkey and probably continued to do so in the Tang. In the Tang, they also boiled the flesh of the proboscis monkey with the five flavors to make a soup that they claimed cured malaria. According to a northern exile, the meat of the white-throated partridge was sweet and plump, superior in flavor to that of chickens and pheasants. Eastern barbarians, the aborigines of China's southeast coast who lived in mountain valleys, ate the native green peacock—it tasted just like duck—not to be confused with the flamboyant Indian peacock. They also made jerky of its flesh.

Southerners also included reptiles in their diet. The locals of many areas relished frogs. They also considered python hash flavored with vinegar a delicacy. Snakes were such common fare in some districts that a northerner who lived there for 10 years had never encountered a single serpent because the locals had eaten them all. The natives of certain areas were fond of eating hornet larvae roasted with salt, cooled, and dried. Wearing protective overcoats made of grass, they smoked out the insects, climbed the trees, and brought down the nests, which had several hundred tiers of combs. Chieftains of southern tribes were in the habit of presenting a sauce of ant eggs and salt to honored guests as a treat.

Another factor in the omnivorous appetite of Tang Chinese was a passion for exotics. Some of the foodstuffs, such as bear's paw, reached the table because they were hard to obtain and had been venerated since antiquity. Others were foreign imports and sometimes difficult to acquire. Golden peaches that came from far-off Samarkand took root in the imperial gardens north of Changan and probably graced the tables only of the emperor and his favorites. Pistachios arrived from as far away as Persia. Tang dietitians contended that eating them made a person fat and robust. By the 9th century, farmers in southeast China were growing them, so they had become a native nut. Korea contributed the best pine seeds and ginseng roots. Dates from palm trees—sweeter than jujubes—and figs made their way from Persia. Both trees took root in the southeast by the 9th century. Mangoes were exotic because they were imported from Southeast Asia and probably were enjoyed only at the tables of exiles banished to the prefectures of the south.

Finally, some dishes were noted for their bizarre preparation. Southerners, always known for their odd customs, stuffed infant mice with honey and let them loose on the table, where they scurried about, peeping. Guests invited to such banquets snatched the "honeyed peepers" with their chopsticks and ate them alive. Southerners also boiled taro and, when the water bubbled, dropped live frogs into the pot. The frogs, attempting to escape the scalding heat, embraced the taro and were eaten when fully cooked. Sometimes bamboo shoots replaced the taro, and the dish became something like an amphibian Popsicle. The range of foodstuffs used by the ancient Chinese shows how omnivorous human beings can be (Benn, 119–26).

FOR MORE INFORMATION

Benn, C. *Daily Life in Traditional China: The Tang Dynasty*. Westport, Conn.: Greenwood Press, 2002.

ISLAMIC WORLD

The populations of the medieval Islamic world benefited from a well-balanced diet. The staple grains in most areas were wheat and, in areas with more saline soil, barley. Because rice could only be cultivated in a few areas, such as along the southern shores of the Caspian Sea, it was a luxury that only the wealthier could afford. Along the Mediterranean coastlands, olive orchards were as thick on the ground as they had been in antiquity. Vineyards were cultivated as well; however, after the Islamic conquests, they eventually became less important to the local diet as more and more of the population converted to Islam and adopted the Islamic prohibition against the consumption of wine. Some of the oasis settlements of Arabia as well as some of the settlements along the rivers in Iraq and Egypt cultivated vast date palm groves. A wide array of fruits and vegetables native to the region were cultivated, and as the trade networks of the medieval Islamic world expanded, a host of new fruits and vegetables that were imported from India and Africa were cultivated. As described by the 10th-century geographer al-Muqaddisi, the diversity of fruits, vegetables, grains, and meats that were available in the medieval Islamic world is truly impressive. The diet of even the lowliest peasant was generally varied and quite healthy, certainly far healthier than what most classes had access to in medieval Europe.

Jerusalem was famous for cheeses, raisins, apples, pine nuts, and bananas. Syria in general was known for olives, oranges, dried figs, raisins, sugarcane, mandrakes, lotus fruit, and carob fruit; Beit Shean for dates and rice; Jericho for bananas; Amman for grain, lamb, and honey; Tyre for sugar; Maab for almonds; Aleppo for dried figs and dried herbs; and Damascus for fresh-pressed olive oil, nuts, dried figs, and raisins.

Fish, dates, and figs caught travelers' attention in southern Iraq. Basra was renowned for 24 varieties of fish and 49 types of dates; Kufa for dates; Hulwan for figs; Wasit for fish. Northern Iraq, whose climate is similar to northern Syria's, was a land of far greater agricultural diversity. Mosul was renowned for grains, honey, dried meats, fats, cheese, honeydew, sumac, pomegranate seeds, and salted fish; Nasibin for chestnuts and dried fruits; Raqqa for olive oil; Harran for *qubbayt* (a preserve made from locust fruit and nuts) and honey; Mal'athaya for dairy products, grapes, fresh fruit, and dried meat.

Egypt was a country of international commerce and a center for the production of textiles, leather, grain, and other foodstuffs. Cairo's foods included vinegar, geese, plantains, bananas, sugar candy, and fish. Upper Egypt was renowned for rice, dates, vinegar, and raisins; Damietta for sugarcane; Fayyum for rice; Busir for shrimp; and Farama and its villages for fish and grains.

Markets throughout the medieval Islamic world were full of local fruits, vegetables, meats, and fish, as well as preserved foods that had been brought from afar. Some of these were preserved by cooling as well as drying. However, the most common method of preservation was to pickle them in vinegar and salt along with a range of condiments, including honey, sugar, lemon juice, olive oil, mustard, nuts, and all sorts of spices and herbs. While any meat can be made into sausage, sausages made from mutton and semolina were preferred. Muhammad is said to have been particularly fond of milk, but given the difficulties of preserving fresh milk, it was converted into a wide variety of soft and hard cheeses.

In the countryside, women generally ground the flour. In the cities, there were mills that ground flour for sale. Because only the wealthiest individuals could afford to have an oven built into their residences, foods prepared at home had to be taken to a local bake house to be cooked. In addition, there were shops that sold breads, pastries, and sweetmeats, as well as restaurants where one could purchase all sorts of prepared dishes.

Whereas most Christian traditions abandoned Jewish kosher regulations entirely, Islamic halal restrictions are limited to but a few items—blood, meats from animals that are not slaughtered properly, carrion, pork, and animals that have been consecrated to pagan gods. During the pilgrimage, in order to remain in a state of ritual purity, one must abstain from all of the above as well as killing or eating game (although fish is permissible). While the Qur'an (Koran) specifically forbids the aforementioned foods, Islamic law recognizes exigent circumstances when one might be forcibly compelled to eat or drink forbidden things.

~*James Lindsay*

FOR MORE INFORMATION

Lindsay, J. *Daily Life in Medieval Islam*. Westport, Conn.: Greenwood Press, forthcoming.

al-Muqaddasi. *The Best Divisions for Knowledge of the Regions: Ahsan al-taqasim fi ma'rifat al-aqalim*. Translated by B. Collins. Reading, England: Garnet, 2001.

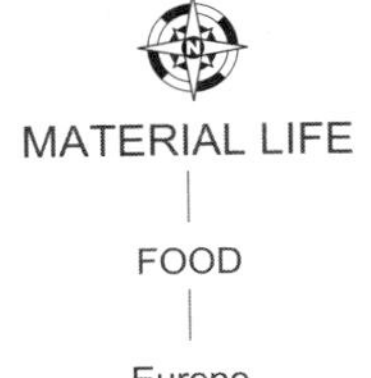

MATERIAL LIFE
FOOD
Europe
Vikings
China
Islamic World
Byzantium
Polynesia

BYZANTIUM

As throughout antiquity, grain was the cornerstone of the average diet in Byzantine times. It was grown across the Mediterranean and Near East and could be easily transported and stored. Soft Roman wheat was cultivated in great quantities in the Nile valley, which supplied the growing population of Constantinople in late antiquity. Hard-shelled durum, barley, and millet more commonly came from western Asia Minor and the Balkans, whereas oats and rye were widely raised for rural consumption and animal fodder. Finely milled and baked in leavened loaves, white wheat bread (*artos katharos*) was preferred across the empire; the blended *mesokatharos artos* and whole-wheat *autopyros* were less widely favored. During the 4th to early 7th centuries, citizens of Constantinople received free distributions of bread (the *panis civilis*) from municipal bakeries. Following the loss of Egypt to the Arabs, this public dole was replaced by charitable distributions organized by the church. The average consumption of bread may have been as much as three to six pounds in late antiquity. Later Byzantine sources suggest a much smaller role for cereal foods, with meat counting for a larger share of the average diet.

Olives and grapes have long been essential components of the Mediterranean diet. Olives were cultivated widely because they can tolerate poor soils and minimal rainfall. Syria and the south coast of Asia Minor produced much of the early Byzantine Empire's supply of olive oil, which was used for cooking, fuel, cleaning, and other household purposes. Its high caloric value made it an indispensable commodity in both town and country. Vineyards were favored in higher, inland areas and produced distinctive regional wines that were distributed across the Mediterranean. Wine was normally mixed at the table with water, but it might also be seasoned with pepper or other spices. It was consumed at home, in taverns, and in the monastery, and on all social levels. The products of certain geographic regions such as Palestine were especially prized; the resin-flavored Athenian *retsina* received both positive and negative comments.

Perishable garden crops were raised on a much smaller scale and were consumed locally. Individual family plots surrounded villages and monasteries, and small kitchen gardens (*kyproi*) commonly were found in cities as well. Eustathios, the late 12th-century archbishop of Thessaloniki, gave his friends peaches, cucumbers, figs, and grapes that he grew in his garden. These family-based operations aimed at self-sufficiency but under favorable conditions could produce a marketable surplus. The 10th-century *Geoponika*, a compilation of earlier agricultural writings, lists a broad variety of popular Byzantine vegetables including cabbage, lettuce, leeks, onions, coriander, cucumbers, peas, and fenugreek. Carrots, beets, onions, radishes, turnips, and garlic were prominent among root vegetables. The broad bean, lentil, and chick-pea appeared among pulses. Orchard fruits included apricots, apples, peaches (also known as "Persian apples"), pears, citron, and especially dates. Dates, figs, and grapes were good market crops because they could be dried, stored, and transported over long distances. The *Geoponika* includes among the hard-shelled fruits pomegranate, almond, walnut, chestnut, and pistachio.

The dietary role of meat (*kreas*) varied with date, place, and social rank. Traditionally regarded as a feature of high status, meat seems to have become an increasingly common feature of the later Byzantine diet. The most widely kept animals were sheep and goats, which provided milk, butter, cheese, and wool in addition to meat. Pigs were not usually raised on such a large scale, and pork seems to have been considered a rustic food. Cattle were intended for labor and hides but were less commonly eaten. Late Byzantine sources indicate that chickens and hens' eggs were common at all social levels; other domestic fowl such as ducks, geese, quails, and pigeons are less well documented. Contemporary authors list a broad range of Mediterranean fish, with mackerel and small tuna readily available in the Constantinopolitan marketplace. Some sources imply that sea catch was preferred to freshwater fish. Letter writers of the 10th to 14th centuries often mention sending fish as gifts. Caviar and sturgeon were among the more exotic delicacies among the aristocracy of the capital. Crustaceans, shellfish, and mussels were widely consumed. Common methods of preserving fish and other meat included drying, salting, smoking, and pickling.

A number of Byzantine recipes survive, especially in treatises dealing with the benefits of a healthy diet. Most meats were roasted, baked, or boiled. Other foods were less often fried than cooked in a deep stewpot or covered casserole. Olive, sesame, and croton oil were commonly used in the kitchen, with vinegar, pepper, cinnamon, and other spices added for seasoning. A fermented fish sauce, derived from the Roman *garum*, was widely known. One popular baked dish was a mixture of fish, cheese, and vegetables known as *monokythron*. Other typical casseroles included lamb baked with garlic and leeks, and salt pork with cabbage. Poultry might be stuffed with almonds or dough balls and drenched with a wine marinade. Fish could be grilled, cooked in soup with dill, leeks, onions, and other vegetables, or baked into rolls.

Honey was the preferred sweetener throughout the Mediterranean, with dates and raisins used as an economical substitute. Cane sugar, which was being refined in Egypt by the 8th century, grew in importance and was produced in quantity in Cyprus during the late Middle Ages. Desserts and honey cakes were made of fine wheat flour with boiled muse (*oinoutta*) or in circular shapes (*krikelos*). Special cakes known as *kollyba* were made of boiled wheat with sugar, dried raisins, pomegranate seeds, nuts, and herbs; these were distributed to the congregation during Lent, usually to commemorate the dead.

An important part of the normal Byzantine diet was its voluntary interruption by periods by fasting. The Great Lent originated in early Christian times in a vigil on Easter eve; by the 7th century, it prescribed a preparatory week known as "cheesefare" followed by a fast lasting 40 days. Lesser observances were recommended before Nativity, Epiphany, the Dormition of the Virgin, and other liturgical festivals. Degrees of fasting varied from total abstinence from food and drink during daylight hours to a restricted diet for a specified term. Meat, wine, cheese, and sweets were most commonly limited, while monastic fasts might allow only an evening meal of bread, salt, and water. Saints' lives celebrate the ability to go without food as a sign of spirituality. Some Byzantine holy men followed the example of John the Baptist and subsisted on acorns, wild berries and plants, and dried locusts.

~*Marcus Rautman*

FOR MORE INFORMATION

Kislinger, E. "Christians of the East: Rules and Realities of the Byzantine Diet." In *Food: A Culinary History from Antiquity to the Present*, edited by J.-L. Flandrin, M. Montanari, and A. Sonnenfeld. New York: Columbia University Press, 2000.

MATERIAL LIFE
FOOD
Europe
Vikings
China
Islamic World
Byzantium
Polynesia

POLYNESIA

Ancient Polynesians were limited in their selection of foods because they had no trade or communication with anyone outside of Polynesia and because their tropical islands grew only what food sources they had brought with them when they first arrived. Of course, there were a few indigenous food plants and animals on the islands, but even when combined with what they brought, their cuisine was still very meager. This does not mean, however, that the Polynesians went hungry. On the contrary, when the European explorers first visited the islands, they were astonished at the amount of food consumed by the average islander. Joseph Banks, the explorer-scientist who traveled with Captain Cook, reported that he saw one Tahitian consume several large breadfruits, 2 fish, 15 bananas, and 15 mangoes all in one sitting.

Polynesians generally ate one main meal a day, early in the afternoon. Mornings were taken up with the gathering and preparing of the food, and the rest of the day was spent in other chores and recreation. Leftovers from the main meal were served as snacks in the evening and as breakfast the next morning. What makes Polynesian food preparation and meals strikingly different from the rest of the world is that their traditional social taboos prevented men and women from eating with one another. Also, men could not eat food prepared by women, and certain foods were prohibited to women. Men did most of the cooking. In fact, the husband had to prepare two different ovens and two different menus—one for himself and one for his wife and small children. Foods touched by women could not be eaten by adult males. Other eating taboos, for example, prohibited sons from eating in the presence of their fathers or other senior male relatives.

Another unique characteristic of Polynesian cuisine was that food was cooked in an underground oven, called an *imu* or *umu*, depending on the dialect. (Polynesians had no metal or ceramic cooking utensils.) The oven was a pit dug about one to two feet deep and five to six feet wide. Firewood and stones (lava stones, if available) were arranged in the pit and the wood set on fire. The stones were turned several times to get them consistently hot. After the wood had burned down, the hot stones were then redistributed around the bottom of the pit, and banana leaves were then carefully placed over them. The various foods (wrapped or unwrapped) were placed at strategic spots on top of the leaves, and then more leaves were added on top of the food. Afterward, the pit and its contents were covered with ashes, dirt, and more leaves. The net effect was a giant steam oven, which cooked the food and prevented its moisture from escaping. The exact cooking time depended on the amount of the food to be cooked. Two hours was the average, but when larger feasts were prepared, it often took overnight. When the cooking was complete, the oven was carefully opened and its contents removed. Food was generally served on large leaves from the banana or ti plants, accompanied with coconut shells full of fresh water (for washing and drinking) and sea water (for its salt content). Boiled foods were prepared by heating stones and dropping them into liquids that had been poured into coconut shells or hallowed-out gourds.

The Polynesian diet consisted of the following food plants.

- Breadfruit (*Artocarpus incisa*) was the staff of life among ancient Polynesians. The fruit grew on large trees that were found abundantly in Polynesia, except in New Zealand. The ripened fruit was gathered year-round, roasted over hot coals or cooked in an underground oven, peeled, and then eaten. It has a starchy consistency similar to the European potato and is quite tasty. It can also be mashed and mixed with other vegetables or fruits. Some Polynesians enjoyed fermented breadfruit. In this case, the rind was cut off, the pulp placed into a leaf-lined pit and covered, where it was left to ferment for several months. The paste (*mehi*) was then taken out and baked or mixed with other ingredients. Some island groups prepared for droughts or famines by making *mehi* in this manner.
- Coconuts (*Cocos nucifera*) were widely used for food. The white "meat" inside the shell can be eaten raw or it can be grated and squeezed and the resulting rich creamy liquid used for seasoning other foods or made into puddings.
- Taro or *kalo* (*Colocasia antiquorum*) was a principal cultivated food. Taro leaves resemble the decorative garden plant called the "elephant ear." Its tubers, which are 10 to 12 inches long, are dug up, baked or boiled, and eaten. Cooked taro has a slight purplish color. Hawaiians mash the cooked taro with water into a delicacy called poi; its consistency depends, of course, on the amount of water added. Hawaiians refer to its varied consistency as one-finger, two-finger, or three-finger poi, and foreign tourists to the islands claim it tastes like children's school paste. Steamed taro leaves were also cooked as a vegetable and taste very much like spinach. Samoans add coconut cream to make an extremely delicious vegetable dish.
- Sweet potatoes (*Ipomoea batatas*) and yams (*Dioscorea alata*) were also well known throughout ancient Polynesia; sweet potatoes were especially popular in Hawai'i, and the yams

were favorites in Tonga. Growing these starchy tubers is labor intensive, and for this reason, they were not as popular in some islands. The ripened tubers are dug out of the ground and cooked, after which their insides become sweet and soft.

- Bananas, mountain plantains (*Musa fehi*), mangoes (*Spondias dulcis*), and Malay apples (*Eugenia malaccensis*) were the basic fruits found in the islands. Plantains were baked in the underground ovens, and the common banana was eaten as we do today.
- Arrowroot (*Tacca pinnatifida*) was grated and used as a thickening starch for making puddings, and the roots of the ti plant (*Cordyline terminalis*) were used for sweetening various foods. Sugarcane (*Saccharum officinarum*) grew wild, and its stalks were chewed for their sweetness.
- Kava (*Piper methysticum*) is common throughout the Pacific. It is a type of narcotic or intoxicant drink, and in ancient times it was drunk with meals. In Tonga, however, its use was ceremonialized, and it became the central focus of most official gatherings that had nothing to do with mealtime. The drink is prepared by mashing the kava root and squeezing it over and over again in water. When finished, it resembles muddy water, and one has to get used to its unusual taste. Drinking too much kava results in a type of stupor rather than drunkenness.

Breadfruit, one of the traditional foods of Polynesia, is a starchy fruit that is roasted and eaten similar to potatoes, or can be mashed and eaten as poi. Photo courtesy of Robert D. Craig.

Protein foods came from various domesticated and wild animals, including the following:

- Pigs, both domesticated and wild, were highly valued as food, but they were usually only eaten on important occasions. The pigs were butchered, cleaned, prepared, and baked (usually whole) in the underground ovens. The fat and moisture together created an extremely tasty delight when it was done. Pig fat was also highly relished, and none of it went to waste.
- Fish and sea crustaceans of all kinds were available to the Polynesians. Men caught a variety of fish in the lagoons either with a fishhook, net, or spear. (Women also fished in the quieter lagoons.) The expert fishermen would frequently go out beyond the reef where they could catch larger fish, such as shark, dolphin, and so on. Fish were then wrapped in banana or ti leaves and cooked in the underground oven; some, however, were eaten raw, and some were dried for future use.
- Dogs were raised, fattened, and sometimes eaten as a delicacy, especially among the chiefly class. Its taste is said to resemble that of lamb.
- Chickens and birds also provided a variety of meat.

~Robert D. Craig

FOR MORE INFORMATION

Ferdon, E. N. *Early Tonga: As the Explorers Saw It 1616–1810*. Tucson: University of Arizona Press, 1987.

Oliver, D. *Ancient Tahitian Society*. 3 vols. Honolulu: University of Hawai'i Press, 1974.

Drink

The start of any discussion of drinks must begin with water. Whether it came from rivers, fountains, rain barrels, wells, or cisterns, it was the staple of life. The

Chinese carefully attributed different health qualities to different water, depending on its origin: from melted hailstones or springs or mineral waters. The Chinese also warned about dangers of pollution and recommended boiling suspect water, which no doubt contributed to their health. In Byzantium, many fountains were built to supply the citizens with water, who prided themselves on the purity of the product. Late in the Middle Ages, snow water was sold in Byzantium and elsewhere as a health cure. Unfortunately, many people who lived by the great rivers in cities of Europe and Baghdad had to make do with water that was already polluted by the cities' inhabitants. The problem of fresh, clean water that is so common today began long ago.

All over the world, most of the poor had to content themselves with drinking only water. A peasant father in a European poem tells his son to be content with water and not long for the wine of the upper classes, but most people longed for stronger drinks when they became available. (The Vikings in the settlement in Greenland never had wine or beer, and theirs was the rare society that did without this kind of beverage.) Even the Polynesians who had neither grapes nor the grains for brewing enjoyed tea from the kava plant, which had a tranquilizing quality.

Beer (really ale, beer without hops) and wine production is as old as agriculture. Beer was made by brewing wheat or oats, barley, rye, millet, or even spelt. Wine is fermented grapes or rice. The Mongols fermented mare's milk to create a preserved intoxicating drink. All these processes served the initial function of preserving the food long after the growing season. In ages without refrigeration or other ways to preserve crops, brewing was essential as a food source.

In fact, ales and wines formed a substantial part of the caloric intake of Europeans. The beer was not as strong as today's brews, and wines were drunk watered so they also were not as strong. Children, too, drank these alcoholic beverages because people believed (in many cases correctly) that brewed beverages were healthier than polluted waters. Both wines and beers were flavored with spices, fruits, and other additives.

Strong alcoholic beverages were not present in the Middle Ages. Making alcoholic beverages required a distilling process instead of the fermentation that produced beer and wine. Alcohol was probably discovered about the 12th century in southern Italy, perhaps in the Salerno school of medicine. Brandy was first made by distilling wine, and it was considered a medicine, not a drink for pleasure. A 14th-century doctor praised brandy as a miracle liquor that preserved youth, "dissipated superfluous body fluids, revived the heart, cured colic, paralysis, toothache and gave protection against plague" (Braudel, 242). However, the dangers of overusing brandy as a cure became readily apparent in the case of the French king Charles the Bad, who died in 1387. Doctors wrapped him in a brandy-soaked sheet sewn up with stitches to fit tightly around the patient so the brandy would seep into his body. A servant held a candle up close to try to break one of the threads, and sheet and patient went up in flames (Braudel, 242). Brandy cures after that were limited to small drinks of the stimulant.

The Chinese had a greater variety of nonalcoholic drinks. They learned to make fruit juices, but the most important beverage was tea. The tea plant was a bush from which the Chinese peasant plucked leaves. The young, small leaves made the best tea—which was sold to the emperors. After being picked, the tea leaves were dried either by heat from a fire to form "green tea" or in the heat of the sun to form "black tea." Today, we recognize the medicinal properties of both kinds of teas, a claim that the Chinese in the Middle Ages had always made. Tea would not be exported to the rest of the world until after the medieval age, when it would become popular all over the world.

~Joyce E. Salisbury

FOR MORE INFORMATION

Braudel, F. *The Structures of Everyday Life*. New York: Harper and Row, 1979.

EUROPE

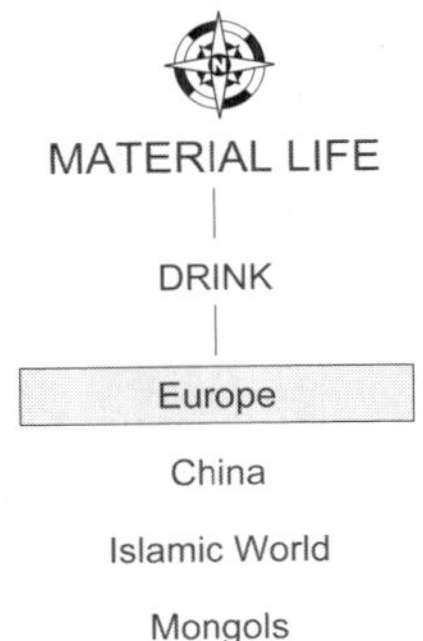

Ale—unhopped beer—was the staple drink of medieval England. It provided a significant portion of people's nutritional intake, women and children included. It was most often brewed from barley malt, but wheat and oats were also used. Because it had no hops, it lacked the bitter edge of modern beer; but it also lacked the preservative properties of the hops, so it did not keep very well. This fragility of the product had one advantage for the women who were primarily involved in making it—they could sell any unconsumed portions for extra income for themselves or their households.

Because beer was an important part of the medieval diet, making it was a significant occupation. First, the seeds were artificially sprouted and then heated to stop growth, and roasted. This process, called "malting," caused the seeds to convert their starch content into soluble starches and helped flavor the ale. The sprouted grain was then ground, boiled in water to extract its contents, and strained to remove the solid matter. Herbal flavorings were added, and the liquid was fermented with yeast, usually from a previous batch of ale.

Daily intake appears to have been substantial, with allowances of one gallon per person being common in the households of the aristocracy, and two to four pints among peasants and laborers. However, medieval ale was not necessarily very strong. After the mash made by boiling the malted grain was poured off, water was poured through the malt several more times. Ale brewed from each successive pouring was progressively weaker. The different strengths of ale were consequently known as ale of the first, second, or third water; ale made from the last washing of the malt was called small ale. Toward the end of the 14th century, ale was beginning to give way to beer in the city, although it remained the predominant drink in the country for centuries to come.

For those who could afford it, wine was also much favored. France was probably the principal source, but wines were also imported from the Rhine valley, from Spain and Portugal, and even from as far away as Greece. Production of wine was simpler than ale. The grapes were pressed to extract the juice, and the resulting liquid was flavored and fermented.

Wines in this period were most often drunk young because they did not keep as well as modern wines. Aged wines were just becoming fashionable at the end of the 14th century. Wine was often watered or sweetened with honey or sugar; sometimes it was spiced to make the drink known as hippocras. Hippocras was reputed to be very good for the health—the name derives from Hippocrates, the Greek physician. Here is the medieval recipe for hippocras:

A tavern scene in medieval Europe. The man in the basement draws wine from the large barrels, while the patrons drink quantities from either flasks or glasses. © The British Library/Topham-HIP/The Image Works.

> Take a half lb. of choice cinnamon, of choice ginger a half lb., of grains of paradise [cardamom] 3 ounces, of long pepper 3 ounces, of cloves 2 ounces, of nutmegs 2 ounces and a half, of caraway 2 ounces, of spikenard [valerian] a half ounce, of galingale 2 ounces, of sugar 2 lb. If sugar is lacking, take a pottle [half-gallon] of honey. (Singman and McLean, 176)

Other drinks included cider (made from apples) and perry (made from pears). In regions lacking these fruits, people developed a popular drink made from fermented honey. This is called mead and is still served today to people who like very sweet beverages. Here is the medieval recipe for mead:

> Take honeycombs and put them into a great vessel and lay therein great sticks, and lay the weight thereon till it be run out as much as it will; and this is called live honey. And then take that forsaid combs and seethe them in clean water, & boil them well. After press out thereof as much as thou may and cast it into another vessel into hot water, & seethe it well and scum it well, and add thereto a quart of live honey. And then let it stand a few days well stopped, and this is good drink. (Singman and McLean, 177)

Distilled liquors—such as brandy—were relatively rare and were generally consumed only for medicinal purposes. People at the lowest end of the economic scale had to rely on water, a drink less flavorful and less healthy than the alcoholic alternatives—particularly in towns, where overcrowding made water pollution a problem. Milk was not much favored by adults, although whey (the thin liquid remaining after the curds are removed from curdled milk) was sometimes consumed in poor households. (See the excerpt of the poem *Meier Helmbrecht* in the "Primary Sources.")

It was important to be able to transport beverages. For trade, drinks were transported in barrels that were carefully made to be watertight. Travelers carried their drink in leather bottles, gourds, or miniature wooden barrels bound with iron (Singman, 53–54; Singman and McLean, 164–66).

To read about drink in Elizabethan England, see the England entry in the section "Food and Drink" in chapter 5 ("Material Life") of volume 3; for 18th-century England, see the England entry in the section "Drink" in chapter 5 ("Material Life") of volume 4 of this series.

FOR MORE INFORMATION

Singman, J. L. *Daily Life in Medieval Europe*. Westport, Conn.: Greenwood Press, 1999.
Singman, J. L., and W. McLean. *Daily Life in Chaucer's England*. Westport, Conn.: Greenwood Press, 1995.

VIKINGS

To read about drink among the Vikings, see the Vikings entry in this chapter in the section "Food."

CHINA

The most common drink of the Tang was water. One medical authority of the early 8th century described the virtues of 26 varieties, from rain to water found in pig troughs. He claimed the latter would heal wounds left by snake bites when applied externally. Dew collected from plants in the autumn improved one's complexion. Frost gathered and melted in the winter could dispel the heat and redness of the face resulting from drinking too much alcohol. Winter snow was an antidote to all kinds of toxins, but spring snow contained "bugs" and was therefore harmful to the health. Tang people also highly prized mineral waters. Streams that flowed through "jade"—actually any sort of prized rock—were thought to possess life-sustaining powers. Drinking from such a brook that cascaded down from Mount Hua just east of Changan prolonged the lives of local people. Quaffing jade water also prevented the graying of hair, a sure sign of advancing old age. Streams flowing from limestone caves with stalactites also promoted health. People who imbibed such waters were fat and robust, and did not grow old. On the southern island of Hainan, where springs and wells were scarce, the natives drank water extracted from creeping vines.

The Chinese also had instant fruit juices in medieval times. They dried jujubes in the sun and boiled them in a wok. After straining out the liquid and mashing the fruit in the bottom of a basin, they would place the pulp in gauze and squeeze out the juice. They then plastered the mash on a plate or the bottom of a bowl and dried it in the sun. After it dried, it could be rubbed into a powder with the fingers. When ready for a drink, a person would mix a spoonful of the powder into a cup of water. This sweet-and-sour drink was just the thing for satisfying the thirst while traveling. There were similar, but simpler, processes for making powders from apricots and crabapples that one could reconstitute as a juice. Vinegar water was another thirst quencher drunk on hot summer days. Some "fruit juices" came directly from the husk. Southerners drank coconut milk, which did not cause intoxication.

Although 80 percent of modern Chinese do not have the enzyme in their stomachs to properly digest milk, it was a beverage in the north during the Tang, perhaps because so many Chinese there had intermarried with the pastoral peoples of the steppes in Tang and pre-Tang times. Tang medical authorities contended that many northerners were plump and robust because they drank cow and goat milk. Milk strengthened and fattened their bodies.

Tea was originally a medicinal substance, but by the 6th century southerners had taken to drinking it as a beverage. The homeland of the plant was in the southwest near the Tibetan border, but it took root in many areas to the east on the lower reaches of the Yangtze River. The habit of imbibing it as a beverage did not reach the north until the early 8th century, when a Buddhist monk on Mount Tai in modern Shandong province sipped it to keep himself awake while he practiced meditation. Barges and wagons carrying the tea from the Huai and Yangtze Rivers supplied the demand of northern aficionados. Lu Yu, a southerner raised in a Buddhist monastery, wrote the oldest surviving manual on tea shortly before 761. His work further popularized the beverage. Tea merchants were so grateful for his assistance in promoting their trade that they had images of him molded in clay and installed on their kilns. They worshiped him as the patron deity of tea.

The processing of tea in the Tang involved plucking the leaves from trees in the spring. Then workers steamed, pounded, patted, and roasted them in ovens or kilns. Afterward, they packed the leaves in paper bags to preserve the flavor and repackaged them in bamboo leaves or tree bark for shipment. Roasting the leaves may have reduced or eliminated the natural bitterness of the foliage and made it palatable to drinkers. Even so, some aficionados took to mixing additives—onions, tangerine peel, ginger, jujubes, pepper, mint, and even clotted cream—to flavor it. In whatever form, everyone appreciated it for its caffeine—a stimulant that relieved depression, drowsiness, and fatigue.

Wine was also known to the Tang people. Centuries earlier, the grape made its way from the West to China, where three varieties—yellow, white, and black—grew. Cuttings for a fourth variety—the purple "mare teat," so called because of its elongated shape—were brought back from central Asia for transplanting in the emperor's park north of Changan. Several districts in north China grew grapes, and a monastery in Changan had a vineyard. There was a small, native variety. Northerners also prepared wine from pears and jujubes. Although the art of making wine had taken root in the lands of the Tang, it was a rare beverage, and drinking it never became a widespread custom.

Jizhou tea bowl. Song dynasty, ca. 960–1279. Tea drinking became widespread during the Tang dynasty and remained popular throughout the Song. The ceramics used in tea drinking were an important part of the ritual. © The British Museum/Topham-HIP/The Image Works.

Northerners, at least in Changan, enjoyed koumiss, fermented mare's milk, a gift from the pastoral peoples of the steppes. Southerners made a wine from the fruit of the "Chinese strawberry," although Tang herbalists warned that it injured the teeth and muscles. Natives of the south also produced toddies from various palms, such as the flowers of the banana and the sap of the areca (betel nut) trees. Among the preferred alcoholic beverages in a list compiled in the 9th century were also three ferments from different species of the myrobalan, a fruit native to India that took root in the vicinity of Canton during the Tang or earlier.

One might occasionally imbibe those exotics, but the real drink of choice for the men of Tang was ale, known best in the West as rice wine. It was an alcoholic beverage made from cereals—millet in the north and rice in the south—in a manner similar to brewing beer. Making wine is a simple process because fruits contain sugar that naturally ferments once the juice has been extracted and bottled. The vintner can sit back and wait for the molds in the juice to convert its sugar to alcohol. The conversion of grains into alcohol is more complicated because its starches must first be transformed into a sugar. This involves the manufacturing of starters—ferment cakes—from airborne molds.

The procedure for making one type of ferment cake called for separately grinding equal measures of raw, steamed, and lightly roasted wheat to a powder and then mixing them. A boy would draw water before sunrise and stir it into the flour. Boys then formed the dough into rounds two-and-a-half inches in diameter and almost an inch thick. They had to complete the task the same day. In a thatched hut with a floor of firmly tamped earth and no loose dirt or moisture, they were to divide the ground into four squares separated and encircled by paths and lay the cakes out to dry. A person was then to make effigies of the gods of the five directions with upturned hands, place jerky, wine, pastry, and broth on their palms as a sacrifice and then pray. The wooden door of the hut was then sealed with mud to prevent drafts from entering. After seven days, one was to open the hut, turn the cakes, and reseal the door. Fourteen days later, one opened the hut again, stacked the cakes, and resealed the door once more. After 21 days, one was to remove the cakes, place them in an earthen jug, cap it, and seal it with mud. Twenty-eight days later, one drilled holes in the cakes, strung them on cords, and dried them in the sun. When the cakes dried totally, they were stored for use.

The process for brewing ale was nearly as complex as the manufacturing of the starter. One method called for grinding the ferment into a fine powder in a mortar and steeping it in a vat of water for three days, until bubbles formed on the top. Then the brewer added half-steamed millet, 21 parts to 1 part of ferment, in four stages over four days, and covered the pot. When the mixture smelled right and ceased bubbling, it was ready to drink. Some varieties took little time to mature.

As with tea, water was a critical factor in brewing ale. River water was the best, especially that collected at the time of the first frost in November or so. If it was drawn in other months, the brewers were to boil it five times before using it. Sometimes rainwater was an ingredient. Thunder ale was a variety of brew that relied on water collected during summer thunderstorms. In localities where it was available, mineral water was a prized element in brewing. Many people used water from limestone caves that had stalactites because its alkaloids cut the acidity of the ale.

Drinkers were not always satisfied with taking their brew straight, so a variety of additives was used to flavor ale during the Tang. One of the drinks favored on New Year's Day was black pepper ale. A recipe for that blend dating from the 3rd century called for powdering 70 kernels of pepper with dried ginger, mixing it with the juice from five pomegranates, pouring it into fine spring ale, and heating it until warm. It was palatable when drunk hot or cold, and it was supposed to prolong life. A man of great capacity could drink a liter or more of it. It had the added virtue of curing a hangover. Another version of the recipe substituted honey for pomegranate juice. One might also flavor ale with ginger, lotus, or bamboo leaves. One aficionado of exotic ingredients served fish ale at the height of winter. He had camphor carved in the form of small fish. When his wine came to a boil, he would toss one of the fish into it, thus imbuing his brew with a fragrance that his contemporaries greatly esteemed (Benn, 138–42).

FOR MORE INFORMATION

Benn, C. *Daily Life in Traditional China: The Tang Dynasty*. Westport, Conn.: Greenwood Press, 2002.

ISLAMIC WORLD

The Qur'an prohibits the drinking of wine or other intoxicating beverages. Although scholars generally extended the Qur'anic prohibition on wine to all alcoholic beverages, it is clear that there was a range of near beers and other "soft" or lightly fermented fruit drinks that could be commonly found throughout the medieval Islamic world. As such, a great deal of ink was spilled defining which types of drinks were in fact "soft" (lightly fermented) and permitted and which were "hard" (real intoxicants) and forbidden.

As one might expect, water was an essential drink, although the quality of water was often determined by how much one was willing and or able to pay a water seller who carried water around in a jug on his back for sale in the market. The wealthiest even purchased snow from snow vendors who brought in snow from afar and kept it in storehouses. Fruit juices mixed with water were very common, including drinks made from lemons, oranges, apples, tamarinds, dates, grapes, and pomegranates.

Various coffees can be found throughout the modern Islamic world, and Arabica beans are a favorite in American coffeehouses. However, coffee was only introduced to the Islamic world from East Africa in the 15th century. There are several legends about who was the first to bring the beans to Yemen, but most of them revolve around one or more Sufis (Islamic mystics) who praised the drink as an inhibitor of sleep and an aide to mystical devotional rituals. Tea is even more ubiquitous in the modern Islamic world but was introduced from India even later, and often from European merchants. For example, a French merchant who had business dealings in East Asia first introduced tea to Morocco around 1700.

~*James Lindsay*

FOR MORE INFORMATION

Lindsay, J. *Daily Life in Medieval Islam*. Westport, Conn.: Greenwood Press, forthcoming.

MONGOLS

Drinking was one of the characteristic traits of the Mongols. The Armenian cleric and historian Kirakos observed firsthand that "Whenever possible they ate and drank insatiably" (Kirakos, 234). Heavy drinking and drunkenness were common and socially acceptable indulgences, and stories of alcohol fuelled excesses are numerous.

Heavy drinking and drunkenness were common and socially acceptable indulgences.

"Drunkenness is honourable among the Tartars, and when someone drinks a great deal he is sick right on the spot, and this does not prevent him from drinking more" (Carpini, 51). So observed the Friar Giovanni Di Plano Carpini (d. 1252), who traveled to Mongolia between 1245 and 1247. A companion of the friar added that they were the more given to drunkenness than any other people on earth, and their drinking bouts were not limited to one session a day but occurred several times throughout the day. Although it did not seem to have induced violence, excessive alcohol consumption has commonly been blamed for the early deaths of many of the leading Mongol rulers.

Although the Mongols drank fresh milk, the favored beverage was a fermented dairy drink still made to this day. This alcoholic concoction is known as koumiss or *qumys* and was generally fermented from mares' milk. William of Rubruck was an unwitting initiate to the pleasures of koumiss, which, upon swallowing for the first time, brought him out in a sweat of "alarm and surprise." However, he admits to finding the drink very palatable.

William of Rubruck devotes a short chapter of his travelogue to the making of koumiss. He describes how the foals of the tribe's horses were tethered to a stretched rope. The mares would seek out their young and then stand peacefully beside their offspring and allow themselves to be peacefully milked. If any mare should prove "intractable," the foal would be allowed to initiate the milking process. The collected milk, "sweet as cow's milk," would be poured into a bag or large skin and then churned with a specially made club "as thick at the lower end as a man's head and hollowed out" until the mix began to bubble "like new wine" and to turn sour and ferment. Churning would continue until butter could be extracted. It was considered ready for drinking when it was moderately pungent. The taste had a sting on the tongue like sour wine but had a very pleasant aftertaste like the milk of almonds. In addition, it produced "a very agreeable sensation inside," a desire to urinate, and intoxication (William of Rubruck, 81–83).

As well as this ordinary koumiss, sometimes dismissively described as white, cloudy, and sour tasting, a superior mare's milk beverage was also fermented. This was known as *qara kumis* or black koumiss and has been described as clear and sweet. Because their mares' milk did not curdle, the churning process was continued until everything solid in the milk sank to the bottom and the liquid that remained on top was very clear. The dregs, which were very white, were then separated and given to the slaves, with, according to Rubruck, a highly soporific effect on them. The clear liquid, black koumiss, was presented to the Mongol lords for their consumption. This drink was very sweet and very potent.

Batu Khan (d. 1255), lord of the Golden Horde of Russia and the Ukraine, was kept supplied with black koumiss by 30 men stationed one day's ride away, around his *ordu* (camp). Each rider would supply the produce of a hundred mares, which means a total of 3,000 mares daily servicing the needs of this Mongol prince. This figure does not include those mares producing the ordinary koumiss. Marco Polo claimed that Kublai Khan (d. 1294) of China needed 10,000 mares daily to satisfy his *ordu*'s demand for black koumiss.

Contact with the sophisticated urban centers of the Islamic west and the Chinese south led to more varied drinking habits, although apparently no less excessive. It was the Mongols who facilitated the introduction of grape wine to China. A colony of Muslim artisans originally from Samarqand, settled in Sīmalī just north of Beijing, cultivated grapes and provided wine for the imperial court throughout the 13th century. The Chinese introduced rice wine to the Persians who called it *tarāsūn*. The Mongols drank both.

Stories of Mongol drinking bouts and excesses are legion. Ögödei (d. 1241), the successor to his father, Chinggis (Genghis) Khan, officially died of excessive drinking, which his brother, Chagatai (d. 1242), had tried in vain to curb.

> Qa'an [Ögödei] was extremely fond of wine, and [he] drank continuously and to excess. Day by day he grew weaker, and though his intimates and well-wishers sought to prevent him, it was not possible, and he drank more in spite of them. Chaghatai appointed an emir to watch over him [Ögödei] and not allow him to drink more than a specified number of cups. As he could not disobey his brother's command, he used to drink from a large cup instead of a small one, so that the number remained the same. (Rashīd al-Dīn, 65)

The il-khan of Mongol Persia, Abaqa Khan, famously died of delirium tremors and hallucinations, while a later il-khan, Geikhatu (r. 1291–95), was remembered primarily for his drinking and other excesses.

> Day and night, he sought his desires . . . in wine and drinking. His desire continued to be for wine, and he dismissed all fear. Whether he was faced by plain or mountain, he had no worldly concern for passing them. Mountain or plain were the same to him, as were strangers or intimate companions. (Ward, 348)

The acclaimed historian and also prime minister of Mongol Iran, Rashīd al-Dīn (d. 1318) recounts some words of wisdom attributed to Chinggis Khan that seem to suggest that in old age the founder of this world empire was well aware of the dangers of the habit that had such a grip on his people.

> When a man gets drunk on wine and *taraāsūn* [rice wine], he is just like a blind man who can't see anything, a deaf man who can't hear when he's called, and a mute who can't reply when he's spoken to. When a man gets drunk he is like someone in a state of death: he can't sit up straight even if he wants to. He's as dazed and senseless as someone who's been hit over the head. (Rashīd al-Dīn, 297)

~George Lane

FOR MORE INFORMATION

Carpini, Giovanni Di Plano. *The Story of the Mongols Whom We Call the Tartars: Historia Mongalorum*. Translated by E. Hildinger. Boston, Mass.: Branden, 1996.

Kirakos Ganjakets_i. *Kirakos Ganjakets_i's History of the Armenians*. Translated by Robert Bedrosian. New York: Sources for the Armenian Tradition, 1986. <http://rbedrosian.com/catalog.html>.

Rashīd al-Dīn. *Rashīduddin Fazlullah: Jami 'u' t-Tawārīkh, Compendium of Chronicles Parts I, II, III*. Translated by W. M. Thackston. Sources of Oriental Languages and Literature 45. Cambridge, Mass.: Central Asian Sources, Harvard University, 1998, 1999.

———. *The Successors of Genghis Khan*. Translated by J. A. Boyle. New York: Columbia University Press, 1971.

Ward, L. J. "Zafarnāmah of Mustawfī." Ph.D. thesis, Manchester University, 1983.

William of Rubruck. *The Mission of William of Rubruck*. Translated and edited by P. Jackson, with D. Morgan. London: Hakluyt Society, 1990.

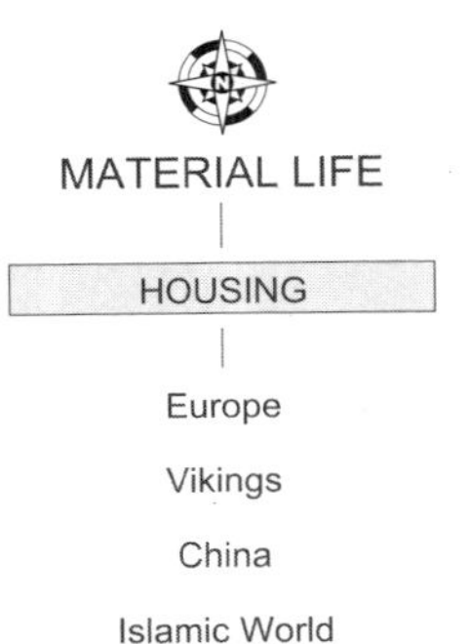

Housing

Shelter is almost as necessary as food and drink, and housing is an essential part of daily life. There are several factors that influence people's houses: (1) the weight of tradition, (2) available building materials, (3) the weather, and (4) the purpose of the house. Looking at these four variables can shed light on people's choices of housing during the Middle Ages.

Tradition and custom strongly influence the shape and layout of houses, and as houses are built and rebuilt—even with different building materials—people usually built that with which they were familiar. For example, the homes of the well-to-do around the Mediterranean usually echoed the shape of the old Roman villas, with rooms around a central courtyard, and this was true of Muslim homes as well as Christian. As Fernand Braudel notes in his famous study of domestic structures, "In short, a 'house' wherever it may be, is an enduring thing, and it bears perpetual witness to the slow pace of civilizations, of cultures bent on preserving, maintaining and repeating" (Braudel, 267).

Sometimes, however, there were dramatic changes in house styles, but these usually accompanied equally dramatic shifts in cultures. The most vivid example is that tribal houses all over the world are customarily round. This is true from the nomad's yurt outside China to the Eskimos' igloo. When tribes are conquered and made part of a larger society and when the tribal people were conquered and more complex political structures prevailed, the corners of houses became squared and houses became square or rectangular. The reason for this changing pattern is still in question.

Building materials obviously shaped the kinds of houses people built. Where wood was available, it was a favored building material. Great beams supported roofs, and wooden walls could be coated with plaster or mud. Vikings in lands with scarce trees built sod houses, and in Egypt and places in the Middle East, people built with baked-mud bricks. In northern Europe, poorer people built houses with mud and wattle (sticks woven together). Roofs were often covered with straw and thick thatch. Nomad tents were made of felt or cloth or skins, all of which were light and portable. The most expensive and durable houses were made of stone, and these made up the defensive castles of the elite. On the Polynesian islands, people used coconut palms and woven matting for their shelters. Housing all over the world shows how creative people have been at using the materials at hand to construct their shelters.

Houses were also constructed with an eye to the weather. On some Polynesian islands, houses had no walls so that they could catch the breezes; temporary mat walls could be erected to keep out the rain. Houses in northern Europe had thick walls (whether of mud or stone) and very small windows. Through the Middle Ages in Europe, virtually no houses had glass windows until the end of the period. Instead, people hung skins across openings to keep in warmth and try to let in some light. In China, people used oiled paper to cover windows; the wealthy used translucent silk. In all these areas, people faced the common problem of dealing with the weather while trying to keep their houses as light and comfortable as possible.

Until the late Middle Ages in Europe, houses had open hearths instead of chimneys. Therefore, houses in the north were very smoky, and fires were a real danger. In Polynesia and parts of China, people separated the cooking into a separate house to reduce the smoke and danger. Once chimneys were added to houses late in the Middle Ages, the quality of the interior air improved dramatically.

The greatest diversity in housing comes from the purposes that they serve. The poorest peasants—wherever they lived in the world—needed relatively inexpensive shelter that would serve the family and their animals. In Greenland, sheep brought into the house during the winter grew so lethargic from lack of exercise that they had to be carried out in the spring and had to practice walking again. Urban houses were more substantial everywhere, but they were also designed to serve the purpose of trade. Often the family lived upstairs or behind the shop that faced the street. The most striking examples of medieval houses were the defensive castles of the nobility. The living quarters of these great edifices were only a small part of the purpose of the building, which was to be warfare.

Throughout history, as people have sought shelter, they have had to adapt to building materials, the weather, and the purpose of the dwelling. At the same time, they have tried to keep to housing styles they found familiar—so that everyone's home might feel like their own castle, no matter how humble.

~Joyce E. Salisbury

FOR MORE INFORMATION

Braudel, F. *The Structures of Everyday Life*. New York: Harper and Row, 1979.

EUROPE

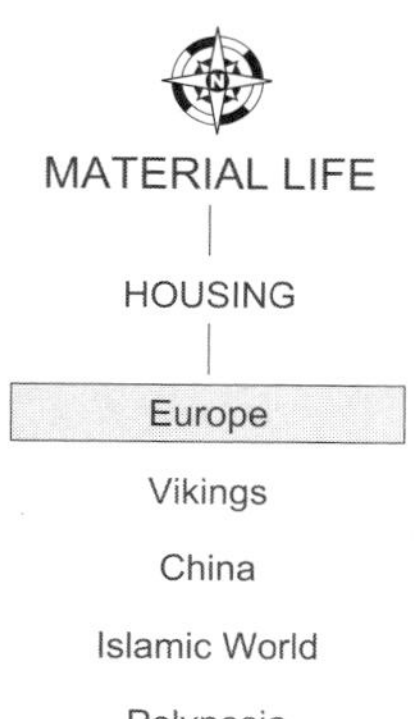

Throughout Europe, peasants, who lived at the lower end of the social scale, lived in homes with very few rooms—probably just one to three—and consisted of two or three bays, or framed construction units, measuring about 15 feet by 15 feet each. In some cases, the structure sheltered not just the family but its livestock as well, albeit in the far end from the human occupants. The frame of the peasant house was of joined timber, and the walls were commonly filled in with wattle and daub. In this technique, the spaces between the posts and beams were filled with wattling: long stakes fixed upright between lateral beams, with flexible sticks woven densely between them. The surface thus created was covered on both sides with daub: clay or loam mixed with straw or some similar fiber for strength. Alternatively, the walls might be made of turf (peat cuttings), cob (unbaked clay), or even stone, although this was beyond the means of the peasant except in places where stone was locally abundant. The roof was thatched with straw or reeds, although wood shingles, tiles, or slate might be used if these were plentiful in the area. The house normally had a packed dirt floor and only one story; boards might be laid across the overhead beams to create a loft for additional space.

The ground on which the house was built was called a toft and might include a cobblestone courtyard and a few additional outbuildings for storage and housing for domestic animals—cows, sheep, goats, pigs, geese, chickens, and the like. Behind the toft was usually a croft, a small garden for herbs, vegetables, and other household plants.

The dwellings of the medieval aristocracy varied as enormously as their incomes, but certain patterns were generally common to them all. Stone was the preferred material of construction, although the lesser aristocracy might have to be content with brick or even with a superior version of wattle and daub. The ideal roof was made of slate or tile; floors and rafters were always made of wood.

The largest room of the aristocratic home was the hall, the most public space of the house. Here the members of the household interacted with each other and with the outside world: it was a place for transacting public business, for holding entertainments, and especially for eating formal meals. It was usually the largest room in the building and was often high as well, with no ceiling but open to the roof. The hall had a "high" and a "low" end demarcated by a raised dais. The area below the dais pertained to the servants and to ordinary guests. At the low end, a wooden partition cut down on drafts; behind it were the main door to the outside and the doors to the service wing of the manor (kitchen, larder, and other areas used by the household staff).

At the high end, on the dais, sat the family itself with its favored guests. From here there was access to the solar (a private room for the family) and other private chambers. These rooms might be located in their own wing of the building or above the hall. Although it was traditional for the family to eat in the hall, aristocrats increasingly chose to have their meals in the private section of the house.

As the manor supported the knight economically, the castle evolved to support him militarily. Castles were defensive fortifications that also served as home to the noble lord and the defenders of the great castle. It provided a base from which a force of knights could strike an opposing force when they saw an opportunity, and to which they could retire for safety when they were at a disadvantage. The earliest castles were built of earthworks and timber, and some of these were still in use in the 13th century, but from the 12th century onward, castles were generally built of stone, and the technology of castle construction was becoming increasingly sophisticated.

The design of castles varied enormously, depending on local topography, the lord's resources, the function of the castle, and the current state of military technology. The most important military and administrative centers lay in strategic locations along rivers, sea coasts, or overlooking valleys that served as communication routes.

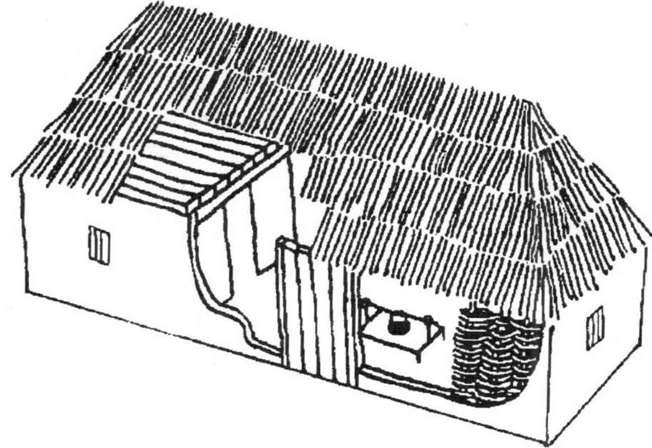

Cutaway reconstruction of a cottage. It is made of wattle-and-daub walls and is roofed with thatch. Inside, the open hearth for cooking is visible. Illustration by Jeffrey Singman.

Many castles were built on a high point in the local terrain, the height improving the garrison's ability to keep watch on the surrounding area, as well as conferring an advantage for the defenders in combat. If built on flat ground, a portion of the castle might be raised on an artificial mound.

Because castles were defensive structures, they were surrounded by one or more walls. Towers were built into the walls at intervals of about 200 feet or less, roughly the range of a bow, ensuring that every point along the perimeter was covered by two towers. The towers rose higher than the wall itself, providing maximum visibility for the defenders, who normally used the towers as their principal bases for defense. Additional defense was furnished by arrow slits in the tower walls. The towers also provided shelter against the weather, an important consideration because rain lessened the effectiveness of the defenders' bows. These towers also served as living spaces for the defenders.

Once a visitor was cleared through the front gate, he or she came into a castle's outer bailey (the space enclosed by the outer wall), which might be divided up into several enclosures separated by fortified walls. The main outer bailey extended around all sides of the inner bailey except the southeast side. This area was probably the principal space for the castle garrison.

The main household of a castle consisted of a large public hall where the castle residents ate, played games, and entertained themselves while gathered around the open hearth in the center of the room. There were also smaller, private chambers where the lord and lady slept, the women of the household did the weaving and sewing, and children were born. In such a private chamber, the lord also stored a strongbox filled with coins and other valuables. In an age with no banking, most nobles guarded their wealth themselves.

By the 13th century, these living quarters were designed for comfort as well as safety. Noble families lived in high towers, where it was safe to have glass windows, and the open hearth was moved to the wall as a fireplace to reduce the smoke in the room. Latrines were built into the walls of adjacent rooms, and pipes brought water to the upper floors.

Different from both peasant and aristocratic dwellings was the townhouse. In construction, the ordinary townhouse resembled the timber-framed peasant dwelling, commonly measuring about 12 feet by 20 feet, with a garden of comparable size behind. Unlike the peasant house, it was two or three stories high and was more likely to have a floor and a cellar as well as a wooden, tile, or slate roof (many towns tried to forbid thatched roofs because of their extreme vulnerability to fire).

If the house belonged to a craftsman or tradesman, the front door would lead into the shop. This shop might extend into the street during the day: wares were placed on display out front, and some tradesmen (notably butchers) actually did their work there. The family lived in a room behind the shop or above it; upper floors could also be used for servants, apprentices, or tenants. The upper floors were accessible by stairs or ladders and sometimes projected over the street to make maximum use of limited urban space. Most urban families probably lived in two rooms and a kitchen or less. Wealthier city dwellers tended to have complexes comparable to aristocratic manors, consisting of several specialized buildings grouped around a courtyard, with a gateway leading to the street (Singman and McLean, 79–83).

To read about housing in Elizabethan England, see the England entry in the section "Houses and Furniture" in chapter 5 ("Material Life") of volume 3; for 18th-century England, see the England entry in the section "Housing and Furnishings" in chapter 5 ("Material Life") of volume 4; for Victorian England, see the England entry in the section "Housing" in chapter 5 ("Material Life") of volume 5 of this series.

FOR MORE INFORMATION

Singman, J. L., and W. McLean. *Daily Life in Chaucer's England*. Westport, Conn.: Greenwood Press, 1995.

VIKINGS

Climatic conditions differ considerably within Scandinavia and in the Norse settlements in the North Atlantic. Accordingly, there was no single pattern of houses in the Viking Age. The mode of constructing houses was determined largely by the surroundings. Treeless regions necessitated use of stone, turf (peat cuttings), clay, straw, and hay, while wooded areas prompted the building of timber houses. In addition, the cold climate of northern Scandinavia, Iceland, and Greenland required considerably more insulation of house walls than did the somewhat milder climate of Denmark and southern Norway and Sweden.

Farmhouses are relatively well known to us from archaeological excavations. Typically, a farm had one main rectangular longhouse, and the length reflected the farmer's social and economic position. And while some houses consisted of only one room, other houses were divided by partition walls into several rooms, which could be closed off. One end of the house was reserved for domestic animals, which helped keep the cold away. The living room and sometimes a room for cooking and storage was at the other end. In Iceland, the plan of the longhouse was extended by adding rooms to it, such as a lobby, kitchen, pantry, and lavatory, and in this way a new pattern was created: a longhouse with annexes. Some farms also had smaller outbuildings with particular functions, such as byres for wintering the animals, barns for their fodder, stables, storehouses, bathhouses, and smithies, which were grouped around the main longhouse.

The houses always had an inner frame consisting of two rows of interior wooden posts situated in pairs and placed in holes dug into the ground. As construction techniques became more sophisticated, the posts were placed on stones to prevent them from rotting. These posts were connected by beams that ran both transversally and longitudinally to a stable frame. Such a construction was sturdy enough to support the roof, which could be made solely of wood or thatched, that is, covered with sod or birch bark. The walls were built in various ways and of various materials. Some were made of logs with wattle-and-daub in-filling. Others were formed of staves or planks standing side by side in wall ditches. Yet others were made only of stone or turf, and in cold regions, these materials—stone and turf—were typically piled up as an outer embankment for insulation purposes. The walls could be either straight or bowed outward. Such houses also had a curved roof ridge and sometimes rounded corners, which made them look like ships turned upside-down. The doors were typically in the long sides at either end. They might be decorated with carvings or iron fittings and could typically be locked with wooden or iron locks. Windows were nonexistent in the longhouses with their thick walls of stone and turf and most likely began in the wooden houses as narrow peepholes protected by inside shutters or glazed with translucent membrane. It is not until the end of the Viking Age that properly glazed windows are recorded. The floors, which were sometimes sunken, were of stamped earth and often strewn with straw or hay.

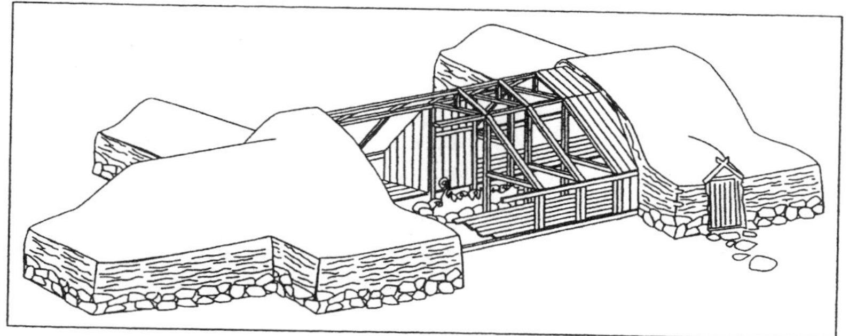

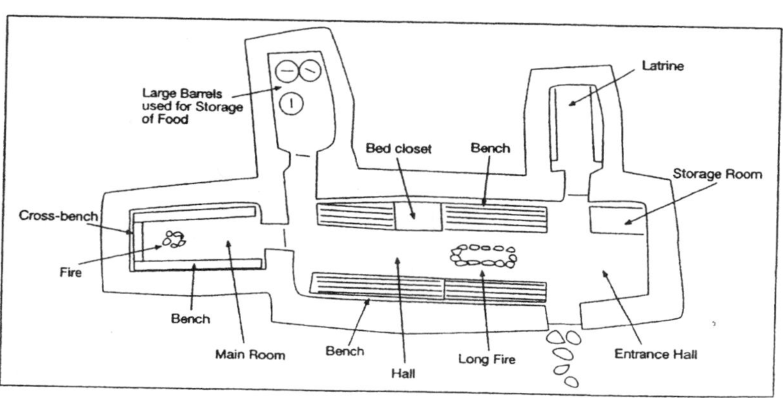

Viking farmhouse at Stong. This shows the cross-section as well as the layout of the farmhouse, which kept the family warm through the long winter.

Houses in urban communities differed in size and construction. Like farm complexes, they were normally situated on a fenced-in plot, usually rectangular in shape, sometimes with one or more additional outbuildings for cooking, commercial purposes, crafts, and the like. Unlike farm complexes, urban houses were packed close together. They could belong to a single owner or be divided into subordinate divisions as tenements or holdings.

Excavations in Hedeby in South Schleswig in the 1930s and again in the 1960s revealed a number of houses from the 9th and 10th centuries. In size the houses varied from 7 by 17.5 meters to 3 by 2.9 meters. Most likely, however, the latter did not serve as living quarters for people. The smallest house believed to have been a home measures 7 by 3.5 meters, an area of only approximately 25 square meters. Some of the houses were constructed of horizontal planking; others were stave-built with vertical planking normally consisting of wedge-shaped portions of tree trunks; yet others were timber framed with wattle-and-daub in-filling. The roofs appear to have been thatched with straw or reeds with a hole either above the hearth in the middle of the house or at the top of the gable end to allow smoke to escape, for, like farmhouses, they had no chimneys. Some of the houses had partition walls. A rather well-preserved house had three rooms: a living room in the middle and two smaller rooms, one containing a bread oven, at either end.

Ibrahim b. Ya'qub al-Turtushi, a 10th-century merchant or diplomat from Andalusia (Muslim Spain), who visited Hedeby, reports that in the town there were freshwater wells. Excavations not only confirm his statement but also reveal that most houses had their own well. Of these wells, which were typically situated behind the houses, there were at least three types: one was box shaped, built of boards around four corner posts; another was circular, built of barrel staves; and a third type consisted of a hollowed-out tree trunk. These wells were often at least two meters deep.

The streets in Hedeby were narrow. In terms of construction, they were simple. They consisted of two parallel rods with a distance of about one meter between them. Across these were placed boards fastened with wooden rivets on either side. The boards jutted out over the beams, making the roads just over one meter wide. No streets were therefore wide enough for vehicular traffic; the broadest street was only about one-and-a-half meters wide. One of the streets crossed a brook via a six-meter-long bridge, of which charred wood remains were found in the bed of the brook itself. In several places, steps led down to the stream, and since a number of hairpins were found in these areas, it is believed that women did their washing there. The remains of a washtub on top of one of these stairs confirms this supposition. In addition to these through streets, most houses had "private roads." The houses were typically built a little back from, but facing, the streets. A catwalk from the entrance in the gable end of the house across the courtyard to the street was therefore necessary; sometimes the wood-block paving of these walks was replaced by stones.

Daily life centered around the fire in the middle of the floor of the living quarters, which gave light and warmth. The fire was on a slightly raised, stone-lined hearth. Because of its rectangular shape, it was called a long hearth or fire. The fire was fed with peat or wood kept outside the house. At night, it had to banked, so that it could be easily relit in the morning. If it went out, it had to be rekindled with flint and steel in tinder. Some houses had a small oven or roasting pit against the wall instead of or in addition to an open hearth. The ovens were made on a framework of wattle and shaped like a dome.

When the light from the fire did not provide sufficient illumination, lamps of soapstone, iron, or clay filled with oil were used. These lamps were simple, open bowls, which stood on a flat surface or were suspended with loops or were mounted on an iron spike stuck in the ground. Wax candles appear to have been a rare and expensive commodity and are known only from wealthy graves, such as at Jelling and Mammen in Jutland, Denmark.

Raised platforms along the long walls of the house served as seats and beds close to the fire, although for sleeping accommodation, some houses had built-in bed closets, which provided at least some privacy. Presumably, these platforms were covered with furs, skins, or woolen blankets. The central section of one platform (usually at the inner end) was the so-called high seat of the head of the household. Although it is referred to in English as the high seat, it was not necessarily higher in elevation, only in honor. The guest of honor was seated opposite the head of the household. The high seat was flanked by pillars, which were often adorned, and from Old Norse literature it is known that the high-seat pillars had religious significance. There are several reports of how men emigrating from Norway to Iceland took their high-seat pillars with them. Once they sighted land, they threw the pillars overboard in the belief that the gods would guide them to the place where they were destined to settle.

~*Kirsten Wolf*

FOR MORE INFORMATION

Wolf, K. *Daily Life of the Vikings*. Westport, Conn.: Greenwood Press, forthcoming.

CHINA

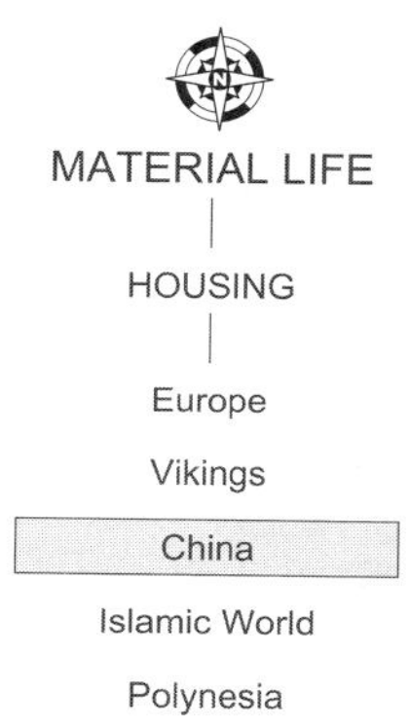

There were all sorts of dwellings in the Tang dynasty. Beyond the Great Wall, pastoral tribes lived in yurts, round tents made of felt that they stretched over wood frames. They could easily dismantle the yurts and move them, loaded on their horses, to greener pastures for grazing their sheep. In northwest China, where trees were scarce and the climate was dry, people lived in artificial caves. The soil of that region was loess, dirt that the winds had blown in from the steppes of the north for centuries. The deposits were 150 or more feet thick and fairly easy to work since they contained few rocks. The inhabitants dug chambers into the sides of hills or excavated deep, rectangular pits at the bottom of which they tunneled into the walls to fashion rooms. Cave dwellings reached a mature stage of development during the Tang. In southwest China, aborigines lived in homes built on pilings to protect themselves and their property from moisture and flooding. Along the Yangtze River, crews of transport vessels spent their entire lives on boats. Their craft even had gardens that produced vegetables for the tables of the boat people. Some merchants in central China had large ships on which they lived with troupes of female entertainers and complements of maidservants. In some southern districts, nearly half of the population lived on boats.

Most of the information about houses in Tang sources concerns the great residences of the patricians in Changan and Luoyang. Ideally, a dwelling of the Tang dynasty faced south so that it received the warmth of the sun and the beneficent forces of fire—the element associated with that direction and a vitalizing force for the inhabitants of the house. This notion, derived from ancient cosmology and geomancy (*feng shui*), determined the location of a dwelling's main gate or door. The Chinese, however, also believed that malevolent forces, such as noxious vapors (*qi*) or ghosts, could enter through the portals. To obstruct such evil invasions, those who could afford to do so had a wall, called a shadow wall, built in front of their gates to prevent calamities from befalling their families.

The mansions of the rich and powerful in Tang China, like those before and after them, consisted of a series of courtyards. Unlike the great houses, châteaus, and villas of the West, they were not single, massive buildings embracing parlors, dining rooms, kitchens, bedrooms, and so forth. Instead, they were compounds containing separate structures for different purposes. In general, the main buildings, or halls, sat on a central axis that ran from north to south and were at the rear of the large courtyards. Smaller buildings sat on the east and west sides of the squares and were joined to the halls by porticos, or covered walkways, that provided shelter from the elements for anyone moving between the structures. The courtyards were fairly self-contained, so that an owner could close one off and rent it to a lodger. The front or outer courtyard was the man's domain. It contained the largest and most formal hall, a parlor where the head of the household received visitors and conducted business. The rear or inner apartments were the woman's realm and were off-limits to men unless they were family members.

Most halls were rectangular with one longer side, the front, facing south. Halls were usually one or two stories high, so mansions presented a horizontal aspect. The halls rested on platforms of rammed earth that prevented floods from damaging the interior and its contents. Sometimes that precaution failed. In 817, a heavy rain in Changan collapsed a pillar in one of the palaces, flooded the markets with three feet of water, and destroyed more than 2,000 homes. That paled in comparison to a flood that struck a city in the northeast during 669. The waters rose to five feet and destroyed more than 14,000 homes.

Mansion of a wealthy family in China, showing the layout of the compound surrounding a courtyard. Illustration by Charles Benn.

The private quarters of a mansion, including its bedchambers, were usually located in courtyards behind the parlor. In one example, a high-ranking official bought a property in Luoyang during the 8th century and had it modified over the years. At the center stood a hall for his first wife, who had died. It was spare and unadorned. To the east of that was one for his elder brother's wife (the brother, presumably, had passed away). To the northeast was another for his elder sisters when they came to visit. It was not uncommon in the Tang for brothers to live together. In that case, the head of the household would allocate a whole courtyard to each so that they could live with their families yet have a degree of privacy. Some halls served special purposes. Aside from the parlor, there were libraries where educated men spent their leisure hours reading and writing or music halls for practicing instruments.

The entire frame of expensive houses—pillars, beams, rafters, and the rest—was made of wood. Pillars, beams, and rafters were often painted bright colors. In some cases, however, roof beams made of cypress timbers were left untouched so that one could admire their fine grains. The eaves of the roof extended beyond the walls to cover porches that surrounded the building and provided shade.

Of all the elements in traditional architecture, the roof was the crowning glory of the hall, its most expensive and striking feature.

Workmen laid semicircular glazed ceramic tiles on roof boards affixed to the rafters. Although much more expensive, tiles had a great advantage over other materials, such as thatch, commonly used in peasant dwellings: they were fireproof. Embers from a nearby blaze blown onto them by the wind would not ignite them.

Windows provided ventilation and light. Glass panes did not exist in Tang China. For those of modest means, paper sufficed for windows, preferably oiled paper because it was translucent and therefore admitted more light. For the more affluent, silk—dyed scarlet, green, or some other hue—might serve the purpose and tint the sunlight falling on the floor inside of the room. In either case, the materials could not withstand the force of strong winds. Consequently, carpenters built wooden lattices to which they glued the paper or cloth. They used pine, wood that was too soft for structural members of the building, for the frames. In exceptional cases, small pieces of glass or mica that sparkled in the sunlight might be inlaid in the frames.

Workers covered the masonry walls inside and out with plaster. The owner of a mansion might have a famous artist paint cranes, horses, a landscape, or a rendering of a famous dance on his walls. A renowned calligrapher might brush a line or two of poetry or prose on the walls of his host's abode during a feast. In all these details, the inhabitants of the houses during the Tang dynasty looked on their homes as pleasing works of art (Benn, 80–83).

FOR MORE INFORMATION

Benn, C. *Daily Life in Traditional China: The Tang Dynasty*. Westport, Conn.: Greenwood Press, 2002.

ISLAMIC WORLD

Housing in the medieval Islamic world included tents, mud huts, reed huts, single-story residences, multistory tenements, and elaborate palaces. In the deserts of Arabia, Syria, Iraq, Iran, and North Africa, tents predominated among the pastoral nomadic populations. These were generally made from the hair or wool of the nomads' herds and flocks, whether sheep, goats, or camels. In the settled oases of the region, most homes were built from mud or reeds simply because wood and stone were rarely available in sufficient quantities to be practicable. In 7th-century Mecca, Muhammad's hometown, homes tended to be huts built of mud bricks, whereas, in other oases, reed huts were more common. In the highlands of Yemen, many residents lived in villages and towns made up of multistory tenement buildings.

In the major cities such as Damascus, Baghdad, and Cairo, wood and stone were the preferred building materials because they were more readily available and because they are far more durable than tents and mud or reed huts. While some residents lived in single-story homes, many lived in multistory apartment buildings. Medieval Muslim rulers also built elaborate stone palaces, mosques, madrasas (schools for study of the Qur'an), caravansaries (inns where caravans stopped at night), bathhouses, and hospitals. Depending on the locale, some of the stones and columns used in constructing such examples of monumental architecture were recycled from Pharaonic, Roman, and Sassanian ruins or from Christian churches and monasteries. Some of the buildings constructed during the Middle Ages still bear the graffiti and other inscriptions of earlier eras.

Typical of most dwellings at the time was a central courtyard or common area of some sort around which salons, bedrooms, and kitchens were constructed. Only the wealthy could afford indoor plumbing or ovens as part of their residences. Outhouses or outdoor latrine facilities of some sort were the order of the day. Men often simply urinated in a street or alley, as was the custom in many places in the ancient world. Public baths were essential to every city. If there was only one in a town, certain days or parts of days were designated for women and others for men. Larger cities had women's bathhouses, which were usually physically separate from the men's bathhouses.

One's home in the medieval Islamic world served as a sanctuary or refuge from the primarily male-dominated public world of the market and the mosque. Most men who were not part of the ruling classes or military spent much of the day outside the home working, studying, or at prayer in the mosque with other men. Women (especially respectable women) spent a great deal of their time at home with their children and other women. Women generally performed their ritual prayers at home. Literate women were usually educated at home, often by their fathers, uncles, brothers, or male cousins. If their mothers or other female relatives were educated, they often studied with them as well. Women who worked for a wage generally labored at home doing piecework as seamstresses or making other handicrafts.

In addition to serving as a refuge from the outside world, the courtyard was a common area shared by the whole family (or families) who lived around it. Among rural and nomadic populations, the courtyard might also serve as a corral for livestock. Women prepared hot meals over a fire in such courtyards or in common neighborhood cooking areas. Meals that required an oven were prepared at home and then taken to a local bake house to be cooked. In the residences of the wealthy and the palaces of the ruling classes, courtyards were often quite elaborate. Many were equipped with fountains, gardens, and sophisticated canopies and trellises that allowed in light but also provided a cooling shade from the hot sun.

The courtyard also served as the public space of the home where guests were welcomed and entertained. In addition to the courtyard, there was often a salon that served the same purpose. In either case, when male guests were involved, the courtyard or the salon became extensions of the outside world in that such gatherings generally were male-only affairs, especially among the wealthy classes. Because hospitality and generosity were notable virtues throughout the Islamic world, food and beverages were served in such instances. In the medieval Islamic world, few things could ruin one's reputation more than being known as stingy or inhospitable.

Because of the strict rules pertaining to sexual segregation, every dwelling had an inviolable space (harem) separate from the rest of the house where the women retreated when male guests were present. In palaces and the homes of the wealthy, this space took the form of well-appointed women's quarters or harems, which only women, children, male kin, and eunuchs were allowed to enter. The women of less well-to-do families retreated to a room or an area separated from the rest of the dwelling by a curtain or some other type of partition. This area served as a harem only when guests were present but was generally used for other purposes, such as cooking, sewing, making handicrafts, study, or sleeping.

~James Lindsay

FOR MORE INFORMATION

Lindsay, J. *Daily Life in the Medieval Islamic World*. Westport, Conn.: Greenwood Press, forthcoming.

al-Muqaddasi. *The Best Divisions for Knowledge of the Regions: Ahsan al-taqasim fi ma'rifat al-aqalim*. Translated by B. Collins. Reading, England: Garnet, 2001.

POLYNESIA

Ancient Polynesians were limited in the construction of their houses because they lacked suitable building materials and because they had no metal tools, utensils, or nails with which to work. Also, the warm, tropical weather allowed the Polynesians to spend most of their time out of doors, so substantial housing was less a requirement as it was elsewhere in the world. Most Polynesian islands and atolls had very few trees from which plank lumber could be extracted. On the other hand, they had substantial amounts of other plants from which housing material could be made. Coconut palm trees, for example, supplied house posts from their trunks, roof thatching and matting from their fronds, and twine (sennit) from the inside husks of the coconut. The common pandanus plant also provided pliable fronds for making finely woven mats, and wild sugarcane and tanglehead grass (*Heteropogon cotortus*) provided roofing materials. All of these materials, of course, were less substantial than the solid wood or stone that were used in other parts of the world, and as a result, the common house in Polynesia resembled what foreigners came to call a "grass hut" or a "grass shack." Despite these facts, however, some of the larger and well-built traditional houses were so skillfully executed that the surviving ones are regarded today as natural treasures.

House size depended on the status, wealth, or energy of the builder. Poorer houses were very small huts that resembled lean-tos, and they were barely large enough for protection against the elements. Most commoner's dwelling huts, however, were generally rectangular—about 16 feet long, 10 feet wide, and 6 to 7 feet high—with gabled roofs. A high chief's house could be as much as three times that size. Some island groups—Tonga and Samoa, for example—preferred their houses rounded at the ends with curved roofs that looked like an egg cut lengthwise and the rounded half placed on supporting posts around the outer edges.

Another characteristic of Polynesian housing was that it consisted of not a single dwelling but of several huts constructed in close proximity and each designed for a different purpose. A well-to-do Polynesian, for example, would have an eating house for the men, separate from and tapu (taboo) to the women; another house where the wife and children lived and not tapu to the husband; a shelter for the wife where she could beat her tapa cloth during inclement weather; a house where the wife lived during her monthly menstrual cycle; a small family chapel where sacred artifacts were kept; a canoe shed if the family lived near the beach; and sometimes a shed where food was stored. Also, houses were generally scattered around the islands along the beaches or in the valleys rather than clustered in large villages. High chiefs' dwellings, however, were generally surrounded by their numerous attendants' and advisors' living quarters that collectively resembled village units.

Building a new house was no simple task. Normally, male members of the family built their own houses. There were no skilled craftsmen or journeymen whose main duty was to construct houses (except, perhaps, in Samoa). Also, a house was supposed to possess a life of its own, and there were many tapus regarding its construction. The builder had to request the services of a priest or diviner to make sure that the house complied with all the proper tapus—for example, a house must face the correct direction, must not be built on tapu land, and must be properly dedicated. After the necessary rituals were completed, the builder collected his materials. His main tools consisted of stone adzes (hard, sharp stones lashed to a handle with twine) and sharpened bone or sea shells for cutting. Trees for the support posts, ridgepoles, and rafters were felled in the forests, sugarcane leaves and tanglehead grass (called *pili* grass in Hawai'i) were collected for the roof, and coconut fronds and lauhala leaves were gathered to be woven into mats for wall enclosures.

A traditionally built community house on the island of Huahine in French Polynesia. Photo courtesy of Robert D. Craig.

First, the earth was leveled and laid out for the house construction. Some floors were raised with a foot of dirt to allow for drainage. (In some parts of Hawai'i, the Marquesas Islands, and the Cook Islands, however, house platforms were constructed from large fitted blocks of basalt stone, and the various dwellings were built on top of these impressive structures.) Corner and side posts were then planted around the perimeter of the proposed building while two main posts were set up within the center of the building to support the main ridge pole of the roof. Heavy beams (plates) were then cut and lashed to the tops of the outer posts to support the lower ends of the rafters. The rafters were poles cut to fit the length between the main ridge pole of the roof and the plates. Smaller, horizontal poles were lashed to the rafters around the whole perimeter of the roof. Lashing the timbers and rafters together was a complex and lengthy job. In more important homes, lashings were often executed in combinations of red, yellow, and black sennit to create a highly artistic design. Once this outer shell was done, the construction looked very much like a bird cage.

Thatching of the roof was a long and tedious procedure. Roof coverings could be made of woven coconut or lauhala mats, closely bound together, lashed onto the rafters, and overlapped so that the house would be rainproof. Other types of roofs consisted of banana or lauhala leaves, or pili grass, carefully tied over short poles, and then the whole unit lashed to the rafters, one overlapping the other, similar to roofing on a modern home.

Walls around the entire house were optional, depending on the purpose of the house and on the island group. Hawai'i and New Zealand, for example, experienced cooler weather, so most of their walls were tightly constructed with very few openings. On other islands, walls were less important, and they were left open to take advantage of the trade winds that helped cool the islands. During inclement weather, portable mats could be set up temporarily for protection against the elements. There were generally no permanent partitions within the houses, but sometimes woven mats, two to three feet wide, set on edge in a circular fashion, or tapa cloth hung from the rafters, could provide privacy when needed.

In poorer homes, the bare earth flooring was simply covered with layers of dried grass and leaves. In other homes, the floor was built up with smooth pebbles gathered from the riverbeds or the seashore. This layer was then covered with finely woven mats. Grass "doormats" were planted around the immediate exterior of the house openings to make sure that no dirt was carried into the house. (Polynesians usually went barefoot.) House utensils generally hung from the ceiling rafters, and there were no fireplaces—all cooking was done outdoors or in a nearby cook house.

After the whole construction was completed, a priest was called in to dedicate the new dwelling. He would take a stone adz and, after chanting several incantations, would trim the long thatching over the main door. After that, the building could be used for the purpose for which it was built (Handy, 69–80; Bellwood, 92–93).

~*Robert D. Craig*

FOR MORE INFORMATION

Bellwood, P. *The Polynesians: Prehistory of an Island People*. London: Thames and Hudson, 1978.

Handy, E. S. *Ancient Hawaiian Civilization*. Rev. ed. Rutland, Vt.: Charles E. Tuttle, 1965.

Clothing

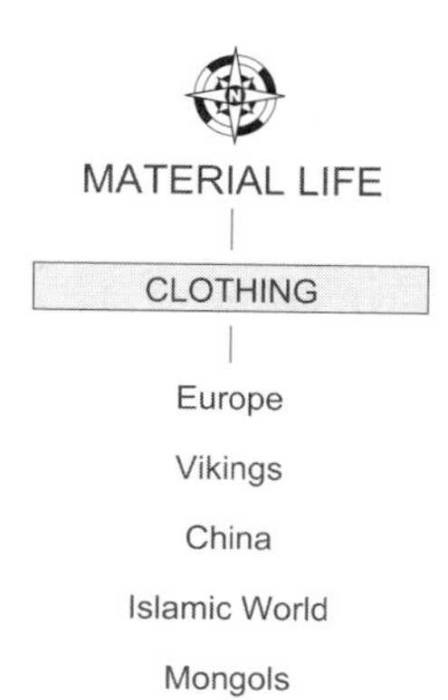

At its most basic level, clothing provides protection from the elements. Fur capes in Europe, felt hoods of the Mongol steppes, or bamboo hats of the Chinese countryside kept off the rain and protected the wearer. The same was true for shoes—leather shoes, wooden clogs, or straw sandals protected the feet in various climates. In the mild climate of Polynesia, people wore very little—children under the age of seven, for example, wore nothing. However, if protection was the whole story, the history of clothing would be much more simple to tell. Instead, clothing also serves as a public statement for the wearer. As such, clothing allows us to define ourselves by gender, social status, and cultural identity. Thus an analysis of the clothes we wear tells us much about who we are.

Most societies make sure that gender is clearly delineated by clothing and general appearance. Polynesian men wore simple loincloths, and women wore skirts. In modern times, we have often used skirts to mark gender, but this was certainly not the case in the Middle Ages. In Scandinavia, in China, and among the Mongols, women could wear trousers just as men did to work or ride horses. In Scotland, China, Byzantium, and Muslim lands, men wore flowing robes as women did. This does not mean gender markers did not exist; they just took different forms.

Headdresses and hairstyles are a basic gender marker in many cultures. In Muslim societies, women were readily recognized by the veils that cover their heads or their full bodies; clothing that was intended as protection from the male gaze quickly defined their gender. Hair, too, was a strong gender marker as well as a sign of the marital availability of women. In Europe, young girls wore their hair exposed, but married women were to modestly veil their hair, although many women found ways to make a token veil as striking and attractive as long, flowing hair. Mongol women shaved their heads from the middle to the forehead when they married. These customs were designed to be sure there was no ambiguity about gender. Viking society even made this a legal regulation:

> If a woman dresses in male clothing or cuts her hair like a man or carries weapons in order to be different from others, the punishment is . . . expatriation for three years. . . . The same is the case if men dress in female [clothes]. (Jochens, 9)

Status was a second important purpose for clothing. People wanted to have their importance recognized at first glance, and this led to differential clothing. Chinese peasants of both genders wore working trousers, and the upper classes of both genders wore silk robes. The emperor of China had 14 different kinds of robes, each for a different ceremonial occasion. In Europe, fashion began to change dramatically in the 12th century, as people wanted to signal their ability to wear new, dramatic looks. One 12th-century commentator lamented: "The old way of dressing has been almost completely thrown over by the new inventions" (Braudel, 317). He was right to worry, for by the 14th century, men wore such short tunics and skin-tight leggings that no one could doubt their gender! Women, too, began to display the tops of their breasts and to wear such elaborate headdresses that they had to cultivate good balance to walk successfully.

European changes in fashion were in striking contrast with much of the rest of the world, in which tradition outweighed innovation as a marker of cultural continuity. In Byzantium, for example, laws were passed in the 4th century to prevent people from wearing furs and trousers in imitation of the Germanic peoples of western Europe. Instead, Byzantium preserved the robes of the late Roman Empire. This preservation was a visual statement of continuity.

Of course, if one *wants* to make a statement of change, clothing is a perfect way to do so. When the Mongols became rulers of China, they began to wear delicately embroidered robes woven with gold and precious stones. They had been transformed. In Europe, during the late Middle Ages, the aristocracy tried to legislate people's clothing by sumptuary laws, to regulate what clothing was appropriate to what social class. In fact, this was an attempt to stop upward social mobility, which was indicated by changing fashions. It was too late—clothes were just the sign of change, not the cause, and people in the Middle Ages as now, wanted to dress for success. For a related topic, see the section "Personal Appearance" in this chapter.

~*Joyce E. Salisbury*

FOR MORE INFORMATION

Braudel, F. *The Structures of Everyday Life*. New York: Harper and Row, 1979.

Jochens, J. "Before the Male Gaze: The Absence of the Female Body in Old Norse." In *Sex in the Middle Ages*, edited by J. E. Salisbury. New York: Garland: 1991.

EUROPE

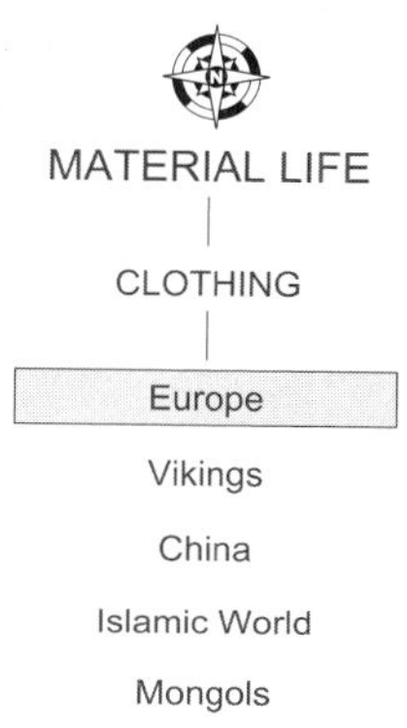

A man's first item of clothing in medieval Europe was his linen breech or braies. Roughly speaking, braies are comparable to a large and loose-fitting pair of boxer shorts or pajama trousers. There was no elastic to hold them up at the waist: after pulling them on, the man would secure them in place with a braiel, which was either a leather belt or a lace comparable to a long shoelace. The braiel was fastened around the waist, gathering the loose upper edge of the braies with it. It might pass through a casing or eyelets in the braies, or the edge of the braies might be wrapped around it to hold them in place. The braies reached to the knees or even lower, and illustrations often show another lace at the bottom that could be used to fasten the braies at the bottom, or tie the loose cuff of the longer braies back up to the braiel when they were being worn without overgarments because of the heat. The braiel might also support a purse, since this was a reasonably secure place to keep money.

The next layer of a man's clothing was a pair of hose. These were two long stockings of woolen cloth, each covering the entire leg. The hose pulled up over the bottom of the braies and came to a point at the top, with a lace attached to tie it to the braiel. Hose were cut on the diagonal for extra stretch, but even so they were loose and given to bunching—a far cry from the tights we usually see in period films. A poor man's hose might not have feet or might have only a strap under the arch of the foot.

Over the braies and hose, the man wore a linen shirt, which reached to the thighs or knees. The shirt had a gusset from hem to crotch to allow greater mobility for the legs. On top, the man wore a longer tunic of similar design. The tunic was usually made of wool and possibly was adorned with decorative trim or embroidery around the collar, cuffs, and hem. Its length depended on the intended use. Labor and other physical activities required a shorter hemline, typically to the knee or so, whereas high-status men in more formal settings might wear long tunics reaching to the feet. Like the shirt, the tunic might have a gusset from hem to crotch or might simply be left open, particularly if the tunic was worn while riding. Because the tunic pulled on over the head, it required a fairly large neck opening, which might be round, square, or triangular. Some had a slit in the middle of the front, fastened at the top with a brooch.

A woman's undergarments were somewhat different from those of a man. Medieval references indicate that she did not wear braies, which were considered a specifically masculine garment. There are occasional references to a "breast-band," perhaps a piece of linen fabric bound around the torso as the equivalent of a brassiere, although it may refer to some sort of sash worn outside the garments. The woman's principal undergarment was her shirt, similar to a man's, but longer, and possibly constructed with triangular inserts in the side seams instead of in front and back. Because her torso garments were longer than a man's, her hose could be shorter, reaching only to the knees, where they were fastened in place with a lace or a buckled leather garter. Her tunic was similar in design to a man's, but it too might have gores instead of gussets and was always long, reaching to the ankles or feet.

Outside their tunics, men and women alike wore a narrow leather belt, useful for suspending a purse, knife, or other necessities. A variety of overgarments were in use. One of the most common was the overtunic, perhaps somewhat shorter skirted and of finer material than the tunic underneath. Some 13th-century overtunics had a vertical slit at the front where the sleeve met the body, allowing the arm to be slipped through while the sleeve was left dangling behind. Overtunics might also have a pocket slit at the waist to allow access to items worn on the belt underneath. The layering of tunics allowed for a fashionable look and also served the practical need for extra warmth.

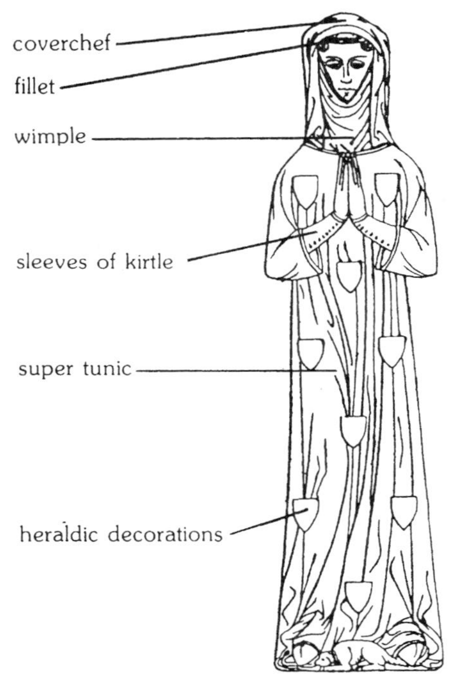

Noble lady in heraldic dress. This 14th-century dress shows how noble women were supposed to cover their heads and necks for modesty. The dress also provides a space for women to display their heraldic arms, which showed their noble ancestry. Joyce E. Salisbury.

There were also looser outer garments of various styles. Some had long sleeves gathered at the top into the shoulder seam, again sometimes with slits for the arms, while others had shorter, bell-shaped sleeves. These loose overgarments sometimes had hoods attached to them. Most were principally male garments, but the plain mantle, the simplest form of overgarment, was worn by men and women alike. The very end of the 13th century saw the appearance of the sleeveless surcoat, a loose overgarment that became very popular in the 14th century. Outer garments were sometimes lined with fur for extra warmth; linings available to ordinary people included rabbit, cat, fox, and fleece. Gloves and mittens were also worn, either for warmth or to protect the hands when working.

For footwear, men and women both wore similar styles of leather shoes and low boots; the latter were particularly favored by working folk. The dominant style of the 12th century relied on drawstring thongs laced around the ankle to keep the shoe on the foot; surviving 13th-century shoes are sometimes fastened with lacings up the inner side or with toggles. The sole was flat, with no additional heel. As the sole wore out, it might be patched with another piece of leather or even removed entirely and a new sole attached to the upper. Medieval shoes were simple in design and did not last long. Shoes were periodically washed and greased to preserve the leather and keep it watertight. Shoes were sometimes worn with pattens, wooden overshoes resembling sandals that helped keep the shoes out of the mud.

Poorer folk sometimes went without hose, wearing their shoes directly against the skin, and the very poor might go entirely barefoot.

Headgear was the single most obvious distinction between male and female attire, and it was also especially subject to the currents of fashion. Men of this period are often depicted bareheaded. The simplest form of male headgear was the coif, a linen bonnet that covered the hair and tied under the chin. The coif kept a man's head warm and his hair clean and was particularly favored by laboring men. Men also wore a variety of caps and hats made of cloth or felt, or perhaps knitted. Agricultural laborers of the period are often shown wearing straw hats in the summer. Ordinary men sometimes wore hoods, usually made of wool but sometimes made of leather. The hood might have a small cape attached to it that draped onto the shoulders. Young aristocrats in the 13th century might wear chaplets (wreaths) of flowers, a style also affected by young aristocratic women.

Women were more likely to keep their heads covered. Like the male coif, the various elements of a woman's head covering were typically made of linen. Ordinary women of the period are often shown wearing a simple head wrap, probably consisting only of a long rectangle of fabric, either tucked into itself or secured in place with a band wrapped twice around the head. Women of slightly higher status wore a veil, an oval or rectangular piece of fabric that lay atop the wearer's hair. This was secured in place with a fillet, also made of fabric, either worn on top of the veil or, more usually, serving as an anchor underneath to which the veil could be pinned. In the mid-12th century some women began to wear a barbette, a strap that passed under the chin and was pinned together at the top of the crown; this too helped anchor the veil. The late 12th century saw the appearance of the wimple, a larger piece of fabric that was draped under the chin, covering the front of the neck; it was probably secured with pins to the fillet or barbette.

Medieval people lived in their clothes much more than we do today. Many people slept naked, but others in colder climates slept in the underclothes they wore during the day, only removing them on Saturday to wash and replace them with a fresh set. Laundry appears to have been done on a weekly basis, at least among those who could afford a second set of undergarments. Linens were washed with water and lye and then laid out in the sun to dry and bleach. Woolen garments were not necessarily washed at all; medieval references generally describe brushing wool clothing to remove the dirt. Wrinkles were smoothed with hemispheres of glass or polished stone that were heated prior to use.

Because cloth was expensive, even a single garment represented a substantial personal investment. An ordinary person probably owned no more than two of each undergarment, perhaps only one outer garment, while the wardrobe of a rich person was no larger, albeit more sumptuous, than that of a middle-income person today. Each garment was treated as a valuable item of property. Holes were mended promptly to prevent further deterioration, and when the condition of the garment was too disreputable for its owner to be seen wearing it, the piece was sold to a used-clothes dealer for resale to a less-fashion-conscious buyer. Ordinary people probably did not often buy new clothes. The thriving trade in used clothes reflects the relative durability of the cloth. Linen clothing might wear out before being resold because it was in constant contact with human skin and was regularly washed. Wool, however, is an outstandingly durable fiber, and a fair number of medieval woolen garments have survived to this day in archaeological contexts. Many garments outlived their owners, and medieval wills commonly make special reference to the disposition of these along with other property of value (Singman, 35–46).

To read about clothing in Elizabethan England, see the England entry in the section "Clothing and Personal Appearance" in chapter 5 ("Material Life") of volume 3; for 18th-century England, see the England entries in the sections "Male Clothing" and "Female Clothing" in chapter 5 ("Material Life") of volume 4; and for Victorian England, see the England entry in the section "Fashion" in chapter 5 ("Material Life") of volume 5 of this series.

FOR MORE INFORMATION

Singman, J. L. *Daily Life in Medieval Europe*. Westport, Conn.: Greenwood Press, 1999.

VIKINGS

During the Viking Age, there was considerably more variety in male clothes than in female clothes, which seem to have been rather undiversified and conservative. It appears that merchants, who traveled widely, liked to introduce new and foreign fashions in their clothing, whereas women, who were evidently less fashion conscious, typically stuck to traditional Scandinavian designs even after they had moved to the colonies in the East and West.

A typical male outfit probably consisted of an undershirt and underpants (long or short) of wool or linen, although concrete evidence for the existence of men's and women's underwear is lacking. On top of the shirt, a knee-length, sleeved tunic or caftan-like jacket was worn, which, if the man was wealthy, might have decorative silk borders and embroideries with gold and silver thread. A bead was sometimes used as a button to close the opening at the neck. Such tunics or jackets could be tight fitting or loose. The small bronze buttons found in graves in Birka on Lake Malaren in Sweden presumably belonged to tight-fitting garments. A belt or sash was worn around the middle, fastened with buckles of bronze or silver. A knife and a purse were normally attached to the belt, although sometimes a knife was carried on a cord around the neck.

A coat or cloak of heavier material—fur, hide, or wool—was worn on top of the tunic, and it was fastened over the right shoulder either by a large brooch, pin, or ties so that the sword arm could be kept free. The cloak might have decorative borders or fur trimmings; the finds in the rich graves of Birka reveal that furs from beavers and martens were used for such purposes. Gloves or mittens and hats or hoods of wool or leather would have completed the outfit of a man in cool weather.

The less fortunate, such as slaves, of course did not have such fancy outer clothes and were more simply dressed in undyed, coarse woolen clothes. One imagines a blanketlike cloak with a hole in the center for the head. Children may have been dressed in a similar way, although very little is known about their clothing.

The fashion in trousers or breeches, which were kept up by a belt, seems to have varied considerably. The Gotlandic picture stones show ankle-length as well as midcalf-length trousers, and narrow as well as baggy trousers. The shorter type was worn with stockings or leggings known as hose. Long hose were held up by cords or laces attached to the top, with which the hose were secured to the breeches belt. Short or knee-high hose were held up by laces or bands wound around the legs. The hose were typically made of wool and worn with shoes or ankle boots, although some were made of hide and therefore did not require shoes.

Boots and shoes were made of leather and to simple patterns that were common all over Scandinavia. The soles were always flat, without heels, but both round and pointed toes are in evidence. A simple slip-on shoe with no fastenings found at Ribe in Jutland, Denmark, is considered a typical Viking Age shoe in its method of manufacture. The upper part was made from a single piece of goat hide, side-seamed at the instep, which was blind stitched to a single-thickness sole. An ankle boot found in York, England, is quite similar in terms of design and was made from a single piece of cowhide blind-stitched to a single-thickness sole. But the heel is finished off by fitting a pointed extension to the sole in a V-shaped cut in the back of the upper. Moreover, the upper has an instep flap which is fastened with the help of a toggle and a loop. Such soles with pointed heels and uppers with instep flaps were common, although other types of fastenings are also in evidence. The ankle boot found in the Oseberg ship burial has a lace that passes through slits or holes in the opening and is bound around the ankle.

Like men, women wore outfits consisting of layers. The first layer was a long woolen or linen chemise with or without sleeves. The chemise might be finely pleated and fastened at the neck with a small disc or brooch. Over the chemise was worn a woolen dress or gown, possibly decorated with bands or borders. It consisted of a rectangular piece of fabric, which was wrapped around the woman's body from armpit to midcalf or longer. The dress, which was tight fitting, was worn suspended from shoulder straps. These straps were sewn on at the back and joined to paired loops attached to the front by a pair of oval brooches, the pins of which passed through the loops. From one of these brooches, usually the right, textile implements such as scissors, tweezers, an awl, or a needle case might hang on straps, and between the brooches festoons of beads might be suspended sometimes with the addition of amber or silver pendants. Around the waist, a belt was worn with knife and purse and, if the woman was a housekeeper, keys to the meal or treasury chest. Married women might also wear a tall headdress or a scarf around their hair.

For outdoors, a woman would wear a shawl or a sleeved cloak, held together either by a brooch, usually equal-armed, trefoil, or disc-shaped, or a pin, and, of course, hose kept up with ties. Footwear as well as gloves or mittens appear not to have differed much, if at all, from those worn by men.

~Kirsten Wolf

FOR MORE INFORMATION

Wolf, K. *Daily Life of the Vikings*. Westport, Conn.: Greenwood Press, forthcoming.

CHINA

Commoners—farmers, artisans, merchants, and scholars not in government service—wore loose, baggy trousers (similar to modern pajama pants), tunics that opened in the front, and sashes tied at the waist. By law, the hems of their tunics, which often had round collars, could not fall below the thigh, and the fabrics used for all of their apparel had to be white hemp cloth. Slippers made of rushes, straw, or hemp thread, and sandals secured to their feet by straps, served as shoes. Some shoes were made of wood. In the fields, peasants wore large-brimmed, bamboo hats that protected them from the sun and rain.

Most of the information about clothing that has survived in Tang sources concerns the attire of aristocrats and mandarins and their women. Ceremonial vestments were numerous and elaborate. There were 14 different regalia for the emperor alone: raiments for worshiping heaven, enthronements, sacrifices to former rulers, offerings to the gods of the seas and mountains, worshiping the deities of soil and grain, audiences on the first day of the moon (new moon), feasting officials, hunting, audiences on the fifteenth day of the moon (full moon), memorial services at tombs, passing legal judgments, horse riding, and funerals. Nobles and officials also had formal dress for religious rituals, audiences with the emperor, and banquets. Ceremonial attire for emperors included mortarboards with chin straps and strings of pearls dangling from the front and rear; robes with embroidered badges depicting dragons, holy mountains, and other symbols; leather belts fastened with jade hooks; ceremonial swords, some of which were embellished with gold and jade; silk pouches for carrying seals; jade girdle pendants; and silk slippers with upturned toes. The stitching of imperial robes was so fine that one could not see the seams. The size, number, color, quality, and decoration of those articles differed according to the rank of the wearer.

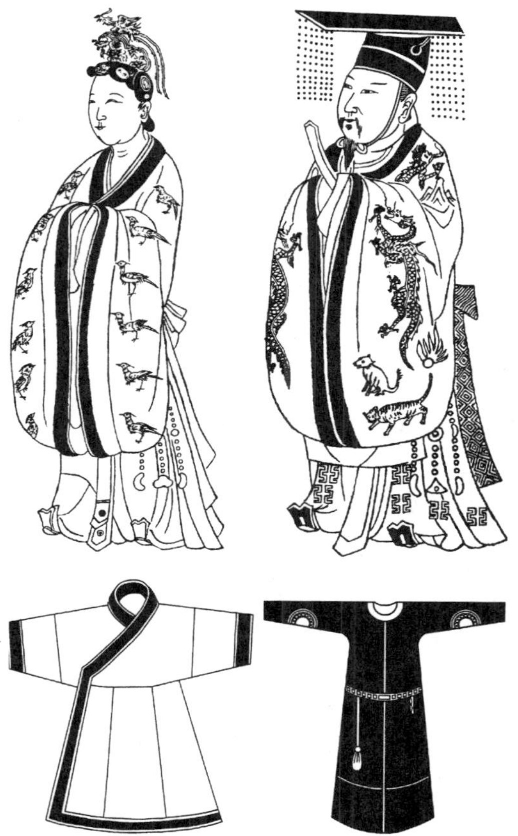

Ritual clothing for men and women during the Tang dynasty. Note the elaborate embroidery on the layered clothing. Illustration by Charles Benn.

Formal dress, whether worn at court or otherwise, resembled modern bathrobes. Gentlemen wore a set of two made of silk. They folded the right lapel of both over the left. The outer was the smaller, so it exposed the lapels and sleeves of the inner. Men wore unlined robes in the summer and lined robes in the winter. A sash or belt secured them at the waist. The sleeves of the clothing were quite voluminous and sometimes hung down from the wrists and forearms to well below the knee. When meeting people, men and women covered their hands with their sleeves. If they needed to use their hands, they folded the sleeves back across their forearms. Those sleeves were ideal places to hide daggers if one had a murderous intent. Men's skirts were tied at their waists. The hems brushed the floor and covered the feet, exposing only the toes of shoes.

The everyday apparel for patricians was much plainer. In fact, it was very similar to that for commoners: baggy trousers and tunics with round collars. However, there were no restrictions on the lengths of the tunics nor on the kind of fabric for them. Silk was the preferred cloth. The standard headgear for men was a cloth cap or turban that wrapped around the forehead and rose up at the back to form projections in various shapes above the head. It was tied in a knot at the back, and the ends of the excess material hung down like tails. Sometimes the ends were starched or lacquered so that they jutted out vertically like wings. Boots were common footwear because horseback riding was an essential mode of transportation for the upper classes. The skin of a deer that roamed the forests of the south supplied the best leather for them. The hides were dyed red before the boot makers set to work.

Peasants wore raincoats made out of reeds or straw that hung down from their necks and covered their bodies. The well-to-do used oiled cloth to protect themselves against downpours. A collection of medical prescriptions had a bizarre formula for waterproofing cloth. One was to place spiders in a pot and feed them pork lard for 100 days and then kill the arachnids and rub the grease exuded from their remains on a towel. Presumably, the towel was placed on the head during storms. Physicians warned that wearing clothes drenched with water or sweat caused sores, rashes, and itchiness. They recommended changing garments immediately and powdering the body.

Women's clothing was similar to the formal wear of men. It resembled the kimono that is still worn in Japan today. In some fashions, the outer skirt was tied across or above the breasts and flared out from the sides of the body. This fashion survives in traditional ceremonial wear for Korean women. At certain times, it was fashionable to bare the shoulders and don a shawl of sheer fabric that fell to floor. Some styles revealed cleavage, an immodesty uncharacteristic for Chinese women. Perhaps they were outfits worn by courtesans or entertainers. Judging from mortuary figures, some female dancers performed topless. When they did not, fluttering the long sleeves of their gowns was an important feature of their choreography.

Western dress became fashionable in the 740s and 750s. It is not clear from which westerners the Chinese adopted the style. They were probably central Asians, but they may also have been Persians. Men sported leopard-skin hats, and the women wore hairpins with trinkets that jingled when they walked. The apparel for women had tight sleeves and collars. After 705, women had adopted masculine attire, boots in particular, according to the customs of the pastoral peoples living northeast of China (Benn, 100–106).

FOR MORE INFORMATION

Benn, C. *Daily Life in Traditional China: The Tang Dynasty*. Westport, Conn.: Greenwood Press, 2002.

ISLAMIC WORLD

Scholars are unsure how women in the early history of Islam dressed. There is a scarcity of contemporary evidence and many Qur'anic passages are allusive (and elusive). Women's clothing is vigorously debated among modern Muslims because of the implications that the practice of the early community has for Muslim women and men today. Fundamental to this discussion is the proper interpretation of the concept of modesty as well as the precise meaning of the Arabic word *hijab* (curtain, veil) used in the Qur'an:

> Enjoin believing men to turn their eyes away from temptation and to restrain their carnal desires. This will make their lives purer. God has knowledge of all their actions. Enjoin believing women to turn their eyes away from temptation and to preserve their chastity; to cover their adornments (except such as are normally displayed); to draw their veils [*hijab*] over their bosoms and not to reveal their finery except to their husbands, their fathers, their husbands' fathers, their sons, their step-sons, their brothers, their brothers' sons, their sisters' sons, their women-servants, and their slave-girls; male attendants lacking in natural vigor, and children who have no carnal knowledge of women. And let them not stamp their feet when walking so as to reveal their hidden trinkets. Believers, turn to God in repentance, that you may prosper. (Qur'an 24:30–31)

In modern Muslim countries and among Muslim communities in the West, the meaning of *hijab* is understood in a variety of ways. Some Muslim women, especially in the West or among more Westernized communities in the Islamic world argue that simply covering one's bosom and dressing modestly (usually according to Western standards of modesty) meets the requirement. Others argue that despite the admonition to "draw their veils [*hijab*] over their bosoms," the subsequent admonition not to "reveal their finery except to their husbands, their fathers" requires not only modest dress but the use of a headscarf or shawl to cover one's hair either partially or completely in the presence of all except those kin, servants, slaves, and impotents mentioned in the passage. Others argue that the proper interpretation of this passage requires the complete covering of a woman's body, hands, feet, hair, and face—even to the point of wearing gloves as well as a veil with sheer material where one's eyes would be so that the woman can see out but that no man can see any aspect of her body, even her eyes.

How was modest Islamic dress defined in 7th-century Arabia? The short and rather unsatisfying answer to this question is that the sources simply make it impossible to provide a definitive answer. However, it does appear that some sort of face veiling was practiced in some pre-Islamic Arabian towns as a sign of high social status. Moreover, the biographical literature on Muhammad (not the Qur'an) records that he required it of his wives as well. In fact, one of the meanings of the phrase *darabat al-hijab* (She took the veil) is, "She became one of Muhammad's wives." Although precisely when face veiling for women became part of broader Islamic practice remains unclear, we do know that both seclusion and veiling were practiced among the urban upper classes in Byzantium and in Sasanian Iran as symbols of economic wealth and high social status. As these areas and their populations were incorporated into the Islamic empire in the first Islamic centuries, it seems plausible that the new Islamic order rather easily adapted this elite urban custom to Islamic standards of sexual morality and segregation of the sexes. Whatever the proper interpretation of this and other Qur'anic passages may be for the modern world, it is clear that the dress—especially the public dress—of women and men in early Islamic history as well as throughout much (although not all) of the medieval Islamic world was modest by any modern American standards and included long robes and cloaks as well as some sort of head covering.

~*James Lindsay*

FOR MORE INFORMATION

Lindsay, J. *Daily Life in Medieval Islam*. Westport, Conn.: Greenwood Press, forthcoming.

MONGOLS

Cloth and clothing held great symbolic significance for the medieval Mongols even before the days of empire. The great number of Muslim weavers transported to China under the Yuan dynasty attest to the importance textiles and dress continued to occupy in Mongol society. Both the wearing and presenting of clothes and items of clothing carried messages and meaning for the peoples of the steppe and the Mongols in particular.

Fur, leather, wool, camel's hair, and felt constituted the basic dress fabric; cotton and silk were also available from their sedentary neighbors. Standard wear was an ankle-length robe cut from a single piece of material. Loose trousers would be worn under this while around the waist a belt made of soft material would be fastened. As protection from the weather, they wore felt capes, fur hoods, and leather boots or buskins made of felt. Friar William of Rubruck, who traveled through Russia to Mongolia between 1253 and 1255, describes their summer wear as being made of silk, gold, and cotton while in winter they wore garments made from a wide variety of furs. He explains that the fur clothes were double layered so that the fur was inside as well as out. These pelts were often obtained from the wolf, fox, or lynx, although the poor used the skins of dogs or goats. Their breeches were also made from pelts with silk lining for the rich and cotton for the poor.

Friar Carpini, an emissary for Pope Innocent IV (although some say spy), traveled east from 1245 to 1247, earlier than William of Rubruck. Carpini's detailed descriptions of the Mongols report that men and women would often be dressed identically and that he had problems telling the sexes apart. They wore tunics of buckram, fine linen, or silk, split open on one side and fastened by cords with the material folded back double over the chest. Married women wore full-length tunics opened at the front.

All reports, including Carpini's, mention *boghta,* the distinctive headdresses worn by married women. Li Chih-Chang, who accompanied the Daoist monk Ch'ang Ch'ung to central Asia to visit Chinggis Khan, described a headdress made of birchbark, some two feet high, covered with black wool or red silk. Later reports describe the *boghta* as a three-foot iron wire frame adorned with red and blue brocade or pearls and later still as frames wrapped with red silk or gold brocade. By the time Rubruck was writing in the 1250s, the *boghta* had become more elaborate and garishly decorated. Peacock and mallard tail feathers along with precious stones now festooned this status symbol of the rich, the whole contraption attached to the lady's head with a fur hood in which was gathered her hair. In addition, the *boghta* was secured around the throat by straps.

The *boghta* could convey more than social status. Chinggis Khan's mother, Hö'elün, signaled her intention to commence an arduous venture by girding her belt and securing her *boghta*. The Mongol ruler of Iran, Arghun Khan (r. 1284–91), signaled his acceptance of Tudai Khātūn (Lady Tudai) as his wife by placing a *boghta* on her head.

The giving and presenting of clothes often held great symbolic significance for the Mongols. When Temüjin (the young Chinggis Khan) presented his powerful uncle, Ong Khan, ruler of the mighty Kereyid tribe, with a black sable coat, it was generally understood that Ong Khan's acceptance of the gift signified that the protection of his tribe had henceforth been extended to Temüjin. The exchange of belts between friends reinforced the friendship and tied them closer, as was the case with the young Temüjin and his neighbor Jamuka, who had already declared themselves *anda* (blood brothers). Gold and silver satins of many colors were always presented to officials on the occasion of royal births. Likewise, to express condolences and loyalty to Mongol custom and tradition, robes and a *boghta* would be presented to a widowed wife even while plots and intrigues were in the making. Such was the case when the third Great Khan, Güyük (1249), died and his wife, Oghul Qaimish, the acting regent, accepted such gifts from her cousins' family, even as they were plotting the annihilation of her whole family line, the Ögödei Ghinggisids. When peace and reconciliation were sought, the presentation of clothes was always expected. Gold, gems, gilded tunics, and gilded hats heavily decorated in jewels and precious stones would be exchanged or offered. Conversely, the taking away of clothes also carried symbolic meaning. Before praying to the sky god, Tengri, Chinggis Khan removed his hat and belt to signify his powerlessness and his need for help. When Chinggis Khan removed his brother Jochi Qasar's hat and belt, he was expressing the ending of his trust in his sibling. During the accession ceremonies of the Great Khans, all those present were expected to remove their hats and drape their belts over their shoulders. Their replacement symbolized the subjects' acceptance of the new order.

Another essential item of clothing for the Mongols, increasingly so as their courts took on an imperial air, was the "robe of honor," or *khilcat*. This was awarded to nobles, princes, sultans, and other rulers who had proved their loyalty to their masters, the Mongols. These robes of honor became more elaborate and splendid as the empire expanded and they are reflective of the value put on fine fabrics and clothing by the Mongol nobility. Ceremonial dress in general was composed mainly of gold-woven brocade.

Recent studies have shown that the need for gold and precious stones, used in the manufacture of the Mongols' ceremonial dress, was one of the driving forces behind the expansion of the Mongol Empire into the settled lines. Sources for the raw materials and artisans to fashion these metals, stones, and fabrics into clothing were a major preoccupation with all the Mongol rulers. The importance of dress in Mongol society has not been fully appreciated until recently.

~*George Lane*

FOR MORE INFORMATION

Allsen, T. T. *Commodity and Exchange in the Mongol Empire*. Cambridge, U.K.: Cambridge University Press, 1997.

Carpini, Giovanni Di Plano. *The Story of the Mongols Whom We Call the Tartars: Historia Mongalorum*. Translated by E. Hildinger. Boston, Mass.: Branden, 1996.

William of Rubruck. *The Mission of Friar William of Rubruck*. Translated and edited by P. Jackson, with D. Morgan. London: Hakluyt Society, 1990.

Fabrics

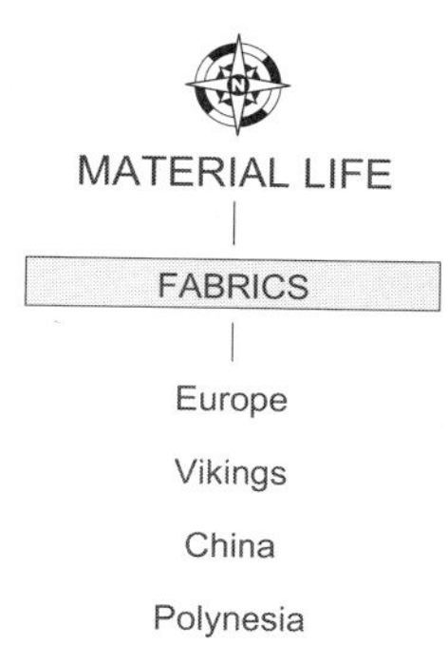

All fabrics in the Middle Ages were made either of plant or animal materials, and all required a large amount of labor to turn it into cloth. Women were responsible for this labor and were deeply identified with all aspects of fabric production. Today, when cloth is produced by machines, synthetic fibers are abundant and clothing almost disposable, it takes an effort of imagination to consider a time when this was not so and when producing cloth was a major part of daily life.

Fibers of some plants can be soaked, pounded to separate the fibers, and then spun into thread. In Polynesia, women spent much time preparing tapa cloth from the inner bark of the mulberry tree. In Europe, linen cloth was made from flax and made a sturdy fabric, good for sacks, peasant trousers, bed linens, and some clothing. It had the advantage of being readily washable and durable. More durable was canvas made from the hemp plant. Cotton was grown in India and spread to China in the 12th century and to the Arab world as well; however, throughout this period, it remained a rare luxury fabric. In China, some more unusual plants were used to make fabric, such as banana fibers in the south.

Animal products made up the most common fabrics throughout this period. Skins from all animals made leather for everything from ox-skin shoes to cat-skin gloves to capes or trousers. Leather was highly durable, although not very washable. Furs were also used to make clothing; Mongols on the cold steppes made cloth with two layers—fur on the outside and leather or linen within. Muslin women wove camel hair for cloaks and rugs.

The most abundant animal product cloth, however, was wool. From ancient times, wool provided the main form of cloth throughout the Mediterranean world, and this continued into the Middle Ages. The domestication of sheep caused them to lose a hair outercoat that covers the wool undercoat in wild sheep. Furthermore, they lost the capacity to shed the wool every summer as wild animals do. This was convenient for people to use the wool without losing it as long as they were willing to shear the sheep each spring. The Vikings were known for their fine woven woolen cloth that was warm and even water resistant in the cold north.

An impetus was given to the European sheep industry in the 12th century by the introduction of merino sheep into Spain from Africa. These sheep had high-grade wool and displaced older breeds in northern Europe. By the 13th century, the wool trade was highly lucrative—especially in England. Representatives to the English Parliament in the Middle Ages sat on wool sacks to remind them of the importance of the wool trade to their prosperity. The Chinese admired the European wool making, for their product was not as high a quality.

The Chinese did develop the precious silk threads that fueled demand for that precious fabric from the time the ancient Romans traveled the Silk Road from the Mediterranean to China. Through the ancient world, the Chinese jealously guarded the secret to weaving silk, but by the 6th century, the Byzantines had smuggled some worms and the essential white mulberries to feed back to Byzantium. The Byzantine emperors kept the monopoly on silk making and grew wealthy. They were never able to make as fine a product as the Chinese, however, and travelers continued along the silk route bringing that precious fabric back across Asia. The attraction of silk is understandable if one imagines how hot it would be to wear even finely woven wool in the hot climates of the Mediterranean and North Africa. By the 14th century, silk production had found a foothold in Italy, and so the Chinese monopoly was broken.

The study of fabrics involves more than the materials themselves, for the threads needed to be spun and woven. For most of this period, women spun the coarse wool or other fiber on spindles to make it into thread. Only late in the Middle Ages did spinning wheels appear to speed up the process. The thread was then placed on a loom to weave, and the skill of weavers everywhere can be seen in beautiful tapestries and fine oriental rugs made in Muslim countries and in China.

Finally, fabrics could be dyed. Colors were highly prized but difficult to attain since people had only natural dyes to use. Blues of various hues were available, as were reds and yellows. The color that conveyed the greatest status, however, was purple. The best purple dye was made from the liquid of a particular decomposed shellfish in the eastern Mediterranean. The Byzantine Empire also had a monopoly on this dye, and money flowed into their coffers from people's desire to wear purple.

~*Joyce E. Salisbury*

FOR MORE INFORMATION

Braudel, F. *The Structures of Everyday Life*. New York: Harper and Row, 1979.
Salisbury, J. E. *The Beast Within: Animals in the Middle Ages*. New York: Routledge, 1994.

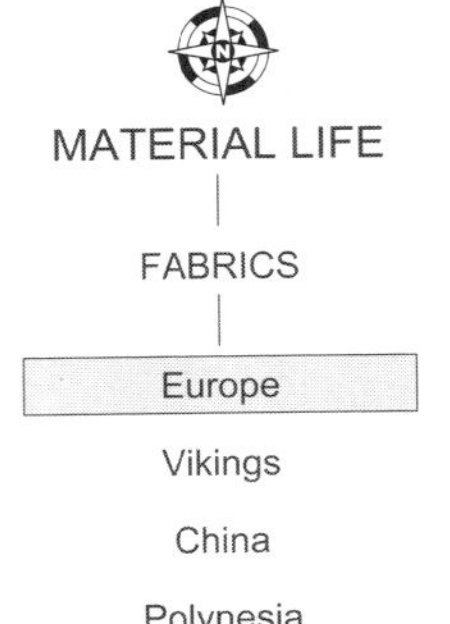

EUROPE

Medieval fabrics were made of natural fibers, principally linen—derived from the fibers of the flax plant—and sheep's wool. Cotton was sometimes imported into Europe, and some even grew in the Mediterranean areas, but the short fibers of cotton were difficult to spin into thread using medieval spinning technology, and cotton was more likely to be used as stuffing or spun in combination with flax. Linen was generally used for inner garments, wool for outer garments, reflecting the respective properties of the two fibers. Linen is soft and absorbent; it soaks up sweat and oils and can be cleaned, properties that make it comfortable and serviceable to wear against the skin. Wool does not clean readily or absorb water well, and it tends to be scratchy, so it is less suitable for wearing against the skin, but it resists water and can be quite warm, both useful qualities in an outer garment. Wool also holds dye better than linen, making woolen cloth well suited for the visible outer layers of an outfit. Linen was nonetheless sometimes used for outer garments, particularly those worn in hot weather. Another relatively common fabric was canvas, a heavy and coarse material made from flax or hemp. Canvas was most often found as lining in garments that needed extra strength. Both linen and canvas were sometimes treated with beeswax to enhance their resistance to water. The finest fabrics were all made from silk. These were imported and very expensive. Fancy shirts were made of silken cloth. Rich fabrics such as satin, velvet, and taffeta were always made of silk.

The preparation of clothing was an extremely labor-intensive process. First, the fiber was harvested, in the case of flax, or shorn in the case of wool. It was then cleaned, purified of unusable fibers, and dressed by combing or carding so that the fibers all ran parallel to each other. The fibers were then spun by hand into thread. The traditional instrument for spinning was the drop spindle, a stick approximately a foot long with a weighted disk at the bottom. The spinner attached the fiber to the spindle and gave it a twist that set it spinning: the spindle twisted the fibers together while its weight drew them out into thread. A more recent invention was the spinning wheel, which was essentially a spindle connected by a drive band to a large drive wheel. This arrangement put more power and momentum behind the spindle, significantly increasing the spinner's speed, although the spinner had to turn the wheel by hand and pull the fiber away from the immobile spindle—the treadle wheel that both twists and pulls did not appear until the 15th century. By the 14th century, there is also some evidence of knitting in Europe, at least for gloves and caps.

Once sufficient thread was spun, it could be woven into cloth. The threads were tied one by one onto a loom, then woven into fabric one cross-thread at a time. This process was facilitated in the Middle Ages by the introduction of the horizontal loom. On the vertical loom, which still dominated in the early Middle Ages, the lengthwise threads hung downward and were pulled tight by weights tied to the ends. On the new horizontal loom, the threads were wound around rollers at each end and kept tight by a ratchet on the roller. The horizontal loom speeded the weaver's work, although the actual weaving was still done by hand.

The weave of most fabrics was of two principal sorts, plain and twill. In plain-woven fabrics, the threads alternate over and under in every direction. Plain weave was used for wool and linen. Plain-weave wool is very durable and sheds water well, so it was especially common among the lower classes. It was often heavily fulled and felted, which made it warmer and more resistant to water, as well as resistant to fraying. In twill fabrics, the threads pass over and under two or more other threads at a time, giving twills their characteristic diagonal look. Twill weave was used for woolen fabrics and was particularly favored for fashionable garments, as it drapes more gracefully than plain weave.

The woven fabric still had to be finished and dyed. The finishing of wool in particular was a complex process, involving cleaning, stretching, and felting: the fibers on the surface would be teased up, then shorn and washed, giving the surface a smooth appearance and increasing the fabric's resistance to wind and rain. The colors available were limited to those obtainable from natural dyes. These dyes tended to yield muted colors that faded with exposure to the sun, so the clothing of most people was probably rather faded in appearance; only the wealthy were likely to overdye or replace faded garments.

The colors of fashionable clothes tended to be bold and bright; ordinary people's clothes were diverse in color but generally muted in tone. All dyes derived from natural sources, usually plants. Blue was derived from the native plant woad and from indigo imported from the East. The native plant madder produced a warm brick red, while imported kermes (made from a Mediterranean insect) dyed a rich scarlet. The plant weld was used for yellow, while other plant sources were used for purple and brown. Dyes could be combined to produce other colors—blue was overdyed with yellow to produce green, for example. Black was difficult to achieve with dyes of the period and was therefore expensive, although not beyond the means of a prosperous gentleman. Coloration could also be provided by the wool itself. Some wools are naturally pigmented black, although they tend to produce a coarse fabric. Other wools are naturally brown or gray. Earth tones and natural tones were the least expensive and were generally worn only by the poor. Bold and long-lasting dyes were generally costly, whereas the cheaper dyes tended to fade fairly quickly.

The outer layers of clothing, such as mantles, gowns, hoods, gloves, and surcoats, were occasionally lined with fur for extra warmth or display. Many of the finest furs came from animals of the weasel family, notably marten, sable (which is dark brown to the point of black), and ermine (the winter coat of the stoat, which is snowy white save for a spot of black at the tip of the tail). Some fine furs came from various species of squirrel. Such high-quality furs were often imported from Scandinavia or Russia, where the cold climate caused especially rich pelts. Less-expensive furs included fox, rabbit, lamb, and even cat (Singman, 35–46; Singman and McLean, 94–96).

FOR MORE INFORMATION

Singman, J. L. *Daily Life in Medieval Europe*. Westport, Conn.: Greenwood Press, 1999.

Singman, J. L., and W. McLean. *Daily Life in Chaucer's England*. Westport, Conn.: Greenwood Press, 1995.

VIKINGS

For clothing during the Viking Age, the primary fabric was wool, which is warm, durable, and water resistant. It also takes well to dyes, although local dyes made from vegetables and minerals were not of a high quality and faded after a short while. Varieties of color could, however, be provided by the wool itself; some wools are naturally shades of gray, brown, and black. Linen appears to have been somewhat less common, although it is reasonable to assume that it was a preferred fabric for undergarments because it is more comfortable on the skin than wool. Canvas, a heavy and coarse material made from flax, is not particularly well represented in the archaeological finds, but it may be because vegetable fibers decompose faster than animal fibers. Silk was a luxury and reserved for the wealthy, for it was imported and costly.

Two women at a loom, mid to late 15th century. © The British Library/Topham-HIP/The Image Works.

The weave of the domestic fabrics was of two kinds, tabby and twill. Tabby is a weave in which the filling threads and the warp threads interlace alternately, forming a checkerboard pattern. In twill, the filling threads pass over one warp thread and then under two or more others, producing a fabric with diagonal parallel ribs. Sometimes short lengths of wool were inserted into the warp during weaving to give the fabric a shaggy look and feel. Such weave was used for cloaks and appears to have been especially common in Iceland, which exported such shaggy cloaks.

A variety of furs were used, in particular for cloaks and trimmings. In addition to fur trimmings, clothes might also be decorated with embroidery of various kinds and tablet-woven bands containing gold or silver threads. A number of such bands have been preserved because of their use of metal threads. In tablet weaving, the warp threads are passed through holes at the four corners of rectangular plaques of wood. These plaques are then moved a quarter-turn at a time to change the position of the warp threads.

In addition to fabric for clothing, Scandinavians loved textile art, and beautiful textiles were as prestigious as gold and jewels. Most Viking textiles were made as handicrafts in local households. However, workshops to produce elaborate decorative textiles—whether woven or embroidered—were established in convents. Most of the surviving embroideries come from churches, but they may not have originally been designed for ecclesiastical use because many of the themes of the images are quite secular, showing knights, battles, and fantastic animals.

On festival occasions, the interior of Viking houses were decorated with long textiles hanging around the walls. Some wall coverings were made of simple woolen cloth, but these were often covered with elaborately woven or embroidered cloths hung on top. These wall hangings would not only be decorative but would also serve as insulation for the cold walls. Ceilings, too, could be decorated with wall hangings, and cushions for benches and chairs also might have textile coverings.

The talented Viking craftsmen and women produced magnificent fabrics that brightened their homes as well as making their clothing. Some of their embroideries as well as their sturdy woolens found their way as trade items as far away as the Byzantine Empire and beyond.

~*Kirsten Wolf and Joyce E. Salisbury*

FOR MORE INFORMATION

Wolf, K. *Daily Life of the Vikings*. Westport, Conn.: Greenwood Press, forthcoming.

CHINA

In 815, an assassin waylaid Pei Du, a chief minister, near his home and struck him on the head. Pei fell off his horse and landed in a drainage ditch. A member of his entourage grabbed the killer from behind and raised the alarm with a loud bellow. The desperado cut off the man's arm and fled before the authorities could apprehend him. Although the blow to his head inflicted a wound, Pei survived the assault because the felt of his hat was so thick. Felt, made from wool, was a tough material, as this anecdote demonstrates. It was used for tents, saddle covers, and boots. In the Tang dynasty, it seems to have been particularly suited for making hats. The original homeland of the fabric was Persia, and it was sent to China from central Asia during the Tang period.

There was a host of fabrics available for making clothes in China. Prefectures in the northwest sent camel hair, a very soft cloth, to the Tang court. The Tibetans presented the throne with a woolen fabric made from otter fur as tribute during the 9th century. Southeast Asia, Tibet, Japan, and Korea sent bombycine, a textile woven from the remnants of the cocoon that the wild tussah moth cut its way out of, to the Tang court. In the southeast, people made fabrics from banana fibers by treating them with lime. They were soft and yellowish-white, inferior to bast fabrics (such as those made from hemp) produced in the rest of China. The Chinese of the Tang knew of cotton, but only as an article of commerce. It was indigenous to Pakistan and India, but made its way gradually along the Silk Road into central Asia. Cotton was expensive to produce and inferior to silk so it was not until the 13th century, when technology improved its manufacture and lowered its price, that it became an important fabric for clothing. Under extreme circumstances, the people sometimes wore garb made of materials not normally used for garments. When a military governor was on his way to Changan to attend an imperial audience in 767, he allowed his troops to plunder a district just east of the capital. They laid waste to an area of 33 miles, stripping it of all its wealth, even clothes. As a result, mandarins and functionaries had to wear apparel made of paper.

One Chinese princess had the imperial workshops make two skirts from the feathers of a hundred birds. When one looked at them from the front, they had one color; from the side, another; in the sun, yet another; and in the shade, a fourth. The dressmakers wove the images of a hundred birds into the "fabric." Afterward, the fashion caught on with officials and commoners. As a result, hunters went into mountain valleys to capture extraordinary birds for sale in the market. The numbers killed in their nets were countless. Nearly all of the extraordinary fowl of the Yangtze River valley and the southeast were exterminated. In 713, Emperor Illustrious August had the princess's skirt burned in front of a palace hall.

All of these fabrics were exotics, and some of them made it no farther than palace warehouses. Except for felt, few played a major role in Chinese clothing of the Tang. In that period, there were really only three types of cloth: wool made from animal fur, linen made from woody (bast) fibers, and silk made from insect filaments. Woolens were probably the easiest to manufacture because there were few steps between shearing the sheep and spinning the thread. Commoners wore clothing made from this fabric during the Tang.

The making of bast fabrics from the fibers of hemp, ramie (a plant of the nettle family), and kudzu (a creeping vine) was more complicated. For example, preparing hemp required soaking the plant in water, peeling the skin off, scraping it, soaking again, washing, drying, beating, combing, splitting, beating again, spinning, steaming, and drying again. Hemp was a northern plant that grew in colder climates and produced seeds that, when pressed, yielded the most prevalent oil for cooking and lighting in the Tang. Hemp cloth was a coarse fabric favored for mourning clothes (sackcloth), bandages, sheets, and shrouds. It was also the cloth for the garments of the lowest classes and recluses. Both ramie and kudzu were southern plants. Ramie was superior to hemp because a farmer could get two to three times the yield from it on the same amount of land. Cloth made from it had a brilliant luster like silk and dried easily in climates of high humidity. Southerners wore it in the summer because it was light and cool and absorbed sweat.

The most difficult and expensive fabric to manufacture was silk. It required, first of all, a grove of mulberry trees. Pickers stood on ladders or platforms to pluck the leaves from the trees. They collected the leaves in baskets and carried them to sheds for feeding the insects. Women took charge of raising the silkworms. When the eggs hatched in the spring, they spread the worms on hemp mats in trays or on shelves so the grubs could feed on the mulberry leaves. The women fed the grubs large amounts of leaves frequently and constantly moved them from one container to another, to clean out their droppings. After about 33 days, the caterpillars would begin to weave cocoons with filaments excreted from the glands located along their sides. They completed their task in about four days. To obtain the best quality of silk thread, reeling began immediately while the moths were alive. The women had to unravel the filaments from the cocoon before the moths started chewing their way out. The women allowed only a select few of the moths to gnaw their way out of the cocoons, which bred and laid the eggs for the next generation of silkworms.

The Bureau of Weaving and Dyeing in Changan recognized 10 types of textiles. Two of them were linens and woolens. The remainder were various types of silk—chiffons, damasks, satins, and the like—differentiated by the character of their weaving. Gauze was one of the finer varieties. It was an open weave in which spaces were left between the warp and woof threads. Gauze was probably the fabric preferred for summer apparel because it was light and permitted air to circulate around the body. In the simplest weaves, the warp threads passed over and under the woof threads. By varying the interlace—for example, passing the warp threads under two woof threads, over three, under two—weavers could create different patterns. Known as figured silks, the designs might include flowers, birds, talons, clouds, or tortoise shells. Brocade was produced when the weaver used threads of different colors to produce the design. Embroidery was yet another method of adorning cloth with images created by threads of various hues.

Color was a very important factor in Tang clothing because it was a mark of status and distinction. The Bureau of Weaving and Dyeing recognized six hues: purple, blue, red, yellow, black, and white. Dyers usually tinted fabrics with vegetable dyes to create the first five colors and used bleaches to produce white. The secretions of the lac insect were used to dye deer skins red. In 630, the emperor issued a decree that fixed the order of hues: the robes of mandarins third grade above were purple; fourth and fifth grades, red; sixth and seventh, green; and eighth and ninth, blue. Wives wore frocks of the same color as their husband's robes. The throne conferred purple robes on men of exceptional distinction, including Daoist priests, Buddhist monks, recluses, and others. White was the prescribed color of garments for commoners. That class included scholars who were candidates for civil service examinations. It was also the color of mourning garments. Commoners in the 7th century apparently were not happy with the color imposed on them by the statute. They took to wearing short, inner tunics of purple, red, green, and blue under their outer garb. Some went so far as to remove their white robes and parade around in their colored underwear when they were in their villages. When the emperor learned this in 674, it upset him because the proper distinctions between the noble (patricians) and the base (commoners) were not being maintained. He ordered everyone to wear inner garments of the same color as their outer garments. During the Sui dynasty, the law required butchers and merchants to wear black, but it is not clear if the rule still applied in the Tang (Benn, 97–100).

FOR MORE INFORMATION

Benn, C. *Daily Life in Traditional China: The Tang Dynasty.* Westport, Conn.: Greenwood Press, 2002.

MATERIAL LIFE
FABRICS
Europe
Vikings
China
Polynesia

POLYNESIA

The production and use of fabrics in ancient Polynesia were determined by two factors. First, the early settlers to these tropical islands brought with them skills and tools associated with prehistoric, primitive societies; and second, the climate and available resources on the islands dictated the way and how they dressed. The most common fabric in Polynesia was bark cloth, called tapa, made from the inner bark of the paper mulberry tree. The second most common was finely plaited matting, usually woven from leaves of the pandanus tree. Loom weaving was unknown in ancient Polynesia.

With the exception of New Zealand, most Polynesian islands lie in the tropics, where the warm, humid climate allowed the inhabitants to wear very little clothing.

Young children up to the age of about seven wore no clothing. Adults wore as little as possible. Most men wore a simple loincloth called the *maro* or *malo* (depending on the dialect). It consisted of a strip of tapa cloth approximately one foot wide and three to four yards long, wrapped around the waist and then down the front covering the genitalia and up the back where it was secured with the waist wrapping. Women wore a skirt called a pareu, probably not much different than the pareu casually worn in modern-day Tahiti. It was a rectangular piece of cloth, approximately 30 inches wide and three to four yards long. It was wrapped around the waist with the free end tucked in to secure it, usually falling to the knees. During inclement weather, both sexes covered their tops with a square piece of tapa cloth with a hole cut out in the middle, similar to a Mexican poncho. Sometimes for important occasions, finely hand-woven matting was worn.

The tedious job making of tapa cloth was predominantly women's work, but men would often contribute their labor when larger pieces of cloth were needed either for gifts or contributions to the chiefs and/or priests. The job began by stripping the outer bark from the trunks of the young paper mulberry tree (*Broussonetia papyrifera*). The more flexible inner bark would then be stripped away from the rough outer bark and soaked in water for two to three days. It would then be cleaned once more, wrapped in banana leaves, and covered with grass for another two to three days. The softened and glutinous inner bark was then ready for further processing. The strip was placed over a wooden board or log and carefully pounded with a wooden mallet until the strip expanded to the required width, sometimes up to seven times its original width. The mallets were usually one foot in length, squared to four equal sides with a short, rounded handle. Three of the squared sides were carved with various longitudinal grooves, and the fourth was usually plain and smooth. The pounding of the tapa mallets by the women was a common sound that could be heard throughout all Polynesian villages. It was a lengthy and laborious task.

Two Tongan women beat strips of the inner bark of the mulberry tree to make tapa, the traditional cloth of Polynesia. Photo courtesy of the Polynesian Cultural Center.

At this point, the tapa was quite fragile and could easily be torn. To add to its strength, strips of tapa would be glued crosswise to each other with a paste made from the arrowroot plant. The damp tapa would then be laid out in the sun for several days to dry and to be bleached white. It would then be rolled up until it was ready for further use. More often, however, the tapa was hand decorated with earth colors made from various native plants and minerals. Designs were painted freehand with a "paint brush" made from the dried fruit of the pandanus tree or the designs were created by placing a stencil-type board under the tapa and the desired dye rubbed over the top of the tapa, thus creating a facsimile replica of the design on the board below.

Even though tapa cloth was reinforced with cross strips in its production, it remained fragile. Cloth left out in the rain for any length of time would practically disintegrate, and the water-based designs would fade and run. Clothing, therefore, could never be washed and had to be replaced frequently, approximately every two months.

Tapa making was something that all women performed—commoners, chiefs, and higher nobility alike. Traditionally, the higher one's status, the better quality of tapa was produced. A high chiefess ("queen") would have felt it derogatory to her position if a woman of lower rank produced a piece of cloth more splendid than hers. A compliment for the maker of a piece of fine tapa was that it looked like one made by the queen herself.

Indeed, tapa was not only used for common-day dress, but it was also used as a type of currency. Polynesian islands had no money economy. Pieces of fine tapa were, therefore, often bartered for other desirable goods, used in the payment of taxes to the chiefs, or used for contributions to temple priests.

A finely plaited mat was the second most common fabric produced in Polynesia. Matting is ranked as a fabric here because these mats could be as pliable as a piece of modern-day, machine-woven calico. They were worth far more than tapa cloth, were passed down through generations of families, and were also used as a type of currency. They generally were plaited from leaves of the very young pandanus plants, and they served as a type of wrap-around clothing (pareu) or for throw-over-the-head ponchos. More coarsely woven mats served as floor coverings, bedding, room partitions, boat sails, and various types of baskets or containers. Mats for clothing were small in size when compared to the larger mats that often measured 12 feet wide by 60 to 100 yards in length.

As already mentioned, the basic plaiting material came from leaves of the pandanus plant (*Pandanus tectorius*), a tree that grows around the rocky and sandy shores of Polynesia's atolls and islands. Other materials could be used as well, such as the inner bark of the mulberry, hibiscus, or breadfruit trees, or from the leaves from the banana and coconut trees, depending on the strength and quality of the finished product. The long pandanus leaves were gathered, their central midribs removed, and their edges trimmed to remove all of their spines. The leaves were then dried either in the sun or more quickly over a fire. The brown, dry leaves were then flattened and rolled together to be used later. When the actual plaiting began, the leaves were cut into equal widths, some as small as one-sixteenth of an inch wide. Extra fine mats were hand plaited with 10 to 20 strands to the inch. Clothing, mats, and baskets were constructed using a diagonal plait, while pillows and other items were made with a square plait. A variety of styles and designs could be created by the use of various widths of leaves and with different plaiting techniques. Mats were then finished off with painted designs, colorful fringes on the edges, or with seeds, shells, and feathers, depending upon their intended use (Oliver, 143–51).

~*Robert Craig*

FOR MORE INFORMATION

Oliver, D. *Ancient Tahitian Society*. 3 vols. Honolulu: University of Hawai'i Press, 1974.

Personal Appearance

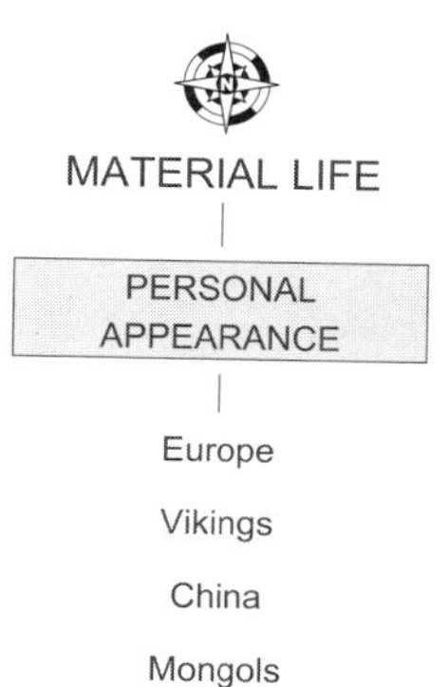

In Western countries today, most people think of hairstyles, cosmetics, and other similar grooming primarily as courting rituals. We want to attract a suitable mate or drive away the competition. In the Middle Ages, hairstyles and bodily adornments mainly served other functions: they defined a person's culture, as well as their social status within society.

Vikings produced numerous grooming artifacts that archaeologists have excavated, but such artifacts don't tell the whole story. Written records of Vikings accuse them of being filthy and ill groomed. Thus we can see that it is hard to really assess people's appearance from so long in the past. Nevertheless, we can tell that things such as hairstyles, jewelry, and other adornments were critically important to people's images.

In the early Middle Ages in Europe, long hair was an important feature for both men and women. Men sported long beards and proudly claimed they could protect their facial hair in battle. The tribe who settled northern Italy were called "Lombards," which means "long beard." When tribes wore similar clothing, they frequently identified themselves by distinctive hairstyles—particular knots, for example. Such distinctions continued into the Middle Ages, even after men began to trim their hair and beards. For example, when the Normans invaded England in 1066, they wore their hair shaved up the back, and they met the Anglo-Saxons, who sported long moustaches. After the Normans won, moustaches quickly fell out of fashion.

The Mongols offer a dramatic example of a group who almost defined themselves by their appearance. During their expansion, men and women alike terrified their opponents by a fierce appearance. Men shaved portions of their hair and left other sections long, and men and women painted their faces. Once they conquered China, however, they quickly took on the aspect of the Chinese, which legitimized their rule.

In all cultures, women's hair was considered attractive, sexual, and a mark of social status. It is precisely because of all these reasons that Muslim women covered their heads or their entire face. Christian and Buddhist nuns shaved their heads as a renunciation of sexual ties to this world. Once women were married, they signaled this status by their hairstyles. For example, once Mongol women married, they shaved the front of their head from the middle to the forehead. In western Europe, women took a less radical approach and simply bound their hair instead of wearing it loose, wearing a veil to cover their heads once they were married.

Hairstyles and other appearance could also reveal social status within society. Chinese women developed very elaborate hairstyles that showed both their status and the leisure and wealth they had to create the complex arrangements. In Europe, since women were limited in how much hair they were supposed to reveal, they adopted elaborate hats and hair coverings to reveal their status. Some during the late Middle Ages were so towering that women had to walk carefully to carry the headdresses. Without a doubt, working women could not wear such devices, so social status was quickly revealed.

Men, too, defined a certain kind of commitment by their hairstyles. In Christian Europe, monks shaved the crown of their heads to mark their vows, and this "tonsure" quickly identified any monk who left a monastery in renunciation of his vows. Buddhists monks shaved their heads, just as the nuns did.

While all cultures used hair as a marker of social status, there was less unanimity in the use of cosmetics and body adornment. Chinese women used elaborate cosmetics to enhance their beauty, but such decoration was frowned upon in Christian and Muslim countries. Therefore, cosmetic use was more limited (although never completely abandoned). Mongol women—before their Chinese phase—used black ash to enhance their eyebrows. In medieval Europe, men abandoned the Germanic practice of tattooing themselves, and in China this body decoration was considered low class and brutal. Yet the practice was never fully forgotten and was occasionally practiced to make a point.

Grooming and appearance were very important parts of people's daily life. Whether one was a poor peasant simply covering her hair with a coarse cloth or a wealthy aristocrat who showed off towering hairstyles or hats, women signaled to the world their social, marital, and economic status.

~Joyce E. Salisbury

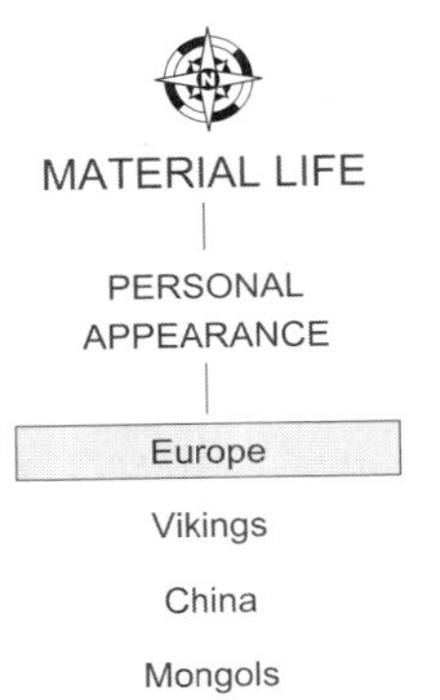

EUROPE

Like clothing, hairstyles in medieval Europe quickly indicated social status. The clergy were instantly recognizable by their "tonsure," or clerical haircut. Their heads were shaven on top, with the rest of the hair worn short, and their facial hair was shaven too. Nuns wore their hair cropped close under their veils. The simplest form of male headgear was the coif, a linen bonnet that covered the hair and tied under the chin. The coif kept a man's head warm and his hair clean and was particularly favored by laboring men. Agricultural laborers of the period are often shown wearing straw hats in the summer. Ordinary men sometimes wore hoods, usually made of wool, but sometimes made of leather. The hood might have a small cape attached to it that draped onto the shoulders. Peasant women covered their heads if they were married. However, the largest variation in hairstyles and head coverings came among women of the aristocracy. Fashions changed quickly as women vied to outdo each other.

Women's hair was not always covered. Fashionable women in the 12th century often wore their hair in two long braids, or they wrapped the two tresses in ribbons or fabric. In some cases, they even extended the wrapped tresses to the ground by weaving false hair into them. In the mid-13th century, fashionable women began encasing their hair in nets. Younger women sometimes wore their hair uncovered, either loose or in a single braid down the back. Most often women's hair was worn rather long, but a few contemporary illustrations from the 14th century show modern-looking cuts no longer than neck-length. Such styles were somewhat coquettish, appropriate for marriageable girls, but generally not for married women, widows, and others from whom a greater degree of modesty was expected.

Women were more likely than men to keep their heads covered because modesty required that married women not show off their hair. Most women wore a simple head wrap, probably consisting only of a long rectangle of fabric, either tucked into itself or secured in place with a band wrapped twice around the head. Women of a slightly higher status wore a veil, an oval or rectangular piece of fabric that lay atop the wearer's hair. This was secured in place with a fillet, also made of fabric, either worn on top of the veil or, more usually, serving as an anchor to which the veil could be pinned underneath. In the mid-12th century, some women began to wear a barbette, a strap that passed under the chin and was pinned together at the top of the crown; this too helped anchor the veil. The late 12th century saw the appearance of the wimple, a larger piece of fabric that was draped under the chin, covering the front of the neck; it was probably secured with pins to the fillet or barbette.

For women, the characteristic headdress of the early 14th century was the veil and wimple. The veil was typically a rectangle of white linen or silk worn draped over the head, trailing in back. The wimple was a similar piece of fabric arranged to fall in folds under the chin and around the neck. Some wimples only covered the front, whereas others surrounded the neck completely. Both veils and wimples were held in place with straight pins, anchored to a headband.

As in modern times, a woman's appearance was often treated as an important personal asset, and many wore makeup or dyed their hair. Moralists considered women's use of cosmetics excessively vain and sometimes condemned it, but the practice never disappeared. Skin was sometimes lightened with powder, and lips and cheeks were reddened. Then as now, curly hair was fashionable among women, who sometimes used curling irons to achieve this effect. The best mirrors were made of glass; a cheaper version consisted of polished metal; all were handheld.

Harold of England talks to Duke William of Normandy. The Anglo-Saxon Harold wears a mustache and can clearly be differentiated from the clean-shaven Normans, with their shaved back hair. © The Art Archive/Musée de la Tapisserie Bayeux/Dagli Orti.

Later in the 14th century, fashionable women ceased to cover the neck and chin, preferring only the veil. These veils were often fastened to a narrow fillet that circled the brow. The fillet also served to support the hair, which was braided, made into two bundles at the side of the face, and wired into place. The fillet might be tablet-woven or of more expensive jeweler's work. The veil might have a frilled edge, and it was often folded so that several layers of frilling framed the face and hair. Older women, as well as the less fashionable, wore the plainer veil. Fashionable women and men might adorn their hair with chaplets—wreathes made from flowers or greenery, or fabric cut to imitate those ephemeral materials, or from jeweler's work. At the end of the century, thick, padded rolls of fabric began to appear on fashionable heads; these were to become very popular in the 15th century for both sexes.

Men wore their hair fairly long—to or past the collar, although not long enough to braid. Beards were common, except for churchmen, who were obliged to be clean shaven. Moustaches had fallen out of fashion after the Norman Conquest and were very rare by the 14th century, although not wholly unknown. Shaving involved a straight razor and basin, in a manner that remained essentially unchanged until the rise of the safety razor in the 20th century; the process is tricky and dangerous and gave employment to a legion of professional barbers. Hair was groomed with a comb; brushes were apparently used only for clothes. Medieval combs had two sets of teeth—one broad to deal with the larger tangles, the other fine to finish up. Ordinary combs were made of wood or horn; expensive ones were made of ivory (Singman, 43–45; Singman and McLean, 109–13).

To read about personal appearance in Elizabethan England, see the England entry in the section "Clothing and Personal Appearance" in chapter 5 ("Material Life") of volume 3 of this series.

FOR MORE INFORMATION

Reeves, C. *Pleasures and Pastimes in Medieval England*. New York: Oxford University Press, 1998.

Singman, J. L. *Daily Life in Medieval Europe*. Westport, Conn.: Greenwood Press, 1999.

Singman, J. L., and W. McLean. *Daily Life in Chaucer's England*. Westport, Conn.: Greenwood Press, 1995.

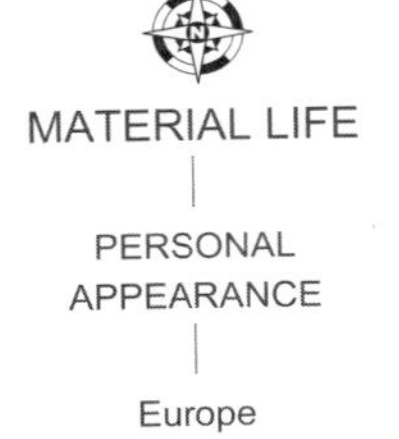

VIKINGS

In appearance, Viking Age Scandinavians were not much different from Scandinavians today, except that they had better teeth and were slightly smaller in stature. The Arab traveler Ibn Fadlan, who in 921 set out as secretary of an embassy from the caliph of Baghdad to the king of the Bulgars of the Middle Volga and who there came into contact with the Rus, Swedish Vikings, claimed that they were tall, blond, with ruddy complexions. Contemporary figurative art suggests that men had moustaches and beards and well-groomed hair, which might be held in place by a band across the head. Young girls and unmarried women wore their hair loose, but married women typically had their long hair gathered into a knot at the back of the head.

Archaeological discoveries of toilet implements, such as ear spoons (for cleaning the ears), tweezers (for removing unwanted hair, although they may also have been used for embroidery with metal threads), toothpicks, combs of antler and bone, and washing bowls, suggest that men and women paid close attention to their general appearance. Indeed, Ibrahim b. Ya'qub al-Turtushi, a 10th-century merchant or diplomat, reported that the inhabitants of Hedeby fabricated artificial eye makeup to enhance their beauty.

Nonetheless, the Viking Age Scandinavian's personal hygiene was probably low, at least by modern Western standards—and also by medieval Muslim ones. Ibn

Fadlan comments on the Rus's lack of sanitary efforts, going so far as to call them the filthiest of Allah's creatures. He notes that they did not wash after urinating, defecating, ejaculating, or eating, and when once a day they did wash, they all used the same water, into which they also spit and blew their noses.

It is, however, possible that within Scandinavia and in the Norse colonies in the North Atlantic, people were a bit more concerned about personal cleanliness. Indeed, the Eddic poem *Havamal* (Sayings of the High One) states that a guest should be greeted at the table with water and a towel, and it also specifies that a man should be washed before going to the assembly. Moreover, Old Norse literature regularly makes reference to saunas and hot baths in Norway and Iceland. In *Eyrbyggja saga* (Saga of the People of Eyri), the sauna at Hraun, Iceland, is described as being partly dug into the ground, with a hole in the top for pouring water on the stove from the outside.

The Viking Age Scandinavians liked splendor, and adorning themselves with jewelry was an important part of their appearance. A considerable amount of jewelry has survived. Most of it comes from hoards and graves. A variety of metals was used. Iron, copper, lead, and tin may have been mined in Scandinavia, but silver, gold, and also zinc, probably already alloyed to produce brass or bronze, were imported.

Brooches were what one may call obligatory jewelry in that they had a function in the costumes as fasteners. Many brooches have been found, ranging from individualized items of precious metals to mass-produced items of base and inexpensive materials. The latter were sometimes gilded to give them the appearance of gold and silver. The domed, oval brooches used by women to fasten their dresses are the most common. Worn in pairs, they are usually 10 to 12 centimeters long, with bold relief decoration and sometimes ornamented with filigree. The ornament is typically a kind of "gripping beast" decoration. Brooches used to fasten a chemise, shawl, or cloak and worn singly are the next most common. Neck rings, arm rings, finger rings, and even toe rings made of silver, gold, or occasionally, jet served the dual function of ornamentation and money. Such rings were typically made according to weight and from hammering out ingots of gold and silver. They normally consisted either of broad bands stamped with patterns or of two, three, or more rods twisted together. In commercial transactions, they could, therefore, easily be cut up. Necklaces, either complete or strung between oval brooches, were frequently used by women. Glass and amber beads, some of which were domestic products, appear to have been the most common, but beads made from imported semiprecious stones, such as crystal, cornelian, and obsidian, were also used. Gold, silver, and bronze beads were considerably less common. Genuine pearls were extremely rare; those that have been found are of poor quality.

Like everyone else in the Middle Ages, Vikings used their appearance to define their social status and to show the world who they were. They used hairstyles and jewelry in addition to their clothing to reveal their public persona.

~*Kirsten Wolf*

FOR MORE INFORMATION

Smyser, H. M. "Ibn Fadlan's Account of the Rus with Some Commentary and Some Allusions to *Beowulf*." In *Franciplegius: Medieval and Linguistic Studies in Honor of Francis Peabody*

Magoun, Jr., edited by J. B. Bessinger, Jr., and R. P. Creed. New York: New York University Press, 1965.
Wolf, K. *Daily Life of the Vikings*. Westport, Conn.: Greenwood Press, forthcoming.

MATERIAL LIFE
PERSONAL APPEARANCE
Europe
Vikings
China
Mongols

CHINA

A pleasing appearance was extremely important to the women of the Tang. It could be obtained naturally or artificially. The natural method involved applying or ingesting animal or vegetable matter that improved the look of the skin. For example, a pharmacologist recommended bat brains applied to a woman's face to remove blackheads, and a manual on aromatics for women in the imperial harem gave the following formula for attaining a fair skin tone: Pulverize dried tangerine peel, white melon seeds, and peach blossoms, strain the powder through a sieve, and ingest a spoonful thrice daily for 30 days. Another facial cream called for steeping three chicken eggs in fine ale, sealing the mixture in a pot, covering the jar tightly, and letting it stand unopened for 28 days. There was an even simpler potion: Smear the face and body with the blood of a black-boned, silky bird on the seventh day of the seventh moon. Apply the gore three times.

Cosmetics were, of course, the artificial means of beautifying the countenance. There were several powders that Tang women applied to their faces to give them color. One of the oldest was ceruse, made of a lead oxide, which tinted the skin white. Women also applied it to their breasts. Poets called such makeup "lead face" and "lead flower." Since the 6th century, Chinese women dabbed their foreheads with a powder containing massicot, a lead oxide, that imparted a yellow color to the brows. They may have used golden arsenic for the same purpose. A yellow forehead was extremely popular in the Tang, perhaps because face readers asserted that a yellow aura around the forehead was extremely auspicious. Conversely, sometimes the character of makeup could be a portent of a calamity. In the early 8th century, Illustrious August's concubines applied ceruse to their cheeks in a pattern suggesting tears. Those in the know considered that to be a bad omen. There was a simple and quick method of perfuming face powders: placing whole cloves in their containers. In the early 9th century, when Tibetan fashions became popular, patrician ladies abandoned face powders and rouges entirely, a change not welcomed by some men.

In ancient China, women applied beauty marks to their chins, cheeks, and foreheads. Painted on with red, yellow, black, and other pigments, they took the form of crescent moons, coins, birds, insects, flowers, leaves, and the like. The fashion was an old custom that dated back to the 2nd century, but it did not come into vogue during the Tang until about 700. A woman who had been enslaved in the palace, and by virtue of her extraordinary literary talents rose to become a secretary to Empress Wu, reintroduced it to high society. It was a means of covering facial blemishes and scars. Beauty marks did not always mask natural flaws or accidental wounds.

It was the habit of women in medieval China to pluck their eyebrows completely and paint in new ones with tinctures. The best-known style was called moth eyebrows because their shape resembled the wings of the insect. It became so fashionable at the court in the early 7th century that officials had to supply a daily ration of 27 quarts of a pigment to the ladies of the emperor's harem. The pigment was derived from conch shells. In the Tang, women seem to have preferred a greenish blue. In the late 8th century, palace women were using indigo, a blue dye of Persian origin. In the early 9th century, under the influence of Tibetan culture, they began to paint thin eyebrows in the form of inverted Vs that gave their faces a sad expression. The style was called "convict," "tear," or "mourning makeup." A decade later, they were drawing three or four red or purple lines above and below their eyes. They called the fashion "blood halos."

Hairstyles for women during the Tang dynasty. Note the elaborate hairstyles for women, which would clearly distinguish one woman from another. Illustration by Charles Benn.

Red was an important color for facial cosmetics. Women brushed rouge on their cheeks directly under their eyes. Cinnabar (mercuric sulfide) imparted the red color to women's lip glosses. A powder ground from the horny plate that closes the shells of mollusks lent an agreeable scent to lip glosses in the Tang. The influence of Tibetan culture briefly led to the abandonment of red glosses. In the early 9th century, black lip glosses became fashionable in high society. Pigment from impatiens, a flowering plant, blended with aluminum sulfate and garlic supplied a dye for women's fingernails. Both men and women wore their nails long. Some medical authorities warned that cutting fingernails and toenails too frequently weakened muscles.

There was a substantial number of hairstyles for women in the Tang. Some were enduring. Others were passing fancies that surfaced for a short time and developed from specific historical or sociological causes. One recent authority has uncovered 24 of the most popular fashions from his study of poems, histories, and other sources, and each had its own name. Three of the most popular were described as follows. *Tall bindings* consisted of hair drawn to the top of the head and formed into "piles" in a large variety of shapes. The height of the hairdo was as much as a foot. The style was the most common in the Tang. In the *conch*, the hair was drawn up to the top of the head, bound at the base with a ribbon, and the ends curled backward into a spiral resembling the shells of certain mollusks. Sometimes women combed their hair into double spirals. In *deserting the family*, the hair at the temples was pulled down along both sides to embrace the face. The fashion came into vogue at the very end of the Tang, when everyone clearly recognized that the dynasty was about to collapse and widespread dislocations of the population would occur in its wake. In all the styles, women often added flowers or jewels to adorn their hair. Combs were essential for keeping the hair in place when tall bindings were worn. The style required as many as 10 combs. Made of gold, silver, jade, rhinoceros horn, and ivory, combs were small and had curved backs. A woman might also insert as many as 12 hairpins to fix her hairdo.

Young girls did not do their hair in tall bindings, perhaps because their elders would not allow it. They did their hair up in a style called "anticipating immortals," which required them to draw two braids up from the back of the neck, pull them over the head, and tie their ends above the hairline to form loops. Girls also wore bangs.

In the Tang, some men also adorned their bodies—especially their skin. In general, the Chinese did not approve of tattooing because it was a mutilation of the body, which ought to be returned to the grave in pristine condition, and because it was a custom practiced by the barbarians. There were, however, some men who defied social conventions. They were mainly the residents of markets, strongmen, and thugs. One of the ruffians in Changan spent a small fortune to have an artist prick his chest and stomach so that he could sport a landscape replete with gazebos nestled in the mountains, pavilions soaring over rivers, trees, birds, and animals. In the 9th century, a band of juvenile bullies, more than 30 in number, terrorized and robbed people by force in the streets of a market at Changan. They entered a tavern carrying snakes and assaulted patrons with the shoulder blades of sheep. All of the hooligans had their heads shaved and tattooed with all sorts of images. The mayor of the capital ordered some ward headmen and their lackeys to apprehend the culprits. After their arrest, he had all of them beaten to death in the market. Thereafter, market people with tattoos had them effaced by burning. At the time, there was a strongman in one of the city's wards who had tattoos on his shoulders. The one on the left read, "In life I do not fear the mayor," and the one on the right read, "In death I will not fear the king of hell." He paid for his insolence. The mayor had him beaten to death as well (Benn, 107, 113).

FOR MORE INFORMATION

Benn, C. *Daily Life in Traditional China: The Tang Dynasty*. Westport, Conn.: Greenwood Press, 2002.

MONGOLS

Many of the early reports of the Mongols that came to the West, both to Europe and the Middle East, in the 13th century carried horrific descriptions of the "barbarian" hordes. These descriptions appeared to confirm the earlier reports of the carnage, savagery, and monstrous invincibility of this "satanic" storm from the East. Even though descriptions and pictures that began to be available later in the 13th century bear more resemblance to reality, these early accounts of the appearance of the Mongols remain of great interest since they convey the emotional impact the devastating appearance of the Mongols made on the medieval societies of Europe and the Islamic world.

The Armenian historian Kirakos of Ganjak (1201–72), a cleric and one-time captive of the Mongols, offered vivid descriptions of his captors, remarking on their clean-shaven and frightful appearance, and their shrill, loud voices. A contemporary of Kirakos, another Christian Armenian cleric, Grigor of Akanc' is more colorful in his depiction of the invaders from the "Nation of Archers," as he called the Mongols:

> They were terrible to look at and indescribable, with large heads like a buffalo's, narrow eyes like a fledging's [young bird], a snub nose like a cat, projecting snouts like a dog's, narrow loins like an ant's, short legs like a hog's, and by nature no beards at all. With a lion's strength they have voices more shrill than an eagle's. (Grigor of Akanc', 295)

A more measured account is given by a Franciscan monk and papal emissary, although some would say a spy, who accompanied Friar Giovanni Di Plano Carpini's party traveling (1245–47) to Qaraqorum, capital of the Mongol Empire. He reports that the "Tatars" are usually

> [o]f low stature and rather thin, owing to their diet of mare's milk, which makes a man slim, and their strenuous life. They are broad of face with prominent cheekbones, and have a tonsure [shaven circle] on their head like our clerics from which they shave a strip three fingers wide from ear to ear. On the forehead, however, they wear their hair in a crescent-shaped fringe reaching to the eyebrows, but gather up the remaining hair, and arrange and braid it like the Saracens [Muslims]. (Skelton, Marston, and Painter, 86)

The Franciscan friar William of Rubruck traveled to the court of the Great Khan Möngke between 1253 and 1255 and on his return sent a full account of his journey to King Louis IX of France. He mentions their shaved heads but describes the bald patch as square rather than round and remarks that the forehead and temples are also shaved of hair, leaving a long tuft of hair hanging from the crown to the eyebrows. William of Rubruck further describes the men as having long hair that they braid in two plaits right up to the ears. He notes that girls, on the day following their marriage, shave their heads from the middle toward the forehead. Interestingly, he adds a detail about hygiene, explaining that in order to wash their hair, the Mongols first take water into their mouths. They then allow this water to trickle from their mouths into their cupped hands which they use to wet their hair and wash their heads.

Although less emotional in his description than others, William of Rubruck is quite pointed in his account of the women:

> The women are astonishingly fat. The less nose one has, the more beautiful she is considered; and they disfigure themselves horribly, moreover, by painting their faces. (William of Rubruck, 89)

Later, he recounts the wife of a local Mongol commander, Scacatai, whose appearance he finds particularly repellent. To enhance her nasal features, the snub nose being a prized sign of beauty, this lady had, it seemed to Rubruck, amputated the bridge of her nose. The horrible result was the almost complete lack of any discernable nose. Worse still, she had apparently applied some black ointment to that disfigured spot as well as to her eyebrows. She "looked thoroughly dreadful," concluded the friar.

However, although the earlier reports of their appearance are rarely very complimentary, the Mongols were ambitious not only for land, conquests, and power but also for the luxuries of the outside world and the fineries of that world with which to adorn themselves. Chinggis Khan is credited by the Persian statesman and historian Rashīd al-Dīn with expressing the following ambition for his wives and daughters:

> To delight their mouths with the sweetness of the sugar of benevolence, to adorn them front and back, top and bottom, with garments of gold brocade. (Allsen, 12)

For his people, Chinggis Khan also wanted a world distant from the frugality and coarseness of the steppe in which he grew up. He foresaw a change in the Mongols' appearance and in the image they projected:

> After us, our posterity will wear garments of sewn gold, partake of fatty and sweet delicacies, sit well-formed horses, and embrace beauteous wives. (Allsen, 12)

To enhance their image and reflect their new status, and no doubt embarrassed by their reputation as primitive, dirty barbarians, the Mongols who ruled in the later 13th century adorned not only themselves but also their living quarters with sumptuous, delicate embroideries and brocades woven with gold and precious stones. The opulence of their palace-tents became legendary and, along with the sophistication of their courts, stood in stark contrast to the appearance they projected when first they emerged from the steppe.

The transformation of the appearance of the Mongols, from their depiction in the annals of the English chronicler Matthew Parris as cannibalistic savages to the later images of imperial splendor that emerged from their appearance in the Yuan (Chinese) courts is aptly illustrated through the words of another European cleric, Friar Odoric of Pordenone (d. 1331), whose extensive travels took him to the Yuan court (Mongol dynasty in China, 1260–1370). Here he describes how the Great Khan rode between his winter and summer palaces:

> The king travelleth in a two-wheeled carriage . . . all [made] of lignaloes [perfumed wood] and gold, and covered with great and fine skins, and set with many precious stones. And the carriage is drawn by four elephants . . . and also by four splendid horses, richly caparisoned. . . . Moreover, he carrieth with him in his chariot twelve gerfalcons; so that even as he sits therein upon his chair of state or some other seat, if he sees any birds pass he lets fly his hawks at them. (Yule, 228–29)

~*George Lane*

FOR MORE INFORMATION

Allsen, T. T. *Commodity and Exchange in the Mongol Empire*. Cambridge, England: Cambridge University Press, 1997.

Grigor of Akanc'. "History of the Nation of Archers," edited and translated by R. P. Blake and R. N. Frye. *Harvard Journal of Asiatic Studies* 12 (1949): 269–399.

Skelton, R. A., T. E. Marston, and G. D. Painter. *The Vinland Map and The Tartar Relation*. 2nd ed. New Haven, Conn.: Yale University Press, 1995.

William of Rubruck. *The Mission of William of Rubruck*. Translated and edited by P. Jackson, with D. Morgan. London: Hakluyt Society, 1990.

Yule, H. *Cathay and the Way Thither*. 3 vols. Hakluyt Society, [1914]. Reprint, Millwood, New York: Kraus Reprint, 1967.

Furnishings

During the Middle Ages, the furnishings of even the wealthiest household would seem sparse by our standards, and the poor had very little indeed. The basic needs inside a household were very simple: a place to sleep, positions to prepare and eat food, and some simple storage. Anything else—even places to sit—were extras.

Beds all over the world ranged from simple mats placed on the floor to mattresses stuffed with straw. The Vikings slept on platforms fixed to the wall, whereas the nobility had "bed closets" to provide some warmth and privacy. As wealth increased, so did a desire for more comfort. Mattresses were filled with feathers to make them softer than straw, which matted and pricked through the woolen covering. The Japanese used wooden pillows to support the head, which seems uncomfortable to Westerners used to a soft pillow. In many parts of the world, mats or mattresses were rolled up during the day to save precious interior space. Fixed beds in Europe were made of a wood frame crossed with ropes to support the mattress.

Storage was usually handled by chests, from simple wood to wicker to Muslim chests of precious cedar wood. Peasants stored their blankets and Sunday clothing and the nobility stored their treasure in the same basic kind of chest. Additional storage might be found on shelves attached to the walls or in recesses in the walls of stucco houses. Late in the Middle Ages, European woodworkers began to design more elaborate storage cupboards and chests carved out of oak. These became the basis for more elaborate furniture that graces many modern houses. Medieval furniture was painted in bright colors, instead of leaving the wood bare, as most prefer today.

The largest difference between furnishings in Europe and elsewhere in the world came with the chair, which dictated how people would comfortably relax. In Islamic countries, India, early China, and Japan, people sat on the floor on cushions or rugs. This caused people to become used to sitting cross-legged or squatting for long periods of time—a posture extremely uncomfortable to Europeans who were used to sitting in chairs. During the Tang dynasty in China, chairs first appeared; their import from outside is noted by their being termed "barbarian beds." At first, chairs in China were reserved for guests of honor or nobility, and simple stools appeared in China in the 9th century.

The arrival of chairs in China led that culture to adopt both methods of interior furnishings. In some households or even parts of a house, everything was adapted to life at floor level—cushions, low tables, and low storage chests. As noted by Fernand Braudel, China experienced "a major expansion of life-styles, accompanied by a separation between seated life and squatting life at the ground level, the latter domestic, the former official" (Braudel, 290). China was one country that adapted to both styles of sitting—the rest of the world chose one over the other, with the result that travel and household comfort was difficult for people traveling to different parts of the world. Imagine riding for long in an ox-cart without a seat as you sit cross-legged in the bottom of the cart.

Tables were very rare in the Middle Ages. In China, bureaucrats had tables on which to write, and the tables would either be low to the ground (like Japanese tables), to accommodate a kneeling scribe, or higher if a chair or stool were available. In Europe, tables were usually only for special occasions. Peasant families would simply help themselves to food from the hearth and sit on the floor or on stools to eat. In noble households, most meals were taken that way as well. For special dinners, great planks of wood were set up temporarily to serve as tables. By late in the Middle Ages, wealthy households began to establish a permanent table, which was a mark of honor.

Within the households of the Middle Ages—East and West—people did the same things: they ate, socialized, and slept. The furnishings were sparse but permitted these activities. Slowly, people began to acquire more items with which to grace their homes, but that development would not fully take place until long after the medieval period had ended.

~*Joyce E. Salisbury*

FOR MORE INFORMATION

Braudel, F. *The Structures of Everyday Life*. New York: Harper and Row, 1979.

EUROPE

The interior of the peasant house in Europe was quite sparse. The floor was no more than packed dirt or clay, perhaps covered with fresh straw from time to time. The house would have a wooden door with iron fittings and possibly even some form of lock. The windows were small to minimize heat loss, with no glass to cover the opening but with simple wooden shutters to close it at night. The discovery of candleholders in some peasant cottages offers evidence that peasants did not always retire to bed when daylight failed, but candles could not be used by the poorest. Light also was provided by the fire on the hearth, placed in the center of the room.

The furnishings of a peasant home were simple and few. Stools and benches provided seating, and there may have been some sort of trestle table, although one text of the period describes the typical peasant eating his meal not at a table but holding his bowl in his lap. For bedding, the peasant used straw, which provided good insulation and a reasonable degree of comfort, although the surface was much harder than a modern bed. The straw might be stuffed inside a sack to make a kind of rough mattress. Bedding straw was a notorious harborer of lice and bedbugs; these unwelcome pests were discouraged by including an herb such as wormwood in the bedding, but the straw still needed to be changed from time to time. Late 13th-century commoners from the English town of Colchester, assessed at a similar value to Richard Bovechurch of Cuxham, owned wooden bedsteads, linen sheets, and coverlets. Woolen blankets would also have been within the peasant's means.

Cooking and eating utensils were few, and because metal was costly, they were more likely made of clay or wood. Clay pots served for cooking food and could also be used for baking after the manner of a Dutch oven, with the dough inside and the pot covered with hot coals. Bowls and drinking vessels were made of clay or wood, and spoons were made of wood as well. Forks were not used at any level of society, but a knife was part of everyone's personal equipment and served as an eating utensil as well as a working tool. Many peasants had brass cauldrons, useful for heating water, as well as cooking tripods, jugs, basins, and hand towels. An English manorial record of the 13th century mentioned peasant tenants bringing a plate, mug, and napkin to a meal.

Storage was provided by simple wooden chests, caskets, cupboards, straw baskets, and coarse fabric sacks; not many were needed to contain the peasant's limited personal possessions. Excavations have turned up keys, suggesting that some peasants had valuables to protect, perhaps money, brooches, or silver spoons that some residents kept in their caskets. The largest part of the household equipment consisted of various sorts of tools for agriculture, dairying, sewing, and spinning. The household probably also had a broom: excavated cottage floors show signs of frequent sweeping.

The only really effective light source was the sun, and people relied heavily on daylight, adjusting their schedules throughout the year to take full advantage of every daylight hour. Indoors, the need for light conflicted with the desire to keep out the cold. In an ordinary household, the windows might be covered with oiled linen cloths that let in some light while cutting down on the draft. A wealthy home might have glass window panes, but even these were cloudy and uneven—the process by which early glass was handblown produced a rippled surface that has contributed to the myth that glass "flows" over time. At night, windows could be shuttered for better insulation.

Windows were larger and more numerous in wealthy households, where the inhabitants could afford more fuel for heating. Even so, the window surface in any given room was significantly less than is usually the case today, and even the wealthy home would look slightly dim to the modern eye. In poorer households, windows were few and small. The interior of an ordinary person's house would be so dark that even in the daytime a person entering from outdoors needed a moment to adjust to the substantially reduced level of light.

At night, people had to rely on fire for light. There was usually a fire on the hearth, which provided a low general level of light, but it would have been unevenly distributed. Various sorts of portable lights provided specific illumination. Candles—a medieval invention—came in two types: wax—made from the honeycombs of bees—and tallow, derived from sheep fat. Both provided a comparable level of light, although wax candles, with their higher melting point, were easier to use—they were also about three times as expensive. Poorer households also used rushlights, made of lengths of rush dipped in fat; these were fairly cheap but offered less light than candles. Various sorts of oil lamps were also used. The illumination afforded by all of these lights was weak compared with modern electric lighting. The lack of artificial light was evident outdoors as well as indoors (Singman, 84–85).

To read about furnishings in Elizabethan England, see the England entry in the section "Houses and Furniture" in chapter 5 ("Material Life") of volume 3; and for 18th-century England, see the England entry in the section "Housing and Furnishings" in chapter 5 ("Material Life") of volume 4 of this series.

FOR MORE INFORMATION

Singman, J. L. *Daily Life in Medieval Europe*. Westport, Conn.: Greenwood Press, 1999.

VIKINGS

The average house in Viking Age Scandinavia had little furniture. Sleeping, sitting, and eating typically took place on the platforms along the walls. Stools and chairs seem to have been uncommon, although they certainly existed. A rectangular wooden board with corner perforations for four legs was found in Hedeby, and three-legged stools are known from Lund, Sweden, and Dublin, Ireland. Of chairs, there were basically two types. One, a bench-type chair with a square back, was found in the Oseberg ship burial in Norway. The other type, round with a swung back made from a thick tree trunk, is known from Sweden. Common to both stools and chairs is that they are quite low.

As for tables, it is known from literary sources that they were used at least on special occasions. Only one table has been discovered, however, in a woman's grave under Horning Church in northern Jutland, Denmark. It is a small table made of oak for a wash basin. It consists of a heavy frame of logs that are slotted into each other and held together with wooden dowels; the top of the table sits in the bottom frame.

Movable beds are also known from archaeological finds, but it is unlikely that they were commonly used, and it may be that they were intended for traveling; well-to-do people would have had bed closets partitioned off from the house. The Oseberg ship burial contained remains of at least five beds, of which the largest measures 2.2 by 1.9 meters at the bottom. It is a substantial and beautifully crafted bed: the bedposts at the head of the bed are high and end in carved, bowed animal heads. Horizontal boards inside the bed suggest that it must have had a mattress, and indeed, mattresses have been found at Tune, Norway. The bedding, or what remains of it, was filled with down. That such luxury was enjoyed also elsewhere in Scandinavia is confirmed by a down-filled pillow found in a grave at Mammen in Denmark.

Cupboards were unknown. Many objects, such as household utensils and weapons, were stored on shelves or hung on the walls. Wooden pails, soapstone bowls, and clay pots were used to store dry foods and liquids. The only kind of furniture for storage was a chest, in which people would keep personal belongings, such as clothing or tools and utensils of various kinds, both while at home and when traveling; it has been suggested that on board a ship, such chests may sometimes have served as rowing benches. Several chests have been preserved, including a very fine specimen found in the Oseberg ship burial. Smaller caskets and boxes were used for valuables, such as jewelry, and they typically belonged to women. Some of them had built-in locks, although barrel-shaped padlocks have also been found.

~*Kirsten Wolf*

FOR MORE INFORMATION

Wolf, K. *Daily Life of the Vikings*. Westport, Conn.: Greenwood Press, forthcoming.

CHINA

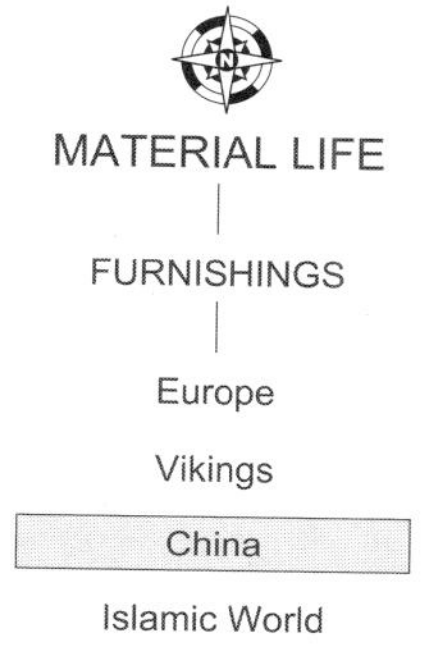

Couches were the primary pieces of furniture in early Chinese parlors. They were low, large, raised platforms, usually made of wood, and had no backs or armrests. People sat on them cross-legged and used low tables for writing and eating. The emperor's throne, called the "dragon couch," was certainly the heaviest and no doubt the most magnificent. It was made of gold and bronze. The throne was mobile in the sense that imperial servitors, probably a good number of them, transported it to various locations for important occasions. On the last day of the moon and during solar eclipses, the attendants carried it to the Altar of Soil, where the emperor attended to state rituals.

Tents, or perhaps more appropriately, curtains with canopies, surrounded couches of the wealthy in formal settings such as parlors. The materials used to make them could be as humble as bamboo or as extravagant as pearls and jade. In 873, the emperor had the finger bone of Buddha brought to the palace and had it ensconced behind drapes of pearls and jade. A chief minister in the late 8th century settled his favorite concubine in a tent with curtains of gold thread. He had another tent made of shark silk. This exotic fabric may have been *pinikon*, a cinnamon-colored cloth made in south Asia from the tough filaments that mussels use to attach themselves to underwater surfaces. Whatever the case, the material purportedly provided warmth in the winter and coolness in the summer.

The Chinese had known of the chair since at least the 1st century C.E. It was a folding seat and clearly of foreign origin, for it was called the "barbarian bed." The fashion of sitting on chairs did not catch on for centuries, perhaps because people preferred sitting cross-legged. Whatever the case, the first true chairs appeared in the Tang. Small, round stools and long benches for sitting at dinner tables also appeared in the home about the 9th century.

Screens were common fixtures in the homes of patricians. They were movable and installed behind seats to block drafts. Their surfaces provided convenient spaces for inscribing texts. Taizong had 10 criticisms of him submitted by a righteous minister affixed to a screen so that he could read them in the morning and evening. He recorded the names of all prefectural governors on another, which he consulted on rising and retiring—apparently so he could memorize the officials' names. Screens were also the objects of aesthetic adornment. A man of means could commission an artist to paint landscapes or scenes of the four seasons on them. Yang Guifei had one on which pictures of beautiful women from former times had been engraved and their clothes inlaid with precious stones.

Beds were couches with poles affixed to their four corners, and curtains hung from the poles. The drapes for imperial use were exquisite. Daoists recommended that beds be at least three-and-a-half feet high, so that damp air and demons emanating from the ground could not attack sleeping people. They also counseled against placing a bed against the northern wall and advocated removing the left shoe first when retiring for the night.

Pillows were made of porcelain, wood, stone, and other hard materials. An official in charge of the government's monopoly on iron and salt had one encrusted with lapis lazuli that he placed on his gold bed. Those made of rosewood were said to cure headaches. Pillows were rectangular, with a dip in the middle for resting the neck. A noble lady in the early 8th century had a "night shining pillow" that glowed in the dark so she did not have to rely on lamps or candles. Pillows, according to the Daoists, should not be too tall because they could diminish the number of years allotted to one. They were also magical in Chinese folklore. The younger sister of Empress Wei had one in the form of a leopard's head to ward off evil, and another in the shape of a prostrate bear to ensure the birth of a male child.

Foreign rugs graced the floors of patrician dwellings in the Tang. At least two ancient centers, Bukhara and Persia, which were renowned for their carpets then as now, sent them as tribute to the court. Such goods were also commercial wares, transported on the backs of camels across the deserts of central Asia to Changan. They made their way to shops in city markets. In a short time, China had its own works for weaving rugs which became big business.

There were four types of implements for lighting in Tang China: torches, oil lamps, candles, and lanterns. Torches provided illumination for courtyards and for travelers. Made of bundles of sticks and installed at the foot of stairs leading into halls, they provided enough light to turn night into day. Without them, nocturnal feasts, polo matches, and hunting were impossible. Lanterns, made of light bamboo frames to which paper or silk was pasted and in which lighted candles were placed, supplied light for short trips in the dark.

Candles and lamps provided interior illumination for halls. The fuel used in lamps—burned in flat metal or ceramic pans—was usually hemp oil. Some exotic fats, such as whale and seal oil, also were used. Medical canons discouraged the use of pork and bear fats for lighting because smoke from their flames was thought to cause nearsightedness. Patricians might have fancy stands made for their lamps. Unlike Europe, where animal fats were the chief constituents of candles, the substance for candles in medieval China was usually an oil derived from the berry of a plant that was mixed with beeswax. Patricians might have aromatic candles that had various fragrances mixed into the wax and that filled their bedrooms with marvelous scents all night. They might also have elegant holders for the candles. Some candles were graduated so that people—probably Buddhist monks performing nocturnal devotions—could determine the passing of time. Buddhists also introduced incense clocks to Tang China. The wood or metal devices had channels in the shapes of Sanskrit characters that were filled with incense. Monks could tell the time because as the incense burned, it passed marks along the channels. Each mark represented one of the night watches: 7 to 9 P.M., 9 to 11 P.M., 11 P.M. to 1 A.M., 1 to 3 A.M., and 3 to 5 A.M (Benn, 85–88, 90).

FOR MORE INFORMATION

Benn, C. *Daily Life in Traditional China: The Tang Dynasty.* Westport, Conn.: Greenwood Press, 2002.

ISLAMIC WORLD

Domestic life in the medieval Islamic world was generally conducted rather close to the ground. As families and friends came inside, they relaxed on large pillows arranged on the floor, and they slept on mattresses also placed on the floor. These habits made a great deal of sense in hot climates, where heat rose in houses and the air was coolest nearest the floor. This pattern of living acquired in the desert formed the basis of furnishings in the Muslim world.

Meals, too, were consumed close to the floor. Families did not sit in chairs around a dining room table at mealtime. Instead, family members and guests sat on a carpet, pillow, or low seat arranged around large serving trays that were set on the floor or on a low stand. People did not eat from individual plates but instead ate directly from the serving trays. Because people generally ate many dishes with their hands and flat breads, clean hands were considered essential. Some utensils were employed; knives were essential for cutting meats, and spoons were needed for eating soups.

While everyone was perfectly comfortable on cushions on the floor, differing status called for different household furnishings. Muslim woodworkers and smiths constructed benches and chairs that were comparable in height to their Western counterparts, but these were used to indicate the rank of high-status individuals (e.g., rulers or the family patriarch), who sat on benches or chairs to place themselves above persons of lower rank. Sitting on sofas, large pillows, or stacks of pillows could both physically and symbolically elevate a person over someone of lesser status and rank.

The heights and kinds of the beds people slept on as well as the kinds of material used to make beds, pillows, and sofas were also indicators of status and wealth. Beds with legs and frames were a sign of the highest status. Beds without them were a step down, sleeping on a mat or carpet a step further, and sleeping on the bare floor was for the poorest as well as for the mendicant Sufis, who considered themselves God's poor ones. Thus, in the Muslim world as elsewhere, household furnishings were as much about wealth and status as they were about domestic comfort.

~*James Lindsay*

FOR MORE INFORMATION

Lindsay, J. *Daily Life in the Medieval Islamic World.* Westport, Conn.: Greenwood Press, forthcoming.

MATERIAL LIFE

TECHNOLOGY

Europe

Vikings

China

Islamic World

Byzantium

Technology

The study of technology usually means to study practical or applied arts, but basically it concerns those artifacts that allow people to do more work more efficiently than they might otherwise have done. Thus the history of technology includes everything from stone tools to modern computers. While we are accustomed to rapidly adopting new technologies (our computer software is almost obsolete the moment we load it), the adoption of new technologies in the past was more complex than simple inventions. A new idea had to coincide with a perceived need, which often depended on other inventions to support it. For example, reading glasses were invented in the Middle Ages but did not spread widely until the printing press and better artificial lights gave more people more to read and more light to do so. Thus to study the progress of technology through history requires us to look closely at intersecting aspects of daily life.

One of the main impulses for the adoption (indeed, invention) of new technology is the lack of power to get things done. Through the ancient world, there were two main sources of power—human and animal. In places where there were large populations (Egypt, China, and India, for example), human labor sufficed for most of the work, even though people are less efficient. For example, people assumed it took about seven men to haul as much weight as one horse (Braudel, 337), but humans were more flexible. After hauling, people could be put to work to build walls, for example, where a horse could not.

Sources of energy also push invention. For example, in preconquest South America, Indians did not develop the wheel even though there were examples of wheeled miniature toys. Why build wheeled vehicles if there were no domestic animals to pull them or good roads? Wheeled vehicles would just mean that people would have to pull heavier loads than they could carry, which was not a good trade-off. Once again, technology is shaped by need and a complex series of available items.

A final determinant of technology is access to raw materials. In Polynesia, people had no metal tools, utensils, or nails. Thus their constructions were limited. Europe and Asia benefited not only from abundant raw materials but from sustained contacts that led inventions to spread. The Chinese invented things as simple and useful as the wheelbarrow, which spread to Europe in the 12th century, to things as complex as suspension bridges. Communication offered great advantage to the spread of technology.

The Byzantine Empire inherited the Romans' technological expertise and at the beginning of the Middle Ages was more advanced than lands farther west. They also had the advantage of being on the crossroads of trade with China and the Muslim world. Late in the Middle Ages, however, their political and economic situation interfered with advances in technology, and western Europe surpassed the Byzantine Empire.

Western Europe experienced a technological revolution in the Middle Ages, beginning in the 11th century. Unlike China, which had a large population to perform labor, Europe had a shortage of labor. Necessity stimulated the invention and wide use of wind and water power to supplement—and in many instances replace—human and animal power. Water mills in particular offered reliable sources of energy all along rivers; these wheels did everything from grinding grain to crushing minerals, pounding cloth, and even powering a mechanical saw that could more easily cut the great oak forests that supplied the materials for castles. Windmills appeared a bit later in Europe and China. They were probably invented in the Middle East, spreading first through Muslim lands.

Beyond power, the heart of the technology of the Middle Ages in Europe and Asia was iron. Iron smelting before the 19th century had remained roughly unchanged from its beginnings about 1200 B.C.E., when metallurgists learned that when iron is repeatedly heated in a hot charcoal furnace, carbon molecules combine with iron molecules to form a reliable metal known as carbon steel. The Chinese, however, had developed ways to smelt the ore at very high temperatures and led the world in producing cast iron and sharp blades. The Muslims quickly learned the techniques of sword making from Asia, and when Western crusaders confronted Muslim armies, their own pounded iron swords were clearly inferior to the Muslims', made of Eastern smelted steel.

The Vikings were in the forefront of technological advance when it came to their magnificent longboats, built to withstand the rough waters of the North Sea. Once again, we can see in this development that necessity yielded invention—these intrepid sailors did what they had to do to navigate their waters.

The Middle Ages may look to the modern reader like an era of very low technology, when people all over the world worked hard with relatively simple tools. Yet this era produced a great technological revolution from China to Europe as people found new sources of energy to do work and new inventions to help them do it. Perhaps more than anything, they awakened the idea that technology could bring positive change—this is the idea that shapes our consciousness.

~*Joyce E. Salisbury*

FOR MORE INFORMATION

Braudel, F. *The Structures of Everyday Life*. New York: Harper and Row, 1979.

EUROPE

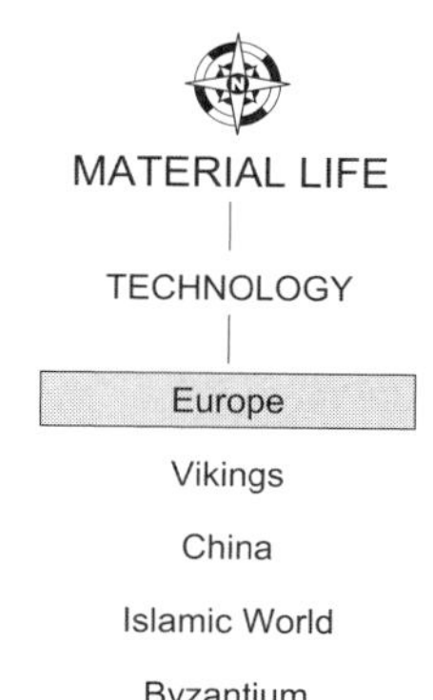

In today's industrialized world, it is hard to envision how much effort it takes to produce even the simplest of goods when each piece must be transformed by hand from raw materials to finished product. Medieval craftsmen made use of a wide range of tools, from the smith's simple hammer to the weaver's intricate loom, but in all cases the amount of human labor involved was enormous.

Even making a fire in the home was labor intensive if someone had not carefully covered the coals through the night so they would remain hot in the morning. Starting a fire from scratch required striking a piece of hardened steel against the sharp edge of a piece of flint. The flint sliced tiny pieces off the steel, heating them red-hot in the process; these sparks were caught in a piece of charred cloth that began to smolder. Step by step, this weak combustion was built up: the cloth would be held against some highly flammable tow (fibers of flax unsuitable for spinning) and blown to produce a small flame; this would be used to ignite small pieces of wooden tinder that in turn ignited larger pieces of wood.

Producing manufactured products was equally difficult. The production of ironwork illustrates the effort involved in medieval industry. Iron was a staple component in medieval material culture, and its use was known in Europe since the first millennium B.C.E., yet its production remained a laborious task. The iron ore had to be extracted from the ground by miners. It then had to be heated to more than two thousand degrees Fahrenheit (although there was no precise way to measure heat) to separate the iron from impurities in the ore, a process involving the consumption of large quantities of fuel in the form of charcoal, itself produced at the expenditure of considerable labor. The iron was then repeatedly heated and beaten to produce the desired carbon content before it could be shaped at the smith's forge—by means of tools themselves made of iron. Because of the enormous amount of labor involved, ironwork was always expensive and was used as sparingly as possible. The same applied to a lesser degree to cheaper, more easily worked metals, such as lead, tin, and copper, and their alloys such as pewter, brass, and bronze. These did not involve as laborious a refining process as iron, and their lower melting temperatures made them easier to work, but they still had to be mined and the ore purified, so that these metals were also somewhat expensive.

Because of the expense of metals, the medieval household made greater use of less-costly materials such as wood and clay. There was also incentive to make full use of natural objects and materials, particularly those available as by-products of other work. When cattle were slaughtered for food, the hide was sold to a tanner for leather, while the bones and horns were purchased by other craftsmen to make small household items. Bone, when highly polished, resembles ivory, and it was used for a variety of items such as knife handles and sheaths, gaming pieces, flutes, pins, and needles. Horn was in some ways the medieval precursor to plastic: it has a smooth surface, it is translucent, and when heated, it can be shaped. Items crafted of horn included combs and inkwells, and lanterns were fitted with panes of horn.

In a world where manufacturing was expensive, people were motivated to make the fullest possible use of manufactured wares. Old goods were not casually discarded. If they had reached the end of their usefulness to an owner but were still functional, they were sold to a dealer in used goods, who mended them as necessary and resold them to someone further down the social scale. Resale of used items was always a significant part of the economy in medieval towns, and regulations had to be promulgated to ensure that refurbished secondhand wares were not passed off as new.

Even those people at the top of the social scale did not waste used materials. When the king of England had the shingles on the royal kitchens at Marlborough Castle replaced with lead roofing in 1260, he ordered the constable to use the old shingles to reroof another building in the castle compound. Old timbers were similarly reused when buildings were taken down, and Roman ruins were often treated as stone quarries for new construction. Because shoe soles wore out much more quickly than the uppers, the uppers were often cut away from worn-out soles and used in new shoes.

Where an object was too worn or too damaged to serve, it might be recycled. Then as now, glass was one of the easiest materials to recycle, and it was also one that medieval technology had a limited ability to produce, particularly in colored varieties. Not only was old glass recycled, but a significant portion of the glass circulating in the Middle Ages actually dated to Roman times. Metals were also regularly recycled: Parisian guild regulations of the 13th century make provision for the reuse of old copper, bronze, and brass for making buckles and prayer beads.

An English water mill. Water mills were a significant technological innovation in the medieval West, and most rivers were dotted with them. Illustration by Jeffrey Singman (after Luttrell Psalter).

Despite the continued low level of technology throughout the Middle Ages, after 1000 C.E., Europe nevertheless experienced something of a small revolution in technology. People began to harness the power of wind and water using mill technology. Water mills provided the major source of mechanical power. In England, for example, in 1086 there were often as many as three mills for every mile of river. Water mills were used to grind grain, forge iron, soften wool cloth, and make beer and wine.

New agricultural techniques and products developed after 1000 also led to a growth in food production (leading to a related population explosion). Padded horse collars (developed in China) permitted horses to plow, and because they work faster than the oxen that once dominated the fields of Europe, more land was cultivated. Peasants also developed new crops, including legumes that improved the soil by adding nitrogen and at the same time added iron to the diets of the people. Technological innovations allowed the population of Europe to double between the 11th and the 13th centuries—from about 37 million to about 74 million people (Singman, 33–35, 47).

To read about technology in 18th-century England, see the England entry in the section "Science and Technology" in chapter 4 ("Intellectual Life") of volume 4; and for Victorian England, see the England entry in the section "Technology" in chapter 5 ("Material Life") of volume 5 of this series.

FOR MORE INFORMATION

Gies, F., and J. Gies. *Cathedral, Forge, and Waterwheel: Technology and Invention in the Middle Ages*. New York: HarperCollins, 1994.

Singman, J. L. *Daily Life in Medieval Europe*. Westport, Conn.: Greenwood Press, 1999.

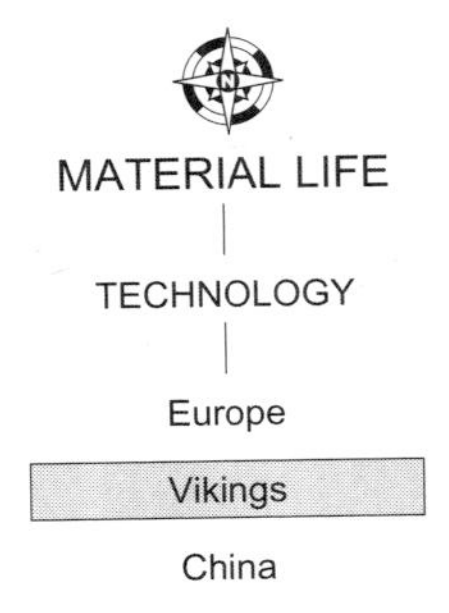

VIKINGS

Boatbuilding and maritime skill were the greatest technological achievements of the Scandinavians in the Viking Age, and the ship was the summit of their material culture. Indeed, the ship has become a symbol of the Viking Age, for it was the ship that facilitated the expansion of the Scandinavians from their homelands and gave them the ability to raid, trade, and cross the open seas.

The best-known and also the best-preserved ships are the two burial ships found at Oseberg and Gokstad on the shores of Oslo fjord in Norway dating from the early 9th century and the late 9th or early 10th century, respectively. Together with the five 11th-century Skuldelev ships excavated from Roskilde fjord in Denmark (the ships had been deliberately sunk to blockade the fjord and thereby protect the town of Roskilde from an attack from the sea), these ships are the primary sources for our knowledge about early Viking Age ships and boatbuilding, although many other ships have been excavated.

All these ships have a clinker-built hull of overlapping planks or strakes, which are fastened with iron nails and caulked with tarred animal hair (to keep the hull watertight). The top planks have a distinctive upward curve at the ends, making the ship higher fore and aft than amidships. The bottom planks are attached to the slightly curved keel, which extends into the curved fore-stem and after-stem at the bow and stem. To stabilize the shape and to add stiffness to the shell, ribs were inserted inside the planking made from naturally curved timbers. The hull was further strengthened with crossbeams placed across the width of the hull, and floor timbers were attached to the planking. The upper crossbeams could be used as rowing benches, with the rower's feet resting on the lower crossbeams. Oar holes were cut at either end or in a continuous line along the length of the ship, and on some ships the oar holes can be closed by wooden covers. The mast was slotted into a hole cut in the keelson (a wooden structure resting on the keel), which distributes the weight of the mast, and additional support was provided by a "mast partner," a heavy block of wood resting on the crossbeam. On some ships, this mast partner has a long opening facing aft, so that the mast could be lowered or raised at will without having to be lifted vertically out of its socket. In later ships, this mast partner was omitted, and the mast was instead supported by an upper crossbeam.

The sail was square, and literary sources suggest that sails were frequently striped. They were made of wool, and for strength a double thickness was generally used. The methods of rigging are obscure and remain open to speculation, for all the ships that have been recovered by archaeologists have been little more than hulls, and contemporary representations of ships are not sufficiently detailed.

A side rudder or steering oar was mounted on the starboard side near the stem. During beaching, the steering oar, which extends below the keel, could be swiveled upward and thereby raised, so that it would not be damaged. Anchors were used, and some iron anchors have been found. They are typically T-shaped in form and with curved arms, which taper to points.

Oak was the preferred timber for boatbuilding. Where oak was not available, as in northern Scandinavia, pine and ash were used, especially, it seems, for the top planks or strakes. As far as possible, timber was matched to the job in hand: the timber whose grain followed the shape of the finished pieces was given preference. Accordingly, stems, keels, and ribs were made from timber with a curve, whereas straight-grained logs were used for planks, keels, masts, and crossbeams. The woodworkers did not use saws and so, using beech or hafted metal wedges, split the log in first 2, then 4, then 8, and finally 16 wedge-shaped planks of uniform breath, which were axed and then scraped to the desired shape.

A substantial amount of wood was necessary to build a ship, for wood was required also for trenails (or wooden pegs), oars, rudders, bailers, gang planks, and other equipment. It has been estimated that for an average-size Viking ship, about 11 trees (approximately 1 meter in diameter and 5 meters in length) and another tall tree (15–18 meters in length) for the keel were required.

The ships served a variety of purposes, ranging from warfare and trade to the transportation of people and cargo across the sea. The warships were built for speed and maneuverability. They were slender, had oar holes in a continuous line along the length of the ship, and had a mast that could be lowered. They also distinguished themselves from other types of ships by having a shield batten on the outer side of the edge of the ship. Some ships were furnished with dragon heads (and sometimes tails), which were attached to the prows (and stems). Warships that had a crew of 40 or 50 men could be classified as longships (a term referring to warships with more than 32 oars). The largest ship recorded in Old Norse literature is the Long Serpent, built for King Olaf Tryggvason of Norway in 998. It is said to have had 34 pairs of oars and to have carried more than two hundred men at the king's final sea battle at Svold in Norway in the year 1000.

Cargo ships were a somewhat later development and reflect an increasing demand for ships that could carry heavy loads. The cargo ships differ from warships in that they did not have the speed and the maneuverability of the warships. They were deeper, wider in the beam, more capacious, heavier, and more suitable for ocean going. They typically had an open cargo hold amidships with a permanent deck and oar holes only fore and aft and either a fixed mast or a more firmly placed mast designed to be lowered only on rare occasions. Cargo ships relied almost exclusively on their sails for propulsion, and the few oars were used only when the ship was becalmed or had to be maneuvered near landing places. Accordingly, they required only a small crew: a helmsman, one or two men to bail (the ships did not have pumps), and a few others to handle the sail. On coastal voyages, a small boat, which was towed astern, enabled to crew to go ashore to sleep in tents or to cook. On voyages across the open sea to, for example, England, the Faroe Islands, Iceland, or Greenland, this would, of course, not have been possible, and the crew and passengers (and livestock) would have had to sleep on the deck and live on the food they brought with them.

Several experiments with replicas of Viking ships show that the ships had virtually no limits as far as seaworthiness is concerned and that they were remarkably fast. Shortly after the discovery of the Gokstad ship in 1880, the first replica of a Viking ship set sail for North America. The ship, called Viking, left Bergen, Norway, on April 30, 1893, with a crew of 12 and reached Newfoundland 28 days later. It skimmed over the waves at an average of 10 knots and achieved 12 knots in fine weather. The rudder (which had seemed peculiar to archaeologists) had proven itself highly efficient even in stormy weather, and the Norwegian captain, Magnus Andersen, also noted the ship's extraordinary flexibility and ability to stay watertight:

Most of the navigation by Scandinavians in the Viking Age was along a coast from one location to another with landfalls made at night. Only the largest trading centers had piers or wharfs, but with their shallow draft, many ships did not need them and could easily be run ashore on beaches. The cargo ships were usually anchored near landing places, and small boats were used to transport cargo and passengers to and from land.

Seafarers combined landmark navigation used in coastal sailing techniques with latitude sailing. That they could fix their latitudes is fairly certain, but there is uncertainty about their methods. It is likely that they relied on simple celestial navigation based on the movements of the sun and, at night, the position of the stars, notably the Polaris, which in Old Norse is called *Leidarstjarna* (lode star). They may also have observed wave and cloud formations, flight patterns of birds, sea creatures, such as whales, and seaweed and used these observations as navigational aids. The question of whether the seafarers had any navigational instruments remains open, although it has been suggested that the sun-seeking property of double refracting cordierite or Icelandic feldspar crystals had been discovered by Norse seafarers. Various sources make reference to an object called a *solarsteinn* (sun stone), but no description of its navigational use is given. Indeed, Viking ships and navigation techniques constitute one of the technological wonders of the Middle Ages.

~*Kirsten Wolf*

FOR MORE INFORMATION

Wolf, K. *Daily Life of the Vikings*. Westport, Conn.: Greenwood Press, forthcoming.

CHINA

Ancient China was considerably more advanced than the West in technology, and for a millennium, inventions slowly made their way from China westward until they reached Europe. Many of the influential technological innovations began in China.

Although China did not learn to work iron until about 513 B.C.E. (long after the West used iron), it was dramatically in the forefront of developing cast iron. Chinese ore had a high phosphorus content, which gave it a lower melting point than other ore, but iron workers learned to use efficient bellows, and by the 4th century B.C.E., they had learned to melt iron and cast it in molds to make tools and weapons. An excavated ironworks of the early Han period (second and first centuries B.C.E.) reveals 17 smelting furnaces, including some blast furnaces. These did not appear in the West until 1,500 years later. By 31 C.E., water power was added to the smelting process to operate the bellows more efficiently.

The Chinese also developed waterwheels, which became widespread in China by the 3rd and 4th centuries C.E. These wheels were used in iron forges, to crush ore, and to hull rice. Floating mills were known in China at least by the 8th century C.E., and they probably inspired another invention: paddle-wheel boats. These boats probably reached their high point in China in the early 12th century, when a shipbuilder constructed a ship that could carry a crew of two or three hundred men, with 11 paddle wheels on either side and 1 in the back (Gies and Gies, 89).

Chinese scientists used the principles of waterwheels to design mechanical clocks. One of the earliest was called the "Water-Driven Spherical Bird's-Eye-View Map of the Heavens," built in the Tang capital of Changan in 725 C.E. It was constructed of a complex mechanism containing, in the words of a contemporary, "hooks, pin, and interlocking rods, coupling devices, and locks checking mutually" (Gies and Gies, 90). This early clock led to centuries of construction of increasingly complex mechanical devices, until the technology was forgotten in the 14th century. (Mechanical clocks were reintroduced in China in the 17th century by Western Jesuits.)

Chinese wheelbarrow, an invention that spread from China all over Asia and Europe and improved rural productivity. Illustration by Charles Benn.

The Chinese also developed more simple, but probably more useful, technologies. Wheelbarrows are described in Chinese sources as early as 230 C.E. and spread to Europe in the 12th century. Suspension bridges were perfected in the 6th century, when Chinese engineers used iron chains to suspend roads.

Magnetic compasses originated in China in the early Middle Ages; a text refers to a geomancer using a "south-controlling spoon." The Chinese carved the arrow on the pointer to point south instead of north, as we do. A reference from the Han dynasty states that "when the people of Cheng go out to collect jade, they carry a south-pointer with them so as not to lose their way" (Gies and Gies, 94). The compass was made more accurate in the 8th century C.E. by floating a magnetized needle on water so it could move freely.

Gunpowder appeared in China as early as the 9th century. Although Chinese did use the powder for fireworks, they also incorporated it into military weapons from about 950 C.E. They built early guns and a kind of rocket to shoot projectiles.

The Chinese developed paper and applied it to many uses. It was widely used by the 3rd century C.E., and it spread outside of China. It was probably first made from rags, but Chinese soon replaced cloth with the bark from the mulberry. The product was improved with dyes and the use of molds. Paper was cheap and light, and it was first used for wrapping. Only by the 3rd century C.E. did it replace silk, bamboo, and wood as a writing medium. The Chinese also used paper for toilet cleanliness. In 851, an Arab traveler commented unfavorably on the Chinese toilet habits, complaining that they did not "wash themselves with water when they have done their necessities; but they only wipe themselves with paper" (Gies and Gies, 96). Paper money originated in the early 9th century and circulated sufficiently to amaze Western travelers such as Marco Polo.

These technological innovations show the range of the imagination and talent of ancient Chinese inventors and engineers. Their products spread slowly outside China to leave their mark on the Muslim and Western worlds.

~*Joyce E. Salisbury*

FOR MORE INFORMATION

Gies, F., and J. Gies. *Cathedral, Forge, and Waterwheel: Technology and Invention in the Middle Ages*. New York: HarperCollins, 1994.

ISLAMIC WORLD

The conquests of the medieval Islamic world connected a vast region from Spain in the west deep into central Asia in the east. The cross-cultural ties created by these conquests generated striking advances in many areas of life. For example, trade expanded and scientific discoveries flourished. However, everyday people's lives were most transformed by the spread and development of new technology throughout the Islamic world. Muslims learned of inventions, both large and small, from as far away as China, and they spread these tools all the way to Europe, where Christians eager for new ideas adopted them. Muslim technology transformed many parts of medieval life.

Warfare in the Middle Ages was dominated by armed knights, who were the best warriors of the time. Heavily armed mounted fighting men depended on the use of a humble artifact—a stirrup—to stabilize the rider as he struck with his weapons. Much historical controversy has arisen over the exact history of the spread of the stirrup, but two facts are indisputable: the mounted people of the steppes of central Asia first developed stirrups, and when Arabs invaded Persia (modern Iran), they did so without stirrups. Muslims seem to have first appropriated stirrups in Persia by the beginning of the 8th century. Western Europeans learned of stirrups from Muslims and then saw their potential for transforming warfare. The medieval knight was born from the invention transmitted through the Muslim lands.

Muslim travelers—whether at sea or across huge deserts—were aided by astrolabes, a device borrowed from the ancient Greeks and improved by Muslim scientists. Astrolabes were used to measure and compute the position of stars and the movement of planets so travelers could locate their positions. Muslims introduced the astrolabe into Europe, where it was used until replaced by the more accurate quadrant and sextant.

Muslims also made great strides in agriculture, which transformed the southern Mediterranean world and spread north into Europe. Muslims borrowed ideas and new crops from India and farther east, added their own creative initiative, and changed the diet of the region. New food and fiber plants were introduced, such as rice, sorghum, sugarcane, cotton, watermelons, eggplants, spinach, artichokes, citrus fruits, mangoes, and many others. Most of these required intensive cultivation and heavy watering, so Muslims modified irrigation techniques they saw in Asia. They built dams, drainage tunnels, canals, and water-lifting machines to irrigate dry fields. These crops and irrigation techniques spread to northern Europe and eventually across the seas to the Americas.

Probably the most influential crop spread throughout the Muslim world was cotton, and Arabic textile production techniques to make cotton cloth would change the world's clothing habits. In the medieval Islamic world, cotton cloth replaced wool as the most important fabric. Royal textile manufacturing was housed in a network of textile workshops known as *tiraz* factories and was closely regulated and strictly controlled. The most highly prized cotton fabrics produced for international commerce came from the *tiraz* cities of Iraq, Persia, and Syria, and Muslim techniques of cloth production spread to North Africa, Spain, Sicily, and southern Italy. When western Europeans reconquered Spain and Italy, they kept the Muslim system of textile production intact.

While Europeans were writing on expensive animal skins—vellum and parchment—Muslims developed advanced techniques of making paper. The Chinese had first invented paper made of vegetable substances, and Muslims adopted and developed the invention. Papermaking required reducing vegetable matter to its crude fibers through pounding, tearing, or stamping. Then the fibers were placed in a water-filled vat and mixed. Papermakers then dipped a mesh tray with as many as 12 wires per inch into the vat to attract the wet pulp. They then lifted the trays out and deposited the wet mass of pulp on felt cloth. They pressed the pulp to remove moisture and hung the individual sheets to dry, sometimes rubbing the sheets with gelatin from the hooves of animals to protect the paper. Such papermaking techniques appeared in Muslim Spain by 1150 and quickly spread.

The list of Muslim technological advances is long. The Muslims developed processes of distillation that eventually fueled the production of hard liquors. Our word *alcohol* derives from the Arabic *al-Kuhl,* showing how influential Muslim techniques of distillation were. Muslim musicians introduced the first bowed instruments—the lute and the rebec, ancestors of the violin. In the 13th century, Venetians bought the secrets of Syrian glassmaking from Muslims and, using Muslim artisans, founded a monopoly of the manufacture of glass. Modern tourists still go to Venetian glass factories to purchase their magnificent wares.

The Middle Ages in the whole Eurasian land mass were marked by a revolution in technology. This technological revolution was fueled in large part by enterprising Muslims who were farsighted enough to recognize good ideas in all parts of their vast lands, modify them, and transmit them to others. Our modern society—so based on technology—owes a large debt to the medieval Islamic world.

~Joyce E. Salisbury

FOR MORE INFORMATION

Gies, F., and J. Gies. *Cathedral, Forge, and Waterwheel: Technology and Invention in the Middle Ages*. New York: HarperCollins, 1994.

Gimpel, J. *The Medieval Machine: The Industrial Revolution of the Middle Ages*. New York: Penguin, 1976.

White, L. *Medieval Technology and Social Change*. London: Oxford University Press, 1962.

BYZANTIUM

Technological development was unevenly pursued over much of Byzantine history. The discoveries of Hellenistic and Roman engineers were studied and refined by Byzantine scholars, who often applied them in creative ways. Military leaders quickly recognized new weapons used by their neighbors and adapted them for their own purposes. Farmers, builders, and craftsmen throughout the empire refined their methods through empirical observation and experiment with materials at hand. Although such modest changes might suggest a lack of inventiveness, Byzantium remained the most technologically sophisticated Mediterranean state until the 12th century. Its cautious approach to innovation reflects practical economic decisions and environmental factors as well as a deeply traditional social outlook.

Agricultural technology saw relatively few advances, and cultivation methods described by Cato, Verro, and Columella were perpetuated with little change into the 15th century. The 10th-century agricultural treatise known as the *Geoponika* gives some sense of medieval farming practices, and manuscripts occasionally illustrate implements and their applications. Fields were prepared with a scratch plow (*gyes*, also known as soleard) with a wood or iron plowshare; the heavy plow developed for turning the rich soils of western Europe was not appropriate in the thin, rocky soils of the east Mediterranean. The iron mattock (*makele*), spade (*lisgon*), and two-pronged hoe (*dikella*) were used for planting and weeding crops. The custom of individual families working small, scattered plots bounded by ditches or rubble walls did not encourage the development of more efficient cultivation methods. Only with the growth of large aristocratic and monastic estates in the 11th to 15th centuries were irrigation methods systematically employed. Fields normally were left fallow in alternate years to conserve ground moisture—a practice that survived into the 20th century. A regime of orderly crop rotation was never devised.

Cereals were harvested with the sickle (*drepanon*) rather than the scythe. Cut sheaves were brought to threshing platforms in the fields or surrounding villages, where they were spread across a hard-packed surface (*alonia*). A flat threshing sled (*doukane*) with embedded flints or iron teeth was dragged over the sheaves by donkeys or oxen. Several kinds of mills were available for grinding grain. The Roman-type mill used two nesting stone grinders that were turned by hand or domestic animals. Water-powered mills (*hydromylones*) were found throughout the Byzantine countryside: a 5th-century overshot mill was excavated in the Agora in Athens, and an undershot mill is depicted in a 6th-century mosaic in Constantinople. Water mills are mentioned frequently in the 7th- or 8th-century *Farmer's Law* and in later archives for Macedonia. The general preference for the less efficient horizontally mounted wheel seems to reflect both the nature of local waterways and the small scale of most Byzantine farmers, who did not see milling as a separate source of income. Wind-powered mills, perhaps derived from Persia, are mentioned in the late Byzantine period.

Vineyards were pruned and harvested using a variety of iron cutting hooks (*kladeuteria*), while olive trees were flailed with sticks. Both grapes and olives were pressed using similar equipment, with a broad stone basin used together with a counterbalance or screw-mounted press. Large numbers of presses have been identified across the Byzantine countryside and resemble those used in recent times.

Land transport remained based on animal-drawn carts that apparently changed little over the Byzantine centuries. Transport by ship, especially over long distances, generally offered a cheaper and safer alternative. Large sailing crafts carried the bulk of commercial goods in late antiquity. About the 7th century, sailing methods changed significantly with the introduction of the lateen sail, which allowed more flexibility in tacking into prevailing winds. Between the 7th and 11th centuries, shipbuilders shifted from constructing mortise-jointed solid-hull vessels to using a skeletal frame to support a shell of overlapping planks; the result was a significant increase in the speed of production.

Byzantine military engineers continued Roman technology while quickly adjusting to the tactics and weaponry of their adversaries. By the 7th century, the stirrup had been picked up from the Avars. The Arab siege of Constantinople in 678 was broken by the timely discovery of Greek fire, believed to be an incendiary mixture of crude oil, bitumen, resin, and sulfur. In the 9th century, Leo the Mathematician built a series of signal towers that used torches and mirrors for rapid communication between the palace in Constantinople and troops along the Cilician frontier. Clashes with heavily armed Turkic armies led to the development in the late 10th century of armored cavalry, known as *kataphraktoi*. The crossbow, heavy armor, and large shields were adopted following contact with the Latin crusaders in the 11th and 12th centuries.

Medieval warfare was characterized by defense. Soldiers wore armor of increasing thickness and complexity. Pictured here is a battle scene during the Hundred Years' War, showing horsemen against foot soldiers from Vigiles de Charles VII, 15th century. © The Art Archive/ Bibliothèque Nationale Paris/HarperCollins Publishers.

Some of the greatest Byzantine technological accomplishments can be seen in the monumental building initiatives of late antiquity. The early development of Constantinople included the construction of a vast urban infrastructure, including a long aqueduct, large cisterns, and extensive harbor facilities. The city's 5th-century land walls include a forward moat, an advance fortification, and a main wall with 96 towers and six gates spread over a length of four-and-a-half miles. The building of the Cathedral of St. Sophia in the 6th century remains a singular achievement. Designed by Anthemios of Tralles and Isidoros of Miletus, the structure employs Roman vaults, pendentives, and domes on a grand scale to enclose an unprecedented interior space. Justinian's simultaneous construction of fortifications, roads, bridges, warehouses, and churches across the empire reflects considerable organizational effort in support of state programs.

Most technological innovation took place in Constantinople under the sponsorship of the imperial palace. Practical and scientific instrumentation included the Hellenistic dioptera for land surveying and the astrolabe for celestial observation.

The heliostat, described by Anthemios of Tralles, was a device for focusing the rays of the sun throughout the day. Public sundials (*horologia*) were set up in the capital and larger provincial cities. Bellows-powered pipe organs, which had been developed in the 2nd century, were featured at chariot races in the hippodrome and as part of imperial ceremonies. Medieval visitors to the palace marveled at elaborate automata. Driven by hydraulic or pneumatic pressure, these machines continued a Hellenistic tradition pioneered by Hero of Alexandria. In the 9th century, Leo the Mathematician was credited with building such fantastic devices as a tree with twittering birds, roaring lions, and a levitating throne for the emperor Theophilos. Official workshops produced embroidered silk costume, decorated silverplate and jewelry, and illustrated books for use by the imperial court.

~*Marcus Rautman*

FOR MORE INFORMATION

Bryer, A. "The Means of Agricultural Production: Muscle and Tools." In *The Economic History of Byzantium*, edited by A. Laiou. Washington, D.C.: Dumbarton Oaks, 2002. <http://www.doaks.org/EconHist/EHB07.pdf>.

Vogel, K. "Byzantine Technology." *Cambridge Medieval History* 4, no. 2 (1967): 299–305.

MATERIAL LIFE: WEB SITES

http://dmoz.org/Arts/Architecture/History/Building_Types/Houses/Country/
http://www.bbc.co.uk/history/lj/conquestlj/colonists_04.shtml?site=history_vikings
http://www.bc.edu/bc_org/avp/cas/fnart/arch/contents_europe.html
http://www.costumes.org/pages/fashiondress/byzantium.htm
http://www.mastep.sjsu.edu/history_of_tech/china.htm
http://www.personal.utulsa.edu/~marc-carlson/shoe/SHOEHOME.htm
http://www.pbm.com/~lindahl/food.html
http://www.quikshave.com/timeline.htm

6

POLITICAL LIFE

The ancient Greek philosopher Aristotle (384–322 B.C.E.) claimed that humans are by definition political animals. By this he meant that an essential part of human life involves interacting in the public sphere with people who are not our intimate families. It is these relationships—along with their complex negotiations—that permit the development of cities, kingdoms, nations, and civilization itself. Throughout history, different cultures have developed different political systems to organize their lives, and all political systems are in constant states of change as they accommodate to the changing needs and interests of the populace. Political life involves two different spheres of influence: organizing the relationship among those within a political unit and negotiating the relations between different political entities (countries or tribes or kingdoms). However, at its basic level, all politics is about power—finding out who has it and who does not.

People create a political system first of all to assure themselves of internal peace and security. As the 17th-century political theorist Thomas Hobbes noted, without a strong authority, people's incessant struggle for power would result in a life that is "nasty, brutish, and short." This is why we want our power structures clear. Our political systems also clarify and solidify our loyalties and allegiances—nationalism has served as a sentiment that can unify people with diverse interests and backgrounds.

The medieval period was born in violence. In the West, Germanic tribes had destroyed the western Roman Empire; in China, warfare tore at the social fabric; and the Byzantine Empire held on in wars against Persia and later the Islamic world. The Islamic world was born in this era, and Muslim armies swept through great reaches of territory bringing some destruction along with their new beliefs. This violence brought people to a strictly hierarchic political organization that perhaps sprang from a desire to bring order to a disorderly land and peace to people's daily lives. In the empires—Byzantine, Muslim, and Chinese—rulers strictly regulated their society. In Polynesia, chiefs claimed complete control over their subjects.

In western Europe, and to some degree in the other areas of Eurasia, men and women were bound to their superiors in contractual ties that we have come to call a "feudal system." As a law issued by a 9th-century French king ruled: "We will that each free man in our kingdom shall choose a lord. . . . We command moreover that no man shall leave his lord" (Cheyney, 18). Such laws bound members of the ruling classes to one another, and other laws bound peasants to their land to serve their lords. Cities that grew up in this time of rigid hierarchy were veritable islands of freedom for those who could find a space to work there. In the 14th century (at the end of the Middle Ages), disasters including the bubonic plague and peasant revolts broke down the medieval structure. Instead of being bound in ties to their lords, more people claimed some of the freedoms of urban dwellers—modern political life was being born.

The tight structure of the Western feudal relationship led (somewhat ironically) to some of our most democratic traditions. All these relationships depended on the rule of law, and thus law was a critical component of the political life of the age. In the West, noblemen insisting on their contractual rights forced King John of England to sign the Magna Carta in the 13th century, which is one of the foundations of Western legal rights. Noblemen advising the kings in councils served as precedent for a parliamentary system that also formed the core of a democratic structure.

As people interact in ever-widening circles, our political life must negotiate the often-difficult relations with other kingdoms, countries, or empires. Diplomacy is the tool of our political life that is meant to smooth these interactions, and war is the breakdown of these negotiations. In war—which has unfortunately dominated so much of human history—we can often see the noblest and worst expressions of our human spirit. In war, we can also definitively see the struggle for power that marks our political life.

All the structures that developed to bring peace and order to medieval life never really solved the violence of the age. Polynesians, too, engaged in relentless warfare with neighboring islanders. In the West, warfare was endemic, and the Crusades brought a new kind of warfare to the world—people began to fight over ideology instead of just power. At the end of the Middle Ages, gunpowder was brought to warfare, and a new age was dawning.

~Joyce E. Salisbury

FOR MORE INFORMATION

Cheyney, E. P., trans. *University of Pennsylvania Translations and Reprints*. Philadelphia: University of Pennsylvania Press, 1898.

Van Evera, S. *Causes of War: Power and the Roots of Conflict*. Ithaca, N.Y.: Cornell University Press, 1999.

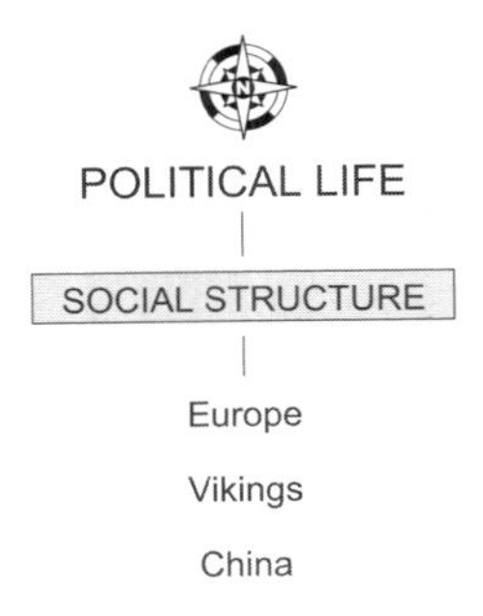

Social Structure

How do we organize our society? In modern times, we often divide ourselves by class, or income, or gender, or work or geography. In the United States (as well as most other parts of the world) in the 21st century, we also cherish individual freedoms and praise those who rise in our social structure. This fluidity and concern for the individual would have been unheard of or at least considered shocking and undesirable in most parts of the world in the Middle Ages. They believed society should be organized differently.

Perhaps ironically, the Muslim world shared more of modern Western values than did any other region. The prophet Muhammad had been a city dweller and a merchant, and thus this lifestyle was praised in the Muslim world. Because the Muslim world was situated at the crossroads of much long-distance trade, the prosperous town life in most Muslim territories existed together with the supporting agricultural life. Because of the importance of trade, there was much geographical mobility, and the prosperity that trade generated led to a good deal of social mobility—here, money could bring status. Careers were open to those with talent, and offices were seldom regarded as being hereditary, so men (and only men) could hope to make their lives different from those of their forefathers. Such fluidity was otherwise unheard of in the Middle Ages.

China was highly stratified and organized by the state, which set and regulated everyone's position in society. The emperor and his family were at the top, surrounded by a hereditary and very powerful aristocracy. This structure was supported by a populous peasantry and many slaves. As strict as this hierarchy was, nevertheless, some people could hope to change their fortunes by entering the extensive bureaucracy that administered the state. There were clerks, accountants, and the like who were needed and respected. The route to this social mobility was through education. This social structure mirrored that of Byzantium, in which a nobility ruled, but the state and an extensive trade offered possibilities to men of talent.

In western Europe, the situation was dramatically different. By the 11th century, European society was organized by "orders," that is, by function. At the top were "those who pray"—the clergy, monks and nuns; next were "those who fight"—the nobility who owed their existence on the need for armies of mounted knights. At the bottom was everyone else, called "those who work." This last class included everyone from the poorest peasant to a wealthy merchant, which served to devalue money as a measure of a man. It would take well beyond the Middle Ages before the middle class would replace "those who fight" as the leaders in society. In the Middle Ages, then, the only route to upward mobility for a talented individual was either through marriage into the nobility or through the church. It is perhaps not surprising that the monasteries and churches of the day received some of the most talented individuals in their ranks.

Another feature of European society was the idea that each person must be bound to some other person by contract and obligation. Serfs were peasants bound to land that was owned by their lords, and they owed a portion of their labor to the nobleman or woman of the manor. Even those who fought bound themselves in service to a lord as they placed their hands between his and promised to be loyal and to fight. Monks and nuns were bound by oaths to their superiors, who in turn were bound to ecclesiastical lords. The only people who were outside this tight hierarchy of contract and promise were townspeople; the medieval social order viewed them with suspicion. Society was supposed to be ordered by the functions people filled and by the ties that bound one person to another.

Even Polynesian society was largely characterized by a strict social stratification. Most islanders were ruled by a nobility of birth, whose genealogy ranked them as practically divine. They were served by laboring commoners who lived on the nobles' land. Beneath them were slaves who either had been captured in war or who had broken a serious taboo (a forbidden act).

The freedoms and the opportunities of the modern world would have seemed very strange—and indeed frightening—to the men and women of the Middle Ages who took comfort in the fact that their societies were clearly structured.

~*Joyce E. Salisbury*

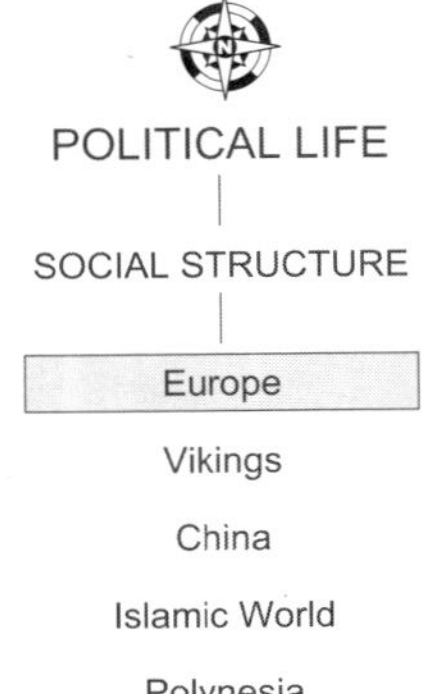

EUROPE

Medieval people understood (and organized) society by function, and by the 10th century, people recognized three "orders" in society, that is, three kinds of people arranged by the functions they filled. At the top were "those who pray," the clergy and monastics who interceded with God for the good of all. The second order was "those who fight," that is, the warrior, noble class who was charged with defending all others. At the bottom were "those who work," and in the medieval mind, this meant people who worked the land to provide a living for all others. In this ordered social structure, men and women alike kept to their places and served their society with their function. Notice that there is no real place in this ideal, ordered world for townspeople and merchants. Medieval people (however incorrectly) viewed them as peripheral to society and did not make a place for them in their theoretical hierarchy.

Within these three orders, society was shaped by personal relationships such as kinship and patronage; these structures were perpetuated not by abstract institutions but by the personal ties of inheritance, tradition, or personal promises. The force of tradition gave these personal relationships some stability, but they were never static. Relationships changed over time in response to changing circumstances, and the actual social structure at any given place and time was an intricate network reflecting a whole history of personal relationships. One peasant might enjoy more rights than his neighbor because one of his forebears had been particularly assertive in his relationship to the manor lord; a baron might be required to provide extra knights for the king's service because his great-grandfather had been a poor negotiator. Historians call these institutions of personal relations "feudalism" and "manorialism"; the first refers to the political alliances of the nobility, and the second refers to the rural structure that included the peasants who worked the land.

Feudalism evolved as a hierarchical system of personal relationships in which land and military power were the principal commodities exchanged. An individual with military power to offer gave his services to a feudal lord. The lord in turn secured his subordinate in the possession of the land that financed his military service. The feudal subordinate was called a vassal, and the vassal's land was termed a fee or fief (*feudum* in Latin, which is the source of the term *feudal*). A vassal who held a great deal of land might in turn grant fiefs to his own feudal tenants, who helped him fulfill his military obligations to his lord. Long-term stability was provided by the principle of heredity, as the feudal relationships between individuals were extended to apply to their heirs.

The feudal transaction was more than a bartering of land for military service. The vassal held some measure of legal jurisdiction and political authority over his holding and subtenants. At the same time, his status as a vassal involved more than just military service. The vassal did homage to the lord, symbolizing his status as his lord's man (*homme* in French), owing him generalized loyalty and political support, while the lord in turn promised his patronage. The king was the supreme feudal power in a kingdom. In theory, he was the owner and ruler of all the land and delegated his authority to his tenants. In practice, his authority was often subject to challenge from his great lords, who together could wield military power comparable to his own. Not all land was held from a king or feudal lord.

Although historians sometimes speak of "the feudal system," feudalism was far from systematic. It evolved locally in response to local situations and varied enormously from place to place. If a system can be perceived, it is because of shared circumstances and because there was a degree of cultural contact and common cultural inheritance. Feudalism was complex, and the details varied greatly. Large landholdings were rarely solid blocks of territory, but scattered patchworks of feudal lands. Military service was commonly for 40 days in the year, but it could be longer or shorter. The basic unit of feudal responsibility was the knight's service, the duty to provide a single mounted knight to serve one's lord. The exact number of services owed varied from fief to fief, depending partly on the value of the land but also on the historical traditions associated with the holding. The distribution of power shifted over time, making new demands possible and old customs unenforceable, and in time these temporary shifts could themselves become established customs.

In medieval Europe, the most visible mark of aristocracy were the castles that served as fortresses for the nobility. © Library of Congress.

Like feudalism, manorialism was based on landholding in exchange for service, but in this case, commoners owed their labor to the nobility. Like the aristocracy, commoners inherited their status from their parents. Most were rural workers, living under the manorial system that mirrored many of the structures of the feudal hierarchy. The manor was the smallest unit of feudal landholding, typically a few hundred acres. It was essentially a holding sufficient to support an aristocratic household, including its most important feudal element, the knight. The manor lord parceled out some portion of his land to peasant tenants, keeping the rest in his own hands as demesne land to be cultivated for his own benefit. Like feudal vassals, the peasants provided service in exchange for their land, in this case, labor service that the lord used to cultivate his demesne. In addition, the lord exercised legal and governmental authority over the manor peasants. The nature of this jurisdiction depended on each peasant's personal status. In general, the medieval commoner was classed as either free or unfree. Like other forms of personal status in the Middle Ages, freedom and unfreedom were inherited. People born of unfree parents were unfree themselves. In mixed unions, the customs varied, but commonly, legitimate children inherited their father's status, illegitimate ones their mother's. Unfree peasants, also called serfs or villeins, were personally subject to their manor lord in a manner that served to guarantee him a stable supply of labor: the serf was obliged to provide certain labor services for the lord, and he had to have the lord's permission to move away from the manor.

Regardless of the serfs' resentment of their status, the distinction between serf and free commoner does not seem to have played a role in determining social status among commoners, and manorial records are full of small acts of resistance to the lord's authority. In the day-to-day life of the medieval commoner, relationships within the local community probably mattered more than the official feudal hierarchy (Singman, 1, 4–7).

To read about social structure and political life in Elizabethan England, see the England entries in the sections "Hierarchy" and "Government" in chapter 6 ("Political Life") of volume 3; for 18th-century England, see the England entries in the sections "Government" and "Social Structure" in chapter 6 ("Political Life") of volume 4; and for Victorian England, see the England entry in the section "Government and Politics" in chapter 6 ("Political and Diplomatic Life") of volume 5.

FOR MORE INFORMATION

Hanawalt, B. *The Ties That Bind: Peasant Families in Medieval England*. New York: Oxford University Press, 1986.

Singman, J. L. *Daily Life in Medieval Europe*. Westport, Conn.: Greenwood Press, 1999.

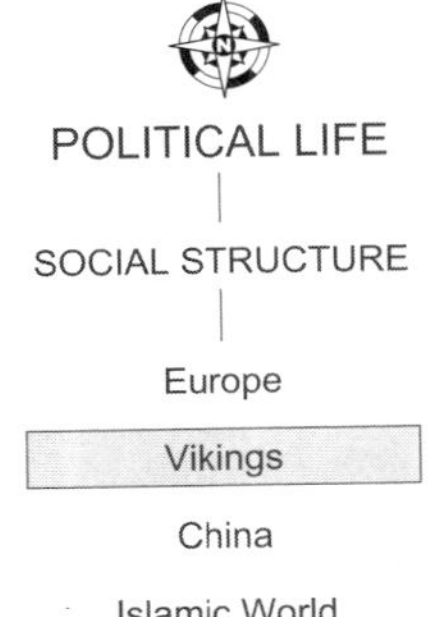

VIKINGS

Abroad, the Vikings let it be known that they were all equal. Dudo of St.-Quentin (d. before 1043) reports in his *De moribus et actis primorum normanniae ducum* (Concerning the deaths and deeds of the first Norman dukes) that when in the late 10th century a messenger from the Franks, who was standing on the bank of the river Eure in France, saluted the approaching Viking ships and asked the name of the Vikings' master, they responded that they did not have any and that they were all equals. The Vikings further argued that they would never submit to anyone nor subject to servitude nor accept favors from anyone.

Nonetheless, there were significant differences, especially between those who were free and those who were not. The general picture of Scandinavian society during the Viking Age is commonly sought in the Eddic poem *List of Rig* (*Rigsthula*), which provides a mythological explanation of the origin of three distinct social classes: slaves, freemen, and nobles. The poem has been assigned by some to the 10th or 11th century, or even the 9th, while others have maintained that it dates from the 11th or 12th century. It survives incomplete in a manuscript from the mid-14th century. The poem tells that Rig—who is in reality the pagan god Heimdall—went on a journey, and as he walked along the seashore he came first to a married couple named Ai (great-grandfather) and Edda (great-grandmother), who lived in a poor hut. They entertained him with coarse bread and boiled calf meat, and Rig spent three nights with them, sharing their bed. Rig went on his way, but nine months later Edda gave birth to a dark-skinned boy named Thraell (thrall), who grew up with rough hands, thick fingers, an ugly face, and a crooked back. He was a physical laborer and married an unattractive woman by the name of Thir (bondwoman). The two had many children who lived a life of hard manual work, their names echoing their disagreeable existence. The sons were called Weatherbeaten, Stableboy, Stout and Sticky, Rough, Badbreath, Stumpy, Fatty, Sluggard and Greyis, Lout, and Long-legs. Their daughters were named equally cruelly: Stumpina and Podgy, Bulgy-calves and Bellows-nose, Noisy, Raggedy-hips, and Crane-legs. The poet claims that slaves were descended from these children.

Next, Rig came to the hall of Afi (grandfather) and Amma (grandmother). There was fire on the floor, and both were at work. Afi, with hair above his brows and a well-trimmed beard, was whittling wood for a cross-beam; Amma, with a headdress on her head, a smock on her body, a kerchief around her neck, and brooches at her shoulders, was spinning. Rig spent three nights with them, sharing their bed, and then went on his way, but nine months later Amma gave birth to a son named Karl (farmer). When Karl grew up, he tamed oxen, worked the harrow, built houses, threw up barns, made carts, and drove the plow. Karl married a woman "with keys at her belt in a goatskin-kirtle," and the couple had children with nice names: Man and Soldier, Lad, Thane and Smith, Broad, Yeoman, Boundbeard, Dweller, Boddi, Smoothbeard, and Fellow. The daughters were equally well named: Lady, Bride, Sensible, Wise, Speaker, Dame, Fanny, Wife, Shy, and Sparky. The poet then claims that farmers were descended from these children.

Finally, Rig came to the hall of Fadir (father) and Modir (mother). The doors were facing south. In he stepped, and the floors were strewn with straw; there sat the couple looking into one another's eyes, Fadir and Modir, busy with their fingers. There sat the householder twisting bow strings, bending elm, and shaping arrows, and the lady of the house was admiring her arms, stroking the material, and straightening the sleeves. Her headdress was set straight, and she wore a pendant on her breast, a short, full cape, and a blue-stitched blouse; her brow was brighter, her breasts more shining, and her neck was whiter than freshly fallen snow. At Fadir and Modir's house, Rig was served at table and lavishly entertained with expensive food and drink. Rig spent three nights with them, sharing their bed, and then went on his way. Nine months later, Modir gave birth to a son named Jarl (earl) and wrapped him in silk. He was very handsome; his hair was blond, his cheeks were bright, and his eyes glittered like those of a serpent. He grew up skilled with the bow, the spear, and the horse. One day, Rig came to him from under a bush; he acknowledged his son, gave him his own name, and taught him the runes. His wife, a "slender-fingered girl, radiant and wise," was called Erna, and they had 12 sons with beautiful names: Son was the eldest and Child the second, Baby and Noble, Heir and Offspring, Descendant, and Kinsman. Young Kon was the noblest of all of them. He knew the runes, could blunt weapons, and understood the speech of birds. The poem is incomplete, and where it breaks off, young Kon, who, as his name implies (Kon plus *ung* [young] equals *konung* [king]), is clearly destined to become king, is about to take off and conquer other lands at the urging of a crow.

Of course, the poem's description of the divinely arranged social structure of Viking Age Scandinavia is somewhat simplistic. Especially the middle group—freemen and women—comprised in reality a wide spectrum of people. There were people who were poor and probably landless living by occasional work and yet were not slaves as well as people, such as chieftains and warriors, who were wealthy and powerful and yet were not nobles. Nonetheless, the tripartite structure that the poem sanctions is a convenient one. The freemen were the backbone of the Scandinavian community, and they formed the bulk of society. They comprised a varied group, and there were different ranks of freemen. The difference in status among freemen, which was largely dependent upon ancestry and wealth, is given clear expression in the laws in terms of the compensation that a man was obliged to pay if he committed a crime or that would be owed to him if he suffered injury at the hands of another man.

Most of the freemen were farmers: independent farmers on inherited land, independent farmers on leased land, and independent farmers on bought land. The independent farmers on inherited family land (called *odal*) made up the most important class, and some of them owned very large tracts of land. Such farmers were typically quite influential and powerful and often served as chieftains. The lawyers and (pagan) priests would also seem to have been drawn from this particular class of farmers. The tenant farmers, who appear to have become quite numerous during the Viking Age, were probably to a large extent made up of freed slaves or freemen with no capital. They usually paid an annual rent in cash or kind to the landowner. Other freemen worked as farmhands or servants or had more specialized occupations, such as craftsmen (smiths, carpenters, weapon makers, jewelers, etc.). The number of craftsmen appears to have gradually increased during the Viking Age as a result of advances in material standards and the growth of towns. Yet other freemen were merchants or professional warriors.

Snapshot

The Viking Sayings of the High One

The Vikings had a list of sayings that reveals their daily life, the violence and courage that marked their society. Here are a few of the sayings, which were attributed to the god Odin:

> Let the man who opens a door be on the lookout for an enemy behind it.
> A coward thinks he will live forever if he avoids his enemies, but old age no man escapes even if he survives the spears.
> A man should never move an inch from his weapons when out in the fields, for he never knows when he will need his spear.
> Beer is not so good for men as it is said to be; the more a man drinks the less control he has of his thoughts. (Brondsted, 249–50)

The freemen had legal protection and played a role in the administration of the law. They also had the right to bear arms, and no doubt the bands of Viking raiders and traders came from this class of people. Such bands were called *felag*. They were essentially partnerships or guilds in which the members owed each other mutual obligations. The *felag* were not limited to raiding and trading activities but could also involve, for example, the sharing of capital in farming ventures or the joint ownership of a boat.

Among the freemen, there were, of course, also poor people. They were the responsibility—at least in theory—of their relatives. The laws required that a man must first maintain his mother, and if he can manage more, then he is to maintain his father. If he can do better, then he is to maintain his children. If he can do better, then he is to maintain his brothers and sisters. If he can do better, then he is to maintain those people from whom he has the right to inherit and those he has taken on by inheritance-trade. It he can do better, then he is to maintain his freedman, one to whom he gave freedom.

It is difficult to know what kind of help or support was available to poor people if there were no relatives or if those relatives were already destitute. Organized poor relief did not come into existence until Christian times. Iceland, in particular, had a sophisticated system to help its financially disadvantaged citizens. The country was divided geographically into *hreppar* (singular *hrepp*), each unit comprising at least 20 farmers. The role of these *hreppar* was among other things to provide for paupers whose relatives were unable to provide economic help. Each farmer had to take care of the pauper for a specific period of time relative to his means. In this manner, the pauper moved between the larger farms in a *hrepp*. The *hreppar* later derived some income for poor relief through the introduction of the tithe law in 1096. This was the first Icelandic tax to be levied according to means. Ten percent of a man's possessions were to be paid to the church, and of this 10 percent, one-quarter should go to the poor. The same *hrepp* system also served as a kind of insurance to circumvent the need for poor relief. If a man lost a quarter or more of his livestock through disease or if he lost three farm buildings (living room, kitchen, and pantry) through fire, the farmers jointly covered half the damage.

The complex requirements for poor relief suggest that the Vikings really did have a kind of egalitarian society even within the hierarchy of social class. Each was responsible for people in their care.

~Kirsten Wolf

FOR MORE INFORMATION

Brondsted, J. *The Vikings*. Translated by K. Skov. Harmondsworth, England: Penguin, 1971.
Wolf, K. *Daily Life of the Vikings*. Westport, Conn.: Greenwood Press, forthcoming.

CHINA

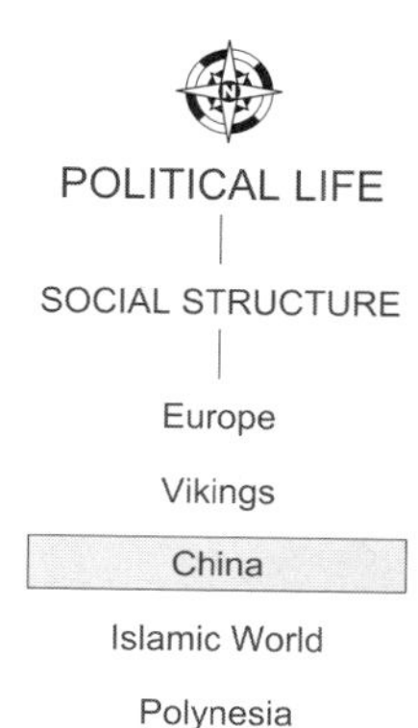

Tang China was a highly stratified, hierarchical society. The state regulated everything—the allocation of resources, access to education and political office, tax obligations and exemptions, legal accountability and punishment, and more—on the basis of an individual's status. Sumptuary laws dictated the quantity, quality, size, and adornment of clothes, transportation, homes, and other facets of life. The notion of equality, so cherished in modern times, did not exist in the Tang.

At the apex of society were, of course, the emperor and his family. The latter included both his nuclear and his extended families: grandfathers, grandmothers, mother, wives, sons, daughters, grandsons, granddaughters, brothers, sisters, uncles, aunts, nephews, nieces, and cousins. The throne bestowed nine ranks of noble titles, from prince to baron, on male relatives. It also conferred the title princess on aunts, sisters, daughters, the consort of the heir apparent, and the wives of princes. The court allocated portions of the annual tax revenues to them. In the first half of the Tang, the government established offices with staffs of officials and clerks for princes. Those agencies coped with the grants and other matters, and over time the revenue received by these imperial nobles grew astronomically.

The emperor and aristocracy remained at the top of a rigidly stratified social structure that led to peasants and slaves at the bottom. However, Tang China had developed a complex bureaucracy that ran most of the business of the land. This bureaucracy not only conducted the empire's business in a generally efficient fashion, but it offered ways for talented men to transform their fortunes and transcend their original place in society in ways remarkable for the medieval world.

In the Tang, there were two types of officials: functionaries and mandarins. Functionaries, known as those "outside the current," were scribes, clerks, warehouse keepers, and other subalterns of the mandarins, those "within the current." They performed the routine tasks of administration—drafting correspondence and reports, compiling records and registers, maintaining inventories, and the like—that were beneath the dignity of the mandarins from whom they received their salaries.

The highest goal for an ambitious man of social standing and/or education was to acquire a position "within the current," to become a mandarin. There were basically three ways to acquire such an office. First, a man could assert hereditary privilege. The sons of officials were eligible for appointment to a post one grade lower than the highest office that their fathers held (or had held, if they were deceased). Second, he could receive a special appointment from the throne. In those cases, the emperor acted on the recommendation of an official or on information, oral or written, that he had received. In most instances, the emperor made his decisions on the grounds that the candidates had superior reputations, special skills, or exceptional qualifications. Last, an aspirant for a bureaucratic position could sit for civil service examinations and receive a post if he passed them.

The Chinese bureaucracy was in many ways a meritocracy because in principle it recruited and promoted officeholders on the basis of learning, skills, and other abilities—not on the basis of social status—and this remained true for the next millennium with some exceptions, notably, mandarins who received appointments on the basis of hereditary privilege. After a man acquired a post, his superior annually rated his character according to four categories of attributes: his virtue and righteousness, integrity and prudence, impartiality, and diligence. The supervisor then assessed the subordinate's actual performance of his duties according to 27 criteria, such as the selection of talented subordinates with good character for his staff, proper training and equipping of troops, just sentencing of convicted criminals, meticulous maintenance of records, prevention of fraud in the market, and rearing the animals under his charge so that they were fat and strong. An official's career depended on favorable evaluations, so he had to conduct himself prudently if he wished to advance.

There was a hierarchy of nine grades for offices and the mandarins holding them. The ladder of success for mandarins—who received elegant titles such as Grandee of Radiant Emolument and Bearer of the Gold Seal with Purple Ribbon on attaining new grades—conferred greater and greater prestige and privileges as they received promotions to offices with higher and higher rankings. The system was also the instrument by which the government fixed salaries, all of them tax exempt, and allocated resources. In addition, the court ennobled high-ranking or meritorious bureaucrats, civil and military. It conferred titles—duke, marquis, count, viscount, and baron—on them and provided them with grants similar to those accorded the aristocracy but smaller in size (the revenues from 50 to 2,000 households).

Many of the Tang's officials were upright, diligent, and competent. Some local officials made efforts to repair schools and encourage students to pursue learning, and others generously cared for the poor and needy. Tang China also had its share of bad officials. The most common form of malfeasance during the dynasty was corruption. For example, when the chief of some aborigines in what is now North Vietnam wanted to take a wife, the Chinese governor of the prefecture demanded 1,000 lengths of fine silk fabric before he would grant his permission. The chief was able to supply only 800 lengths, so the governor seized the bride-to-be and had his way with her for three days before returning her. Because he had deflowered the woman, the chief would not marry her. The throne took a particularly dim view of such offenses and often had mandarins found guilty of the crime beaten to death before officials standing in the courtyard of the audience hall, to serve as a warning (Benn, 23–27).

To read about government and society in 19th-century China, see the China entry in the section "Government and Politics" in chapter 6 ("Political and Diplomatic Life") of volume 5 of this series.

FOR MORE INFORMATION

Benn, C. *Daily Life in Traditional China: The Tang Dynasty*. Westport, Conn.: Greenwood Press, 2002.

Loewe, M. *Everyday Life in Early Imperial China*. London: Fromm International, 1968.

ISLAMIC WORLD

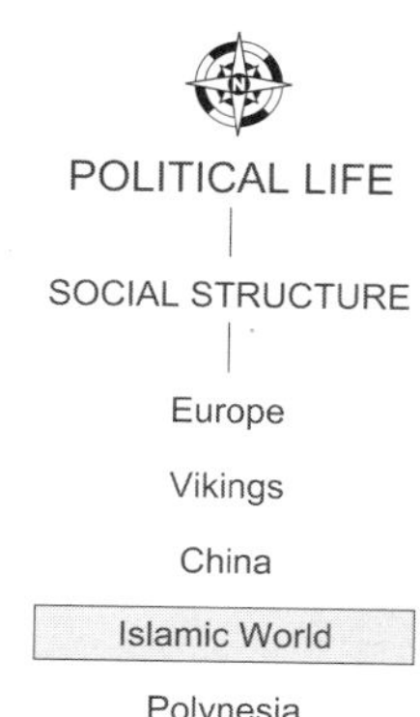

From the death of Muhammad (632) until the Mongol destruction of Baghdad (1258), Islamic societies looked to the institution of the caliphate for guidance, protection, and inspiration—at the very least, for a sense of unity among the community of believers as a whole. The institution of the caliphate and debates about it figured into nearly every aspect of Islamic life in the premodern period, and it has from time to time informed political and religious debates in the modern period as well. Hence it is useful at this point to treat some of the basic issues surrounding the institution of the caliphate as well as make some comments about the nature of medieval Islamic societies in general.

Islam began with a religious and political leader—Muhammad—who was believed to possess a divinely appointed right to govern the community. In fact, the Qur'an (Koran) contains very little political material at all—it simply envisages a community led by a prophet. Initially, the Islamic community was constituted as a voluntary community. After Muhammad's death, the *umma* agreed on the need for a leader and selected Abu Bakr as Muhammad's first successor. Our sources refer to the holders of this office by three titles: (1) *Khalifat Rasul Allah* (caliph—deputy or successor of the Messenger of God), (2) *Amir al-Mu'minin* (commander of the believers), and (3) *Imam* (religious leader).

For all intents and purposes, these titles simply emphasize different aspects of the caliph's political, military, and religious authority. Whatever the title, there was a general consensus about the basic responsibilities of the office: (1) the caliph should be the sole leader of the community, (2) all political power was to be invested in this one man, and (3) this office was to be a lifetime office. Most of the major Muslim sects agreed with these three positions. The basic problem concerned the criteria for determining who was qualified to hold this important office. While there was and remains a great deal of diversity of opinion within the Muslim community on this issue, three broad groupings—Sunni, Shi'ite, and Kharijite—deserve consideration here.

The Sunnis represent the majority of Muslims in the premodern and modern world. The name *Sunni* is derived from the formal title of this group—*ahl al-sunna wa'l-jama'a* (people of tradition and unity). At the risk of oversimplification, one can say that one of the highest values of the Sunni community was the maintenance of the broad unity of the *umma*. As such, the general position that developed among Sunni theorists was that the caliph needed only to be good enough politically to do the job and maintain the unity of the community. Hence the Sunnis are often referred to as "caliphal loyalists."

The second major group is referred to as the Shia or Shi'ites. This name derives from the fact that they belonged to the party or faction (*shia*) of Muhammad's cousin and son-in-law, 'Ali ibn Abi Talib. The Shi'ites believe that prior to his death, Muhammad designated 'Ali ibn Abi Talib as his successor; therefore, the acclamation of Abu Bakr as the first caliph was an illegitimate usurpation on its face. There are two basic doctrines that developed among the Shi'ites that are worth noting as well. First, the rightful caliph or imam had to be a lineal descendant of the Prophet, in particular through the line of 'Ali and Fatima, Muhammad's daughter. The second, and more controversial, is that the caliph or imam was not only the political head of the community but an infallible religious teacher—guaranteed to be without error in matters of faith and morals. Because of this emphasis on the religious and theological role of the head of the community, Shi'ite texts tend to use the title Imam for this office more frequently than caliph or *Amir al-Mu'minin*.

The third group is referred to as the Kharijites (Ar. *Khawarij*)—that is, "the seceders." This group disagreed with both the Sunni and the Shi'ite positions. They were the purists in that their principal criteria for leadership of the community was piety—genealogy did not matter to them, nor did the practical consideration of maintaining the unity of the community. For them, moral purity was far more important than political unity. However the Islamic community was defined, full membership and participation in it was based on religion. This was an absolutely universal idea in the world of late antiquity, whether in Byzantium or Sasanian Iran. That is, if one had any hopes of being a full participant in Byzantine society, he had to be an Orthodox Christian; if one had any hopes of being a full participant in Iranian society, he had to be Zoroastrian.

To read about political and social structures in the Islamic world in the 19th century, see the Islamic World entries in the sections "Empire" and "Reform Movements" in chapter 6 ("Political Life") of volume 5; for the 20th century, see the sections "Government" and "Reform" in chapter 6 ("Political Life") of volume 6 of this series.

~*James Lindsay*

FOR MORE INFORMATION

Lindsay, J. *Daily Life in Medieval Islam*. Westport, Conn.: Greenwood Press, forthcoming.
Roberts, R. *The Social Laws of the Quran*. Atlantic Highlands, N.J.: Humanities Press, 1990.

POLYNESIA

Most ancient Polynesians lived in highly stratified societies where extreme, rigid class structures were established. Some islanders, however, lived in a more equalitarian society, such as the New Zealand Māoris, or in a warrior-dominated one, such as Easter Island or Mangaia. The two major classes in the highly stratified societies consisted of a powerful ruling class of nobles (called the *ali'i, ari'i, ariki,* or *'eiki*) and a laboring class of commoners (called *maka'āinana* in Hawai'i, *manahune* in Tahiti, and *tu'a* in Tonga). Almost everywhere, the two major classes were separated by a wide gulf, with the aristocracy having all of the privileges of government, rule, ownership of land, and priestly functions. In essence, Polynesian societies resembled the social structure of medieval Europe with its two classes of nobles and serfs, but unlike Europe, the members of the noble class in Polynesia were considered practically divine.

Noble rank in Polynesia depended on genealogical descent from some powerful, high-ranking chief, and some royal pedigrees even claimed descent from the gods themselves (the Tu'i Tonga, or king of Tonga, for example). So powerful were these high chiefs that no one could have the same name as his during his lifetime, and no commoner could utter his name out loud. He had to be carried around on the backs of his servants or on a dais so that his feet would not touch the ground of another's property; otherwise, that property would become his. If he ever entered the home of a commoner, that home had to be burned to the ground. The lower classes had to prostrate themselves in his presence or bare their shoulders out of respect. Children conceived between members of these two widely separated classes were usually put to death at birth. Countless other taboos regulated the complex relationships between the high chiefs and the rest of society. (See details of the chiefly class in the Polynesia entry in the section "Aristocracy" in this chapter.)

Commoners in Polynesia consisted of the laboring masses—the cultivators of the soil, fishermen, hunters, craftsmen, and their families. They lived on land belonging to the high chiefs, and they were expected to provide food and labor to the chiefs whenever called upon. In wartime, they had to gather their weapons and join the fighting between the chiefs of the island. Their treatment by the chiefly class was often regarded as harsh, and tales of chiefly cruelty abound, but most chiefs seem to have been generous and concerned about the welfare of the people under their rule. Commoners could usually transfer their allegiance from one chief to another by simply picking up and moving to another district (unlike the serfs in medieval Europe). Although they were regarded as a lower class by the chiefs, they were not considered degraded or full-time servants or slaves, nor were they restricted in the kinds of work they wanted to do. They were generally free to live their lives as they wished. Some commoners entered the priesthood, but in most of these cases, they remained adjuncts or assistants to the more prestigious high priests who were members of the chiefly class.

Shown here are two Tongan dancers dressed in their traditional clothing of finely woven mats, tapa cloth, and other finery. The dancer in the foreground wears modern (cotton) woven materials. Photo courtesy of the Institute for Polynesian Studies.

There were two other groups in Polynesian societies that sometimes were considered classes, and the early explorers to the islands referred to them the "middle class" and the "slave class," although their terminologies and descriptions are often conflicting. The middle class was referred to as the "gentry," "gentlemen," or "landed proprietors." The emphasis was on being landowners who held their land through hereditary right and from whom it could not be confiscated. Members of the middle class often provided their ruler with substantial support both in peace and war, and they were often called upon to be his spokesmen. They were also placed in charge of distributing food gifts for the chiefs; they served as warriors, and some were appointed as governors of small islands. On occasion, these governors became subordinate chiefs, and their positions were inherited by their sons.

The lowest class of individuals in Polynesian society included the slaves and outcasts. Some of these individuals had lost their freedom through war—their chiefs had been defeated, and they had become the property of the conquerors. They were often kept to become the human sacrifices needed in the most important religious ceremonies. Others may have broken important taboos and were enslaved, while some may have been descended from earlier peoples who had inhabited the islands before the coming of the last waves of conquerors to the island. Whatever the case may have been, these outcasts were without land and personal rights within the community and were generally despised by the rest of the population.

~*Robert D. Craig*

FOR MORE INFORMATION

Goldman, I. *Ancient Polynesian Society*. Chicago: University of Chicago Press, 1970.

Aristocracy

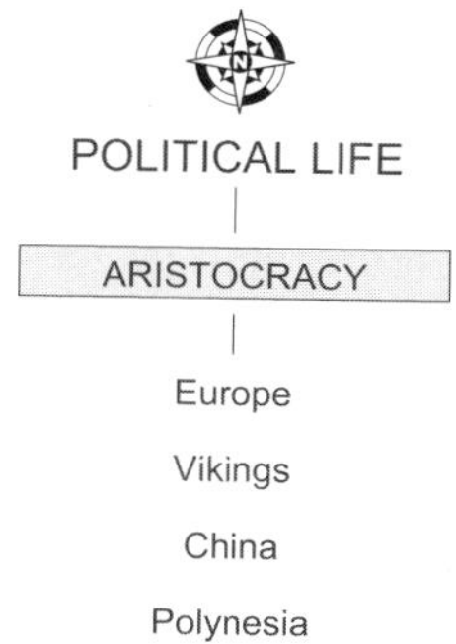

All the cultures of the Middle Ages were ruled to some degree or another by an aristocracy. This was a class whose members thought themselves descended from nobility, so they gained their privileges through the accident of their birth. In Europe and China, it was also a class of landed fighting men who used their estates as the basis of their wealth and power and served the functions of warriors for that society. While the aristocracy shared these general definitions, the realities of their lives varied widely.

The Polynesian chiefs achieved a level of respect that perhaps even exceeded that of the Chinese emperors. Many of these chieftains claimed divine descent, which they often preserved by brother-sister marriages to avoid diluting their royal blood. Subjects bowed to the ground in respect at the presence of these semidivine chiefs. The aristocracy of Europe never achieved anywhere near this level of respect during the Middle Ages.

Early in the Middle Ages, and probably as late as the 10th century, the daily life of the aristocracy would not have looked strikingly different from that of agricultural workers. They lived in houses with few furnishings. Most of the castles had only two rooms, a hall—where the lord, lady, and all their retainers ate and worked—and a chamber, where the lord and lady retired to sleep. Life was crowded, food simple, and cleanliness hard to come by. The aristocracy of this period set themselves apart only by their birth and by their function in society, which was warfare. The men fought, and the women supervised the household and produced more heirs to continue the line.

Throughout the Middle Ages, we see a slow and continuous process by which the aristocracy separated itself from the classes below and subdivided itself. The aristocracy began to differentiate itself on the basis of wealth, power, and leisure. While the aristocracy derived its wealth from the land, some lords began to figure out how to collect more rents and make more money. With this, manor houses and defensive castles became more differentiated, and so did the aristocracy. There seemed to be little in common with great nobles, who lived well and controlled huge tracts of land, and knights, who owned little more than the strength of their arms. However, both shared the order of "those who fight," and as such they were of the aristocracy.

The separation of the aristocracy from the other orders did not only take the form of material life; the aristocracy in medieval Europe developed new values to set itself apart from other classes, as well as to preserve identity within a group that ranged from a landless knight to a king. By the late Middle Ages, the aristocracy embraced a code of chivalry that claimed their fighting was a sacred duty, bound by religious sanction and secular honor. This calling began to include learning how to be gracious in love and courteous to noble ladies. The 12th-century *Art of Courtly Love* is a fascinating document that details how the nobility was purportedly set apart by its capacity to engage in romantic love. This work also shows the degree to which the nobility separated itself from the peasantry, for it suggests that if a noblemen should feel drawn to a peasant girl, he should simply rape her and then move his affections more appropriately to one of his own class.

This distinction continued through the Middle Ages, as aristocrats defined themselves apart from the lower classes. In the West, peasants ate with their fingers, and noblemen began to adopt forks; peasants wore homespun wool, and aristocrats imported silk; peasants continued to live in one or two rooms just as aristocrats expanded their castles and manor houses. As middle-class urban dwellers began to stress frugality, the nobility asserted their right to waste. For example, instead of eating everything on their plate, noble men and women would consciously leave some to prove they had consumed enough.

Throughout the Middle Ages, the aristocracy in the West continued to try to demonstrate that they were different from peasants or the growing middle class. By the end of the period, they passed sumptuary laws, which regulated the kinds of clothing lower classes could wear. In China, these regulations took the form of state-mandated laws. The appearance of such laws indicates that the aristocracy had lost their privileged position and were desperately trying to hold on. The modern age was coming, when the aristocracy could no longer claim privilege simply on the basis of birth.

~*Joyce E. Salisbury*

FOR MORE INFORMATION

Anderson, R. T. *Traditional Europe: A Study in Anthropology and History*. Belmont, Calif.: Wadsworth, 1971.

Andreas Capellanus. *Art of Courtly Love*. Translated by J. J. Perry. New York: Columbia University Press, 1990.

EUROPE

Toward the end of the early Middle Ages in Europe, the mounted knight emerged as the predominant force on the battlefield, and the class of arms-bearing freemen was gradually redivided. Those who served as knights on horseback were assimilated into the aristocracy, often receiving land as a means of supporting their expensive military equipment, and the aristocracy itself came to be seen as society's warrior class. The rest, whose military service was now of minimal importance, lost status and were increasingly assimilated into the category of the unfree.

The power and distinctive status of the warrior aristocracy were perpetuated by ongoing social realities. As the warrior class, the aristocracy had the power to acquire and hold wealth and its sources, while advances in military technology further concentrated power in their hands. Improved armor raised the cost of military equipment while widening the gulf between the effectiveness of a peasant spearman and a fully equipped warrior. Even more important was the introduction of the stirrup, which made possible a new form of warfare based on the power of the mounted knight. The knight was enormously expensive to train, maintain, and equip, but he was virtually unbeatable on the battlefield until the rise of the longbow and pike in the 14th century. The aristocracy had the resources to take advantage of the new technology, and their hold on those resources was reinforced by the technology itself.

Aristocratic status was inherited, and this reflected the force of tradition as well as the natural inclination of parents to use their resources to benefit their children. Many of the medieval aristocracy had their ancestry among the Germanic warriors who had invaded the Roman Empire during its declining days, taking over the land as their own and in some cases adopting the positions of the former Roman landlords. Others belonged to families who had entered the aristocracy more recently through some combination of military, political, and economic success. The line between aristocrat and commoner was never so firm that it could not be crossed through prosperity or decline, although the transition usually took more than a single generation.

There was enormous variation in wealth, power, and status among aristocrats. The wealthiest aristocrats in England in the 13th century might have an annual income of 5,000 pounds, about five hundred times more than the poorest. At the top were the kings and upper nobility, whose extensive networks of patronage placed them in authority over large territories and populations, allowing them a major political role at the national and international level. Below them were aristocrats whose authority was more limited, some having only a few other aristocrats under their power, others at an even lower level, having authority only over commoners; this last group corresponded to landowning knights. The very lowest tier of the aristocracy was made up of those who had no governmental authority at all—professional warriors of aristocratic families who could only support themselves by taking military service with a greater aristocrat. Such men had significantly less wealth and power than the upper levels of commoners, and vastly less than the upper levels of their own class.

Within its own ranks, the aristocracy was highly stratified. A simple knight who rose through good fortune to join the titled nobility would be regarded as an upstart by other noblemen. Yet relative to society as a whole, the aristocracy shared a common culture and social image that associated the mighty duke with the landless knight rather than with the wealthy merchant. Both duke and knight were officially warriors, born to the role by right of inheritance and claiming generations of ancestors who had been born to this status before them. Both maintained their elite status by participating in a courtly culture that became increasingly elaborate over the course of the Middle Ages. This culture involved not only the cultivation of martial skills such as swordsmanship and riding but also an appreciation of arts such as poetry and music, familiarity with courtly pastimes such as hunting and chess, and command of an ever-changing code of fashion and etiquette. Wealthy commoners in search of social status, always latecomers to the world of privilege, were perpetually playing a game whose rules had already been set by the aristocracy.

Aristocratic couple holding hands. Both the knight and his lady wear heraldic clothing that shows their family crest and proves their aristocratic family ties. Joyce E. Salisbury.

All in all, the aristocracy of the High Middle Ages probably constituted about 1 percent of the population, but their power and influence were far greater than their actual numbers. In particular, the distinctively medieval institution of feudalism was dominated by the aristocracy, and as the framework of medieval law and government, it shaped the lives even of those who did not participate in it directly (Singman, 2–4).

To read about aristocracy in Elizabethan England, see the England entry in the section "Hierarchy" in chapter 6 ("Political Life") of volume 3; for 18th-century England, see the England entry in the section "Social Structure" in chapter 6 ("Political Life") of volume 4; and for Victorian England, see the England entry in the section "Government and Politics" in chapter 6 ("Political Life") of volume 5 of this series.

FOR MORE INFORMATION

Gies, J., and F. Gies. *Life in a Medieval Castle*. New York: Harper and Row, 1974.

Singman, J. L. *Daily Life in Medieval Europe*. Westport, Conn.: Greenwood Press, 1999.

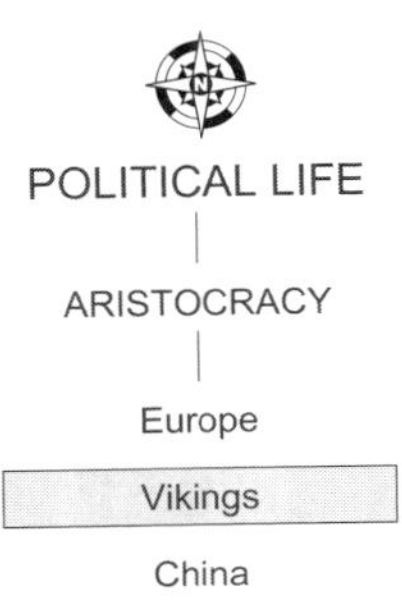

VIKINGS

The top of the Scandinavian social structure in the Viking Age consisted of aristocrats. They were the ruling caste, and to this group belonged the people with wealth, land, and rank. At the top of the aristocracy was the king, and the nobility served him.

It is generally assumed that before the Viking Age, there was a considerable number of petty kingdoms and independent earldoms in Scandinavia. Very little, if anything, is known about these petty kings and kingdoms; we do not know the extent of the kings' powers or the size of their territories. Presumably, they were warriors who had gathered bands of men around them and united areas of the country. The title of king was probably used quite freely, although certainly some regulations applied as to how and on whom it could be bestowed. The succession pattern reveals two principles. One required that a king be related by blood to a previous king. This principle may have its origin in the belief that the kings were descended from pagan gods. The other principle, election, gave leading chieftains the privilege of choosing a suitable candidate. Often, there were two or more contenders for the title, and joint rule was by no means uncommon. It was not until the very end of the Viking Age, when Denmark, Norway, and Sweden had taken shape as kingdoms, that the notion of vertical lineage within a single dynasty was promoted. The aim was succession through primogeniture, but it was not achieved until well after the Viking Age.

The king was the head of state in international relations and served as a representative of his country. He functioned primarily as a military leader, although it was not until the end of the Viking Age that Scandinavian kings themselves led and participated in attacks on the British Isles. Their kingdoms were too unstable to permit them to be away for long periods of time. The king's main duty was to maintain peace at home and protect his subjects not only from foreign attacks but also from unruly local chieftains. As a military leader, the king's powers were secured by his *hird,* an Anglo-Saxon word meaning "household" that had become adopted in Scandinavia by the 11th century as a term for the retinue accompanying kings, earls, or other rulers.

The *hird* was essentially a private warrior organization—a nucleus of armed followers—and most of its members probably lived in close proximity to the king. Although some form of contract must have existed between the king and the members of his *hird,* the fundamental tie was that of personal loyalty to the king. The king's bodyguards and standard-bearer (an especially talented man whose task it was to keep the standard from falling) were almost certainly drawn from the *hird.*

The most detailed information about the composition of the *hird* is found in the *Hirdskra,* a Norwegian code from about 1270. By that time, the *hird* was a three-tier organization of knights, officials, and servants. The knights or so-called *hirdmen* caroused with the king in his hall and received gifts of booty from the royal hand. This group was hierarchical and divided into *hird* officials, who were the elite and typically drawn from leading families, landed men, *skutilsveinar* (men who served at the royal table), and ordinary *hirdmen.* The officials, who were called *gestir* (guests), were of a lower order and received less pay. They functioned as a kind of police force. The servants were referred to as *kertisveinar* (candle boys). They were young men or boys, apprentices, recruited from the better families in the kingdom, who served as pages. In essence, the *hird* served as protection for the king.

The king also served as a religious leader. In pagan times, it was the king who conducted the major sacrifices to the gods to ensure peace and prosperity in the country. We know that Lejre on Zealand in Denmark, Uppsala in Sweden, and Trondheim in Norway were important religious centers, and these locations may also have served as permanent royal estates. Generally, the king was held responsible for peace and good harvests in his country.

The king had no absolute authority as law maker and judge. Laws were established and decisions were made by freemen at the assemblies (*things*), although it is reasonable to assume that the king played an important role in the maintenance of law and order and in the execution of legal decisions. The conversion of the three Scandinavian countries to Christianity, for example, seems to have taken place largely at the independent initiative of the respective king and his immediate circle of aristocrats, who served as advisors and diplomats.

Royal structures, such as the Danish fortresses and the Jelling monuments, suggest that the king must have had considerable funds at his disposal. The economic foundation of the crown was primarily revenues from land ownership and buildings on estates throughout the country, some of which may have served as temporary royal residences during the king's travels around the kingdom, but income was also derived from trading, fines, shares of property confiscated from outlaws, and minting at home and tributes and tolls abroad.

~*Kirsten Wolf*

FOR MORE INFORMATION

Jones, G. *A History of the Vikings*. Oxford: Oxford University Press, 1984.
Wolf, K. *Daily Life of the Vikings*. Westport, Conn.: Greenwood Press, forthcoming.

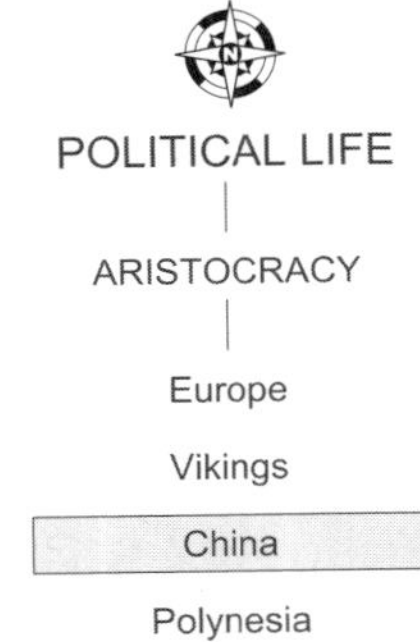

CHINA

The aristocracy formed the highest rank in Tang China, with the exception only of the emperor and his close family. There were two kinds of aristocrats. The first came from the imperial family, and the emperor gave noble titles to his relatives. These nobles received an income from the imperial taxes. These grants came to be quite large and a drain on the economy. In 709, one of the emperor's ministers calculated that taxes from 600,000 households, about 8 percent of the tax-paying population, were going to pay for the incomes of the imperial nobility. He reckoned that aristocrats received more silk from levies than the imperial treasury did. In the same year, a report to the throne concluded that there were 140 nobles receiving incomes from 54 prefectures, roughly 15 percent of the empire. After Illustrious August ascended the throne and launched his program of austerities, he cut the incomes of the nobility, and the fiscal health of the government improved.

The second kind of aristocrat came from the extremely powerful clans who had monopolized high government positions in the dynasties before the Tang. Some of them, four from the northeast in particular, professed to have the finest Chinese pedigrees, married only among themselves, and considered the Lis (the royal house of the Tang) to be parvenus. As late as the early 9th century, an emperor complained that a marriage to two of those families was considered superior to one with the imperial family. The members of those clans who held noble titles did not acquire them by virtue of their birth. The throne bestowed them for meritorious service or as expressions of favor. The power of the clans rested solely on social prestige and tradition. That strength was sufficient to secure them high-ranking positions in the bureaucracy until the end of the dynasty.

Except in the worst of times, the aristocracy lived comfortably. In the best of times, they lived lavishly and extravagantly. Some princes were dissolute, indulging in hunting, drinking, and entertainment. In the early 8th century, the son of one prince died suddenly because of overindulgence in wine and women. Zhongzong's daughters, however, outdid all others in the prodigal expenditure of the enormous wealth that they had acquired by selling ordination certificates and office titles. Princess Anle expropriated the estates of commoners west of Changan to build a pleasure park. She spent enormous sums on adorning the grounds. Workers excavated a lake 16 miles in circumference. Laborers piled stones to create a mountain resembling Mount Hua—a sacred peak and scenic wonder east of the capital—dug a river channel in the form of the Milky Way, installed bridges, and paved roads with stone. Carpenters erected pavilions and covered walkways. Artisans decorated the structures with gold and silver and inlaid them with pearls and jade. After the execution of the princess in 710, the government seized the property and turned it into a public park. Citizens of the capital visited it daily and kept it as a constant example of the excesses of some aristocrats.

In the Tang dynasty, aristocrats were prominent officers in imperial armies, preserving the warrior tradition in the imperial family, at least in the early years of the dynasty. It was also the custom of the Tang court, especially in the first half of the dynasty, to appoint princes and other nobles to government posts. In many cases, the aristocrats held these posts in absentia and never performed the duties assigned to their offices or even left their mansions in the capital. In some cases, however, nobles actually went to the provinces and administered their districts as true officials. A few of them acquitted themselves admirably. One acquired a reputation for his fairness in adjudicating important legal cases. Another was so uncorrupt and severe in administering justice that criminals fled his jurisdiction. Yet another distinguished himself by quelling a rebellion of aborigines in southeast China without resorting to force. Others, however, were cruel governors. One prince who was serving as the governor of a prefecture assaulted a county commandant under his authority for no just cause. When one of his subordinates dared to reprove him for trampling the crops of peasants while hunting, the prince beat him.

Some aristocrats took to learning and the arts. Others fostered scholarship. An emperor appointed one of his sons to the post of director of the imperial library because he was so fond of learning. A prince in the early 7th century used his wealth to collect a large library that contained very fine editions as well as rare calligraphy and copies of stone inscriptions. In 641, another prince published a large historical geography of the empire compiled by a literary academy of scholars that he had established with imperial consent.

Sometimes the character of aristocrats left something to be desired. Some were arrogant, overbearing, or self-indulgent. Others were ignoble, their behavior unseemly, criminal, indecent, or depraved. In 672, a son of an ailing prince took advantage of his father's weakened state to molest one of the prince's concubines. Afterward, the prince learned about the harassment and rebuked his son. Unrepentant, the son deprived his father of food and medicine so that he died of starvation. One of Illustrious August's nephews and three of his friends murdered a man in the capital, partly to obtain his riches and partly to settle a grudge. In broad daylight, they bludgeoned the man to death, boiled his flesh, and ate it. When the crime came to light in the summer of 739, the throne banished the nephew. It then ordered him to commit suicide when he reached a rapid relay station east of Changan.

These examples show that the range of aristocratic behavior was as varied as humans themselves. Those at the top of the social structure sometimes acquitted themselves well and at times abused the power they received (Benn, 19–23).

To read about government and society in 19th-century China, see the China entry in the section "Government and Politics" in chapter 6 ("Political Life") of volume 5 of this series.

FOR MORE INFORMATION

Barfield, T. J. *The Perilous Frontier: Nomadic Empires and China*. Cambridge, Mass.: Cambridge University Press, 1989.

Benn, C. *Daily Life in Traditional China: The Tang Dynasty*. Westport, Conn.: Greenwood Press, 2002.

POLYNESIA

Ancient Polynesian societies were generally divided into two major classes—chiefs and commoners—although several minor classes were often described by the early explorers who first visited the islands in the late 18th and early 19th centuries. These early explorers and the later Christian missionaries were fascinated by the unique chiefly class that ruled these islands, devoting pages of descriptive writings to it.

Polynesian chiefs were called *ali'i, aliki, ari'i, ariki,* or *ÿeiki*. They claimed lineal descent from a powerful, ancient ancestor or from the gods, and for that reason, they assumed power and authority far beyond any other rulers in the Pacific Ocean. The Japanese emperor, who claimed divine descent from the sun goddess, and the early modern European rulers, who ruled by "divine right," could never assume the power possessed by the Polynesian high chiefs because their powers were held in check by other forces in society—religion, law, and other powerful lords. The position of the Polynesian high chiefs, however, was so divine that brother-sister marriages were common (especially in Hawai'i) so that they could better preserve their impeccable royal pedigrees, similar to the royal marriages in ancient Egypt.

The dense population on the high volcanic islands of Polynesia allowed for the evolution of a more centralized authority than existed on the smaller islands and atolls in the Pacific. When Europeans first came into contact with Polynesia, two island groups—Hawai'i and Tonga—were well on their way to developing a centralized hierarchy of government, ruled by a single authority, which the Europeans called "king." The smaller islands of Polynesia, however, were ruled by district chieftains, none of whom held political power over any of the other district chiefs on the island. The small atolls were generally characterized by being even more egalitarian.

Anciently, Polynesian islands were politically divided into geographical sections or districts, each resembling a pie slice with the tip of the "pie" at the top of the inland mountains and the larger outer edge along the seashore. Commoners who lived in the districts were usually members of the same tribe and were related to some degree. They lived in huts scattered throughout the district, and they had access to the ocean for fishing, the inland valleys for agriculture and fresh water, and the mountains for hunting. Each district was ruled by a chief who claimed that title by genealogical descent or by right of conquest. Descent was determined through the firstborn son (primogeniture), who was usually given special treatment as a child because he was being groomed to be the next ruler. This was especially true regarding the highest-ranking chief on the entire island or island group. These chiefs were superior and sacred and often called *akua* (gods). Others did all the work for them. In New Zealand and Tahiti, for example, the *Tumu-whakare* and the *Ari'i nui* were so sacred that they had to be carried on the shoulders of a servant lest the lands of others they touch became theirs. Their names were so sacred that they could not be uttered by the lower classes, and no other person under their rule could have that same name during their lifetime. In Tonga, everyone stripped down to their waist or prostrated themselves when the Tuÿi Tonga (king of Tonga) approached. There was even a special form of speech that had to be spoken in his presence.

Although male descent was the general rule, firstborn daughters also claimed powers of their own and frequently might claim higher rank than the ruling chief and oppose his laws. In New Zealand, for example, the *Tapiru* (the firstborn daughter of a high chief) assumed the duties of high priestess of the tribe and could participate in ceremonies and religious rites not normally open to any other woman. She was so sacred that no one could eat in her presence. In early modern times, the Tongan princess Sinaitakala outranked her younger brother and ruled jointly with him. Her children by a Fijian chief were still considered of higher rank than the Tu'i Tonga, but they did not rule. A similar incident occurred in Tahiti, where Chieftess Tetuaehuri claimed higher genealogical descent than the ruling high chief, and she refused to recognize one of his laws. He proclaimed war and invaded her lands. His forces were crushed, however, and Tetuaehuri's son Teu became the highest-ranking chief on the island. His son, Pomare I (1751–1803), became Tahiti's first crowned "king."

Although genealogical descent determined basic ranking among Polynesian chiefs, there was a Polynesian personal characteristic that sometimes allowed a junior line to come to the fore. That characteristic was called *mana,* a spiritual power inherited from a powerful ancestor or acquired through heroic deeds done in one's lifetime. High chiefs were expected to have the highest degree of *mana,* and on occasion a dying chief might pass over his legitimate heir in favor of a younger son whom he thought best to rule. That son would then inherit his father's *mana.* In Hawai'i, for example, Chief Kamehameha (1758–1819) was trained in warfare during his early childhood. When the ruler of the island of Hawai'i died and passed his authority to his legitimate heir, Kamehemaha declared war, usurped his authority, and became the ruling high chief. His *mana* far outstripped his rival, the legitimate heir to the position. Kamehemaha spent the next 20 years establishing sovereignty over all of the other Hawaiian islands by right of conquest and was eventually crowned Hawai'i's first king. But, surprisingly, Kamehemaha was outranked by Ka'ahumanu, his favorite wife. It is said that when he entered her hut, he had to crawl on his hands and knees for she outranked even him—this powerful and formidable king of Hawai'i.

~Robert D. Craig

FOR MORE INFORMATION

Craig, R. D. *Historical Dictionary of Polynesia.* London: Scarecrow Press, 2002.
Goldman, I. *Ancient Polynesian Society.* Chicago: University of Chicago Press, 1970.
Handy, E.S.C. *Ancient Hawaiian Civilization.* Rev. ed. Rutland, Vt.: Charles E. Tuttle, 1970.

Peasants, Serfs, and Slaves

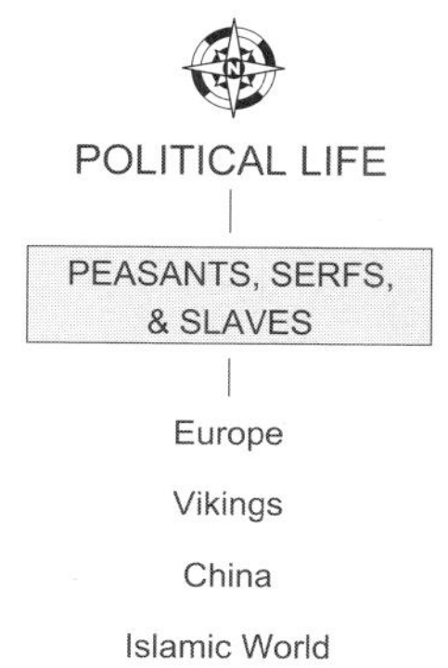

Throughout the Middle Ages all over the world, the vast majority of the population worked the land. Between 80 and 90 percent of the population were rural workers, all of whom shared a low standard of living and a low status in society. The names given to these rural dwellers vary somewhat to reveal a differing legal status among them. Some were "freeholders," that is, people who owed no labor obligations to the landlord. They might or might not own the land itself, but they did own their own work. Freeholders would usually owe taxes, whether in money or in a portion of their produce. In the Middle Ages, where people were bound closely in ties of obligation, this was the rarest form of landholder.

More common were serfs—men and women who were personally free but who were bound to a particular plot of land and who owed labor obligations to the landlords. They were not free to leave their land without permission from the lord, and they usually spent their lives in one small region. In Europe, serfs might owe two to three days a week to the lord. They would spend this time either working the lord's fields or repairing roads, erecting buildings, and performing similar labor. Women, too, owed labor obligations, spinning or weaving for the lady of the manor. In addition to labor, serfs owed a portion of whatever they produced, from crops to animals to eggs to cloth. In China, all the rural dwellers owed periodic labor to the state as they were available for conscription at any time for special building projects.

There were always serfs who were dissatisfied with their servile condition. In China, some were willing to risk the hazards of flight to travel to the south and find land that was uninhabited to establish free farms. In Europe, some serfs fled to the towns to gain their freedom after hiding there a year and a day; others gained some freedom by agreeing to move to new lands with a lord anxious to carve out a new manor. However, until late in the Middle Ages, these options were rare, and most lived out their lives bound in servitude.

Slavery existed in the Middle Ages in Byzantium, the Islamic world, and China. In these great, centralized states, they continued to enslave captives of war or even to purchase slaves from traders outside their borders. In the Muslim world, slaves were even used as elite cavalry warriors. In China, family members of enemies of the state were enslaved. Slaves differed from serfs in that they were not even personally free. In western Europe, on the other hand, slavery died out, and people whose families had been slaves in the early Middle Ages ended up as serfs. In the West, it was too much work to hold slaves; it was easier for lords to let people govern their own lives and simply collect rents and labor. (Slavery would reappear in western Europe during the 15th and 16th centuries.)

The most general name for most of the rural agricultural workers of the Middle Ages is *peasant*. Peasant refers to agricultural workers who live in villages and move out to their fields to work, rather than living in the middle of their fields and periodically traveling to town. (These were "farmers," who had their own social structure.)

As we have seen, peasants from freeholders to serfs owed a great number of obligations to their lords, but within their own villages, they had a good deal of freedom to govern themselves. Village life was usually guided by elders who periodically gathered in the square or the local "public house" (the equivalent to our bars; known as "pubs" in England). Here, they took care of everything from disputes among neighbors to when to plant to how to handle a vicious dog in the village. Peasants rarely referred conflicts to the lord; they were perpetually (and probably quite rightly) suspicious of getting a good deal from the owner of the land. They trusted their own traditions to preserve their ways of life.

In the 14th century in western Europe, the political life in the villages changed dramatically. In that century, plague swept through western Europe, leaving a disabling shortage of labor. Desperate lords tried to increase their customary—and already excessive—labor requirements in an effort to farm their lands. Peasants all over western Europe revolted in waves of violence. In France, the Jacquerie (the name of the peasant revolt) was particularly violent, with reports of even cannibalism circulating as angry peasants stormed the manor houses of those they believed had repressed them. In time, all the revolts were suppressed, with many peasants and their leaders massacred. Yet the violence, the labor shortages, and the prevailing belief that things were changing had begun to erode the old manorial system. Over time, peasants who owed only rent gradually replaced serfs who had owed labor. For these new peasants, their labor was now their own, giving them more freedom and opportunities to work for their own profit. The medieval rural social structure was changed, and the modern world of the peasantry was introduced in western Europe. The rest of the world would take longer to free rural country workers.

~Joyce E. Salisbury

FOR MORE INFORMATION

Hilton, R. *Bond Men Made Free*. New York: Methuen, 1973.

Potter, J. M., M. N. Diaz, and G. M. Foster. *Peasant Society: A Reader*. Boston, Mass.: Little, Brown, 1967.

EUROPE

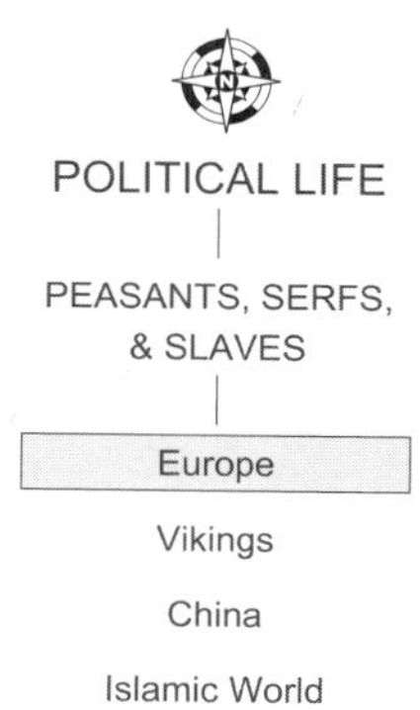

The rural inhabitants of medieval Europe had varying degrees of freedom, based on tradition and old contracts. All, however, shared in the manorial system in which they owed labor and/or rents to noble landlords who ruled. By the High Middle Ages, it was no longer considered appropriate for Christians to own other Christians as slaves, and true slavery persisted only at the margins of Europe where Christians were in contact with non-Christian societies.

Most of the medieval rural workers were serfs (known in England by the term *villein*). The institution of serfdom had some of its roots in the older practice of slavery, and the serf's status was in some ways akin to that of a slave. Serfdom, however, had been shaped by centuries of customs that tended to ease some of the serf's disadvantages, so they were not slaves. Serfs were personally free but were bound by obligations they owed their lords. Serfs owed services to their lord, but these were limited by custom. A serf could be bought and sold, but the buyer acquired only the lord's traditional rights over the serf, not complete ownership. A serf's personal property in theory belonged to the lord, but in practice lords only collected traditional rents, fees, and fines from their serfs.

The obligations placed on villeins depended on local tradition, but most of them were designed to ensure that the manor lord had control over his labor supply. Villeins were forbidden to depart from the manor without the lord's permission; this permission could usually be acquired by payment of *chevage*, an annual fee exacted for permission to dwell outside of the manor. Fees also had to be paid for a girl to marry someone not belonging to the manor or for a boy to enter the clergy. Local custom might place additional impositions on villeins. In one English manor, for example, custom stated that a villein could not "give his son or daughter in marriage or sell a cow that has calved nor a plucked male pullet . . . without permission of his lord. And whenever he brews he must pay one penny" (Singman, 73). In principle, a villein held his land at his lord's pleasure and might be turned out at will, but over the centuries it had become customary to treat the landholding as heritable property.

Villeins were forbidden to depart from the manor without the lord's permission.

The rent for a villein's land was principally in the form of labor services owed to the lord, which the lord used to farm his own lands (called the "demesne"). The services owed depended on the customs associated with the landholding, but the customs recorded for Richard East in England in 1298 were typical:

> He will plow and harrow at his own expense a fourth of an acre. And throughout the year he will work every second day, either carrying or mowing or reaping or carting, or doing some other work according as the lord or his bailiff commands him, except on Saturdays and major church holidays. And at harvest time he will find two men to reap for two days for the customary additional work at his own cost, that is two men on each day. And at the end of harvest time he will reap with one man for the whole day at his own cost. (Singman, 74)

The ordinary weekly work requirement came out to approximately two days. This labor also entailed obligations on the lord's part, as an English contract explains:

> All the aforesaid villeins at the end of mowing will have sixpence for beer and a loaf of bread apiece. And he must provide three bushels of wheat for the aforesaid bread. And each of the aforementioned mowers will have one small bundle of hay each evening, as much as he can mow with his scythe. (Singman, 74)

A free peasant was not subject to the various obligations and restrictions imposed on the villein, but his economic status was not necessarily better. Some free peasants were tenants of freehold land. The freeholding was fully heritable: when the holder died or chose to relinquish the holding, the right to occupy it passed on to his heirs. The tenant of a freehold might even sell the holding, transferring the tenancy to the buyer, provided he had the lord's consent. The tenant paid a fixed rent, generally in cash or in kind, although some freeholdings had minor labor services attached to them. The rent varied substantially: some tenants paid under a shilling an acre, others over two shillings. Freeholdings were not necessarily more valuable than unfree land. Freeholdings tended to be polarized between larger holdings that offered significant prospects for financial advancement and small ones that were insufficient to support a family. Small freeholders, like villein cottagers, had to hire themselves out as laborers to make up the shortfall; such free peasants were generally at an economic disadvantage relative to the substantial villein landholder, and if they leased a holding that traditionally had been a villein tenement, they ran the risk of being reclassified as villeins themselves.

The position of a peasant in the community had more to do with his economic status than with his standing as a villein or freeman. One of the principal determinants was the size of the landholding. The landholding required to support a household depended on the quality of the land and the size of the family. Roughly speaking, a holding of about 10 to 15 acres was sufficient to support a household. It might produce a surplus in good years but could fall short if the harvest was bad. Such subsistence farmers may have constituted about a quarter to a half of agricultural landholders, and a higher proportion among landholding villeins. Peasants who held about 20 acres or more could regularly produce a surplus and achieve a fairly high standard of living relative to their neighbors, with prospects of economic advancement if they invested their earnings well. Perhaps a fifth of landholding peasants fell into this category, with a tiny proportion holding over 40 or even over 60 acres of land. Most of these very prosperous peasants tended to be freeholders, who had greater flexibility in making their investments. At the bottom end of the scale, a holding of about five acres or less was insufficient to support a family, and peasants in this position worked as part- or full-time laborers. Both free peasants and villeins were in this class.

Although serfs were not necessarily subject to the kinds of social or economic disadvantages that plagued ancient slaves, they nonetheless perceived serfdom as an undesirable state. Numerous court cases of the period document the efforts of individual peasants to prove that they were not serfs, and resentment of serfdom was a factor in the Peasants' Revolt that erupted in England in 1381; one of the principal demands of the rebels was the abolition of serfdom. The revolt was unsuccessful, but social and economic trends were already causing serfdom to decline. In the increasingly monetary economy of the High Middle Ages, many lords and serfs agreed to convert labor services into monetary payments. Some serfs were given their freedom outright, or they purchased it from their lords. As a result, the unfree portion of the population declined over the course of the Middle Ages. In some places in the mid-11th century, serfs may have constituted 90 percent of the peasantry, but by the early 14th century, the figure may have been closer to one-half (Singman, 7–8, 72–76).

To read about peasants and farmers in Elizabethan England, see the England entry in the section "Hierarchy" in chapter 6 ("Political Life") of volume 3; for 18th-century England, see the England entry in the section "Social Structure" in chapter 6 ("Political Life") of volume 4; and for Victorian England, see the England entry in the section "Urban and Rural Environments" in chapter 3 ("Economic Life") of volume 5 of this series.

FOR MORE INFORMATION

Singman, J. L. *Daily Life in Medieval Europe*. Westport, Conn.: Greenwood Press, 1999.

Sweeny, D., ed. *Agriculture in the Middle Ages: Technology, Practice, and Representation*. Philadelphia, Penn.: University of Pennsylvania Press, 1995.

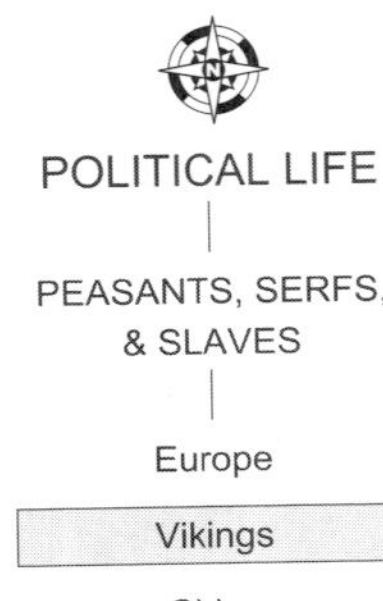

VIKINGS

The early Vikings were clearly preoccupied with social class. Poets and others were sympathetic to the freemen, the farmers, who are mentioned with respect in the sources. The slaves, on the other hand, are portrayed as crude, almost bestial, creatures. Indeed, in Viking Age Scandinavia, the slaves were at the very bottom of the social scale. Slaves had no legal rights whatsoever. They could own nothing and were property, like livestock. It is not uncommon to find a sacrificed slave in a Viking Age grave. Excavations of a 10th-century grave near Stengade on the island of Langeland in Denmark, for example, revealed a wealthy farmer who had been accompanied by a decapitated slave; and in the royal mound of Oseberg in Norway, a noble lady was similarly accompanied by what must have been a young slave woman. Slaves could be purchased and sold and used to pay off debts. The price of a slave varied according to his or her skills, age, health, and looks. They were not protected by law against violent abuse; the laws did not punish owners for injuring or killing their slaves, and if someone injured or killed another man's slave, he had to pay market-value compensation to the slave's owner and not to the slave's relatives. By extension, the owner was accountable for injuries committed by his slave unless the slave had escaped, although for some minor crimes slaves were physically punished.

Some areas of Scandinavia recognized slave marriage, but generally it appears to have had little, if any, legal standing. Children born to slaves belonged to the mother's owners or were split between the mother's and father's owners. Because slavery was hereditary, the children of slaves also became slaves. The number of slaves must have increased by the addition of captives once the Viking raids became common, although most of these slaves were sold in European or Eastern markets. The many references to slaves in the literary sources suggest that they were an important segment of society. Unfortunately, archaeology can tell us nothing about their numbers and very little about their living conditions. Most likely, only the more privileged had slaves on their estates, where they were members of the household. Most likely, they did more or less the same work as family members or hired laborers and served in a variety of capacities, including that of cook, cleaner, washerwoman, farmhand, craftsman, messenger, and companion. The more unpleasant types of work, such as dunging fields, herding pigs, and digging peat, were probably reserved for slaves. It is also possible that slave labor was used in such large construction or building projects as Danevirke and the circular fortresses.

Occasionally, slaves were freed by their owners. A rune stone from Horning in Jutland, Denmark, was raised by a freed slave. In the inscription, the freed slave, Toki, acknowledges his gratitude to his master, who not only set him free but evidently also helped him financially to get established as a smith.

Slaves could also purchase their own or their relatives' freedom. Most of the freed slaves, who had lower status than the fully free, probably lived as cottagers or as landless farm workers or servants for their former owners.

~*Kirsten Wolf*

FOR MORE INFORMATION

Logan, D. F. *Vikings in History*. New York: Routledge, Chapman, and Hall, 1992.
Wolf, K. *Daily Life of the Vikings*. Westport, Conn.: Greenwood Press, forthcoming.

CHINA

All Chinese dynasties regarded farming as the fundamental occupation, and rightly so since the economy was overwhelmingly agrarian. Farmers and their families constituted 80 to 90 percent of the population. The government relied on them to produce the revenues that enriched the royal treasury, supported the nobility, supplied salaries for officials, maintained armies, and funded public works, among other things. Consequently, during the early Tang, the state took steps to ensure a minimum standard of living for the peasants and to bind them to their land. The latter required registration of the entire rural population. Local officials revised the registers every third year, taking a sort of census, to make sure that farmers still occupied their assigned plots. From the registers, they then compiled tax rolls.

Adult males of rural households grew grain in their fields: wheat, barley, and millet in the relatively dry north and rice in the wet south. They also raised vegetables as well as domestic animals, especially pigs, cattle, and chickens. In addition, the men hunted and fished to augment their diets. The Tang law code permitted private citizens to possess bows, arrows, swords, shields, and short spears. If the peasant had enough money to buy or the skill to manufacture them, he could supply himself with the tools for bagging game. There was a division of labor in farming families. The wives and daughters were responsible for weaving textiles. That task required them to process plant fibers and draw out silk from the cocoons of silkworms.

The peasant suffered from a large number of afflictions, both natural and man-made. Natural disasters were the worst. Floods as deep as 40 feet inundated as many as 60 prefectures, or one-sixth of the empire. Some destroyed as many as 10,000 homes, forcing people to live on boats or nest in trees. They drowned thousands and laid waste to crops and farmland. Droughts struck as often as four years in a row. The government undertook measures to relieve the distress of the peasants. It had a system of granaries situated at strategic sites throughout the empire. The granaries collected about three-and-a-half bushels of grain from each landholder annually. When a natural disaster struck, causing famine, officials distributed the stored cereals to the starving population in the affected region.

Peasants also suffered greatly at the hands of their fellow men. There were large displacements of population in the north because the wars with the Khitan and Turks during Empress Wu's reign and the rebellion of An Lushan had devastated farmlands. Peasants also deserted their fields and fled to evade compulsory labor and conscription. Even when it involved public works, such as constructing dikes or repairing roads, that the farmer might benefit from, forced labor took him away from his land and family for extended periods. Conscription into the army was even more terrible because the term of service was three years, it might mean serving far from home on the frontiers, and it involved the risk of injury or death.

War and compulsory labor were not the only banes of the peasant's existence. Aristocrats, mandarins (both those in the capital and in the provinces), and eunuchs, as well as military governors, army officers, and merchants, were major sources of misery for free farmers. Beginning in the second half of the 7th century, powerful families, especially those in the region around Changan, built landed estates at the expense of independent peasants. Under such difficult circumstances, the peasant had two options. First, he could stay where he was and become a tenant farmer or agricultural laborer. That was not an appealing alternative. Tenant farmers, as many as two hundred families on a single estate, constituted the bulk of the landowner's labor force. The tenant paid half of the crops that he harvested as rent to the landowner, a sum much larger than the taxes he would have paid to the government had he been free. In addition, when the estate supplied him seed and food, it expected repayment and charged him a high rate of interest. It also imposed levies on other commodities, such as textiles, that he produced. Finally, the landowner required him to perform labor services, such as constructing or repairing walls, bridges, and buildings.

The peasant's second option was flight. Although that choice involved a certain amount of hardship initially—leaving one's ancestral home was excruciating, and traveling was hazardous—the peasant was better off in the end. The south was the preferred destination because there were still extensive regions of rich land that had not been occupied.

At the bottom of society were the slaves. There were two types: official and private. The imperial court and the government acquired official slaves from several sources. During the early years of the Tang, large numbers of slaves were foreign soldiers and civilians captured in victorious campaigns that Tang armies conducted in Korea, Inner Mongolia, central Asia, and northern India. The second source came from family members of men sentenced to death for rebellion and sedition. The court confined the womenfolk of the condemned in the Flank Court, the western section of the central palace within the walls of Changan, and called them palace ladies. This no doubt accounts for the enormous size—40,000 women—of Emperor Illustrious August's harem. The third source of official slaves was foreign tribute, the obligation that monarchs and chieftains of subject states or tribes owed the Chinese emperor, who was their liege lord. Those gifts included skilled artists and entertainers.

Private slaves were supplied by merchants to wealthy customers for a price. Most of their human traffic were foreigners or aboriginal peoples living in the southern districts of China. The foreigners included Turks from the northwest, who were prized for their abilities to ride horses and handle livestock; Persians captured by Chinese pirates in the southeast; and Korean women, whose beauty made them a popular commodity in the households of the well-to-do. It had been taboo since ancient times to sell Chinese, and the Tang law code imposed a stiff penalty for doing so. Kidnapping a person to sell as a slave was a capital offense requiring execution by strangulation.

This law applied, however, only to those who were enslaved against their will. Chinese debtors and tenant farmers who could not meet their obligations sold themselves or their sons for fixed periods, even for life, to relieve themselves of their burdens. Furthermore, the law did not apply to aborigines living in the southern prefectures of the empire. Those regions supplied the largest number of slaves in the Tang. Traders considered the native inhabitants of those regions to be barbarians, beyond the pale of Chinese civilization, and therefore not subject to the law prohibiting their abduction and sale. Neither the emperor nor local officials could stop the trade.

Slaves in the Tang, as elsewhere, were property. The Tang law code accorded them a status equal to that of domestic animals and inanimate possessions. Consequently, if a man abducted another man's slave, it prescribed a severe punishment of exile to the distant reaches of the empire. The same rule applied to someone who caught a runaway slave and failed to turn him in to the authorities within five days (Benn, 32–36, 38–40).

To read about government and society in 19th-century China, see the China entry in the section "Government and Politics" in chapter 6 ("Political Life") of volume 5 of this series.

FOR MORE INFORMATION

Benn, C. *Daily Life in Traditional China: The Tang Dynasty*. Westport, Conn.: Greenwood Press, 2002.

Creel, H. G. *The Birth of China*. New York: Ungar Publishing, 1937.

ISLAMIC WORLD

One of the remarkable features of the medieval Muslim world was the use of slaves as elite soldiers, called mamluks. It is in the early 9th century as well that we see the establishment of the mamluk institution as a means of recruiting and training elite cavalry units, largely comprised of mounted archers who had been enslaved as young boys and raised to the profession of arms.

The ʿAbbasid caliph al-Muʿtasim (r. 833–42) is credited with establishing the first effective mamluk corps. Al-Muʿtasim's predominantly Turkish mamluk troops represented a major change in the ʿAbbasid military structure. No longer would the military be composed largely of men who could trace their lineage back to the Arabian Peninsula. Rather, it would increasingly be the preserve of ethnic minorities—Turks, Berbers, Armenians, Daylamis, and others recruited from the fringes of the empire. Al-Muʿtasim even built a new city—Samarra—to house his new troops. Located some 80 mile north of Baghdad on the Tigris, Samarra served as the ʿAbbasid capital through the late 9th century.

Although *mamluk* is an Arabic word that means "one who is owned," it is almost always used as a technical term for a particular type of military slavery designed to produce an elite force of mounted warriors. *ʿAbd* and *khadim* are the words generally used to describe field hands and domestic servants, images of slavery and servitude that more closely resemble the history of slavery in the agrarian slave societies of the southern United States. In fact, there is plenty of evidence that the kinds of abuses that one equates with slavery in the United States were inflicted on field hands and domestic servants in Islamic history as well. In the medieval Islamic world, however, having been enslaved as a young boy and raised to the profession of arms was anything but degrading. In fact, mamluks served in a number of important offices on behalf of the ruler—personal attendants, cup bearers, equerries, falconers, and even provincial governors. Moreover, being a mamluk was a position of privilege that opened the door to many avenues of wealth and position in society, even to the highest offices in the regime. It appears that in the 9th through the 11th centuries, it was not required for mamluks who rose to such high positions to be freed. Thereafter, it was much more common that they were.

While some were incorporated into mamluk regiments as adults, the preferred route was to purchase boys and to train them in barracks apart from the rest of society in the sciences of horsemanship, warfare, and religion. According to Islamic law, a free person could only be enslaved if he were a non-Muslim and resided outside the Abode of Islam; that is, in the Abode of War. Hence military slaves were recruited from just about every group along the frontiers of the Abode of Islam—sub-Saharan Africans, eastern Europeans, Greeks, Armenians, Circassians, Indians, and so on. However, the preferred practice was to purchase boys from the slave markets along the central Asian frontier north of the Oxus River.

To increase their supply of slaves, caliphs undertook policy that was a dramatic departure from the traditional practice of slave procurement. That is, they levied a rather peculiar tax on their Balkan Christian subjects in the form of children. This tax, called the *Devshirme*, produced the elite janissary corps as well as so many high government officials in the Ottoman regime that there are instances in which Muslim families in the Balkans presented their own children as Christians so that they too might benefit from such prestigious and lucrative opportunities.

From the outset, purchasing Turkish boys had at least three advantages for their owners. First, given the high rates of infant mortality in the prevaccination age of the medieval Islamic world, to purchase children at a younger age was simply a bad investment. However, once a boy reached age 10 to 12 or so, had survived his childhood diseases, and had built up considerable immunities, he was more than likely to live a relatively long and healthy life. Second, because they were taken from their families and homes at such a young age, they were still quite amenable to the kind of training designed to produce an elite force of mounted warriors with a high level of esprit de corps and intense loyalty to their commander. Finally, it was a commonplace at the time that Turks were by nature tough and loyal, but also superior horsemen and archers. Therefore, because the goal was to produce elite mounted warriors, purchasing Turkish boys who already were quite skilled in horsemanship and archery by the time they were 10 to 12 years old was an intuitively obvious choice and certainly saved a great deal of effort and expense with respect to basic training in the necessary skills.

Muslim slave traders. This 13th-century manuscript shows merchants at a slave market in southern Arabia dealing in black slaves captured in sub-Saharan Africa. Art Resource, NY.

Modern anthropologists have demonstrated quite convincingly that the kind of racial and ethnic theories so common in the premodern world have no basis in actual science. Nevertheless, such views were common about most groups in the medieval Islamic world. The prolific 9th-century author al-Jahiz (777–869) wrote a number of such essays. In his essay "The Merits of the Turks and of the Imperial Army as a Whole," al-Jahiz writes, among other things, that al-Mu'tasim knew what he was doing when he recruited Turks because Turks have four eyes (two in front and two in back), are expert with a lasso, are inveterate hunters, are skilled at veterinary science, can withstand extreme weather conditions, and are superb archers who can shoot their arrows while their horses race at full gallop in any direction. In addition, "the Turk is at one and the same time herdsman, groom, trainer, horse-dealer, farrier and rider: in short, a one-man team." Turks also carry two or three bows and everything they might need on their horses, can ride for days, sleep in the saddle, change mounts at a full gallop, and over the course of their lifetimes spend more time in the saddle than with their feet on the ground. According to al-Jahiz, the Turks are to warfare what the Greeks are to philosophy and the Chinese to craftsmanship (al-Jahiz, 91–97).

Of course, al-Jahiz is engaging in a bit of hyperbole here—at least the part about the four eyes. But his essay conveys very eloquently the dominant sentiment that there was no better horseman than a Turk. Because horse societies did not exist in sub-Saharan Africa, the military slaves recruited there for the North African regimes tended to serve as infantry and were referred to as *'abid;* mamluk was a term reserved for cavalry.

Mamluks frequently referred to their *ustadh*—commander-trainer—as father, and it was not unusual for an *ustadh* to feel a bond of kinship with his mamluks and make them his heirs. Even when manumitted, the mamluk's loyalty to his *ustadh* remained strong; despite his manumission, he remained a part of the *ustadh*'s family. In addition to the sciences of warfare, the mamluks were taught the sciences of the Islamic religion. Many learned to speak Arabic; some even learned to read and write it as well. One of the clear strengths of the mamluk system was that it produced superb cavalry forces who were intensely loyal to one another as well as to their *ustadh*.

However, this strength also proved to be a weakness in large part because the loyalty that mamluks felt toward their *ustadh* did not always transfer to his sons upon the *ustadh*'s death; for while it was the *ustadh* who made the mamluks, in many fundamental ways it was the mamluks who made the son. An early and dramatic example of this occurred when some of the 'Abbasid Turkish troops assassinated the

ʻAbbasid caliph al-Mutawakkil in December 861 because they felt that their positions of privilege under al-Mutawakkil's predecessors were threatened.

To read about political and social structures in the Islamic world in the 19th century, see the Islamic World entries in the sections "Empire" and "Reform Movements" in chapter 6 ("Political Life") of volume 5; and for the 20th century, see the Islamic World entries in the sections "Government" and "Reform" in chapter 6 ("Political Life") of volume 6 of this series.

~*James Lindsay*

FOR MORE INFORMATION

al-Jahiz. *The Life and Works of al-Jahiz*. Translated by C. Pellat. Berkeley: University of California Press, 1969.

Lindsay, J. *Daily Life in Medieval Islam*. Westport, Conn.: Greenwood Press, forthcoming.

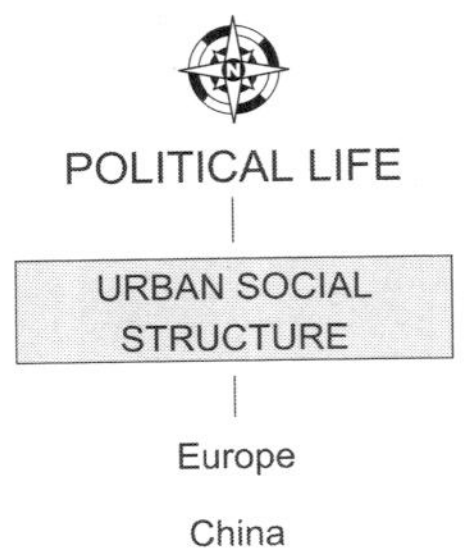

Urban Social Structure

In the political life of the medieval centuries, cities posed particular problems. They did not neatly fit into political structures that had been developed to govern vast tracts of rural inhabitants who supported a military elite. This was true to some degree all over Eurasia. There were two kinds of cities in this large zone—administrative and commercial centers—and each developed its own kind of governance structure and social stratification.

Most of the cities in western Europe began as commercial centers. Men and women in these towns had little in common with the feudal society that surrounded it, as they were islands of relative freedom in a world in which each person was tied to someone else. To escape the many requirements imposed on village serfs, towns negotiated charters with the lords on whose land the town stood. These charters granted townspeople freedom from labor obligations and freedom to travel at will. They also protected the growing town profits from unreasonable taxation and seizure, and some charters allowed the towns to run their own law courts. Cash-strapped landlords were willing to grant these privileges to towns in return for money. Thus, these commercial centers were independent islands within the feudal structure.

Within the commercial cities, townspeople had to develop structures with which to govern themselves. Many townspeople (who came to be called "burgers" or "bourgeoisie") joined together in sworn associations called "communes" to govern themselves. The communes elected their own officials, regulated taxation within the town, and generally conducted the business of running the urban centers. The communes were not democratic because people accepted as natural the principle that the wealthy should conduct the people's business, and thus the wealthiest merchants took the offices of mayor or the equivalent post.

As the major business of these commercial towns was trade, merchants and craftsmen formed organizations called guilds to protect their own interests and control the manufacturing in the town. These guilds represented the various trades—goldsmiths, bread makers, weavers, and such—and the guild members decided on their own membership, regulated prices, and ensured quality control.

Cities in the Byzantine, Muslim, and Chinese empires were not as free. Most of these cities were established by royal patronage as administrative centers, so rulers had more of a direct stake in the politics of the towns. All cities in China were seats of government administration, so the bureaucrats had high status, and the merchants never gained the control they did in the West. In fact, merchants were considered to be on the lowest rung of the social hierarchy.

The Muslim cities, by contrast, favored merchants and proudly allowed them to feature their wares in the center of the city—even administrative cities. Nevertheless, the caliphs never let anyone forget who was in charge. See also in this volume, chapter 3 ("Economic Life"), sections "Urban Economic Life" and "Great Cities."

~*Joyce E. Salisbury*

EUROPE

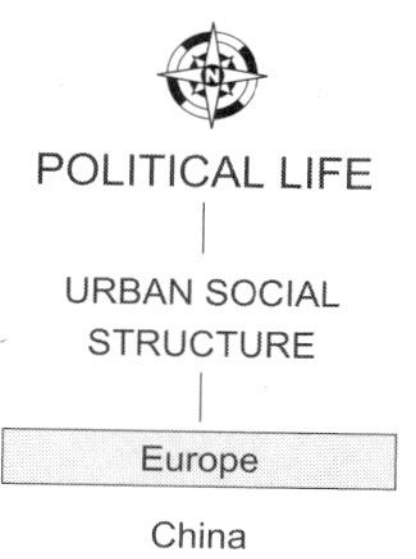

Urban life in Europe slowly reestablished itself over the course of the early Middle Ages. By 1200, cities and towns were numerous and prospering, and although the number of city dwellers was small in relation to the population at large—probably no more than 10 percent at any time in the Middle Ages—the towns wielded social and cultural influence well beyond their size. These medieval towns were outside the standard medieval social organization and thus developed their own social structures. While still dominated by stratification (like all of medieval society), towns nevertheless offered more freedoms and room for individual initiative than other parts of society.

One of the features of urban life was a diversity of population that was not present in rural areas; townspeople moved about. Urban populations were boosted by immigration from neighboring rural areas or, in the case of larger towns, from various countries. Immigration was stimulated by various economic forces. The 11th and 12th centuries were a period of rapid growth in the rural population. As the rural population grew, opportunities shrank, prompting many to seek their fortunes in the towns. The consequent growth in town populations in turn spurred immigration from smaller towns to major cities such as Paris and London. Urban centers, for their part, were a rich market for the surplus population of the country. Poor urban living conditions kept the death rate above the birth rate, so that the medieval town was perennially unable to maintain its numbers without constant immigration.

Immigration to a town offered particular advantages for serfs. According to a custom widely observed from the 12th century onward, anyone who lived in a town for a year and a day became free. Even if a serf's lord caught up with him within that time, the lord still had to prove the serf's status before he could be returned. It was also possible for a serf to live in a town with his lord's permission. Although this arrangement did not lead directly to freedom, it might in time loosen the manorial bond.

Urban populations were rising significantly in the 12th and 13th centuries, reflecting the new dynamism of town life. In 1100, the largest Western cities, with populations generally numbering around 25,000, were mostly in the south. These included Florence, Genoa, Milan, Venice, Padua, Bologna, Naples, and Palermo in Italy and Barcelona, Cordova, Seville, and Granada in Spain. London at the time had only about 10,000 inhabitants. By the early 14th century, the population in all of these towns was upward of 50,000, and Milan had reached 100,000 (Singman, 174).

At the low end of urban development was the ordinary market town, consisting of a cluster of houses grouped in a few dirt streets. The smallest of these towns might have fewer than 500 inhabitants, making them less populous than the largest villages. Such a town was distinguished from a village not by its size but by its facilities. The town would have a large open area that served as a marketplace, as well as a range of tradesmen's shops not represented in a village. In many cases, there were also establishments catering to travelers.

Although town dwellers were usually free commoners by definition, their society was highly stratified. At the top were the wealthy and powerful who dominated city politics. Some of these were great merchants, men whose fortunes were made by major commercial enterprises. Others were important administrative officials who derived their power from the feudal or ecclesiastical hierarchy. The elite in a town might also include resident aristocrats, particularly in Italy and Spain, where many of the aristocracy had their primary homes in the town.

The middle layer of the urban hierarchy consisted of independent heads of smaller commercial establishments. Some were artisans, producing manufactured goods for sale to local buyers—whether from within the town or from the hinterland—or for export to other urban centers. Others were tradesmen such as lesser merchants, food sellers, and tavern keepers. People at this level were considered citizens of the town, with commercial privileges and usually some degree of participation in municipal government. They enjoyed a reasonable measure of comfort and security and possessed the means to support themselves, but they were still far below the opulence of the upper stratum and lacked the substantial capital and political influence that made the fortunes of the urban upper classes. The middle and upper echelons of urban society required the labor of a lower stratum of hired staff. Some of these might be fairly prosperous themselves, if they were well-placed functionaries in the pay of the upper classes. Among those who worked for the middle layer of urban society, the most fortunate were the journeymen and apprentices. Apprentices were usually teenagers, placed in service to a master for a certain term of years in order to learn a trade. On completion of their apprenticeship, they became journeymen, entitled to sell their services to any master, typically for a daily wage (in French, *journée*, day). The journeyman might in principle achieve economic independence because, as a fully qualified practitioner of his trade, he could eventually set up his own shop. In practice, opportunities were limited by the journeyman's access to capital and working facilities, and unless he was heir to an established tradesman, he might well spend his working life in the employ of others. Not every employee had even these prospects for social and economic advancement.

In addition to the skilled labor represented by journeymen and apprentices, a town drew on a pool of unskilled workers employed as day laborers and servants. This class constituted a majority of the population in a medieval town, and in an age when labor was cheap and plentiful, such people led a hand-to-mouth existence, with minimal employment security and little surplus income to make provision against unemployment, disability, or old age. Some would be household servants and chambermaids assigned such tasks as waiting on the family, cooking the food, and maintaining the home. Others would be hired hands in shops.

At the lower end, the laborers shaded into the class of the chronically poor—the unemployed, the underemployed, and the unemployable. Many of the poor were dependent on charity. The most fortunate might a find a place in one of the town's charitable foundations, generally administered as religious institutions on behalf of lay founders. Yet even the numerous charitable houses of cities such as Paris were insufficient to address the needs of the poor. Many who did not find places in charitable establishments lived by begging. Those who were not obviously disabled were unlikely to receive charity at all, since alms were generally reserved for those who lacked the capacity to support themselves, such as orphans, widows, the elderly, the handicapped, and the infirm. In an age when rural populations far exceeded the opportunities for rural labor, the surplus gravitated toward the more fluid economy of the town, but many of them found insufficient work even there and ultimately contributed instead to urban crime (Singman, 171–76).

FOR MORE INFORMATION

Lilley, K. D. *Urban Life in the Middle Ages*. New York: Palgrave, 2002.
Singman, J. L. *Daily Life in Medieval Europe*. Westport, Conn.: Greenwood Press, 1999.

CHINA

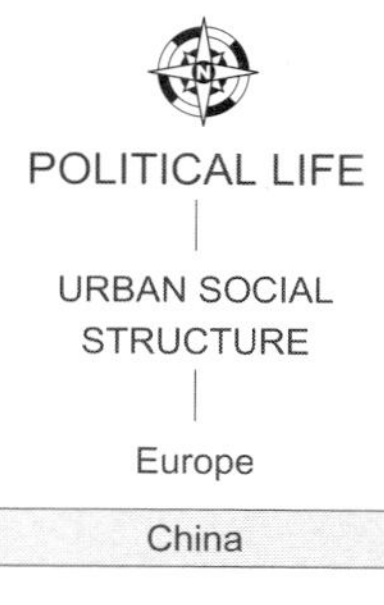

The word for "city" in Chinese literally means "walls and markets," an adequate if somewhat minimal definition of a traditional urban settlement. All cities in Tang China theoretically had ramparts and bazaars. Officially, according to the census of 754, there were 1,859 cities—321 prefectures and 1,538 counties—throughout the empire. The actual figure was somewhat smaller because prefectures were also the seats for some counties. A number of the prefectures and counties were located in poor backwaters that had neither the resources to afford nor the strategic value to justify the construction of outer walls. They also had populations too small to warrant labeling them "cities." Those settlements had bamboo fences or palisades instead of walls.

All cities—capitals, prefectures, and counties—were seats of government administration. Commerce, industry, transportation, and communication were important but secondary facets of their character. Cities never enjoyed any significant autonomy from the central government. Nor were they independent from the countryside that surrounded them. The figures for populations of county seats included both the citizens within their walls and the inhabitants of the villages within their jurisdictions, and most Chinese in ancient times thought of themselves as residents of villages or urban wards where their families originated, and where their ancestral graveyards were situated in the adjacent countryside. City walls were purely defensive; they did not serve as rigid boundaries between the rural and the urban.

Aside from slaves and vagrants, the classes most subject to discrimination in the Tang were artisans and merchants, especially the latter. The basis for the prejudice against merchants on the part of the state, officials, and intellectuals was that traders were "leeches" who produced nothing. They lived off the surplus that the peasantry generated by dint of its hard labor. Furthermore, their pursuit of wealth was contrary to conventional ethics that frowned on materialism. Finally, their wandering lifestyle made it difficult for the government to control them. For those reasons, merchants and artisans—the latter was grouped with merchants because, although they were producers, they sold their wares for profit—occupied the lowest rung in the traditional hierarchy of classes. The government and the upper classes accepted them only because they were necessary for the operation of the economy.

Because of that bias, the government enacted statutes that discriminated against merchants and artisans. The law prohibited them from having dealings with officials and banned the upper echelons of the bureaucracy from entering urban markets. It forbade merchants and artisans to sit for civil service examinations and therefore to hold public office. They had no access to political power. The state did not allocate land to them except in regions where there were vacant tracts, and even then it allowed them to occupy only half of the amount that it normally granted to peasants. It also forbade them to ride horses.

Despite the discrimination and exploitation, some merchants made immense fortunes. In 734, when the state confiscated the property of a merchant living in Changan, his fortune amounted to 600 million coppers. The government took a similar action against another merchant residing in a city on the Grand Canal in the early 9th century and seized 10 billion coppers from him. Those men were among the tycoons, a very small number of traders. There was a host of small vendors and peddlers who eked out a hard living with little return and never struck it rich.

In the late 8th century, aristocrats and officials who had previously been reluctant to sully themselves with mercantile activities openly engaged in commerce. By 780, they had set up shops to trade commodities in Yangzhou, the great center of commerce and industry. At the time, military governors and inspector generals in the south also got involved in establishing businesses. Under the guise of making money for their armies, they actually made a profit for themselves. By 831, even soldiers had established shops along the avenues of Changan.

In the same period that some officials were becoming merchants, some merchants were becoming officials. Although still despised by the upper classes, merchants were indispensable for producing revenue at a time when older sources, especially land taxes, were drying up. In their ceaseless search for funds, local governors, warlords, and others sought out merchants and employed them because they had the talent to make money. Even the central government was not above using them. Furthermore, although a merchant might not take civil service examinations, it appears that by 803 large numbers of their sons were doing so, and also occupying most of the seats in the state colleges at the capitals.

The lowest inhabitants of cities were the impoverished, who lived wherever they could find shelter and sought sustenance by begging from those better off than themselves. An impoverished woman and her father sang songs in the streets of wards to eke out a living. A general was so smitten with her voice that he took her as one of his private entertainers. Not all panhandlers were human. A clever artisan who was in charge of the imperial factories once carved a Buddhist monk from wood and placed it in the market of a provincial city. The automaton carried a bowl in its hand, was able to move on its own, and begged for money. When its bowl was full of coppers, a mechanized bolt abruptly shot out, locking the coins in the dish so that no one could filch them. The wooden monk could speak on its own and say "Alms." The market folk flocked to see the spectacle. Because they wanted the automaton to speak, the donations made to watch it perform filled the bowl several thousand times each day.

Emperors were not happy to have derelicts roaming the streets of the capitals. They considered the cities to be their own special domiciles. In 734, the throne banned beggars from the streets of the metropolises and consigned them to the wards for the sick, Buddhist foundations that cared for the ill, aged, orphaned, and poor. The government oversaw the wards, and capital officials provided the money for their maintenance from their own funds. In 738, the emperor also assigned revenues from newly opened fields near Changan for the relief of the poor and of commoners who had returned to their lands after fleeing (Benn, 36–38, 45–46, 58).

FOR MORE INFORMATION

Benn, C. *Daily Life in Traditional China: The Tang Dynasty.* Westport, Conn.: Greenwood Press, 2002.

Creel, H. G. *The Birth of China.* New York: Ungar Publishing, 1937.

Law

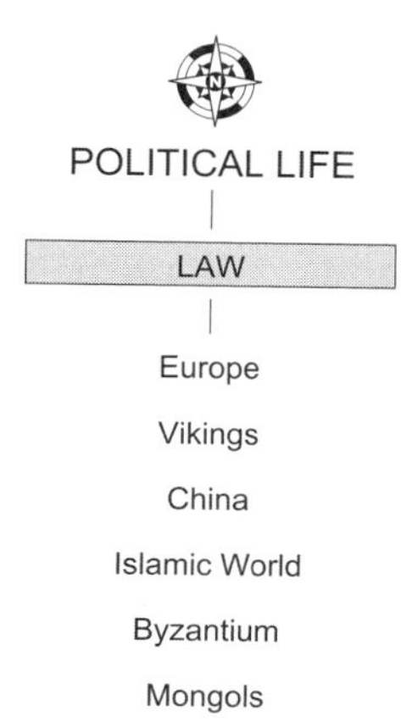

All the peoples of the Middle Ages governed themselves within a strong legal framework. Within that framework, however, there were a number of different opinions about what the law actually was and what it was trying to achieve. For example, Byzantium looked back to Roman legal traditions and believed that there was an abstract justice and that the law and lawyers were to strive to achieve this abstract justice. As Justinian's code claimed: "Justice is the constant and perpetual wish to render every one his due. Jurisprudence is the . . . science of the just and the unjust" (Sandars, 7). This legal concept approximates the modern American view of law with the idea that there is justice and that each of us deserves it. (Whether we get it or not is another question.) However, in the Middle Ages there were other concepts of law. The Muslims believed that law was based on the Qur'an and the interpretations of God's law within it. This idea of law as God's continues to inform Muslim legal traditions.

The Germanic law codes and the Chinese law codes placed society above either the individual or any abstract concept of law. The Germanic tribes and the Vikings that followed them were more interested in determining the worth of the individual hurt or killed (the *wergild*) and restoring that worth to society than they were in deciding who was at fault. So, they did not question who started a fight, for example, but they wanted to know how much to pay the damaged man. The Chinese code organized "Ten Abominations," which forbade antisocial actions from offending the emperor, the state, or families. Again, the issue here was whether society had been damaged, not whether the individual should be protected. The Mongol laws that emerged in the 13th century show a borrowing from many places—from Islamic law to Chinese law to ancient Mongol tribal traditions.

Whatever the source of law, societies had to deal with those who broke the law. The investigative procedures differed dramatically among the groups. During the Middle Ages, people looked to old Germanic principles to ascertain guilt and innocence. For example, they used the practice of compurgation, in which people would testify to the worth of the person charged, even if the witnesses had no knowledge of the crime (much like "character witnesses" in the American legal system). When this was not enough, medieval investigators might turn to "trial by ordeal," in which they believed God decided the case. A person charged with a crime might have to do battle to prove his innocence, or pick up a hot poker in his bare hand and see if the resulting wound festered. The Chinese used more modern means of investigation—interrogating accusers or suspects and try to determine who might be lying. The Chinese and the European Inquisition (the church court charged with investigating religious beliefs) institutionalized the use of torture to ascertain the truth.

Finally, societies had to decide on punishments for the guilty. Most lenient were the early Europeans who were willing to take cash payments in return for even murder. In the absence of payment, they relied on exile to remove criminals from their midst. (Long-term imprisonment was very rare and used for aristocratic political prisoners more than anyone else.)

Most societies of the Middle Ages—including the Europeans by the 11th century—used harsh and public punishments. They believed both would serve as deterrents for other would-be criminals. The Chinese and the Muslims regularly administered public beatings, and all groups administered public executions. The executions could take gruesome forms—for example, Europeans used "drawing and quartering," in which the condemned's intestines were pulled out and burned while the poor prisoner still lived, and then his body was cut into four parts (quartered). The Mongols, too, used horrible means of execution to deter others. The decapitated heads of executed prisoners were regularly displayed in public to warn people of the consequences of crime.

Societies today face the same problems as those of the Middle Ages. All have to decide what the laws of the land should be, and what principles should be protected. Then, inevitably, some will break the laws, and societies have to decide what to do about the criminals. There has been no good solution for crime and punishment in the past, and societies can only hope to do better in the future.

~Joyce E. Salisbury

FOR MORE INFORMATION

Sandars, T. C. *The Institutes of Justinian*. London: Longmans, Green, 1874.

EUROPE

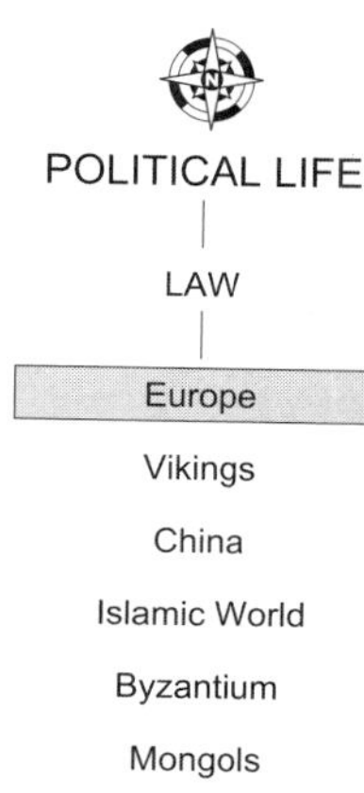

Medieval Europe inherited two different, but both strong, traditions of law. As Germanic tribes settled in the old Roman Empire, they confronted the long tradition of written Roman laws, which forms one of the pillars of modern legal theory. Romans—and their lawyers—envisioned an idea of abstract justice, and written law codes were supposed to implement these abstract notions of justice. Through their long history, Romans had accumulated a whole body of laws and legal opinions that formed precedent for subsequent legal ideas.

The Germanic tribes had their own unwritten traditions of law. Laws were not legislated by king or council but instead were considered as customs of the past enforced by individuals and their families. Laws were thought of as traditions that helped preserve the families, clans, and tribes and keep them intact in the face of violent intrusions into their peace.

When disputes arose, instead of appealing to written law codes, leaders of Germanic tribes gathered in assembly to assess the matter. Instead of considering evidence as our modern courts do, these assemblies developed different means of ascertaining the correct outcome. For example, they might consider the character (or value to the community) of the accused, and in a practice called compurgation, 12 honorable men would testify to the character of the accused, even if they had no knowledge of the facts of the matter under discussion. In this case, the decision would likely go in favor of the most valuable member of the community. If compurgation could not resolve the dispute, the assembly might call for a trial by ordeal (the word originally meant "judgment"). In this instance, the disputing parties might engage in a trial by combat, in which case the stronger was considered right. Other kinds of ordeals appealed to the supernatural. For example, an accused might have to pick up a red-hot iron or immerse his hand in boiling water. If the hand healed cleanly, he was innocent; if it festered, he was guilty.

As Germanic tribes began to settle in the old Roman Empire, they at first kept two separate legal traditions: Romans were governed by Roman law, and Germans by Germanic legal traditions. In time, this dual system became unworkable. By the late 5th century, Germanic kings began to codify their people's laws, and they were helped by Roman subjects trained in classical law. These written law codes began the process of blending the two traditions into one. Germanic ideals of compurgation and ordeal became part of the written codes of law.

The heart of ancient Germanic law was the concept of wergild—which means "man-gold." In this system, the value of an individual (or a piece of property) was determined, and when this value was violated (or reduced), then the offending party could make up for the violation by paying a price. This was supposed to reduce the violence in society because it precluded the family of the injured party from taking vengeance, which was dear to the heart of the Germanic tribes. The law codes used the techniques of ordeal and compurgation to determine who should pay the wergild.

The early medieval law codes list a bewildering range of wergild assessments. The Lombard laws (in Italy), for example, give a price for cutting off noses, ears, arms, hands, and fingers and for knocking out teeth (Drew, 62–63). Laws also indicate the price of injury to women, children, animals, and trees in the forest. They even offered a price for such things as insults or watching a woman urinate behind a bush.

Although these law codes that so precisely reveal the details of life in the early Germanic kingdoms may appear strange to us because they put a price on everything from an insult to a toe injury, they were intended to bring peace and order to the kingdoms. Nonetheless, they were only partially successful. Despite efforts by kings to record laws, the 8th and 9th centuries remained an era of rampant lawlessness, largely because these laws were too difficult to enforce. At any time, laws were only as effective as the enforcement mechanisms.

The growth of feudalism with its complicated feudal contracts led to increased emphasis on contract law. Lords owed vassals specific things—for example, maintenance, protection, and "good faith"—and vassals on their part owed their lords specific things: military service, advice, and special payments. Vassals meeting together to give advice to their king led to the growth of parliaments and important modern representative traditions. Disputes about feudal obligations under King John of England in the early 13th century led to a revolt in which the king had to promise that he indeed was bound by the laws of the feudal contract. He was forced to sign the Magna Carta in 1215, in which he promised to adhere to the old agreements. This document forms the core of modern American legal rights. (To memorialize this important legal document the American Bar Association erected a monument at Runnymeade in England where King John signed the Magna Carta.)

The legal situation in medieval Europe became even more complex in the late 11th century as the church began to exert claims for leadership over broad areas of society. Even in the early Middle Ages, church courts claimed jurisdiction over wills as part of their care for widows and orphans, but after the Investiture Controversy, in which popes began to claim jurisdiction over many more areas of life, church law became increasingly influential.

In about 1140, the influential church lawyer Gratian issued his "Decretum," a collection of church law—canon law—that showed that church canons could form as complete a structure of jurisprudence as secular law. This influential collection with its commentaries quickly became accepted as church law. This collection argued that the pope was the supreme judge and legislator, and several subsequent popes were canon lawyers who used the papacy as a supreme court. They argued that the popes had jurisdiction over any religious matter, which for them covered many things, including marriage, contracts, vows (including the important feudal relationships), education, poverty, and almost any area of life. Criminal law, for example, concerned morality, so it was claimed to be in the purview of canon law.

Late in the 12th and early 13th centuries, groups of canon lawyers, called the Decretalists, reconciled old texts with new legislation and continued the growth of canon law. This group formulated complex jurisprudence. This growth of the church as a secular power could not help but generate some controversy.

A monk and a nun are being punished by having to spend time in public restrained in stocks. Thomas Wright, *History of Domestic Manners and Sentiments in England during the Middle Ages,* 1862.

Toward the end of the Middle Ages, kings began to reclaim legal jurisdiction from church courts. Through this process, much of canon law became incorporated into secular law codes. For example, some morality legislation—such as prohibitions of some sexual activities—became part of secular law for the first time. Our legal heritage from medieval Europe shows the complexity of the legal developments that combined sources as disparate as Germanic tribal law, Roman law and canon law.

To read about law and crime in Elizabethan England, see the England entry in the section "Justice and Legal Systems" in chapter 6 ("Political Life") of volume 3; for 18th-century England, see the England entry in the section "Law, Crime, and Punishment" in chapter 6 ("Political Life") of volume 4; and for Victorian England, see the England entry in the section "Law and Crime" in chapter 6 ("Political Life") of volume 5 of this series.

~Joyce E. Salisbury

FOR MORE INFORMATION

Drew, K. F. *The Lombard Laws.* Philadelphia: University of Pennsylvania Press, 1973.

Musson, A. *Medieval Law in Context.* Manchester, U.K.: Manchester University Press, 2001.

VIKINGS

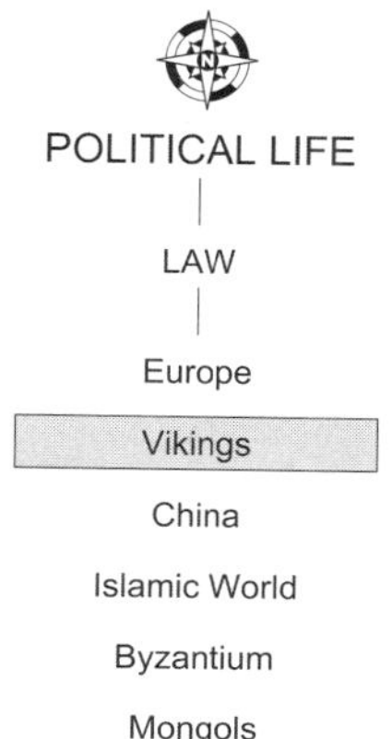

About the legal systems of the Viking Age Scandinavians we know next to nothing. Contemporary primary sources have little, if anything, to say about their laws, and no vernacular legal codes from the Viking Age survive. The written laws were not codified until the 12th and 13th centuries. The earliest legal text is the Norwegian law of the Gulathing, which was established about 950 and held in Gulen south of the mouth of the Sogn Fjord in western Norway. The text survives in a version from the second half of the 13th century. The earliest Swedish and Danish law codes that have been preserved are of an even later date. It is, of course, probable that these laws contain older provisions reflective of Viking Age customs and regulations, but it is difficult to identify and extract the old material from the new.

That laws were important to Viking Age Scandinavians is beyond doubt. The modern English word *law* is an Anglo-Saxon loan of the Old Norse *log*, meaning what was laid down or settled. Only for Iceland do we have an account of how a legal code came into existence and was accepted. It is related in the *Book of Icelanders* that when Iceland had been widely settled, a Norwegian by the name of Ulfljot was sent home to Norway to lay the basis of the Icelandic legislation using the law of the Gulathing as his point of departure. The *Book of Settlements* tells that he returned to Iceland after three years with a collection of laws that he had adapted for the conditions in Iceland.

From references in the literary sources, it is evident that in the Viking Age, the laws were based on the proceedings of the *thing*, the assembly of freemen. Slaves and children did not participate, and women only occasionally participated as companions. The *things* were normally held in the open air within a fenced-off area. They were held at regular intervals and could be weekly, biweekly, quarterly, or annual. In densely populated areas, the *things* were typically held more frequently than in sparsely populated regions. The *things* could also be convoked by a secular or religious authority.

The *thing* could be an assembly of all freemen in a district or a representative assembly of a larger region or province, and it convened for special purposes. The local *things*, about which little is known, were presumably convoked to decide on matters such as pasture rights, use of forests, construction of bridges, and to settle disputes between neighbors or families. Moreover, each community obviously had an interest in agreeing upon a tariff of payment for manslaughter (wergild) as an alternative to the traditional blood feud among the families concerned. The regional *things* were comprised of local chieftains, and such *things* made decisions regarding jurisdiction and defense, and they also decided on cases that could not be agreed upon at local *things*. Only Iceland had a national *thing* in the Viking Age.

There does not seem to have been any kind of proper trial or specific procedure relating to trial, for in small communities the nature of the crime and the identity of the criminal were usually well known. But the proceedings were nonetheless quite ritualistic, and accusations and responses were made using traditional formulas. Proof of innocence or guilt was demonstrated by producing witnesses, usually two or three freemen, who were formally called in by a principal in the suit. In some cases, compurgation, that is, the practice of clearing an accused person of a charge by having a number of people swear to a belief in his innocence, was resorted to in order to strengthen a testimony. Another, though probably less common, method was to subject the accused to an ordeal in order to determine his or her innocence. The most frequent type was the ordeal of carrying hot iron, which was probably introduced from abroad. For women, the ordeal of taking stones from the bottom of a cauldron of boiling water seems to have been the norm. Decisions could also be reached by a duel (*holmganga*) between parties to a dispute. As the name *holmganga* (island-going) implies, the duel was typically held on an island, and it was governed by very specific rules. Weapons varied, but the sword seems to have been common. Dueling was often occasioned by the breakdown of the legal proceedings or a judgment unacceptable to one party. In essence, therefore, dueling was an acknowledgment that the dispute had to be settled by a superior force or by the intervention of the gods.

The *things* had no executive power. The individuals who won a legal judgment against others were responsible for enforcing the penalty. The intended effect of the laws and regulations was therefore dependent upon pressures from the society at large. This society was based on a system of kinship, and relatives protected and avenged one another. An injury or insult inflicted by an outside party against a member of a family was considered an injury or insult against the family as a whole, and it fell to the head of the family to take legal action or revenge. The revenge could be inflicted on the perpetrator, but it could also be inflicted on one of his relatives. If a woman or a child committed a crime, the husband or guardian was responsible. The same applied to slaves, for whom the owner was liable.

The most common punishment for a crime or an offense that could be imposed was a fine. Large portions of the Old Norwegian law, the Danish and Swedish provincial laws, and the laws of the Icelandic free state are devoted to cataloging the fines that could be imposed for different infractions. The imposition of fines evidently functioned as an important method of settling disputes, especially between two families. The fines also served as a means of limiting insult and violence and circumventing informal retribution for injuries, that is, blood vengeance, which, judging from the Sagas of Icelanders, was very common in Iceland. Because most crimes were, at least originally, considered to be an encroachment on a person's property, reputation, or rights, fines were granted to the party instituting the suit both as financial compensation for the damage he had suffered and as moral satisfaction.

Outlawry could amount to a death sentence, for an outlaw could be killed with impunity.

Another kind of penalty that could be imposed was outlawry. It was used primarily for crimes that could not be atoned for with fines, although sometimes fines did replace outlawry. Similarly, outlawry could be imposed if fines were not paid. The literary sources distinguish between two types of outlawry. One is "full outlawry." The laws of the Icelandic free state call it *skoggang* (forest-going), which clearly refers to outlaws' hideouts in the wilderness as outcasts from society. In Iceland, full outlawry was the ultimate punishment, for the laws made no provisions for the imposition of capital or corporal punishment. In fact, outlawry could amount to a death sentence, for an outlaw could be killed with impunity, that is, with no vengeance expected, even if he managed to escape abroad. If he succeeded in leaving Iceland, he could never return. The outlaw also lost his property, from which compensation to the prosecutor was paid as well as an allowance for the outlaw's dependents; any remaining funds probably went to the local inhabitants. A full outlaw was denied burial in a churchyard, and children born to an outlaw had no inheritance rights. In certain cases, full outlaws could obtain reduction of their sentences or reprieve by killing other outlaws. Such rules probably created distrust among outlaws and kept them from banding together.

The other type of outlawry was more restricted in that it banished an individual from a specific region or province. Curiously, this type of outlawry is not mentioned in *Gragas* (the Icelandic legal collection), which instead refers to "lesser outlawry." It involved payment to a chieftain, forfeit of the lesser outlaw's property, and a three-year exile from Iceland. While abroad, the lesser outlaw had legal immunity from attack, and when he returned to Iceland he could resume his position as a full member of society. If a lesser outlaw failed to leave the country within three years, he became a full outlaw.

The infliction of capital punishment was practiced in Denmark and Sweden for rapists, robbers, slanderers, and adulterers. The Danish and Swedish provincial laws list beheading, hanging, breaking on the wheel, burning, stoning, and live burial as forms of capital punishment. To this may be added drowning or sinking in a bog, which—in Norwegian law—was prescribed for sorcery. The execution was probably undertaken, at least originally, by the prosecutors. Immediate revenge by the offended party was permissible when the criminal was caught in the act of, for instance, adultery, rape, or theft.

Corporal punishment, such as flogging or mutilation, was mainly reserved for slaves, although in the Swedish provincial laws it appears to have been the most common punishment after fines. Later, corporal punishment also appears to have been used as a penalty for petty theft, outstanding debts, and specific sex crimes.

~*Kirsten Wolf*

FOR MORE INFORMATION

Sawyer, P. H. *Kings and Vikings*. New York: Routledge, 1993.
Wolf, K. *Daily Life of the Vikings*. Westport, Conn.: Greenwood Press, forthcoming.

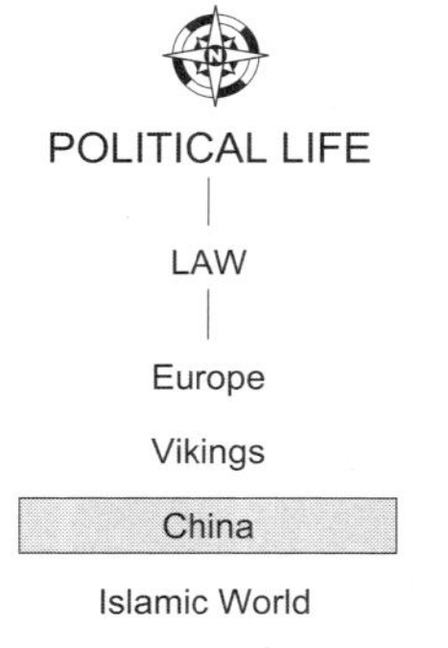

CHINA

The Chinese had a long tradition of law codes and a deep respect for the traditions of law and justice. However, traditional Chinese law is dramatically different from that of the modern West in that it was designed to preserve the social order rather than defend any rights of individuals. The Tang law code—organized by offenses—reflects this idea.

The Ten Abominations were the most heinous offenses in the Tang law code and covered four categories of crimes, the largest number of which pertained to the emperor. Threats to the sovereign's person included not only plotting or carrying out a rebellion but also endangering his life or health through incompetence or malpractice. Servitors guilty of the latter offenses included physicians who failed to follow the proper formulas when composing the emperor's medicine and palace chefs who violated proscriptions in the *Food Canons* when preparing the emperor's meals. The *Food Canons* were dietary manuals that enumerated cooking taboos, such as mixing soft-shell turtles with greens or jerky with glutinous millet. Other crimes against the throne were acts that undermined the emperor's authority, such as unfounded criticism of the sovereign or forging his seals, as well as acts that involved the destruction or theft of his property—palaces, carriages, quilts, cushions, clothes, and the like.

The second "abominations" encompassed crimes against the state: switching allegiance to a foreign ruler, betraying a city to a rebel, attempting to flee China, and killing a superior civil or military official. Because the emperor was the embodiment of the state, most of these were also offenses against him.

The third involved offenses against the family: beating or murdering grandparents, parents, uncles, aunts, elder brothers or sisters, and husbands; selling close relatives into slavery; lodging accusations against paternal grandparents, parents, or husbands; and failing to provide elders with adequate support; and incest. The power of elders was the same as that of the emperor and his governors, who thought of themselves as the parents of the people. In the interest of maintaining social stability, the state made every effort to maintain the authority of household heads. Legally, it was perfectly acceptable for a father to flog his son, but a son found guilty of whipping his father was subject to death.

The final category comprised depraved crimes. Those offenses included slaying three or more members of a household if they were not guilty of a capital crime; dismembering or burning a body before, after, or in the process of murdering the victim; and sorcery with special reference to *gu* poison. *Gu* poison was made by placing venomous creatures such as snakes, toads, scorpions, spiders, and centipedes in a pot. According to tradition, the animal that survived combat with the others and devoured them was the most noxious, by virtue of having absorbed the others' toxins. When the sorcerer or sorcerers decided to kill someone, he or she secretly injected the feces of the creature in the intended victim's food or drink. The poison then destroyed the victim's organs and caused him to vomit blood. No one who consumed it survived. Sorcery included other forms of black magic as well. Carvers of dolls who stabbed the hearts, nailed the eyes, or bound the feet and hands of their effigies to inflict harm on their intended victims were subject to the death penalty. So too were conjurers who uttered curses to cause misfortune and death.

A trial began with the incarceration of a suspect whom thief catchers had caught in the act or with the lodging of an accusation by a victim, witness, or informant. Magistrates had to take great care in cases initiated by allegations because many accusers filed false charges for personal gain, vengeance, or other reasons. In most cases, the officials responsible for conducting trials in the first instance were the county or market commandants. County commandants in particular were busy men charged with all governmental affairs in their districts—tax collection, famine relief, military defense, and public works, to name a few. Most of them probably spent little time on legal matters, delegating most of those duties to subordinates: the marshals and provosts of law, as well as constables, bailiffs, jailers, detectives, and court reporters. Few of those men, including the commandant, had any specialized legal training. There were no lawyers, prosecutors, or judges in the modern sense. The presiding officer, the magistrate, could, however, avail himself of manuals that contained hypothetical judgments.

Investigation of a crime involved examining evidence and interrogating accusers or suspects. Nearly all trials included a confrontation between the magistrate and the defendant. Except in cases of murder, robbery by force, flight, and rape of a good woman, the law required magistrates to conduct those hearings on three different days. During the first, he took the suspect's statement. That document served as the basis for the judge's oral questions during the second and third sessions. There were five ancient principles for conducting such interrogations. Judges were to examine the accused's statement to discover complications or inconsistencies in it; observe his face to find any signs of blushing; watch his respiration to detect irregularities in his breathing; test his ears to ascertain if he could hear the questions addressed to him; and look into his eyes to see if they were clear. The first three were techniques for detecting lies, and the last two methods were for determining the competence of accusers or suspects to stand trial.

If, when a magistrate completed his investigation, the facts of the case were in doubt and the defendant refused to admit his crime, the magistrate could, with the approval of his superior or colleagues, apply judicial torture to extract a confession. Under those circumstances, a conviction required an acknowledgment of guilt from the accused not only as evidence of his wrongdoing but also as a sign of his contrition and willingness to reform. The only legitimate form of torture was scourging with the interrogation rod, and the law code imposed limitations on its use. It prohibited more than three thrashings and a total of no more than two hundred blows. It also stipulated that the three beatings had to be administered at least 20 days apart. Furthermore, the code prohibited the thrashing of dwarfs, mutes, morons, the disabled, and relatives of high-ranking officials who were over 69 years of age or younger than 14. If the suspect still did not confess, then the magistrate had to release him.

Once the defendant had been convicted, the magistrate passed sentence on him. The law required the magistrate to assign punishments in accordance with provisions in the code or other collections of statutes. To ensure that all officials were well versed in the laws, the throne ordered that the laws be inscribed on walls of offices so that officials could study them while taking breaks from their duties.

The duty of apprehending culprits fell to the Gold Bird Guards in the capitals and to thief catchers in the prefectures and counties. After arresting suspects, thief catchers hauled them off to jail. In 754, there were somewhat less than 1,900 prisons with well over 10,000 administrators throughout the empire. Incarceration in Tang China was not a form of punishment in itself. Jails were simply places for holding the accused while the authorities investigated the crime and imposed the sentence, a period rarely more than a few months. Because Tang jails were not the formidable stone, concrete, and iron dungeons of the West, escape could not have been difficult. To prevent that, the law required wardens to keep dangerous inmates in fetters. The restraints for male prisoners charged with capital crimes were *cangues* (wooden collars) and wooden handcuffs. Women subject to the death penalty and all suspects charged with crimes punishable by exile or penal servitude wore *cangues* only. There were exceptions to the rules. Mandarins ranked seventh grade or higher enjoyed the right of wearing chains only. Dwarfs, pregnant women, the disabled, and inmates over 79 years of age awaited judgment unfettered.

After the trial, if the prisoner was found guilty, then the state imposed a punishment. In its first chapter, the Tang law code lists five major forms of punishment. The first was thrashing with the thin rod and had five degrees: 10, 20, 30, 40, and 50 blows. Magistrates who failed to pass sentences according to the laws were subject to 30 blows. Failure to report a fire or assist in putting it out was punishable by 20 blows, and illegal entry into a home during the night, by 40 blows. The law prescribed 40 blows for masters of mad dogs that they did not kill, as well as for owners of domestic animals and dogs that gored, kicked, or bit people. Furthermore, the code required that the owners cut off the horns, hobble the legs, and cut off the ears, respectively, of the offending creatures.

Chinese prisoner being executed by strangulation. Illustration by Charles Benn.

In 630, while examining an anatomical illustration, Emperor Taizong noticed that the internal organs of humans were located just under the skin of the back. To spare his subjects suffering, he ordered that magistrates apply thrashings only to the buttocks and thighs when punishing criminals.

The second major form of punishment was scourging with the thick rod and had five degrees: 60, 70, 80, 90, and 100 blows. Shooting arrows toward a city, home, or road was punishable by 60 blows. The maximum penalty for debtors who failed to repay loans worth one foot of cloth within 100 days after the date stipulated in a contract was 60 blows. Eighty blows was the punishment for sticking objects into another person's ears, nostrils, or other orifices when the objects obstructed the passage, as well as for pulling out a square inch or more of an adversary's hair during a fight. Gambling on games of chance was punishable by 100 blows except in cases when the wager was food and drink or the contest involved archery and other martial arts.

The third punishment was penal servitude and had five degrees: one, one-and-a-half, two, two-and-a-half, and three years. One year of penal servitude was the punishment for destroying tombstones and for peering into an imperial palace from a high place. Possession of armor and crossbows was punishable by one-and-a-half years, and possession of military treatises by two years. Artisans who failed to paint or embellish imperial boats were subject to two years. Three years was the sentence for persons who burned coffins while attempting to smoke foxes out of tombs. (The folklore of traditional China depicted foxes as evil creatures.)

In the capitals, magistrates sent men sentenced to penal servitude to labor on the construction of buildings, and women to toil at sewing for the court. In the provinces, judges set criminals to work on city walls, moats, granaries, and warehouses or employed them for miscellaneous tasks in their offices. In either case, the convicts were confined at the offices of the agency involved. The law required that prefects review all sentences to penal servitude that county or market commandants imposed.

The fourth punishment was exile and had three degrees: 666, 833, and 1,000 miles, with compulsory labor added in some cases. Those who submitted anonymous accusations or lodged them under false names were subject to banishment at a place 833 miles from their homes, as were thieves who stole armor or crossbows and Chinese men who married aliens (Persians, Indians, and the like).

The most forbidding destination for an exile was Lingnan, the southernmost region of the empire that included Hainan Island and northern Vietnam. Imperial decrees referred to it as that "distant, evil place." Although Chinese had largely settled the region by Tang times, the aborigines remained a constant threat and frequently attacked the immigrants. The climate of the area was intolerably hot and periodically suffered devastating typhoons. The objectives of exile were to send offenders far from the capital and the imperial court, to separate them from their clans and hometowns, and to prevent them from performing their sacrificial duties to their ancestors.

The fifth, and gravest, of punishments in the Tang was execution. There were two forms, strangulation and decapitation. According to the law code, there were 144 crimes punishable by the former and 89 by the latter. The emperor had to personally approve all executions. Strangulation was the punishment for lodging an accusation against grandparents or parents with a magistrate, scheming to kidnap and sell a person into slavery, or opening a coffin while desecrating a tomb. Executioners throttled the condemned by placing a noose around the convict's neck and twisting the rope until he suffocated. In Tang China, hanging was a means of committing suicide, not a form of capital punishment.

In Tang China, hanging was a means of committing suicide, not a form of capital punishment.

Although strangulation entailed more prolonged pain and suffering, it was preferable to decapitation for most Chinese. They believed that their bodies were gifts from their parents and that it was most disrespectful to their ancestors to die without returning the gift to the grave intact. In the capitals, most executions took place at the western market because in Chinese cosmology, metal, the executioner's sword, was the element of the west. However, on occasion, authorities used the eastern market, post road stations, palace halls, ball fields, and various other sites for that purpose. Nearly all executions were public, to warn citizens of the dire consequences that would befall them if they should contemplate committing capital crimes. It is not unlikely that they were also a form of entertainment, spectacles that titillated thrill seekers. After decapitations, the heads were displayed on poles or spears and the bodies thrown on the ground beneath. When local authorities beheaded criminals, they boxed the heads and sent them to the capital to confirm the identity and death of the culprit.

As always, rank had its privileges. When a high-ranking minister, fifth grade and above, received a death sentence, the throne might grant him a special dispensation by bestowing suicide on him in lieu of imposing strangulation or decapitation. The strong-willed accepted such "gifts" gracefully by bathing, composing themselves, and writing a last statement before killing themselves. The weak-willed could not bring themselves to take their own lives.

When the state sentenced a convict to decapitation for rebellion or sedition, it also imposed punishments on his relatives—whether they were guilty or innocent of participating in the crime—by reason of association. Fathers under the age of 79 and sons over the age of 15 were strangled. Sons under the age of 15, mothers, daughters, wives, concubines, grandfathers, grandsons, brothers, and sisters were enslaved. The women were imprisoned in the Flank Close, and the sons were sent to the service of the provost of agriculture. Uncles and nephews were banished to the farthest reaches of the empire. Finally, the government confiscated all slaves, personal retainers, fields, homes, and movable property owned by the condemned. On occasion, the throne also ordered the tombs of their ancestors leveled and had their coffins destroyed and their bones scattered.

The number of people condemned to strangulation, exile, or slavery by virtue of association with a relative convicted of rebellion could be quite large. In 688, judicial authorities sentenced 5,000 persons in a single district to those punishments because they were related to a Tang prince who revolted against Empress Wu. Only the intervention of a humane governor, who informed the empress that the verdicts were erroneous, saved them.

There were other forms of punishment besides the five listed at the beginning of the Tang code. The law demanded restitution when the crime involved the destruction of property. Arsonists and reckless drivers who injured or killed domestic animals had to compensate the injured parties for their losses. For minor infractions, the law required mandarins to resign their posts for one year. For more severe offenses, the state revoked all of the officials' titles for six years. Some forms of punishment were extralegal. The government fined officials by docking their salaries when fires broke out in their agencies. The throne often demoted mandarins to posts outside the capital, generally for political rather than criminal transgressions. Demotion was actually a mild form of exile, for it did not entail dismissal from all offices. Occasionally, the demoted sneaked back into the capital, dressed as women to avoid detection, and restored themselves to the good graces of the throne.

At least two types of capital punishment were extralegal. Throughout the Tang, scourging to death with the thick rod was a common form of execution applied especially in cases of gross corruption. On occasion, the throne also employed it to make an example. In the spring of 716, the emperor ordered his brother-in-law beaten to death in front of all his officials for having ambushed and assaulted a man in the lane of a ward at the capital. In that instance, the emperor imposed the sentence to serve as an apology to the bureaucratic corps for the misbehavior of his relative. By far the most brutal sort of execution was truncation, cutting in two at the waist with a fodder knife. The condemned, who had committed some crime considered to be particularly treacherous or repugnant, slowly and painfully bled to death.

By modern standards, the legal system of the Tang may seem to have been inhumane and discriminatory, but it was also incredibly merciful. Status played a role in the granting of leniency. Except in cases involving the Ten Abominations or the death penalty, the code established an automatic reduction of one degree in the punishment for crimes committed by relatives of the emperor; men of great talent, virtue, and achievement; and mandarins ranked seventh grade or higher. Criminals under 15 or over 68 years of age and the impaired were exempt from all punishments except the death penalty; those under 7 or over 88 were exempt even from the death penalty. The impaired included the mentally ill. Those exclusions did not, however, apply to those sentenced by reason of association with convicts condemned to decapitation. The law also conferred on all of those groups immunity from judicial torture and the right to redeem their punishments by payments of copper.

Common criminals who did not enjoy such privileges could expect to have their sentences nullified or commuted by one of the numerous pardons that emperors bestowed as acts of benevolence. The throne absolved individuals; groups of individuals, such as officials forced against their will to serve rebels, defeated barbarians, or soldiers serving on military campaigns; classes of convicts such as exiles; and all offenders in a specific district. Emperors also regularly reduced the sentences of criminals, commuting the death penalty to exile and exile to penal servitude.

The vast majority of criminals, those who had not committed a heinous or political crime, could expect some modification of their sentences, either by pardon or by commutation. The convicts who benefited most from imperial indulgences in the Tang were those condemned to penal servitude or exile because their sentences were the longest. The extent of clemency in the Tang was far greater than that in modern times (Benn, 198–212).

To read about law and crime in 19th-century China, see the China entry in the section "Law and Crime" in chapter 6 ("Political Life") of volume 5 of this series.

FOR MORE INFORMATION

Benn, C. *Daily Life in Traditional China: The Tang Dynasty*. Westport, Conn.: Greenwood Press, 2002.

Ch'ü T'ung-tsu. *Law and Society in Traditional China*. Westport, Conn.: Hyperion Press, 1961.

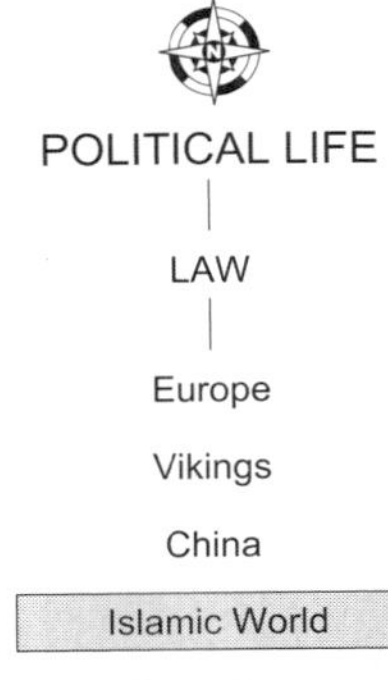

ISLAMIC WORLD

Islamic law is called Sharia and is based on the teachings in the Qur'an. Beause matters inevitably arise that are not directly dealt with in the Prophet's words, legal scholars had to develop ways to apply religious laws.

The science of working out the Sharia can be divided into two basic categories, and because the Arabic language is fond of agricultural metaphors, these categories are referred to as the roots of jurisprudence (*'usul al-fiqh*, legal theory) and the branches of jurisprudence (*furu' al-fiqh*, practical application). Because knowledge of the Qur'an and the sunna (sayings or actions) of Muhammad were essential to the sciences of jurisprudence, and because proper jurisprudence was essential to working out what it meant to be a good Muslim, the entire educational system of the period was based on memorizing the Qur'an as well as thousands of these hadiths (traditions of the Prophet) along with a list of transmittors of these traditions (or *isnads*).

Scholars employed (at least in theory) a five-step process to determine whether a given practice was acceptable or not. First, if the Qur'an specifically commanded or prohibited something, there really was nothing to discuss. Second, if the Qur'an addressed an issue, but without specific guidance, they turned to the sunna of Muhammad for clarification of the Qur'anic commandment. For example, Muslims are admonished repeatedly in the Qur'an to pray; however, it is only because of the sunna of Muhammad that Muslims know to pray five times per day, to perform specific ablutions and in which order, and to perform certain prostrations and in which order. Third, because Muhammad is understood to have been preserved from gross moral error (*ma'sum*), if an authentic hadith spoke specifically to an issue not addressed at all in the Qur'an, Muslims could be assured that if they followed the admonition of that hadith, they would be acting in obedience to God. Fourth, when neither the Qur'an nor the sunna addressed an issue, scholars argued that they must employ their reason to extrapolate what was the proper response based on the principles set forth in the Qur'an and the sunna as a whole.

Because most aspects of life are in this fourth category, and because this category is most open to interpretation, it is to this category that the scholars devoted most of their energies and their arguments. In fact, they developed a range of categories of reasoning that could be employed in this enterprise. Not surprisingly, the various traditions did not always agree on which methods of reasoning were legitimate.

Finally, the scholars used the principle of consensus (*ijma'*) to determine whether a doctrine or decision was legitimate in these instances. This principle of consensus is rooted in a hadith in which Muhammad is purported to have said that his community would never agree upon an error. In practical terms, the scholars identified the community as themselves in that when there was no scholar of good repute holding a contrary position on a particular issue, the issue was considered settled.

Modern scholars tend to be skeptical about the authenticity of even the hadiths in the authoritative collections. They also tend to be skeptical about when or even if the methodology just described was actually employed or whether it was simply used after the fact to legitimate practices and decisions that were really rooted in Arabian tribal custom or in the local practice of Kufa, Basra, Damascus, Baghdad, or elsewhere. In any case, it is clear that the formal positions of the Sharia reflect the life of the cities and towns in the medieval Islamic world, for it is in the urban centers that the scholars were studying the religious sciences and working out the details of the Sharia in response to the questions that arose in the urban environments in which they lived. Moreover, it was in the urban centers that there were actual judges (*qadis*) and the mechanisms to enforce judges' decisions. In the countryside and among the pastoral nomadic groups, the, at times, arcane details of the Sharia tended to take a back seat to local custom. In these circumstances, a person was helpless to contest a violation of Sharia because there was no judge to hear his or her case nor was there anyone to enforce it. If there was an Islamic "scholar" there, he most likely was an ill-educated preacher who was not well versed in the intricate details of Islamic jurisprudence.

Whether the methodology of jurisprudence described here was actually employed consistently or even at all need not concern us. The fact that it was supposed to be employed illustrates the importance that Muslims attached to following the dictates of the Qur'an and the teachings of Muhammad in their daily lives. In short, the Sharia in all its manifestations comprises the entire body of duties and obligations incumbent on all believers covering every aspect of daily life imaginable. It is that straight path by which the individual believer can know that he or she is walking according to God's will.

To read about law and crime in the Islamic world in the 20th century, see the Islamic World entry in the section "Law and Crime" in chapter 6 ("Political Life") of volume 6 of this series.

~*James Lindsay*

FOR MORE INFORMATION

Lindsay, J. *Daily Life in Medieval Islam*. Westport, Conn.: Greenwood Press, forthcoming.

von Grunebaum, G. E. *Medieval Islam*. Chicago: University of Chicago Press, 1953.

BYZANTIUM

One of the great contributions of the ancient Romans to modern society was in the field of the law. Romans had developed abstract notions of justice, a respect for written laws, and a tradition of interpreting the law by lawyers and jurors. Since the earliest days of the Roman Republic, this law had been growing and changing to meet new conditions. Therefore, the body of law that had accumulated by the Middle Ages included legislation by the Senate and emperors, decisions made by judges, and comments by leading lawyers and jurists (legal scholars).

By the third century C.E., the mass of law that had accumulated was known as the *jus vetus* (old law). From the 4th century onward, nearly all legislation was by imperial edict—laws issued by the increasingly powerful Byzantine emperors. This body of law was known as the *jus novum* (new law). This full body of Roman law dealt with all aspects of human interactions, but because it had grown up over such a long period of time, it was full of obscurities and internal contradictions. The emperor Justinian (r. 527–65) decided to consolidate and clarify the laws.

In 528, Justinian assigned his jurists to begin to codify the *jus novum*, and they quickly produced the *Codex Justinianus*. In 530, the emperor took on the larger task of tidying up the massive body of the *jus vetus*. This was a formidable project, but the work was finally completed. It created the *Digest*, 50 books of law. Justinian completed the work by publishing the *Institutes*, a summary of the main principles of Roman law that was intended for use as a textbook. Justinian's codification was to be of the highest importance for the future of jurisprudence.

The Byzantine emperors—like Justinian himself—were autocrats. They believed they were ordained by God to rule as they liked. However, the Roman laws declared that the power of the emperor was derived from the people and that even an emperor was expected to rule in accordance with the law. Thus, in later centuries, Roman law as codified by Justinian, was used to support democratic theories of the state.

Justinian (483–565), Byzantine emperor, surrounded by his court, from a 14th-century Latin manuscript of The Institutions of Justinian. Justinian's codification was rediscovered in western Europe at the end of the 11th century, and it exerted a profound influence on medieval law and political theory. © The Art Archive/Biblioteca Capitolare Padua/Dagli Orti.

Justinian's codification was rediscovered in western Europe at the end of the 11th century, and it exerted a profound influence on medieval law and political theory. It formed the basis of religious law (canon law), and through that it influenced the legal systems of the growing national states. In the area of law, the contribution of the Byzantine Empire to the future history of the West and East was immense.

To read about law in ancient Rome, see the Rome entry in the section "Law" in chapter 6 ("Political Life") of volume 1 of this series.

~Joyce E. Salisbury

FOR MORE INFORMATION

Mango, C. *Byzantium: The Empire of New Rome*. New York: Macmillan, 1980.
Moorehead, J. *Justinian*. Boston, Mass.: Addison-Wesley, 1994.

MONGOLS

The term *yasa* is a Mongol word meaning law, order, decree, judgment. As a verb, it implied the death sentence; for example, "some were delivered to the *yasa*" usually means that an official execution was carried out. It was once generally accepted that Chinggis (Genghis) Khan had laid down a basic legal code called the "Great *Yasa*" during the *Quriltai* (Great Council) of 1206 and that written copies of his decrees were kept by the Mongol princes in their treasuries for future consultation. This code, the so-called Great *Yasa*, was to be binding throughout the lands where Mongol rule prevailed, although, strangely, the actual texts of the code were to remain taboo in the same way as the text of the *Altan Debter* (an official Mongol chronicle accessible only to Mongol nobles) was treated. This restriction on access to the text explains the fact that no copies of the Great *Yasa* have ever actually been recorded. Although it never existed in any physical sense, in later years many assumed that these collected Mongol edicts, known as the Great *Yasa*, had been compiled by Chinggis Khan.

The Great *Yasa* became a body of laws governing the social and legal behavior of the Mongol tribes and the peoples of those lands that came under their control. Initially, it was based on Mongol traditions, customary law, and precedent, but it was never rigid and it was always open to very flexible and liberal interpretation and quite able to adapt, adopt, and absorb other legal systems. Speaking of the *yasas*, the Muslim Juwaynī (d. 1282), historian and governor of Baghdad under the Mongol il-khans, was able to declare, "There are many of these ordinances that are in conformity with the *Sharīʿat* [Islamic law]" (Juwaynī, 25). The Great *Yasa* must therefore be viewed as an evolving body of customs and decrees that began long before Chinggis Khan's *Quriltai* of 1206. His son Chagatai was known to adhere strictly to the unwritten Mongol customary law, and many of his strictures and rulings would have been incorporated into the evolving body of law. Many of the rulings which appear to be part of this Great *Yasa* are based on quotations and *biligs* (maxims) of Chinggis Khan that are known to have been recorded. Another source of the laws that made up the Great *Yasa* is the Tatar (member of the Turco-Mongol tribe of Tatars) Shigi-Qutuqu, Chinggis Khan's adopted brother, who was entrusted with judicial authority during the 1206 *Quriltai*. He established the Mongol practice of recording in writing the various decisions he arrived at as head *yarghuchi* (judge). His decisions were recorded in the Uighur script in a blue book (*kökö debter*) and were considered binding, thus creating an ad hoc body of case histories. However, this in itself did not represent the Great *Yasa* of Chinggis Khan, and it must be assumed that such a document never existed, even though in the years to come the existence of just such a document became a widespread belief.

With or without the existence of a written Great *Yasa*, the Mongols, especially under Chinggis Khan, had a strict set of rules and laws to which they adhered, and their discipline was everywhere remarked on and admired. An intelligence report prepared by Franciscan friars led by Friar Giovanni Di Plano Carpini, who visited Mongolia in the 1240s comments as follows:

> Among themselves, however, they are peaceable, fornication and adultery are very rare, and their women excel those of other nations in chastity, except that they often use shameless words when jesting. Theft is unusual among them, and therefore their dwellings and all their property are not put under lock and key. If horses or oxen or other animal stock are found

straying, they are either allowed to go free or are led back to their own masters. . . . Rebellion is rarely raised among them, and it is no wonder if such is their way, for, as I have said above, transgressors are punished without mercy. (Skelton, Marston, and Painter, 97–98)

Even the Muslim historian Jūzjānī (d. 1260) does not hold back:

> The Chinggis Khan moreover in [the administration of] justice was such, that, throughout his whole camp, it was impossible for any person to take up a fallen whip from the ground except he were the owner of it; and, throughout his whole army, no one could give indication of [the existence of] lying and theft. (Jūzjānī, 144)

Nor does he refrain from treating Chinggis Khan's son and successor, Ögödei, who was generally credited with having shown compassion and great sympathy for his Muslim subjects, with respect and positive treatment.

Religious tolerance became enshrined in the *Yasa*, although some would say that the Mongols were just playing safe by safeguarding religious leaders of all faiths. Priests and religious institutions were all exempted from taxation. Water was treated with great respect, and it was strictly forbidden to wash or urinate in running water, streams and rivers being considered as living entities. Execution was the punishment for spying, treason, desertion, theft, and adultery, and persistent bankruptcy in the case of merchants. Execution could take on various horrific forms. One particularly gruesome example was recorded by Rashīd al-Dīn (d. 1318), a prime minister of Iran during the Mongol il-khanid period. A rash Kurdish warlord had attempted to double-cross Hülegü Khan. He was apprehended and received this fate:

Kings and the particularly mighty were wrapped in carpets and kicked to death.

> He [Hülegü] ordered that he [Malik Salih] be covered with sheep fat, trussed with felt and rope, and left in the summer sun. After a week, the fat got maggoty, and they started devouring the poor man. He died of that torture within a month. He had a three-year-old son who was sent to Mosul, where he was cut in two on the banks of the Tigris and hung as an example on two sides of the city until his remains rotted away to nothing. (Rashīd al-Dīn, 510–11)

Reflecting the Mongols' respect for and superstitious fear of aristocracy, they were fearful of shedding the blood of the high-born upon the earth. They therefore reserved a special form of execution for kings and the particularly mighty. Such nobles, in recognition of their status, were wrapped in carpets and kicked to death.

Often portrayed as barbarians, the Mongols are not frequently credited with the discipline and law-abiding nature of their society. Although anarchy often followed in their wake, once established, serious measures were invariably enacted to ensure that the rule of law governed all members of their society.

~George Lane

FOR MORE INFORMATION

Juwaynī, ʿAt ā Malik. *Genghis Khan: The History of the World Conqueror.* Translated by J. A. Boyle. Manchester: Manchester University Press, 1997.

Jūzjānī, Maulānā Minhāj al-Dīn. *T abakāt-i-Nās irī*. Translated by H. G. Raverty. Calcutta: The Asiatic Society, 1995.
Morgan, D. *The Mongols*. Oxford: Blackwell, 1986.
Rashīd al-Dīn. *Jami'u't-tawarikh: Compendium of Chronicles*. 3 vols. Translated by W. M. Thackston. Cambridge, Mass.: Harvard University Press, 1998–99.
Skelton, R. A., T. E. Marston, and G. D. Painter. 2nd ed. *The Vinland Map and the Tartar Relation*. 2nd ed. New Haven, Conn.: Yale University Press, 1995.

Warfare and Weapons

The Middle Ages dawned with violence and warfare that broke out everywhere. Just as in the ancient world, people killed each other for reasons that were similar wherever they were: people fought for wealth, power, and vengeance. This was true in China, Europe, and the far reaches of Polynesia. However, the Middle Ages introduced several new features in the history of warfare. Perhaps the most important was the notion that wars should be fought in the name of religion: that warfare is not just something that breaks out because of rage or greed, but is something that is justified from above.

The Muslim world began in warfare as Muhammad fought for the survival of the new religion and then spread it through the armies of Allah. The Muslims developed an idea of "holy war" or jihad, which continues to stir controversy and make the headlines into the 21st century. Even in the medieval world, Muslims did not all agree on what *jihad* actually meant, whether it was an internal struggle or a war, but they did agree that the Muslim world was separate from the rest, and separated by religion. Christians quickly adopted this notion of fighting for faith: Charlemagne forcefully converted the Saxons by the sword, and Christian armies marched in Crusades against the forces of Islam. This precedent begun in the Middle Ages extends unfortunately into modern times in places as disparate as Ireland, Israel, and elsewhere. Even medieval China, while not advocating fighting for ideology, thought about warfare; Sun-Tzu was the first author to write a comprehensive text on the subject—*The Art of War*. War was no longer something that broke out spontaneously.

Armies between the 8th and 12th centuries were extremely small by modern standards. For example, when William of Normandy conquered England in 1066, he was probably accompanied by about 7,000 men. To defend his land from the English invasion in 1214, Philip II of France put about 27,000 men into the field. The largest army ever mustered for the defense of the Latin kingdom of Jerusalem in 1183 numbered no more than 15,000 men. For comparison, during the United States Civil War (1861–65), the northern forces under two generals, Meade and Sherman, numbered 185,000 during one battle (Beeler, 250). Medieval armies were small and for the most part similarly armed.

The whole Eurasian land mass quickly shared a similar technology of warfare. This may be compared with isolated areas such as Polynesia, where they continued to fight mostly naked armed only with wooden weapons. In Eurasia, by contrast, military weapons spread rapidly. Armies are all too ready to adopt something that works. For example, the stirrup, probably developed in Persia, spread to the Muslim world and then to Europe, making the mounted soldier a viable and fierce fighter. Before the use of the stirrup, mounted soldiers could only use their horses as transportation; if they tried to engage an enemy while mounted, they would too easily fall off. With the use of the stirrup, mounted knights took over as the warriors in the West. The Byzantine Empire marked an exception to the rapid weapon spreading because they were able to preserve the secret to their dreaded "Greek fire" with which they could burn ships and people alike.

From China to northern Europe, soldiers were armed with iron weapons; swords were favored, but axes in Scandinavia were also lethal. Soldiers also fought with maces and weapons designed to crush, rather than cut, the opponent. Chinese and Muslims were highly advanced swordsmiths, and their weapons held a blade much longer than those of the Europeans. The mounted warriors were supported everywhere by archers, and through most of the Middle Ages, crossbowmen held sway. In the 14th century, weapons changed dramatically. The English longbow, with its greater range and firepower, replaced the crossbow and even unseated the fierce knights. The 14th century also witnessed the development of gunpowder, and foot soldiers began to see the benefits of a long pike against horsemen. By the beginning of the 15th century, the seeds of modern warfare were set. The future lay with large armies of foot soldiers with guns rather than mounted knights with swords.

Medieval warfare was also characterized by defense. Soldiers wore armor of increasing thickness and complexity—chain mail was layered over thick padding, and plate mail later was placed on top of the chain. Cities were surrounded by walls to keep out soldiers, and defensive castles grew larger and larger as armies increased the effectiveness of their siege engines. Only at the end of the Middle Ages, with the advent of gunpowder, did armies—and societies—begin to trust their safety to offense rather than defense. Security lay with a larger gun and more soldiers, not with a thicker wall.

~Joyce E. Salisbury

FOR MORE INFORMATION

Beeler, J. *Warfare in Feudal Europe, 730–1200.* Ithaca, N.Y.: Cornell University Press, 1971.

EUROPE

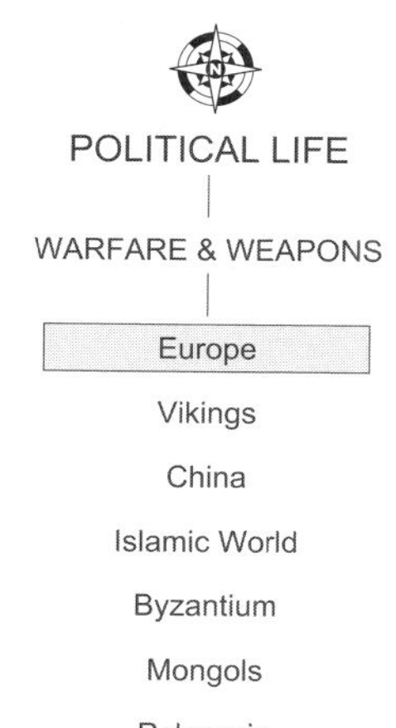

Warfare was never very far from daily life in the Middle Ages. Many people either had served in person or had friends or relatives who had served in the almost-incessant wars. Much of the structure of medieval life in Europe was to defend against wars: cities were walled to keep out marauders, and countrysides depended on a fortified castle to defend the villages in the vicinity. Most warfare consisted of long sieges during which offensive armies tried to take these fortified positions. Noble youth spent years training for lives spent in fighting, and villagers frequently had to recover from the periodic warfare that destroyed property, lives, and peace of mind. At a fundamental level, military structures pervaded medieval society—the entire feudal system was theoretically a form of military organization.

From the 10th through the 13th centuries, the most valuable soldier was the mounted knight. Once the use of the stirrup had spread from the East to western Europe (probably in the early 8th century), leaders saw the advantage of using a mounted force of soldiers who could put the force of horse power behind the thrust of a lance or the strike of a sword. From this moment on, the resources of the Western kingdoms were placed in training and fielding an army of mounted, heavily armed knights, known as "men-at-arms." The man-at-arms was by definition a man of means. He was expected to provide his own equipment, and this equipment was expensive. A full "harness," or set of armor, cost upwards of 2 pounds, as much money as a laborer made in a year. An ordinary war horse cost 5 pounds, and a good one could cost 10 times as much.

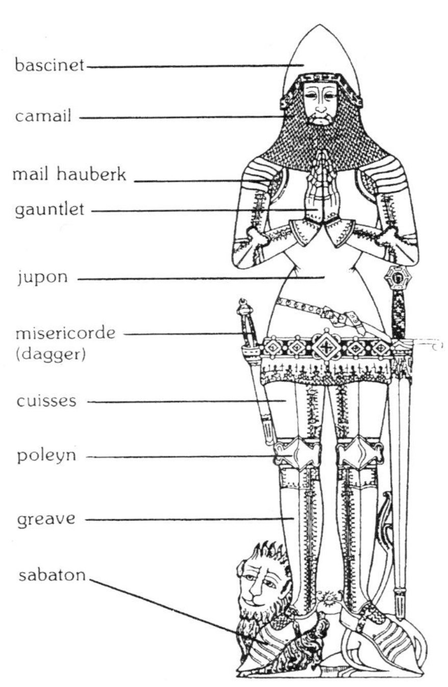

14th-century armor. This shows the development of plate armor that came about in the 14th century. The chain mail that had dominated during the Middle Ages can still be seen under the knight's arms and on his neck. Joyce E. Salisbury.

While the knight was the pride of the medieval army, he was supported by various types of soldiers, with sharp distinctions of class and income among them. The highest paid were archers. During the early Middle Ages, crossbowmen were an important component of support because their bolts could penetrate armor. They could not fire very quickly, but their weapons were important in situations such as defense of fixed positions or castles. Other footmen were armed with weapons for hand-to-hand combat: spears, axes, and other pole arms. Common soldiers were generally more lightly armored than men-at-arms and therefore relatively vulnerable at close quarters against fully armored opponents, although the man-at-arms was still vulnerable to archers at a distance. In battle, troops of the same type usually fought together; but for purposes of recruitment, muster, and pay, they were organized as retinues comprising all these sorts of troops (sometimes containing only a few men), each troop under the command of the man-at-arms that raised them.

At the base of the military hierarchy were irregular troops called brigands, ribalds, pilars, or coutiliers. Often their only weapon was a long knife. They stayed out of the front lines but generally made themselves useful by foraging, skirmishing, pillaging, and finishing off the wounded. There were also a host of servants whose duties included camp chores and holding the horses of the dismounted men-at-arms. Such servants sometimes made a useful contribution to the fighting—as at Otterburn in 1388, where they defended the Scottish camp as their masters armed themselves. However, they were equally likely to panic and run off with the horses.

In the 14th century, during the Hundred Years' War between England and France, new warfare techniques came into play that served to reduce the importance of the mounted knight. The English fought on French soil, so their knights were outnumbered. The English forces, however, developed new strategy and used new weapons—they brought archers trained to use a longbow, originally used by the Welsh, that not only could fire many more arrows a minute than the old crossbow but had a longer range as well. These developments caused the foot soldier to be more significant, and the English mounted knights also learned the advantage of fighting on foot.

During the Hundred Years' War, an English man-at-arms rode a horse to battle, but he usually fought on foot. Early in the century, the English had discovered that they could win battles by dismounting their knights. All other things being equal, in a face-to-face contest, properly trained and equipped men on foot have the advantage against an equal number of comparably equipped horsemen. The reason lies in geometry and the psychology of horses. Men on foot can hold a denser formation, outnumbering mounted opponents at the point of impact; and they are, once properly trained, much less likely than horses to whicker nervously and edge away once the yelling and shouting starts. The man-at-arms was by definition a well-equipped, trained warrior, so the only real disadvantage of having such troops fight on foot was the reduced battlefield mobility.

During the Hundred Years' War, kings also made more use of mercenary armies who fought for pay and who used the new weapons—including the newly developed guns and cannons. These trends marked the end of medieval warfare. No longer was warfare fought among noble specialists who spent more time in defensive sieges than in offensive attacks. From then on, future battles depended increasingly on large numbers of troops who could overwhelm an opposing force with offensive weapons. The knight in shining armor had given way to large numbers of common foot soldiers.

From about the 8th century, medieval weaponry in Europe emphasized defensive armor that allowed mounted soldiers to serve as shock troops in an army highly dependant upon heavily armed cavalry. During the 12th and 13th centuries, the knight's equipment remained relatively constant.

The knight's main body armor consisted of a long tunic of mail, called a hauberk, generally reaching to the knees, with a slit from hem to crotch in front and back, allowing him to sit in a saddle. Mail consisted of a tightly packed surface of small steel rings, each interlocking with several of its neighbors in each direction and riveted shut for added strength. Mail was particularly good at resisting the bite of a sword's edge, but it offered somewhat less protection against the crushing force of a blow, and it could be penetrated by the highly concentrated power of a crossbow bolt.

Underneath the hauberk, a knight wore a padded cloth tunic, called an aketon, which provided some of the impact absorption that the mail lacked. From the late 12th century, the knight's hands were protected with mail mittens built into the hauberk, with slits at the wrists that allowed him to free his hands when needed. On his legs, the knight wore long stockings of mail, protecting everything from his feet to his thighs. In the 13th century, this armor was beginning to be supplemented with solid plates of steel at crucial points, particularly over the torso and knees. Additional protection was afforded by a shield strapped to the knight's left arm.

The head required the most protection because of its importance and vulnerability. The innermost layer of head protection was a padded coif, secured in place by ties under the chin. Over this the knight wore another coif of mail, this one a full hood attached to the hauberk and covering the entire head, leaving only the face exposed. On top of this, the knight wore a steel helmet. The helmet of the 12th century was generally only a conical cap with a bar projecting downward in front of the nose, but in the 13th century, it became common to wear a larger "barrel" helm that covered the entire head, with a horizontal slot in front of the eyes and a grille of breathing holes in the area of the mouth and nostrils.

The barrel helmet weighed some 6 pounds, and the hauberk about 25 pounds. The combined bulk of the hauberk and aketon tended to impede mobility, as did the multiple layers of head protection, but they provided significant protection in close combat, and the knight's training gave him strength and skill to compensate for his encumbrance.

The knight's most powerful weapon was his lance. This was a wooden spear about 9 to 11 feet long, with a steel point at the end. Medieval battle tactics typically began with a concentrated charge by the knights with their lances. A group of knights with lances tucked hard under their arms charging at their enemy en masse could deliver an enormously powerful initial shock, and it was axiomatic that no body of foot soldiers could withstand such an onslaught. Once combat was joined at close quarters, the lances were useless and were discarded.

Some knights relied instead on a mace, a wooden or iron club with a heavy, weighted end.

The most common secondary weapon was the sword. The typical knightly sword of this period weighed about two-and-a-half to three-and-a-half pounds and had a blade a bit over 30 inches long. With a weighted pommel at the end of the grip to counterbalance the weight of the blade, it was a fairly handy weapon, and a well-trained swordsman could handle it with grace and skill. Some knights relied instead on a mace, a wooden or iron club with a heavy, weighted end. The mace's strength was its ability to deliver powerful crushing blows, taking advantage of the weakness of mail in protecting against impact, but the weapon was unwieldy compared with the sword, and its principal advantage was against armored opponents.

For centuries, the mail shirt had been considered adequate body protection, but by the 14th century, warfare had changed, limiting the usefulness of the mail shirt. Chain mail began to be supplemented by solid iron plates. The move toward plate body armor began with the "coat-of-plates," which 14th-century Englishmen probably called a "jack," "plates," or "a pair of plates." There were many variations on the coat of plates, but most were constructed of rectangular iron plates riveted inside a cloth or leather "coat."

Over time, the coat-of-plates evolved in two different directions. On some armors, the plates became smaller and more numerous, allowing greater flexibility but sacrificing a degree of protection. References to "brigandine" appear as early as 1368, and it is likely that then, as later, the term referred to this sort of armor. The name came from its popularity among mercenary foot soldiers known as "brigands," although even knights wore this type of protection. Other coats-of-plates developed in the opposite direction. All other things being equal, a large plate spreads the force of a blow better than several small ones and is less likely to catch the point of a weapon. By the middle of the 14th century, some coats-of-plates included a large oval plate directly over the chest. By the 1370s, this plate commonly covered the entire front of the rib cage.

Knights also developed plates to cover their arms. At the top was the rerebrace, which covered the upper arm. The rerebrace did not always extend all the way around; some examples covered only the back of the arm. Full rerebraces enclosed the entire upper arm, with a hinge to allow them to be opened and straps and buckles to fasten them shut. Finally, the man-at-arms donned gauntlets and helmet. Iron gauntlets in this period had a distinctive hourglass shape, with a narrow wrist and flaring cuff to protect the wrist while allowing it to move freely. The knuckles were sometimes equipped with metal spikes known as gadlings.

By far the most characteristic style of helmet in the 14th century was the bascinet. It resembled a kind of steel hood, with a point somewhere above the crown of the head; it covered the entire head above the neck, except for the face. The bascinet evolved from a hemispherical skull cap worn in the 13th century and was already well developed by the 1320s. Toward the end of the century, the point became more pronounced. Typically, a light crest ran up the front to the point, continuing about one-third of the way down the back; as with the breastplate, this was designed to help deflect blows.

For extra protection, the face opening could be fitted with a visor. The most characteristic form of visor was the so-called hounskull, characterized by its pointed snout; others had a more rounded face. The visor most often pivoted on bolts at the temples, although some had a single hinge at the forehead. Visors were usually attached to the side pivots by a hinge-and-pin arrangement that allowed the visor to be removed.

In addition to its distinctive snout, the hounskull visor had eye slits and an angular mouth slit. In the later part of the 14th century, the mouth was fashionably cut in vertical slits suggesting teeth. Breathing holes were usually pierced on the right side only, and additional holes were often put around the mouth opening. The vision and ventilation afforded by this style of visor left something to be desired, and many contemporary illustrations show soldiers fighting with the visor open.

The typical 14th-century shield was made of wood; this was covered with canvas, leather, or both and then covered with a gypsum-based sealant called gesso and painted. A gentleman's shield usually bore his personal emblem or "arms." The man-at-arms used a fairly small shield, about two feet long, often curved and shaped like the bottom of an iron (whence its modern name, a "heater"). Ordinary infantry shields were larger. They were either circular, oval, or rectangular and equipped with a simple pair of straps, or strap and handle, for the arm. Small round shields called "bucklers" had a single handle in the center behind a protruding iron boss or spike.

During the 14th century, weapons evolved to meet the advances in armor. As plate armor improved, the thrust became more important. It could find the weak points in a harness; moreover, a thrust driven by the force of both arms, when concentrated on the tiny area struck by an acute weapon point, could pierce the heaviest plate. For this reason, the spear was highly popular and effective throughout the period, wielded either from horseback or on foot. The basic spear was an ash shaft 9 to 12 feet long topped by a steel head. Sword design also changed to emphasize the thrust. The older, parallel-sided, blunt-pointed blades, substantially unchanged since Viking times, began to be replaced by stiffer, more pointed blades.

Sword pommels, designed both to make the grip more secure and to help balance the weight of the blade, were also an opportunity for decoration. Some were of round or oval shape, but the "fig" shape, sometimes faceted, became increasingly common, being easier to grip with a second hand.

Other weapons relied on sheer force to smash through plate armor. The deadliest of these was the poll-axe (sometimes called a poleax today). With a heavy head on the end of a shaft five feet or longer, it possessed tremendous leverage. The head was often backed by a spike, fluke, or hammer head and topped by a spike as well. The bottom of the shaft was also used for thrusting; it was strengthened with a ring or spike. This type of axe was closely related to the pole-hammer, which bore a hammer head backed by a spike or fluke. Great heavy-headed mallets at the end of long shafts could also deal terrible blows. Single-handed weapons in this class included the mace, a single-handed club with a flanged steel head, and shorter versions of the poll-axe and hammer.

Daggers were ubiquitous during this period. They were worn by men of all classes, either with civilian clothes as the only weapon or with armor, opposite the sword. The most common form was the "baselard"; this had a wooden handle, quillon, and pommel forming an H-shape. The blade was usually double-edged, of diamond section, and varied in length from a few inches to two feet.

One of the most significant weapons on the 14th-century battlefield was the English longbow, which consisted of a six-foot bowstaff made of elm, ash, or (ideally) yew, with a bowstring of wax-coated linen. The arrows were a yard long. For war, they were equipped with a small pointed tip that could penetrate mail or even—at close range with a solid, well-placed hit—plate armor. An experienced archer might wield a bow of 80 pounds draw or more, even as much as 150 pounds; the maximum range of the weapon was about 400 yards. Such bows were used almost exclusively by the English; because they required enormous strength in certain muscles, they were only effective in the hands of an archer who had practiced intensely for a long time.

Other armies relied on the crossbow instead. Early in the 14th century, the crossbow typically had a bowstaff made of wood reinforced with horn and sinew; by midcentury, it was largely replaced by a more powerful steel staff. The crossbow had a far lower rate of fire than the longbow because it was much harder to load. Lighter ones had a foot stirrup in front: the bowman attached the string to a hook on his belt, crouched down to place his foot in the stirrup, and used the strength of his legs to string the bow. Other crossbows had to be strung with a lever or a small winch. The crossbow had much more power than a longbow, but its principal advantage was that it required little training to use.

During the course of the 14th century, a new form of missile weapon made its appearance in battle—the cannon, or "gun." Large versions were used on board ships and to assail fortifications, but there were also smaller hand cannons resembling a small cannon barrel mounted on a staff. Such weapons were as yet not a major factor on the battlefield, but they would eventually give rise to the firearms that rendered obsolete the armored knight of the Middle Ages (Singman, 120–24; Singman and McLean, 138–58).

To read about warfare in 18th-century England, see the England entry in the section "Warfare" in chapter 6 ("Political Life") of volume 4; and for Victorian England, see the England entry in the section "War and Military" in chapter 6 ("Political Life") of volume 5.

FOR MORE INFORMATION

Singman, J. L. *Daily Life in Medieval Europe*. Westport, Conn.: Greenwood Press, 1999.

Singman, J. L., and W. McLean. *Daily Life in Chaucer's England*. Westport, Conn.: Greenwood Press, 1995.

VIKINGS

In all of the Scandinavian countries, the art of war was based on the *leidang* (levy) system. The term designates any military expedition, but because of the topography of the three countries—mountainous barriers in Norway, impenetrable forests in Sweden, and extensive stretches of woodland in Denmark—the military attached to the sea, and the *leidang* was essentially a maritime organization, a naval levy.

The *leidang* may be characterized as a public fleet levy consisting of the freemen of the three countries under the leadership of the monarch, who was the chief military leader. The *leidang* system was founded upon a division of the country into districts. The farmers in each district were required to provide a ship of approximately 40 oars, along with men, equipment, and supplies for a ship. A shipmaster was selected to be in charge of the ship, its crew, the armament, and the provisions, and he was also the commander of the ship at sea.

Generally, it seems that for defensive purposes, the entire levy was required to convene. When the ships had gathered, it was then a question of awaiting news of the enemy's attack and the planned place of assault. Once such information was available, the main function of the fleet was to swiftly deliver fighting units to that location. Here they would be supported by locals, for every man was obliged to turn out to fight off invaders. Even slaves were allowed to fight under such circumstances, and a slave who killed an enemy was by law granted freedom. For offensive purposes, only a part of the *leidang* was selected, since obviously some forces had to remain at home to defend the country if necessary.

Battles on sea did not differ much from battles on land. In Scandinavian waters, the ships were lined up and roped together side by side to create one, two, or more lines of ships directly facing the enemy. The battle was typically begun with a volley of arrows against the enemy followed by an attempt to initiate hand-to-hand fighting on the enemy's deck with swords, spears, and axes. The victorious force was the one that succeeded in reducing the opposing force's resistance to such an extent that its ships could be cleared and taken over. The *leidang* system obviously owed much of its success to the quality of the ships. They were capable of moving swiftly and could be propelled by both oars and sail. Moreover, they were so light that they could be hauled overland from one river to another.

When battles were fought on land, the forces were arranged in lines with a center and wings that moved forward to hand-to-hand melee. The literary sources make reference to the deployment of forces in a wedge-shaped formation called *svinfylking* (pig-formation); those in the forefront were called *rani* (the snout). As with naval battles, the battles on land were initiated by a volley of arrows probably accompanied by war cries to encourage fellow warriors and terrify the enemy. According to the literary sources, it was also common for military leaders to incite their men with speeches before the battle began. Troops trained to fight on horseback appear to have been virtually nonexistent in battles during the Viking Age, and cavalry does not play any significant role until the early 12th century. The outcome of the battle was determined by the flight of the forces and/or the death of the leaders on one side. When the combat had ended, the wounded men were tended to by healers and the dead were buried. The plunder was then gathered and apportioned.

All freemen were required to own weapons and were permitted to carry them. According to the Norwegian provincial laws, a man's armament reflected his social status. A poor freeman would have only an axe and a shield, while a wealthy man would have a shield, a helmet, and a coat of mail, in addition to the Viking Age Scandinavian's three main weapons: sword, spear, and ax.

Of all weapons, the sword was the most prestigious and took pride of place. Swords were praised in poetry, and a great number of kennings (poetic metaphors) were devised for them, including "snake of wounds" and "flame of Odin." Some of the more special swords were even given names, such as *Brynjubitr* (Byrnie biter) and *Fotbitr* (Leg biter). The fact that sword hilts (that is, the guard made of bone, antler, ivory, or metal) were often decorated with animal motifs inlaid with copper, silver, or gold further demonstrates the glamour of the sword in Viking Age society.

Of all weapons, the sword was the most prestigious and took pride of place.

Double-edged swords were by far the most common. The total length of a normal sword was about 90 centimeters, the iron blade being typically 80 centimeters long and the tang 10 centimeters long. The blade was usually broad and tapered toward the blunted tip, for the sword was a cutting and not a thrusting weapon made for use in one hand. Many blades were made with the so-called pattern-welding technique—a laborious process that entailed welding together bars of iron, bending them, and then compressing them into a thin plate or sheet—which gave the blade an ornamented look. To this middle section, edges made of specially treated iron would be welded. A groove down the center of the blade on either side served to reduce the weight of the sword and give it flexibility. The sword was carried in a scabbard suspended on the left side from a strap across the right shoulder. The scabbard was made of thin wood covered with leather and lined with wool or fabric.

Apart from the sword, the most common weapon found in Viking Age graves is the spear, although spears are represented almost exclusively by their spearheads (the wooden shafts are seldom preserved). There were two main kinds of spear: the heavy throwing spear and the somewhat-lighter thrusting spear. Both were used for fighting and hunting. The blades, which are typically leaf-shaped with shoulders toward the socket, are up to 50 centimeters long and have a distinct midrib and a hollow cone-shaped socket to fit the end of the shaft. Some of the spears had pattern-welded blades and sockets richly inlaid with silver patterns.

The third main weapon, the ax, is the one with which the Viking Age Scandinavians are typically associated in popular culture. The importance of the ax may be somewhat overrated, however, for axes are not often found with other weapons in graves, and they are not celebrated to any significant extent in poetry. Several types of axes were used, and some of the ones that have been found in connection with settlements were probably tools rather than weapons. The earliest axes were simple woodworker's axes, but over time broad-bladed axes intended specifically for battle were manufactured. The characteristics of the battle ax are its broad neck and thin blade, which thickens immediately behind the edge. Some of the ax heads are beautifully ornamented.

Like spears, bows and arrows were used for both hunting and fighting, and it is reasonable to assume that they played an important role in battles, for they are often referred to in literary sources. Finds of Viking Age bows and arrows are rare, however. In fact, only one complete Viking Age bow has so far been discovered. It is a bow, about 192 centimeters long and made from a bough of yew, found in Hedeby. Arrowheads are frequently found in graves sometimes alongside the dead in bundles. Arrowheads were made of iron, and most of them are tanged, although some have sockets. The arrowheads take various forms, but a long leaf-shaped blade seems to have been the most common shape. The shafts were made of wood with a tied-on feather. The arrows were carried in cylindrical quivers.

The most important means of self-defense was the shield. Not many complete shields have been preserved, but they are well known from contemporary pictorial representations and from literary sources. The shield board was usually round and flat with a hole at the center for the handgrip covered by a hemispherical iron boss. Such shields hung in rows along the gunwales of the Viking ships.

Other protection in the form of helmets and mail shirts appears to have been less common and reserved for wealthy warriors. The most complete surviving Viking Age helmet comes from the 10th-century Gjermundbu grave from Ringerike in Norway. The helmet is made of iron and has the shape of a rounded cap. It consists of a series of iron plates riveted together with binding strips, and projecting below the helmet is a piece of iron that frames and protects the nose and eyes.

The best-preserved remains of a Viking Age mail shirt also comes from the Gjennundbu grave, although it is still difficult to get a clear idea of what it looked like in its original form. It is possible that it was knee-length and had sleeves. The shirt is made up of small rings with overlapping ends, but that other designs also existed is clear from a fragment of a chain mail found at Lund in Scania, consisting of closed rings each linking four others, and another fragment found in the fortress at Birka, consisting of small iron plates tied together.

Their weapons, warfare techniques, and fierce courage made Viking warriors a feared force all over Europe.

~*Kirsten Wolf*

FOR MORE INFORMATION

Sawyer, P. H. *Kings and Vikings*. New York: Routledge, 1993.
Wolf, K. *Daily Life of the Vikings*. Westport, Conn.: Greenwood Press, forthcoming.

CHINA

Like other ancient societies, China had a long history of war, but unlike most other societies, Chinese scholars developed a theory of warfare. The most famous treatise of military practice was written by Sun-Tzu (ca. 400–320 B.C.E.), *The Art of War,* in which he lays out the strategies that would lead to victory. His chapters include a discussion of topics that are present in modern military manuals: terrain, movement, timing, formation, offensive strategies, and even espionage. He recognizes five key factors to victory: morale, weather, terrain, command, and organization (Bradford, 135). It is not surprising that this treatise remained central to Chinese military life throughout the Middle Ages and continues to be used today.

Chinese warfare was influenced by more than treatises on strategy, however. Warriors were also influenced by technology and by their enemies. These things had as much influence on Chinese warfare as anything else. In China's earliest history, warfare was fought by individualistic warriors—heroes who delighted in showing their prowess. They approached battles and performed early skirmishes in two-wheeled chariots drawn by four horses. Three men rode the chariot: the driver, spearman, and archer. The battles assumed the nature of a duel with each chariot choosing to fight another individually. The end of the battle came when losing chariots fled or surrendered.

By 337 B.C.E., these early heroic, polite duels were over. The government had been centralized into several warring provinces, and warfare took on a larger scale. The crossbow was introduced in the later 4th century B.C.E., and iron was used for weapons. The chariot was replaced by horse cavalry in 307 B.C.E. as the Chinese faced seemingly endless wars with the Huns of Mongolia, whose mounted archers easily outstripped the more ponderous chariots. At this point, each leader had his own cavalry and a standing army drafted from peasants. Now armies developed siegecraft and catapults.

One famous example of a battle between the Chinese and the Huns took place in 99 B.C.E. The emperor sent 30,000 cavalry to attack the Huns, and the commander Li Ling requested that he be allowed to take an infantry force armed with crossbows to make a diversionary attack on the Huns. As he traveled with his force into the territory of the Huns, he was surrounded by a cavalry force of 30,000 Huns. Li Ling circled his wagons and arranged his forces with men with shields and lances in front and those with bows and crossbows behind. Li Ling's strategy was effective, and the Huns retreated to get reinforcements. The Huns attacked Li Ling's position by setting fires, and the Chinese started counterfires. The Huns had the weight of numbers, however, and the last of Li Ling's men (only 3,000 survivors) ran out of arrows. They used wagon spokes to use as clubs, but in the night the survivors slipped back. Only 400 made their way home, and Li Ling was captured (Bradford, 150). This episode shows several things about ancient Chinese warfare: the use of the various kinds of weapons, the importance of the numbers of combatants, and the advantage of mobility offered by the Huns. It also shows the weight the Chinese gave to good generals like Li Ling.

During the Han and later the Tang dynasties, these general policies continued—as did the threats from the Huns in the north. The Han dynasty built walls to protect its borders, and the walls continued to be built until they formed the Great Wall of China, that characteristic feature of ancient Chinese military culture. Defense remained at the heart of Chinese military strategy.

To read about warfare in 19th-century China, see the China entry in the section "War and the Military" in chapter 6 ("Political Life") of volume 5 of this series.

~Joyce E. Salisbury

FOR MORE INFORMATION

Bradford, A. S. *With Arrow, Sword, and Spear: A History of Warfare in the Ancient World.* London: Praeger, 2001.

ISLAMIC WORLD

By the time Muhammad died in 632, he had become the ruler of the Hijaz and had established tributary alliances with a number of the outlying tribes in Arabia. Sources make it clear that Muhammad achieved his goal of establishing a society that lived in accordance with God's commandments in part by persuasion but also by coercion and even warfare. While violence in the name of religion tends to make modern Westerners uncomfortable, the idea that brutality could be an expression of piety was neither new nor unique in the 7th-century Near East. The Bible is replete with stories in which the ancient Israelites slaughtered their enemies in the name of God.

One of the most controversial aspects of Muslim warfare is the idea of jihad. Jihad is an Arabic noun that conveys the idea of struggle or struggling. In the Qur'an, jihad is usually used as part of the phrase "jihad fi sabil Allah" (struggle in the path of God). Some Muslims, especially followers of the mystical (Sufi) traditions and other more piety-minded scholars, argued that there were two types of jihad—the greater jihad and the lesser jihad. For them, the greater jihad was that internal struggle within oneself against temptation and evil. This greater jihad is also referred to as the jihad of the tongue or the jihad of the pen: that is, the jihad of piety and persuasion. According to this position, military jihad was the lesser jihad, also known as the jihad of the sword, which is the type discussed here.

Jihad in the Qur'an is spoken of as offensive warfare against idolaters, polytheists, and infidels, but also defensively against those who fight against Muhammad, his followers, and right religion in general.

> Will you not fight against those who have broken their oaths and conspired to banish the Apostle? They were the first to attack you. Do you fear them? Surely God is more deserving of your fear, if you are true believers. Make war on them: God will chastise them at your hands and humble them. He will grant you victory over them and heal the spirit of the faithful. He will take away all rancour from their hearts: God shows mercy to whom He pleases. God is all-knowing and wise. (Qur'an 9:13–14)

In addition to this and other Qur'anic passages, Muslim scholars also appealed to a host of hadiths that extolled the merits of jihad against the enemies of right religion (however defined) and the rewards that awaited those engaged in it. According to one such hadith, Muhammad said:

> If anyone is pleased with God as Lord, with Islam as religion and with Muhammad as messenger, paradise will be assured to him. . . . There is also something else for which God will raise a servant in paradise a hundred degrees between each of two of which there is a distance like that between heaven and earth. . . . [That is], "jihad in God's path; jihad in God's path; jihad in God's path." (Al-Tibrizi, 817)

Since Muhammad found himself at war with the Meccans and others after his Hijra (Hegira) to Medina, it is easy to see the relevance of this and other statements to his immediate situation. After his death, his followers used these and many similar statements to form the basis for the ideology of jihad in the medieval Islamic world. They inspired many of the faithful during the first century of conquest even as others were undoubtedly inspired merely by booty and glory in battle. Once the frontiers of the new Islamic empire were more or less stabilized, the caliphs maintained an expansionist jihad ideology by leading or ordering raids along the Syrian Byzantine frontier. Many a caliph strengthened his own religious and political *bone fides* by leading the raids himself. The ʿAbbasid Harun al-Rashid (r. 786–809) is one of the most famous to have done so.

As Islamic scholars honed their understanding of right religion, they divided the world into two broad spheres in an effort to clarify the role of jihad and warfare in Islam—the Abode of Islam (*dar al-Islam*) and the Abode of War (*dar al-harb*). The Abode of Islam was comprised of those territories under Islamic political domination. The Abode of War was comprised of everywhere else. This division did not mean, however, that Muslims were at all times engaged in a state of open warfare against the Abode of War. Formal truces did exist. Moreover, for purely practical reasons of inertia, military capability, and political calculation, expansion of the borders of Islam waxed and waned over time.

During the Seljukid period, Turkoman bandits legitimated their raiding and pillaging throughout eastern and central Anatolia with the ideology of jihad. Such activities led to the disastrous defeat of the Byzantines at Manzikert in 1071, and the beginnings of the process of Anatolia becoming "Turkey." These disruptions along the Byzantine frontier were one of the reasons Urban II invoked when he called the First Crusade at Claremont in 1095, which resulted in the Frankish conquest of Jerusalem in 1099. Additional territories in Syria were lost to the crusaders, but Muslim forces regained all of them by the end of the 13th century.

On the other hand, territories in Iberia that had been under Muslim control since the 8th century were permanently lost to the Christian reconquest by the early 16th century.

Throughout the Middle Ages, Muslim armies fought successfully to expand the borders of the Islamic world in central Asia, India, Africa, Anatolia, and Europe. At other times, Muslim armies fought against other Muslim armies within the Islamic world to restore a particular vision of proper Islamic religion and government. We see this in the civil wars that plagued the early Muslim community during the Rashidun (632–61) and the Umayyad Caliphates (661–750). We see this also in the ʿAbbasid Revolution in the late 740s that established the ʿAbbasid Caliphate, which endured until the Mongols sacked Baghdad in 1258.

While the concept of jihad established abstract principles of Muslim warfare, in fact, it was the history of actual wars that created the practical reality of medieval Muslim warfare. At the very beginning, Muhammad had to fight to occupy his home town and establish himself as the direct ruler of Mecca and Medina, and these early battles teach us something about the nature of warfare in early Islamic history, including the role of raids, camels, horses, infantry, weapons, women in battle, siege warfare, exile and even the execution of one-time allies.

Whether in relatively minor raids, in pitched battles among archers, infantry, or cavalry, or when one side laid siege to another, sources indicate that combatants generally were outfitted with similar body armor and weapons. Literary sources employ a range of vocabulary to describe military equipment, which included coats of mail, helmets, shields, swords, spears, lances, knives, iron maces, bows, arrows, and *naft* (Greek fire). Because each person was expected to provision himself, only the wealthiest were outfitted completely. For example, despite its critical role as body armor, it is likely that only a small percentage of soldiers could actually afford a coat of mail, given the great expense and craftsmanship involved in producing one. In fact, we learn that seven decades after Muhammad's death (704 C.E.), the province of Khurasan in eastern Iran had a military force of some 50,000 men but only 350 coats of mail (Kennedy, 169–70).

Helmets were crucial for protection as well. Many were constructed with pieces of mail or other fabric that hung down from the back to protect the neck. There is even the occasional mention of helmets with nose guards. It should come as no surprise that some fought without helmets for reasons of expense; others did without them for other reasons. Before he met his fate as a Meccan champion at Badr, one officer looked for a helmet to put on his head; because he could not find one that would fit him, he wound a piece of cloth he had around his head.

Swords were the principal weapons used at this time. They were straight, hilted, and carried on straps around the shoulder or waist. The earliest evidence of curved swords or scimitars is from the 9th century and among the soldiers in Khurasan. A great deal is made of swords in early Arabic literature, and according to our sources, the best swords came from India followed by those made in Yemen and Syria after the Indian fashion. Given the number of stories of severed legs, arms, hands, and heads, these swords appear to have been put to use effectively. Very few early Islamic swords have actually survived, but those that have correspond to the descriptions in the sources as about 100 centimeters in length, 6 to 9 centimeters in width and 1.15 kilograms in weight.

Most battles were fought among infantry and archers, in part because of the general scarcity of horses. However, it is clear that horses were critically important to those who had them. Because of their scarcity and importance, horses tended to be led to battle and only mounted when hostilities broke out. Sources indicate that horses were outfitted with some sort of protection as well. Although it is unclear what materials were used, there is no evidence that horses were outfitted with mail or any other sort of iron armor. Given the disparity of coats of mail to soldiers, one can assume that it was simply far too expensive to outfit one's horse in such a fashion at this early date.

In the process of the early Islamic conquests, Muslim armies captured far more horses than were available to them in Arabia. They also adopted new equipment as a result of their encounters. Sources indicate that one of the principal innovations borrowed from the Persians in the late 7th century was the iron stirrup. Leather loop stirrups were not unknown in Arabia, and sources portray mounted archers as very effective even without the benefit of stirrups at all. The adoption of the iron stirrup in the late 7th century encouraged the widespread use of the mounted archer and the replacement of infantry by cavalry as the dominant force on the battle field by the early third of the 9th century.

Siege warfare was known in 7th-century Arabia, but the residents of the Hijaz were not very good at it and preferred to fight out in the open. The early Muslim armies of course laid siege to cities and even took refuge behind fortifications such as the trench dug by Muhammad at Medina in 627. However, the sources indicate that during the conquest period as well as during the Umayyad and early ʿAbbasid Caliphates, many preferred to fight in the open and found that fighting from behind walls was too restrictive. Others even deemed it dishonorable to seek refuge behind walls. When the early Muslim armies actually deployed siege engines and other techniques of siege warfare, it tended to be against non-Muslim fortresses along the frontiers. By the time of the crusader period, much had changed.

A significant turning point in Muslim warfare (as well as in long-term relations between the West and the Muslim world) took place in the late 11th century, when Pope Urban II called the First Crusade at Claremont in 1095, which resulted in the Frankish conquest of Jerusalem in 1099. The crusader enterprise in the Near East (1095–1291) represents a major turning point in the discussion of daily life in the medieval Islamic world, for it is during the crusader period that one can really begin to speak of world history in an integrated sense. That is, political institutions, religious trends, military adventures, technological advancements, and a host of other developments in western Europe, the Italian city-states, Byzantium, North Africa, the Near East, central Asia, India, Mongolia, and elsewhere converge at one time or another during the 12th and 13th centuries in the eastern Mediterranean.

There is evidence that some Syrian preachers and scholars decried the loss of Jerusalem and even undertook missions to Baghdad for assistance from the ʿAbbasid caliphs and Seljukid sultans. But neither was in a position to respond favorably to such requests. It was not until 1144, when a Turkish commander named Zengi captured the Frankish city of Edessa (ostensibly on behalf of his ʿAbbasid overlords), that we find the first successful Muslim counteroffensive against the Franks. His son Nur al-Din (d. 1174), after occupying Damascus in 1154, was able to unite the Muslim controlled areas of Syria and undertook his own jihad against the Franks. He also dealt the Franks a decisive defeat at the Battle of Hattin in 1187 and retook Jerusalem shortly thereafter.

While the styles of weapons varied from place to place and time period to time period, the warriors of the crusader period generally employed many of the same types of weapons used during the early period already discussed—coats of mail, helmets, shields, swords, spears, lances, knives, iron maces, lassos, bows, arrows, and *naft* (Greek fire). In addition, although the Fatimid navy in Egypt was able to acquit itself fairly well in the early 12th century, there was essentially no naval resistance to the Franks from Syria. In the end, what distinguished the Muslim forces during the crusader era was the absolutely crucial role of cavalry forces (both freeborn and mamluk regiments) as well as the improved techniques of siege warfare. (See the Islamic World entry in the section "Peasants, Serfs, and Slaves," in this chapter for a discussion of the mamluks).

~James Lindsay

FOR MORE INFORMATION

Al-Tibrizi. *Mishkat al-Masabih*. Vol. 3. Translated by James Robson. Lahore: Ashraf Press, 1972.

Hillenbrand, C. *The Crusades: Islamic Perspectives*. Edinburgh: Edinburgh University Press, 1999.

Holt, P. M. *The Age of the Crusades: The Near East from the Eleventh Century to 1517*. New York: Longman, 1986.

Kennedy, H. *The Armies of the Caliphs*. New York: Routledge, 2001.

Lindsay, J. *Daily Life in Medieval Islam*. Westport, Conn.: Greenwood Press, forthcoming.

Riley-Smith, J. *The Crusades: A Short History*. New Haven, Conn.: Yale University Press, 1987.

BYZANTIUM

Byzantium owed its long survival to both military power and diplomatic efforts to avoid committing it in decisive engagements. The extensive territories of the early empire, which reached from the Near East across the Mediterranean, ensured that Byzantine military strategy would be primarily defensive in nature. The shift in the early 4th century from a frontier-based defense to mobile field units brought few major changes to the battlefield. Repeated conflict with the Persians and Avars led to the Byzantine development of a well-equipped cavalry supported by archers. Contemporary observers and historians provide much information about military affairs and planning. Important treatises include the late 6th-century *Strategikon* of the emperor Maurice, the *Taktika* of Leo VI (ca. 905), and the *Sylloge Tacticorum* of the later 10th century. These documents cover history, exercises, and strategy, as well as the weaponry and support equipment needed for successful field operations. Illustrations of weapons and armor appear in several late Byzantine books, especially a 12th-century manuscript of John Skylitzes (now in Madrid), but these may not accurately represent current practice. Few surviving examples of weapons have actually been identified.

Byzantine field equipment continued the main types of Roman weaponry. The basic implement was the *spathion*, a long two-edged sword that was worn on a belt or baldric over the shoulder by foot soldiers and cavalrymen. Swords used during the 10th century are thought to have measured about 36 inches long, including the hilt. A curved saber-like sword (*paramerion*) of similar length was used by the cavalry.

Foot soldiers and horsemen carried a variety of long weapons. The *kontarion* or infantry spear was essential. In the 10th century, infantry spears stood about 13 feet long and were tipped by an iron point. The *menaulion* was an especially sturdy infantry spear or pike with a 20-inch-long blade that was used against armored cavalry. Similar *kontaria* were used by the cavalry. During the 6th and 7th centuries, cavalry lances had a thong at midshaft and a pennant. Shorter javelins and simple slings were widely employed as well.

Iron axes, clubs, and maces were used for throwing and close-quarter combat. The hand ax had a single curved or straight blade, sometimes with a thick spike on the opposite side. This seems to have been the weapon of choice among northern mercenaries, including the Rus and the Varangian Guard.

Both infantry and cavalry troops used a light composite reflex bow. The large infantry bow was strung against the bow's natural flex, which was reinforced with animal sinew and horn, and had an estimated range of almost a thousand feet. The smaller cavalry bows, which stood about 45 to 48 inches tall, were designed for greater accuracy at short distances. Arrows were about 27 inches long. A portable crossbow (*solenarion*) seems to have had a hollowed wooden stock for simultaneously launching multiple short arrows, known as "mice" (*myias*). The Western type of crossbow apparently was introduced by the crusaders for it was unknown before the late 11th century.

Shields were carried by both foot soldiers and cavalrymen. A small round shield (*thureos*) with a diameter of 12 to 30 inches was carried by ground troops and horsemen. The heavy infantry shield (*skuta*) consisted of a large oval or rectangle measuring about three by four feet; it was made of wood covered with iron or leather, sometimes with a central spike. The 10th-century *Sylloge* also mentions large kite-shaped shields, which were worn strapped to the shoulder. Later manuscript illustrations regularly depict Western-style triangular shields.

Several kinds of body armor were worn by Byzantine soldiers, even though the mountainous terrain and warm Mediterranean climate limited its effectiveness. Infantrymen were protected by corselets and short cloaks made of felt, wool, boiled leather, or horn lamellar. Foot soldiers and cavalrymen alike might wear reinforced arm guards, greaves, padded caps, and iron helmets, sometimes with chain-mail attachments along the back and sides; altogether this armor could weigh over 33 pounds. Cloaked horses and armored riders were deployed against the Persians as early as the 4th century, but heavy cavalry forces were not widely used until developed by the emperor Nikephoros II Phokas in the late 10th century. These *kataphraktoi* wore long felt cloaks over their lamellar or chain-mail armor, wore heavy iron helmets, and wielded both mace and saber. Large groups of these mounted troops were deployed in wedge formations with the aim of smashing through infantry lines.

Larger field weapons were used in siege operations. The simple trebuchet-type catapult (*petrobola*) was used widely in the east Mediterranean. This consisted of a beam mounted asymmetrically on a crossbar, which was pulled by attached ropes to hurl stones or other projectiles from a sling. Smaller stones or arrows could be fired by a stationary crossbow (*cheiroballistron*), which used a high-tension locking string. Mobile wood towers (*helepoleis*) and battering rams (*krioi*) were built at the site of siege by military engineers.

The manufacture of weaponry was an important state responsibility. Weapons, armor, and uniforms were made in a series of imperial factories (*fabricae*) located throughout the early Byzantine Empire. In later times, these became geographically consolidated but continued to operate in both the capital and provinces. On occasion, new recruits were expected to bring their own equipment purchased from private suppliers.

The most-feared Byzantine weapon was the incendiary device known as Greek fire. The first recorded account of the "liquid flame" (*hygron pyr*) dates to 678, when the Byzantine navy used it to repel the Arab fleet then besieging the capital. It was used with equal success in sea battles against the Arabs in 717 and the Kievan Rus in 941, as well as with land-based siege machinery on other occasions. Although naphtha and other flammable substances were known earlier, the nature of this spectacular weapon remained a carefully guarded secret throughout Byzantine history and continues to stir debate. Modern consensus holds that it probably involved a mixture of crude oil, bitumen, resin, and sulfur, which was heated and sprayed through a firing tube (*strepton*) before being ignited. Some technical skill was needed to deploy the weapon effectively; supplies captured by the Bulgars could not be successfully used by the enemy. Other incendiary materials may also have been contained in explosive ceramic "grenades" found by archaeological excavations in the Near East. The lack of gunpowder and saltpeter, however, left the Byzantines unable to respond to the Turkish cannons used to besiege the capital in the 15th century.

~*Marcus Rautman*

FOR MORE INFORMATION

Haldon, J. F. *The Byzantine Wars. Battles and Campaigns of the Byzantine Era.* Charleston, S.C.: Tempus, 2001.

Heath, I. *Byzantine Armies, 886–1118.* London: Osprey, 1979.

MONGOLS

The army was the backbone of Mongol rule during its days of empire. Immediately after the *Quriltai* (grand council meeting of the Mongol nobility) of 1206, which

confirmed him as Qa'an or Great Khan, Chinggis Khan began to consolidate power and reorganize his army in anticipation of expansion from the Steppe into the Sown, the settled lands southeast and southwest of his homelands. He introduced the process of decimalization, where military units were divided into decimal units. In addition, where possible, he broke up tribal structures and rewarded with command postings those who had been loyal to him during the lean years of his rise to power. The breakup of the tribal makeup of his fighting force was to have profound effects on the loyalty, discipline, and effectiveness of his army. Family and clan had been replaced by unit, and loyalty was given first to the unit and its commander and, indeed, ultimately to the Great Khan himself. Strict discipline and a well-defined chain of command with duties and responsibilities itemized and standardized gave every soldier a position in the brave new world that the Mongols were carving out for themselves.

The *ordu* (base camp) was a tightly regulated unit, and its layout and organization were often uniform so that visitors would immediately know where to find the armory, the physician's tent, or the chief. The fighting men, which included all males from 14 to 60 years, were organized into the standard units, named *arbans* (10 men), *jaguns* (100 men), *minghans* (1,000 men), and *tümens* (10,000 men); these units were overseen by the *tümen* quartermaster, called the *jurtchi*. Such an organization meant that no order would ever have to be given to more than 10 men at any one time. Transfers between units were forbidden. Soldiers fought as part of a unit, not as individuals. Individual soldiers, however, were responsible for their equipment, weapons, and up to five mounts. Their families and even their herds would accompany them on foreign expeditions.

Soldiers wore protective heavy silk undershirts, a practice learned from the Chinese. Even if an arrow pierced their mail or leather outer garment, the arrow head was unlikely to pierce the silk. In this way, even though a wound might be opened up in the flesh, the actual metal would be tightly bound in the silk and so would be prevented from causing more extensive harm and would also be easier to withdraw later. The silk undershirt would be worn beneath a tunic of thick leather, layered armor-plate or mail, and sometimes a cuirass of leather-covered iron scales. Whether the helmet was leather or metal depended on rank. Contemporary illustrations depict helmets with a central metal spike bending backward; others end in a ball with a plume and wide neck-guard shielding the shoulders and the jaws and neck. Shields were leather-covered wicker.

The Mongols were famous for their mastery of firing their arrows in any direction while mounted and galloping at full speed. Strapped to their backs, their quivers contained 60 arrows for use with two bows made of bamboo and yak horn. The light cavalry was armed with a small sword and two or three javelins while the heavy horsemen carried a long lance (4 meters) fitted with a hook, a heavy mace or ax and a scimitar (an Asian sword with a curved blade broadening toward the point).

On campaign, all fighting men were expected to carry their equipment and provisions as well as their weaponry. A horsehair lasso, a coil of stout rope, an awl, needle and thread, cooking pots, leather water bottles, and a file for sharpening arrows would be among the utilities possibly carried in an inflatable saddlebag fashioned from a cow's stomach. When fording rivers, this saddlebag, if inflated, could double as a float.

The *nerge* or hunt was not only a source of entertainment and food but was vital in the training of the Mongol army as a disciplined and coordinated fighting force.

Propaganda and terror were also tools of the Mongol army. So terrible was their reputation that victory was often achieved without actual fighting. They deliberately exaggerated and encouraged the horror stories to ensure speedy surrender. This ploy was so effective that it is this element of their conquests that shapes their reputation to this day.

Chinggis Khan and his cavalry chase retreating forces. This indicates the importance of cavalry to the Mongol forces and shows their round shields and impressive swords. © Bibliothèque Nationale, Paris, France/Bridgeman Art Library.

The *yam* was the Mongols' imperial communications network, the efficacy of which ensured the unity and cohesiveness of the empire and its armies. It is first mentioned during the Great Khan Ögödei's reign (1229–41). The network was run by the army, and therefore it crisscrossed the whole expanse of Mongol-controlled territory from eastern Europe to the Sea of Japan. Post houses were established every three or four *farsangs* (3 to 4.5 miles), and each *yam* had at least 15 horses in good condition and ready to go; according to Marco Polo (d. 1324), the Venetian merchant who served at the court of the Great Khan Kublai, each had between 200 and 400 ready mounts. Rashīd al-Dīn (1248–1318), the historian and prime minister to the Mongols in Iran, puts the figure at 500 mounts, but it can be assumed that different routes would have different requirements. *Īlchis* (messengers, representatives) would be authorized to make use of these waiting horses as well as replenish their supplies or seek shelter if their journey was to be continued by another waiting *īlchi*. Although the army was entrusted with operating and replenishing these numerous *yam* stations, it was the local peasantry who supplied the food, fodder, and generous provisions that were made available to the *īlchīs* and others passing through. Officially, only persons on official business and in possession of a tablet of authority, a *paiza*, made of wood, silver, or gold and engraved in the Uighur script with a tiger or gerfalcon at its head, were permitted to make use of the *yam* services.

Chinggis Khan succeeded in transforming a disparate group of feuding bandit tribes into a united and mighty fighting force by revolutionizing steppe society and regulating and controlling those skills his people excelled at, namely, horsemanship, archery, mounted warfare, and battle discipline. Later, he added the military skills and techniques of the people he had conquered; an international force that his sons led to further conquests.

~George Lane

FOR MORE INFORMATION

Chambers, J. *The Devil's Horsemen*. London: Weidenfeld and Nicholson, 1979.
Morgan, D. *The Mongols*. Oxford: Blackwell, 1986.
Turnbull, S. R. *The Mongols*. Men-at-Arms Series no. 105. Oxford: Osprey Publishing, 1985.

POLITICAL LIFE
WARFARE & WEAPONS
Europe
Vikings
China
Islamic World
Byzantium
Mongols
Polynesia

POLYNESIA

Warfare was common among ancient Polynesians, and all district chiefs devoted much of their time training and preparing for war. Some island groups with more centralized governments—Tonga, for example—experienced fewer wars than others, but even then, ancient warfare was frequent, fierce, and savage. Wars broke out between families, districts, islands, and sometimes between different neighboring island groups where those island groups lay close to each other (Tonga and Samoa, for example). The reasons for going to war were many, just as in modern times—breaking of a mutual treaty, murdering a visitor or messenger from a different district, rebelling against an unjust leader, jealousy between district leaders, competition for the love of a beautiful woman, greed over another chief's lands, and so on.

From their early childhood, young Polynesians grew up hearing minute details of the battles their fathers had participated in, and their daily sports consisted of mock skirmishes and exercises to increase their fighting abilities. Certain dances were even choreographed to promote the fighting agility of both boys and girls. Although no professional armies were known throughout Polynesia, there were often skilled fighters (called *toa* or *koa*) who were attached to a district chief and who could be assembled at a moment's notice. The rest of the fighters consisted of any adult male who could be called up to aid in the battle when needed.

A New Zealand Māori warrior with a hand-carved club (patu), a traditionally styled facial tattoo, and other decorations, poses in front of a Māori community house (whare whakairo). Photo courtesy of the Institute for Polynesian Studies.

When a chief believed that he had been wronged or injured, he would generally call a council of his advisors, subordinate chiefs, and temple priests. The appointed speakers would sit at one end of the council, with the high chief and his advisors at the other. Subordinate chiefs would sit in a row to the left of the two groups and the priests in another to the right facing the chiefs. Speakers would stand in the center of the assembly and discuss the issue, after which the chiefs would discuss the number of men and the amount of provisions they could muster from their districts for the proposed war. Priests were then asked to seek divine guidance in the matter through trances or dreams, through auguries—the reading of the entrails of sacrificed animals—or through various other omens that were revealed by the gods. Human sacrifices might be required if the outcome of the battle was significant. Once all had been said and done, the final decision rested with the high chief. If the decision was war, the council would be dismissed and the whole district would prepare for the forthcoming battle. Heralds traveled throughout the districts to announce details of the impending conflict.

District chiefs would then call up their men. They would bring their personal war weapons and whatever other victuals they could and camp out around the chief's dwelling in small lean-tos or grass huts until the designated time of the battle. Women and children would often accompany the men into battle to act as caretakers, and frequently, many wives could be seen fighting alongside their husbands. War weapons consisted of handmade slings, javelins, spears, scythes, and clubs, all of various lengths and sizes. Slings were easily tucked into one's belt and brought out at a moment's notice. Stones could often be picked up on the field of battle, or more formidable ones could be honed at home and brought along. Slings and stones were often more destructive than the common bow and arrow found among other cultures. Javelins, spears, and clubs were carved from wood (iron was unknown in those days), and they ranged in size from 5 to 20 feet in length. They were often carved with barbs and notches and embedded with shark teeth in order to disembowel the enemy in one fell swoop. Some had ropes attached to their ends so that they could be retrieved after they had been thrown at the enemy.

The normal war dress among most Polynesians was as little as possible, consisting of a simple loincloth and perhaps a type of protective turban around the head; in Tahiti, however, the warriors wore their finest capes, helmets, and neck gorgets. Just as on festive occasions, fighters would lubricate their skin with coconut oil and attach colorful feathers and flowers around their heads, wrists, and ankles.

About three days prior to the intended battle, temple priests would check again for any omens that might foretell the outcome of the battle. God images would be taken from their storage containers and exposed fully to the public for the duration of the three-day ritual. If the battle was significant enough, human sacrifices might be offered to the gods. On other occasions, a long banana shoot, resembling a human being, would be sufficient. After prayers, feasting, and prophecy, the god images would be returned to their safe, and often-secret, resting places, so that they could not be found and destroyed by the enemy. In Hawai'i, however, the priests carried their national war gods into battle and shouted at the tops of their lungs to let the enemy know that their gods were accompanying them.

Meanwhile, the warriors set up protection against invasion throughout the district. Fortifications were set up at various strategic passes in the mountains; protective embankments were built from trees hewn down and piled over with sand and earth; and women, children, the aged, and infirm were secreted away to hiding places in the mountains.

On the day of the battle, the armies would face off. Sometimes each side would send a single warrior before it to confront a rival competitor from the opposite side. The two champions would taunt each other with boastful chants until they clashed together in hand-to-hand combat while their comrades spurred them on with their shouts of encouragement and support. When one fell in battle, another would rise and take his place. It was considered dishonorable for anyone else to interfere in the duel competition. This type of battle might go on for hours and days before the two sides considered a truce or decided that the time had come for all-out war.

Very little strategy was usually exhibited in the fighting. Normally, one side rushed the other without regard to any preconceived notion of what to expect. Sometimes, however, the warriors would be marshaled up into a crescent body with their chiefs located in the protective center. Other formations included individual groups of warriors that advanced together, or perhaps even solid lines were drawn up facing each other. In most instances, however, the method of attack by both sides was amicably agreed upon prior to the actual confrontation, similar to the medieval "gentlemen's battle." But different from the medieval knight who stood his ground to the last, the Polynesian who fled the fastest when the stakes were down was considered the bravest warrior.

When an enemy was routed, the victorious army pursued its survivors and cut them down without mercy. Prisoners (both men and women) who were taken captive were considered slaves. The victors buried their dead and let the corpses of the enemy rot on the battlefield. The enemy's lands were seized and reapportioned among the victorious chiefs.

Peace truces were sometimes called when both sides considered winning no longer possible. Messengers were then sent to each side with tokens of peace (a banana shoot and a ti leaf branch) to negotiate a peace treaty. If all was agreed, a pig was sacrificed and a symbolic wreath of two vines, plaited together, was placed in the temple. After that, both sides entered into festivities that included feasting, dancing, and public games. Each then returned home where religious ceremonies were conducted to offer up thanksgiving to the gods for their success. Prisoners of war were usually sacrificed and their heads laid on the religious altars. Food sacrifices were also offered to the gods, and the whole district then commemorated their victory with great feasting, dancing, and entertainment.

~*Robert D. Craig*

FOR MORE INFORMATION

Ferdon, E. N. *Early Tonga as the Explorers Saw It, 1616–1810*. Tucson: University of Arizona Press, 1987.

Handy, E.S.C. *Ancient Hawaiian Civilization*. Rev. ed. Rutland, Vt.: Charles E. Tuttle, 1965.

Henry, T. *Ancient Tahiti*. Honolulu: Bernice P. Bishop Museum, 1928.

POLITICAL LIFE: WEB SITES

http://es.rice.edu/ES/humsoc/Galileo/Things/inquisition.html
http://www.byu.edu/ipt/projects/middleages/LifeTimes/People.html
http://www.deremilitari.org/resources.htm
http://www.jajz-ed.org.il/juice/2000/jerusalem/j3k-9,k-9.html
http://www.pbs.org/wgbh/nova/lostempires/trebuchet/race.html

7

RECREATIONAL LIFE

RECREATIONAL LIFE

SPORTS & GAMES

HUNTING

MUSIC & DANCE

ENTERTAINMENT

Play is serious business. All mammals play, but humans have cultivated recreation to a high art. After family and work, most of our energies and time are devoted to recreational activities, and as any modern sports enthusiast knows, we can play with as much passion as we work. What are recreational activities? There are several characteristics that all play shares. First, it is voluntary—one can't be forced to play. As such, it is in fact the very essence of freedom, and even slaves and prisoners have treated themselves to games or music or dance for the sheer voluntary quality of the activities. Second, recreation is outside of "real" life, limited in time, duration, and space. Thus, playtime by contrast almost defines "work" time; recess at school not only offers a break from study—it marks the serious times when one is to learn. Third, recreation has its own rules that are more rigorous and predictable than anything we can find in our more complex "real lives." At the end of the game—and there is a definitive end—there is a winner and loser, and the rules are clear. Of course, cheating is always a possibility (archaeologists have even found loaded dice in Anglo-Saxon settlements), but even unsportsmanlike conduct is recognizable. It may be that we love games precisely for the clarity of the rules. Finally, recreational life builds a group identity among the "players," and this is true even of individual sports such as archery or bicycling, for "archers" see themselves as linked with others who share the pastime.

While recreational activities throughout history share these general characteristics, the particular forms of play we choose shed light on who we are and what we value. In play, we prepare ourselves for the rest of our lives. For example, games from the Olympics to chess hone our skills for war, while music and art stimulate our creativity. Violent sports from dog fights to boxing steel us to face violence in life, and team sports like American football prepare us to work together in an economy of separation of skills. In studying the games people play, we can more fully understand the society they are creating.

Recreation usually takes one of two forms: participatory and spectator. Most medieval recreation was participatory. People of all classes engaged in active sports outdoors and games indoors. Modern people would find many of the games familiar—archery, ball games, chess, backgammon and cards—all filled the lives of medieval people all over Eurasia. Just as now, recreational activities divided along class lines. The nobility had the leisure to cultivate elaborate hunting for pleasure. It takes years to train a hunting hawk or skilled hunting dog, and the nobility prided itself on this kind of recreation that they believed enhanced their skill in warfare. Men of the lower classes played at wrestling, which required little preparation. (The exception to this was the highly trained sumo wrestlers in Asia.)

In some ways, medieval recreation was significantly different from ours. Much medieval recreation was dangerous and violent. The mock battles of the nobility so regularly caused injury that the church constantly tried (with little success) to ban them. Spectator sports were even more violent—people cheered as dogs, chickens, bears, or other animals fought to the death. Most of these sports—with the exception of bullfights—are banned today in most parts of the Western world, but they were greatly beloved in the Middle Ages.

Like today, medieval people of all classes loved music and dance. Talented musicians were invited to courts and cheered in town squares. Without recorded music, people needed more musicians who played instruments live, but it also meant that everyone was prepared to sing, dance, and play rudimentary instruments to accompany themselves. Music was much more of a participatory recreation in the Middle Ages than it is now.

Medieval recreation was also different from ours in the degree to which people bet on the results. Players of all games from China to Scandinavia to Polynesia enjoyed the game more if they could gamble on the results. People placed wagers on everything from a favorite dog in a fight to a wrestler to a chess game. Modern societies try to regulate gambling to protect somewhat the players, but medieval rulers had no such inclination. Recreation was always a gamble.

~Joyce E. Salisbury

FOR MORE INFORMATION

Huizinga, J. *Homo Ludens: A Study of the Play Element in Culture*. Boston, Mass.: Beacon Press, 1964.

Sports and Games

Medieval people enjoyed a wide variety of sports and games, perhaps even more than we do, since much recreation in the 21st century focuses on visual entertainment in television or movies. Without such electronic media, medieval people all over the world created many games.

One category of sports included outdoor participatory sports, and these often involved honing skills for warfare. European aristocracy loved tournaments and jousts during which mounted knights engaged in mock battles with blunted weapons. These were dangerous, and people were frequently injured—as late as the 16th century, King Henry II of France died of infection when a lance splintered during a joust and a fragment of the wood gouged his eye. Danger notwithstanding, the European aristocracy loved their sporting battles. Commoners, too, engaged in mock battle games. In Europe, they had archery contests and fought each other with sticks or cudgels. They also engaged in wrestling matches. In China, sumo wrestling was practiced and raised to an art form that continues to be widely admired today.

Ball games were also popular sports, and unlike today where more people watch than play, in the Middle Ages more people played. In the West, people played early versions of tennis, badminton, baseball, and bowling. From China to England, people played a form of soccer with a ball that was often filled with feathers. The Chinese developed polo, which was played on horseback and which often led to injury of both animal and rider; the Muslims quickly took up this game. Ball games were so popular that they were briefly banned in England in 1363 as a way to make commoners engage in archery to improve their military skills.

Medieval people loved to wager on games, and betting was a major feature of the spectator sports as well as the participatory ones. From the earliest years of the Middle Ages, people enjoyed playing dice—and gambling on the results. Archaeologists have even discovered "loaded" dice with which players could cheat unsuspecting participants.

Favored spectator sports appear very violent to modern eyes, and most have been banned. People loved to watch bull and bear baiting, where dogs would fight with the larger animals. Bulldogs were bred with a short muzzle so they could breathe while gripping tenaciously to a bull's nose to slowly weaken the beast. Dog fights, too, were well attended. Cockfighting was popular from China to Europe, and fierce roosters were armed with sharp spurs to tear each other apart during a fight. Bull fighting is the only medieval blood sport that remains popularly played today, although other animal fights do continue.

People also played a number of indoor games to while away the evening hours. Board games were very popular from China to the northern reaches of Scandinavia. Archaeologists have found pieces for games similar to backgammon and *Go*, but the favored aristocratic game was chess. Chess seems to have begun in India and spread from there to Persia. By the 8th century, it had become widely popular throughout the Muslim world, and caliphs invited chess champions to palace matches. Skilled women played chess and even in the Muslim world were invited to participate in champion matches. Chess mimicked the endless warfare of the period, and players believed they honed their strategic skills by playing. Chess was so popular everywhere that great amounts of money were spent on magnificent chess sets.

In the 14th century, the Turks had developed playing cards, which would revolutionize indoor games. They had four suits like modern decks, and the variety of games that were available made the cards so popular that they rivaled chess as the favored pastime. Playing cards spread from the Muslim world through Italy from Venetian traders and from there north throughout Europe.

The sports and games of the Middle Ages look very familiar to modern eyes. It seems that humans everywhere love to challenge themselves physically and mentally, and to challenge each other as well. We have not lost our love for games—even though today many of them are played on computers.

~Joyce E. Salisbury

EUROPE

One favorite aristocratic pastime in Europe was the tournament, along with related martial sports. The oldest form was the tournament proper, which involved a mass of armored horsemen fighting as two teams. Combat took place within a limited area, typically about the size of a modern football field, surrounded by heavy barriers. The two sides might initially charge each other with lances and then fight out the combat with blunt swords, maces, or clubs. The awarding of prizes was in the hands of judges, often a panel of ladies. Somewhat less chaotic was the joust, which gained favor as the tournament lost it. The joust pitted armored horsemen against each other one by one, charging with sharp or blunt lances. At any given occasion, a number of horsemen would challenge each other, often divided into two teams of "holders" and "comers." In other forms of single combat, the participants might fight on foot with swords, axes, or daggers. Such contests were extremely dangerous and were generally only fought up to a certain number of blows in order to reduce the risk.

Commoners practiced martial sports too, although they were less elaborate. Their favorite weapons were cudgels, quarterstaves, and sword-and-buckler (the buckler being a small round shield). As with aristocratic combat, such pastimes could be very dangerous—or even more so, since commoners did not wear armor. Somewhat less risky was wrestling, another favorite among commoners. Play could be full contact or it could allow grasping an opponent's clothes or a cloth sash worn over one shoulder. The aim could be either to give the opponent a simple fall, to pin him, or to throw him outside a circle. People also engaged in what is now called chicken fighting, with two wrestlers mounted on the shoulders of two supporters, each trying to throw his opponent off.

Some entertainments were pure demonstrations of athleticism. Men exhibited their strength by casting axles and heavy stones, or they showed their speed in foot races. In the winter, people skated on frozen rivers and lakes on skates made of bone.

Ball games existed in a number of variations. An edict of 1363, attempting to stem the decay of English archery, forbade other sports including "handball," "football," "stickball," and "cambok." Medieval football was similar to its modern European namesake, known in the United States as soccer. The game was invariably rowdy and sometimes extremely dangerous. Similar in structure was the game of cambok, a sort of field hockey, named for the cambok or cammock, the curved stick often carried by shepherds. Variants (or other names) included goff and bandy. A rather more dangerous ball game was camp ball, comparable to rugby and American football. There were two goals, which might be miles apart; each team would score by bringing the ball to the other team's goal. The ball could be conveyed by any means chosen: some versions of this game even included horsemen, and serious injury was common.

One family of ball games was related to tennis. Commoners played a simple game called handball, and aristocrats played an early version of tennis in which the ball was struck with the hand. Closely related was the game of shuttlecock, the medieval equivalent of badminton, played with wooden paddles. Other ball games involved sticks or bats and were related to baseball and cricket. A 15th-century text mentions stoolball, which in later centuries involved one player pitching a ball at a stool and another attempting to ward it off, either with his hand or with a bat.

Another type of ball game was bowls, in which the players would try to cast their balls as close as possible to a target. In the game of quoits, the players cast flat round stones at a target. Somewhere between medieval bowls and modern 10-pin bowling was the game of kailes or loggats, in which a number of wooden or bone pins would be set up and the players would attempt to knock them over by casting a stick at them.

Several popular games involved some sort of violence between or against animals. Bulls and bears were "baited," which involved setting dogs against them and betting on the outcome of the fight. Cockfighting was also popular: two cocks were set to fight each other, and the onlookers bet on which would win. Cocks were often the objects of violent sports. Not only were they used in cockfighting and as archery targets, but there was a sport called "cockthrashing," in which a blindfolded person would attempt to hit one with a stick.

Some games seem to have been particularly the pastimes of children. Such was prisoner's base, known as base, or post and pillar, a game that had to be forbidden in Westminster because the noise it generated disturbed the deliberations of the government. Another was the whip-top, a form of top beaten with a scourge to make it turn. Quite a few children's games were based on the giving and receiving of blows. In the game later known as hot cockles, one player sat and took the head of the player who was "it" in his lap, to keep him from peeking; the other players took turns slapping the victim's rear, and if he correctly guessed who had struck the blow, that person became "it." Closely related was hoodman's blind, or bobet, the ancestor of blindman's buff (also called bear-baiting, after its more bloodthirsty cousin). In this game, a hood was pulled over the eyes of one player, who then tried to catch one of the other players in order to change places with him or her. This was complicated by the fact that at the same time the other players were hitting the hooded player with their own hoods tied in a knot, or even with sticks—it is from these "buffets" that the game received its modern name. As in hot cockles, the object may sometimes have been to identify who had given the last blow. A similar game was frog in the middle, in which the player who was "it" crouched on the floor: the rest would try to touch, pinch, or slap the player—anyone he or she caught would be "it." All these games were popular among both boys and girls.

Snapshot

A Medieval European Fishing Game

The northern pike was a popular game fish in medieval Europe. It is a voracious predator—they called it the "water wolf"—and consequently puts up a good fight when hooked. One fishing treatise offers the following sport designed to amuse the human watchers more than the animal participants:

> If you want to have a good sport, then bait a hook with a frog. Tie the cord with the baited hook to a goose's foot and toss the bait in the water. You shall see a good tug-of-war, and you can wager on whether the goose or the Pike shall get the better of it. (Hoffman, 72)

In addition to the physical games already mentioned, there were a number of popular table games. Chess occupied a prestigious position and was particularly favored as an aristocratic pastime. After chess, perhaps the most popular class of board game was tables, a family of games of which backgammon is the only surviving descendant. The board and pieces were essentially the same as in modern backgammon. Backgammon itself was not invented until the 17th century—in the 14th century, there existed a variety of games at tables, each with different initial set-ups and conditions for victory.

One of the most simple, popular, and morally suspect forms of play was dicing, a practice that required almost no space and minimal equipment—two or three dice (bone was an inexpensive and popular material; ivory was used by the wealthy)—and something to play for. The spots on the dice had special names borrowed from French: ace, deuce, trey, cater, sink, and sise. Dice games were generally very simple, involving pure chance and almost no strategy, so their interest resided in the gambling.

Two women playing backgammon. Folio 75v of *Book of Games,* a manuscript written in 1282 by Alfonso X the Wise (1221–84), king of Castile and Leon. © The Art Archive/Real biblioteca de lo Escorial/Dagli Orti.

Although games tend to be conservative, every now and then a real change occurs. One major example was under way during the 14th century with the introduction of playing cards to Europe. These arrived from the Near East, perhaps through Venetian trade with the Mamluk Turks. The first clear references to playing cards in Europe occur in 1377, from which date onward there survive numerous references from France, Italy, Spain, Switzerland, Germany, and the Low Countries. Visual evidence suggests that the first playing cards in Europe were of the Italian suit system of coins, cups, swords, and batons, similar to the suits found on modern Tarot decks. One of the first references in Europe is the *Tractatus de moribus et disciplina humanae conversationis*, written by a Dominican friar from Basel in 1377. The text describes the deck as having four suits, three court cards in each suit, and 10 number cards in each suit. The number cards, as now, bear a number of pips of the suit sign equal to their value (i.e., twos have two pips, fives have five, and so on). This description exactly parallels modern decks. The earliest surviving decks have the same pip cards as in a modern deck (1 to 10), but the face cards might include a knight as well as the knave (the modern jack), queen, and king.

One important difference between medieval and modern games is the role of betting. Physically demanding sports might be played for the pleasure of exercise, and chess for the intellectual challenge, but most other games were likely to involve some form of wager. Moralists railed against the vice of gambling, and social reformers saw it as a destructive vice (particularly among commoners, who were supposed to be working for their living), but the excitement provided by a stake was treated as an integral part of play. Even relatively poor people gambled, and for the aristocracy it was practically a way of life. Most table games involved some degree of gambling. In fact, the practice of gambling pervaded all sorts of games. Some, such as animal fights, were gambling sports by definition, and many other classes of games might be enlivened by the addition of a wager.

The penchant for gambling may well be related to the interest in sports that were inherently dangerous, such as jousting or fencing with sword and buckler. In general, medieval people seem to have been quite willing to risk serious personal injury in the pursuit of entertainment. After all, games gave meaning and interest to people's lives. Perhaps because medieval society was quite static, people vented a natural desire for excitement and challenge by deliberately choosing risky forms of play. In fact, games were very much a part of people's everyday lives (Singman and McLean, 184–91).

To read about sports and games in Elizabethan England, see the England entry in the section "Games and Sports" in chapter 7 ("Recreational Life") of volume 3; for 18th-century England, see the England entry in the section "Games" in chapter 7 ("Recreational Life") of volume 4; and for Victorian England, see the England entry in the section "Sports" in chapter 7 ("Recreational Life") of volume 5 of this series.

FOR MORE INFORMATION

Hoffman, R. C. "The Protohistory of the Pike in Western Culture." In *The Medieval World of Nature: A Book of Essays*, edited by J. E. Salisbury. New York: Garland, 1993.

Reeves, C. *Pleasures and Pastimes in Medieval England*. Oxford: Oxford University Press, 1998.

Singman, J. L., and W. McLean. *Daily Life in Chaucer's England*. Westport, Conn.: Greenwood Press, 1995.

VIKINGS

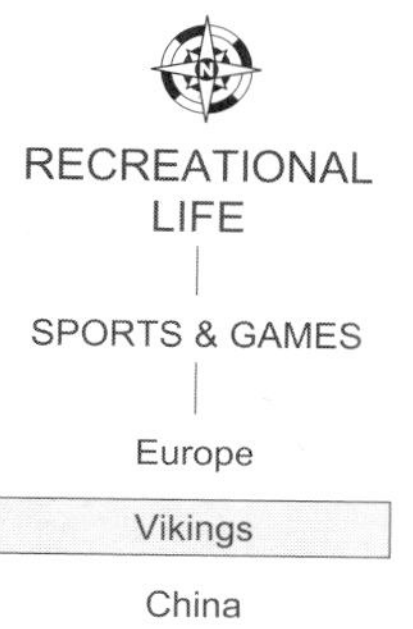

Both climatic and occupational conditions must have allowed the Norsemen a fair amount of leisure time. Indeed, both literary and archaeological sources provide evidence of a great variety of both indoor and outdoor activities that pleasantly occupied people's free time.

The Icelandic saga writers often mention athletic achievements when offering character portrayals of their protagonists. Although their descriptions are often exaggerated, it is clear that physical fitness and skills in sports were regarded as admirable qualities. The author of *Njal's saga*, for example, says this about the saga hero Gunnar Hamundarson:

> He was big and strong and an excellent fighter. He could swing a sword and throw a spear with either hand, if he wished, and he was so swift with a sword that there seemed to be three in the air at once. He could shoot with a bow better than anyone else, and he always hit what he aimed at. He could jump higher than his own height, in full fighting gear, and just as far backwards as forward. He swam like a seal, and there was no sport in which there was any point in competing with him. (Hreinsson, 3:24)

Weapon training was a favorite sports activity and probably essential for young men. Swordplay, archery, and the throwing of spears are frequently referred to in the sources. Gunnar was said to have been able to throw a spear with either hand, but the art of throwing spears with both hands at the same time and catching a spear in the air seems to have been practiced as well. Stone throwing also formed part of the training of future warriors, and it is often mentioned as being used in battles. For stone throwing, a sling was sometimes used.

Tests of physical strength included wrestling, fist-fighting, and the lifting of heavy stones. Among activities that involve a high degree of physical agility and balance, the sources mention mountain climbing and the ability to step from oar to oar outside the railing of a ship while it was being rowed. King Olaf Tryggvason of Norway (d. 999/1000) was hailed as a master of both arts and was said to have excelled also in juggling with knives.

Running and jumping were activities in which children also participated. Much the same applied to swimming, which appears to have been practiced also by women, although probably not for competitive purposes. Skiing and skating were the primary winter sports; among adults, skis and skates were also important means of transport on snow and ice. A passage in Snorri Sturluson's saga about the sons of the Norwegian king Magnus shows the use of skates (called "ice-legs") in sporting contexts and as tests of masculine courage.

Horse racing and horse fighting were probably common, although only the latter is mentioned in the sources and usually because of the dissension that often occurred among the owners of the horses. The rules of horse fighting are unclear, but it seems that two stallions were pitted against one another within sight and smell of fenced-off mares. The fight frequently resulted in the death of one of the stallions.

Hunting as a sport was limited to Denmark, where it was not a particularly important source of food or wealth. A great variety of sea birds appear to have been hunted; among terrestrial birds, partridges were the most important. Deer and hare were the main animals hunted for meat, whereas foxes were hunted for their furs and because they killed domestic animals. The weapons used were bow, spear, and later, crossbow. Stalking was the most common form of hunting, although the practice of chasing game, usually with dogs, was by no means uncommon. In addition, a variety of traps and snares were used. The right to hunt generally belonged to the owner of the land. The majority of hunters were farmers; professional hunters were found only at the courts. Gradually, hunting became a privilege of princes and nobles, who would reserve certain geographical areas for themselves; it is, however, doubtful that this had any noticeable effect on the hunting activities of the farmers.

Icelandic sources often refer to a ball game akin to hockey called *knattleikr*. The game is not known in the other Nordic countries, and it is believed to have come to Iceland via Norwegian emigrants from England. The rules of the game, which was popular among both children and adults, are unclear, but it is known that it was played with a bat and a little, hard ball usually on a smooth field of ice. The game could be played by two individuals or two teams, but it had to be played person against person. The game was a tough one, which often resulted in injuries, and like horse fighting, it appears to have attracted many spectators.

Board games, called *tafl*, were a favorite indoor pastime, and archaeological finds reveal that they were played all over Scandinavia. The pieces were made of glass (clearly imported), amber, clay, stone, or more commonly, bone. The colors vary, but it is likely that each game had pieces in two colors. It is not known how many pieces a complete set required, primarily because very few boards have been preserved, and hardly any intact.

There were at least three varieties of board games: *hnefatafl*, which is probably the oldest game; *skaktafl*, which first appears in the 12th century and may have come to Scandinavia from France and England; and *kvatrutafl*, which seems to have been less common. *Hnefatafl* was at type of hunting game, in which one or more pieces tried to escape from a larger number of "hunters." *Skaktafl* was a kind of war game similar to modern chess. *Kvatrutafl* appears to have been analogous to modern backgammon. Of the three games, *hnefatafl* and *kvatrutafl* were certainly played with a dice, and excavations of graves have revealed a fair number of dice (usually made of bone) from all over Scandinavia. Games of dice appear to have been so common that on occasion, legal intervention was considered necessary with the result that in some areas the games, especially if they involved money, were forbidden.

~*Kirsten Wolf*

FOR MORE INFORMATION

Hreinsson, V., ed. *The Complete Sagas of Icelanders Including 49 Tales*. 5 vols. Reykjavik, Iceland: Leifur Eiriksson, 1997.

Wolf, K. *Daily Life of the Vikings*. Westport, Conn.: Greenwood Press, forthcoming.

CHINA

Football was an ancient game in China that was still popular in the Tang. There were football fields in the palaces of the emperor and the heir apparent at Changan. The ball was probably a leather sphere filled with feathers, as it had been in previous times. As in modern soccer, the objective of the game was to keep the ball in the air by kicking it with the feet. The players, who performed for the pleasure of the throne, were often soldiers in imperial armies or members of the Gold Bird Guard. One military official could loft the ball halfway up the height of a pagoda. Intellectuals might also indulge in the game, but when a courtier had no skill at it, he might ask the emperor to appoint him scorekeeper.

Polo, a sport imported from the west (Persia or Tibet) in the 7th century, was immensely popular among the upper classes in the Tang. There was a polo field in an imperial park and another at a palace in Changan. Some mansions of the upper classes in the capital also had such facilities. At the imperial court, two teams of 16 men dressed in elegant outfits competed in a match to accompaniment of music provided by a military band. Astride well-trained horses, competitors struck the ball with mallets that had crescent-shaped heads. The objective was to put the ball through a circular goal one foot in diameter that was set 10 to 30 feet above the ground. The sport was also played on asses. Imperial armies selected talented troops to engage in the sport for the emperor's amusement. However, virtually anyone—eunuchs, officials, graduates of the civil service examinations—could play if he had a horse and riding habit. One remarkable player could set up a string of 10 or more coppers on a playing field and, at a gallop, strike each with his mallet, knocking them 60 or 70 feet in the air.

Polo was a dangerous sport for man and animal. In the early 8th century, a prince who fell off his horse was knocked unconscious. In 826, the emperor held polo and sumo matches at a palace. The entertainment continued into the night and resulted in cracked heads and broken arms. Emperor Illustrious August was something of a fanatic about the sport. In 710, before he assumed the throne, Zhongzong ordered him and three others to compete against a Tibetan team of 10 that had defeated the court's team. Illustrious August charged east and west so quickly that no one could get in front of him to block his shots. As a result, he and his teammates vanquished the Tibetans. During his reign, he pursued his passion to such a degree that horses suffered injuries and died.

Sports that involved pitting animal against animal—ducks, geese, dogs, and elephants—were quite common in the Tang. In the late 9th century, a prized male goose was worth 500,000 coppers. The most popular form of such entertainment was cockfighting. In the early 7th century, all royal princes were aficionados of it. One emperor established special coops for more than a thousand of the birds in Changan and assigned 500 young soldiers from his armies to train and care for them. As usual, aristocrats and even citizens of Changan emulated the throne and took to the sport, sometimes going broke in pursuit of their amusement. At the beginning of a match, their keepers led the cocks out, and the birds arrayed themselves in a row, raising their feathers and flapping their wings. Then they went into battle with metal spurs attached to their legs. A single bird might fight more than once in a day. A keeper might revive an injured gamecock by spraying water from his mouth on it. When the contests were finished and the keepers led them out, the winners took the lead with the vanquished trailing in the rear. A superior bird could fetch 2 million coppers in the late 9th century, when most emperors were fond of the sport and at least one was fond of gambling on the matches.

Pitch pot was one of the oldest games in China. A Confucian classic supplied an early set of rules for playing it. It required a bronze pot one foot tall with a mouth three inches in diameter. Attached to the neck of the vessel were two ears, tubes that were one inch in diameter. The base of the pot was heavy and filled with beans to prevent it from tipping over when struck and to keep arrows from bouncing out. Each player received 12 arrows at the beginning of the game. Made from mulberry branches, the arrows were two feet, four inches in length. Two men sat on mats and alternately tossed missiles at their pots, to the accompaniment of zither music. The total number of arrows landing in the pot and the difficulty of their placement—missiles falling into the ears counted more than those penetrating the mouth—determined a player's tally. A guest kept track of the points with counters, and 120 was a winning score. Although it appears to have originated as some part of military training, pitch pot was a gentlemen's game, an amusement for parties, and it required dexterity and hand-eye coordination. Some players were amazingly adept at it. One who excelled at it in the early Tang boasted that his arrows never missed. He could toss the missiles over his shoulder into a pot behind him. For every 100 throws, 100 arrows struck home. His tosses were like "dragons rising and hawks soaring."

Board games were also popular in the Tang, and one favorite has remained popular today. This was *weiqi* (encirclement chess), better known in the West by its Japanese name, Go. The game requires a board and stones, or round pieces. The board has a grid of 19 vertical and 19 horizontal lines that yields 361 intersections. There are 361 stones: 181 black and 180 white. The game begins when the player having the black stones places one at an intersection, and it proceeds with black and white taking alternate turns. Stones never change their positions or leave the board unless captured. The winner is the player who surrounds the most territory and captures the largest number of his opponent's pieces. It is a purely intellectual game of strategy (Benn, 172–75).

FOR MORE INFORMATION

Benn, C. *Daily Life in Traditional China: The Tang Dynasty*. Westport, Conn.: Greenwood Press, 2002.

Qifeng, F. U. *Chinese Acrobats throughout the Ages*. Beijing: China Books and Publications, 1985.

BYZANTIUM

For sports and games in the Byzantine Empire, see the Byzantium entry under the section "Entertainment" at the end of this chapter.

Hunting

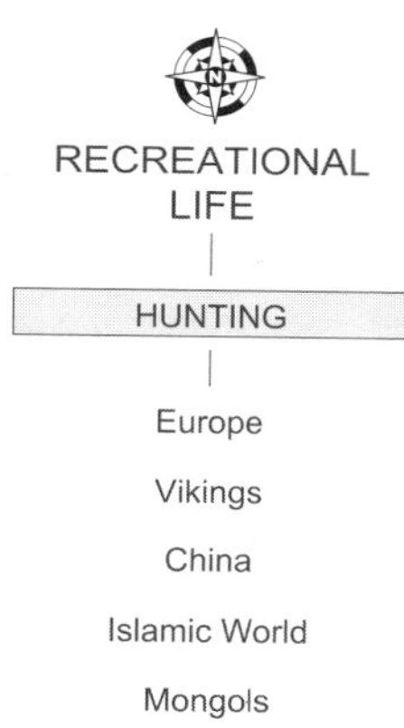

There are two reasons to hunt wild game: for food and for sport. By the late Middle Ages, sport far outweighed the need for food (although the hunters did eat the results of their day's activities). Hunting was a logical training for warfare, in which the hunters honed their skills with weapons and, indeed, with their animal partners. Thus, hunting was an activity of the aristocracy, whose job was warfare. When peasants were permitted to catch wild game, by the late Middle Ages, they usually trapped rabbits or other small game. Skill with weapons was for the warrior classes.

The relationship between hunting and warfare is perhaps most clearly seen with the Mongols. Chinggis (Genghis) Khan formalized a Great Hunt specifically as a military exercise. He organized his troops in large lines to round up huge amounts of game. This hunt called for communication, horsemanship, skill with arms, and a great deal of discipline. The Mongol skill at coordinating large numbers of men in a hunt served them well as their armies swept through Asia into Europe.

In Europe, the Muslim world, and China, the aristocracy favored hunts in which the skill of the individual—not the movement of armies—was featured. Many of the wealthy kings and aristocrats created game parks or forest preserves as their own hunting ground. The Chinese emperor kept a huge park north of Changan. A favored animal everywhere was the stag—a large deer. These animals ran swiftly, making the chase exciting, and made a delicious feast after the kill. Other animals were hunted simply because they were fierce (even though the meat was not desirable). In western Europe, wild boars were the most dangerous animals. These huge beasts could weigh more than 500 pounds and charge with such single-minded ferocity that a hunter would not get two chances to bring it down. Bears were also popular animals because of the danger they posed, even though people usually did not eat bear meat. Harun al-Rashid and other caliphs near Baghdad favored hunting lions, which were as fierce as wild boars. The hunters who brought down such wild animals were considered great warriors and were valued for armies.

Part of the skill of hunting lay in training animal partners to share in the chase just as they did in war. Just like the Mongols, hunters (and warriors) everywhere else in Eurasia depended on their horses to carry them to the chase. Caliphs used specially trained horses that could overcome their fear as they chased lions, and it was extremely difficult for any hunter to get a horse to stand still for the charge of a boar.

Dogs were also crucially important to a hunt, and from the earliest years of the Middle Ages, the sources indicate a bewildering range of breeds of dogs. Breeds were distinguished less by appearance (as is true today) and more by function. There were tracking dogs (comparable to modern hounds) to find the prey, and running dogs (that resembled greyhounds) to chase it down. Running dogs were so valued that in northern Europe, the owner of the running dog was allowed to keep the hide of a killed deer. There were also fierce mastiffs and wolfhounds that were expected to engage and fight the prey. In Muslim lands, the richest hunters unleashed trained cheetahs to bring down prey; the cheetahs were so graceful and skilled that even poets sang the animal's praises.

The final hunting partners for the aristocrats of the Middle Ages were raptors—birds of prey that had been trained to hunt with their owners. Birds of prey were very costly because they could not be bred in captivity to hunt, so they had to be caught in the wild. Even eagles were used to hunt, although it took a strong arm to handle such a huge bird. Hawks and falcons were more commonly used, and traders came from far afield to satisfy noble cravings for these birds. It took a long time to train a raptor to hunt. First, the wild bird was calmed by sealing its eyelids: a stitch was placed in the lower lid, which was threaded with linen thread and then pulled up to blind the bird until it was tamed. Then the bird had to slowly learn to respond to human signals. These birds usually hunted other birds, bringing down doves or even cranes, which would then find their way to the noble dinner tables. The great eagles, however, could hunt fairly large game on the ground. Men and women alike enjoyed a day of hunting with the tamed raptors on their wrists.

In many ways, medieval nobility defined themselves by their noble pastime of hunting. It trained them for war and constantly validated their military skills. As noble households gathered at the tables, the game that was spread before them marked their status as warriors.

~*Joyce E. Salisbury*

FOR MORE INFORMATION

Clot, A. *Harun al-Rashid*. New York: New Amsterdam Books, 1989.

Salisbury, J. E. *The Beast Within: Animals in the Middle Ages*. New York: Routledge, 1994.

EUROPE

RECREATIONAL LIFE
HUNTING
Europe
Vikings
China
Islamic World
Mongols

One pastime was particularly held for the aristocracy in Europe—hunting. In fact, it was generally illegal for commoners to hunt, as the rights to use land for hunting were usually reserved for the aristocratic holders. Aristocratic hunters used these opportunities to develop their skills for war as well as to show off their lands and the animals under their control. There were two main methods of hunting large forest game, and both required a close partnership between humans and dogs. The oldest form of the hunt depended on hounds to find the scent of a large animal (usually deer) and work with mounted hunters to drive the game toward hidden archers. In this kind of hunt, large numbers of deer were killed, and this was an effective way to provide food for the noble tables (or the noble armies). The poet of the 14th-century poem *Sir Gawain and the Green Knight* describes the result of such a hunt: the king "killed so many no one could count them. Huntsmen and keepers came together, proud, and quickly collected the bodies in a pile" (*Sir Gawain*, 90).

The most popular hunt was the elaborate hunt of a stag. This tapestry depicts the ritual presentation of severed right foreleg of stag to the guest of honor during stag hunt. From a later 15th-century Flemish tapestry (detail). © The Art Archive/Château de Langeais/Dagli Orti.

A second form of hunt was much more ritualized and conducted less for food than for entertainment. In this hunt, a huntsman went ahead (the day before, probably) and with a specially trained hound that would track without baying, located a suitable animal. Many dogs were then released to chase the animal while their handlers followed, guiding and encouraging the hounds with calls and horns. Once the dogs had brought the animal to a standstill, they held it at bay while one of the hunters killed it with a sword or spear.

The most valued prey was either a stag or a boar. Wild boars were the most dangerous animals to hunt because they would charge with such anger that they were unstoppable unless killed. The bravest hunter would face such a charging animal on foot with his spear braced on the ground ready to stab the charging animal. If the hunter missed a vital spot, he would be ripped by the raging boar before he could be saved by his companions. The hunter would be rewarded for a successful killing of the boar by being given the boar's testicles to eat. Medieval people believed that the power of the boar would come to the hunter who consumed this food. Hunters kept their dogs in training for hunting deer or boar by having them chase hare, which provided a challenging run for the dogs.

The hunt required careful partnership between the humans and their dogs, and hunting dogs were carefully bred and trained. Some dogs were designated as "tracking hounds," presumably because they could follow the scent of the game. Other dogs were called "running dogs," and illustrations indicate that they resembled modern greyhounds. These dogs ran the prey to the ground. Other dogs were trained to help kill prey such as wolves or bear, and these large, fierce animals seem to have resembled modern mastiffs or wolfhounds.

Another kind of hunt favored by the aristocracy was conducted with hawks and other raptors. It took a good deal of time and patience to train a wild hawk in order to turn it into a hunting partner. First, the trainer calmed the wild bird by sealing its eyelids: a stitch was placed in the lower lid, which was threaded with linen thread. The thread was then tied over the bird's head, keeping the lid closed. The temporarily blinded bird then became accustomed to human voice and touch and to depend on humans for food. Once it was tamed, the trainer slowly restored the bird's sight by adjusting the thread. Then the bird began training for the hunt. It was taught to respond to a lure and always look to humans for food. The best birds were trained to hunt large birds, such as ducks, geese, and even cranes and herons.

For a hawk to hunt a crane required the kind of interaction between human, hound, and hawk that warmed medieval hearts. As cranes rose, two falcons attacked one crane and brought it to the ground. Then greyhounds ran to the prey to kill the crane before its thrashing could damage the more delicate hawks. Finally, the hunter claimed the crane, which would likely become his dinner. But first, he rewarded his hunting partners. The hawks received the crane's heart and some bone marrow, perhaps served ritually on a white gauntlet. The hound received its customary reward of the bird's entrails and blood. This type of hunt was difficult but rewarding to proud aristocrats. Women also engaged in hunting with raptors.

To read about hunting in Elizabethan England, see the England entry in the section "Outdoor Pursuits" in chapter 7 ("Recreational Life") of volume 3 of this series.

~Joyce E. Salisbury

FOR MORE INFORMATION

Salisbury, J. E. *The Beast Within: Animals in the Middle Ages*. New York: Routledge, 1994.

Sir Gawain and the Green Knight. Translated by B. Raffel. New York: Mentor, 1970.

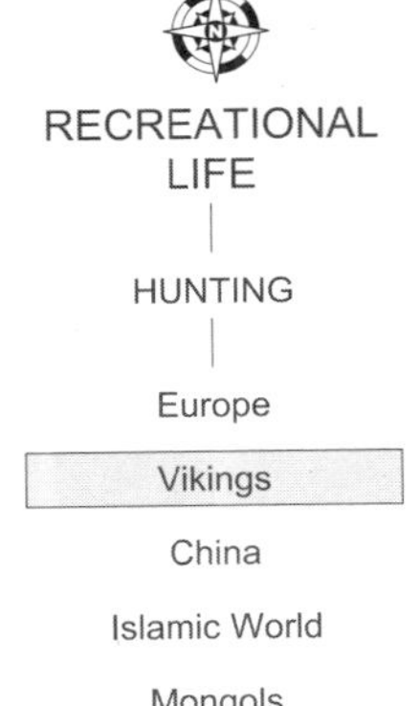

VIKINGS

Hunting and sea and freshwater fishing were important in all parts of Scandinavia, but especially in areas where people lived in marginal farming territories. The fish resources along the North Atlantic shores of Scandinavia are unique not only because they are very rich but also because they are relatively close to land. Accordingly, fish could be caught with simple fishing equipment—spear, net, and line—and in small boats by the farmers. In the coastal areas of Norway and in northern

Sweden, where grain cultivation and cattle and sheep breeding were minimal because of the climatic conditions, fishing was a staple of the economy. Indeed, traces of fishing stations consisting of small huts or buildings have been found along the coastlines. The finds in these huts have included fishing hooks, line sinkers, potsherds, knives, and bones of various fish. Lakes and rivers in Scandinavia also contained a variety of fish, of which salmon was the most important.

In Denmark, hunting was not a significant source of food or income, but in large areas of Norway and Sweden, it gave farmers an extra and often necessary supply of cash and meat. On land, squirrel, ermine, marten, fox, and—in Norway and Sweden—bear were mostly hunted for fur and hides, while deer, elk, reindeer, and hare were also hunted for meat. From the elk and reindeer, people took antlers, which were used to fabricate combs, spindle whorls, spoons, arrowheads, and other small objects. The northernmost part of Scandinavia, which was inhabited by tribes of people often called Lapps, but who call themselves Sami, lived almost exclusively by fishing and hunting, especially reindeer, which provided them with meat, skins for clothing, boats, and tents, and antler for implements and ornaments. Bows and spears were the weapons used to hunt animals. Reindeer, elk, and deer were typically chased over cliffs or into trenches dug in rows across the tracks of the animals. In addition, snares and a variety of traps were used.

The sea animals that were hunted comprised whales, seals, and walruses. Whales were hunted in most of Scandinavia, and especially in Norway. Several forms of whaling were practiced, the most primitive being cutting the blubber off beached whales. Other forms of whaling involved harpooning the whales on the open sea and scaring them to shore, where they would be killed with spears and knives. Seals were hunted all over Scandinavia and were typically clubbed or harpooned. Both whale and seal meat was eaten, but the most important product derived from these sea animals was their blubber, which was eaten as an alternative to butter. In addition, seal oil was used instead of tar to smear boats and in oil lamps. Sealskins were used for gloves, shoes, bags, and the like. Walrus was hunted especially northeast of Norway, around Murmansk, for their valuable ivory and hides, from which strong ropes could be made.

In addition, wild birds were netted and lured or shot with bows and arrows, and their eggs were collected with a variety of methods. It is also known that peregrine falcons were tamed and trained to hunt ducks and seabirds. The birds provided not only meat but also feathers and down used for insulation purposes.

~*Kirsten Wolf*

FOR MORE INFORMATION

Wolf, K. *Daily Life of the Vikings*. Westport, Conn.: Greenwood Press, forthcoming.

CHINA

Hunting as entertainment was a sport for aristocrats and mandarins. In the early Tang, they pursued it with passion. One prince declared, "I can go without eating for three days, but I can't go without hunting for a single day" (Benn, 171). The grandest hunts were the emperor's, which took place in the Forbidden Park north of Changan. The walls of the Forbidden Park encompassed the ruins of the ancient capital of the Han dynasty and pavilions where the emperor entertained his guests. It was also a reserve where wild animals such as white deer roamed free, so that this emperor and his guests, foreign envoys in particular, could enjoy themselves hunting. The game they shot usually provided meat for sacrifices, especially those at the imperial ancestral shrine. The park had mews for hawks, eagles, and other raptors, as well as kennels for hounds that were employed in the hunt to chase down or catch quarry. It also had pens for exotic creatures—lions, leopards, elephants, and rhinoceroses—sent as tribute by foreign nations. A Tang manual on government states that there was not a bird, animal, vegetable, or fruit that was not raised there.

The royal court and favored aristocrats also could hunt in regions close to the capital, or in wilderness areas near a city that the emperor visited. In all cases, the court went with him and set itself up at a clearing. Beaters drove the game toward the open field where the emperor and the courtiers shot it down. Some of the rulers excelled at the sport. Taizong once shot four arrows at a herd of wild pigs charging from the woods and brought down four of the animals. Illustrious August once bagged two wild boars with one arrow. Afterward, he ordered an artist to paint a scene of his remarkable feat on a wall of the palace's northern gate.

Like medieval Europeans, the upper classes of the Tang used raptors to bring down prey for them. Because of their size, they used eagles to hunt large mammals such as foxes, wolves, and small deer. Their falcons, which knocked victims from the sky with clenched talons, attacked fowl; the saker took herons and larger birds, while the smaller peregrine struck down ducks and smaller game. Goshawks were the most favored of all the raptors during this period because they were fierce and the most competent in attacking prey, usually rabbits and pheasants. Sparrow hawks, smallest of the raptors, killed their prey, usually lesser fowl such as quail, by gripping them with needle-sharp claws and pinning them to the ground.

Naturally, the throne had the finest collection of raptors, along with the best hounds and hunting leopards. Their keepers, eunuchs, were not always scrupulous. In 806, they released goshawks in the mansions of wealthy families in Changan and then demanded handsome compensation for retrieving them. The fact that the wealthy were willing to pay for the capture of the raptors (instead of just killing them) testifies to the value the aristocrats placed on hunting and their animal partners (Benn, 171–72).

FOR MORE INFORMATION

Benn, C. *Daily Life in Traditional China: The Tang Dynasty*. Westport, Conn.: Greenwood Press, 2002.

ISLAMIC WORLD

Hunting in the medieval Islamic world was done for sport as well as for food. Given the specific regulations for butchering domesticated animals for them to be halal, that is, permitted according to Sharia, or Islamic law, Muslim scholars devoted their attention to determining which game was permissible for consumption and when. Essentially, any wild animal killed by a hunter was considered halal, with the notable exception of pigs, which are forbidden under any circumstances. However, it is forbidden for pilgrims to eat game during the annual pilgrimage (*hajj*). Finally, whereas according to the Jewish tradition only fish with scales are considered kosher, all fish and seafood are permissible to Muslims at any time.

Hunting was a common theme in medieval Islamic literature, whether in poetry or in descriptions of a ruler's fondness for spending time on his horse as he and his companions pursued hares, partridges, quail, geese, and other small game with their hunting falcons and hounds. In his memoir, Usamah Ibn-Muhqidh (1095–1188) includes a section about his father's exploits as a hunter near the family estate at Shayzar in the mountains between Hama and the Syrian coast. Because his family was well-to-do, they had broad access to land on which to hunt. In fact, Usama reports that in Shayzar, "we had two hunting fields, one for partridges and hares, in the mountains to the south of town; and another for waterfowl, francolins, hares and gazelles, on the bank of the river in the cane fields to the west of town" (Hitti, 228).

Falcons and hawks are birds of prey that were essential to a successful hunt; so too were hunting hounds. In fact, Usamah's father often dispatched some of his men to distant lands to purchase choice falcons as well as pigeons to feed them. He even sent some of his aides as far as Constantinople, the Byzantine capital, to purchase falcons and hounds. Falcons and hawks were also purchased from locals who had set up trapping stations nearby to meet the demand for birds. While falcons and hawks were excellent hunters of small game and other birds, cheetahs were often used when hunting larger game, such as gazelles, antelopes, deer, wild donkeys, and wild boar.

Falcons, hawks, hounds, cheetahs, and horses were a keeper's livelihood, as well as essential to his employer's successful hunts. Hence, a great deal of care and attention was paid to a man's hunting animals. In fact, it was not uncommon for a hunter to keep his birds of prey in his home. Usamah reports that his father even kept his prize cheetah in their house.

> He had a special maid who served it. In one side of the courtyard she had a velvet quilt folded, with dry grass beneath. In the wall was an iron staple. After the hunt, the cheetah trainer would bring it to the door of the house in which its couching place lay, and leave it there. It would then enter the house and go to that place where its bed was spread and sleep. The maid would come and tie it to the staple fastened to the wall. (Hitti, 237)

Usamah also reports that gazelles, rams, goats, and fawns were born in the same courtyard, but that the cheetah was so well behaved it never touched them.

~James Lindsay

FOR MORE INFORMATION

Hitti, P. K., trans. *An Arab-Syrian Gentleman and Warrior in the Period of the Crusades: Memoirs of Usamah Ibn-Muhqidh.* 1929. Reprint, Princeton, N.J.: Princeton University Press, 1987.

Lindsay, J. *Daily Life in the Medieval Islamic World*. Westport, Conn.: Greenwood Press, forthcoming.

MONGOLS

From an early age, all Mongol children learned horsemanship and archery. This was prescribed by law. The maneuvers and battlefield tactics were drilled into the Mongol citizenry by constant practice. Chinggis Khan formalized the Great Hunt, the *nerge*, as a military training exercise. The *nerge* was a vast, highly organized, and strictly regulated hunt that at its most basic, replenished the tribe's meat supplies for the coming winter. However, as Juwaynī (d. 1282), an eyewitness historian and later governor of Baghdad for the Mongol il-khans, was quick to note, this chase was far more than a Mongol "shopping" trip:

> Now war—with its killing, counting of the slain and sparing of the survivors—is after the same fashion, and indeed analogous in every detail, because all that is left in the neighbourhood of the battlefield are a few broken-down wretches. (Juwaynī, 29)

The *nerge* was training practice for war and battle. Stealth, tight communications, horsemanship, and coordination were all essential skills honed and perfected during the *nerge*. The Mongols learned the disciplined teamwork for which they were both admired and feared from these annual events. The *nerge* would be held in winter and would last three months; every soldier, most of the tribe, would participate. It served as a morale booster and excellent practice for the real thing. All military skills were honed during the course of the Great Hunt, particularly discipline, coordination of units, and most essential, close effective communications.

The overall strategy and development of the hunt was usually the same. A starting line, possibly 80 miles long, would be established by huntsmen, who would plant flags at various assembly points to position the *tumans* (units of 10,000) who would be taking part in the *nerge*. Another flag, hundreds of miles distant, would be planted to mark the suitable finishing point. On a signal from the khan, this vast line of fully armed, battle-ready troops would begin to move forward, and before them all wildlife would flee. Over the next few weeks, as the amount of game and other animals increased, the two flanks of this vast army would move ahead and slowly close in on their prey. The two wings would aim to pass the finishing flag and then move closer in order to eventually meet up with each other, thereby trapping the increasingly frantic animals in a circle. The hunters would form a vast ring over a huge expanse of land. This human ring would then slowly contract, driving every living beast within its circumference toward its center. Shifts would be employed to ensure that a vigil was kept at all times, with even the sleeping troops fully clothed and ready for action. Any hunter who allowed any game to escape the diminishing circle could expect severe punishment, as could anyone who killed any animal before the allotted time:

> And if, unexpectedly, any game should break through, a minute inquiry is made into the cause and reason, and the commanders of thousands, hundreds, and tens are clubbed there-

fore, and even put to death. And if . . . a man does not keep to the line . . . but takes a step forwards or backwards, severe punishment is dealt out to him and is never remitted. (Juwaynī, 28)

The initial line of fully armed mounted men, which may have been as long as 130 kilometers before the flanks had formed, would now be compressed into a tightly knit human stadium with an arena of hysterical and highly dangerous animals at its core. The khan would be waiting with his own smaller line of troops at a predetermined spot chosen for its suitability for the final entrapment possibly hundreds of miles from the starting line.

Here there becomes massed together an extraordinary multitude of wild beasts, such as lions, wild oxen, bears, stags, and a great variety of others, and all in a state of the greatest alarm. For there is such a prodigious noise and uproar . . . that a person cannot hear what his neighbour says; and all the unfortunate beasts quiver with terror at the disturbance. (Yule, 235)

When the frantic roaring and screeching horde of terrified animals was finally massed together, the khan would make the first kill; this would be the signal for the massacre to commence. Animals destined for the kitchens and cookhouses might be cleanly and swiftly killed, while others would have to earn their deaths. Sometimes the Great Khan with some of his retinue would disport themselves killing game before the lesser princes would be allowed to start. When these princes in turn had tired of their sport, the ordinary soldiers would be let loose on the unfortunate captives. All knew that the Great Khan and commanders were present and witnessing the fun; therefore the *nerge* was seen as an opportunity for the soldiery to demonstrate their skills and valor against often very ferocious animals. Unarmed combat, sword and knife fighting, on foot and on horseback, and other martial skills would all be demonstrated in the hope of attracting the attention of the commanders to the dexterity and talents of the individual soldier.

Some animals would be retained for breeding, and some would be symbolically released, although most would end up with the kitchen staff. A Mongol tradition had young princes and old soldiers come before the khan to plead for the life of remaining animals, and the khan's subsequent act of clemency signaled the end of the hunt. After the *nerge*, nine days of feasting and revelry would ensue. The remaining food would be distributed throughout the various units to ensure that all who had participated in the event had their due share of the booty.

The Great Hunt or *nerge* perfected the Mongols' communications system, which used frequent couriers, flag waving, torch burning, and an efficient, highly effective network of staging posts (see the Mongols entry in the section "Warfare and Weapons" in chapter 6) called the *yam*, for which history has long recorded its admiration. It provided provisions for the tribe and entertainment for all. Most important, perhaps, was the *nerge*'s ability to provide battle experience for the troops, the worth of which has been proved many times.

~*George Lane*

FOR MORE INFORMATION

Chambers, J. *The Devil's Horsemen*. London: Weidenfeld and Nicholson, 1979.
Juwaynī, 'At ā Malik. *Genghis Khan: The History of the World Conqueror*. Translated by J. A. Boyle. Manchester: Manchester University Press, 1997.
Morgan, D. *The Mongols*. Oxford: Blackwell, 1986.
Yule, H. "The Travels of Friar Oderic." In *Cathay and the Way Thither*, vol. 2. 1913. Reprint, New York: Klaus Reprint, 1967.

Music and Dance

Music is everywhere in our modern society. Radios, compact discs, and electronic instruments have filled almost every moment of our lives with music, and its ubiquitous nature tells us how important music is to us. It is difficult to imagine a time when music was rare and treasured, but that is how things were in the Middle Ages.

People everywhere believed that music offered a window into a cosmic or sacred world. In Europe, for example, scholars linked music to mathematics as revealing a sacred order. As educated Europeans thought about the universe, they believed the turning spheres in which planets and stars were embedded played magnificent celestial music. The Chinese believed that music not only revealed the order of the universe but was essential to maintaining the order in society. The Polynesians thought music and dance were created by various gods and goddesses. While these theoretical concepts about music came from scholarly reflections, in fact, music and dance served several purposes in society.

Some music and dance served a military purpose. Horns and drums spurred warriors on in battle, but even once the battle was done, music sometimes had a military component. Young men in the early Middle Ages executed complex sword dances to build their skills and show their courage, and in China, dance was regularly a part of military training. Today's remnants of this kind of musical use are military bands that accompany marching soldiers.

Religion offered an even more common use of music and dance. In Europe, chants by choirs in church enhanced the religious experience and drew the faithful into contemplation. Church music in the Middle Ages began with quite simple compositions but by the 12th century became extremely complex with many voices singing in various harmonies. During the early Middle Ages, priests encouraged dancing in the church with congregations holding hands and moving rhythmically through the church. One contemporary claimed that dance steps leaped up to God just as prayers. Polynesian islanders would have understood this concept readily, because many of their graceful dances accompanied religious ceremonies.

Finally, music and dance played a prominent role in secular celebrations. Village life everywhere was held together by the community singing and dancing together, and aristocrats, too, enjoyed musical diversions in their manor houses. After the 12th century, minstrels could look to lucrative patronage as they performed in castles or town squares. Dances in the Middle Ages were carried out by groups of men and women (sometimes just one gender at a time), and most were chain dances with the dancers holding hands as they danced through intricate patterns.

Singing usually formed the heart of music (and dance), but some musical instruments were popular accompaniments. Instruments were either wind, string, or percussion. In most of the Polynesian islands, musicians favored percussion instruments—various kinds of drums. They also had nose flutes to play a melody, but they lacked string instruments. In Europe and Asia, musicians had a wider range of instruments. European wind instruments included flutes of varying kinds and bagpipes, which produced a loud enough sound to be heard from a long distance. China, too, enjoyed a number of pipes.

String instruments were even more diverse because they were either plucked or played with a bow. Throughout Europe and in China, musicians used instruments that resemble modern mandolins, harps, and fiddles. Percussion instruments ranged from drums of various sizes to bells and chimes. The great bells cast for European churches dominated towns with their peals.

In general, medieval music from East and West sounds strange to modern ears because their rhythms and melodic intervals are not ours. However, listeners today can get a sense of how popular this music would have been—the religious chants are moving and the dance music is vivid and exciting.

~*Joyce E. Salisbury*

EUROPE

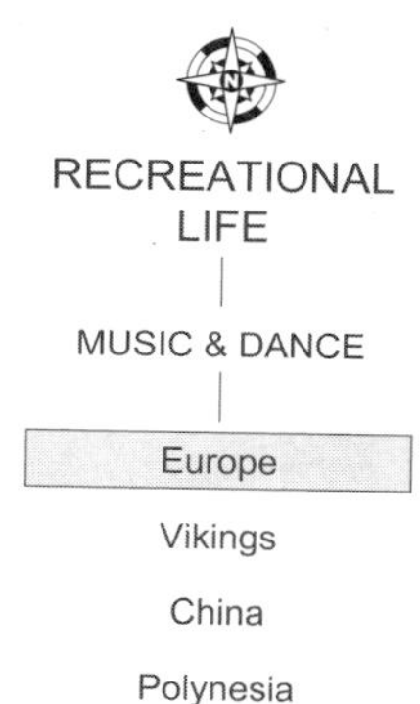

Music was a pervasive form of entertainment in Europe, and in ages before electronic reproduction of music, live musicians formed an important part of people's lives. From the beginnings of Christianity, church music provided a significant (and much valued) part of people's experience. The Gregorian chant sung by monks and nuns filled the churches with haunting, meditative melodies. By the 12th century, church singers had developed polyphony, where the simpler melodies were made complex by weaving together different lines of melody. Without a doubt, some people went to church services to enjoy the complex beautiful music.

Other music grew from the celebrations of daily life. Some of it was provided by professional musicians, who were often hired by the aristocracy and rich townsfolk, but ordinary people could scarcely afford such a luxury. However, while they might occasionally have the opportunity to hear traveling musicians, most people had to create most of their music themselves. It was common for people to sing for their own entertainment, sometimes as part of holiday revelry, sometimes during work to make the labor go more easily. The subjects of songs were diverse: there were love songs, drinking songs, and religious songs, songs about historical events and current politics, satirical songs about money or sex, and even nonsense songs.

People also enjoyed instrumental music. Medieval instruments were generally different from those used today. Bagpipes were one of the most popular instruments, especially among commoners: they were easy to hear at an outdoor festival, and their driving sound made them excellent for dancing. Also popular was the "pipe and tabor": the pipe was a three-hole recorder played with the left hand while the musician beat a drum (the "tabor") with the right. This provided both melody and rhythm at once and was especially favored among common folk. Simple flutes and recorders were also in use, as was the shawm, an extremely loud double-reeded ancestor of the oboe.

There were several sorts of bowed instruments. The most familiar was the fiddle, which was about the size of a modern viola, more plain in construction, and held against the chest rather than under the chin. The rebec was a smaller cousin, about the size of the musician's forearm, with a rounded back. The psaltery was a triangular box with strings running across it, comparable in appearance to a modern hammer dulcimer; it might be played with a bow or plucked with a plectrum. Other stringed instruments included the harp and the gittern, a plucked instrument vaguely comparable to a mandolin. Percussion was provided by drums, especially for dance music. Somewhere between percussion and wind instruments was the instrument known today as a Jew's harp, an inexpensive and common instrument in medieval England.

Woman playing a harp (center). The other musicians and instruments in this manuscript illustration indicate the variety of instruments that were played during the period. Scala/Art Resource, NY.

The sounds of all these instruments were generally coarser and harsher than is favored today, and many medieval instruments were quite loud. All this helped to ensure that the instrument would be audible. There were no amplifying systems, and one could not always count on good acoustics. The rhythms of 14th-century music were less rigid than in later centuries.

One common way of enjoying music was through dancing, which was widely popular throughout society and seems to have been fairly consistent at all social levels. It was especially common for women to dance together at all levels of society, while male-only dances seem to have been most popular among common folk. The music for the dance might be provided by musicians, but often the only music was the singing of the dancers themselves, a custom still found in a few parts of Europe.

Although there are no detailed descriptions of medieval dances, scholars have assembled reconstructions of dances based on visual evidence compared with later treatises of dances. A typical dance was a circle or chain dance, called a carol. Reconstructed carols could be done in two forms, the "single bransle" (pronounced "brawl") and the "farandole."

The single bransle is one of the most archaic dance forms in Europe—versions are still danced in places from the Faeroe Islands to the Balkans. The dancers form a circle or a chain without regard to gender. They may be all men, all women, or a mixed group, and not necessarily of even numbers. There were a number of possible grips: the dancers could link hands, link hands and elbows, or hold onto kerchiefs or garlands. The dance is very simple: it consists of two steps to the left and one to the right in time with the music, repeated throughout the dance. The farandole is more complex because the dancers must follow a leader, who conducts the linked chain of dancers to create various figures. For example, in the "snail," the leader leads the chain around into a circle, then spirals inward to the center. Once there, the leader may turn back and spiral out again, or he or she and the second dancer may lift their joined hands to make an arch under which the rest of the dancers pass. The dance may be as complex as the imagination of the leader (Singman and McLean, 182–83, 212–13).

To read about music and dance in Elizabethan England, see the England entry in the section "The Arts" in chapter 7 ("Recreational Life") of volume 3; for 18th-century England, see the England entry in the section "Arts and Hobbies" in chapter 7 ("Recreational Life") of volume 4; and for Victorian England, see the England entries in the sections "Music" and "Leisure Time" in chapter 7 ("Recreational Life") of volume 5 of this series.

FOR MORE INFORMATION

Reeves, C. *Pleasures and Pastimes in Medieval England*. Oxford: Oxford University Press, 1998.

Singman, J. L., and W. McLean. *Daily Life in Chaucer's England*. Westport, Conn.: Greenwood Press, 1995.

VIKINGS

Little is known about the musical life of the Norsemen in the Viking Age, but literary sources tell that music was recognized as an art and that musical proficiency was considered an accomplishment fitting for a cultured man. The *Saga of the Orkney Islanders*, for example, tells that Earl Rognvald Kali Kolsson (d. 1158) included harp playing among his primary skills. Evidently, music was considered an accompaniment to merrymaking, for in the mythical-heroic *Saga of Bosi*, it is related that Bosi (in the guise of King Godmund's harp player) played tunes at the wedding party held at King Godmund's court. According to the saga, Bosi played with such vigor that knives, dishes, and everything that was not held down began to move, and many people started to dance. Although the harp is the musical instrument most commonly mentioned, we also hear of fiddles, lyres, and lutes. No instrumental music has survived from the Viking Age, and probably none was ever committed to writing.

The sources describe several musical instruments. There were a variety of string instruments, including harp, lyre, lute, and fiddle. Sources also name a variety of wind and percussion instruments, but it is usually hard to represent exactly what these instruments looked like. There seem to have been a number of wandering musicians, and they must have been indispensable to weddings, public festivals, and market gatherings.

After the arrival of Christianity, music in Scandinavia—as in Christian Europe—became a regular feature of church services. As early as 1080, a king made a provision for a cantor in his endowment for the Church of St. Lawrence in Lund, and a French clerk was hired in Iceland to teach church music in the school founded in 1107. From this point on, Scandinavian music followed the pattern of European music.

As evident from the *Saga of Bosi*, dancing certainly existed, and the custom of dancing at weddings is believed to be old. The practice of dancing during a wake and after a successful birth is also considered to have originated in pre-Christian times. The latter was a woman's feast, which in addition to dancing entailed drinking and mocking of a male figure made of straw. During the 12th century, the European ring dance became established in Scandinavia, where it remained popular for centuries.

~*Kirsten Wolf*

FOR MORE INFORMATION

Jones, G. A *History of the Vikings*. Oxford: Oxford University Press, 1968.
Wolf, K. *Daily Life of the Vikings*. Westport, Conn.: Greenwood Press, forthcoming.

CHINA

Chinese philosophers including Confucius (551–479 B.C.E.) regarded music as essential in maintaining order in the universe and in human society. Because music was regarded as so essential, ancient Chinese musicians developed a science of acoustics and produced a five-tone scale similar to modern Western music. Chinese texts mention various kinds of instruments that were carefully tuned for music. These instruments include tuned chimes, drums, bells, wind instruments, and string instruments.

String instruments included both bowed and plucked strings. The bow instruments included the *erhu*, with two strings and a range of about three octaves, and the *gaohu*, which is higher pitched than the *erhu*. These bowed instruments were refined and transformed slightly over time. The plucked string instruments included the *pipa*, which produced the most common music and which resembles a pear-shaped Spanish guitar with four strings, to be plucked with long fingernails. Other plucked instruments (including the *ruan* and the *sanxian*) varied the pitches. Wind instruments included various pipes, the oldest of which is the *sheng*, which consisted of a bundle of between 17 and 36 pipes seated on a small wind chamber. The melodies produced by these instruments were accompanied by various drums and chimes.

Dancing was an important form of entertainment, especially among the nobility. Among the most popular kinds of dances were "vigorous dances," through which the nobility memorialized and celebrated great military victories. These dances show the close relationship between dance and theater in ancient China.

Imperial princes received instruction in vigorous dances at a very early age. For example, in 690, when he was five years old, Emperor Illustrious August performed "The Long-Lived Lady" during a banquet given by Empress Wu. At the same feast, another prince, who was four years old, danced "The Prince of Lanling." The Prince of Lanling was a northern general of the 6th century who won a great victory. Afterward, his troops composed a song called "The Prince of Lanling Breaks through the Battle Formation" to celebrate his triumph. During the Sui and Tang dynasties, this air evolved into a dance pantomime. By the early 8th century, it depicted the general as having the face of a beautiful woman, so he wore a mask to strike terror in the minds of his foes when he went into battle. In the course of its performance, the dancer brandished a weapon as though thrusting and stabbing at his adversaries. By the 9th century, a whip replaced the weapon, and the performer wore a purple costume with a gold girdle. It was a "vigorous" dance in the Tang's system for classifying music.

Another vigorous dance was "The Prince of Qin Smashes Battle Formations." After Taizong, then prince of Qin, defeated a rebel army in 622, his troops composed an air with that title to commemorate his triumph. Entertainers first performed it at a banquet in 627. In 633, Taizong drew a diagram for a dance that had a round formation to the left and a square one to the right. He ordered one of his courtiers to train dancers to perform it according to his drawing. The piece had three movements, each consisting of four formations. Clad in silver armor and carrying crescent-shaped spears, 128 boys pummeled and pierced to simulate the ebb and flow of battle. After the first performance in that year, the emperor had his ministers compose lyrics for it and renamed it "The Dance of Seven Virtues."

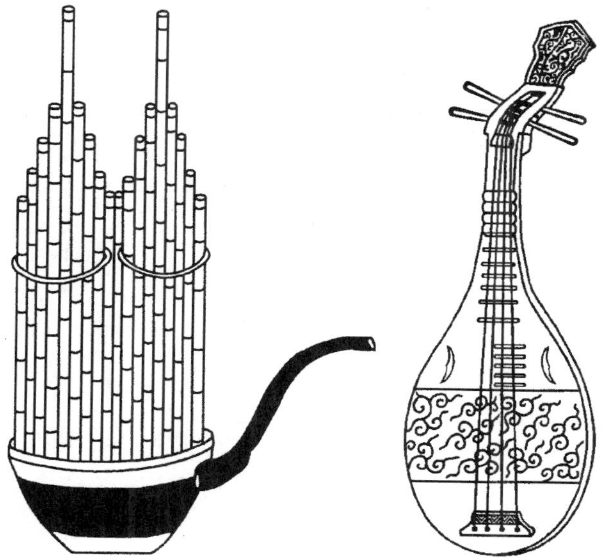

Two Chinese musical instruments: A complex mouth organ and a balloon guitar. Illustration by Charles Benn.

Military men also learned the art of dancing. In fact, dancing may have been part of their training to handle weapons. In early 622, a rebel commander captured Governor-General Li. The rebel admired the governor's talents and wanted to make him a grand general in his army, but Li refused. Some of Li's former subordinates regaled him with food and ale, perhaps as a farewell before his execution. At the feast, he said to them, "Gentlemen, you wish to console me with food and ale because you lament my difficulty and disgrace, so I shall carouse with you one last time." When they were all quite inebriated, Li spoke to the guards who had him in custody. "I can perform the sword dance. Would one of you be willing to loan me a blade?" One of them handed him a rapier. When he finished dancing, Li heaved a great sigh. "How can a great man, who has proved himself incapable of protecting that which he was entrusted with to defend, live and breathe with honor in this world?" Then he seized the sword and stabbed himself. His blood gushed out of his stomach, and he died (Benn, 168).

In the early 8th century, General Pei Min asked Wu Daoxuan to paint some murals on the walls of a Buddhist monastery in Luoyang. The artist agreed to do it on the condition that the general inspire him by performing the sword dance. Pei leapt on his horse. At a gallop, he wheeled to his right and then to his left, brandishing his rapier. Then he abruptly tossed the sword hundreds of feet in the air. As it descended, he extended his scabbard to catch it, but it fell through a roof instead. Wu seized his brush and executed a mural that was the wonder of the world. Earlier, the general had put his skills to a more practical purpose when he found himself surrounded by the Turks during a campaign in the north. He did his dance standing on the back of a horse and cut down arrows shot at him by the enemy. They were so awestruck by the feat that they left the field of battle.

A form of the sword dance was performed by women. The greatest of its artists—indeed, the only one said to have truly mastered it—was a lady in Emperor Illustrious August's troupe during the early 8th century. She taught the secrets of her craft to at least one other woman. Entertainers of that sort may have brandished two swords, but some writers report that they wielded silk ribbons with luminous objects at each end instead.

The grandest of the "supple dances" was "The Air of the Rainbow Robe and Feathered Skirt." Despite the legends of Emperor Illustrious August acquiring it from the moon palaces, it was in reality a form of entertainment that he adapted from Indian music. He often had it performed on his birthday. The female dancers wore costumes made of kingfisher feathers—hence its title—and necklaces made of gems. They were supposed to look like immortal maidens. In the 9th century, they also wore hats with strings of pearls hanging down. A single dancer, or a troupe of dancers might dance it. In 836, 300 women under the age of 19 from the emperor's Ward of Instruction performed the act at court. The ballet was largely a palace entertainment, but occasionally the emperor bestowed on meritorious ministers treatises that contained instructions on how to perform it (Benn, 167–69).

FOR MORE INFORMATION

Benn, C. *Daily Life in Traditional China: The Tang Dynasty*. Westport, Conn.: Greenwood Press, 2002.

Grady, M. "Making Chinese Music," 2002. <http://www.mi-reporter.com/sited/story/html/93353>, accessed November, 2003.

"Instruments of the Chinese Orchestra," *Chinese Musical Instruments*. <http://www.bigskymusic.com/b-world.htm>, accessed November, 2003.

POLYNESIA

Music and dance played major roles in the cultural life of ancient Polynesian societies. Although the number of musical instruments in the island groups was extremely limited, Polynesians played them with an expertise that impressed all of the early European explorers to the islands. Likewise, Polynesian dances, performed singly or in a chorus, were intricately and remarkably executed. Anciently, Polynesian music and dances were performed not only for entertainment but for religious ceremonies as well, and in modern times, Polynesian music and dance have become famous throughout the world.

The traditional musical instruments consisted primarily of drums, slit gongs, and nose flutes, although not all were found in every island group. (For example, drums were not found anciently in New Zealand and western Polynesia until the 19th century.) Wooden drums were typically cylindrical in shape with a sharkskin membrane stretched over the hollowed end and secured with *sennit* (a type of twine made of coconut fibers) through slotted holes in the drum's base. Drums ranged in size from the small knee drum (unique to Hawai'i) to the tall, slender drums with elaborate carvings found in Tahiti and other central Polynesian islands. Drums were traditionally beaten by fingers and the full hands in a variety of percussion rhythms, depending on the desired sound. The drums of Bora Bora are particularly well known today, and a number of recordings of different songs are available.

Slit gongs are found throughout the world, and the early Polynesians brought the knowledge of their construction and use with them when they entered the South Pacific. The slit gong (sometimes called the slit drum) is made by hollowing out an elongated tree trunk or branch, leaving a narrow slit as an opening and keeping the two ends closed. The percussive sound is made by beating the slit gong with various-sized sticks or logs. A large slit gong hit with a log can be heard for a great distance and can be used to communicate messages from one place to another or to summon members of the community to congregate for social or religious gatherings. Smaller slit gongs are struck with a variety of sticks at various speeds and rhythms to accompany performers in their dances.

Nose flutes are made from one section of bamboo about a foot long and up to an inch in diameter. (Mouth-blown flutes were hardly known in ancient Polynesia.) Nose flutes have a hole on one side at one end and up to six holes on the other side. The performer places the thumb of the right hand against the right nostril and holds the flute with the right fingers up to the left nostril, through which air is blown. Covering and uncovering the other holes produces a variety of notes. Its sound is described as soft and plaintive, but its range is extremely limited, consisting of three to four notes; unlike Western music, it may include half and quarter notes on the scale. The flute accompanied both singing and dancing.

Other minor musical instruments included the panpipes (Samoa and Tonga), stamping tubes made of bamboo sections (Hawai'i), ankle rattles (Hawai'i), gourds, and a type of Jew's harp made from a coconut leaf and bamboo.

Dance is one of Polynesia's most treasured and unique art forms. Anciently, dances were performed for religious ceremonies or for entertainment by a single performer or in groups of both men and women. They were thought to have been introduced into the world by various gods and goddesses, and Polynesian mythology abounds with stories of the many demigods and heroes who excelled in dance competitions with their rivals. Dances were usually accompanied only by percussion instruments—drums, slit gongs, and the human body (hitting parts of the body with the hands, for example), and the early explorers who first witnessed them described them as graceful, eloquent, and diverse. Dances in some areas of Polynesia, how-

A contemporary Tahitian dancer wears a flower crown on her head and a lei around her neck. Photo courtesy of Robert D. Craig.

ever, were also described as obscene, lascivious, and immoral. As a result, the early Christian missionaries to the islands banned their performance, and it is surprising that they survived at all. In the 19th and 20th centuries, Western music and tourist demands led to significant changes in the dance, but beginning in the later 20th century, there has been an ever-increasing interest and revival of the traditional dances.

Polynesian dance is best described as a visual extension of sung poetry (chanting), using complex hand, arm, hip, and leg movements either in a standing or sitting position, and performed by both men and women. Each island group—Hawai'i, Tahiti, New Zealand, Samoa, and Tonga, for example—has particular characteristics that set it apart from the others. Western Polynesian dancing (Samoa and Tonga) is characterized by the rhythmic pulsating of the legs and lower body and hand clapping, whereas eastern Polynesia (Tahiti and Hawai'i) is characterized by the swaying of hips and the varied movements of the hands, wrists, and arms.

Because of the wide diversity of traditional dances, it is not possible here to describe any in great detail, but three examples can help to explain the differences. In ancient Hawai'i, hulas were performed to a *mele* (song) sung by a chanter, who would most often accompany him- or herself with a gourd, whose percussion sound was made by hitting the gourd on the ground and hitting it with one's hand. The dancers interpreted the words to the *mele* with appropriate arm, hand, and hip motions while at the same time moving side to side with their feet. Sometimes the dancers would carry percussion instruments—feather-decorated gourd rattles, split-bamboo sections, sticks, and stones (used as castanets)—to accompany themselves. In Tahiti, the performers usually danced to a rapid beating of several slit gongs and/or drums; characteristic of these dances, the women rapidly moved their hips while keeping their feet and outstretched arms almost motionless. In Tonga, a large group of men perform an ancient dance called the *Me'etu'upaki* (a paddle dance), which has come down to us virtually unchanged. One man stands apart and acts as a type of director. He indicates the end of one stanza and the beginning of another. The skillful dancers sometimes move as a single group, or they split into two or three groups while twirling their paddles (*paki*) and making numerous turns of their bodies. The rows of men alternately change so that they move from front to back in quick transitions. The men accompany the percussion of the large slit gong with their own singing as one large chorus.

While dancing, men usually wore only a loincloth, whereas the women wore a variety of clothing, ranging from very little or nothing to yards of traditional *tapa* (bark cloth) wound about them. Almost all wore festive feathers, colorful flower leis, and wood ferns around their heads, arm, and legs.

~*Robert D. Craig*

FOR MORE INFORMATION

Kaeppler, A. L. *Poetry in Motion: Studies of Tongan Dance*. Vava'u, Tonda: Vava'u Press, 1993.

McLean, M. *Weavers of Song: Polynesian Music and Dance*. Honolulu: University of Hawai'i Press, 1999.

Entertainment

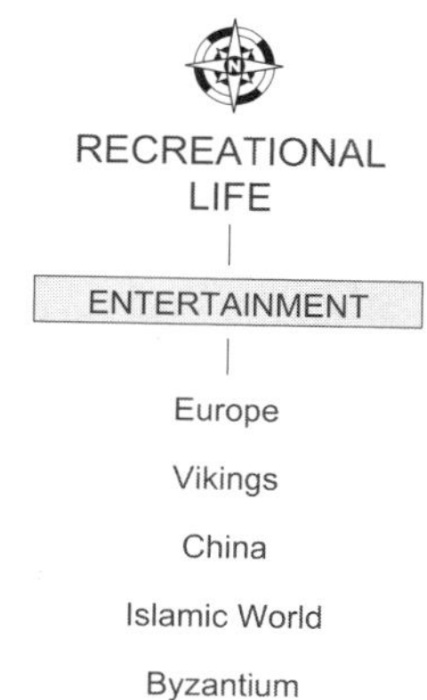

One of the characteristics of human beings is that we can become bored. Medieval monks called deep boredom *accidie*, which would distract a monk from his spiritual endeavors, and modern students fear boredom almost more than any other hazard that we might plausibly face. Many aspects of our daily lives are designed to prevent boredom: we crave new foods, we travel to new places, and we seek entertainment.

In earliest societies, entertainment probably took place at home. This was particularly true for Viking society. Entertainment—especially through the long winters—involved feasting, drinking, and telling stories and poems. This kind of entertainment is as old as human society. As the world became more complex, and urban, entertainment, too, became more complicated.

In today's life, we are accustomed to bringing entertainment into our homes in the form of television. In the medieval world, the wealthy could also hire entertainers to come to their homes, but most people had to go somewhere to seek out entertainment. In the Byzantine Empire, the great chariot races drew crowds until the 13th century. This entertainment was the center of public life in Byzantium. In the West, the best opportunity for entertainment took place at fairs where many people gathered (and where there was money available to reward the entertainers). As towns grew larger, entertainers might be found in the town square. Finally, church services sometimes offered entertainment as a way to bring the faithful to God.

Entertainment depends on novelty, so we seek out those things that are new to us. This can be anything from an unusual object to a rare talent. An early medieval author even described with wonder an entertainer who drew crowds because he could pass gas in a tune on command. People also gathered to stare at those who had been born deformed in some way. Most entertainment, however, surrounded various talents that had been cultivated.

Some entertainment took the form of musical performances. However, just as popular were acrobats and jugglers. In China, acrobats were particularly skilled, often performing death-defying acts on high poles or ropes. Women frequently performed these feats. The fairs of Europe also featured jugglers and acrobats of all kinds. There is a charming tale of a European acrobat who entered a monastery to seek a spiritual life but found he had no skill that could contribute to monastic life. Instead, every day he secretly performed acrobatic feats before a statue of the Virgin Mary. In time, his skills were rewarded when the other monks witnessed a miraculous appearance of Mary rewarding her acrobat (Mason, 53–66).

More formal entertainment took the form of theatrical productions. The Byzantine Empire preserved the strong theatrical tradition of the classical world, but western Europe had to reinvent this form of entertainment. The first plays took place in churches, during which actors reenacted biblical tales. This kind of play soon went to the marketplaces as wandering players traveled performing what became called "miracle plays." These beginnings of theater in western Europe would bear fruit in the Renaissance with the flowering of this kind of entertainment.

~*Joyce E. Salisbury*

FOR MORE INFORMATION

Mason, E. *Aucassin and Nicolette and Other Mediaeval Romances and Legends*. New York: E. P. Dutton, 1910.

EUROPE

Entertainment in the Middle Ages was somewhat more ritualized than it is today. This was partly because for most people the heavy schedule of work forced entertainment into certain restricted settings. For the medieval commoner, entertainment activities were concentrated on festival occasions, especially Sundays and holy days after church. Although people's opportunity for entertainment depended on their social status, the entertainments themselves were less stratified than were other aspects of medieval life. A few entertainments belonged especially to one class or another—hunting, for example, was an aristocratic pastime, whereas wrestling was more popular among common folk. Yet for the most part, entertainments seem to have crossed class boundaries more readily than other activities. The courtly poetry of the aristocracy may have been more refined than the folk verse of the commons, but both lord and peasant enjoyed many of the same stories; the dice used by the peasantry may have been made of simple bone or wood, but commoners played many of the same sorts of games as the nobility played with their dice of ivory.

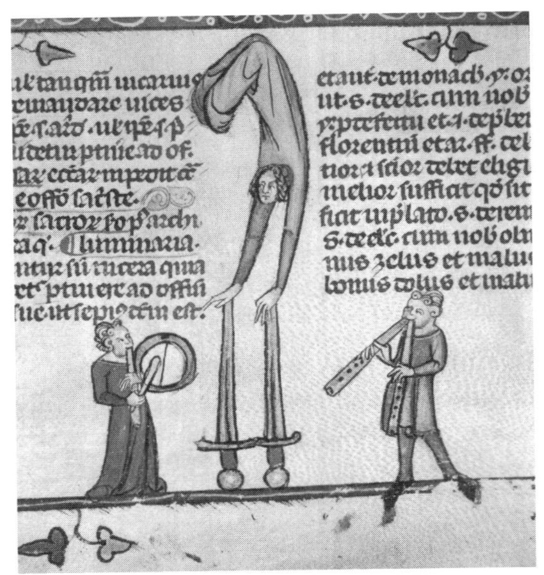

Acrobat doing a handstand on two swords, accompanied by two other entertainers playing musical instruments. © The British Library/Topham-HIP/The Image Works.

The most popular entertainments took place at fairs where people could enjoy jugglers, acrobats, and musicians. In an age when there was no electronic media, people depended upon the talented among them to provide entertainment. Nobility engaged and supported wandering musicians and poets to entertain in the great halls of the manor houses and castles.

The medieval church also inadvertently developed entertainment in the form of dramatic presentations. By the 10th century, plays were produced within churches to teach people about the Bible and to offer other moral lessons. There were a number of plays written and produced, but one of the earliest playwrights who has been identified is the German nun Hrotswitha of Gandersheim (ca. 935–73), who wrote six Christian plays loosely modeled after the Roman comedy dramatist Terence. Through the 11th and into the 12th centuries, plays were performed as part of church services and included music, props, and costumes. There were two kinds of plays: Mystery plays that depicted Gospel events and miracle plays that dealt with saints' lives. (Hrotswitha's plays were miracle dramas.) These plays were staged to awe (and entertain) the audience and teach them the importance of good and pious deeds. At the same time, these presentations included humor. For example, in one of Hrotswitha's plays, *Dulcitius*, the evil character is humiliated into imagining that pots and pans are beautiful women, and surely the audience laughed as he embraced these kitchen artifacts.

Soon, however, the popular dramatic presentations moved out of the churches to the marketplaces of the towns. The performances were staged by guilds who took on the task of performing and organizing these play. As the plays were presented outside, more and more of them began to include bawdy references to increase the entertainment.

Religious entertainment of the theater provided a creative outlet for talented people. It encouraged music, drama, acting, and writing. Furthermore, it offered entertainment for many of the common people who had no access to the entertainers performing in noble households. Furthermore, these miracle plays planted the seeds that were to flourish in the Renaissance theater of Shakespeare and others (Singman and McLean, 180).

To read about entertainment in Elizabethan England, see the England entries in the sections "Games and Sports" and "The Arts" in chapter 7 ("Recreational Life") of volume 3; for 18th-century England, see the England entries in the sections "Games" and "Arts and Hobbies" in chapter 7 ("Recreational Life") of volume 4; and for Victorian England, see the England entries in the sections "Music" and "Leisure Time" in chapter 7 ("Recreational Life") of volume 5 of this series.

FOR MORE INFORMATION

"Drama in Medieval Times." <www.geocities.com/Athens/Forum/5161/page8.htm>, accessed November, 2003.

Singman, J. L., and W. McLean. *Daily Life in Chaucer's England*. Westport, Conn.: Greenwood Press, 1995.

Tydeman, W. *English Medieval Theater*. London: Routledge, 1986.

Wilson, K., trans. *Hrotsvit of Gandersheim: A Florilegium of Her Works*. Cambridge, U.K.: Brewer, 1998.

VIKINGS

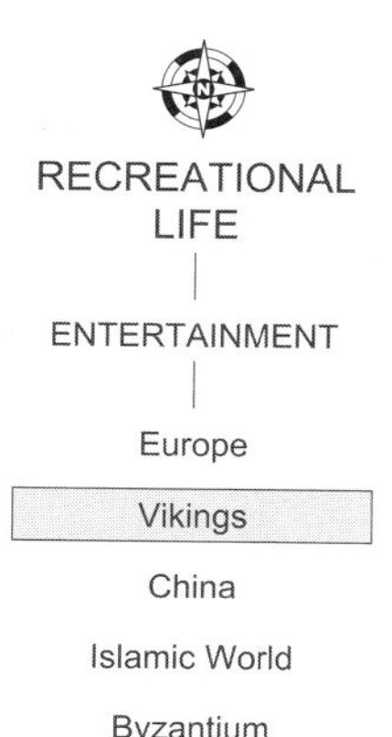

Feasting was the most common social diversion in the Viking Age. It provided respite from labor and opportunities for relaxation. The feasts included seasonal celebrations and commemorations of personal events. In origin, both were associated with pagan sacrifices, and although Christian leaders tried to purge these ceremonial feasts of pagan elements, they retained their timing and associated them with commemorative days of Christianity or the feast days of saints. Typical of this endeavor is the story of King Olaf Tryggvason of Norway, of whom it is reported that he abolished heathen sacrifice and libations and replaced them, to please the populace, with festival toasts at Christmas and Easter of midsummer ale, and autumn mead at

Michaelmass. It is telling that the pagan name for the midwinter feast, Yule, is still used to refer to Christmas.

Hospitality and generosity were qualities especially appreciated by the Norsemen, and these virtues were given expression in the hosting of parties for friends and kinsmen. Of course, the size and grandeur of the feast depended on the occasion and the host's social and economic status. A royal feast would no doubt have been quite extravagant, with an elaborate spread of food and drink and lasted several days. In his *Gesta Hammaburgensis ecclesiae pontificum*, Adam of Bremen says about King Sven Estridsson of Denmark that he indulged in feasting as was the custom among the barbarians. He also mentions that the alliance treaty between King Sven and the archbishop of Hamburg-Bremen had been confirmed and celebrated by a sumptuous feast that lasted eight days.

The feasts probably did not differ substantially from those held elsewhere in western Europe, but there is reason to believe that they were rowdier and involved heavier drinking. Drinking is often referred to in Icelandic sources but was probably more common in Scandinavia than in the Norse colonies in the North Atlantic, which may have had somewhat limited supplies of alcoholic beverages. The Sagas of Icelanders, for example, relate more details of games and entertainment in Iceland but reveal more drunkenness in Norway. The appropriate way to drink was without inhibition, and competitive drinking appears to have been common. When the drinking horn was passed, a man could not refuse unless he was old or sick; if someone tried to refuse, he was penalized by being forced to drain an extra cup. The sources are silent on the matter of hangovers, but they do include descriptions of vomiting as a result of excessive drinking. A spectacular example of projectile vomiting is given in *Egil's Saga*, where it is told that when Egil realized he could not tolerate more alcohol, he went over to his devious host, put both hands on his shoulders, and pressed him hard against a pillar. He then heaved up a vomit of massive proportions that gushed all over his host's face, into his eyes, nostrils, and mouth, and then flooded down his chest so that the host was almost suffocated. How fully women participated in drinking is unclear, but certainly they were involved in the drinking culture as serving women.

Alcohol loosens the tongue, and verbal contests appear to have been a common consequence of intoxication. As a man became drunk, he was likely to make statements he otherwise would have kept to himself. He might brag about himself and his leader and insult others, and such provocations would inevitably lead to new and probably more contemptuous replies. Soon a verbal duel or contest would be taking place that would increase in intensity as the men became more and more intoxicated. The goal was to improve verbal skill and performance without showing the effects of alcohol. Old Norse-Icelandic literature distinguishes between two types of verbal contests: *senna* and *mannjafnad*. The former is generally defined as a formal exchange of insults and threats; here one individual assails another in a verbal duel both by the insults themselves and by the wit through which they are created. The latter is defined as a formal exchange of boasts; here two individuals attempt to eclipse each other with boasting accounts of their own accomplishments.

The recital of poetry, which is closely related to verbal contests, was also a favorite form of entertainment and is also commonly associated with the consumption of alcohol. After all, Odin, the god of drink, was also the god of the poet, and Odin's mead was poetic inspiration. Storytelling, on the other hand, probably required soberness on the part of the performer, for the stories, whether new or old ones about living kings, distant ancestors, or mythical beings, could be long and intricate. The Icelanders in particular were known for their ability to tell stories and were often asked to entertain at royal courts abroad.

~*Kirsten Wolf*

FOR MORE INFORMATION

Brondsted, J. *The Vikings*. Translated by K. Skov. Harmondsworth: Penguin, 1971.
Christiansen, E. *The Norsemen in the Viking Age*. Oxford: Blackwell, 2002.
Wolf, K. *Daily Life of the Vikings*. Westport, Conn.: Greenwood Press, forthcoming.

CHINA

The Chinese term for the performances of the independent entertainers can be translated literally as the "hundred acts." As the phrase indicates, it encompassed a host of diversions—including snake charmers, sword swallowers, fire eaters, and weight lifters, as well as more dignified music, singing, dance, and acting. Dwarfs played a role in the variety shows and were permanent fixtures at the Tang court, as well as in the mansions of the patricians. No more than three feet tall, they came from a southern prefecture. The district sent them to the emperor as tribute until the late 8th century, when the throne abandoned the practice at the instigation of an upright governor.

There were a number of acrobatic acts, two of which fell into the death-defying class. The first was tightrope walking. Some performers, most of them women, sauntered along the line with wooden platform shoes on their feet; others paced it on painted stilts, five or six feet in length, bound to their shins. In one act, the acrobats formed a human tower of three or four performers, and the anchor man nimbly danced along the rope in time to the music. In another, the acrobats in the pyramid somersaulted off the shoulders of those below, one after the other, and landed on the rope without falling to the ground. Still others juggled balls, turned somersaults, or fenced with double-edged swords.

The second, and more spectacular, type of death-defying act were the pole acts. These feats required an anchorwoman—most of the names for the performers that have survived are feminine—who placed a tall, painted pole, 70 to 100 feet long, on her head. The shaft normally had a crossbar affixed to its top on which slim young girls performed acrobatic moves such as hanging by their chins or doing handstands and somersaults. In one act, the pole was crowned with a wooden mountain carved to resemble the fairyland of the immortals. A child climbed to the top and cavorted among the peaks while singing and dancing. In another, five young girls balanced themselves on five taut bowstrings stretched across a frame at the top of a shaft. They performed a martial dance that involved manipulating lances and spears. While all of that was going on aloft, the burly anchorwoman walked about, weaving back and forth to enhance the suspense in the audience.

Other acrobatic acts—juggling props such as swords, plates, pillows, or pearls—involved feats of dexterity. Some performers kept small bells in the air by kicking them with their feet. The best of the entertainers must have been an armless panhandler in Luoyang who lived in the second half of the 8th century. He begged money from passersby at a bridge in the city by inscribing texts with a writing brush that he grasped between the toes of his right foot. Before he set his pen to paper, the mendicant tossed the brush a foot or more into the air two or three times and never failed to retrieve it with his foot before it fell to the ground. His calligraphy was not inferior to that of official scribes.

Magic was most popular with Tang spectators. According to ancient historians, masters of illusion made their way to China from India when the Silk Road was opened in the 2nd century B.C.E. In the early 4th century, an Indian who could sever his tongue as well as spit fire arrived in south China. The residents of the area gathered to observe his act. When he was about to cut off his tongue, he would stick it out to show the audience. Then he severed it, and his blood flowed out, covering the ground. He placed the amputated piece in a bowl and passed it around to show the people. The spectators could see both it and the stump still in his mouth. Afterward, he replaced the tip of his tongue and rejoined it to the stump. Then he sat down to permit the gathering to see that his tongue was just as it had been before. China had its own well-developed tradition in the arts of illusion, a tradition as old as the 2nd century B.C.E. A Chinese magician who flourished between 670 and 674 had a trick in which he suspended a water jug from a beam and chopped the rope with a knife. Although he severed the rope, the jar did not fall. He also installed a jug of water in an empty room, placed a sword horizontally across the top of it, and closed the door tightly. Sometime later, spectators entered the room to have a look. There they saw the dismembered body of the magician that had been cut into five pieces (torso, arms, and legs). The jug no longer contained water. Instead it was full of his blood. After they left and closed the door, the magician reassembled his body and appeared to them in his original state. He sold fortunes in a market and made 100 coppers a day. Later someone filed charges against him at court. The magistrate sentenced him to death. While he was being led to the market for execution, the expression on his face was composed, and there was not the slightest sign of fear on it.

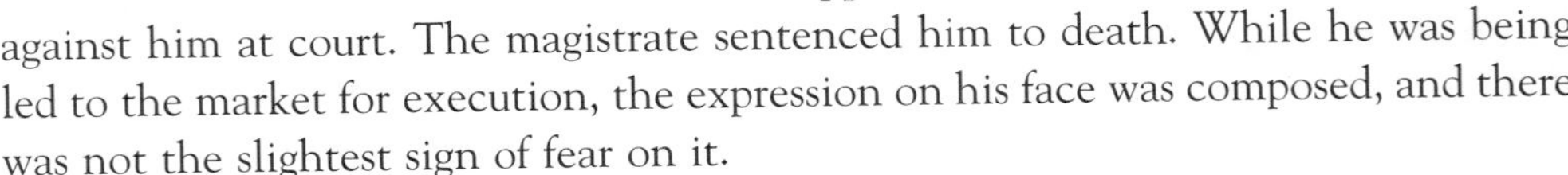

A troupe of musicians from southwest Asia performing on an elephant. Such entertainers traveled to the capital during the Tang dynasty. © The Art Archive/Private Collection Paris/Dagli Orti.

Animal acts played an important role in carnivals and elsewhere. The largest and most awesome were those involving elephants. Although some of the creatures still survived in southern China, those that performed at entertainments in the capital were probably tribute sent from the countries south of the empire to the court in Changan. When they arrived in the metropolis, the throne assigned two grooms to care for them and supplied them with rice, soybeans, and salt for feed. Because the animals could not tolerate the cold of the north, their keepers clothed them in sheepskins and felt during the winter. When the emperor called on them to entertain—in particular at the New Year's levee—they danced and bowed in homage to the strains of music. Incredibly, there were also tamed rhinoceroses that performed the same act as their fellow pachyderms. When Changan fell to An Lushan in 756, he had the beasts brought to Luoyang, his capital. To impress envoys from foreign lands, he declared that the animals had rushed north in response to his having received the mandate of Heaven. They would dance and pay homage to him as their sovereign by bowing. Then he ordered his servitors to lead in the elephants. However, when they arrived, the pachyderms stared at him in anger and refused to perform. Chagrined and enraged, An ordered his attendants to herd them into a pit and roast them alive. The fate of the rhinoceroses is unknown.

Perhaps the most amusing of all animal acts were those involving monkeys because their cavorting most closely resembled the behavior of humans. They performed pole acts, at which they were most adept, as well as somersaults. A man from western China excelled at training them and had at any given time more than 10 of the creatures, large and small, in his care. Purportedly, they were able to utter human speech because he fed them mercury sulfide. In one act, wearing hats and boots, they rode dogs. Spurring their mounts on with whips in their hands, they shouted as they passed from the front to the rear of a hall. They also performed a skit in which they emulated drunks and fell to the ground.

All these examples indicate that the range of entertainments was limited only by the imagination of the performers. The Chinese audience was insatiable for varied entertainment, and indeed they had more than a "hundred acts" (Benn, 157–67).

FOR MORE INFORMATION

Benn, C. *Daily Life in Traditional China: The Tang Dynasty*. Westport, Conn.: Greenwood Press, 2002.

Loewe, M. *Everyday Life in Early Imperial China*. London: Froma International, 1968.

ISLAMIC WORLD

Common children's entertainments in the medieval Islamic world included puppet theaters and see-saws, as well as games played with balls, dolls, and toy animals and birds. Board games, such as chess and backgammon, and card games were popular among all sectors of society. Entertainments that involved tests of physical prowess were also popular, including wrestling, races, polo, mock military competitions, and other displays of horsemanship.

Medieval manuscript illumination, *Two Arabs Playing Chess in a Tent.* This illumination comes from the Spanish medieval manuscript *Book of Games,* by Alfonso X, the king of Spain. © The Art Archive/Real biblioteca de lo Escorial/Dagli Orti.

Not all popular entertainments involved toys, puppets, or physical competitions. One of the most popular events at trade fairs in 7th-century Arabia was the poetry competition among the leading poets of the clans present. The best poet not only won a financial reward, but his entire clan benefited from the prestige of his poetic prowess. Arabic poetry performances continued to be extremely popular throughout the medieval Islamic world and remain so today, often selling out large auditoriums. Persian reemerged as a language of literature and administration in the 10th century. Public recitations of Ferdowsi's (ca. 940–1020) *Shahnameh* (Book of Kings)—one of the earliest and greatest examples of new Persian epic poetry—were popular throughout the Persian-speaking world. Turkish poetry began to gain popularity by 1400 after the rise of the Ottoman house in Anatolia and southeastern Europe.

Poetry often dealt with themes of honor, glory, and heroism among men, but also addressed the beauty of one's beloved, the passions of unrequited love, and the romantic benefits of wine. Among the ruling elites, as well as among the wealthy classes, poetry performances were often accompanied by music and performed by singing girls, many of whom were slaves purchased expressly for their beauty, voices, and dancing abilities.

~James Lindsay

FOR MORE INFORMATION

Lindsay, J. *Daily Life in the Medieval Islamic World*. Westport, Conn.: Greenwood Press, forthcoming.

Spuler, B. *The Muslim World*. 2 vols. Trans. F.R.C. Bagley. Leiden: E. J. Bull, 1960.

Byzantium

BYZANTIUM

Forms of entertainment changed a great deal over the life of the Byzantine Empire. Many of the popular pastimes of Greek and Roman culture continued through late antiquity but gradually were transformed or abandoned under economic and religious pressures. Literary sources for the 10th to 15th centuries mention a variety of public engagements and private activities that reflect contact with neighbors to east and west.

Public sporting events were among the main entertainments of inhabitants of Constantinople and the provincial cities during late antiquity; but by the 7th century, they had declined in the face of changing tastes and rising costs. Gladiatorial events were banned during the 4th century, and violent animal combats (*venationes*) gradually shifted to staged fights and exhibitions of leopards, lions, and other exotic animals, which continued in Constantinople as late as the 12th century. Hunting and falconry remained popular pursuits of aristocrats and emperors into late Byzantine times. The emperor Theodosios sought to suppress the games at Olympia around 393, although elsewhere they are known to have continued into the 5th century. Wrestling, boxing, running, jumping, discus throwing, and archery competitions remained a feature of the capital.

Chariot racing was the most popular of these public activities and drew huge crowds to hippodromes across the empire. The largest of these structures stood next to the imperial palace in Constantinople, where the emperor sponsored races and appeared before his public. The complex was approximately 1,500 feet long by 260 feet wide. Banks of seats with a capacity of perhaps 60,000 to 80,000 surrounded the track. Admission was free to male spectators (women did not attend), who could watch as many as 25 races in a single day. Events normally saw four teams of horse-drawn chariots in a race of seven laps. Partisan factions, known as the Blues, Greens, Whites, and Reds, enthusiastically supported their teams, which occasionally led to violent clashes with each other and civil authorities. During the 6th century, the triumphs of Porphyrios and other successful charioteers were commemorated by public monuments displayed on the track's high central median (*spina*). Despite its widespread popularity, chariot racing succumbed to its high costs and the opprobrium of the church. Races continued to be held through the 12th century but at a much reduced scale, on festival days and other special occasions. Other equestrian games included a form of polo (*tzykanion*), which was brought from Persia by the emperor Theodosios II in the early 5th century. In the 12th century, Western mercenaries introduced jousting tournaments (*tornemen* and *dzoustra*). Throughout this period, the hippodrome remained the capital's main assembly site and place of public spectacles, punishments, and executions.

A second public entertainment inherited from Rome was the theater. At least four theaters stood in the early Byzantine capital. Classical dramatic productions had been replaced much earlier by exhibitions of acrobats, jugglers, illusionists, mimes, and pantomimes. Costumed actors and mimes performed broad slapstick routines and were roundly condemned by the church even while they performed at court. Leading churchmen were especially critical of pantomime, in which a solo dancer employing a series of masks reenacted mythological stories. The imperial prohibition of pantomime in the early 6th century boosted the popularity of chariot racing and led to the decay of theater buildings everywhere. In later times, bands of acrobats, jugglers, storytellers, and other entertainers performed in towns and villages. Religious liturgy, funerary oratory, and palace ceremonial were the main scenes of late Byzantine theatrical display. A surviving example of liturgical drama is "The Three Holy Children in the Fiery Furnace," which was performed in Constantinople in the 15th century.

Attending the public baths, with their facilities for exercise, athletic competitions, lectures, and relaxation, was another Roman diversion that withered during late antiquity. By the mid-5th century, Constantinople was equipped with more than 150 private baths and 8 public baths, including the baths of Constantine and Zeuxippos near the imperial palace. These were large heated facilities lavishly decorated with classical statuary. Despite water shortages, some of these baths were maintained into the 8th and 9th centuries. Later baths were built on a much smaller scale and were privately run, or else formed part of the imperial palace, aristocratic houses, or monasteries.

Civil and religious festivals and fairs were popular occasions that were observed across the empire. Military triumphs were marked in the capital by a procession led by the returning emperor or general from the Golden Gate in the city walls to the hippodrome and imperial palace. Large cities such as Constantinople and Rome had their own municipal celebrations, including the Brumalia (festival of Dionysos observed on November 24) and Lupercalia (marking the foundation of Rome on February 15). These generally were accompanied by street processions, masquerades, displays of exotic animals such as bears, lions, and elephants, and general carousing. Other festivals were sponsored by urban guilds and confraternities. During the later period, large commercial fairs (*panegyreis*) accompanied festivals of certain saints, such as St. Demetrios at Thessaloniki or St. John at Ephesus. Contemporary writers describe the crowds, livestock, wares, food, games, and other diversions found at these fairs. Such events were held among tents and stalls that were set up outside the city walls and could last for several days. Smaller periodic fairs were held near rural market towns.

As in earlier Roman times, inns and taverns were popular gathering places for public relaxation in town and country alike. Urban taverns could include wine markets and other shops (*kapeleion*) where one could buy wine and food. Contemporary writers note the liveliness of these places, whose hours in the capital were restricted according to the religious calendar. The inward orientation of later Byzantine society ensured that special occasions were celebrated primarily within the home. Children usually were born at home and were welcomed with gifts and feasting. Wedding celebrations included a banquet at the house of the groom accompanied by drinking and dancing that lasted until dawn; in aristocratic circles such festivities could last for weeks.

Other domestic pastimes included playing board games. Chess (*zatrikion*) apparently was introduced from the East and by the 12th century had become popular among the Byzantine nobility. Anna Komnene noted that her father, the emperor Alexios I, played the game with family members in the palace. Other writers mention games such as dice, backgammon (*tablia*), and checkers, although the differences are not always clear. Less formal kinds of gambling, knucklebones, and other games were enjoyed across the empire.

~*Marcus Rautman*

FOR MORE INFORMATION

Mango, C. "Daily Life in Byzantium." *Jahrbuch der Österreichischen Byzantinistik* 31, no. 1 (1981): 337–53.

Schrodt, B. "Sports of the Byzantine Empire." *Journal of Sport History* 8, no. 3 (1981): 40–59, <http://www.aafla.org/SportsLibrary/JSH/JSH1981/JSH0803/jsh0803d.pdf>.

RECREATIONAL LIFE: WEB SITES

http://www.pbs.org/holomaipele/hula1.html
http://www.geocities.com/MedievalWorld/LibraryHunting.html
http://www.hypermusic.ca/hist/medieval.html
http://www.regia.org/games.htm
http://www.sdcoe.k12.ca.us/score/chinin/chininsg5.htm

8

RELIGIOUS LIFE

The human world is made up of more than the material and social environments that surround us. Throughout history, people have left records of their recognition of and longing for something larger than themselves, and this desire to transcend the daily life forms the basis for people's religious faith. Religions have two intertwined components—belief and rituals—and the second derives from and preserves the former. Thus, through careful enactment of rituals, the faithful believe they can rise above the mundane realities of day-to-day life, and historians find the study of religious practices offers a window into people's spiritual beliefs.

Religious beliefs have served to help people make sense of the natural world—from its beauties to its disasters. For example, an ancient Egyptian pharaoh (Akhenaton) and a medieval Christian saint (Francis of Assisi) both wrote magnificent poetry praising the blessings of this world. In addition, the Buddha and the Hebrew scriptures' Book of Job both address the deep sufferings of this life. In these ways, religion has always helped people make sense of the world that surrounds them.

The Middle Ages are known as an "Age of Faith" because religious beliefs shaped people's lives in many ways. In the Middle Ages, two of the great monotheistic religions—Christianity and Islam—came to prominence and created a cultural division in the Mediterranean world all the way into Asia. This cultural divide erupted into violence in the Crusades that continues to generate remembered animosity into the 21st century. Christianity, too, split into Roman Catholic and Greek Orthodox, and both churches survive today. In China, religion also shaped society as Confucianism, Buddhism, and Daoism had an impact on the educational system as well as on people's daily faith and ethics.

The powerful religious faith stimulated the establishment of many religious institutions. Great church buildings dominated the urban landscapes from England to China. Church bells in the West and the calls of the Muslim muezzins to prayer filled the cities and defined communities as people identified with everyone within the sound of the religious call. Monasteries, too, were influential institutions in the East and West. Here, men and women retired to seek God but ended up being tremendously influential in society.

Religious rituals also serve the needs of society. The faithful reinforce their social ties by worshiping together, and sociologists of religion argue that religion is the symbolic worship of society itself. Sacred songs, dances, and feasts have always served to bind communities closer together, and in these ways the religious and secular lives of the people mingle. This intimate relationship between religious beliefs, rituals, and societies makes the study of religious life a fruitful one. The complex nature of societies also yields complexities in religious beliefs and practices. Throughout history, we can follow the reforms and indeed revolutions in religious ideas that have profoundly shaped our past.

Religious rituals shaped the calendar years of people in the East and West. Cycles of work and leisure were marked by religious holidays, and when people engaged in their greatest celebrations, they were religious ones. Religions also surrounded death rituals to a much greater extent than is true today. Indeed, people's lives from birth to death were guided by the religious rituals that served their faith. Religion in the Middle Ages also defined the afterlife in ways that continue to be familiar to us. Unlike people in the ancient world, medieval people expected an afterlife that would be a strong continuity with their life on this world. They expected to be rewarded or punished in an afterlife that finally brought a justice that seemed too often lacking in this world, and this hope prevailed whether one was Muslim, Christian, or Buddhist.

Through the study of religious life, we can thus learn about how people viewed the natural and supernatural, how rituals organized people's daily lives, and how beliefs brought out the best (and the worst) in people. At the same time, we can glimpse the deep longing in the human souls that has generated some of peoples' noblest thoughts. And perhaps more than in any other arena, it is in religious life that modern people are different from their medieval counterparts.

~Joyce E. Salisbury

RELIGIOUS LIFE
RELIGIOUS BELIEFS
Europe
Vikings
China
Islamic World
Byzantium
Mongols
Polynesia

Religious Beliefs

The religious of the world in the Middle Ages can be divided into two main streams: polytheism (the belief in many gods) and monotheism (the belief in one god). The first was the older tradition, and the latter represented the Judeo-Christian-Muslim tradition, who all worshiped the same one God. Beyond these two great divisions, all the religions established specialized leaders to teach and guide the faithful. These general religious beliefs influenced everyone's daily life.

The Polynesians had been isolated for millennia, so their religious beliefs were the oldest—they seem to have been virtually unchanged for 3,000 years. Polynesians were polytheistic and believed generally in "animism," which means they believed that supernatural forces animated the whole universe. One of the Chinese religions—Daoism—also held that people should live by the laws of an animated nature. The other great Chinese religions—Confucianism and Buddhism—were also polytheistic in that they did not restrict worship to one deity. The Vikings were polytheistic when they emerged into the European culture, but within a few centuries, they converted to Christianity.

Christians and Muslims, on the other hand, were monotheistic. Both were, as the Muslims said, "People of the Book," which means that they valued Hebrew scriptures and the New Testament as the divinely inspired word of God. Muslims add the Qur'an (Koran) to that list of scriptures, for they believe that to be God's word to the prophet Muhammad. One of the tragedies of the Middle Ages was that during this time, these believers in the same God engaged in violence with each other: Jews were killed in pogroms (large-scale persecutions), and Christians and Muslims went to war for two hundred years in Crusades over the control of Jerusalem and the land that was holy to both.

During the Middle Ages, Christians experienced the first split in the Christian Church: Christians in the Byzantine Empire began to split from those in western Europe. The two churches began to differ on language, ritual, and leadership. In 1054, the split was made formal, and Eastern Christians became the Orthodox Church while Western ones were Catholic. This split continues today.

One facet of most religions is an emphasis on ethics, or correct action. Polynesians were surrounded by forbidden actions that were considered taboo. Chinese Confucianism and Buddhism stressed ethical behavior or, in Buddhism, the "eightfold path" that could govern one's life. By stressing practice over belief, the Chinese avoided many of the kinds of divisive struggles that split the Christian West. Christians and Muslims, too, had ethical requirements. For example, Muslims, like Jews, had dietary requirements and were forbidden pork, and Christians had periodic fasting days during which they could not eat meat.

Ritual practices shaped Muslims' lives even more than it did Christians'. Muslims had to pray five times a day, for example, whereas Christians were expected to go to church once a week. Both Christians and Muslims hoped to go on pilgrimage to holy sites at least once in their lives. Muslims went to Mecca and Medina and perhaps Jerusalem, and Christians went to various shrines of saints—Santiago de Compostella in Spain was the most popular in the Middle Ages—or to Rome or Jerusalem. This movement of peoples on pilgrimage gave a great stimulus to the exchange of ideas; for example, Gothic churches spread from France to all over Europe.

Most religions have a hierarchy of leaders that are expected to mediate between people and God. Christians in the West had a hierarchy of priests, bishops, archbishops, and the pope (the bishop of Rome) to guide them. Christians in Byzantium looked to priests and patriarchs to guide them under the direction of an emperor who ruled church and state. Muslims looked to scholar-jurists to interpret divine law and teach the faithful. The educated Chinese clergy even set the school curricula to ensure the transmission of their ethical ideas. Polynesians had powerful priests who mediated with the vast spiritual world. In all these religions, women were excluded from religious leadership and were expected to serve God more privately and quietly.

It is impossible to overstate the importance of religion in the Middle Ages. Everywhere, this was an age of faith, when people believed their role was to follow

God's will. Sometimes that desire created magnificent products of faith, and sometimes it brought about religious violence. However, everyone from Buddhists to Christians recognized that this was an imperfect world (in Christian terms, a "fallen" world), so they could not expect perfection here—they could only continue to strive for it.

~*Joyce E. Salisbury*

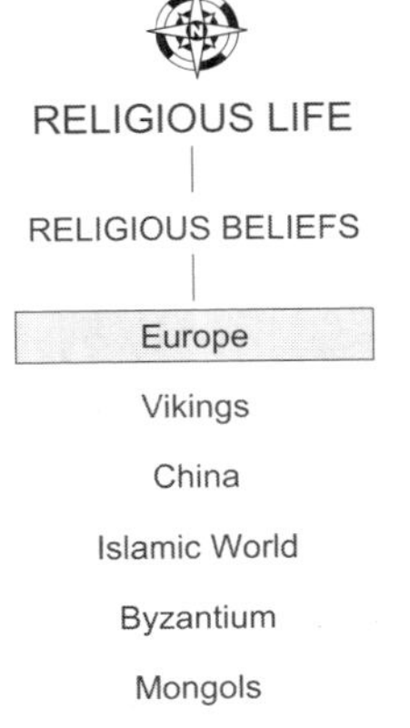

EUROPE

The Middle Ages have often been called the "Age of Faith" because the society and culture was based on religious beliefs and the institution of the Catholic Church. The Roman Empire first accepted Christianity when Emperor Constantine issued the Edict of Toleration in 313, allowing Christian worship within the empire. He further stimulated that worship by supporting Christian churches and taking an active interest in Christian doctrine. The emperor Theodosius I (r. 379–95) completed the process of acceptance when he declared Christianity the *only* religion of the empire. Christianity was thus declared "universal" (at least for the Mediterranean world), and the "Roman Catholic Church" was born. When the Roman Empire fell in the early 5th century, the church remained as an institution, and as Germanic tribes converted and medieval civilization was born, Christian beliefs and institutions remained at the heart of people's daily lives.

The core of Christian beliefs lay in the Gospels that detailed the life, death, and teachings of Jesus, accepted as the resurrected savior to the faithful. Even before Christianity had been accepted by the Roman Empire, Christians gathered in the house-churches of believers and celebrated the central mysteries of Christianity: baptism, during which people were accepted into the community of the faithful; communal prayers and celebrations; and the Eucharist, during which Christians reenacted the Last Supper of Jesus by ritually eating bread and wine that were (or symbolized) the body and blood of Jesus who had been sacrificed to redeem the sinners of the world. As church services moved from the small congregations to increasingly large churches of the Middle Ages, these central celebrations continued.

As Christianity embraced more and more people, it is perhaps not surprising that differences arose as to the specific beliefs of the religion. As early as the 4th century, Constantine had to preside over church councils to resolve disputes. Christians argued over such matters as the relationship between Jesus and the Father or how Christ's humanity and divinity were united. These and other disputes were resolved by the issuing of council resolution and the drafting of creeds—such as the Nicene Creed—that expressed the increasingly complex doctrine that represented Christian belief.

The emperors in the eastern part of the old Roman Empire could not retain the influence over the church that earlier emperors such as Constantine had wielded. The church in the West went its own way, and during the early Middle Ages it was unclear who would lead this church: the bishop of Rome (who became known as the pope) or kings or emperors. This struggle came to a head in the 11th century when the popes and Holy Roman Emperors of German lands struggled over who should lead (and reform) the church. By the early 13th century, popes had emerged victorious, and they established an imperial papacy that exerted power over political as well as religious fields. One of the high points of papal power was the Crusades, when Christian armies marched to fight to reclaim the Holy Land. This leadership continued until new struggles emerged in the 14th-century that eventually broke the secular power of the popes. But for the Middle Ages, a strong papacy was a feature that shaped people's lives.

The development of religious doctrine became a regular feature of medieval life as people continued to raise questions about Christian belief. The most influential medieval council was the Fourth Lateran Council, which met in 1215 and issued a number of influential decrees. One of the most important was that church leaders fixed the number of sacraments—vehicles of God's grace—at seven: (1) baptism, when an individual formally enters the church; (2) confirmation, when the soul receives the Holy Ghost; (3) communion, the taking of the Body and Blood of Christ; (4) marriage; (5) penance, the confessing and forgiveness of sins; (6) extreme unction, when the sick and the dying are reassured of salvation; and (7) ordination, when priests are blessed to administer the sacraments. These seven sacraments would be challenged during the waning of the Middle Ages and attacked by Christian reformers during the Reformation.

The development of this established church and its ideas did not go unchallenged through the Middle Ages. The history of religious beliefs during this time is equally one of religious dissent during which people and groups disagreed with the direction of the church. Some people questioned many aspects of the medieval church and its beliefs: whether the popes should be in charge, whether the church should be rich, whether confession was required, whether people should read the Bible and preach, and many other questions. Some dissenters were able to find expression for their beliefs by entering various monastic and other religious movements that offered people religious options. For example, people in the 13th century who wanted to give up all their goods and follow a Christian life by being poor and begging could become Franciscan Friars, who approached God in this way.

However, other dissenters were repressed, sometimes in brutal ways. In the 13th century, the church established the court of the Inquisition, which was to determine whether people's thoughts about religion were in error. Ostensibly designed to correct errors, in reality this court used tortures and other abuses to try to make sure dissenters did not prevail. Although the church did not exact capital punishment, when the Inquisition determined that someone was unrepentant, it turned him or her over to the secular government, which then sometimes executed the offender.

The religious beliefs of the Middle Ages were complex and encompassed all aspects of society. The medieval church generated some of the most beautiful products of the Middle Ages, from great cathedrals to magnificent mystical writings. The church was also responsible for some of the worst excesses of the times, from the Crusades to the Inquisition.

To read about religion in Elizabethan England, see the Protestantism (England) entries in the sections "Deities and Doctrines" and "Priests and Rituals" in chapter

8 ("Religious Life") of volume 3; for 18th-century England, see the England entries in the sections "Religious Beliefs" and "Religious Practices" in chapter 8 ("Religious Life") of volume 4; and for Victorian England, see the England entries in the sections "Morality" and "Religion" in chapter 8 ("Religious Life") of volume 5 of this series.

~*Joyce E. Salisbury*

FOR MORE INFORMATION

Barraclough, G. *The Medieval Papacy*. New York: 1968.
Hamilton, B. *The Medieval Inquisition*. New York: 1981.
Lynch, J. H. *The Medieval Church: A Brief History*. New York: Longman, 1992.

RELIGIOUS LIFE
RELIGIOUS BELIEFS
Europe
Vikings
China
Islamic World
Byzantium
Mongols
Polynesia

VIKINGS

During most of the Viking Age, the majority of Scandinavians shared a system of beliefs and mythology that Christians derogatorily labeled heathenism or paganism. The Scandinavians themselves had no specific word for their religion. The closest word for the concept was the Old Norse *sidr,* meaning custom, which shows how integrated religion was in everyday life. Unlike Christianity, the pagan Scandinavian religion was fluid and it never appears to have undergone the processes of open codification that characterized Christianity from its earliest stages.

Most Vikings believed in a pantheon of 12 gods, excluding Odin, the all-father and head of the Aesir (the group of deities). Odin was the god of poetry, secret wisdom, and magic; the patron of warriors and aristocrats; and the creator of the human race, for he gave life and breath to Ask and Embla, the first man and woman, whom he made from tree trunks. Odin dwelled in Valholl with his wolves, Geri and Freki, and his ravens, Huginn and Muninn, who flew over the world every day and brought him tidings from afar. His weapon was the spear Gungnir, and he rode an eight-legged gray horse named Sleipnir. Odin's legitimate wife was the goddess Frigg, who knew the fates of men, and with her he sometimes sat on his throne looking over all the worlds. By Frigg, Odin was the father of Baldr, the most eloquent and the gentlest among the Aesir, whose death was brought about by the blind god Hod through the machinations of Loki, a cunning schemer, who both helped and hindered the gods. Part god and part demon, Loki was the son of the giant Farbauti and married to Sigyn, with whom he had a son, Nam, but he also had issue by a giantess Angrboda, and they turned out to be a sinister brood: the death-goddess Hel, the wolf Fenrir, and the Midgard serpent Iormungand. When the gods realized that these three siblings were being raised in the realm of the giants, they pursued oracles and learned that the siblings would bring them disaster. Accordingly, Odin threw Iormungand into the depths of the ocean, where he remained encircling the inhabited world; Hel he threw into the underworld; and Fenrir was fettered with a deceitful chain.

Another son of Odin was Thor, whose mother was Jord (Earth). Thor was a warrior god and the defender of the Aesir against their natural enemies, the giants and giantesses. His weapon was the hammer Mjollnir, with which he held the forces of chaos in check. He also possessed a pair of iron gloves with which to grasp the hammer and a belt, and when he girded himself with it, his divine strength was doubled. Thor lived in Thrudheim (World of Might). He was married to the goddess Sif, about whom little is known except that she had a son, Ull, who appears to have been a sky god, and that her hair was of gold.

Other sons of Odin included the courageous Tyr, a god of justice and war, who lost his hand when, as a sign of good faith, he put it into Fenrir's jaws, as the wolf was chained up; Bragi, god of poetry and husband of the goddess Idunn, who kept the precious apples of eternal youth, which prevented the gods from growing old; and the enigmatic Heimdall, who is called the white god and is said to have been born by nine maidens, all sisters. Heimdall dwelt in Himinbjorg (Rocks of Heaven) beside Bifrost, for he was the gods' watchman, guarding Asgard from the frost-giants. He owned Gjallarhorn (the ringing horn), whose note could be heard throughout all worlds; at the first signs of Ragnarok, during which he and Loki kill each other, he blows his horn.

Two other gods and one other goddess lived in Asgard but were of the race of the Vanir, deities of fertility and wealth, with whom the Aesir were once at war. These were Njord and his twins, Freyr and Freyja. The twins were born to Njord by his sister when he lived among his native tribe, which permitted incestuous unions. Njord's son Freyr also took his wife, Gerd, from the giant world, but in contrast to his father's marriage, Freyr and Gerd's union was a happy one; indeed, the story of Freyr's passion for Gerd as related in the Eddic poem *Skirnismal* (Skirnir's Journey) is one of the most charming Norse myths. Freyja, a goddess of love, who was known chiefly for her loose morals, married a character by the name of Od. Od, about whom nothing is known, is generally thought to be a doublet of Odin, who shared with Freyja the men who fell in battle and who learned from her the kind of magic called *seid,* which enabled its practitioners to see into the future, cause death, misfortune, and sickness, and deprive men of their wits. Freyja is sometimes referred to as the chief of the *disir,* who were tutelary goddesses attached to a person, a family, or a neighborhood, and closely connected with *fylgjur,* guardian spirits or fetches of an individual or a clan and representative of what one today would regard as inherent qualities.

In essence, Scandinavian mythology is about the continuous struggle between the gods and the giants, who may be regarded as personifications of the forces of order and chaos. The struggles are typically between individual gods and giants, and most of them involve Odin and Thor, the two most famous and powerful of the Aesir. However, the two stand in sharp contrast to one another, and in their combats with the giants they use very different means, which serve to throw light on their character.

The Norwegian and Icelandic poets present Odin as the foremost god. Their reason for doing so is obvious: Odin was the patron of aristocrats and poets, who were responsible for the formal poetry that has been preserved from the pagan era. But there are also indications that the cult of Odin spread and was especially practiced during the Viking Age. Unpredictable, deceitful, and cynical, Odin was the god of war, and his human clientele consisted of kings, earls, chieftains, warriors, and poets. He would thus have appealed to the Vikings and the Viking style of life. Judging from place-name evidence, Odin was especially worshiped in Denmark and southern Sweden.

The hierarchy of the gods in terms of worship is not entirely clear, but it seems that whereas the upper classes favored Odin, the farming freemen showed preference for Thor, a guardian of their communities and of the stability and law of these communities. Although the place-names of western Norway and Iceland, where he was particularly popular, show that his cult was firmly established in the latter part of the 9th century, it appears that his popularity increased and that he rose in eminence especially in the late pagan period. Thor defended gods and humans against giants and monsters, and so he was considered the best suited to defend paganism against the aggression of Christ. Thor ruled in the sky and governed thunder, lightning, winds, rain, fair weather, and produce of the soil, and the Swedes sacrificed to him if there was danger of pestilence or famine. Although there is little indication of Thor's role as a divine promoter of fertility in Icelandic and Norwegian myths, it may account for his popularity in communities built on agriculture and fisheries. Freyr is generally the god standing for powers of fertility, peace, and prosperity, and his idol in Uppsala was fashioned with a gigantic penis.

The Scandinavians had known of Christianity for several hundred years before the conversion took place. They had become acquainted with it in the course of their raids, Anglo-Saxon and German monks had come to Scandinavia as missionaries, and some of the Scandinavians who settled abroad had even permitted themselves to be baptized.

For a long time, people mixed the two religions; a practice that is discernible in archaeological finds. Representations of Thor's hammer and Christian crosses appear side by side, and a 10th-century soapstone mold for making both cross and Mjollnir amulets found in Denmark indicates the close association of the two symbols toward the end of the pagan era. A 10th-century amulet found at Foss in southwest Iceland seems to be a hybrid of a hammer and a cross, perhaps the creation of a man of a mixed religion.

As the Scandinavians became better acquainted with Christianity, they gradually came to understand that Christianity meant that only one god could and should be worshiped—but Christian concepts of guardian angels and saints probably filled the roles of several of the pagan gods and supernatural beings. Some of the latter, such as the elves and land spirits, have, however, survived into modern times and figure prominently in folktales collected in the 19th century.

Although the conversion of the Scandinavian countries was a long process of contacts between the Scandinavians and their Christian neighbors in the south and west, it may for practical purposes be said to have taken place when the kings of the individual countries, who were closely linked with the traditional cults, decided to abandon pagan sacrifices in favor of Christian rites.

The King Harald Klak of Denmark was the first Scandinavian king to be baptized. The ceremony took place in Mainz in 826, but because Harald Klak was exiled a year later, his conversion had little effect. Nonetheless, in the century that followed, Christianity made considerable progress: many people converted, and several churches were built, not least a result of the missionary activities of Ansgar. However, the German priest Poppo is the one normally credited with converting the Danes and their king, Harald Bluetooth (d. ca. 985), to Christianity. This is considered to have occurred around 960. The Saxon Widukind, a contemporary writer, relates that Poppo demonstrated the superiority of Christ by carrying a bar of red-hot iron in his bare hands without suffering any harm. By this ordeal, King Harald Bluetooth decided to convert, and on the greater Jelling rune stone he declares himself responsible for introducing Christianity into Denmark.

Although Hakon the Good (ca. 920–60), who had been fostered in England at the Christian court of King Aethelstan of Wessex, was Norway's first Christian king, the conversion of Norway is generally associated with King Olaf Tryggvason (d. 999/1000), who had led great Viking raids to the British Isles, where he had been baptized. When in 995 he became king, he set out to Christianize Norway and managed to make the entire coastal area of Norway convert. It was not only in Norway, however, that King Olaf tried to spread Christianity. His pressure on the Icelandic chieftains was probably one of the main reasons that the Icelanders accepted the new faith at the Althing, their parliament, in 999–1000. He also made the Norse colonists in Greenland accept Christianity. The conversion of Norway was completed by Olaf Tryggvason's successor, King Olaf Haraldssson (d. 1030), who was declared a saint shortly after his death.

The conversion of Sweden is less clearly documented. Olaf Skotkonung (d. 1022), king of the Gotar and Svear, is generally recognized as the first Christian king, and probably most people in Vastergotland were Christian by the mid-11th century. Indeed, under Olaf Skotkonung, a bishopric was established from Hamburg-Bremen, at Skara in Vastergotland. However, paganism remained entrenched in Uppland, Gotland, and Smaland, and pagan cults continued to be celebrated at Uppsala for many decades. Most likely, the cults were abandoned early in the 12th century, at which time it is believed that Sweden was predominantly Christian.

~Kirsten Wolf

FOR MORE INFORMATION

DuBois, T. A. *Nordic Religions in the Viking Age*. Philadelphia: University of Pennsylvania Press, 1999.

Turville-Petre, E.O.G. *Myth and Religion of the North. The Religion of Ancient Scandinavia*. New York: Holt, Rinehart and Winston, 1964.

Wolf, K. *Daily Life of the Vikings*. Westport, Conn.: Greenwood Press, forthcoming.

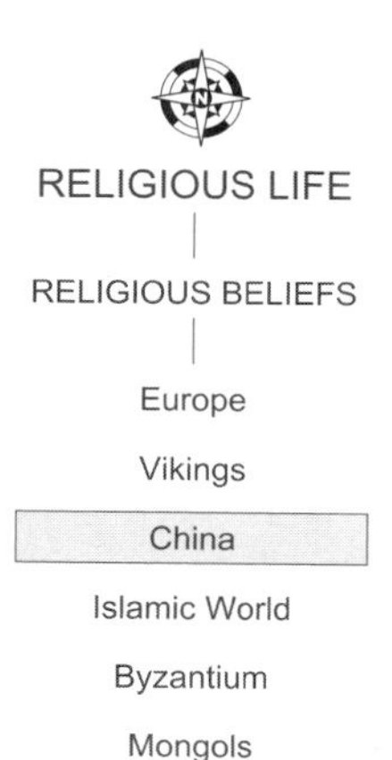

CHINA

In the 6th and 5th centuries B.C.E., three great religious leaders developed ideas that would form the core of religious beliefs during the Tang dynasty—Confucius and Lao-tzu in China, and Buddha (Gautama) in India. The three religions coexisted comfortably in China, and people did not need to select just one to follow; they drew ideas from all three.

Confucius taught that the most important thing to guide human's lives was a moral order. He believed that developing a moral character was central not only to achieving a just society, but to personal development. As Confucius wrote, "It is Goodness that gives to a neighborhood its beauty" (Thompson, 93). Thus if people constantly strive to behave well, the world will be a better place.

This development was acquired through strict rules of behavior that honored ancestors and ancient rituals. The heart of Confucius's teachings is found in the *Analects*, the Confucian sacred book. The *Analects* contains a collection of short ethical sayings and proverbs attributed to or concerning Confucius. The master's disciples arranged these sayings in a rather informal order following Confucius's death in 479 B.C.E., and this work remained at the center of the educational curriculum during the Tang era. Perhaps the most representative aspect of Confucian thought is summed up in the following anecdote: "A follower asked, saying 'is there any single saying that one can act upon all day and every day?' The Master said, 'Yes, it is the saying about altruism—Never do to others what you would not like them to do to you' " (Thompson, 93).

A statue of Buddha. These statues spread from India all over the East as more people followed the path of Buddhism. The statue was to remind people of the peace that came with contemplation. © Library of Congress.

The second great Chinese religion—Daoism was attributed to Lao-tzu but was developed more fully by Chuang Tzu (ca. 300 B.C.E.). Dao, which means "The Way," focuses on a way of looking at life that would yield a happy, balanced life. While Confucianism emphasized correct behavior in this world, Daoists focused on more abstract, mystical wisdom. In a purported conversation between Confucius and Lao-tzu (which probably never took place), the Daoist author points up this difference: Confucius is said to ask "what is the great Dao?" Lao-tzu replied, "Throw away your sage wisdom! Dao is dark and elusive, difficult to describe" (Thompson, 98). Thus the Daoist sage repudiates the reasoned rules of Confucius.

Daoists believe that everyone should understand and live by the laws of nature (more than the regulations made by people). They believe that the central law of nature is harmony and balance that is symbolized by the principles of yin and yang. (Chinese medicine was based on the Daoist belief of harmony among these two elements.) Yin is associated with the dark, negative, patient, and female side of nature, whereas yang is associated with the light, positive, active, and male side. Neither one nor the other was considered bad; it was important to have an appropriate balance of both.

Most of the Daoist writers were fond of paradoxes that were to reveal the truth of nature and religion. For example, a poet writes:

My teachings are very easy to understand and very easy to practice,
But no one can understand them and no one can practice them. (Thompson, 96)

Generations of Daoist spiritualists have meditated on these and other paradoxes to try to understand the way that would lead to harmony with nature.

The third great religion in China—Buddhism—had spread from India, where it had been founded by Prince Siddhartha Gautama (553–483 B.C.E.). The young prince had been raised in pampered surroundings, but he was shocked and saddened when he discovered that the world was filled with the suffering of old age, sickness, and death. He began to travel to discover the solution to these sufferings. He traveled for six years throughout India, but one day while meditating, he arrived at understanding. At this point he earned the title the Buddha, which means "Awakened One."

Although the Buddha agreed with the Hindus on these basic principles of reincarnation and karma, he disagreed about the methods by which the final goals were to be achieved. He did not approve of the spectacularly ascetic practices of the Hindu experts, and he also disapproved of the Hindu caste system, believing that everyone was equal in spiritual potential. Instead, he taught what he called the Middle Way between asceticism and self-indulgence, and he taught the Path, which is a practical way to behave to achieve a good life and perhaps escape the cycles of rebirth and achieve "nirvana," an impersonal ultimate salvation. (The Middle Way is the Noble Eightfold Path, described in the sidebar box.)

Practicing these precepts required meditation and a dedication to right living. Buddhists are vegetarians because they believe it is forbidden to kill even animals. The perfect practice of these principles could only be done by monks who dedicated their lives to striving for enlightenment. These monks were extremely influential in spreading the ideas of Buddhism to China and elsewhere.

Snapshot

The Basic Tenets of Buddhism

Buddhism's Four Noble Truths

1. Life is full of pain and suffering.
2. Suffering is caused by desire.
3. Suffering can be ended by ending desire.
4. To stop desire, people must follow the Eightfold Path.

Buddhism's Eightfold Path

1. Right knowledge
2. Right intention
3. Right speech
4. Right conduct
5. Right means of livelihood
6. Right effort
7. Right mindfulness
8. Right concentration

Buddhists (like Hindus) believe in reincarnation, during which the reborn soul would pay for the deeds enacted in a previous life. (This is *karma*.) The final goal for Buddhists was to achieve nirvana, a state of perfection that allowed the practitioner to escape the cycle of birth, death, and rebirth by detaching from all commitment to the desires of this world that led to suffering.

To read about religion in 19th-century China, see the China entries in the sections "Morality" and "Religion" in chapter 8 ("Religious Life") of volume 5 of this series.

~Joyce E. Salisbury

FOR MORE INFORMATION

Mote, F. W. *Intellectual Foundations of China*. New York: McGraw-Hill, 1989.
Thompson, E., ed. *The World's Great Religions*. New York: Time, 1957.

ISLAMIC WORLD

Islam was founded by the prophet Muhammad (c. 570–632), who received a series of visions, which were written down in the Qur'an, the holy book of Islam. Muham-

mad followed the same God as the Jews and Christians, but his visions were seen as a completion of those earlier religions.

For the vast majority of Muslims, the Qur'an is the eternal uncreated speech of God flawlessly communicated to mankind through his messenger, Muhammad. The revelations Muhammad received and delivered to the people of Mecca (ca. 610–22) and Medina (622–32) are referred to as *Kitab Allah* (the book of God) as well as *Qur'an* (recitation). The traditional Muslim account places the compilation of the Qur'an into a single manuscript during the reign of the third Caliph, ʿUthman ibn ʿAffan (r. 644–56), some two decades after Muhammad's passing. Because, according to Muslim dogma, the Qur'an represents God's uncreated speech and not Muhammad's human teachings, it is believed to be without error. Therefore, for the believer, the text of the Qur'an cannot be called into question in any way, shape, or form. Translations, of course, are another matter because according to Muslim dogma, the Arabic Qur'an is simply untranslatable. Therefore, Muslims refer to all translations of the Qur'an as interpretations of or commentaries on the Arabic text.

Muhammad was born in Mecca around the year 570 to a woman named Amina. Although accounts differ, most indicate that his father, ʿAbd Allah, died before Muhammad was born. Muhammad's mother died while he was a young boy, after which he came under the protection of his father's brother, Abu Talib, the leader of Muhammad's clan, the Banu Hashim—an honorable, though certainly not the most important, branch of the Quraysh. The dominant group in Mecca at the time, the Quraysh derived much of its prestige and wealth from two things. First, they were the custodians of the principal pagan shrine of the town—the *kaʿaba*—which focused on the god Hubal, an Arabian god of war. Second, they were involved in regional trade. It is doubtful that Mecca was a major player in long-distance trade at the time, but its trading activities and shrine custodianship did serve as the basis for the Quraysh's relations with outlying tribal confederations in the Hijaz and other regions of Arabia.

Page from the Qur'an. This shows the beautiful calligraphy of the Arabic letters and demonstrates how strikingly different the Arabic alphabet is from the Greek and Latin scripts that dominated in the West. © The Art Archive/Turkish and Islamic Art Museum Istanbul/Dagli Orti (A).

Muhammad's prophetic career spanned some two decades, beginning around the year 610 when he was about 40 years old and lasting up to the year of his death in 632. The sources agree that Muhammad was a rather reluctant prophet when the angel Gabriel brought him the first revelation. However, he soon realized that he was a prophet in the mold of the ancient Hebrew prophets, and like Isaiah and Jeremiah of old, he knew that he could not refuse to preach. After all, in a world where people still believed very concretely in the supernatural, and were aware of at least the gist of the biblical stories of God's powerful and miraculous dealings with the Children of Israel and their enemies, one simply could not ignore a summons from the very creator and sustainer of the universe. Like Abraham, Isaac, Jacob, Moses, and Jesus—to name but a few of the biblical prophets—Muhammad is portrayed as having a prophetic pedigree. He, too, could trace his lineage back to Abraham, although unlike the biblical prophets, his genealogy went through Abraham's son Ishmael rather than Isaac. In addition to genealogy, contemporary sources include numerous stories in which Christian and Jewish holy men give their stamp of approval to Muhammad's prophethood. What better ways to prove to one's audience that God's chosen messenger was indeed who he claimed to be? Not only did he belong to a long line of prophets, but the very holy men who had access to the special knowledge that only holy men possess agreed that he was in fact who he claimed to be.

Muhammad's prophetic career can be divided into two roughly equal periods. The first took place in his home town of Mecca from circa 610–622. By 622, he had fallen out of favor with the leaders of Mecca and negotiated a move for himself and his followers to the oasis settlement of Medina some 250 miles to the north. This move from Mecca to Medina in 622 is referred to as his Hijra (Hegira, migration) and is of such importance to his prophetic career that the year 622 of the Gregorian Christian calendar marks the year one of the Muslim calendar. Those early Meccan converts who moved to Medina with Muhammad are referred to as *Muhajirum* (emigrants). The people of Medina who embraced Muhammad and his message and who welcomed him to Medina are referred to as *Ansar* (helpers). These two groups and their descendants played major roles in the course of Islamic history both during Muhammad's career in Medina and after his death in 632.

The most common theological doctrine in the Qur'an is God's mercy and compassion. In fact, all but one of the 114 chapters of the Qur'an begin with the same phrase, "In the name of God, the Merciful, the Compassionate." At the same time, one of the most common themes in the Qur'an is humankind's duty to obey God. Unlike the Hebrew Bible (especially the books of Leviticus and Deuteronomy), the Qur'an contains very little legal material. While the commandments, prohibitions, and punishments that are in the Qur'an are quite specific, they do not even come close to covering the many possibilities Muslims might encounter in 7th-century Arabia, let alone the cosmopolitan centers of the Muslim empires in the centuries to come. If the early Muslim community was to determine God's will in every aspect of life after the divine revelations ceased with Muhammad's death, it needed to find authoritative guidance outside the text of the Qur'an itself. Initially, this was found in the practice or tradition (*sunna*) of the early community. Because the early community (especially the early community in Medina) was seen to be the best community by virtue of its firsthand encounter with the Messenger of God, its example could be used to answer questions that were not dealt with specifically in the Qur'an.

Not surprisingly, as the sunna of the early community and Muhammad came to be seen as authoritative, many hadiths (anecdotes attributed to or about Muhammad) were put into circulation that purported to be the words of Muhammad but were in fact made up out of whole cloth for political and sectarian purposes. In response to these fabrications, scholars devised a methodology for determining which hadiths were authentic and which were fabrications. Scholars began to argue that only those hadiths that were transmitted by an unbroken chain (*isnad*) of reliable transmitters reaching back to Muhammad himself could be deemed authentic. Scholars were well aware that it was just as easy to fabricate an *isnad* as it was to fabricate a hadith. Nevertheless, by the end of the 9th century, there had emerged a general consensus about which hadiths were authentic. By the same time, the followers of a given teacher began to refer to themselves as a *madhhab*, another

Arabic word conveying the idea of pathway. *Madhhab* is generally translated as "school of law," in the sense of a "school of thought," not a physical building. By the 11th century, there remained only four Sunni *madhhabs* to speak of (Hanafi, Hanbali, Maliki, and Shafiʿi). Each was named after the scholar whose teaching the *madhhab* followed, although he may not have founded a school in his lifetime. There were several *madhhabs* of the Shiʿite variety as well.

It is customary for a father to whisper the shahada in the ear of his newborn child.

There are five pillars of Islam. The first of the five pillars, the *shahada* or statement of belief, is a simple two-part statement that is at the center of Islamic belief, ritual, and worship—*la ilaha illaʾllah* (there is no god but God) and *Muhammadun rasul Allah* (Muhammad is the messenger of God). The inscriptions on the Dome of the Rock in Jerusalem (ca. 692) provide additional early examples of the sentiments of the *shahada*, although again not the specific *shahada* formula per se. One inscription reads, "There is no god but God alone; He has no partner with Him; Muhammad is the messenger of God." Another reads, "Muhammad is the servant of God and His messenger whom He sent with the guidance and the religion of truth. . . . " This latter phrase is the same phrase that we find on Umayyad coins after the reign of ʿAbd al-Malik (685–705), the Umayyad caliph who built the Dome of the Rock. When precisely the *shahada* became a widespread ritual formula used by Muslims is not clear and for our purposes, not all that important. Even though the specific formulaic expression of the *shahada* is missing from the earliest Islamic coins as well as the first major example of monumental architecture in Islamic history, it is clear that the sentiments of the *shahada*—that there is no god but God and that Muhammad is his messenger—were part of the Qur'an and Islamic doctrine from very early on.

The *shahada* is the simplest of the five pillars to perform because of its brevity; it is arguably also the most important of all, for to recite the *shahada* with proper intent is to accept one's obligation to perform the remaining four as well. While one need recite the *shahada* but once to be a Muslim, in practice, observant Muslims recite the *shahada* throughout the day and on all manner of occasions. It is also used in an abbreviated form (*la illaha illaʾallah*) to invoke God's blessing, aide, protection, and so on throughout the day in any and all circumstances. It is customary for a father to whisper it in the ear of his newborn child, and children are often taught to recite the *shahada* as soon as they are able to speak. Of course, neither a newborn nor a small child is expected to understand the words let alone the meaning of the *shahada* at such a young age. But the act of reciting and hearing is what is important as much for the parent as it is for the child.

Although one can make the case that the *shahada* is the most important of the five pillars, in practice, it is the second pillar, the *salat*—the ritual prayer performed five times per day—that is the ubiquitous symbol of Islamic ritual and piety. What the Qur'an does not indicate are the precise number of times per day one should perform the *salat*, the specific times of the day in which *salat* should be performed, the specific ablutions necessary to make one ritually clean (*tahara*) so that one's prayers can be valid, the specific words that should be said in the ritual prayers, or the specific prostrations that should be performed. Rather, these things come—and in great detail—from the biographical literature about Muhammad's life and teachings.

The sources tell us that in Mecca, Muhammad had instructed his followers to pray toward Syria, which was understood to mean toward Jerusalem. Muhammad continued this practice after his arrival in Medina as well. The sources give few details about Muhammad's specific relations with the Jews of Medina during this very early period in Medina, but according to Ibn Ishaq, when Muhammad received a revelation to change the direction of prayer (the *qibla*) toward Mecca "at the beginning of the seventeenth month after the apostle's arrival in Medina" (February 624), a number of the leading Jews of Medina asked him why he had done so. They told him that if he changed it back to Jerusalem, they would follow him. Ibn Ishaq goes on to tell us that they only did this "to seduce him from his religion."

Because for Muslims (as in the Jewish tradition) a day begins in the evening, the first of the five designated prayer times is the evening prayer, followed by the night, the morning, the noon, and the afternoon prayers. Each prayer is to be performed during specific periods determined according to the position of the sun, not an hour on the clock. That is, the evening prayer can be performed at any time after sunset and before the disappearance of the last light over the horizon. The night prayer can be performed at any time between the end of the time period for the evening prayer and beginning of the time period for the morning prayer, which begins with the crack of dawn and ends at sunrise. The noon prayer is to be performed when the sun is at its midpoint, not at 12:00 noon. The afternoon prayer is usually performed when some item's shadow is slightly longer than itself. Although each prayer is valid during its appointed time frame, it is best to perform the *salat* shortly after the call to prayer (*adhan*) itself.

The five daily prayers may be said in the privacy of one's home (the customary practice among women), although it is more meritorious to say them in congregation with others in a mosque, especially on Friday. While the Arabic word for mosque (*masjid*) literally means "place of prostration," its function was essentially the same as a synagogue or a church in the ancient world; that is, it was a place for the formal worship and assembly of the community of faith. In early Islamic history, the entire male Muslim population was required to worship together during the Friday noon prayer in its local congregational mosque (*masjid al-jami'a*).

The practical reason for choosing Friday (long known in Arabic as *yawm al-jum'a;* day of assembly) was that it was the major market day in Medina and as such, the bulk of the local population was already congregated in Medina for purposes of commerce. The choice of the hottest part of the day in one of the hottest climates in the world for the congregational prayer has a practical explanation as well. Because most of the population was already in town on Fridays, and because the day's trading was largely completed by noon because of the heat, holding the congregational worship at that time made perfect sense from a practical standpoint, despite the numerous anecdotes of people dozing off during the sermon because of the heat. Of course, since the authors of most of the sources were, in fact, religious scholars of some sort, they may have had reason to attribute drowsiness to heat rather than the occasionally less than impressive sermon.

Although one could find slight differences from region to region and among the various sects within the Islamic tradition, the rituals and requirements of the five daily prayers were practiced in much the same fashion throughout the medieval Islamic world, whether in Cordoba, Cairo, Damascus, Baghdad or Delhi. In Islamic countries today and with the benefit of modern audio technology, one can hear a muezzin's voice begin to sound forth from one mosque, then another, and another, until there is a chorus of voices and loudspeakers calling the faithful to prayer throughout an entire city. Beginning with the proclamation that "God is greatest," the muezzin then invokes the *shahada*, "I bear witness that there is no god but God; I bear witness that Muhammad is the messenger of God." The faithful are then summoned to prayer, "Hurry to the *salat*. Hurry to salvation. God is the greatest. There is no god but God." In the morning call to prayer, the muezzin usually adds the phrase, "Prayer is better than sleep" after "Hurry to salvation." Obviously, muezzins in the medieval Islamic world did not have access to powerful loudspeakers, but one certainly could hear the call to prayer (*adhan*) in the precincts surrounding the central congregational mosque in any town or city.

Before one could actually perform the *salat*, he or she needed to perform a series of major or minor ablutions to enter into a state of ritual purity (*tahara*). Therefore, it was essential that mosque complexes at the very minimum had access to clean water. The minor ablution (*wudu*ʿ) is required after one has entered a state of minor ritual impurity from a range of unavoidable daily activities such as sleeping, relieving oneself, and passing gas. The minor ablution involves washing certain body parts with water in the following order: hands, mouth, nose, right forearm, left forearm, face, head, ears, right foot, left foot. Both the major and the minor ablutions can be performed with sand or with a stone in those instances where one has no access to clean water or if one should not touch water for medical or other reasons.

Once one has performed the appropriate ablution, he or she is ready to perform the *salat*. The act of ritual prayer is the same whether one performs it by oneself or in congregation with others. It consists of a series of precise bowings and prostrations, which together are called a *rak*ʿ*a*, or "cycle." In a congregational setting, those performing the *salat* line up behind an imam (prayer leader) in rows facing the direction of Mecca (the *qibla*). Men line up behind the imam; if women are present, they line up at the back of the mosque behind the men or in an antechamber of some sort.

The third pillar of faith is almsgiving—*zakat*—although the Qur'an does not specify what percentage of one's wealth should be given as *zakat* beyond that one should give "what you can spare" (Qur'an 2:219). As in the case of ritual prayer, it is from the biographical literature on Muhammad as interpreted by legal scholars in subsequent generations that we learn that the *zakat* should be paid from one's profit, not necessarily the totality of one's wealth. The portion of one's profit that should be given as *zakat* can range any where from 2.5 percent of one's gold, silver or merchandise to 10 percent of one's crops, to be paid at harvest time. How the *zakat* was actually collected or distributed is difficult to ascertain. While the Qur'an speaks of giving *zakat* to those "engaged in the management of alms," individuals could legitimately give their *zakat* directly to the deserving recipients. Of course, throughout Islamic history, there have been occasions when one regime or another sought to take control of the collection of *zakat* ostensibly as a means of enhancing its own religious bona fides, but also simply as another means of collecting revenue for the state. Some scholars and reformers even argued that the *zakat* was the only legitimate form of taxation of Muslims. However, regimes that sought to rely solely on *zakat* collections soon learned that they needed to impose other kinds of taxes as well.

The fourth pillar of faith was fasting. Fasting as an integral part of religious observance certainly was not new with Islam in 7th-century Arabia. It had long been part of the religious observances of ancient Rome, Greece, Babylon, Egypt, and India. Moreover, it was essential to the religious life of ancient Israel and the early Christian church as an act of repentance, contrition, atonement, mourning, prayer, supplication, and devotion. Based on the interpretation of passages in the Qur'an, Muslims were to fast during the day for one month—the month of Ramadan. Ramadan came to take on a special sanctity in Islamic religious practice as well. According to the Qur'an, it was during the month of Ramadan that Muhammad received his first revelation.

Muslims fast during the day for one month—the month of Ramadan.

During the fast, one is to abstain from food and drink, but also from swallowing spittle that could be expectorated, as well as from inhaling tobacco smoke. Sexual relations with one's spouse are forbidden during the fast. Menstruation, and bleeding in the wake of childbirth, and deliberate seminal emission all invalidate one's fast. Those who cannot perform the fast because of illness, travel, warfare or other exigent circumstances are to make up the fast at a later time. The same applies to women who are pregnant or nursing. Those who simply break the fast without good reason are required to fast for two months to make up for each day.

The Ramadan fast begins at dusk on the first of day of the ninth month of the Islamic lunar calendar; that is, when the new crescent moon is sighted. It ends with the festival of fast breaking (*'Id al-Fitr*), when the next crescent moon is cited at the beginning of the tenth month, Shawwal. Because lunar months generally last 29 or 30 days, if the skies are too cloudy to see whether there is in fact a crescent moon, the first day of Ramadan is deemed to be 30 days after the first of the preceding month.

The fifth pillar of faith is pilgrimage, called the *hajj*. It takes place in and around the precincts of Mecca, it begins on the eighth and ends on the thirteenth day of the last lunar month of the Islamic calendar, Dhu'l-Hijja (the *hajj* month), and it is incumbent upon only those Muslims who are able to undertake it and withstand the many physical and financial hardships required of the pilgrims who come from the entirety of the Islamic world. As such, the *hajj* is the single act of devotion that most represents the egalitarian nature that the Islamic religion claims for itself.

Along the major arteries well outside of Mecca, stations were established where pilgrims (after months, or even years, in transit) removed their regular clothes, performed the necessary ablutions, and donned a special garment consisting of two rectangular pieces of unstitched white cloth, called an *ihram*. The men wrap one piece of cloth around their waists. This piece should be large enough that it reached down to the ankles. The second piece of cloth is wrapped around the torso and draped over the left shoulder. The *ihram* is worn throughout the entire *hajj*. Pilgrims either go barefoot or wear sandals without heels. Instead of the *ihram*, women wear clean, modest and plain clothes. Women cover their heads, but they do not wear a face veil.

According to the Qur'an, Abraham and his son Ishmael built the Ka'ba. It covers the black stone, which is about 12 inches across, and today is in a silver setting. Today the Ka'ba is an irregular cubicle that stands some 50 feet high and is in the center of the massive courtyard of the Haram mosque that was refurbished in the 20th century in order to accommodate the millions of pilgrims who (because of the ease of modern transportation) are now able to make the pilgrimage.

After completing the seven circumambulations, the pilgrim proceeds to the *Maqam Ibrahim*, or Station of Abraham, which is opposite the Ka'ba. Standing behind the station, the pilgrim performs two *rak'as*, which are called the circumambulation prayer. After completing the two *rak'as*, he or she then goes to well of Zamzam, drinks some of the water, and performs additional ablutions. Despite the well's brackish water, the waters of Zamzam are believed to possess special healing qualities. According to Islamic tradition, it was at Zamzam that the angel Gabriel miraculously brought forth water for Hagar and Ishmael after Abraham had left them in Mecca and headed out in the desert.

Next the pilgrim leaves the Haram complex by the southeastern gate and proceeds to a small hill called Safa; he or she then runs or jogs about a quarter mile to another rise, called Marwa. The pilgrim repeats this seven times, all the while reciting prayers in commemoration of Hagar's frantic search for water. Today, pilgrims run between Safa and Marwa in an enclosed causeway. In Naser-e Khosraw's day, pilgrims ran the length of the bazaar.

The pilgrims then travel east through the desert some four miles to Mina, where they spend the night on the eighth day of Dhu'l-Hijja. They set out the next day for the plain of 'Arafat, some seven miles further east. While during medieval times the wealthier could afford to hire camel transport, most walked the whole way. Some even walked barefoot as an act of piety. Despite the sanctity and inviolability of the pilgrimage month, it was not unheard of for Bedouin raiders to plunder the procession. At noon on the ninth day of Dhu'l-Hijja, pilgrims begin the part of the *hajj* that is called "The Standing." That is, they keep vigil around the Mount of Mercy until sundown, all the while reciting "What is Your Command? I am Here!" and listening to sermons preached from the summit where, according to Islamic tradition, the first man, Adam, had prayed and where Muhammad preached his farewell sermon to his followers prior to his passing.

At sunset, the pilgrims pack up and begin their return to Mecca. By tradition, the pilgrims wait until they have reached Muzdalifa, some three miles back toward Mina, to perform their evening prayers. Those who are physically able run as fast as they can to Muzdalifa. While most of the pilgrims bed down at Muzdalifa for the night, women, children, and the infirm can continue on to Mina. At Mina on the tenth of the month, the pilgrims begin what is called the Feast of Sacrifice (*'Id al-Adha*) in remembrance of God's instruction to Abraham to sacrifice a ram instead of his son.

At Mina, three stone pillars are located east to west along the valley. The first ritual act at Mina is to throw pebbles at the westernmost pillar. For the pilgrim, this "stoning of the devil" is a symbolic identification with Abraham, who threw stones at the devil as he sought to convince Abraham not to sacrifice his son as God commanded. After the stoning, the pilgrim then purchases a goat or a sheep (or a camel if he or she can afford it) to sacrifice. The pilgrim turns the face of the animal toward Mecca and then slits its throat as did Abraham. Slitting the throat of the animal is the final act of the *ihram* phase of the pilgrimage. Pilgrims then return to Mecca where they circumambulate the Ka'ba once again. The solemn rites of the *hajj* are now completed. In the remaining days of the *hajj*, pilgrims return to Mina to throw pebbles at all three pillars, sacrifice additional animals, and enjoy the festivities with fellow pilgrims. Before they depart for home, they return to Mecca to perform a farewell circumambulation as their final ritual act. Although it is not required, many pilgrims also make the trek northward to Medina to visit Muhammad's mosque there before returning home.

To read about religion in the Islamic world in the 19th century, see the Muslim entries in the sections "Morality" and "Religion" in chapter 8 ("Religious Life") of volume 5; for the 20th century, see the Islamic World entry in the section "Religion" in chapter 8 ("Religious Life") of volume 6 of this series.

~James Lindsay

FOR MORE INFORMATION

Andrea, T. *Mohammed, the Man and His Faith*. New York: Harper and Row, 1960.
Lindsay, J. *Daily Life in Medieval Islam*. Westport, Conn.: Greenwood Press, forthcoming.

BYZANTIUM

During the late Roman Empire, Christianity had linked the faithful of many regions and backgrounds together in one worship. However, this unifying force began to weaken between the 7th and 11th centuries, leading to a separation between the Roman Catholic Church and the eastern church, which would come to be called the Greek Orthodox Church (later to be called the Russian Orthodox or Eastern Orthodox Church).

In part, the religious separation had its roots in the language difference between the eastern and western portions of the Mediterranean basin. As the official language of the Byzantine Empire became Greek, it made sense for church services and religious administration to be conducted in Greek. In the West, on the other hand, Latin continued as the language of church services.

The question of who should lead the church posed another problem. In the West, the bishops of Rome—who came to be called "popes"—emerged as political and religious leaders since the Roman Empire in the West had fallen, taking with it strong secular leaders. In the East, however, the self-styled sacred emperors led both the church and the state. Emperors appointed "patriarchs," which were the Eastern equivalents of the highest-ranking archbishops in the West, and this power of appointment gave the emperors a good deal of control over the church.

The Eastern emperors also guided the church by presiding over church councils to decide the religious questions of the day. When bishops argued about the origin of Christ, Constantine called the Council of Nicaea in 325 and issued the Nicene Creed, which continues to be recited in many churches today. When Byzantium seethed with arguments about the relationship between the human and divine natures of Christ, Emperor Marcian called the Council of Chalcedon in 451, which decided the question. The conclusions of these councils were largely accepted in the East and the West, but all decisions guided by emperors did not contribute to the unity of Christendom.

In the 8th century, a religious controversy convulsed the East and brought the growing differences between the Latin and Greek churches to the forefront. In the previous centuries, the worship of the faithful particularly in the Eastern church had centered on icons—images of Jesus, Mary, and the saints. People viewed these depictions as more than simple portrayals; they believed that the images contained spirituality that had become material and could thus bring divine help. Byzantine monasteries in particular had amassed huge wealth by painting and selling icons. In the West, men and women also venerated images of saints, but not to the same degree.

Perhaps in response to Muslim criticism about "worshiping" idols, or perhaps to control the growing power of the Eastern monks, the Byzantine emperor Leo III (r. 717–41) ordered all icons destroyed, and in the autocratic style of the emperors, he intended his decree to apply to all of Christendom, East and West. The followers of the emperor's policy were called *iconoclasts* (which means icon destroyers), and this controversy raged for a century in the East, during which time many mosaics in Byzantium and Asia Minor were destroyed. The Western popes never acknowledged the emperor's authority in this matter, and the tensions resulting from this struggle strained relations between the Eastern and Western churches even further.

Over the centuries, the two branches of Christianity grew more and more apart until they became two separate churches—the Catholic West and the Orthodox East. The Orthodox Church rejected the concept of papal supremacy that was growing in the West and preserved the idea that the church should be led by five bishops—the patriarchs—who presided in the five major cities: Rome, Constantinople (Byzantium), Jerusalem, Alexandria, and Antioch. Each of the five patriarchs—called the pentarchs—exerted jurisdiction in his own area and met with the other patriarchs in council to regulate matters of dogma and church discipline. Over time, they rejected decisions made outside these councils by the popes alone.

Questions of language, theology, hierarchy, the wording of the creeds, and even the date of Easter finally severed ties between East and West. In 1054, the two churches broke apart. The pope and the patriarch of Constantinople excommunicated each other, and the original unified Christian church became two. (The mutual excommunications were finally withdrawn, but not until 1965.)

The split between the two churches had implications for all of eastern Europe as pagan tribes that moved into that area were converted to Orthodox (rather than

Roman) Christianity. For example, in 863, the Byzantine emperor Michael III sent two missionaries, Cyril and Methodius, to convert the Slavic tribes to the north. In the course of their missionary work, the two developed a Slavonic written language that was based on the Greek alphabet. Their mission was successful. Serbs and Russians embraced Greek Christianity and the alphabet that Cyril and Methodius developed to transmit the religion became known as the "Cyrillic alphabet" (named after Cyril). It is still used in Russia and in portions of the Balkan Peninsula today.

Like its Byzantine counterparts, the Catholic Church also sent missionaries who successfully converted some tribes in portions of the east. The Poles, Bohemians, Hungarians, and Corats adopted Catholic Christianity and the Latin alphabet that came with it. These divisions in religion, loyalty, and alphabet divided eastern Europe, and indeed, cultural divisions established during this period have continued to color the politics of the region into the 21st century.

When the Byzantine Empire fell to the Turks in 1453, the center of Greek Orthodox religiosity moved north to Moscow and the newly strengthened Russian Empire. The patriarchs of Moscow replaced those of Constantinople as the leaders of the church, and they served in the shadow of the Russian czars who replaced the Byzantine emperors.

~Joyce E. Salisbury

FOR MORE INFORMATION

Conte, F. *The Slavs*. New York: Columbia University Press, 1995.

Hussey, J. M. *The Orthodox Church in the Byzantine Empire*. New York: Oxford University Press, 1990.

MONGOLS

In the Mongol Empire, religious orders generally thrived. The Mongols were known for their liberality regarding the faiths of those under their rule, and the treatment of clerics and divines who fell into their hands was usually respectful. However, this attitude may not have been entirely altruistic. The Mongols were probably hedging their bets and playing spiritually safe. In addition to this liberal attitude, it was the wish of the Great Khan that all his subjects should pray for him and his well-being; to this end, the Mongol rulers courted the religious classes. Whoever was ruling in the heavens, the Mongols were determined to keep that god's good-will. As a result of this policy, Islamic judges, clerics, and Islamic foundations, Christian priests and monks, and Buddhist lamas and monks were all exempted from forced labor and taxes.

The religion that many Mongols traditionally practiced has been described as shamanism. Shamanists believe in the existence of various spirits that interact with the temporal world and that can be contacted and influenced by holy men, or shamans. The shaman held a very powerful position in Mongol society and was respected and often feared by the whole tribe, in some cases more so than the tribe's own khan or chief. There was frequently political rivalry between the shaman and the khan, as Chinggis (Genghis) Khan found during his rise to power with his dealings with the shaman Teb-tengri, who sought to challenge his authority. Shamanism was in essence a practical religion concerned with the material needs of its adherents. The shaman was there to advance the material well-being of the tribe and the individual.

The Mongols believed in a sky god, Tenggeri, who resided in heaven, and also an earth goddess, Itügen, who represented fertility. However, much of the practice of their religion revolved around ancestor worship and contacts with the spirits of the dead. The family would often keep expensively dressed effigies of their ancestors in specially assigned places in their yurts (tentlike structures made of felt on a fixed circular wooden frame). When they traveled the effigies, which the Mongols called *ongghod*, would be placed in a special wagon under the supervision of the shamans. No one other than the shamans would be allowed access to these wagons containing the ancestors' effigies. These *ongghot* were made of felt. Both the master and mistress of the tent had an *ongghot* hung on the wall of the yurt above their designated position, while other smaller effigies would be placed nearer the entrance on a cow's and mare's udder in recognition of the importance of the milk from these animals. The *ongghot* would always receive sprinklings of drink and genuflections before drinking sessions commenced.

Public religious worship played no part in Mongol society, although various social formalities, practices, and taboos held religious significance. The common assertion that the Mongols were godless and irreligious originated because of the absence of religious services in Mongol society. The Mongols would often commune with their god by climbing a high mountain. They would remove their hats and sling their belts over their shoulders as a sign of submission. Mountain tops and flowing water both held spiritual significance. Taboos regarding water and washing created great problems in their contact with "settled" peoples especially in the earlier decades. Flowing water was not allowed to be polluted on pain of death. Washing the body, clothes, dishes, or cooking utensils was forbidden. Ögödei (r. 1229–41) demonstrated the softening of these strictures in various well-known anecdotes reported during his reign. The Muslim historian Juwaynī (d. 1282), who served as a minister under Hülegü Khan, the Mongol ruler of Iran (r. 1256–65) records many stories in which Ögödei found ways of excusing those who had inadvertently transgressed the strict religious taboos of the Mongols. Finding a Muslim washing himself in a river, Ögödei's brother Chagatai, a strict upholder of Mongol tradition, insisted that the man be punished. Ögödei arranged that some gold be placed in the river and instructed the unfortunate Muslim to claim that he had been in the water to retrieve the gold. In this way, the transgressor escaped punishment.

An important part of Mongol life and an essential duty of the shaman was divination. The shaman was the intermediary with the spirit world, and he could intercede and also foretell what the spirits had planned and what the future still held for the tribe. Dressed in white robes and riding a white horse, the shaman, with his insignia of staff and drum, was charged with various duties for the tribe including exorcism, the recital of blessings, and prophecy. Prophecy could be performed while in a self-induced trance or through the ritual burning and interpreting of sheep's shoulder blades. The cracks and splits that appeared in the bones after ritual burning would have special significance, which only the shaman could determine, although Mangu Khan (r. 1251–59) was recorded as being able to read them by himself.

With increasing contact with other religions, the Mongol tribes often converted or adapted the practices of other religions. Buddhism increased its influence as the Mongol Empire spread south across China. Nestorian Christianity (the doctrine that Christ was two distinct persons, divine and human, implying a denial that the Virgin Mary was the mother of God) had converts among the Turco-Mongol tribes from at least the 11th century. Such powerful Mongol tribes as the Kereyit and Naiman were predominantly Christian. Other Mongol tribes such as the Merkits and Öngüt had many Christian followers. Hülegü Khan's major wife, Dokuz Khātūn, was an active Christian, as was the Byzantine wife of his son, Abaqa (r. 1265–82). The Mongols cynically exploited their Christian credentials when they sought European allies in the fight against the Muslim mamluks of Egypt.

Islam increasingly gained ground among the Mongols as they moved west. The Turks of central Asia had long had contact with Islam, but with the conquest of Persia and the forcible movement of the subject peoples eastward to man the bureaucracy of the empire, Islam began to take root. Berke Khan (r. 1257–67) of the Golden Horde, which ruled Russia and the western steppe lands, was a Muslim. Many of the Mongols in Iran converted to Islam before the Mongol state itself, the il-khanate, became officially Muslim in 1295. The close cultural, trade, and political links between Iran and China in the 13th and 14th centuries ensured that Islam became entrenched throughout the empire.

With a tradition of shamanism, the Mongols were open to the more sophisticated religious systems that they encountered as they spread their power bases outward. Often they adapted rather than adopted the beliefs that they encountered, but as their own culture drew away from its nomadic roots, so too did their religious practices lose their anchorage in the steppe and the mountain top.

~George Lane

FOR MORE INFORMATION

Heissig, W. *The Religions of Mongolia*. Berkeley: University of California Press, 1980.

Morgan, D. *The Mongols*. Oxford: Blackwell, 1986.

William of Rubruck. *The Mission of Friar William of Rubruck*. Translated and edited by P. Jackson, with D. Morgan. London: Hakluyt Society, 1990.

POLYNESIA

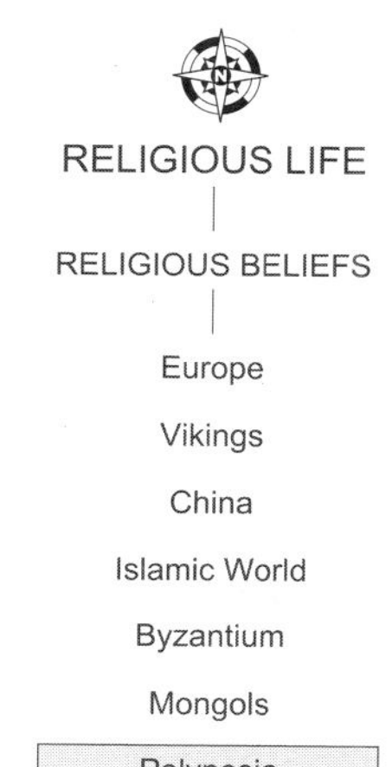

When the early Polynesians entered the Pacific from their original homelands in Southeast Asia three thousand years ago, they brought their religious beliefs and customs with them. Once established in the far-flung islands of the Pacific, Polynesians became isolated from the rest of the world. As a result, their cultures and religion went through very little change until the arrival of the European explorers in the 18th and 19th centuries. It is mainly through the eyes and ears of these early explorers and the later Christian missionaries that we learn details of the ancient beliefs of the Polynesians. Specific details vary widely from one island to another and from one island group to another, but there are some generalizations that can be gleaned from these early texts and from the mythology that has survived to the present day.

Similar to most primitive cultures throughout the world, Polynesians believed in animism—the conviction that supernatural forces animate and organize the universe, that natural objects such as trees, mountains, and the sky have souls or consciousness, and that humans have souls that leave them at death. Polynesians were polytheistic; they believed in innumerable deities, the majority of which were male. Within their pantheon of gods and goddesses, there was a hierarchy or an order of importance from the first ranking gods who had created the universe down to the simple deified ancestor of a family that lived on a remote island.

Polynesian mythology tells at least two different beliefs in the creation of the heavens—the creation by a single god and a more popular belief of the pairing of male and female entities that produced generations after generations of creation. As an example of the first, Tahitian chants tell of the great god Ta'aroa who awoke from an eternal sleep, peered out of his shell into the vast universe, saw that nothing existed, and began the act of creation. From one part of his shell, he made "foundation earth" and from the other, he made the sky. He then created fellow gods and goddesses who dwelled with him in total darkness. He created land, called Havai'i, the birthplace of all lands. He then shook off his feathers, and they became trees and vegetation. Space was formed, and it was separated from earth by raising it up on pillars above the mountains. Myriads of other deities and creations were brought forth. Finally, the first man, Ti'i, was created from the earth; he married the goddess Hina, and from that union sprang the high chiefs of Tahiti. The common people were simply conjured up by Ti'i and Hina.

A more popular account comes from Hawai'i, where the lengthy Kumulipo chant tells of an evolutionary process in the creation of the world. It begins in deep darkness (*pō*) and then, in a process of conception and birth, it continues from one generation to another, moving from the depths of the ocean to the creation of land, the separation of the sky and earth, the creation of land animals, and finally, to the creation of humans, recording them generation by generation down to high chief Ka-'i-'i-mamao (living about 1700).

Some of the important gods recognized throughout Polynesia are Ta'aroa (Kanaloa), Tū (Kū), Kāne (Tāne), and Rongo (Lono); the two important goddesses are Hina (the universal woman) and Pele (the volcano goddess, known primarily in Hawai'i). Numerous Polynesian legends tell of the varied tales of these famous and infamous deities. They also tell of the great demigods and heroes of ancient Polynesia—Māui, the challenger of the gods; Tinirau, the romantic hero and god of the oceans; Tahaki, the perfect chief; and Rata (Laka), the irreverent vagabond, to mention only a few.

Similar to other peoples around the world, ordinary Polynesians generally designated certain humans (priests) to act as mediators between them and the gods. It was their duty to organize rituals, rites, and ceremonies to mark certain significant events in the life of an individual or a community. Priests usually came from the aristocratic (high chiefly) families; in some island groups, priests were trained from childhood to carry out these duties. New Zealand, for example, had official schools where novices endured strict discipline for years before becoming an officially recognized priest. The Tongans, however, did not have an exclusive class of priests, and the will of the gods became known through "trances" encountered by any chief who might be included in the council circle of the high chief.

Shown here is a contemporary tiki (a statue of a god or ancestral hero), carved in the highly stylized and traditional manner of the Marquesas Islands. Photo courtesy of the Polynesian Cultural Center.

Official priests used certain natural objects to assist them in their ceremonies—colorful bird feathers and rosewood leaves to wave around to catch the attention of the gods, animal or human blood to sprinkle over the altars, banana stalks in lieu of human sacrifices, sacred ti plants and tapa cloth for wrapping god images, and seawater to sprinkle over objects or persons. In some areas of Polynesia, large outdoor temples (*marae* or *heiau*) were built to house sacred objects and for official ceremonies. These were open only to the male members of the community. Women were excluded from all public religious ceremonies. Prostration or the baring of one's shoulders was required when one was in the presence of a god image or a high chief (since high chiefs were considered to be descended from the gods).

Polynesians participated in numerous religious ceremonies throughout their lives. At birth, the umbilical cord was cut by a priest who prayed for the child's good health and long life. At marriage (usually the nobility), a priest would wave sacred objects over the couple's head and recite various charms and incantations. Sickness and death both required elaborate rituals. Sickness was believed to have been caused by a sorcerer, and a priest was summoned to find out who the sorcerer was and what had to be done to lift his curse. Pains in the body were treated by priests who touched the painful part with sacred sticks so that the gods could lift the swelling or pain through the sticks. Hundreds of other spells and charms were used for the various ills of the body.

Death required elaborate mourning ceremonies. Prior to a natural death, the family would retain the services of a priest who would sit outside the compound reciting prayers and charms. Upon death, the body would be placed upright against an inside post of the house for several days while the priests continued his rituals and while members of the family appeared and expressed their grief through wailing, crying, and lacerating their bodies with sharks' teeth or sharp stones. Little is known of burial rites since this sacred ceremony was performed in secret so that no outsider ever knew exactly where the body had been laid to rest. After death, a person's spirit made its way to the underworld, where it might lead a pleasurable life, but that was not guaranteed because all kinds of evil spirits and demons lay in wait to snatch the spirit and gobble it up. Polynesian religion was not ethical; that is, a person's activities on earth had nothing necessarily to do with religion or with a reward or punishment in the life hereafter, except where a particular type of behavior might displease a certain deity. Polynesians were highly religious in that individuals would recite a variety of personal charms and invocations to bring good luck or ward off evil, but not as a guarantee for some future reward in the hereafter.

~*Robert D. Craig*

FOR MORE INFORMATION

Beckwith, M. *Hawaiian Mythology*. New Haven, Conn.: Yale University Press, 1940.
Best, E. *Maori Religion and Mythology*. Vol. 1. Wellington: Te Papa Tongarewa Museum of New Zealand, 1995.
Craig, R. *Dictionary of Polynesian Mythology*. New York: Greenwood Press, 1989.
Luomala, K. *Voices on the Wind*. Honolulu, Hawai'i: Bishop Museum Press, 1955.

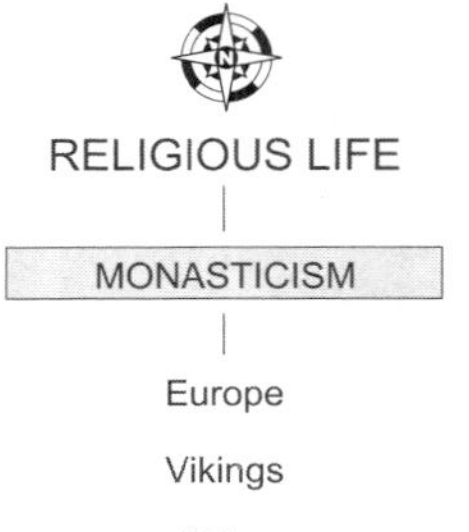

Monasticism

Throughout history, there have always been those who have wanted to devote their lives completely to seeking God or to living a life particularly dedicated to spirituality. Buddha, for example, left his wealthy life to meditate and seek "enlightenment," or an attainment of spiritual truth. From the earliest days of Buddhism, many followers of the movement became monks and nuns. They established monasteries, and by the Middle Ages, there were many Buddhist monasteries throughout China. The impulse to withdraw from society in search of religion was not limited to followers of Eastern religions.

As early as the second century C.E., some Christians left their communities to live in solitude in the deserts of Egypt and Syria. Thousands of men and women chose this life of physical renunciation and prayer. Some sought solitude in different ways: Stylite monks lived 20 years and more on a platform erected on a high pole, and some holy women sealed themselves into small rooms, with only one small opening to receive a bit of bread and water. Perhaps not surprisingly, ordinary Christians gave a great deal of respect to these holy men and women who seemed able to transcend the everyday world and reach a higher level of spirituality.

By the 7th century, Christian society and church hierarchy was sufficiently organized that these individualistic holy people seemed out of place. Reformers established monasticism as a regulated way to allow men and women to dedicate their lives to God. Within monasteries, men and women followed a "rule" that strictly regulated all aspects of life from food to clothing to work and sleep. Men and women who entered monasteries had to take vows of poverty, chastity, and obedience and promised never to leave the monastery. They lived under a strict vow of obedience to the abbot or abbess—the ruler of the monastery.

These monasteries were very popular throughout the Middle Ages, both in the West and in the Byzantine Empire. They offered an attractive life to those who felt called to the life of the spirit or even of the mind. Less positively, they provided a place for parents to dedicate unwanted children, who would then grow up serving God whether they wanted to or not. Local people who lived in the vicinity of monasteries believed that the institutions brought great benefit to the neighborhood, both from the prayers of the monks and nuns and from the charity they provided.

Perhaps not surprisingly, monasteries became wealthy. Individual monks and nuns (whether Christian or Buddhist) might have taken vows of poverty, but monasteries themselves began to accumulate a good deal of wealth. In part, this came from the money made from labor done by the monks—whether copying manuscripts or creating icons (religious pictures) in Byzantium or operating oil presses in China. Because the monks lived frugally, the wealth accumulated.

Periodically, the accumulation of wealth led to reform movements. In the Christian West, for example, one reform movement—the Cistercian—told monks they could not accept money for praying but instead needed to work the land in service. In a perhaps predictable irony, however, Cistercian monks also grew wealthy as they began to practice agricultural innovations. Francis of Assisi established another reform that stated that followers of his order could not even own a purse, much less a building. Franciscans were supposed to wander and beg so that they would not accidentally become wealthy.

Buddhist monks engaged in pawnbroking and charging interest on debts. The emperor tried to regulate the huge profits that came into the coffers of the Buddhists, but with little success. Like Francis of Assisi, some Buddhists tried to avoid contact with money and only wander and beg as their spiritual path.

Although many people criticized the wealth that monks and nuns accumulated, nevertheless, they were committed to performing acts of charity for the faithful in their community. In this way, monasteries served a central role in the medieval economy. But they also served as strong religious reformers, reminding people that a spiritual life was possible and even desirable. However, at the end of the Middle Ages, enough corruption was visible in the Western monasteries that reformers would do away with these spiritual specialists. However, that would only happen during the Reformation (see volume 3 of this series).

~Joyce E. Salisbury

EUROPE

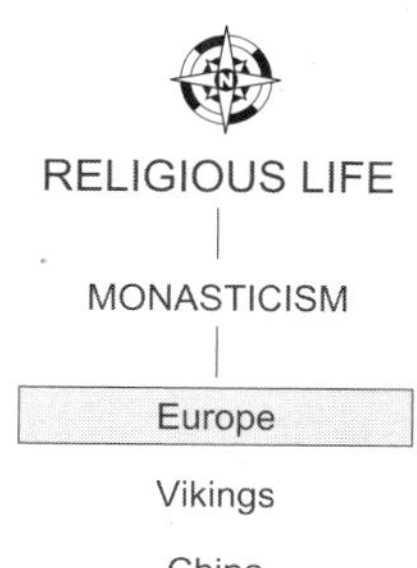

Medieval political theory commonly divided European society into three estates, consisting of the aristocracy, commoners, and clergy. The clergy, unlike the others, was not born into its class but entered into it as a career, whether by choice or compulsion. Clerics were in large measure drawn from the aristocracy, particularly at the upper levels of church administration, but a clerical career was also one of the few avenues of advancement open to the lower levels of society. Like the aristocracy, the clergy constituted only a tiny fraction of the population, perhaps another 1 percent.

The clergy was divided into secular and regular clerics. The secular clergy ministered directly to the public at large (in Latin, *seculum,* the temporal world). The most common secular cleric was the parish priest who conducted religious services at the local church for the residents of the area, in some cases with the assistance of a staff of lesser clerics. Above the parish priest was a vast administrative hierarchy that covered all of Europe. The bishop administered a diocese that was composed of hundreds of parish churches. He was assisted in his duties by a substantial staff of church officers, notably, a body of priests called canons who conducted religious services in the cathedral, or episcopal church, and took part in the administration of the diocese. Above the bishop was the archbishop, whose authority might extend over a half-dozen to a dozen dioceses, and at the head of the church as a whole was the pope. Both archbishops and the pope had large administrative staffs of their own, also drawn from the clergy.

Marriage and its legal ramifications fell under the jurisdiction of the church.

The church wielded influence comparable to that of the aristocracy. The importance attached to so small a group reflects the status of religion in medieval society. There was no distinction between church and state, or even between church and community: to be a part of society was to be part of the church. This aspect of medieval society had roots in the ancient world. The Roman Empire required its subjects to honor the state religion in addition to their own local deities, and among the barbarians religion was closely tied to a tribe's communal identity. Christianity was oriented more toward personal spirituality than were the older pagan religions of Europe, but in becoming the official religion in Europe, it also took on the social roles once occupied by paganism.

The medieval church constituted a kind of second social system, sharing governmental authority with the feudal hierarchy and occasionally coming in conflict with secular lords over disputed rights. Every community and neighborhood was under the auspices of a parish. The church had its own law code, called canon law, and a system of church courts to enforce it, exercising authority over many aspects of people's lives. Marriage and its legal ramifications fell under the jurisdiction of the church, and wills were also solemnized and enforced by church authority. The church was also responsible for what today would be termed moral legislation, including such matters as adultery, fornication, and blasphemy.

The regular clergy was originally limited to monks and nuns, who sought spiritual perfection by withdrawing from the secular world and living communal lives according to a codified rule of organization and conduct (in Latin, *regula,* rule). In time, other clerics became regular clergy by taking on the communal mode of life under a rule, while continuing to interact with the secular world. Many groups of cathedral canons adopted rules, and eventually houses of regular canons were established independent of cathedrals. Regular canons enjoyed the strengths of monastic discipline and organization while still being permitted to interact with the world at large, a combination that made them extremely useful to both the church and secular society. During the High Middle Ages, there arose new regular orders called mendicants or friars, who also lived communally under a rule but existed specifically to minister to the secular world. The regular clergy, like the secular, was ultimately subject to the authority of the pope.

Monks and nuns were sworn to a life of personal poverty, but this does not mean that they were recruited from among the poor. In fact, they were predominantly drawn from the aristocracy. Recruits were expected to bring a significant donation to their monastery, and it was the upper classes who had land and money to offer. While monks and nuns were individually poor because they were not permitted to own personal property, the monastery collectively was a rich institution, and these regular clergy enjoyed a standard of living far above that of ordinary medieval people. They had regular and sufficient meals regardless of the state of the harvest; they had wine to drink and occasional fine foods. Most lived in well-constructed stone facilities with good sanitation, and there was ample provision for them in illness and old age. The monastic way of life was austere, but it offered enough advantages that there was always a demand among the aristocracy for monastic positions.

Aristocratic parents with multiple sons and daughters needed to find an appropriate career for the younger ones, and sending them to monasteries was a good option, offering an acceptable standard of living, a stable future, and even prospects of prestige and power. Of course, this practice of treating monasticism as a career rather than a vocation meant that many monks were not deeply committed to the monastic ideal, to the detriment of monastic discipline.

The monk's vows were considered permanently binding, and new monks and nuns were in principle bound to the monastery for the rest of their lives, not even permitted to pass the cloister gate without permission, or to talk with any layperson. Everything they needed for the rest of their days was provided within the precincts of the monastery. In this way, the monastic residents could leave behind the outside world. In practice, however, many monks did have contact with the world beyond the cloister. Monastic officers were required by their work to interact with laymen and spend time in the outer areas of the monastery, or even beyond the monastery walls, serving as ambassadors from the monastery or administering its business affairs. Nuns, on the other hand, tended to stay more restricted within the walls, sometimes so much that the convents ran out of supplies.

In some cases, a monk or nun was permitted to transfer to a new monastery, either for his or her own spiritual benefit or to provide experience or expertise for an institution in need. During the 13th century, with rising educational standards in the secular world, many monasteries began to send monks to universities, and some monasteries established houses at universities to serve as residences for members of their order. Nuns continued to be educated in their own institutions.

Western monasticism was given a definitive shape by Saint Benedict of Nursia in the 6th century. Benedict, an Italian abbot, laid out a plan for monastic life and organization that ultimately became the standard in western Europe. Benedictine monasticism was ascetic, requiring monks to live with minimal possessions, simple food, and austere accommodations; yet it avoided the excesses of heroic self-denial, stressing instead the role of communal cooperation as a means of achieving personal spiritual improvement. The Benedictine monk sought communion with God through a combination of physical labor and a daily cycle of communal worship that came to be known as the Divine Office. Over time, the Divine Office took precedence over other monastic activities, although some forms of work, particularly reading and writing, continued to play an important part in the monastic routine and ethos.

For most of the early Middle Ages, the Benedictines were the only monastic order in western Europe. Over the centuries, monasteries of the order became lax in applying the rule and less vigorous in their sense of religious vocation, and in the 10th century a major reform movement was initiated with the founding of Cluny. Cluny's first abbot brought a renewed sense of zeal and discipline to the monastic world. Over the next two centuries, many new monasteries were established under Cluny's guidance, and older ones were placed under the authority of Cluny to help them reform. Partly in response to Cluny, a new reform movement arose toward the end of the 11th century at the nearby abbey of Cîteaux. These Cistercians established a new rule of their own, rejecting the opulence of the traditional Benedictine monastery and its reliance on income from feudal manors. The new Cistercian monasteries were much plainer in decoration, and the monks made their living by farming their own lands through hired labor and lay brothers—members of the monastic community who lived semimonastic lives but were not actually monks.

The monastery also provided hospitality for travelers in an age when inns were not always easy to find. Many of the monastery's visitors were aristocrats, particularly lay patrons and other important figures, but others were ordinary folk, in many cases pilgrims making a journey to a shrine. Also important was the monastery's role in learning and literacy. Christianity was a religion based on written texts, and literacy was essential to allow the monk to fulfill his spiritual obligations. Monastic schools were especially influential during the early Middle Ages, at a time when other educational institutions were practically nonexistent; even some secular students acquired their learning in schools run by monasteries outside the cloister. A part of the intellectual importance of monasteries was their contribution to the study, preservation, and composition of written texts. The Benedictine rule made provision for work as an integral part of monastic life. Saint Benedict envisaged manual labor as an important part of monastic work, but by the High Middle Ages, the aristocratic population of the monasteries had largely abandoned physical work in favor of the more genteel occupations of reading and writing.

In sum, the monastic life was an essential one in the Middle Ages. As men and women sought a spiritual life, they ended up fulfilling many other roles in society. It is perhaps not surprising that as time passed, some monks and nuns forgot their spiritual roles and focused on more secular activities, leading to much criticism at the end of the medieval period (Singman, 11–13, 146–47, 138–41, 155–56, 167–69).

FOR MORE INFORMATION

Eco, U. *Name of the Rose*. New York: Harcourt, 1983.

Knowles, D. *Christian Monasticism*. New York: McGraw-Hill, 1969.

Singman, J. L. *Daily Life in Medieval Europe*. Westport, Conn.: Greenwood Press, 1999.

VIKINGS

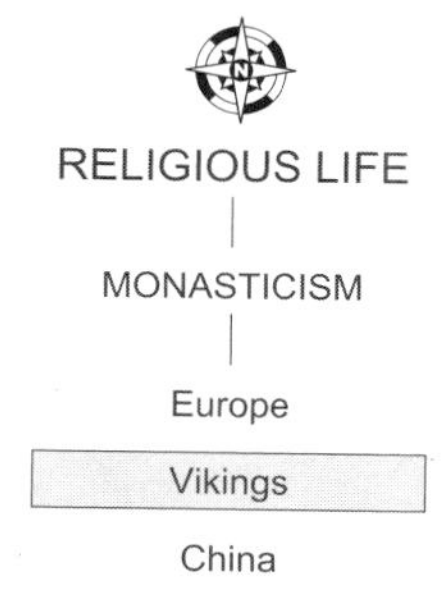

Following the conversion of the Scandinavian countries to Christianity, monasteries were eventually founded there, in which men (and later women) could seclude themselves from the secular world and dedicate themselves to austere lives devoted to prayer and contemplation in order to achieve greater personal perfection and sanctification than is normally possible in the world. During the Viking Age, this kind of life probably did not appeal to very many people, and we know of only a few monasteries founded before 1100. Around 1095, the Benedictine monastic chapter of Odense on Fyn in Denmark was established. It was a daughter house of Evesham Abbey in England and was founded by monks from Evesham at the request of King Erik Ever-good of Denmark (r. 1095–1103). The church in Odense was where the Danish king (and later saint) Knud the Holy (r. 1080–86) was martyred, and it was dedicated to Saint Alban, the protomartyr of Britain. It is also known that around 1100, the monastic centers of Selja near Bergen and Nidarholm on an island outside of Trondheim in Norway were established. Generally, it is impossible to determine the date of the foundation of the early Scandinavian monasteries, however. The ones near the cathedral towns of Ribe, Schleswig, and Lund may also date from shortly before the end of the Viking Age.

Monasteries in Scandinavia served the same functions as those in western Europe—providing a spiritual outlet for some individuals as well as serving educational functions to bring learning and literacy to the northern lands. In the late Middle Ages (after the end of the Viking Age), Scandinavian monasteries were as integrated into society as they were in southern Europe.

~*Kirsten Wolf*

FOR MORE INFORMATION

Wolf, K. *Daily Life of the Vikings*. Westport, Conn.: Greenwood Press, forthcoming.

CHINA

One of the largest privileged groups in Tang society was the clergy. In 845, there were 360,000 monks and nuns throughout the empire. The church attracted novices not only because of their devotion to the faith but also because, once ordained, they were exempt from taxes and compulsory labor. It also attracted many landlords who wished to evade those obligations. Those "bogus monks" remained laymen, acquired ordination certificates, but did not practice celibacy, lived with their families, and reaped the profits from their fields or other enterprises.

The power of Buddhism rested on its control of land, industrial works, and money that were often tax-exempt. Its doctrines of compassion and salvation were the forces that led to the acquisition of wealth and property. Compassion required the clergy and laity to assist those less fortunate than themselves: the indigent, the frail, and others. That tenet of faith compelled the laity to donate portions of their wealth to the church as a kind of sectarian welfare. Salvation was individual and particular, in contrast to compassion, which was universal and altruistic (i.e., compassion applied to all people, regardless of their status or relationships). The motive of donors was to improve their lot and that of their ancestors in purgatory, and to elevate themselves or their ancestors to a superior station during their rebirth in the next state of existence. The notion was that a gift could redeem sins committed in this life and thereby reduce or eliminate punishment in the afterlife. The size of such gifts was sometimes astronomical. In 767, a eunuch not only granted the church his estate, a prime piece of real estate east of Changan, but also contributed a billion coppers for the construction of a monastery on the manor.

The donors belonged to all classes of society from the emperor to the peasant and gave all manner of property—land, mills, coppers, silk, slaves, and more. In addition, monasteries increased their holdings by purchasing fields and confiscating lands when debtors defaulted on loans. Except for Chan (Zen) Buddhists, the ordained clergy did not work the land. According to the Indian notion of nonviolence, the monastic rules of discipline forbade them from digging, irrigating, and harvesting because such actions might result in the killing of living things, in particular, insects and microorganisms. Consequently, monasteries entrusted the working of the land to novices, tenant farmers who paid rent that was 10 to 20 times the tax obligation that they would otherwise have paid to the government, bond servants who indentured themselves to pay off debts, and slaves. In 845, at the height of the persecution of Buddhism, the government confiscated 150,000 slaves from Buddhist establishments. The slaves did not fare well. The army took possession of those who had martial skills, civil offices took the old and enfeebled, and the government sold the young who had no skills. Officials divided their families, sending fathers in one direction and sons in another. In the provinces of central China slaves had no food or shelter. Corrupt officials or wealthy merchants often illegally seized them.

From the earliest days of Buddhism (from the 6th century B.C.E.), many followers of the movement joined monastic communities where they dedicated themselves to the search for enlightenment. Supported by charity, monks spent their time preaching the beliefs of Buddhism (see the section "Religious Beliefs" in this chapter) and encouraging people to follow the Noble Eightfold Path in their daily lives. During the centuries following the Buddha's death, the monastic organization served to win converts to the faith and spread the belief as far away as China. By the Tang dynasty, monks were an integral part of the life—and economy—of ancient China.

Monasteries augmented the revenue they received from their land with income from industrial enterprises. The most important were mills for hulling grains or grinding them into flour. These installations, operated on water power, were built along irrigation canals in uplands and were far too expensive for peasants to construct. The clergy entrusted their construction and maintenance to millwrights and the production to millers. The millers, who may have been serfs, had to pay rent for the use of the mills. The revenues collected went into the coffers of the monastery.

Monasteries operated oil presses that extracted oil from sesame (hemp) seeds. As with the mills, they owned the equipment and were responsible for its maintenance, but they entrusted the operation of the presses to laymen. They charged the operators rent for use of them. Contracts entitled them to seize the property of the lessees should they fail to pay the prescribed fees. Like millers, the oil producers were free to sell to the public any surplus in excess of the rents they owed, but the monastery imposed a tax on such sales. They were probably the greatest consumers of oil because they kept lamps perpetually burning in their Buddha halls.

The wealth accumulated by the church through donations, rents, and industries went first to the maintenance of monasteries and the support of the clergy. However, the normal expenditures of monasteries apparently required only one-fourth to one-third of their income. Some of the surplus went to the construction of new facilities and to the commissioning or purchase of paintings, murals, statues, and bells, as well as furnishing supplies for festivals. However, the monks employed a large portion of it to increase their revenues through commercial transactions. The first of them was pawnbroking, which appeared in Buddhist monasteries in the 6th century. A peasant in need of seed at the beginning of spring would deposit a valuable object, such as an iron cauldron, with the monastery as security for a loan of grain. If he failed to redeem the property by returning the seed after the autumn harvest, he agreed to forfeit all of his movable property. The monks charged him no interest for the transaction. If, however, the person was of a higher station and the transaction involved money, such as a woman who pawned her comb for 500 coppers, he or she had to return the principal with interest to redeem the pledge. Buddhist pawnshops did a thriving business. One monk in the early 9th century set up establishments that lent out more than 1 billion coppers a year against security. This astonished the emperor, who issued a decree in 817 that prohibited the nobility, officials, Daoist priests, and Buddhist monks from holding more than 5 million cash at a given time.

The second commercial activity was lending. There were basically two types of loans. The first type was short-term loans, usually for seven months, extended to peasants and consisting mostly of seed grain. Some farmers, either because they exhausted their stores during the winter or they had used their surplus to celebrate the New Year, did not have enough to begin sowing in the spring. If the borrower was a monastery's tenant, it advanced the grain to him without interest. He agreed, however, to forfeit his movable property if he failed to repay the loan after the autumn harvest. If the borrower was a free farmer, the monastery charged him interest, generally 50 percent, when he returned the principal. The second type consisted of loans extended to individuals of some station, officials or aristocrats. They were advances of silk, money, or processed commodities, such as oil and flour. The interest rates were substantially higher than those charged peasants. One contract established the rate for a loan of 1,000 coppers at 200 cash per month, for a total of 1,200 coppers interest when the loan fell due in six months. In other words, the borrower paid a rate of 120 percent when he returned the principal. The reason for such exorbitant rates of interest may be that the risk was higher, both because the value of the loans was greater and because there was a greater chance of default. Some officials failed to pay their debts, and monasteries were relatively powerless to compel them to make good. To reduce the risk, the monks usually drew up contracts with borrowers,

Pawnbroking appeared in Buddhist monasteries in the 6th century.

including peasants, that were signed by guarantors who promised to make restitution should the borrowers default.

The income from commercial transactions must have been substantial. The ledgers of two monasteries in central Asia record that 33 and 55 percent of their income came from interest. The returns to some prominent churches in the capitals and other large, prosperous cities in China proper were even greater. By and large, Buddhists lived off the labor and product of the peasantry and other lower classes. However, they returned much of their income to the community as charity (Benn, 28–32).

FOR MORE INFORMATION

Benn, C. *Daily Life in Traditional China: The Tang Dynasty*. Westport, Conn.: Greenwood Press, 2002.

Groot, J.J.M. de. *The Religious Systems of China*. 6 vols. Leiden: J.J. Brill, 1892–1910.

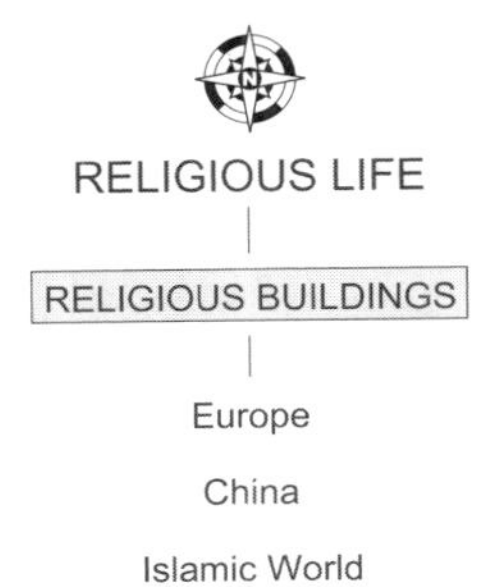

Religious Buildings

Ancient religions that emphasized a worship of nature tended not to build buildings for worship. This was true of the Polynesians, who designated large outdoor temples to house their sacred items, and the ancient pagan Celts, who worshiped in oak groves. However, in the Middle Ages, Western cultures were more influenced by the Greco-Roman heritage that called for buildings to express their religious aspirations and to serve as the center of worship. In China, too, a centralized authority helped foster a proliferation of religious buildings. While all had this impulse in common, each religion created buildings that expressed their own specific characteristics, and thus the religious buildings serve as a mirror for each religion.

There were two main architectural styles of church in western Europe, and each reflected the times in which they were built. Early medieval Romanesque architecture led to churches that were sold and dark. These were sanctuaries in a violent, uncertain world. In the 12th century, however, the growth of cities brought money, pilgrims, and the need for a new kind of church building. Architects in France first designed "Gothic" architecture for grand new cathedrals. These lofty buildings reached heights never before imagined in the West, and they were large enough to hold congregations of 10,000 people and more. These buildings served as showcases for carved statues and magnificent stained glass that portrayed scenes of daily life as well as those of religious significance.

As the faithful entered these Gothic cathedrals, the building was supposed to evoke feelings of awe and majesty. As colored light filtered down through the stained glass, men and women were supposed to be reminded of heavenly spirit, and as people were surrounded by statues and carvings, they were to feel members of the Christian community, past and present. The buildings themselves expressed all these values while they gloried in the new wealth of the cities that built them. The tall Gothic spires rising above the centers of town marked the heart of the medieval city, and they do so still.

The greatest Byzantine church was Hagia Sophia, built by Emperor Justinian in the 6th century. This great domed building is dramatically different from anything in the medieval West, and throughout the Middle Ages, members of the Orthodox Church looked to this building as the focus of their worship. Byzantine churches—again unlike most of those of the West—were decorated with magnificent mosaics. These brilliant images of gold showed pictures of saints and biblical accounts, and many of the faithful seemed to worship the image instead of what it represented. The feelings of awe stirred by these images led to the 9th-century "iconoclastic" (icon-breaking) movement during which many magnificent old images were destroyed. Later, images were again permitted in Byzantine churches, leading to a flourish of art production that continues to mark the churches of Russia today.

The Muslim world theoretically had no need for a special religious building because Muhammad urged people to pray anywhere. Nevertheless, Muslims developed a distinctive architecture for their mosques—or church buildings. All mosques have a central courtyard with a pool for ritual washing, which is enclosed by covered arcades with a roofed prayer hall on the side facing Mecca. Mosques have tall minarets—towers from which the muezzin calls the faithful to prayer. Muslims believed that Christians had fallen into idolatry by decorating their churches with images, so such imagery is forbidden in mosques. Instead, mosques are decorated with patterns that were to remind the faithful of the infinite pattern of the universe. Many mosques are filled with columns that not only hold up the roof but also represent the many faithful joined in prayer. Thus, mosques, like Christian churches, visually portray the ideals of their faith.

All the great cities of medieval China had many religious establishments, from monasteries to temples. Monasteries were designed for people to come and worship, so, more than in the West, they served as public buildings. The most prominent design of Buddhist monasteries was the pagoda, and architectural design intended to imitate sacred mountains. Just as in Western churches, these pagodas were designed to draw the mind and the eye up to the heavens.

For all the difference in religious architecture around the world, these buildings have one major thing in common: they express the deep spiritual hopes of the builders and of the people who frequent them.

~Joyce E. Salisbury

EUROPE

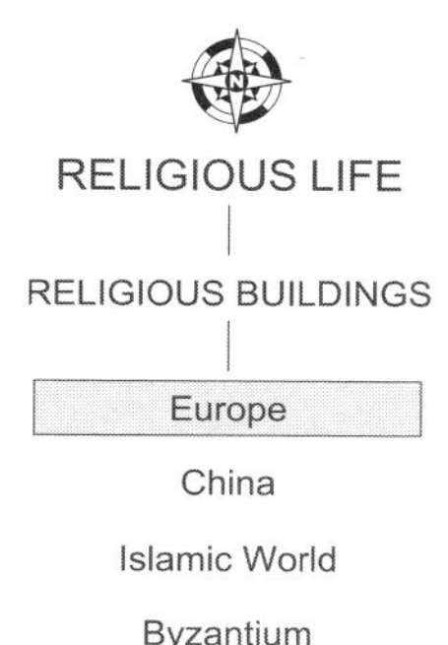

In medieval Europe, religion was at the center of people's lives, and consequently, the church buildings that served people in all walks of life were central features of their daily life. Each building was developed with an architecture that suited its purpose, and the development of church architecture—from small parish churches to Romanesque monastic churches to Gothic city cathedrals—is one of the influential features of the Middle Ages.

The parish was the fundamental local division of the church. Most parishes encompassed one village, but others extended over two or more villages. By late in the Middle Ages, a parish was often considered to extend to the range of a church bell. When towns grew large, competing bells echoed throughout the town calling to each one's parishioners. The parish church was tiny and plain in comparison with the great cathedrals, yet still an impressive building relative to other structures in the village. A typical church was built of stone and might measure about 35 feet long, 35 feet tall, and 24 feet wide, with a bell tower over the entrance measuring about 12 feet by 12 feet. The church's overall volume was probably about four times that of the more substantial peasant cottages that stood near it. The building was distinguished by its materials and decoration as well. Apart from the manor lord's solar, it was the only large stone building in the village. The interiors of many parish churches were limewashed and decorated with murals depicting biblical stories and other religious themes, and they were richly furnished relative to the simplicity of the peasant cottage. Churches were built with entries facing west (from where they expected Christ at the second coming) and its altar at the east—this was the origin of our term "orientation."

The church was an important focal point in the community: the children of the parish were baptized in the font, couples were married at the door, and the dead were buried in the yard. The building also served as a meeting place because it was the only public building in the village large enough to hold a significant number of people.

Nobles who lived in castles and large estates had their own churches. Most castles had only chapels, although many castle lords tried to elevate their chapels to parochial status since as a parish church it would be entitled to receive the tithes of its parishioners. The church probably ministered to the garrison and staff at large, and the enclosure in which it stood is likely to have served as a residential area for the castle's civilian population.

Monastic churches were primarily for the use of the monastic community, although at some monasteries it served as the parish church as well. At Cluny in France, for example, the church was accessible to the public, although visitors were allowed only in the nave, at the western end of the church, where they had no contact with the monks in the choir at the eastern end. In monastic churches, the choir was elongated and had stalls equipped with seats to allow the monks to rest during the Divine Office. The church was lit in the day by 160 windows, and at night by four large chandeliers with wax candles. Additional candlelight was provided at ground level close to the monks, to allow them to read their chants.

As towns grew larger, they developed their own styles of churches. Before the 12th century, the church architecture of monastic churches and the largest churches in the cities was Romanesque. The Madeleine was one of the most important churches in Paris, and it is one of the most impressive examples of Romanesque architecture. Architects of these churches wanted height and size while continuing to build with round arches in the old Roman style. To keep the heavy roofs from falling in, they had to make the stone walls very thick and thicken key points of the outside walls with fixed buttresses (extra supports attached to the walls). The interior of the churches were dark, solemn, and lit with candles like the monastery church at Cluny.

Medieval towns often had monastic houses as well as secular religious establishments, and many towns had the impressive churches of the Knight-Templar, a crusading order of warrior-monks. London's Templars church was built as an octagon in the style of the Church of the Holy Sacrament in Jerusalem, and the buildings of the Temple in Paris included an enormous fortified keep.

In the 12th century, Abbot Suger in France had a revolutionary idea for church architecture. He wanted a church that was filled with light—which he saw as symbolizing the presence of God, and he still wanted the church to be tall, reaching up to the heavens. Under his guidance, architects developed the Gothic style, which would revolutionize the look of the large city churches. In Gothic architecture, builders used pointed arches (instead of the round Romanesque ones), which allowed the weight of the roof to be brought down massive columns. This freed up the walls, allowing them to be filled with stained-glass windows that let in colored light. The exterior was given further support by flying buttresses that further opened up the space of the walls. This form of architecture spread rapidly all over Europe as the growing cities vied with each other to build greater and greater cathedrals to house their bishops. These became characteristic of the church architecture of the High Middle Ages.

Detail from a Milan cathedral, showing the flying buttresses that are characteristic of Gothic architecture. © Library of Congress.

These new architectural techniques that developed in the 12th century allowed cathedrals to become the skyscrapers of their day, and the Cathedral of Notre-Dame towered over the city, dwarfing every other building in Paris; it was visible for miles around the city. The interior vaults of Notre-Dame rose to a height of 110 feet (equivalent to about 10 stories today), the towers to 210 feet, and the spire over the body of the church to a dizzying 325 feet above the ground—this in an age when even an unusually tall secular building, such as the keep at the castle of Dover, measured less than 90 feet.

As a result of the Gothic revolution in architecture, churches such as the Cathedral of Notre-Dame had a grace and delicacy unlike any other buildings of their day, with large open interiors and enormous windows; in contrast, other contemporary structures' rooms were usually small and dimly lit. Only a large castle could begin to compare with Notre-Dame in scale, and none matched it in beauty. Perhaps most important, the cathedral was a public space, accessible to people who might never see the inside of a castle. Notre-Dame can easily accommodate nine thousand people and has been known to accommodate significantly more. For medieval people, this outstanding feat of architecture and decoration must have been an overwhelming sight (Singman, 92, 153, 189–90).

FOR MORE INFORMATION

Adams, H. *Mont Saint Michel and Chartres*. New York: Penguin, 1986.

Singman, J. L. *Daily Life in Medieval Europe*. Westport, Conn.: Greenwood Press, 1999.

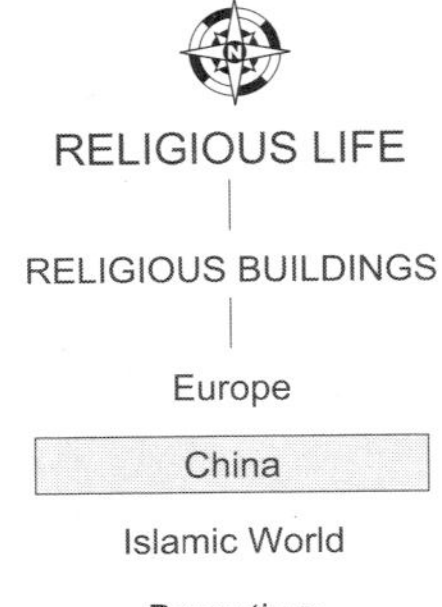

CHINA

All great cities in the Tang had religious establishments of one sort or another. In the early 8th century, Changan had 91 Buddhist monasteries (64 for monks and 27 for nuns), 16 Daoist temples (10 for priests and 6 for priestesses), 2 Christian churches, and 4 Zoroastrian shrines. Those figures do not include small Buddhist chapels or the ancestral shrines of powerful families. Some of the monasteries and temples were immense, occupying entire wards in the capital. One of the Buddhist establishments there had more than 10 courtyards with 1,897 bays (the space between pillars) where 300 officially ordained monks resided.

The size and magnificence of the churches in Changan were the result primarily of patronage from the throne, nobility, and eminent political figures, who usually endowed the churches in order to earn merit toward salvation for themselves and their ancestors. In one example, the mother of an emperor in the mid-9th century endowed a Buddhist monastery with 200,000 coins and three carts laden with embroidered cloth to accrue merit for her son's deceased wife. In another case, the most powerful eunuch of the early 8th century donated his mansion in Changan for conversion into a Buddhist monastery. After the casting of a bell for the church, he convened a vegetarian feast for members of the imperial court. He demanded that his guests contribute 100,000 coppers each time they struck the bell. Someone who wished to curry the eunuch's favor struck the bell 20 times and forked over 2 million cash. It was also the habit of the throne to have buildings in palaces dismantled and given to churches, which reassembled them to construct religious halls. In 730, the emperor bestowed perhaps the largest of such gifts when he wanted a Daoist abbey erected with utmost speed. He ordered four palace halls dismantled to construct two halls for venerating the gods, a meditation chamber, and gates.

The wealth of Buddhist monasteries in Changan was enormous. In the early years of the dynasty, a monk set up an Inexhaustible Treasury—so named because its assets could earn interest indefinitely—in a monastery. Men and women of high standing brought cartloads of coppers and silk as acts of repentance. They left their riches on the premises and then departed without giving their names. By the middle of the 7th century, the wealth derived from those donations was incalculable. The monastery used the interest it earned from loaning the riches it accumulated to pay for the restoration of other monasteries throughout the empire, to feed the starving, and to sponsor religious rites.

All monasteries had at least one hall for worshiping Buddha: offering prayers, burning incense, and chanting scriptures. Some were enormous. A hall dedicated to the Buddha Who Is to Come was 150 feet high. Every hall had a statue of the Buddha, one of which was 30 feet tall. They were usually made of bronze but also could be of precious metals and stones. One monastery in Changan had 600 small silver Buddhas, one figure of pure gold that was several feet high, and another of silver over six feet tall. A church in the capital had a statue carved from jade that came from central Asia. Occasionally, emperors bestowed statuary from the palace collection on monasteries. In such cases, they sent the images forth in corteges having one thousand painted carriages escorted by troupes of palace musicians, singers, and dancers.

The most prominent structures of Buddhist monasteries were pagodas, a unique form of architecture developed by the Chinese. Purportedly based on Indian stupas, they more closely resembled ancient towers that had been the vogue in architecture centuries before the Tang. Pagodas were artificial imitations of the sacred mountain and were the only high-rise buildings in traditional times. Two, the Large Goose and the Small Goose, that rise to 210 feet and 149 feet, respectively, and are built of brick, are the only structures that survive from Tang Changan. The upper stories of pagodas provided excellent views of cities and became urban landmarks.

Some of Changan's monasteries were repositories for Buddha's relics; four of his teeth were preserved in four different cloisters. One of them, which a Chinese pilgrim brought from India, was three inches in length. Those monasteries put the purported artifacts on exhibit with offerings of food, flowers, and incense. Citizens donated cereals, coppers, and other items as pledges of their reverence. The most revered of the relics was part of Buddha's finger bone, preserved in a cloister about one hundred miles west of the capital. On three occasions in the late 8th and the 9th centuries, the throne had it brought to Changan, escorted by a grand cortege with monks and nuns trailing behind (Benn, 59–64).

FOR MORE INFORMATION

Benn, C. *Daily Life in Traditional China: The Tang Dynasty.* Westport, Conn.: Greenwood Press, 2002.

Groot, J.J.M. de. *The Religious Systems of China.* 6 vols. Leiden: J.J. Brill, 1892–1910.

ISLAMIC WORLD

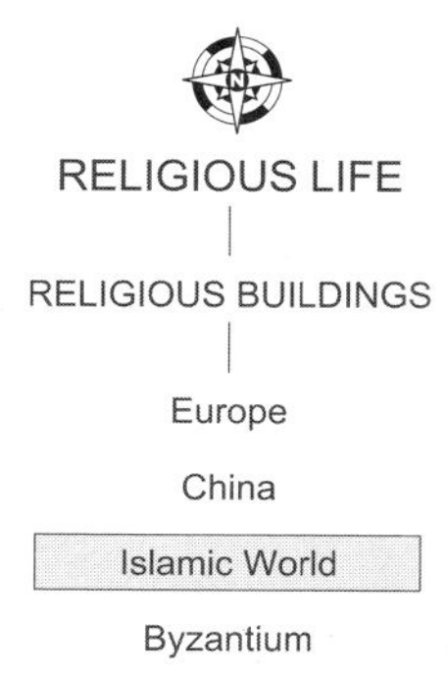

Daily life in the medieval Islamic world revolved around its religious buildings—called mosques—and its markets, two institutions essential to the life of every city and town. The main congregational mosque—the center of official religious and political life—was always located within or next to a market. The Arabic word for mosque (*masjid*) literally means "place of prostration," yet its function was essentially the same as a synagogue or a church; that is, it was a place for the formal worship and assembly of the community of faith. Although Friday was not established as an Islamic day of rest, it did take on an air of sanctity similar to that associated with Saturday and Sunday in Judaism and Christianity as evidenced by admonitions that people should take care to bathe completely on Fridays, wear their best clothes, perfume themselves, and eat special dishes.

Mosques all have the same basic layout, although the scale differs depending on how large the building is. The design of mosques was established early by the conquering armies of Islam. As soldiers stopped for the day, they created a space to offer their prayers: They established an open field with a ditch and a small prayer shelter on the *kibla* side—that is, the wall facing Mecca. As Muslims began to establish permanent religious buildings, they kept the same basic design.

Mosques have a large open court enclosed on three sides by covered arcades, which provide shade from the desert sun. On the *kibla* side is a roofed prayer hall with a central niche (called the mihrab) in the wall to further point to the direction of Mecca. To the right of the mihrab was a pulpit, called the *minibar* from which a leader conducted readings from the Qur'an or offered sermons. The faithful brought rugs on which to kneel as they were offering their prayers.

Pilgrims at Mecca, from a treatise manuscript on laws of religious observance by Muhammad ibn Halva, ca. 1410. Note the tall minaret of this mosque. © The Art Archive/British Library/British Library.

Muhammad had indicated that the faithful should be called to prayer by the human voice. (Christians were called by bells and Jews by horns.) To facilitate this, mosques have tall, slender towers, or minarets, attached to them from which the man who called the faithful—the muezzin—could chant his call. (Today, these calls are enhanced by microphones or even recorded.) There was no mandatory number of minarets, but no mosque was allowed to have exactly seven; that number was reserved for the great mosque in Mecca. The muezzin begins by proclaiming four times that "God is greatest." The next five lines are repeated twice each. "I bear witness that there is no god but God; I bear witness that Muhammad is the messenger of God. Hurry to the *salat*. Hurry to salvation. God is the greatest." The last line, "There is no god but God," is said only once. In the morning call to prayer, the muezzin usually adds the phrase, "Prayer is better than sleep" after the phrase, "Hurry to salvation." The call to prayer according to the Shiʿite tradition is the same as that just described but concludes with the phrase, "Hasten to the best of deeds."

The interior of mosques looked very different from Christian churches. Many were huge but lacked the specific focal points that characterized Christian churches. The great mosque in Cordoba, for example, was dominated by 856 columns that led to arches holding up the roof. Because mosques were not allowed to have images of any kind, they were decorated instead with geometric patterns. These patterns were intended to remind the faithful of eternity and of the infinite patterns that make up God's universe. The patterns are beautiful and varied, and this patterning is continued in magnificent carpets that are valued all over the world today.

~*Joyce E. Salisbury*

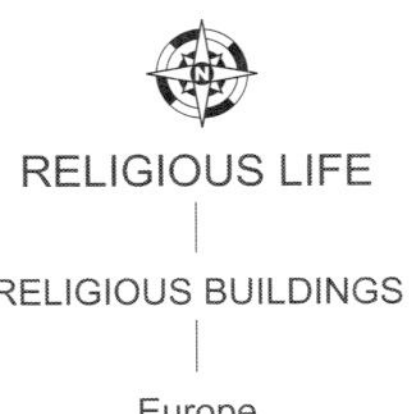

RELIGIOUS LIFE
RELIGIOUS BUILDINGS
Europe
China
Islamic World
Byzantium

FOR MORE INFORMATION

Creswell, K.A.C. A *Short Account of Early Muslim Architecture*. New York: Penguin, 1958.
Stewart, D. *Early Islam*. New York: Time-Life Books, 1967.

BYZANTIUM

Churches are the most distinctive and best-preserved kinds of Byzantine buildings. From small rural chapels to urban cathedrals, religious structures dotted the landscape and shaped the daily lives of its inhabitants. Most of these buildings are known only by fragmentary foundations recovered by archaeological excavation, but a number of churches still stand and many continue to serve as centers of orthodox worship. Descriptions provided by contemporary observers give an impression of how many of these operated in Byzantine times.

Churches varied widely by date, location, and function. The rapid spread of Christianity during the 4th through 6th centuries triggered the construction of churches in all parts of the empire. Large assembly halls were erected to serve the growing populations of major cities. These buildings served as local models for other churches that then were set up in nearby towns and villages. The pace of construction slowed amid the political and cultural troubles of the 7th and 8th centuries, but many new churches were founded between the 10th and 15th centuries. The surviving buildings preserve a number of regional architectural traditions, ranging from the brick-faced walls of north Italy to the fine limestone masonry of north Syria and the mud-brick constructions of upper Egypt. Even within the reduced borders of the later Byzantine state, one can differentiate the mortared rubble work of western Asia Minor from the carefully built cloisonné masonry found in central Greece. Equally broad distinctions can be drawn among the intended functions of Byzantine churches, between the large urban cathedrals and specialized pilgrimage centers that handled large crowds in late antiquity, and the much smaller churches built after the 9th century. Many of these late structures were founded by private patrons in their ancestral villages and often served the needs of small monasteries.

The Christian basilica took shape during the 4th through 6th centuries. Like its widespread Roman predecessor, the basic form of the basilica church consisted of a long hall or nave that was subdivided into parallel aisles by two (sometimes four) rows of columns. Windows were set in the side walls and in the clerestory above the colonnades, and a pitched tile roof on a timber frame covered the interior. A vestibule or narthex, sometimes accompanied by an open court, served as a gathering place for worshipers in front of the hall. Processions led from the narthex down the length of the nave to the altar, which was placed in a broad semicircular apse at the opposite end of the building, which usually was oriented to the east. In many cases, interior walls were covered with paintings or mosaics depicting stories from the Old and New Testaments. The tall semidome above the altar soon received its own distinctive thematic treatment, which echoed and reinforced the liturgy that was celebrated below.

The construction of most Byzantine churches was supervised by local masons and craftsmen, rather than professional architects. Builders generally approached their task in a pragmatic way that allowed considerable experimentation. The basic timber-roofed basilica could be readily adapted to suit the needs and resources of the local community. In some cases, builders turned to more complex architectural forms, such as a central plan with a vaulted superstructure. The most ambitious of these experiments resulted in the new cathedral of Constantinople, St. Sophia, which was built by two theoretical engineers, Anthemios of Tralles and Isidoros of Miletus, for the emperor Justinian in 532–37. Covering an area of almost 58,000 square feet, St. Sophia was one of the largest interior spaces of the medieval world. Its plan consisted of a broad central nave with flanking aisles and upper galleries. Most important, the interior was covered by an enormous dome supported by monumental pendentives at a height of about 100 feet. Windows in the base of the dome, semidomes, and nave walls brought light into the interior, which was surrounded by polished marble revetment. In its audacious design and unprecedented scale, St. Sophia set an enduring precedent for later Byzantine and Islamic builders. It continues to impress visitors to modern Istanbul.

The most characteristic churches of the 10th through 15th centuries translated the soaring dome of St. Sophia into the intimate setting of the later Byzantine monastery. The typical monastic church was located within a walled enclosure that included the monks' cells, refectory, storage rooms, workshops, and stables. The church, known as the *katholikon*, was a compact, freestanding structure. One entered this building by a low vestibule or narthex that extended the full width of the church. From here, one moved into the main hall or *naos*, whose vaulted superstructure was supported by a combination of walls, piers, or columns and usually included a tall central dome. The sanctuary to the east had three distinct parts: the *bema* with the altar standing before the main apse, the *prothesis* on the north side where the elements of the Eucharist were prepared, and the *diakonikon* or supporting sacristy to the south. Larger churches could include subsidiary chapels located at the ends of the flanking aisles.

Interior view of Hagia Sophia. The interior of this magnificent church made medieval visitors think of heaven. © The Art Archive/ Dagli Orti.

This complex liturgical space was covered with a set of images that were organized according to clear principles of hierarchy and function. Frontally arranged paintings of standing saints lined the lower walls. Looking onto this central congregational space, these soldiers, monks, and clerics represented the historical community of believers of which the Byzantine monk formed a living part. Painted figural panels, or icons, depicting Christ, the Virgin Mary, John the Baptist, and other special saints were displayed on a high continuous frame known as an *iconostasis*. This formed a visual barrier separating the *naos* from the sanctuary, to which only officiating clergy had access. Biblical narratives were displayed on the upper walls and vaults of the church, with special emphasis given to those stories commemorated in the major liturgical festivals, running chronologically from the Annunciation and Nativity through the Passion and Pentecost. The image of the Virgin, who was recognized as the *Theotokos* (Bearer of God) in Byzantine thought, occupied the semidome over the altar and provided visual evidence of the incarnation. The dome offered the highest and most central part of this complex interior and invariably was occupied by an image of Christ. The popular image of the all-ruling *Pantokrator* figure presented an eloquent visual summation of Byzantine theology, which incorporated the individual worshiper within a carefully structured liturgical environment.

~Marcus Rautman

FOR MORE INFORMATION

Demus, O. *Byzantine Mosaic Decoration: Aspects of Monumental Art in Byzantium*. London: Kegan Paul, 1948. Reprint, New Rochelle, New York: Caratzas, 1976.
Mango, C. *Byzantine Architecture*. New York: Harry N. Abrams, 1976.

Festivals and Holidays

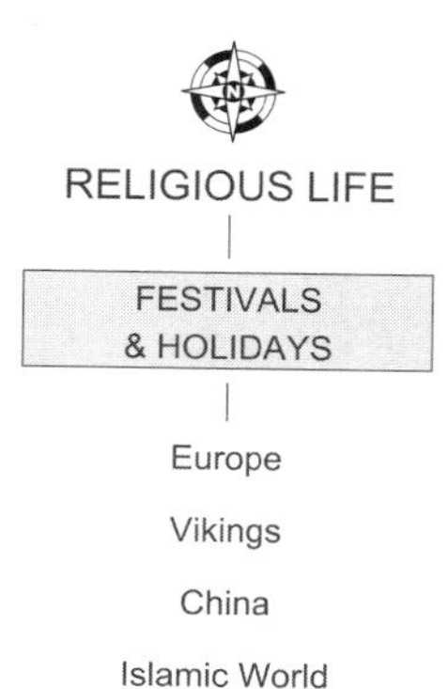

The word *holiday* comes from "holy days" and shows the medieval link between festivals, days off work, and religious observances. In the Middle Ages, there was really no such thing as a secular holiday; the calendar of work and play was a religious one.

The cycle of the holidays of the Christian year coincided with natural rhythms of nature, for as one might expect, celebrations that involved food and drink could not be held during times when food was scarce. The pagan Viking holidays were scheduled to align with the cycles of the seasons. In our modern world, when many people can buy fresh strawberries in the middle of winter, we have to imagine a time when this was not so. In medieval Europe, holidays were carefully scheduled around the cycles of planting and harvesting.

Spring began the holiday cycle with the celebration of the movable feast of Easter (which comes each year on the first Sunday after the first full moon after the vernal equinox). Easter was never celebrated as a large feast, however, because food was still somewhat scarce after the winter. Instead, people usually killed a lamb or a piglet, both newly born with the spring. May, June, and July were months of hard agricultural work. Only beginning in late July did the promise of spring come through with harvests, so from August through December, the cycle of festivals escalated. Saints' days were celebrated with feasts, and the fall cycle culminated with the Christmas celebration.

The Christmas season brought a full 12 days of leisure and celebration, with feasts, music, and dance. England celebrated an unusual tradition of appointing a boy as bishop to preside over the church for a week or two. This festival was often raucous and irreverent, but much enjoyed. Many of the celebrations in the Middle Ages involved a "feast of fools," during which the regular order of the world was inverted—as with boys being appointed bishops. During such feasts, men dressed as women or as beasts, and a clown was made king. These reversals were intended to preserve the order of the world by using up all the disorder at one time.

After the Christmas season, few holidays were celebrated during the winter months. Lent, which marks the 40 days before Easter, was observed as a time of fasting, which often made a virtue of necessity during the time of year when food was scarce.

Most Chinese holidays also were linked to annual cycles of nature. For example, the Chinese celebrated solar turning points of the winter and summer solstices. They also celebrated lunar holidays, which were much more numerous. The lunar festivals came with such frequency that a month did not go by without a festival. They were celebrated with different degrees of abundance depending on how much food was available.

Muslims celebrated fewer major holidays throughout the year. Instead, they focused their celebrations during two major times. The first was during the pilgrimage month, when the faithful went to Mecca. At the end of the pilgrimage, the faithful celebrated the Great Festival, a four-day period of feasting and gift giving. This celebration included parades with musicians. Muslims also celebrate during Ramadan, the month of fasting. It may seem counterintuitive that a month of renunciation and fasts should also be a time of rejoicing, but it is true. The fasting takes place only during daylight hours; after dark, people break their fast with much celebration. During this month, Muslims recognize the reality that feasting and fasting are two sides of the same coin and that the pattern of life includes both. These Muslim celebrations recognize the principle that holidays are linked to holy days and that festivals are matters of religion.

Only after the Middle Ages did festivals and holidays become separated from the religious impulses that created them. Now, we consider vacations and time off work as a secular right, separated from any religious obligation. In this, modern holidays are very different from their medieval counterparts.

~*Joyce E. Salisbury*

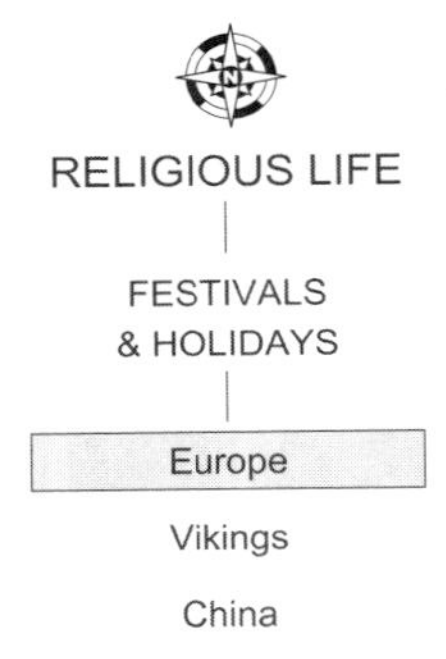

EUROPE

Medieval people navigated through time by a complex system of signposts based on natural cycles, religious rituals, and cultural traditions. The seven-day week was a part of ordinary life, since Sundays, and in many cases Saturday afternoons, were occasions of leisure.

People in medieval Europe organized their year around the cycle of religious holy days—days that served as occasions for secular merrymaking as well as religious observations. The countess of Leicester's daily accounts from Dover fixes dates as "the Monday before the feast of St. Margaret" and "the eve of St. Botolph." Manor courts in Cuxham were held "on the next Friday after the Conversion of St. Paul" or "on Wednesday the morrow of St. Augustine." Even in the more modern urban environment of Paris, the bakers paid their taxes to the king at Christmas, Easter, St. John's Day, and Martinmas. The repertoire and sometimes the actual dates of holy days varied from place to place, but the following calendar gives the major feasts that were probably celebrated throughout Europe. These were observed as a holiday and required a fast on the previous day.

January	1	Circumcision of Christ
	6	Epiphany

February	2	The Purification (Candlemas)
	24	St. Matthias the Apostle
Movable feasts		
	Shrove Tuesday	The day before Ash Wednesday
	Ash Wednesday	The Wednesday before the sixth Sunday before Easter. This day marked the beginning of Lent, a period of penitence observed by abstinence from meat.
March	25	The Annunciation of the Virgin Mary
April	25	St. Mark the Evangelist
Movable feasts		
	Maundy Thursday	The Thursday before Easter
	Good Friday	The Friday before Easter
	Easter	The first Sunday after the first full moon on or after March 21; if the full moon was on a Sunday, Easter was the next Sunday.
May	1	SS. Phillip and James
	3	Discovery of the Cross (Holy Rood Day)
Movable feasts		
	Rogation Sunday	Five weeks after Easter
	Ascension	The Thursday after Rogation Sunday
	Pentecost	Ten days after the Ascension
	Trinity Sunday	One week after Pentecost
June	24	St. John the Baptist (Midsummer)
	29	The Death of Peter and Paul the Apostles
	30	The Commemoration of Paul the Apostle
July	22	St. Mary Magdalene
	25	SS. James the Greater and Christopher
August	1	St. Peter in Chains
	10	St. Lawrence
	15	St. Bartholomew
September	8	Nativity of the Virgin
	14	Exaltation of the Cross
	21	St. Matthew
	29	St. Michael (Michaelmas)
October	28	SS. Simon and Jude
November	1	All Saints (Hallowmas)
	11	St. Martin of Tours (Martinmas)
	30	St. Andrew
December	6	St. Nicholas
	25	Nativity of Christ (Christmas)

26	St. Stephen
27	St. John the Evangelist
28	The Holy Innocents (Childermas)

The major festivals of Christmas and Easter brought days of holidays from work. The Christmas season brought a holiday for the full 12 days from Christmas Eve to Epiphany. This was a time when the need and opportunity for farmwork was at a low ebb, and villagers took the opportunity for a rare holiday. Easter, too, brought a respite in the cycle of labor, lasting through the week following Easter and into Hocktide, the Monday, Tuesday, and Wednesday of the subsequent week.

A medieval feast, at which aristocrats celebrate with food, wine, and music. Illustration by Will McLean.

With the addition of a number of local celebrations for various saints' days, the religious observances for medieval people amounted to many celebrations throughout the year. The cycles of life were framed by these religious holidays (Singman, 219–23).

To read about festivals and holidays in 18th-century England, see the England entry in the section "Holidays" in chapter 7 ("Recreational Life") of volume 4; for Victorian England, see the England entry in the section "Holidays and Festivals" in chapter 7 ("Recreational Life") of volume 5 of this series.

FOR MORE INFORMATION

Reeves, C. *Pleasures and Pastimes in Medieval England*. Oxford: Oxford University Press, 1995.
Singman, J. L. *Daily Life in Medieval Europe*. Westport, Conn.: Greenwood Press, 1999.

VIKINGS

During their pagan period, Vikings celebrated three major religious festivals each year: one in the fall after harvest, one in midwinter (Yule), and one at the beginning of spring. Sometimes there was a fourth festival in midsummer. Their purpose was primarily to placate the gods, avert catastrophes, secure success in the campaigns or raids planned, and promote fertility and peace. No doubt, systematic attention was paid to oracles in these circumstances, and the casting of lots and performing of other rites to learn about the future in connection with the sacrifices was probably common.

The central part of the festivals was the sacrifice. Sacrifices could be inanimate (agricultural produce, utensils, weapons) or animate (sheep, horses, even human beings). Animal sacrifices were connected with a sacrificial meal meant to establish a communion between the divinities and the participants. On such occasions, toasts were also drunk to individual gods and in memory of deceased kinsmen. Most likely, there were also hymns to the gods and dances, although the sources are virtually silent on these aspects of the festivals.

It is known that very large, official celebrations were held at Uppsala in Sweden and Lejre in Denmark, and in both places, large monuments are still visible. It is likely that they were somehow associated with royal power. The Uppsala cult was described by Adam of Bremen, who tells of contemporary conditions, while the Lejre cult was described by the German Thietmar of Merseburg around 1000, that is, about half a century after the Christianization of Denmark. According to both accounts, people gathered every nine years, and both human beings and animals were sacrificed to the gods. In Lejre, 99 humans and 99 horses along with dogs and cocks were sacrificed; in Uppsala, 9 males of every creature were slaughtered, and Adam says that a Christian informant had seen as many as 72 carcasses hanging there side by side in a grove next to the temple. Adam further relates that this feast was for all the provinces of Sweden and that no exemption from attendance was allowed; those who had embraced Christianity could, however, buy themselves out from participation. According to Adam, priests were assigned to perform the offerings in the temple, which, Adam claims, was adorned with gold. His description of the temple is, however, believed to have been inspired by Christian worship because temples of such splendor are not known from earlier sources. Moreover, priesthood as a sacral office appears not to have been in existence. To be sure, there were pagan Scandinavian priests in the sense of persons with priestly functions. The Sagas of Icelanders mention both men and women who performed specific tasks at cult celebrations. But priestly function appears to have been only part of a man's secular position as the head of a household or community. Women were no doubt central to domestic cult practices. Indeed, fall or midwinter sacrifices to the *disir* (tutelary goddesses) appear to have been particularly associated with women's religious expression. But in this they were probably only fulfilling the duties of the more senior household members.

The introduction of Christianity brought with it many changes. Conversion meant accepting not only Christian beliefs but also the regulations and rituals of the Christian Church. Every Christian was required to know at least the *Pater noster*, the Creed, and probably also the formula for baptism (in emergency cases). Moreover, every Christian was expected to show respect for the rules of the liturgical year through periodic abstention from work and certain foods and to receive communion at least annually. The pagan practices of eating horse meat and exposing children (leaving unwanted newborns outside to die) were forbidden, marriage within certain degrees of kinship became unlawful, and the burial of the dead was now to take place in consecrated ground.

By the 12th century, Scandinavians had joined Christian Europe, and their festivals paralleled those celebrated in the Christian south.

~*Kirsten Wolf*

FOR MORE INFORMATION

Jones, G. *A History of the Vikings*. Oxford: Oxford University Press, 1968.
Wolf, K. *Daily Life of the Vikings*. Westport, Conn.: Greenwood Press, forthcoming.

CHINA

Tang statutes recognized 28 holidays for which the government granted a total of 58 days of leave to all mandarins throughout the empire. The rest of society—peasants, merchants, and artisans—also celebrated festivals, although probably with less time off. Regulations provided officials with one day off every 10 days (a Tang week). In addition, the state gave its high-ranking employees 15 days off in the fifth moon as a "farming holiday" and another 15 days in the ninth moon as a "holiday for the bestowal of robes." In all of those instances, government offices closed, permitting their personnel to spend their free time at home or in places of amusement. Finally, there were irregular vacations granted to officials individually, including the following:

1. 30 days off every three years for a visit to their parents, if they lived more than a thousand miles away, or 15 days, if they lived more than 167 miles away (travel time not included)
2. 9 days for the wedding of a son or daughter, and 5, 3, or 1 day for the nuptials of other close relatives (travel time not included)
3. 3 days for a son's capping (manhood) rite or 1 for another close kinsman's ceremony

In addition to these holidays, there were two sorts of festivals in Tang China. The first were solar, such as the summer and winter solstices. The second and more numerous were lunar and often fell on double digits such as the third day of the third moon. (Because it is the convention to refer to the 12 divisions of the year in the solar calendar as months, the term *moons* is used here to designate the 12 divisions of the lunar year.) The lunar calendar began sometime between mid-January and mid-February, the exact date differing from year to year. There was scarcely a moon without festivals to cheer the lives of the people.

The first day of the first moon, also called the day of the chicken, was New Year's, the grandest of all festivals, a holiday of seven days for government officials. It was an occasion for reviewing the omens and disasters or blessings of the preceding year, for displaying the tribute submitted by prefectures and foreign nations, and for the presentation of candidates whom provincial governors had recommended for national examinations in the capitals.

Throughout the land, however, New Year's was mostly a private affair celebrated in the home. It was a festival for dispelling evil, to ensure a fortuitous future in the coming year. Householders rose at cockcrow and threw segments of bamboo into fires that they had lit in a courtyard or in front of their houses. When the heat expanded the air captured inside the segments, the bamboo exploded with a loud bang. Folk beliefs maintained that the noise drove away a malicious, one-legged specter that was somewhat over a foot tall, was unafraid of humans, and caused chills and fevers. After the 11th century, firecrackers replaced the bamboo segments. To further protect their abodes, people hung willow branches on their gates to prevent ghosts from entering the premises. Some county officials took extraordinary measures by slaughtering a sheep, hanging its head on a gate, and covering it with a butchered chicken. The sacrifice of the sheep, which ate the sprouts, and the chicken, which ate the seed, would enable crops to grow. On New Year's Day, it was the custom for people to drink an ale called Killing Ghosts and Reviving Souls, into which special herbs had been mixed. Imbibing the brew would ensure that they would not contract any illnesses in the coming year. They also ate a platter of five bitters—onions, garlic, leeks, and the like—because it fortified their internal organs.

The next festival, the Lantern Festival, was a three-day event, held on the fourteenth, fifteenth and sixteenth days of the first moon. It was the only occasion when the government lifted the curfew so that citizens could freely stroll the streets outside their wards during the night. The Lantern Festival was a festival of light when the moon was full, and patricians sought to outdo each other in providing the grandest lamps.

On the third day of the third moon (double-three), the Chinese celebrated a one-day festival called Lustration. In ancient times, this had been an occasion for repairing to a river and bathing in waters scented with the aromatic orchid plant. It was a rite for dispelling evil and washing away defilement. By the Tang dynasty, the festival had become a time for merrymaking, specifically for drinking ale, feasting, and writing poetry.

The "Cold Food Festival" was so named because custom forbade the lighting of fires for three days and therefore people ate cold food. This was a solar celebration that fell on April 5. On this occasion, people went to the tombs of their ancestors to sweep them, sacrifice to their forebears, and have a picnic. It was also a time for indulging in diversions. Women amused themselves on swings. Palace women as well as new graduates of the civil service examinations played football. Cold Food Festival also had something of the character of Easter in the West because it was the custom in the Tang to dye chicken and duck eggs during this festival.

The fifth day of the fifth moon was an official one-day holiday that commemorated the suicide of a upright statesman in the 3rd century B.C.E. who seized a rock and leaped into a river because his king had banished him for his criticisms. According to folklore, witnesses to the statesman's drowning boarded skiffs and rushed out in a futile attempt to save him. That tradition was apparently the reason for the boat races, now called dragon boat races, during that festival in Tang times. The special food for the fifth day of the fifth moon was a dumpling made of glutinous millet or rice wrapped in leaves and boiled. If it was raining on the fifth day, some people cut a piece of bamboo to make a tube for collecting the "divine water." Then they mixed rain water with the liver of an otter to form a ring that they ate to cure certain illnesses.

The seventh night of the seventh moon was a one-day holiday for officials, celebrating the love affair between the cow herder—the deity of the star Altair in the constellation Aquila—and the weaver maid, the spirit of the star Vega in the constellation Lyra. Separated by the Milky Way, they could cross it only once a year on a bridge of magpies. When they finally met, they consummated their relationship during the evening. The festival was basically for women, who prayed for enhancement of their skills at sewing and weaving.

The All Souls' Feast on the fifteenth day of the seventh moon, developed from the legend of the bodhisattva (savior) Mulian, who found his sinful mother suffering in the purgatory of hungry ghosts. There she starved, because when she put food in her mouth, it changed into burning charcoal. When Mulian informed Buddha, the latter instructed him to make a sumptuous offering, especially of fruit, on the fifteenth day of the seventh moon for monks everywhere. The collective virtue of the clergy was powerful enough to effect the salvation of seven generations of ancestors from hell, from existence as hungry ghosts, and from rebirth as animals. By dint of his effort, Mulian saved his mother. Thereafter, he asked Buddha to make the day a permanent festival, and Buddha agreed. The story became the subject of a sutra translated into Chinese during the third century and was the basis for the custom of the devout laity making offerings to monks. Monasteries took the opportunity of All Souls' Feast to make ostentatious displays of their treasures, probably to attract large numbers of donors. They also gave dramatic performances for the diversion of the crowds.

The midautumn festival of the fifteenth day of the eighth moon was a three-day vacation for officials. Today, Chinese call it the Moon Festival. In Tang times, it was an occasion when gentlemen admired the moon during the night, at least when the weather was clear enough to see it. They saw in the moon not an old man but a hare who was hard at work grinding ingredients for an elixir, using a mortar and pestle. (This was a Daoist image, for alchemy was Daoism's special field of endeavor.) Not everyone agreed on what the craters and plains of the lunar surface depicted. Some saw a toad there. The moon was also the site of the ice palace for the moon goddess and her court. Whatever the case, patricians and plebes alike enjoyed the festival. Those who lived in the country, where the curfew did not apply, might repair to a mountain to drink and feast throughout the night.

The ninth day of the ninth moon was another three-day holiday. This was an occasion, like the Cold Food Festival, for picnicking in the countryside, specifically, on a high elevation such as a mountain. Urban dwellers might convene their feasts at the top of a pagoda or at the Serpentine River park in Changan. There was an intimate association between the festival and the chrysanthemum. The plant was thought to promote longevity because it blooms in the autumn and mimics the life-giving sun with its yellow center and white petals. During the Tang, it was the custom to imbibe chrysanthemum-blossom ale during the festivities. The stems and leaves of the plant were gathered on the ninth day of the ninth moon, added to fermenting grains, and allowed to brew for an entire year. Drinking the ale on the festival the following year prolonged one's life.

On the last day of the twelfth moon, the well-to-do invited Buddhist monks or Daoist priests to recite scriptures at their homes. Then they prepared ale and fruit to send the god of the stove on his way. It was that deity's duty to record the sins of the family throughout the year and report them to heaven on the last day of the year. Families hung an image of the god painted on paper above their stoves on New Year's Day, and it remained there all year long, noting all the transgressions committed by the householders. On the eve of the last day of the twelfth moon, the god of the stove left the home and journeyed to the celestial realm. That was not a pleasant thought to families, so they rubbed the dregs of ale on the mouths of their images to get the deity so drunk that he could not make his report to heaven (Benn, 149–54).

FOR MORE INFORMATION

Benn, C. *Daily Life in Traditional China: The Tang Dynasty*. Westport, Conn.: Greenwood Press, 2002.

Loewe, M. *Everyday Life in Imperial China*. London: Fromm International, 1968.

ISLAMIC WORLD

The greatest festival of the Muslim world is the annual *hajj* or pilgrimage to Mecca, which begins on the eighth and ends on the thirteenth day of the last lunar month of the Islamic calendar, Dhu'l-Hijja (the *hajj* month). It is one of the five pillars of Islam, but it is required only of those Muslims who are able to undertake it and withstand the many physical and financial hardships required of the pilgrims who come from the entirety of the Islamic world.

Adherents to the Shi'ite branch of Islam had an additional obligation. Pilgrimage to the tombs of the Shi'ite imams was essential to Shi'ite piety. According to Shi'ite doctrine, all of the imams save the twelfth died as martyrs. Some, like the first imam, 'Ali ibn Abi Talib (Muhammad's cousin and son-in-law), were slain in battle; others were poisoned or died in prison. The most dramatic martyrdom is that of 'Ali's son and Muhammad's grandson, Husayn, at the Battle of Kabala' in Iraq on 10 Muharram 61 (October 10, 680 C.E.). Because all the imams are seen as the "sinless ones," their suffering and martyrdom is understood to exemplify their willingness to voluntarily take on a portion of the suffering and punishment of humankind. That is, because of their suffering, humankind can be spared the severity of God's justice. Moreover, the imams' martyrdom qualifies them to serve as intercessors between the faithful and God himself. Therefore, according to the Shi'ite view, the suffering of the imams benefits the faithful only for the specific sins they have committed. (The majority of Muslims are Sunnis, who reject the Shi'ite doctrine of the imamate as well as the idea that the imams play any redemptive role at all.)

The Shi'ite faithful can benefit from the imams' suffering and martyrdom by their willingness to become martyrs themselves but also by pilgrimages to the tombs of the imams and weeping over them. There are reports of the faithful weeping over Husayn's grave almost immediately after his tomb was constructed. Over time, elaborate rituals developed as part of the faithful's visitation and public mourning at the imams' tombs, whether at Husayn's tomb in Karbala or 'Ali's tomb in Najaf, or at the tombs of the imams buried in Baghdad, or Samarra, or Medina, or Mashhad in Iran.

The most elaborate rituals are those associated with Husayn. The oldest of these rituals is for pilgrims to Husayn's tomb to request a sip of water in commemoration of one of Husayn's final acts prior to his martyrdom. Near the end of the battle, as Husayn pleaded for water for his infant son (whom he held in his arms), an arrow pierced the baby's throat and killed him. Undeterred by the death of his child, Husayn continued to fight until he was finally slain. The elaborate passion plays and the public processions during which mourners beat and cut themselves in identification with Husayn's suffering and that are so common in modern Iran, Iraq, and Lebanon appear to date from the Safavid (1501–1722) and Qajar (1779–1925) periods in Iran.

In addition to the major and minor pilgrimages to Mecca and the Shi'ite pilgrimages to the tombs of the imams, there were countless local pilgrimages to the tombs of Sufi saints throughout the medieval Islamic world. Jerusalem and other sacred sites associated with pre-Islamic prophets such as Abraham, Moses, Joseph, and Jesus in Syria and Egypt were also extremely popular. Finally, the tombs of some of the more venerated rulers became local pilgrimage sites as well.

See the section "Religious Beliefs" in this chapter for details on this pilgrimage.

~James Lindsay

FOR MORE INFORMATION

Lindsay, J. *Daily Life in Medieval Islam*. Westport, Conn.: Greenwood Press, forthcoming.
Momen, M. *An Introduction to Shiite Islam*. Oxford: George Ronald, 1985.

Death and the Afterlife

Everyone dies, and all societies have had to deal with that reality. The Middle Ages are located at a point that is significant for those who study attitudes toward death and the dying. On the one hand, the period is markedly different from what went before with regard to views of an afterlife. On the other hand, it is significantly different from modern views of the process of dying and the moment of death itself. By looking at medieval attitudes, we can see the roots of modern attitudes toward the afterlife, while contrasting our views of the dying.

The coming of Christianity and Islam opened up a new world of the afterlife. No longer was death the passageway to a dim, shadowy world as it had been in the classical era, nor was it the pagan hall of victors of the Vikings. For Christians, the afterlife was as rich and fraught with danger as this world. By the Middle Ages, Christians believed in the resurrection of the flesh, which fulfilled the promise of Jesus' resurrection. However, they also began to believe that the soul left the dying body and began to enjoy an afterlife while it waited for the Last Days, when the body would rise again and reclaim its soul. As Christians added questions of justice to this image of the afterlife, they believed in a hell, in which the damned would be tortured forever. This hell became the abode of damned souls while they waited for their condemned bodies to join them in the hereafter. By the 11th century, this geography of the afterlife was made more complex by the development of the idea of purgatory—a third place for souls to await their bodies. Souls of people who had neither sinned enough to go to hell nor been virtuous enough to go to heaven entered purgatory. There they would be punished enough to cleanse them of their sins before they could enter heaven. After the Middle Ages, the idea of purgatory would be challenged by reformers who wanted to simplify the afterlife. In the medieval world, however, it remained highly complex.

Muslims shared the Christian view of a paradise to be enjoyed by the virtuous and a hell for the damned. Muslim ideas of Holy War were enhanced by the idea that those who died during such battles would go immediately to heaven to enjoy the pleasures of paradise. These ideas influenced Christians, who also began to claim that crusaders in a Holy War could go to heaven without paying for their sins.

Polynesians also believed the souls went to an afterlife, but their image of it was less highly developed. They did sometimes kill wives and slaves of high chiefs in the expectation that they could care for their master in the afterlife.

Buddhists in China had varied views of the afterlife. Some believed people were immediately reincarnated unless they had reached a sufficiently high level of enlightenment that they could go to nirvana (a kind of a heaven but without a sense of individual salvation) and escape reincarnation. Others believed in a paradise that was similar to the Christian and Muslim notions where an individual could enjoy a happy afterlife. Buddhist views of hell were more similar to a purgatory, in which a soul is punished and cleansed for a fixed period before being reborn.

These perceptions of the afterlife are familiar to us in the modern world. However, the scene at the deathbed was very different from our own. Death in the Middle Ages was considered deeply sad but natural. The dying person was surrounded by the living—including children—who stayed by his or her bedside waiting for the moment of death. Polynesians took the dying outside to die because they believed that if anyone died inside a house, the house had to be destroyed. But in the West and China, all the loved ones prepared themselves for the death at the bedside.

The dying person also made preparations. In Christian Europe, priests were summoned to take a last confession and administer the last rites to help pave the way to the afterlife. Buddhists too offered prayers at the bedside. Death was not a surprise.

After death, bodies were carefully washed and dressed for burial. These ceremonies were surrounded by ritual and requirements, and the community mourned in expected fashions. In the medieval West, the dead were buried in the churchyard very close to the living. (In the ancient world, the dead were buried farther away for fear of pollution.) Both in Polynesia and in the West, the dead were exhumed after a few years when the decomposition had been completed, and the bones were moved to another location.

Death marked a disruption. Families and communities lost loved ones and developed rituals to mark the passing and heal their grief. In today's world, this remains true. What has changed is that we treat death as an accident and separate it from our homes. People die in hospitals trying to be saved instead of at home with families.

~Joyce E. Salisbury

FOR MORE INFORMATION

Ariès, P. *Western Attitudes toward Death*. Baltimore, Md.: Johns Hopkins University Press, 1974.

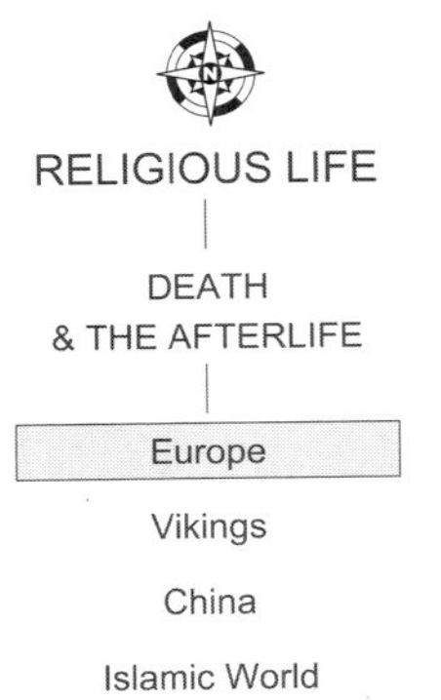

EUROPE

In a world with high rates of mortality at every age, death was a familiar occurrence, and although an object of fear, it was perhaps less a matter of mystery than it is today. Medieval people typically died as they were born and as they were conceived: at home in bed. The parish priest was summoned to administer to the dying person the rite of extreme unction, the last of the sacraments of the church. After death, the body was washed, wrapped in a cloth, and carried to the church for burial. Most people were buried in the churchyard, without a coffin or grave marker. Traditionally, only priests were buried in the church itself, but by the 13th century, some aristocrats were buried there as well. The wealthiest might be laid in coffins of stone, and in the 13th century, important graves were adorned with brass images of the deceased. The churchyard that served for burial was often an important public space in the community, serving not just as a repository for the dead but as a place of public assembly, a marketplace, and even as a playing field.

Through the Middle Ages, Christians developed a rich and complex view of the afterlife. From the earliest centuries of Christianity, most of the church leaders believed (and taught) that the soul was immortal and thus left the body at death. The ghostly soul that kept the shape and imprint of its body went immediately to an afterlife. Echoing modern Islamic beliefs, Tertullian, the 3rd-century fierce advocate of martyrdom, claimed that martyrs went directly to paradise to receive their reward and that they were the only souls who could do so. Tertullian believed the souls of nonmartyrs went to Hades and began accounting for their deeds on earth. This model of an afterlife drew much from the ideas of the classical world that had gone before. What was strikingly new in Christianity was the believers' insistence that the body, too, would be resurrected, not just the soul. After all, Jesus' physical resurrection promised the same for his followers.

As even Tertullian noted, this model raised the question of why there had to be a resurrection of the flesh at all if the corporeal soul was already being punished or rewarded after death. The theologian answered his critics by falling back again to his deep sense of justice. The soul participated in sins by its will or its thought—all the intangibles that lead us to action. The body on the other hand *performed* those acts, so the body had to be resurrected on the last day to participate in the promised justice. So the souls of the dead—whether they were already suffering punishment or not—waited to be reunited with their bodies on Judgment Day.

At the end of the world, Christians believed that Christ would come again to judge the dead and the living. At this time, all the dead bodies that had been turned to dust (or even had been eaten by animals) would be reassembled and reunited with their souls. Christ would then judge them, and they would go on to their final reward. Sinners went to hell to be punished forever, and the faithful went to heaven.

Visions of hell varied, but all imagined dramatically physical punishments for the bodies that had sinned on earth. While modern images focus on eternal burning in a fiery pit, medieval images more often imagined a body forever eaten. For example, a 12th-century knight describes his fearful vision of hell:

> Fiery dragons were sitting on some of them [the tormented souls] and were gnawing them with iron teeth, to their inexpressible anguish. Others were the victims of fiery serpents, which, coiling round their necks, arms, and bodies, fixed iron fangs into their hearts. Toads, immense and terrible, also sat on the breasts of some of them and tried to tear out their hearts with their ugly beaks. (Salisbury, 73)

The most famous vision of hell is Dante's in the *Divine Comedy*, written in the 14th century. Dante describes hell as a huge pit with souls suffering physical punishments to fit their crimes on earth. For example, adulterers endlessly swirled in storms of lust and gluttons starved.

Domenico di Michelino, *Dante Standing before the City of Florence* (1465). This painting shows the most famous medieval view of the afterlife, that portrayed in Dante's *Divine Comedy.* In the background are souls in hell and purgatory, hoping to ascend to the heaven above. © The Art Archive/Duomo Florence/Dagli Orti (A).

Visions of heaven also varied. Some followed the biblical Book of Revelations in imagining heaven as a magnificent city; others pictured a beautiful garden. Dante describes heaven as an elaborate rose in the sky with the saved arrayed on the petals of the rose. All the visions of heaven shared with hell the idea that salvation would be a physical sensation.

By the late 11th century, many of the faithful—including church leaders—believed that this binary vision of heaven or hell, salvation or damnation, was too simple. They understood that people's actions in this world did not fall neatly into categories of good and bad. Thus, at that time an idea of a third place in the afterlife arose: purgatory. Souls who were not evil enough to be damned forever, yet not good enough to go immediately to heaven, went to purgatory, where they were punished for the sins they committed in the expectation that in time they would be received into heaven. Dante describes purgatory as a mountain with various levels of sinners working off their sins. By late in the Middle Ages, the idea of purgatory was so accepted that people believed their prayers and good deeds might help free their loved ones from time in purgatory.

Medieval Christians had vivid images of an afterlife. They believed that souls of the dead began their journey in the next life right at death, while at the same time they believed that their own bodies would be resurrected to rejoin their souls. People died in company of friends and family, and the prayers of these same loved ones followed the dead. It was a complex vision that would be challenged during the Reformation after the Middle Ages ended. Nevertheless, it is a vision that continues among many people today.

To read about death and the afterlife in Elizabethan England, see the Christianity entry in the section "Sacred Story: Beginnings and Endings" in chapter 8 ("Religious Life") of volume 3 of this series.

~*Joyce E. Salisbury*

FOR MORE INFORMATION

Ariès, P. *Western Attitudes toward Death*. Baltimore, Md.: Johns Hopkins University Press, 1974.

LeGoff, J. *The Birth of Purgatory*. Translated by A. Goldhammer. Chicago: University of Chicago Press, 1984.

McDannell, C., and B. Lang. *Heaven: A History*. New Haven, Conn.: Yale University Press, 1988.

Salisbury, J. E. *The Beast Within: Animals in the Middle Ages*. New York: Routledge, 1994.

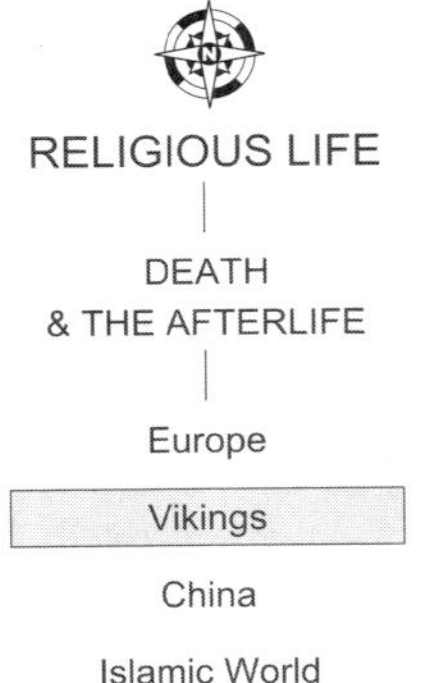

VIKINGS

Concerning beliefs about death, there was in Viking Age Scandinavia no consistency. Different people held different beliefs, and a person might well hold views that were logically inconsistent. Some believed that life went on after death, either in the grave or burial mound or in the underworlds known as Hel or Niflheim or in Odin's Valholl. Others believed that death was simply the end.

Although a belief in the afterlife was not universal, the many graves excavated in Scandinavia and elsewhere nonetheless testify to a widespread notion of some form of existence after death. So too does the information available about the treatment of the dead, who typically drew their final breath either on the battlefield or at home as a result of warfare, accident, illness, or in the case of women, as a consequence of childbirth.

The profession of undertaker is a relatively modern phenomenon; in the Viking Age, it was generally the duty of the relatives to prepare the body for funeral. When someone died, the first act was usually to close the nostrils, mouth, and eyes. Often, the body was washed and the head wrapped in a cloth. If the death occurred at home, the body was sometimes carried away by a special route to the place of burial. The latter was a precaution taken if it was feared that the dead person would become an evil dead walker, who might return and harm the living. Although the dead were generally regarded as guardians watching that the family's members upheld the rights and responsibilities incumbent upon the clan, persons who had disgraced themselves in death became outcast ancestors and would typically roam as ghosts.

The pre-Christian burial customs testify to the belief in the continued existence of the dead. Many people were buried with possessions for use in the afterlife; grave goods ranged from food and drink and clothing to weapons and tools of various kinds. Sometimes the dead were accompanied by their dogs, and there is also evidence that on occasion slaves were sacrificed to attend their masters or mistresses. Other grave goods had a more symbolic function; they include horses, boats, and wagons to represent the journey to the otherworld. But when it comes to notions about the otherworlds that might receive the dead the beliefs are varied and often hazy. Some clearly believed that the home of the dead was in the grave or burial mound. The belief in Valholl belonged to the kings and warriors of the Viking Age, although it is possible that it had its origin in the idea of mountains as a dwelling place for the dead. The fact that the name is applied to certain rocks in southern

Sweden that were believed to house the dead certainly points in that direction. The medieval Icelandic poets, however, present Valholl not as a rock but as a magnificent palace, in which dead kings and warriors gathered.

Native sources provide very little information about funeral rites in Viking Age Scandinavia. The most detailed description comes from the pen of the Arab traveler Ibn Fadlan, who in 922 witnessed the funeral of a Rus chieftain at the river Volga in Russia. According to Ibn Fadlan, when the chieftain died, he was placed in his grave for several days while his clothes were being cut out and made ready. The chieftain's slaves and servants were then asked who would die with him. When one had volunteered, she (in this case, it was a female) was held to her word and treated like a princess. Meanwhile, a ship was drawn up on posts on the shore. A bier was placed on it, and an old woman called the Angel of Death covered it with fine tapestries and cushions. This woman was also in charge of embalming and preparing the dead man. The chieftain's body was then raised from the grave and dressed in splendid garments. It was carried into a tent on the ship and laid on the tapestry. Food and alcohol were placed next to the dead man, and two horses and two cows were cut into pieces with a sword and thrown into the ship.

While these events took place, the woman who was to die with the chieftain went to each tent in the camp and had sexual intercourse with each owner. She was then raised three times from what looked like the frame of a door. On the third occasion she claimed that she saw her master in paradise and asked to be sent to him. Accordingly, she was taken to the ship, where she took off her jewelry, drank two beakers of alcoholic beverage, and sang. The Angel of Death led her into the tent, followed by six men, who all had intercourse with her. The woman was then laid by the side of the dead chieftain. Four men held her hands and legs while the Angel of Death put a rope around her neck and gave it to two men to pull. The Angel of Death repeatedly stabbed her in the chest with a dagger while the two men choked her with the rope.

The dead chieftain's closest relative, who was naked, now lit a fire under the ship. Others threw burning wood on it, so that everything was burnt to fine ashes. Then they built a mound on the place where the ship had stood, raised a large post in the middle of it with the names of the chieftain and the king of the Rus on it, and went away.

Ibn Fadlan adds that a man of the Rus tribe, who was present, had commented that the Arabs were stupid to place their beloved in the earth where worms would eat them instead of burning them, so that the dead would go instantly to paradise.

Although some details in this account, such as the Angel of Death and the naked kinsman, have no parallels in Norse sources, archaeological finds confirm several of the funeral rites described by Ibn Fadlan. Both cremation and inhumation burial were practiced in Viking Age Scandinavia, although the former was more common in Denmark than elsewhere.

Normally, the dead was buried in a coffin or, more elaborately, in a chamber. Those who lived in the country buried their dead on their estates, whereas city dwellers usually buried them in a communal cemetery inside or, more commonly, outside the city walls. The graves were usually marked by mounds (although flat graves are not infrequent), wooden posts, or stone settings of various shapes—oval (boat-shaped), round, square, or triangular. Rune stones are generally not associated with graves.

The mounds could be large or small. Some of the small mounds are no more than 2 or 3 meters in diameter and no more than 0.15 meters high; the largest mound in Scandinavia, the pre-Viking Age Raknehaug in Norway, is 95 meters in diameter and about 19 meters high. The large mounds were typically reserved for the royalty. Notable examples of large Viking Age mounds are the two royal mounds at Jelling, Denmark, the northern one with a large wooden burial chamber, and the mounds of Gokstad and Oseberg, Norway, containing unburnt ship burials, which were common in Norway and Sweden but rare in Denmark, Iceland, and the colonies.

The Oseberg ship burial is without question the most spectacular grave in Scandinavia. The site was excavated in 1904, and the grave has generally been dated to around 800. The burial was placed in a ship 21.6 meters long and 5 meters wide, and originally the bodies of two women were placed in the burial chamber built onto its deck. One was of a woman 50 to 60 years old with bad arthritis; the other was between 20 and 30 years old. In addition to the ship, a wagon and four sledges were found, as well as wooden artifacts including troughs, ladles, chests, boxes, a plain work sledge, a hoe, a dung fork, and shovels. Oseberg also contains textiles, both imported and local, tools for textile work, metalwork, and plant remains. Because of the wealth of the burial, it is believed that it must have been for a member of the ruling dynasty, who was evidently accompanied by a female servant.

Such splendid burials as the Oseberg ship burial are, however, the exception rather than the rule, and it can be said generally that the Scandinavian graves reveal a high degree of social stratification: graves vary according to the status and wealth of the deceased. This stratification is especially evident in market towns such as Hedeby in South Schleswig, in which rich grave mounds filled with valuables lie beside the humble graves of peasants containing only insignificant grave goods or none at all.

As Christianity gradually came to replace the pagan Scandinavian, inhumation burial in a consecrated churchyard became the norm along with a more minimalist approach to interment. The dead was shrouded simply in a sheet and placed in a plain earth or wooden grave oriented east-west, devoid of grave goods.

~*Kirsten Wolf*

FOR MORE INFORMATION

Jones, G. *A History of the Vikings*. Oxford: Oxford University Press, 1968.
Wolf, K. *Daily Life of the Vikings*. Westport, Conn.: Greenwood Press, forthcoming.

CHINA

Because the Chinese believed that breath, *qi*, was the vital energy on which life depended, they took the cessation of breathing as evidence that death had occurred. A family member, friend, or outsider leaned over and placed his or her face close to the mouth of the unconscious person in order to determine if there was any movement of air coming from the lips. As soon as the family determined that their loved one was dead, they began to wail. After exhausting their grief, they undressed the corpse, washed it with perfumed water, placed a piece of jade in its mouth to prevent the body from decaying, clothed it in grave garments, and placed it in a coffin. Coffins, at least those of the upper classes, were made of sturdy wood and sealed tightly because the family kept the corpse in the home for some time or sent it to a storage area in the city. The reason for the delay in most cases was that burial had to take place on a proper day according to the almanac or that the tomb had not been completed. On the day of death or shortly thereafter, the family made a sacrifice to the deceased. For the humble, the offering consisted of a simple meal with ale to nourish the soul in the afterlife. For the nobility, the sacrifices were opulent.

Funerals, too, were elaborate for the wealthy. There were firms, at least in Changan, that provided exorcists, singers, hearses, and other equipment for funerals when the family had the means to pay for them. Furthermore, if a bureaucrat died in the course of a military campaign, while serving as a member of the imperial entourage when the court traveled, or when carrying out public business on a commission, the government supplied a coffin for him and paid for shipping his remains back to his home. When the man was not an official, his family bore the entire burden of the funeral expenses. According to Tang statutes, if a man died without family (male heirs), his daughter or nearest relative had to sell his slaves, shops, homes, and other property to pay for his funeral and burial. If he had neither a daughter nor close kinsman, then an official undertook the task, presumably drawing the money from government funds.

Graves were almost always in the countryside rather than in cities. According to the religious beliefs of premodern Chinese, the land beneath ground level belonged to the gods, and digging into it to construct tombs offended them unless the family of the deceased purchased the site from the deities. Consequently, the deceased's kinsmen drew up a contract to buy the plot. They deposited the document in the sepulcher to resolve any legal problems that might arise for the departed in the afterlife.

Mourning continued after the burial of the dead, its length determined by the relationship of the mourner to the deceased. According to ritual regulations, a man was supposed to mourn for his brother's son for one year, and his uncle's grandson for five months. The longest period, "three years," was for parents and grandparents, except in the case of army officers, when it was 100 days. The three-year mourning period was actually only 27 months but imposed great hardships nonetheless. All mandarins had to resign from their posts the moment they learned of their parent's or grandparent's death, don mourning dress, and remain in retirement for the duration of the period. The official lost his salary and had to find other means of supporting himself and his family in the interim. At the end of 27 months, he could return to government service at the same rank that he held before. Failure to inform one's superior or to mourn was an offense punishable by exile to a place 666 miles from his place of residence.

Custom and the law demanded that the son or grandson adopt an austere lifestyle during the 27 months. Removing mourning clothes and donning ordinary garments was punishable by three years of penal servitude. So was listening to or performing music. The Tang law code defined music as playing instruments, singing, and dancing, but the proscription undoubtedly applied to other forms of amusement, such as the variety acts of the independent entertainers.

Ancient Chinese believed that a multiplicity of souls inhabited the human body. A time-honored medical canon contended that each of the five viscera—liver, lungs, heart, spleen, and kidneys—had its own spirit. Religious Daoists went to extremes in their beliefs about the residents of the body. They claimed that it was the abode of 36,000 gods. The consensus, however, was that there were only two. They represented, and were produced by, the cosmological forces of yin and yang.

The *po* soul was a manifestation of yin—earth, water, and the dark. It was the governor of the physical, animal nature of humans and gave form to the fetus in the womb. The *po* was fixed to the body and after death returned to earth, where it moldered in the soil and lodged in the bones at the grave. The *hun* soul was a manifestation of yang—heaven, fire, and light. It governed the intelligence. The *hun* governed the character of people: their benevolence, righteousness, decorum, knowledge, and trustworthiness. The *hun* was *qi*, breath, and therefore not attached to the body. It was free to roam, in life as well as in death. Some of its wanderings occurred during sleep when a person had dreams. At death, it returned to heaven, but when summoned, it visited its family for sacrifices at the home or its grave.

The different religions in China had different beliefs about the afterlife. The highest state of spiritual attainment for Buddhists was nirvana, a state of extinction attained by suppressing all desires and delusions in order to terminate suffering, obliterate karma, and escape from the perpetual cycle of rebirth. It was a form of individual salvation that required a monk or nun to live a life of asceticism, self-denial, and meditation in near-total isolation from his or her family.

One school of Buddhism offered another image of the afterlife. This school claimed that heaven was Pure Land, a paradise located somewhere to the west of the world. From its gold ground sprang jeweled trees that make music when their branches are moved by gentle breezes. Stairs adorned with gold, silver, lapis lazuli, and crystal lead down into bathing pools filled with cool, sweet, thirst-quenching water. In beds of gold dust, blue, red, white, and yellow lotus blossoms grow. Four times a day, flowers rain down from above, and flocks of birds—peacocks, egrets, and parrots—with elegant plumages sang songs expounding Buddhist tenets. It is a paradise of pure bliss in which nothing unpleasant exists. Dwellers there are free from all suffering, having escaped from the endless cycle of rebirth.

Buddhism not only brought to China the belief in a paradise for the faithful; it also introduced the notion of three woeful modes of existences for sinners: rebirth as a hungry ghost, as a denizen of hell, or as an inferior being in a future life. The belief in hungry ghosts was very old in China, but the notion had no stigma attached to it. The famished spirits were simply unfortunate souls who had no descendants to supply them with sustenance. Buddhism saw them in a different light. Starving specters were suffering as punishment for violating religious ethics.

The Buddhist notion of hell was different from that in the West. It was not an inferno of eternal damnation for sinners. Instead, hell was a kind of purgatory in which the damned suffered torment for limited, albeit lengthy, terms. Hunters received the worst punishments because the taking of life was an anathema to Buddhists. As one story relates, archer Li slew enormous numbers of animals with his arrows and caught countless fish. In 645, he died after being ill for several days. A ghost led him to hell, where he entered a walled courtyard full of flying birds and running animals. The creatures pressed closer and closer to the bowman and demanded his life for having slaughtered them. A dog whom he had shot dead came straight up to him, bit his face, and then gnawed his body until there was not an inch that was free of wounds. After sinners completed their sentences in hell, officials of the unseen world assigned them new destinies among the living. If their transgressions were minor, they stood a good chance of being reborn as human beings of prominent social standing or as gods. Sometimes their sins were so trivial that they passed straight through hell without suffering any punishment whatsoever. If the transgressions were grave, the mandarins in the netherworld might consign the sinner to an animal's body. Regardless of whether one was reborn as an animal in this world or as a deity in the netherworld, reincarnation was always something of an unwelcome event because it did not liberate one from suffering.

Daoism differed from popular Chinese religion and Buddhism in its belief that both *po,* the body, and *hun,* the spirit, survive after death. For the vast majority of its adherents, salvation meant resurrection of the body and the soul. After death, the corpse underwent refining in a realm at the northern reaches of the universe. The process destroyed all of its corruptible substances, the agents of aging and dying, and transformed it into imperishable matter. The person then became an immortal, and therefore qualified to hold office in the bureaucracy of the other world. Those who did not perform good deeds during their lifetime passed into a netherworld, where they perished (Benn, 265–89).

FOR MORE INFORMATION

Benn, C. *Daily Life in Traditional China: The Tang Dynasty.* Westport, Conn.: Greenwood Press, 2002.

Wan Zhongshu. *Han Civilization.* Trans. K. C. Chang. New Haven, Conn.: Yale University Press, 1982.

ISLAMIC WORLD

Muslim burial rituals are fairly simple and, if possible, should occur on the day the person died. First, the corpse is washed and wrapped in a shroud in preparation for burial. After the ritual prayer (*salat*) is performed (ideally in a mosque), funeral prayers (*janaza*) are recited. After a procession, during which the shrouded corpse is carried through the streets on a kind of stretcher to the cemetery, the body is interred.

According to most Muslim scholars, cremation was not an acceptable practice. Traditionally, it had also been held unacceptable by Jewish and Christian scholars.

The necessity of belief in the one God and in the Last Day (the Day of Judgment or Resurrection) are two of the most frequent themes in the Qur'an. The importance of these themes is made abundantly clear in Qur'an 7:171, which describes an event that occurred ostensibly at the beginning of human time. God brought forth Adam's descendants from the loins of his children and made them testify that He was their Lord so that on the Last Day they could not claim ignorance of His oneness or that they were blameless in their polytheism or idolatry because they learned such false beliefs from their parents.

Although only God knows when the Last Day will be, certain events or signs are expected to occur prior to it, such as natural disasters and the arrival of the "Deceiver." Jesus, who, according to Qur'an 4:157, only appeared to die on the cross, will also return to do battle with the Antichrist (*al-Dajjal*), after which Jesus will die (for the first time) and be buried in a tomb near Muhammad's tomb in Medina. A messianic figure from Muhammad's family called the Mahdi will come and defeat God's enemies, the world will be destroyed, and a new millennial age ushered in. Prior to the Day of Judgment, the physical resurrection of the dead must occur. The righteous and the wicked will then be summoned before God, their vices and virtues will be recited by angels who recorded them in special books, and God's final judgment will be given. Essentially, God's final judgment is a formal, ominous, and public vindication of the reward or punishment He decreed for each person at the moment he or she died.

According to Muslim scholars, the final judgment will occur in the Valley of Jehosephat to the east of Jerusalem (as it will in Judaism and Christianity), and the Ka'ba will be transported from Mecca to witness it. The reward for the righteous and the punishment for the wicked also parallel those found in Judaism and Christianity. The righteous are rewarded with a garden (*janna*), while the wicked are condemned to the fire (*nar*), which they will access via Gehenna (*gehinom* in Hebrew and *jahannam* in Arabic), a place south of Jerusalem that is associated with the city's smoldering garbage dump. The Qur'an speaks of two gardens "for those who fear to stand before God" (Qur'an 55:46) and "two more gardens" beyond them (Qur'an 55:62). Some commentators expanded the number from four to seven gardens or "heavens," culminating in the "Garden of Eden." Qur'an 47:15 contrasts the rewards of the righteous with the punishments of the wicked: "This is the Garden which the righteous have been promised. Therein shall flow rivers of water undefiled, and rivers of milk forever fresh, rivers of wine delectable to those that drink it, and rivers of clarified honey. They shall eat therein of every fruit and receive forgiveness from their Lord. Is this like the lot of those who shall abide in the Fire forever, and drink scalding water which will tear their bowels?"

~*James Lindsay*

FOR MORE INFORMATION

Lindsay, J. *Daily Life in the Medieval Islamic World.* Westport, Conn.: Greenwood Press, forthcoming.

Roberts, R. *The Social Laws of the Quran.* Atlantic Highlands, N.J.: Humaniteus Press, 1990.

POLYNESIA

Ancient Polynesians believed that humans might have lived forever had the demigod Māui been successful in his encounter with the goddess of the underworld. But his defeat and death by the goddess caused all humanity to suffer a similar fate. Since then, death has been a natural occurrence among humans.

Polynesians believed that a human being consisted of the body, an animating force within the body, and a spirit or soul. Thus, they believed that a person's spirit could leave the body during sleep and wander about while at the same time the animating force within the body remained, keeping the body alive. Dreams and nightmares were thus explained, and when the spirit returned to the body, the sleeper generally awoke. Upon death, the spirit left the body permanently. Sometimes, however, one's spirit hovered above the body like a butterfly, and an expert priest could "catch" the spirit and through prayer and by massaging the body with certain herbs, "force" the spirit to return to its body, usually by reentering through the toes and working itself through the rest of the body.

When a sick man was dying, his relatives moved him from his house to the outside where he could make his last wishes known because any house in which a person died became taboo and had to be destroyed, usually by burning. Some Polynesians believed that normal death came at the same hour of the day as when the person was born. In New Zealand, the Māoris would lay the dying man on a mat outside his hut, his head toward the north and his feet to the south. His wife would sit at the head of the burial mat, and the male relatives would sit on one side and the females on the other. Each would tie a thin line of flax to the woven mat and hold the opposite end. When death was near, the gathered mourners would collectively give a tug on the lines northward to indicate that the spirit could now leave the body and head off in a northerly direction to its next destination.

When death was finally announced, the attendants began their mourning. Loud dirges and crying began that lasted for days. Close relatives took sharp knives or stones and gnashed their faces and bodies and cut their hair while blood flowed everywhere. Sometimes an attendant slave was slain in order that the deceased might have an attendant to accompany him on his journey. If the deceased was a high chief, his wives might strangle themselves out of affection and in the belief that they could prepare his food along the way.

The body of the deceased was then placed in a sitting position and wrapped in finely woven mats. His weapons were placed nearby, and the visiting mourners from other villages brought mats and gifts and placed them at his feet. The mourning continued for several days, during which time the family usually fasted and continued their wailings and laments.

Slaves and commoners were generally buried in the ground immediately, but chiefs' bodies were carried a distance away into the forest where they were placed on sacred structures and left to decompose. After a period of time, their remains would then be buried in the ground for two years. The body would then be exhumed, the bones cleaned of all bodily remains and the bones removed to a permanent, secret burial ground, often high upon the sides of the mountains. Frequently, the skull of the deceased would be kept by the family as a memento and placed with their other ancestral heirlooms in the sacred places of their homes.

Most Polynesians believed that the departed spirit journeyed to a specific "jumping-off" point somewhere in their island group overlooking the sea, where the spirit jumped to its final destination—the underworld, called the *pō*. In Tahiti, these spirits would make their way to Tata'a Point, the northern tip of the island, where they would dive into the sea and swim to the neighboring island of Mo'orea. From there, they would ascend Mount Rotui and then fly to Mount Temehani on the sacred island of Rā'iātea, where they would meet their eventual destiny. Hawaiians say their underworld lies far to the west, under the ocean, while the Tongans believe it lies northwest of their island chain. The Māoris believe it rests at the foot of Cape Reinga (the extreme north point of New Zealand).

A wide variety of beliefs regarding the underground permeated ancient Polynesia, and when the Christian missionaries arrived, they attempted to identify the *pō* as a Christian hell where all the lost souls of the Polynesians had gone. According to most ancient beliefs, the *pō* is presided over by the goddess Miru, and it is conceived as being a type of paradise possessed of streams, forests, vegetation, and animal life similar to the upper world. Those who made their way there participated in activities very much like they did on earth—they would enjoy themselves by eating, drinking, dancing, and conversing with their friends. But the uncertainty of its existence and the uncertainty concerning whether one's soul would actually make it there caused Polynesians great fear when facing death (Tregear, 386–401; Cunningham, 151–53).

~*Robert D. Craig*

FOR MORE INFORMATION

Cunningham, S. *Hawaiian Religion and Magic*. St. Paul, Minn.: Llewellyn, 1995.
Tregear, E. *The Maori Race*. Wanganui, New Zealand: A. D. Willis, 1904.

RELIGIOUS LIFE: WEB SITES

http://www.britannia.com/church/monlist.html
http://www.fsmitha.com/h1/ch28.htm
http://www.newyorkcarver.com/cathedrallinks.htm
http://www.ucalgary.ca/applied_history/tutor/islam/
http://www.wizardrealm.com/norse/holidays.html

PRIMARY SOURCES

JEAN FROISSART, EXCERPTS FROM *THE CHRONICLES* (CA. 1388)

Often hailed as one of the greatest of medieval European writers, Froissart is well known for writing *The Chronicles*, which primarily deals with battles between England and France during the first phase of the Hundred Years' War in the 14th century. The excerpts here describe two of the most famous battles of the war—the Battle of Crecy and the Battle of Poitiers.

BATTLE OF CRECY, 1346

Then anon the air began to wax clear, and the sun to shine fair and bright, the which was right in the Frenchmen's eyes and on the Englishmen's backs. When the Genoways were assembled together and began to approach, they made a great leap and cry to abash the Englishmen, but they stood still and stirred not for all that: then the Genoways again the second time made another leap and a fell cry, and step forward a little, and the Englishmen removed not one foot: thirdly again they leapt and cried, and went forth till they came within shot; then they shot fiercely with their cross-bows. Then the English archers stept forth one pace and let fly their arrows so wholly (together) and thick, that it seemed snow. When the Genoways felt the arrows piercing through heads, arms, and breasts, many of them cast down their cross-bows and did cut their strings and returned discomfited. When the French king saw them fly away, he said: "Slay these rascals, for they shall let and trouble us without reason." They ye should have seen the men of arms dash in among them and killed a great number of them: and ever still the Englishmen shot whereas they saw thickest press; the sharp arrows ran into the men of arms and into their horses, and many fell, horse and men, among the Genoways, and when they were down, they could not relieve again, the press was so thick that one overthrew another. And also among the Englishmen there were certain rascals that went afoot with great knives, and they went in among the men of arms, and slew and murdered many as they lay on the ground, both earls, barons, knights, and squires, whereof the king of England was after displeased, for he had rather they had been taken prisoners.

The valiant king of Bohemia called Charles of Luxembourg, son to the noble emperor Henry of Luxembourg, for all that he was nigh blind, when he understood the order of the battle, he said to them about him: "Where is the lord Charles my son?" His men said: "Sir, we cannot tell; we think he be fighting." Then he said: "Sirs, ye are my men, my companions and friends in this journey: I require you bring me so far forward, that I may strike one stroke with my sword." They said they would do his commandment, and to the intent that they should not lose him in thed press, they tied all their reins of their bridles each to other and set the king before to accomplish his desire, and so they went on their enemies. The lord Charles of Bohemia his on, who wrote himself king of Almaine and bare the arms, he came in good order to the battle; but when we saw that the matter went awry on their party, he departed, I cannot tell you which way. The king his father was so far forward the he strake a stroke with his sword, yea and more than four, and fought valiantly and so did his company; and they adventured themselves so forward, that they were there all slain, and the next day they were found in the place about the king, and all their horses tied to each other.

BATTLE OF POITIERS, 1356

Then the battle began on all parts, and the battles of the marshals of France approached, and they set forth that were appointed to break the array of the archers. They entered a-horseback in the way where the great hedges were on both sides set full of archers. As soon as the men of arms entered, the archers began to shoot on both sides and did slay and hunt horses and knights, so that the horses when they felt the sharp arrows they would in no wise go forward, but drew aback and flang and took on so fiercely, that many of them fell on their masters, so that for press they could not rise again; insomuch that the marshals' battle could never come at the prince. Certain knights and squires that were well horsed passed through the archers and thought to approach the prince, but they could not. The lord James Audley with his four squires was in the front of that battle and there did marvels in arms, and by great prowess he came and fought with sir Arnold d'Audrehem under his own banner, and there they fought long together and sir Arnold was there sore handled. The battle of the marshals began to disorder by reason of the shot of the archers with the aid of the men of arms, who came in among them and slew of them and did what they list, and there was the lord Arnold d'Audrehem taken prisoner by other men than by sir James Audley or by his four squires; for that day he never took prisoner, but always fought and went on his enemies.

Also on the French party the lord John Clermont fought under his own banner as long as he could endure: but there he was beaten down and could not be relieved nor ransomed, but was slain without mercy: some said it was because of the words that he had the day before to sir John Chandos. So within a short space the marshals' battles were discomfited, for they fell one upon another and could not go forth; and the Frenchmen that were behind and could not get forward reculed back and came on the battle of the duke of Normandy, the which was great and thick and were afoot, but anon they began to open behind; for when they knew that the marshals' battle was discomfited, they took their horses and departed, he that might best. Also they saw a rout of Englishmen coming down a little mountain a-horseback, and many archers with them, who brake in on the side of the duke's battle. True to say, the archers did their company that day great advantage; for they shot so thick that the Frenchmen wist not on what side to take heed, and little and little the Englishmen won ground on them.

From Jean Froissart, *The Chronicles of Froissart,* ed. G. C. Macaulay, trans. J. Bourchier (London: MacMillan, 1895).

EXCERPTS FROM *GREENLAND SAGA* AND *ERIK'S SAGA*, MEDIEVAL ICELANDIC SAGAS OF NEW WORLD EXPLORATION (13TH CENTURY)

The *Greenland Saga* and *Erik's Saga* are medieval Icelandic sagas that discuss Viking exploration westward across the Atlantic. Among the stories are descriptions of landing on Iceland, Greenland, and North America centuries before Christopher Columbus. The selections reproduced here describe the encounters of Norsemen with the land and inhabitants of that New World.

GREENLAND SAGA

They went ashore and looked about them. The weather was fine. There was dew on the grass, and the first thing they did was to get some of it on their hands and put it to their lips, and to them it seemed the sweetest thing they had ever tasted. Then they went back to their ship and sailed into the sound that lay between the island and the headland jutting out to the north.

They steered a westerly course round the headland. There were extensive shallows there and at low tide their ship was left high and dry, with the sea almost out of sight. But they were so impatient to land that they could not bear to wait for the rising tide to float the ship; they ran ashore to a place where a river flowed out of a lake. As soon as the tide had refloated the ship they took a boat and rowed out to it and brought it up the river into the lake, where they anchored it. They carried their hammocks ashore and put up booths. Then they decided to winter there, and built some large houses.

There was no lack of salmon in the river or the lake, bigger salmon than they had ever seen. The country seemed to them so kind that no winter fodder would be needed for livestock: there was never any frost all winter and the grass hardly withered at all.

In this country, night and day were of more even length than in either Greenland or Iceland: on the shortest day of the year, the sun was already up by 9 A.M., and did not set until after 3 P.M.

When they had finished building their houses, Leif said to his companions, "Now I want to divide our company into two parties and have the country explored; half of the company are to remain here at the houses while the other half go exploring—but they must not go so far that they cannot return the same evening, and they are not to become separated."

They carried out these instructions for a time. Leif himself took turns at going out with the exploring party and staying behind at the base.

ERIK'S SAGA

Then, early one morning in spring, they saw a great horde of skin-boats approaching from the south round the headland, so dense that it looked as if the estuary were strewn with charcoal; and sticks were being waved from every boat. Karlsefni's men raised their shields and the two parties began to trade.

What the natives wanted most to buy was red cloth; they also wanted to buy swords and spears, but Karlsefni and Snorri forbade that. In exchange for the cloth they traded grey pelts. The natives took a span of red cloth for each pelt, and tied the cloth round their heads. The trading went on like this for a while until the cloth began to run short; then Karlsefni and his men cut it up into pieces which were no more than a finger's breath; but the Skraelings paid just as much or even more for it.

Then it so happened that a bull belonging to Karlsefni and his men came running out of the woods, bellowing furiously. The Skraelings were terrified and ran to their skin-boats and rowed away south round the headland.

After that there was no sign of the natives for three whole weeks. But then Karlsefni's men saw a huge number of boats coming from the south, pouring in like a torrent. This time all the sticks were being waved anti-clockwise and all the Skraelings were howling loudly. Karlsefni and his men now hoisted red shields and advanced towards them.

When they clashed there was a fierce battle and a hail of missiles came flying over, for the Skraelings were using catapults. Karlsefni and Snorri saw them hoist a large sphere on a pole; it was dark blue in colour. It came flying in over the heads of Karlsefni's men and made an ugly din when it struck the ground. This terrified Karlsefni and his men so much that their only thought was to flee, and they retreated farther up the river. They did not halt until they reached some cliffs, where they prepared to make a resolute stand.

Freydis came out and saw the retreat. She shouted, "Why do you flee from such pitiful wretches, brave men like you? You should be able to slaughter them like cattle. If I had weapons, I am sure I could fight better than any of you."

The men paid no attention to what she was saying. Freydis tried to join them but she could not keep up with them because she was pregnant. She was following them into the woods when the Skraelings closed in on her. In front of her lay a dead man,

Thorbrand Snorrason, with a flintstone buried in his head, and his sword beside him. She snatched up the sword and prepared to defend herself. When the Skraelings came rushing towards her she pulled one of her breasts out of her bodice and slapped it with the sword. The Skraelings were terrified at the sight of this and fled back to their boats and hastened away.

Karlsefni and his men came over to her and praised her courage. Two of their men had been killed, and four of the Skraelings, even though Karlsefni and his men had been fighting against heavy odds.

They returned to their houses and pondered what force it was that had attacked them from inland; they then realized that the only attackers had been those who had come in the boats, and that the other force had just been a delusion.

The Skraelings found the other dead Norseman, with his axe lying beside him. One of them hacked at a rock with the axe, and the axe broke; and thinking it worthless now because it could not withstand stone, they threw it away.

Karlsefni and his men had realized by now that although the land was excellent they could never live there in safety or freedom from fear, because of the native inhabitants. So they made ready to leave the place and return home.

From M. Magnusson and H. Palsson, trans., *The Vinland Sagas, The Norse Discovery of America: Graenlendinga Saga and Erik's Saga* (London: Penguin, 1965).

GUIBERT DE NOGENT, EXCERPTS FROM A *MONK'S CONFESSION* (EARLY 12TH CENTURY)

Written in the early 12th century, *A Monk's Confession: The Memoirs of Guibert de Nogent* provides a glimpse into the life of a monk living in northern France. Guibert's writing is unique in that it is primarily autobiographical, which is rare for the time. Obsessed with his own sinfulness, Guibert, in the following passages, provides useful information about medieval childhood.

There was a little before that time, and in a measure there is still in my time, such a scarcity of grammarians that in the towns hardly anyone, and in the cities very few, could be found, and those who by good hap could be discovered, had but slight knowledge and could not be compared with the itinerant clerks of these days. And so the man in whose charge my mother decided to put me, had begun to learn grammar late in life and was the more unskilled in the art through having imbibed little of it when young. Yet of such sobriety was he, that what he wanted in letters, he made up for in honesty. . . .

Placed under him I was taught with such purity and checked with such honesty in the excesses which are wont to spring up in my youth, that I was kept well-guarded from the common wolves and never allowed to leave his company, or to eat anywhere than at home, or to accept gifts from anyone without his leave; in everything I had to show self-control in word, look or act, so that he seemed to require of me the conduct of a monk rather than a clerk. For whereas others of my age wandered everywhere at will and were unchecked in the indulgence of such inclinations to their age, I, hedged in with constant restraints, would sit and look on in my clerical chasuble at the troops of players like a beast awaiting sacrifice. . . .

Although, therefore, he crushed me by such severity, yet in other ways he made it quite plain that he loved me as well as he did himself. With such watchful care did he devote himself to me, with such foresight did he secure my welfare against the spite of others and teach me on what authority I should beware of the dissolute manners of some who paid court to me, and so long did he argue with my mother about the elaborate richness of my dress, that he was regarded as exercising the guardianship not of a master, but of a parent, and not over my body only, but my soul, too. As for me, considering the dull sensibility of my age and my littleness, great was the love I conceived for him in response, in spite of the many weals with which he marked my tender skin so that not through fear, as is common in those of my age, but through a sort of love deeply implanted in my heart, I obeyed him in utter forgetfulness of his severity. . . .

Now it so happened that at the very beginning of that lawful union conjugal intercourse was made ineffective through the bewitchments of certain persons. For it was said that their marriage drew upon them the envy of a step-mother, who, having nieces of great beauty and nobility, was plotting to entangle one of them with my father. Meeting with no success in her designs, she is said to have used magical arts to prevent entirely the consummation of the marriage. His wife's virginity thus remaining intact for three years, during which he endured his great misfortune in silence, at last, driven to it by his kinfolk, my father was the first to reveal the facts. Imagine how my kinsmen tried hard in every way to bring about a divorce, and their constant pressure upon my father, young and raw, to become a monk, although at that time there was little talk of such orders. This, however, was not done for his soul's good, but with the purpose of getting possession of his property. But when their suggestion produced no effect, they began to hound the girl herself, far away as she was from her kinsfolk and harassed by the violence of strangers, into voluntary flight out of sheer exhaustion under their insults, and without waiting for divorce. Meanwhile she endured all this, bearing with calmness the abuse that was aimed at her, and, if out of this rose any strife, pretending ignorance of it.

When, therefore, that bewitchment was brought to naught with the aid of a certain old woman, my mother submitted to the duties of a wife as faithfully as she had kept her virginity when assailed by so many reproaches. Happy as she was in all else, she laid herself open to the chance, if not the certainty, of endless misery when she, whose goodness was ever growing, begat a son never else than wicked, worse sinner than myself. Yet Thou knowest, Almighty One, with what purity and holiness in obedience to Thee was my upbringing, what care of nurses in infancy, of masters and teachers in boyhood, she gave me, with no lack even of fine clothes for my little body, putting me on an honourable quality with sons of princes and nobles. And not only in my mother, O Lord, didst Thou put this love for me, but didst inspire with it other far richer persons, so that rather through the affection they had for me than under the obligations of kinship, they lavished on me careful tending and nurture.

O God, Thou knowest what warnings, what prayers she daily poured into my ears not to listen to corrupting words from anyone. She taught me, as often as she had leisure from household cares, how and for what I should pray to Thee. Thou alone knowest with what pains she travailed that the sound beginning of a happy and honourable childhood guarded by Thee, might not be ruined by an unsound heart.

From Guibert de Nogent, *The Autobiography of Guibert, Abbot of Nogent-Sous-Coucy*, trans. C. C. Swinton Bland (London: George Routledge and Sons, 1926).

HILDEGARD OF BINGEN, EXCERPTS FROM *CAUSES AND CURES*, A MEDICAL TREATISE (12TH CENTURY)

Born in 1098 as the tenth child in a wealthy family, Hildegard of Bingen joined a hermitage near a Benedictine abbey at the age of seven. The hermitage grew to become a house for nuns, and Hildegard became the abbess at age 38. She went on preaching journeys, wrote extensively, and maintained an active public life. The excerpts here are from *Causes and Cures*, an important treatise on medicine, and the first text to address the conditions of women.

Why menstruation. When the flow of cupidity entered Eve all her blood vessels were opened for the flow of blood. Therefore every woman suffers an upheaval in her blood so that she holds back and pours out the drops of her blood, similar to the restraint and effusion of the moon, and all the members of her body that are fastened by blood vessels are opened. For as the moon waxes and wanes, so for woman the blood and the humors are purged at the time of menstruation. Otherwise she could not survive because she is moister than man and would incur serious infirmity.

For a virgin, modesty is the lock of her integrity because, not knowing the act of a man, she has disregarded it. Therefore, menstrual blood from a virgin is more sanguineous than a woman's because the virgin is still closed. When a virgin has been deflowered she has thereafter, because she has been deflowered, more *livor* in her menstrual blood than she had earlier when she was still a virgin. When a girl is still a pure virgin, her menstruation comes in drops, so to speak, from her blood vessels. But after she has been deflowered the drops flow like a rivulet because they have been released through the act of a man. So they are like a rivulet because the blood vessels have been opened through intercourse. For when a virgin's lock of integrity is broken this breaking releases blood. Indeed, woman is made such that she must receive and retain man's semen with her blood. Therefore she is also weak and cold, and the humors in her are infirm. As a result, she would always be infirm if her blood were not purged through menstruation, just as food in a pot is purged when it discharges foam. . . .

TREATMENT

Migraine. A person who suffers from migraine should take aloe and twice that amount of myrrh. Grind both into a very fine powder. Then add wheat flour, add poppy oil to all of this and make a mixture similar to dough. Cover the entire head with this dough, down to the ears and to the neck, put a cap over it, and leave this on the head, day and night, for three days. For the warmth of aloe and the dryness of myrrh well tempered by the mildness of wheat flour and the coldness of poppy oil relieves this headache, and a dough prepared in this manner supplies fattiness to the brain.

From Hildegard of Bingen, *On Natural Philosophy and Medicine: Selections from Cause et Cure*, trans. M. Berger (Cambridge, England: D. S. Brewer, 1999).

IBN FADLAN, EXCERPTS FROM *THE RISALA*, AN ACCOUNT AMONG THE PEOPLE OF RUSSIA (EARLY 10TH CENTURY)

As an emissary sent from Baghdad to Asia in 921, Ibn Fadlan witnessed the life of a tribe he calls the Rus. The collected writings of Ibn Fadlan's journeys are titled *The Risala*, excerpts of which are included here. Of particular significance are the entries regarding cleanliness and hygiene.

§ 80

I have seen the Rus as they came on their merchant journeys and encamped by the Volga. I have never seen more perfect physical specimens, tall as date palms, blonde and ruddy; they wear neither tunics nor caftans, but the men wear a garment which covers one side of the body and leaves a hand free.

§ 81

Each man has an axe, a sword, and a knife and keeps each by him at all times. The swords are broad and grooved, of Frankish sort. Every man is tattooed from finger nails to neck with dark green (or green or blue-black) trees, figures, etc.

§ 82

Each woman wears on either breast a box of iron, silver, copper or gold; the value of the box indicates the wealth of the husband. Each box has a ring from which depends a knife. The women wear neck rings of gold and silver, one for each 10,000 dirhems which her husband is worth; some women have many. Their most prized ornaments are beads of green glass of the same make as ceramic objects one finds on their ships. They trade beads among themselves and they pay an exaggerated price for them, for they buy them for a dirhem apiece. They string them as necklaces for their women.

§ 83

They are the filthiest of God's creatures. They have no modesty in defecation and urination, nor do they wash after pollution from orgasm, nor do they wash their hands after eating. Thus they are like wild asses. When they have come from their land and anchored on, or tied up at the shore of the Volga, which is a great river, they build big houses of wood on the shore, each holding ten to twenty persons more or less. Each man has a couch on which he sits. With them are pretty slave girls destined for sale to merchants: a man will have sexual intercourse with his slave girl while his companion looks on. Sometimes whole groups will come together in this fashion, each in the presence of others. A merchant who arrives to buy a slave girl from them may have to wait and look on while a Rus completes the act of intercourse with a slave girl.

§ 84

Every day they must wash their faces and heads and this they do in the dirtiest and filthiest fashion possible: to wit, every morning a girl servant brings a great basin of water; she offers this to her master and he washes his hands and face and his hair—he washes it and combs it out with a comb in the water; then he blows his nose and spits into the basin. When he has finished, the servant carries the basin to the next person, who does likewise. She carries the basin thus to all the household in turn, and each blows his nose, spits, and washes his face and hair in it.

§ 86

An ill person is put in a tent apart with some bread and water and people do not come to speak with him; they do not come even to see him every day, especially if his is a poor man or a slave. If he recovers, he returns to them, and if he dies, they cremate him. If he is a slave, he is left to be eaten by dogs and birds of prey. If the Rus catch a thief or robber, they hang him on a tall tree and leave him hanging until his body falls in pieces.

From Ibn Fadlan, *The Risala*, <http://www.vikinganswerlady.com/ibn_fdln.htm#Risala

JEAN DE JOINVILLE, EXCERPTS FROM *CHRONICLE OF THE CRUSADE OF ST. LOUIS* (LOUIS IX OF FRANCE) (13TH CENTURY)

Jean de Joinville lived in France and left on a Crusade with St. Louis in August 1248. He wrote his account of his adventures five decades later. His *Chronicle of the Crusade of St. Louis* is an excellent historical source for the last of the Western Crusades. Three subjects are mentioned in the excerpts reproduced here: a description of St. Louis, Joinville's perspective on the Crusades, and an introduction to the Old Man of the Mountain and his Assassins.

WHAT ST. LOUIS THOUGHT ABOUT FAITH

The holy king endeavoured with all his power—as you shall here be told—to make me believe firmly in the Christian law, which God has given us. He said that we ought to believe so firmly the articles of faith that neither from fear of death, nor for any mischief that might happen to the body, should we be willing to go against them in word or deed. And he said that the Enemy is so subtle that, when people are dying, he labours all he can to make them die doubting as to some points of the faith. For he knows that when he can in no wise deprive a man of the good works he has done; and he knows also that the man is lost to him if he dies in the faith.

Wherefore we should so guard and defend ourselves from this snare, as to say to the Enemy, when he sends such a temptation: "Away!" Yes, "Away!" must one say to the Enemy. "Thou shalt not tempt me so that I cease to believe firmly all the articles of the faith. Even if thou didst cause all my members to be cut off, yet would I live and die in the faith." And whosoever acts thus, overcomes the Enemy with the very club and sword that the Enemy desired to murder him withal.

He said that the Christian faith and creed were things in which we ought to believe firmly, even though we might not be certain of them except by hearsay. On this point he asked me what was my father's name? And I told him his name was Simon. And he asked how I knew it. And I said I thought I was certain of it, and believed it firmly, because my mother hand borne witness thereto. Then he said, "So ought you to believe all the articles of the faith, to which the Apostles have borne witness, as also you chant of a Sunday in the Creed."

THE CRUSADERS EMBARK, AUGUST 1248

In the month of August we entered into our ship at the Roche-de-Marseille. On the day that we entered into our ship, they opened the door of the ship and put therein all the horses we were to take oversea; and then they reclosed the door, and caulked it well, as when a cask is sunk in water, because, when the ship is on the high seas, all the said door is under water.

When the horses were in the ship, our master mariner called to his seamen, who stood at the prow, and said: "Are you ready?" and they answered, "Aye, sir—let the clerks and priests come forward!" As soon as these had come forward, he called to them, "Sing, for God's sake!" and they all, with one voice, chanted: "*Veni Creator Spritus*."

Then he cried to his seamen, "Unfurl the sails, for God's sake!" and they did so.

In a short space the wind filled our sails and had borne us out of sight of land, so that we saw naught save sky and water, and every day the wind carried us further from the land where we were born. And these things I tell you, that you may understand how foolhardy is that man who dares, having other's chattels in his possession, or being in mortal sin, to place himself in such peril, seeing that, when you lie down to sleep at night on shipboard, you lie down not knowing whether, in the morning, you may find yourself at the bottom of the sea. . . .

THE BEDOUINS

. . . The Bedouins do not believe in Mahomet, but they believe in the law of Ali, who was uncle to Mahomet; and so also believes the Old Man of the Mountain, who entertains the Assassins. And they believe that when a man dies for his lord, or in any good cause, his soul goes into another body, better and more comfortable; and for this reason the Assassins are not greatly concerned if they are killed when carrying out the commands of the Old Man of the Mountain. . . .

One of the points taught by the law of Ali is, that when a man gets himself killed doing the commands of his lord, his soul goes into a pleasanter body than before; and therefore the Assassins do not hesitate to get themselves killed when their lord so orders, because they believe they will then be in better case after they are dead.

Another point is this: that they believe no man can die until the day appointed for him; and this belief no man should hold, seeing that God has power to prolong our lives, or to shorten them. And on this point the Bedouins accept the law of Ali, for which reason they will not put on armour when they go into battle, since by so doing they think they would be acting contrary to the commandment of their law. And when they curse their children they say: "Let there be upon thee the curse of the Frank, who puts on armour for fear of death."

From Geoffrey de Villehardouin and Jean de Joinville, *Memoirs of the Crusades*, trans. F. Marzials (New York: Dent, 1908).

MARCO POLO, EXCERPTS FROM *THE TRAVELS OF MARCO POLO* (13TH CENTURY)

With his father and uncle, Marco Polo set out on his adventures at the age of 17, traveling from his native Venice, across central Asia, to the China of Kublai Khan, grandson of the Mongol conqueror Chinggis Khan. Years later, while imprisoned in Genoa, Polo dictated this account of his travels. The author tells of wondrous new cities and ports. The selections here describe one of these ports and the women of the Kublai Khan's court.

Tauris is a large and very noble city belonging to the province of Irak, which contains many other cities and fortified places, but this is the eminent and most populous. The inhabitants support themselves principally by commerce and manufactures, which latter consist of various kinds of silk, some of them interwoven with gold, and of high price. It is so advantageously situated for trade, that merchants from India, . . . as well as from different parts of Europe, resort thither to purchase and to sell a number of articles. Precious stones and pearls in abundance may be procured at this place. The merchants concerned in foreign commerce acquire considerable wealth, but the inhabitants in general are poor. They consist of a mixture of various nations and sects, Nestorians, Armenians, Jacobites, Georgians, Persians, and the followers of Mahomet, who form the bulk of the populations, and are those properly called Taurisians. Each description of people have their peculiar language. The city is surrounded with delightful gardens, producing the finest fruits. The Mahometan inhabitants are treacherous and unprincipled. According to their doctrine, whatever is stolen or plundered from others of a different faith, is properly taken, and the theft is no crime; whilst those who suffer death or injury by the hands of Christians, are considered as martyrs. If, therefore, they were not prohibited and restrained by the powers who now govern them, they would commit many outrages. These principles are common to all the Saracens. When they are at the point of death, their priest attends upon them, and asks whether they believe that Mahomet was the true apostle of God. If their answer be that they do believe, their salvation is assured to them; and in consequence of this facility of absolution, which gives free scope to the perpetration of everything flagitious, they have succeeded in converting to their faith a great proportion of the Tartars, who consider it as relieving them from restraint in the commission of crimes. . . .

[Kublai] has four wives of the first rank, who are esteemed legitimate, and the eldest born son of any one of these succeeds to the empire, upon the decease of the grand khan. They bear equally the title of empress, and have their separate courts. None of them have fewer than three hundred young female attendants of great beauty, together with a multitude of youths as pages, and other eunuchs, as well as ladies of the bedchamber; so that the number of persons belonging to each of their respective courts amounts to ten thousand. . . . Besides these, he has many concubines provided for his use, from a province of Tartary named Ungut, having a city of the same name, the inhabitants of which are distinguished for beauty and features and fairness of complexion. Thither the grand khan sends his officers every second year, or oftener, as it may happen to be his pleasure, who collect for him, to the number of four or five hundred, or more, of the handsomest of the young women, according to the estimation of beauty communicated to them in their instructions. . . . Upon the arrival of these commissioners, they give orders for assembling all the young women of the province, and appoint qualified persons to examine them, who, upon careful inspection of each of them separately, that is to say, of the hair, the countenance, the eyebrows, the mouth, the lips, and other features, as well as the symmetry of these with each other, estimate their value at sixteen, seventeen, eighteen, or twenty, or more carats, according to the greater or less degree of beauty. The number required by the grand khan, at the rates, perhaps of twenty or twenty-one carats, to which their commission was limited, is then selected from the rest, and they are conveyed to his court. Upon their arrival in his presence, he causes a new examination to be made by a different set of inspectors, and from amongst them a further selection takes place, when thirty or forty are retained for his own chamber at a higher valuation. These, in the first instance, are committed separately to the care of the wives of certain of the nobles, whose duty it is to observe them attentively during the course of the night, in order to ascertain that they have not any concealed imperfections, that they sleep tranquilly, do not snore, have sweet breath, and are free from unpleasant scent in any part of the body. Having undergone this rigorous scrutiny, they're divided into parties of five, one of which parties attends during three days and three nights, in his majesty's interior apartment, where they are to perform every service that is required of them, and he does with them as he likes. When this term is completed, they are relieved by another party, and in this manner successively, until the whole number have taken their turn; when the first five recommence their attendance. But whilst the one party officiates in the inner chamber, another is stationed in the outer apartment adjoining; in order that if his majesty should have occasion for anything, such as drink or victuals, the former may signify his commands to the latter, by whom the article required is immediately procured: and thus the duty of waiting upon his majesty's person is exclusively performed by these young females. The remainder of them, whose value had been estimated at an inferior rate, are assigned to the different lords of the household; under whom they are instructed in cookery, in dressmaking, and other suitable works; and upon any person belonging to the court expressing an inclination to take a wife, the grand khan bestows upon him one of these damsels, with a handsome portion. In this manner he provides for them all amongst his nobility. It may be asked whether the people of the province do not feel themselves aggrieved in having their daughters thus forcibly taken from them by the sovereign? . . . [T]hey regard it as a favour and an honour done to them; and those who are the fathers of handsome children feel highly gratified by his condescending to make choice of their daughters. "If," say they, "my daughter is born under an auspicious planet and to good fortune, his majesty can best fulfill her destinies, by matching her nobly; which it would not be in my power to do." If, on the other hand, the daughter misconducts herself, or any mischance befalls her (by which she becomes disqualified), the father attributes the disappointment to the malign influence of her stars.

From Marco Polo, *The Travels of Marco Polo the Venetian*, ed. E. Rhys, trans. J. Masefield (New York: Dent, 1908).

EDWARD, SECOND DUKE OF YORK, EXCERPTS FROM *THE MASTER OF GAME* (EARLY 15TH CENTURY)

Edward, the second duke of York, was a cousin of King Henry V, for whom York fought and died at the Battle of Agincourt in 1415. The duke's treatise *The Master of Game* is the oldest surviving book on hunting. It cannot be dated precisely, although it was probably completed between 1406 and 1413. The passages reproduced here explain how a hunter should live.

Now shall I prove how hunters live in this world more joyfully than any other men. For when the hunter riseth in the morning, and he sees a sweet and fair morn and clear weather and bright, and he heareth the song of the small birds, the which sing so sweetly with great melody and full of love, each in it's own language in the best wise that it can according that it learneth of it's own kind. And when the sun is arisen, he shall see fresh dew upon the small twigs and grasses, and the sun by his virtue shall make them shine. And that is great joy and liking to the hunter's heart. After when he shall go to his quest or searching he shall see or meet anon with the hart without great seeking, and shall harbour him well and readily within a little compass. It is great joy and liking to the hunter. And after when he shall come to the assembly or gathering, and he shall report before the Lord and his company that which he hath seen with his eyes, or by scantilon (measure) of the trace (slot) which he ought always of right to take, or by the fumes (excrements) that he shall put in his horn or in his lap. And every man shall say: Lo, here is a great hart and a deer of high meating or pasturing; go we and move him; the which things I shall declare hereafter, then can one say that the hunter has great joy. When he beginneth to hunt and he hath hunted but a little and he shall hear or see the hart start before him and shall well know that it is the right one, and his hounds that shall this day be finders, shall come to the lair (bed), or to the fues (track), and shall there be uncoupled without any be left coupled, and they shall all run well and hunt, then hath the hunter great joy and great pleasure. Afterward he leapeth on horseback, *if he be of that estate, and else on foot* with great haste to follow his hounds. And in case peradventure the hounds shall have gone far from where he uncoupled, he seeketh some advantage to get in front of his hounds. And then shall he see the hart pass before him, and shall shout and rout mightily, and he shall see which hound come in the van-chase, and in the middle, and which are parfitours, according to the order in which they shall come. And when all the hounds have passed before him then shall he ride after them and shall rout and blow as loud as he may with great joy and great pleasure, and I assure you he thinketh of no other sin or of no other evil. And when the hart be overcome and shall be at bay he shall have pleasure. And after, when the hart is spayed and dead, he undoeth him and maketh his curee and enquireth or rewardeth his hounds, and so he shall have great pleasure, and when he cometh home he cometh joyfully, for his lord hath given him to drink of his good wine at the curee, and when he has come home he shall doff his clothes and his shoes and his hose, and he shall wash his thighs and his legs, and peradventure all his body. And in the meanwhile he shall order well his supper, with *wortes* (roots) *and of the neck* of the hart and of other good meats, and good wine *or ale*. And when he hath well eaten and drunk he shall be glad and well, and well at his ease. And then shall he take the air in the evening of the night, for the great heat that he hath had. And then he shall go and drink and lie in his bed in fair fresh clothes, and shall sleep well and steadfastly all the night without any evil thoughts of any sins, wherefore I saw that hunters go into Paradise when they die, and live in this world more joyfully than any other men. . . .

WHAT MANNER AND CONDITION A GOOD HUNTER SHOULD HAVE

Thous, Sir, whatever you be, great or little, that would teach a man to be a good hunter, first he must be a child past seven or eight years of age or little older, and if any man would say that I take a child in too tender age for to put him to work, I answer that all nature shortens and descends. For every man knoweth well that a child of seven years of age is more capable in these times of such things that he liketh to learn than was a child of twelve years of age (in times that I have seen). And therefore I put him so young thereto, for a craft requires all a man's life ere he be perfect thereof. And also men say that which a man learns in youth he will hold best in his age. And furthermore from this child many things are required, first that he love his master, and that his heart and his business be with the hounds, and he must take him, and beat him when he will not do what his master commands him, until the time that the child dreads to fail. And first I shall take and teach him for to take in writing all the names of the hounds of the hues of the hounds, until the time that the child knoweth them both by the hue and by the name. After I will teach him to make clean every day in the morning the hounds' kennel of all foul things. After I will learn him to put before them twice a day fresh water and clean, from a well, in a vessel there where the hound drinks, or fair running water, in the morning and the evening. After I will teach him that once in the day he empty the kennel and make all clean, and renew their straw, and put again fresh new straw a great deal and right thick.

From Edward, Second Duke of York, *The Master of Game*, ed. W. A. Bailie-Grohman and F. Bailie-Grohman (New York: Duffield, 1909).

EXCERPTS FROM *AUCASSIN AND NICOLETT*, A 13TH-CENTURY SATIRE OF MEDIEVAL ROMANCES

The following is an excerpt from a 13th-century story that was probably written as a gentle satire of the popular medieval romances. Instead of an active knight doing great deeds for his passive princess in a tower, it has an active heroine escaping from her tower, while the knight is weeping in prison. It is a charming, funny tale that comments on gender roles and love in the Middle Ages. Its fresh look at relationships suggests to some critics that the author may have been a woman.

[The work begins with the two lovers, Aucassin and Nicolett, forcibly separated by the young man's father, who imprisons his son to keep him away from Nicolett.]

Aucassin was cast into prison as ye have heard tell. Now it was summer time, the month of May, when days are warm, and long, and clear, and the night still and serene. Nicolette lay one night on her bed, and saw the moon shine clear through a window, yea, and heard the nightingale sing in the garden, so she minded her of Aucassin her lover whom she loved so well. Then she arose, and clad her in a mantle of silk she had by her, very lovely, and took napkins, and sheets of the bed, and knotted one to the other, and made therewith a cord as long as she might, so knitted it to a pillar in the window, and let herself slip down into the garden, then caught up her raiment in both hands, behind and before, and kilted up her kirtle, because of the dew that she was lying deep on the grass, and so went her way down through the garden.

Her locks were yellow and curled, her eyes blue and smiling, her face neatly fashioned, the nose high and fairly set, the lips more red than cherry or rose in time of summer, her teeth white and small; her breasts so firm that they bore up the folds of her bodice as they had been two apples; so slim she was in the waist that your two hands might have clipped her, and the daisy flowers that brake beneath her as she went tip-toe seemed black against her feet, so white was the maiden.

She came to the postern gate, and unbarred it, and went out through the streets of Biaucaire, keeping always on the shadowy side, for the moon was shining right clear, and so wandered she still she came to the tower where her lover lay. The tower was flanked with buttresses, and she cowered under one of them, wrapped in her mantle. Then thrust she her head through a crevice of the tower that was old and worn, and so heard she Aucassin wailing within, and making dole and lament for the sweet lady he loved so well. And when she had listened to him she began to say:

Nicolette the bright of brow
On a pillar leanest thou,
All Aucassin's wail dost hear
For his love that is so dear,
Then thou spakest, shrill and clear,
"Gentle knight withouten fear
Little good befalleth thee,
Little help of sigh or tear,
Ne'er shalt thou have joy of me.
Never shalt thou win me; still
Am I held in evil will
Of thy father and thy kin,
Therefore must I cross the sea,
And another land must win."
Then she cut her curls of gold,
Cast them in the dungeon hold,
Aucassin doth clasp them there,
Kissed the curls that were so fair,
Them doth in his bosom bear,
Then he wept, even us of old,
All for his love!

[Nicolette escapes into the forest and builds a beautiful hut, where she waits for Aucassin. When he is freed from his prison, he finds the hut, and once again, the knight is shown to be clumsy and the woman competent.]

"God!" quoth Aucassin, "here was Nicolette, my sweet lady, and this lodge builded she with her fair hands. For the sweetness of it, and for love of her will I alight, and rest here this night long."

He drew forth his foot from the stirrup to alight, and the steed was great and tall. He dreamed so thick on Nicolette his right sweet lady, that he slipped on a stone, and drove his shoulder out of his place. Then knew he that he was hurt sore, nonetheless he bore him with what force he might, and fastened with the other hand the horse to a thorn. Then turned he on his side, and crept backwise into the lodge of boughs. And he looked through a gap in the lodge and saw the stars in heaven, and one that was brighter than the rest; so began he to say:

"Star, that I from far behold,
Star, the Moon calls to her fold,
Nicolette with thee doth dwell,
My sweet love with locks of gold,
God would have her dwell afar,
Dwell with him for evening star,
Would to God, whate'er befell,
Would that with her I might dwell.
I would clip her close and strait,
Nay, were I of much estate,
Some king's son desirable,
Worthy she to be my mate,
Me to kiss and clip me well,
Sister, sweet friend!"

When Nicolette heard Aucassin, right so came, she unto him, for she was not far away. She passed within the lodge, and threw her arms about his neck, and kissed him.

"Fair sweet friend, welcome be thou."

"And thou, fair sweet love, be thou welcome."

So either kissed the other, and fair joy was them between.

"Ha! sweet love," quoth Aucassin, "but now was I sore hurt, and my shoulder twisted, but I take no force of it, nor have no hurt therefrom since I have thee."

Right so felt she his shoulder and found it was wrenched from its place. And she so handled it with her white hands, and so wrought in her surgery: that by God's will who loveth lovers, it went back into its place. Then took she flowers, and fresh grass, and leaves green, and bound these herbs on the hurt with a strip of her smock, and he was all healed.

"Aucassin," saith she, "fair sweet love, take counsel what thou wilt do. If thy father let search in this forest tomorrow, and men find me here, they will slay me, come to thee what will."

"Certes, fair sweet love, therefore should I sorrow heavily, but, an if I may, never shall they take thee."

Anon gat he on his horse, and his lady before him, kissing and hugging her, and so rode they at adventure.

Aucassin the frank, the fair,
Aucassin of the yellow hair,
Gentle knight, and true lover,
From the forest doth he care,
Holds his love before him there,
Kissing cheek, and chin, and eyes,
But she spake in sober wise,
"Aucassin, true love and fair,
To what land do we repair?"
Sweet my love, I take no care,
Thou art with me everywhere!"
So they pass the woods and downs,
Pass the villages and towns,

Hills and dales and open land,
Came at down to the sea sand,
Lighted down upon the strand,
  Beside the sea.

[The couple travels to a land where men bear the children and wars are fought with food instead of weapons. After more adventures in which the two are separated, they finally come together and live happily ever after.]

From Anonymous, *Aucassin and Nicolett,* trans. A. Lang (New York: Thomas Y. Crowell, 1905).

WERNHER DER GARTENAERE, EXCERPTS FROM *MEIER HELMBRECHT,* AN EPIC POEM ON LIFE IN 13TH-CENTURY GERMANY

Written in 13th-century Germany, the poem *Meier Helmbrecht* by Wernher der Gartenaere describes the life of peasants in a time of changing social structures. The poem tells the story of a young man in conflict with his family and tradition. The selections reproduced here capture this turmoil and specifically look at the role of food in the lives of the people.

Now Gotlint, Helmbrecht's sister, won
The favor of this pretty nun
By giving her a fine fat cow.
Skilled with her hands, the latter now
Repaid them, as so well she could:
Made Helmbrecht both a suit and hood.
When Gotlint gave the cow to her,
Hear what further did occur:
The mother gave, the nun to please,
So many eggs and so much cheese,
The while in convent halls she ate
She ne'er had been thus satiate
With foods—so many eggs to crack,
And such fine cheeses without lack. . . .
"Stay here, dear son, and do not go!
For Peasant Ruprecht, as I know,
Will give to you his daughter's hand;
Ten cattle, too, I understand,
And swine and sheep, both young and old.
At court you'll hungry be, and cold.
Your bed will often be most hard,
You'll win no favor nor regard.
Now follow my admonishment,
'Twill bring you honor and content;
For seldom does it come to pass

That one can rise above one's class. . . .
"For if *you* steal a peasant's food,
Dear son of mine, beloved and good,
If once he gets you in his hand,
You're pledge and hostage, understand,
For all who've robbed of him before.
On you he'll settle each old score. . . .
"Live here on what I live on too,
And on what mother gives to you.
Drink water, dearest son of mine,
Ere you with booty buy your wine.
Our meal-cake, even in Austria, son,
Is much enjoyed by everyone.
Both wise and stupid relish it,
For noblemen they deem it fit.
Do you, dear child, eat of it too,
Before you go so far that you
Exchange your stolen oxen when
You're hungry, for a paltry hen.
Each week day mother here can make
The best of soups, and no mistake!
Fill up your maw with that! 'Twill aid
You better than to give in trade
For someone's goose your stolen horse.
If you will only take this course
You'll live in honor, son, like me,
No matter where you chance to be.
Son, mix a little bit of rye
Together with your oats, and try
To be content with this good dish
Before you eat of stolen fish. . . . "
"You drink your water, father mine,
And I shall quench my thirst with wine.
Enjoy your groats, if you so wish,
But I prefer a better dish
Of chicken, boiled deliciously;
It cannot be forbidden me.
And I shall eat, until I'm dead,
The finest, whitest wheaten bread.
The oats are proper food for you. . . . "
All, just the same, our Helmbrecht took,
The peasant Helmbrecht's ill-starred son.
He'd take a horse from anyone,
Or cow, and scarce a spoonful leave.
Of sword and doublet he'd relieve
A man—of mantle and of coat.
He took his kid, he took his goat,
He took the sheep, the ram beside;
He paid it later with his hide! . . .
When Helmbrecht had awaked again
The dinner was prepared, and then
He washed his hands. I'll now relate

What food was placed before his plate.
I'll name the course they first set down
(Were I a man of high renown
I'd always most contented be
If this same dish were served to me):
As fine-cut kraut as you will find;
And fat and lean (there was each kind)
Came with this dish—the best of meat.
Now hear what food he next did eat:
A soft and ripe and fatty cheese
Was served and cut, the youth to please.
A third dish followed then, to wit,
As fat a goose as e'er on spit
Was roasted at a kitchen fire.
(The parents did not seem to tire,
They did all this with best of will.)
This fowl had grown so large until
'Twas big as ever buzzard is,
And now the youth could call it his.
A boiled hen and a roasted one,
As Helmbrecht's father ordered done,
Were now brought on the groaning board.
Such food would surely please a lord;
He'd glad enough eat just the same
While in his blind he ambushed game.
Many other dishes, too,
The like a peasant never knew,
Foods fine and good as could be had,
Were now served up before the lad.
The father said: "If I had wine
We'd drink it now, dear son of mine.
Instead, loved Helmbrecht, take for drink
This fine spring water, best, I think,
That ever from the earth did flow. . . .
Schluckdenwidder poured the wine.
Hollensack, the next in line,
Seated the guests, both strange and known;
As steward, bright his talent shone.
And he, unsteady, fickle swain,
Ruttelschrein, was chamberlain.
Kuhfrass, kitcheners, served the meat;
He gave them all that they could eat,
And whether roast, or boiled instead.
Mausdenkelch passed round the bread.
The banquet passed without alarm.
Wolfesgaum and Wolfesdarm
And Wolfesrussel, at their wish,
Emptied many a well-filled dish,
Drained many a brimming goblet, too,
Ere the wedding feast was through.
Before the lads, food disappeared
With a rapidity quite weird,

As though there'd come a sudden gust
That carried it away like dust.
Each banqueter consumed in haste
All of the foods the stewart placed
Before him—everything he saw.
And did the dogs thereafter gnaw
Meat from the bones when they were through?
No, this a dog could hardly do.
For, as the wise have often said,
A man gulps down his meat and bread
More greedily than e'er before
When death is standing at his door.
And so they now ate greedily—
It was their last festivity—
Last time they sat in merriment
And ate their food to their content. . . .
What fate decrees is bound to be!
God seldom spares a man, when he
Does evil deeds he should not do.
In Helmbrecth this we see come true.
To avenge the father, I surmise,
The sheriff pierced out Helmbrecht's eyes.
Nor was the punishment yet through;
For they avenged the mother, too,
By lopping off a hand and foot.

CUMULATIVE INDEX

Boldface numbers refer to volume numbers. A key appears on all verso pages.

1: Ancient World	4: 17th and 18th C.
2: Medieval World	5: 19th C.
3: 15th and 16th C.	6: Modern World

1: Ancient World	4: 17th and 18th C.
2: Medieval World	5: 19th C.
3: 15th and 16th C.	6: Modern World

1: Ancient World	4: 17th and 18th C.
2: Medieval World	5: 19th C.
3: 15th and 16th C.	6: Modern World

1: Ancient World 4: 17th and 18th C.
2: Medieval World 5: 19th C.
3: 15th and 16th C. 6: Modern World

1: Ancient World	4: 17th and 18th C.
2: Medieval World	5: 19th C.
3: 15th and 16th C.	6: Modern World

1: Ancient World	**4:** 17th and 18th C.
2: Medieval World	**5:** 19th C.
3: 15th and 16th C.	**6:** Modern World

1: Ancient World	4: 17th and 18th C.
2: Medieval World	5: 19th C.
3: 15th and 16th C.	6: Modern World

1: Ancient World	4: 17th and 18th C.
2: Medieval World	5: 19th C.
3: 15th and 16th C.	6: Modern World

1: Ancient World	**4**: 17th and 18th C.
2: Medieval World	**5**: 19th C.
3: 15th and 16th C.	**6**: Modern World

1: Ancient World	4: 17th and 18th C.
2: Medieval World	5: 19th C.
3: 15th and 16th C.	6: Modern World

1: Ancient World	4: 17th and 18th C.
2: Medieval World	5: 19th C.
3: 15th and 16th C.	6: Modern World

1: Ancient World	4: 17th and 18th C.
2: Medieval World	5: 19th C.
3: 15th and 16th C.	6: Modern World

1: Ancient World	4: 17th and 18th C.
2: Medieval World	5: 19th C.
3: 15th and 16th C.	6: Modern World

1: Ancient World	**4**: 17th and 18th C.
2: Medieval World	**5**: 19th C.
3: 15th and 16th C.	**6**: Modern World

1: Ancient World	4: 17th and 18th C.
2: Medieval World	5: 19th C.
3: 15th and 16th C.	6: Modern World

1: Ancient World	4: 17th and 18th C.
2: Medieval World	5: 19th C.
3: 15th and 16th C.	6: Modern World

1: Ancient World	4: 17th and 18th C.
2: Medieval World	5: 19th C.
3: 15th and 16th C.	6: Modern World

1: Ancient World	4: 17th and 18th C.
2: Medieval World	5: 19th C.
3: 15th and 16th C.	6: Modern World

1: Ancient World	4: 17th and 18th C.
2: Medieval World	5: 19th C.
3: 15th and 16th C.	6: Modern World

1: Ancient World	4: 17th and 18th C.
2: Medieval World	5: 19th C.
3: 15th and 16th C.	6: Modern World

1: Ancient World	4: 17th and 18th C.
2: Medieval World	5: 19th C.
3: 15th and 16th C.	6: Modern World

1: Ancient World	4: 17th and 18th C.
2: Medieval World	5: 19th C.
3: 15th and 16th C.	6: Modern World

1: Ancient World 4: 17th and 18th C.
2: Medieval World 5: 19th C.
3: 15th and 16th C. 6: Modern World

1: Ancient World	4: 17th and 18th C.
2: Medieval World	5: 19th C.
3: 15th and 16th C.	6: Modern World

1: Ancient World	4: 17th and 18th C.
2: Medieval World	5: 19th C.
3: 15th and 16th C.	6: Modern World

1: Ancient World	4: 17th and 18th C.
2: Medieval World	5: 19th C.
3: 15th and 16th C.	6: Modern World

1: Ancient World	**4:** 17th and 18th C.
2: Medieval World	**5:** 19th C.
3: 15th and 16th C.	**6:** Modern World

1: Ancient World	4: 17th and 18th C.
2: Medieval World	5: 19th C.
3: 15th and 16th C.	6: Modern World

1: Ancient World	**4:** 17th and 18th C.
2: Medieval World	**5:** 19th C.
3: 15th and 16th C.	**6:** Modern World

1: Ancient World	**4**: 17th and 18th C.
2: Medieval World	**5**: 19th C.
3: 15th and 16th C.	**6**: Modern World

1: Ancient World	4: 17th and 18th C.
2: Medieval World	5: 19th C.
3: 15th and 16th C.	6: Modern World

1: Ancient World	4: 17th and 18th C.
2: Medieval World	5: 19th C.
3: 15th and 16th C.	6: Modern World

1: Ancient World	4: 17th and 18th C.
2: Medieval World	5: 19th C.
3: 15th and 16th C.	6: Modern World

1: Ancient World	**4:** 17th and 18th C.
2: Medieval World	**5:** 19th C.
3: 15th and 16th C.	**6:** Modern World

1: Ancient World	**4:** 17th and 18th C.
2: Medieval World	**5:** 19th C.
3: 15th and 16th C.	**6:** Modern World

1: Ancient World	4: 17th and 18th C.
2: Medieval World	5: 19th C.
3: 15th and 16th C.	6: Modern World

1: Ancient World	4: 17th and 18th C.
2: Medieval World	5: 19th C.
3: 15th and 16th C.	6: Modern World

1: Ancient World	4: 17th and 18th C.
2: Medieval World	5: 19th C.
3: 15th and 16th C.	6: Modern World

ABOUT THE CONTRIBUTORS

General Editor and Volume Editor

Joyce E. Salisbury is Frankenthal Professor of History at University of Wisconsin–Green Bay. She has a doctorate in medieval history from Rutgers University. Professor Salisbury is an award-winning teacher: she was named CASE (Council for Advancement and Support of Education) Professor of the Year for Wisconsin in 1991 and has brought her concern for pedagogy to this encyclopedia. Professor Salisbury has written or edited more than 10 books, including the award-winning *Perpetua's Passion: Death and Memory of a Young Roman Woman, The Beast Within: Animals in the Middle Ages*, and *The West in the World*, a textbook on western civilization.

Additional Contributors

Robert D. Craig, Alaska Pacific University
George Lane, University of London, School of Oriental and African Studies
James Lindsay, Colorado State University
Marcus Rautman, University of Missouri–Columbia
Paula Rentmeester, University of Wisconsin–Green Bay

I would also acknowledge the following authors of Greenwood Publishing's "Daily Life through History" series, whose books contributed much to entries in this volume:

Charles Benn, *Daily Life in Traditional China: The Tang Dynasty*, 2002.
John J. Butt, *Daily Life in the Age of Charlemagne*, 2002.
James Lindsay, *Daily Life in Medieval Islam*, forthcoming.
Jeffrey L. Singman, *Daily Life in Medieval Europe*, 1999.
Jeffrey L. Singman and Will McLean, *Daily Life in Chaucer's England*, 1995.
Kirsten Wolf, *Daily Life of the Vikings*, forthcoming.